ebXML:
The Technical
Specifications

AARON E. WALSH
EDITOR

Prentice Hall PTR
Upper Saddle River, NJ 07458
www.phptr.com

ISBN 0-13-034798-1

90000

9 780130 347985

Library of Congress Cataloging-in-Publication Data

Walsh, Aaron E.
  ebXML : the technical specifications / Aaron Walsh.
    p. cm.
  Includes bibliographical references.
  ISBN 0-13-034798-1
    1. XML (Document markup language) 2. Web sites--Design. 3. Internet programming.
  4. Electronic commerce. I. Title.

  QA76.76.H94 W32 2002
  05.2'76--dc21

2001056581

Production Supervision: *Donna Cullen-Dolce*
Acquisitions Editor: *Tim Moore*
Editorial Assistant: *Allyson Kloss*
Manufacturing Buyer: *Maura Zaldivar*
Cover Design: *Talar Boorujy*
Cover Design Director: *Jerry Votta*
Marketing Manager: *Debby van Dijk*

Prentice Hall books are widely used by corporations and government agencies for training, marketing, and resale.

The publisher offers discounts on this book when ordered in bulk quantities.
For more information, contact: Corporate Sales Department, Phone: 800-382-3419; Fax: 201-236-7141; E-mail: corpsales@prenhall.com; or write: Prentice Hall PTR, Corp. Sales Dept., One Lake Street, Upper Saddle River, NJ 07458.

Printed in the United States of America
ISBN 0-13-034798-1

Pearson Education LTD.
Pearson Education Australia PTY, Limited
Pearson Education Singapore, Pte. Ltd.
Pearson Education North Asia Ltd.
Pearson Education Canada, Ltd.
Pearson Educación de Mexico, S.A. de C.V.
Pearson Education—Japan
Pearson Education Malaysia, Pte. Ltd.

Contents

CHAPTER 2
Technical Architecture Specification v1.0.4   35

CHAPTER 3
Business Process Specification Schema v1.01   **79**

CHAPTER 6
Collaboration-Protocol Profile and Agreement
Specification v1.0   377

Preface

You hold in your hands the first book in the world to present all seven ebXML technical specifications in printed form, which is more than appropriate considering that Electronic Business Extensible Markup Language (ebXML) is itself a "first" in the world of electronic business.

ebXML is a joint initiative of the United Nations (UN/CEFACT) and the Organization for the Advancement of Structured Information Standards (OASIS). UN/CEFACT and OASIS started the ebXML initiative in the fall of 1999 with a mission to *"provide an open XML-based infrastructure enabling the global use of electronic business information in an interoperable, secure and consistent manner by all parties."*

In May 2001, following an 18-month self-imposed deadline, the initiative publicly unveiled the seven technical specifications found in this book in addition to a number of technical reports and white papers found in the companion to this book, *ebXML:The Technical Reports* (Prentice Hall PTR). With barely a toe in the doorway of the new millennium, ebXML 1.0 was born, ushering in the first and only open global electronic business framework.

Rooted in XML and based on open standards (such as HTTP, TCP/IP, MIME, and other open and public standards), ebXML is a landmark of technological evolution that promises to spark a revolution in electronic business. As a set of related specifications developed by more than 75 companies spanning the globe, ebXML was designed specifically for business in the Internet age. By enabling entirely digital business transactions that are modular, transport-independent, and loosely coupled by design, ebXML effectively brings Electronic Data Interchange (EDI) to the Internet and World Wide Web.

More than 2000 individuals from over 30 countries ultimately contributed to ebXML 1.0 to ensure that the standard solved the fundamental business requirements established by a wide range of participants. Although it is possible to run EDI over public networks, doing so is typically off-limits to many small and medium-sized businesses because of the high cost associated with implementation, infrastructure, and support. ebXML, on the other hand, was designed from the onset to run over public networks using open and publicly available standards, making ebXML a viable and cost-effective solution for small, medium, and large companies. Consequently, ebXML deployment costs are expected to be minimal as compared to EDI and proprietary electronic business framework alternatives.

Although ebXML is relatively new, especially when compared to EDI (which has been with us for nearly 30 years), it's already proving to be a success worthy of the effort it took to develop it. As this book went to press, a variety of organizations have made strides toward embracing ebXML as a solution for Business-to-Business (B2B) electronic commerce, and many more were poised to jump headfirst into the swelling ebXML pool.

The true value of ebXML as an agent of revolution will be seen downstream as new and innovative business models develop around the framework specified in this book. In the meantime, early adopters are already finding ebXML to be an exciting and cost-effective solution based on past successes with EDI and open standards. Whatever your interest, I believe that you'll find the wealth of technical information in this book invaluable as you dive into ebXML. Welcome to the future of electronic business—come on in, the water's fine.

Aaron E. Walsh

Introduction

ebXML was developed by several project teams working in concert with one another over an 18-month period. Version 1.0 of ebXML was brought to fruition by the following project teams, each of which had its own set of deliverables and schedule: ebXML Requirements, Business Process Methodology, Technical Architecture, Core Components, Transport/Routing and Packaging, Registry and Repository, Quality Review, Proof of Concept, Trading Partners, Marketing Awareness, and Ta-Security.

About UN/CEFACT and OASIS

UN/CEFACT (http://www.unece.org/cefact) is the United Nations body whose mandate covers worldwide policy and technical development in the area of trade facilitation and electronic business. Headquartered in Geneva, it has developed and promoted many tools for the facilitation of global business processes, including UN/EDIFACT, the international EDI standard. Its current work program includes topics such as Simpl-EDI and Object-Oriented EDI, and it strongly supports the development and implementation of open, interoperable, global standards and specifications for electronic business.

OASIS (http://www.oasis-open.org) is the international, not-for-profit consortium that advances electronic business by promoting open, collaborative development of interoperability specifications. OASIS operates XML.ORG, the noncommercial portal that delivers information on the use of XML in industry. The XML.ORG Registry provides an open community clearinghouse for distributing and locating XML application schemas, vocabularies, and related documents. OASIS serves as the home for industry groups and organizations interested in developing XML specifications.

How This Book Is Organized

This book consists of all seven ebXML 1.0 technical specifications produced by the ebXML initiative, as well as an official glossary that defines terminology and jargon specific to ebXML. You'll notice that every chapter name is followed immediately by a version number, such as v1.0 or v1.06, which indicates the official version of the document presented in that chapter. All chapters fall under the "1.0 family" of ebXML specifications, which was the most current version of ebXML as this book went to print.

Book Contents Overview

Following is a brief description of each chapter and appendix that appears in this book. Each chapter corresponds directly to an official ebXML technical specification, which should come as no surprise because this book is a printed rendition of the electronic documents produced by the ebXML initiative.

Chapter 1: Requirements Specification v1.06

This chapter corresponds to the ebXML specification document named *ebREQ*. Created by the ebXML Requirements Project Team, working in cooperation with representatives of international business and accredited standards organizations, the ebXML Requirements Specification defines ebXML and the ebXML effort, articulates the fundamental business requirements for ebXML, and defines specific requirements that all ebXML project teams must follow when preparing their deliverables.

Chapter 2: Technical Architecture Specification v1.04

This chapter corresponds to the ebXML specification document named *ebTA*. Although intended primarily for ebXML project teams, to help guide their work, this chapter details architectural aspects of ebXML that software implementers, international standards bodies, and other industry organizations will find invaluable when it comes to understanding the technical underpinnings of ebXML. Specifically, this chapter describes the underlying architecture of ebXML. It provides a high-level overview of ebXML and describes the relationships, interactions, and basic functionality of ebXML. As such, it should be used as a roadmap to learn: (1) what ebXML is, (2) what problems ebXML solves, and (3) core ebXML functionality and architecture.

Chapter 3: Business Process Specification Schema v1.01

This chapter corresponds to the ebXML specification document named *ebBPSS*, which describes the ebXML specification schema in Unified Modeling Language (UML) form as well as in Document Type Definition (DTD) and XML schema forms. The specification schema supports the specification of business transactions and the choreography of business transactions into business collaborations. Each business transaction can be implemented using one of many available standard patterns. These patterns determine the actual exchange of business documents and business signals between partners to achieve the required electronic commerce transaction. This chapter begins with an introduction to general concepts and semantics, after which it applies these semantics in a detailed discussion of each part of the model, and ultimately concludes by specifying all elements using UML, DTD, and XML schema representations.

Chapter 4: Registry Information Model v1.0

This chapter corresponds to the ebXML specification document named *ebRIM*, which specifies the information model for the ebXML Registry. The Registry provides a stable store where information submitted by a submitting organization is made persistent. Such information is used to facilitate ebXML-based B2B partnerships and transactions. Submitted content may be XML schema and documents, process descriptions, core components, context descriptions, UML models, information about parties, and even software components.

The Registry Information Model found in this chapter provides a blueprint, or high-level schema, for the ebXML Registry that implementers of ebXML follow. It does so by defining the types of objects stored in the Registry and how stored objects are organized in the Registry. In short, this chapter describes in detail what information is in the Registry and how that information is structured and organized. Whereas this chapter specifies the information model for the ebXML Registry, the next chapter (Chapter 5, "Registry Services Specification v1.0") describes how to build Registry services that provide access to the information in the ebXML Registry.

Chapter 5: Registry Services Specification v1.0

This chapter corresponds to the ebXML specification document named *ebRS*, which defines the interface to the ebXML Registry services as well as the interaction protocols, message definitions, and XML schema. The ebXML Registry provides a set of services that enables the sharing of information between interested parties for the purpose of enabling business process integration between such parties based on the ebXML specifications. The shared information is maintained as objects in a repository and is managed by the ebXML Registry services defined in this chapter (note that Chapter 4, "Registry Information Model v1.0," describes the types of metadata that are stored in the Registry as well as the relationships among the various metadata classes).

Chapter 6: Collaboration-Protocol Profile and Agreement Specification v1.0

This chapter corresponds to the ebXML specification document named *ebCPP*, which contains detailed definitions of the Collaboration-Protocol Profile (CPP) and Collaboration-Protocol Agreement (CPA).

As defined in Chapter 3, "Business Process Specification Schema v1.01," a business partner is an entity that engages in business transactions with another business partner(s). Each partner's capabilities (both commercial/business and technical) to engage in electronic message exchanges with other partners may be described by a document called a Trading-Partner Profile (TPP). The agreed interactions between two partners may be documented in a document called a Trading-Partner Agreement (TPA). A TPA may be created by computing the intersection of the two partners' TPPs. The message exchange capabilities of a party may be described by a Collaboration-Protocol Profile (CPP) within the TPP.

The message exchange agreement between two parties may be described by a CPA within a TPA. Included in the CPP and CPA are details regarding transport, messaging, security constraints, and bindings to a Business-Process-Specification (or for short, Process-Specification) document that contains the definition of the interactions between the two parties while engaging in a specified electronic business collaboration.

Chapter 7: Message Service Specification v1.0

This chapter corresponds to the ebXML specification document named *ebMS*, which defines the ebXML Message Service Protocol that enables the secure and reliable exchange of messages between two parties. Generally speaking, ebXML is a set of related specifications that realizes the vision of creating a single global electronic marketplace where enterprises of any size and in any geographical location can meet and conduct business with each other through the exchange of XML-based messages.

The Message Service Specification found in this chapter defines a communications protocol-neutral method for exchanging electronic business messages. It defines specific enveloping constructs that support reliable, secure delivery of business information. Furthermore, the specification defines a flexible enveloping technique that permits ebXML-compliant messages to contain payloads of any format type. This versatility ensures that legacy electronic business systems employing traditional syntaxes (e.g., UN/EDIFACT, ASC X12, or HL7) can leverage the advantages of the ebXML infrastructure along with users of emerging technologies.

Appendix A: ebXML Glossary

This appendix corresponds to the ebXML specification document named *ebGLOSS*, which defines terminology and jargon specific to ebXML.

Styles Used In This Book

Throughout this book, specific font styles and type faces have been employed to make it easy for you to distinguish between normal text and source code. The main text of the book is set in 10-point Palatino, while source code is set in 9-point Courier. The text you are reading this very moment, for example, is formatted using the style applied to the main text, which is used throughout the remainder of this book.

The following source code example, on the other hand, appears in the style applied to all source code listings in this book. Example of source code:

```
<?xml version="1.0"?>
<!DOCTYPE html PUBLIC "-//W3C//DTD XHTML 1.0 Strict//EN"
"http://www.w3.org/TR/xhtml1/DTD/xhtml1-strict.dtd">
<html xmlns="http://www.w3.org/1999/xhtml">
<head>
  <title>Welcome</title>
</head>
<body>
  <p>Welcome to this book!</p>
</body>
</html>
```

CHAPTER
1

Requirements Specification
v1.06
Requirements Team
11 May 2001

TABLE OF CONTENTS

1 Status of this Document

This document specifies an ebXML Technical Specification for the eBusiness community.

Distribution of this document is unlimited.

The document formatting is based on the Internet Society's Standard RFC format.

This version:
www.ebxml.org/specs/ebREQ.pdf

Latest version:
www.ebxml.org/specs/ebREQ.pdf

2 ebXML Participants

We would like to recognize the following for their significant participation to the development of this document.

Mike Rawlins	Rawlins EC Consulting - Team Leader
Mark Crawford	Logistics Management Institute - Team Editor
Don Rudie	Dun & Bradstreet
Thomas Warner	The Boeing Company
Kenji Itoh	Japan Association for Simplification of International Trade Procedures
Jean Kubler	UN/Economic Commission for Europe
Kathleen Tyson-Quah	KTQ Consulting Limited
David R.R. Webber	XML Global
Garrett Minakawa	Oracle Corporation
Turochas Fuad	Sun Microsystems Incorporated
Dr. Marcia McLure	McLure-Moynihan Inc.
Norbert Mikula	Data Channel
Christopher Lueder	Mitre Corporation

Scott Hinkelman	International Business Machines
Ravi Kackar	Kraft Foods
Doug Hopeman	XML Solutions
Gaile L. Spadin	Data Interchange Standards Association
Sangwon Lim	Korea Institute for Electronic Commerce

Additionally, valuable input was provided from the Team Leaders and various members of the other ebXML Project Teams.

3   Document Introduction

3.1   Summary of Contents of Document

This *ebXML Requirements Specification* represents the work of the ebXML *Requirements Project Team*. It defines ebXML and the ebXML effort, articulates business requirements for ebXML, and defines specific requirements that SHALL be addressed by the various ebXML project teams in preparing their deliverables.

The keywords MUST, MUST NOT, REQUIRED, SHALL, SHALL NOT, SHOULD, SHOULD NOT, RECOMMENDED, MAY, and OPTIONAL, when they appear in this document, are to be interpreted as described in Internet Engineering Task Force (IETF) Request For Comments (RFC) 2119.

3.2   Audience

The target audiences for this document are:

▼ ebXML Project Teams, as a foundation for developing their technical specifications

▼ Other interested parties, as a means to convey the purpose, scope, and vision of ebXML

3.3   Related Documents

ebXML Invitation
http://www.ebXML.org/documents/199909/ebXML_invitation.htm

ebXML Terms of Reference (TOR)

http://www.ebXML.org/documents/199909/terms_of_reference.htm

Recommendations for ebXML Kickoff Meeting -
UN/CEFACT/TMWG/N104

http://www.ebxml.org/documents/contributions/tm104.pdf

Technical Reports and Publications, World Wide Web Consortium,
http://www.w3.org/TR

3.4 Documentation Conventions

The following highlighting is used for non-normative commentary in this
document:

Note

General comments directed to all readers.

4 General Introduction

Electronic Business Extensible Markup Language (ebXML) is an international initiative established by the United Nations Centre for Trade Facilitation and Electronic Business (UN/CEFACT) and the Organization for the Advancement of
Structured Information Standards (OASIS) with a mandate to undertake a 15-18
month program of work. As identified in the ebXML Terms of Reference, the purpose of the ebXML initiative is to research and identify the technical basis upon
which the global implementation of XML can be standardized. The goal is to provide an XML-based open technical framework to enable XML to be utilized in a
consistent and uniform manner for the exchange of electronic business (eb) data
in application to application, application to human, and human to application
environments—thus *creating a single global electronic market.*™ [1]

ebXML is based on international standards and is itself intended to become an
international standard. A key aspect for the success of the ebXML initiative is

---

[1]"creating a single global electronic market" is a trademark of the ebXML Working Group
Key words for use in RFCs to Indicate Requirement Levels - Internet Engineering Task Force,
Request For Comments 2119, March 1997 *http://www.ietf.org/rfc/rfc2119.txt?number=2119*

adherence to the use of the W3C suite of XML and related Web technical specifications to the maximum extent practical. Although these specifications may not provide the optimal technical solution, acceptance of ebXML by the business community and technical community is tied to XML. However, certain key elements of the ebXML technical framework may require adopting alternative technologies and technical specifications—such as those of the Internet Engineering Task Force (IETF), International Organization for Standardization (ISO), Institute of Electrical and Electronics Engineers (IEEE), International Electrotechnical Commission (IEC), UN/CEFACT, OASIS, and the Object Management Group (OMG).

ebXML operates under the procedures identified in the ebXML Terms of Reference.

Note

4.1 ebXML Vision and Scope

4.1.1 ebXML Vision

The ebXML vision is to deliver:

> *"A single set of internationally agreed upon technical specifications that consist of common XML semantics and related document structures to facilitate global trade."*

These ebXML technical specifications are intended to create a *Single Global Electronic Market.*™ To create this single global electronic market, this single set of ebXML technical specifications:

▼ SHALL be fully compliant with W3C XML technical specifications holding a recommended status[2]

▼ SHALL provide for interoperability within and between ebXML compliant trading partner applications

▼ SHALL maximize interoperability and efficiency while providing a transition path from accredited electronic data interchange (EDI) standards and developing XML business standards

▼ SHALL be submitted to an appropriate internationally recognized accredited standards body for publication as an international standard

4.1.2 ebXML Scope

The ebXML initiative is targeted at every sector of the business community, from international conglomerate to small and medium sized enterprises engaged in

---

[2] Technical Reports and Publications, World Wide Web Consortium http://www.w3.org/TR

business-to-business and business-to-consumer trade. With that audience in mind, the ebXML initiative is committed to developing and delivering specifications that will be used by all trading partners interested in maximizing XML interoperability within and across trading partner communities.

4.2   ebXML Requirements Specification Purpose and Scope

The *ebXML Requirements Specification* purpose and scope are defined in the following sub-sections.

4.2.1   ebXML Requirements Specification Purpose

This *Requirements Specification* has two primary purposes. The first of these is to provide clearly articulated requirements from representatives of international business and accredited standards organizations. These requirements are intended to serve as a foundation for all other ebXML specifications and SHOULD assist the ebXML project team members in developing their deliverables in a consistent manner. This specification is also intended to convey to interested parties the purpose, scope, and vision of ebXML.

4.2.2   ebXML Requirements Specification Scope

This *ebXML Requirements Specification* applies to the work underway within the current ebXML project teams. Each project team has provided input to this document to ensure consensus with its contents. In addition to the *Requirements Project Team*, project teams currently chartered by the ebXML Steering Committee are:

▼ Business Process

▼ Technical Architecture

▼ Core Components

▼ Transport/Routing and Packaging

▼ Registry and Repository

▼ Trading Partner

▼ Proof of Concept

In addition, the following special management support teams are chartered by the ebXML Executive Committee:

▼ Quality Review

▼ Marketing Awareness

4.3   General ebXML Principles

General ebXML principles to be followed in developing ebXML deliverables are to create technical specifications that:

▼ Enable simple, easy and ubiquitous electronic business through the use of XML

▼ Use W3C XML technical specifications holding recommended status to the maximum extent practicable

▼ Provide a global cross-industry open, interoperable standard for business-to-business and business-to-consumer trade

▼ Coalesce the structure and content components of divergent XML initiatives into a single useable XML business standard

▼ Provide impetus so that common resources currently engaged in short-term vertical solutions SHALL be marshaled to reach a common long-term, horizontal solution

▼ Support vertical and horizontal segments of industry and business participants

▼ Avoid proprietary solutions that impose financial or software requirements constraints on ebXML users to buy, install or programmatically support any ebXML unique software products in the conduct of business information exchange

▼ Strive to minimize costs of doing business electronically

▼ Provide multi-lingual support

▼ Accommodate national and international trade requirements

▼ Provide a migration path from accredited EDI and developing XML business standards

▼ Apply when possible the simplification principles of SIMAC Business Requirements[3]

---

[3]*SIMAC Future Vision Statement* - UN/CEFACT Ad Hoc Working Group on Simple-EDI and Forms and Web Based EDI (SIMAC) - UN/CEFACT, TRADE/CEFACT/1999/CRP.12 http://www.unece.org/trade/untdid/download/99cp12.pdf

5 Business Requirements

This section describes the business requirements for business to be conducted electronically. The business requirements identified in this section are oriented toward using XML for electronic business, but most of the requirements are applicable to implementation with other technologies as well.

The scope of the ebXML business requirements is to meet the needs for the business side of both business-to-business (B2B) and business-to-consumer (B2C) activities. Consumer requirements of the B2C model are beyond the scope of the ebXML technical specifications. Application-to-application (A2A) exchanges within an enterprise may also be able to use the ebXML technical specifications, however ebXML A2A solutions SHALL not be developed at the expense of simplified B2B and B2C solutions.

Note For ease of reading, the term business is to be interpreted as interchangeable with for-profit, non-profit, not-for profit, and government entities.

Note For the purposes of this document, Application-to-Application is defined as the computer-to-computer exchange of business information without human intervention both within and across enterprise boundaries.

The business requirements to be addressed by the ebXML initiative are divided into nine core areas - General Business, Electronic Business, Globalization, Openness, Usability/Interoperability, Security, Legal, Digital Signatures, and Organizational. Each of these requirements is identified in the following sections.

5.1 General Business Requirements

Business has a real need to use new technology with minimized investment to gain competitive advantage. The advent of the Internet and World Wide Web has proven to offer such benefits. However, realizing these benefits requires a functionally neutral standard method of exchanging data. Specifically, business needs a solution that provides:

▼ A single, consistent, simple approach to using XML for electronic business processes in both the B2B and B2C environments

▼ A process and recommendation for ebXML conformance

▼ Support for both vertical (e.g. industry, functional, organizational) and horizontal (e.g. cross-industry, multi-functional, organizationally neutral) solutions regardless of the sophistication of the user

▼ Support for a range of implementations from basic, low cost solutions appropriate for Small and Medium Enterprise (SME) deployment, to comprehensive, complex implementations using all optional features appropriate to large enterprises

▼ A range of usage from using core features in ad hoc, informal exchanges to highly formal, structured exchanges

▼ A single consistent modeling language and methodology

▼ Support for current business models and practices as well as new ones developed through business process modeling

▼ A business process metamodel that supports individually developed business process models

▼ Design rules for developing ebXML compliant XML documents that are based on approved W3C schema specifications

▼ Syntactically neutral core components

▼ XML syntax based boilerplate schemas and tags to support individual trading partner business processes that -

    ▼ eliminate duplication of effort
    ▼ provide support for XML metadata
    ▼ clearly identify core, mandatory features, and optional features
    ▼ provide a mechanism for full specification of semantic meaning

▼ Fully interoperable transport, routing, and packaging solutions

▼ Security solutions that meet business confidentiality requirements

▼ A single recognized international standards organization to oversee continued ebXML work

▼ An open development process with no barriers to entry

▼ Open, readily accessible, perpetually free technical specifications and standards

▼ A solution that minimizes costs for development, maintenance, and use

Note

> Business looks to XML as a means of gaining competitive advantage through leveraging new technology. Minimizing the cost of doing business electronically is a key element in achieving a competitive advantage. The cost of doing business electronically can be grouped into acquisition, development, deployment and customization, integration with business applications, and operations and support. It is expected that using XML for electronic business will be less costly than traditional forms of EDI and other existing electronic commerce technologies in each of these areas. This expected cost reduction is a driving force for considering XML over traditional EDI technologies.

5.2   Conducting Electronic Business Using ebXML

Business applications need to be able to exchange structured business documents (encoded in XML) with a corresponding application of another enterprise to support a business process. This exchange may either be completely without human intervention, as is the case with traditional EDI, or with some level of human intervention to correct missing or erroneous data. Business applications may also need to exchange structured business documents with intermediaries such as portals and brokers. Because a majority of businesses do not have sophisticated IT architectures, business applications will need to exchange structured business documents with trading partners who will be limited to viewing and manually processing both inbound and outbound transactions. Business applications also require information exchange mechanisms that provide for the exchange of pure XML payloads but may also support plug-and-play, shrink-wrapped, syntactically-neutral solutions.

Additionally, business applications may also need to:

▼ Be able to generate business documents encoded in XML and other syntax structures that can be used in traditional computer to computer exchanges as well as being displayed using an associated style sheet keyed to a specific presentation format; such as the appropriate U.N. Layout Key for Trade Documents or a trading partner specified format.[4]

▼ Enable data entry of business documents using a specified presentation format; such as the appropriate U.N. Layout Key for Trade Documents or a trading partner specified format. The data entry SHALL result in an ebXML compliant encoded document representing the business information.

---

[4]*United Nations Layout Key for Trade Documents, Recommendation No. 1, second edition,* adopted by the Working Party on Facilitation of International Trade Procedures, Geneva, UN/ECE, ECE/TRADE/137, March 1981 http://www.unece.org/cefact/rec/rec01en.htm

5.3 Globalization

Global solutions are critical in today's ever expanding marketplace. The underlying purpose of ebXML is to facilitate international trade. To achieve *"a single global electronic market"* that such facilitation implies, it is critical to simplify existing exchange standards methodologies and harmonize divergent approaches. This simplification and harmonization can be achieved through developing a business metamodel in conjunction with syntax neutral core components. Both of these deliverables SHALL accommodate divergent national and multi-national process requirements, and SHOULD support backward compatibility with the developing ebXML technical framework.

To simplify development efforts, all work SHALL use English. To support globalization, all ebXML technical specifications SHALL be translatable into other natural languages. Translation into other natural languages is the responsibility of the intended user, although such translations SHOULD be supported in the ebXML repository. Regardless of language, and in keeping with the requirements of W3C XML 1.0, all work SHALL be compliant with Unicode and ISO/IEC 10646 for characters, IETF RFC 1766 for language identification tags, ISO 639 for language name codes, and ISO 3166 for country name codes.[5 6 7 8 9 10 11 12]

5.3.1 Openness

Openness is a critical aspect of ebXML. Business requires the ability to easily access ebXML technical specifications without regard to "membership", or payment of access and/or use fees. ebXML technical specifications SHALL be

---

[5]*Extensible Markup Language (XML) 1.0, (Second Edition)*, World Wide Web Consortium, October 2000 http://www.w3.org/TR/REC-xml

[6]*Information technology — Universal Multiple-Octet Coded Character Set (UCS) — Part 1: Architecture and Basic Multilingual Plane*, International Organization for Standardization, ISO 10646-1:1993(E), 1993 http://www.iso.ch

[7]*Tags for the Identification of Languages*, Internet Engineering Task Force, Request For Comments 1766, March 1995 http://www.ietf.org/rfc/rfc1766.txt

[8]*Code for the Representation of Names of Languages*, 1st Edition, International Standardization Organization, ISO 639-1, 1988 http://www.iso.ch

[9]*Codes for the Representation of Names of Languages: Alpha-3.* 1st Edition. Geneva: International Standardization Organization, ISO 639-2, 1998 http://www.iso.ch

[10]*Country codes,* International Standardization Organization, ISO 3166-1,1997 http://www.iso.ch

[11]*Country Subdivision Code*, International Standardization Organization, ISO 3166-2, December 1998 http://www.iso.ch

[12]*Code for formerly used names of countries, International Standardization Organization,* International Standardization Organization, ISO 3166-3, March 1999 http://www.iso.ch

completely open to all potential users so as to eliminate the barriers for entry. Openness requires several key components to ensure viability. Chief among these is an open, easily accessible registry and repository for the ebXML technical specifications.

5.3.2   *Registry and Repository*

A registry is required to allow process owners to submit, classify, register and up-date mapping templates, business process specifications, and data interchange specifications. This registry MUST have an interface that supports access by humans as well as computer applications. This registry MUST support an agreed upon security protocol.

A repository is required for storage and retrieval of various items that support performing business electronically. There are two distinct sets of business requirements on the repository: a set dealing with managing the workflow of developing standard components that are stored in the repository, and a set dealing with application usage of the repository. Additionally, the repository MUST support the information needs of the ebXML work group and project teams, as well as ebXML technical specification users with respect to glossaries and products.

Note

> A registry is a mechanism whereby relevant documents and metadata about them can be registered such that a pointer to their location, and all their metadata, can be retrieved as the result of a query. A repository is a location or a set of distributed locations where documents pointed at by the registry reside and from which they can be retrieved by conventional (http / ftp) means, perhaps with additional authentication/permission layers.

The ebXML Registry and Repository SHALL support the concept of a network of registries and repositories that can intercommunicate via the interfaces specified by the ebXML *Registry and Repository Project Team.* A registry can be established by an industry group or standards organization and can intercommunicate with any number of repositories. In addition, content with a repository can reference content within another repository. The concept of a single repository is not scalable, nor does it promote the idea of a global web.

If ebXML is to exist beyond its initial 18-month timeframe, then ebXML SHOULD maintain responsibility for ebXML technical specifications, ebXML work group deliverables, and ebXML glossaries in an ebXML-supported repository. However, if the decision is made that ebXML will not exist after the initial set of deliverables, or that ebXML will not maintain or support its own repository, then ebXML MUST determine if repository oversight responsibilities for ebXML technical specifications SHOULD transition to UN/CEFACT, OASIS, or some other existing XML business standards organization or consortium.

5.4 Usability/Interoperability

Usability and interoperability of the ebXML technical framework are critical business requirements. Components of usability and interoperability are architecture; transport, routing, and packaging; extensibility; and leveraging existing technology. Each of these is addressed in the following sub-sections.

5.4.1 Architecture

This is a primary requirement of the ebXML initiative. To maximize interoperability, the ebXML architecture SHOULD support

▼ Common Business Processes - Both entities involved in the exchange of data MUST be engaged in executing the same transaction in the context of a business process

▼ Common Semantics - Common meaning, as distinct from words, expression, or presentation

▼ Common Vocabulary - A direct correspondence between words and meaning

▼ Common Character Encoding

UNICODE, which is specified in the W3C XML Version 1.0 technical specification, provides this.

▼ Common Expression - Common set of XML element names, attributes and common usage of those attributes, common approach to document structure

▼ Common Security Implementations

▼ Common Data Transfer Protocol

▼ Common Network Layer

As with other non-functional requirements, some aspects of achieving interoperability may conflict with other non-functional requirements. Where a requirement is not met, software can usually be developed to provide a bridge. However, such bridges may increase costs of development, implementation, or both, and conflict with cost minimization. In other cases, achieving interoperability enhances other requirements. For example, maximizing interoperability helps to achieve platform independence.

5.4.2 Transport, Routing and Packaging

Any exchange of business information requires fully described transport, routing, and packaging methodologies. These descriptions MUST be based on a program language definition independent of the service interface required for systems to control the messaging system for the purpose of sending and receiving messages. These descriptions SHOULD identify the behavior of the messaging system required to:

▼ Realize reliable secure sending and receiving of messages over any network capable of carrying XML

▼ Support syntax-neutral definition of the information that needs to be retained

▼ Detail the format and structure of the wrapper, header, and any other data within the message - to include signatures and encryption

▼ Query ebXML servers (such as ebXML compliant message handling systems or registries) for the services they support

5.4.3 Extensibility

Businesses seek solutions that provide for a certain level of customization beyond core standards. This extensibility is necessary to ensure internally unique business process requirements can be addressed beyond the scope of standards used for information exchanges between businesses. One example of this requirement is customization beyond core standards to support exchanges within an enterprise. Another is customization to support application/database to human exchanges. ebXML MUST ensure extensibility is facilitated while ensuring conformance with core standards.

5.4.4 Leveraging Existing Technology

Leveraging existing technology encompasses both the ability to inter-operate with existing technology as well as the ability to migrate to the new technology. Each of these is discussed in the following sub-sections.

5.4.4.1 Compatibility with Existing Technology and EB Standards and Practices

Businesses already have in place extensive EDI architectures and business solutions based on accredited EDI standards; and customized sub-sets in the form of implementation conventions based on those standards. Additionally, many businesses are implementing XML solutions that are based on the technical specifications issued by the World Wide Web Consortium (W3C) and the XML-based business standards of various competing XML groups—such as RosettaNet, BizTalk, XML.ORG, the Open Applications Group (OAG). Although the ebXML solution will facilitate a single global electronic market, and although its technical framework will provide a single set of technical specifications, businesses will still require the ability to inter-operate their existing EDI and XML solutions with solutions built on the ebXML framework.

As part of compatibility, businesses require a technical framework that reuses common elements regardless of syntax. To ensure a syntax neutral solution, ebXML MUST identify and define those items considered common across XML business data exchanges. Common items are semantic units at any level that stay consistent across contexts, and therefore are reusable both within and between business exchange messages. Business process models will help define common items and provide their context. This context will in turn define the precise use of common items in messages exchanged among parties. ebXML MUST describe these items in terms that are independent of implementation syntax. This syntax neutral approach will enable their reuse for not only XML documents, but other syntax-based transactions as well.

The ebXML technical framework MUST adopt—or if needed, develop—a methodology to consistently build or derive core components, including methods to encourage reuse and provide for extensions. ebXML MUST identify element names that can apply across business processes and contexts yet still allow for translation into leading spoken languages. All ebXML work SHALL generate the content of core components independent of implementation syntax, but with references to data structures in XML messages and EDI transactions. The ebXML solution SHALL identify attributes that describe the context of the components also in terms independent of syntax.

5.4.4.2 Migration from Existing EDI and XML Solutions

Businesses seek maximum interoperability between their applications and trading partner applications. This can be achieved by a single way of doing business electronically, i.e., a single standard for using XML for electronic business. However, many businesses also have a considerable investment in existing standards-based EDI and emerging XML business approaches. These businesses require a mechanism and migration path for accommodating legacy EDI solutions based on accredited standards and XML solutions already in progress or implemented. Although migration from existing EDI and XML solutions is a key element of ebXML, the ebXML solution will ensure maximizing interoperability takes precedence in developing the ebXML technical specifications.

> **It is beyond the current scope of the ebXML initiative to develop specific migration and transformation methods to include mapping services, communication channels, and architecture support from traditional EDI architectures.**

Note

5.5 Security

Businesses have a high level requirement that appropriate security technology be applied to protect information involved in business processes. Aspects of security may be required at various layers of a business process; at an outsourcing/transaction layer, at a session layer (i.e., for the duration of a network session in which data is exchanged) or applied to a single, stand-alone document instance. In addition, application of security to a particular exchange or document instance MUST be determined by the business needs, and allow unrestricted and unsecured interchanges if the business process requires this. All, some, or no security features may be required in any particular exchange of business information. The following requirements are general security definitions:

▼ Confidentiality - Only sender and receiver can interpret document contents

▼ Authentication of sender - Assurance of the sender's identity

▼ Authentication of receiver - Assurance of the receiver's identity

▼ Integrity - Assurance that the message contents have not been altered

▼ Non-repudiation of Origin - The sender can not deny having sent the message

▼ Non-repudiation of Receipt - The receiver can not deny having received the message

▼ Archiving - It MUST be possible to reconstruct the semantic intent of a document several years after the creation of the document

The understanding of these security requirements is also subject to the following related requirements; Legal, Digital Signatures, Interoperability, and Third Party Trust relationships. For example; The Archiving, Authentication, and Non-Repudiation of Origin and Receipt may be performed by a trusted third party through which the Parties to a transaction agree to channel transaction messages in order to provide independent historical proof that the transaction took place at a specific time and on specific terms. This time period is subject to the archiving and record retention requirements of particular situations. In general, businesses might require archiving and retrieval of up to 30 years after document creation.

5.5.1 Legal

Beyond the security requirements identified in section 6.5, the following additional legal requirements exist:

▼ Comply with the requirements of UN/CEFACT recommendation 14 - Authentication of Trade Documents by Means Other Than Signature[13]

▼ Provide versioning support to facilitate reconstructing the semantic meaning of transactions in accordance with the underlying transaction format used

▼ Ensure full audit capability is supported

▼ Ensure all transmitted data is well defined by a minimal set of metadata

▼ Ensure a mechanism provides for identifying completeness of a transaction

5.5.2 *Digital Signatures*

Digital signatures, or electronic signatures, have security and legal implications that directly affect electronic business requirements. As more and more government bodies define digital signatures, and enact legislation that adopts such techniques as having the same force of law as traditional signatures, new technology solutions MUST accommodate these business requirements.

The following definition and statement of compliance requirements is taken from Article 6 of UN Commission on International Trade Law, Working Group on Electronic Commerce, Draft Guide to Enactment of the UNCITRAL Model Law on Electronic Signatures (A/CN.9/WG.IV/WP.88):

1. Where the law requires a signature of a person, that requirement is met in relation to a data message if an electronic signature is used which is as reliable as was appropriate for the purpose for which the data message was generated or communicated, in light of all the circumstances, including any relevant agreement.

2. Paragraph (1) applies whether the requirement referred to therein is in the form of an obligation or whether the law simply provides consequences for the absence of a signature.

3. An electronic signature is considered to be reliable for the purpose of satisfying the requirement *referred to in paragraph (1) if:*

   a.) *the signature creation data are, within the context in which they are used, linked to the signatory and to no other person*

   b.) *the signature creation data were, at the time of signing, under the control of the signatory and of no other person*

---

[13]*Authentication of Trade Documents by Means Other Than Signature*, Recommendation No. 14, second edition, adopted by the Working Party on Facilitation of International Trade Procedures, UN/ECE, TRADEWP.4/INF.63, March 1979 http://www.unece.org/cefact/rec/rec14en.htm

> c.) *any alteration to the electronic signature, made after the time of signing, is detectable; and*
>
> d.) *where a purpose of the legal requirement for a signature is to provide assurance as to the integrity of the information to which it relates, any alteration made to that information after the time of signing is detectable.*

The ebXML technical framework MUST support electronic transactions that provide for electronic signatures at an appropriate level within the transaction to meet requirements of both the sender and receiver in keeping with the forgoing definition and attributes.

5.6 Management

If ebXML is to be successful in both the short and long term, and if the ebXML technical framework is to be adopted by the international business community, then management issues associated with both organizational structure and participation MUST be addressed. The following sub-sections identify the business requirements for each of these areas.

5.6.1 Organizational Structure

The ebXML initiative is an eighteen-month effort to develop a technical framework. To ensure efficiency of operation and success in achieving the ebXML vision, sufficient organizational controls MUST be put in-place as quickly as possible. Further, there exists the possibility that ebXML will become more than a short term initiative. As such, long-term requirements for managing ebXML MUST be defined and addressed in the near term to ensure a smooth transition from short- to long-term management. Further, if such a long-term organization becomes reality, processes MUST be adopted for recasting ebXML as an internationally accredited standards body.

5.6.2 Participation

The ebXML initiative relies heavily on technical expert participation. This participation MUST be free of organizational requirements that restrict or otherwise inhibit participation of anyone. Further, participation SHOULD be limited to the individual and not at the organizational level. This will ensure each technical expert is given an equal footing in the organization, management, and work effort of ebXML.

6 ebXML Technical Framework Requirements

This section identifies specific requirements for achieving the ebXML technical framework through the work of each of the ebXML project teams. These requirements have been developed in close coordination with those project teams to ensure consensus on their content. These high level requirements are closely aligned with the business requirements in section two of this document and are consistent with the vision, purpose, scope and guiding principles contained in Section Five. These high level requirements are carefully designed to provide a road map for the respective project teams as they drill down to more detailed requirements in preparation for developing their ebXML deliverables. As each of these deliverables becomes a reality, they will contribute to the developing ebXML technical specifications as part of building the ebXML technical framework as illustrated in Figure 6-1.

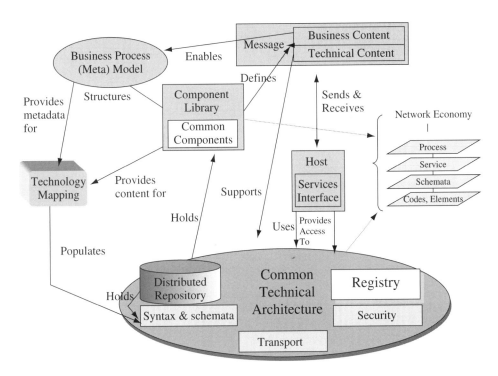

FIGURE 6-1 ebXML Technical Framework

6.1   General Requirements

The following general requirements, in conjunction with the business requirements stated in Section Six, apply to each project team. Deliverables for each of the project teams MUST -

▼ Be developed in compliance with the purpose, scope, and guiding principles identified in Section Five

▼ Meet the business needs articulated in Section Two

▼ Be fully compliant with approved ebXML technical specifications

▼ Clearly identify core, mandatory features, and optional features

▼ Clearly define conformance requirements

▼ Support the requirements of each project team as identified in the following sub-sections.

6.2   Requirements

The *Requirements Project Team's* initial task was to produce this *ebXML Requirements Specification*. In addition, the *Requirements Project Team* SHALL:

▼ Develop follow-on requirements documents in support of the ebXML Executive Committee and ebXML Steering Committee that meet the requirements contained in section 4 of this document

▼ Review, evaluate, and assimilate follow-on requirements submitted by external organizations for consideration by ebXML

▼ Provide assistance as required to the *Quality Review Team* on ebXML requirements issues to include at a minimum a requirements traceability matrix

6.3   Business Process

The *Business Process Project Team* detailed requirements and deliverables SHALL:

▼ Provide a technical specification for business process definition (BPDS), enabling an organization to express its business processes so that they are understandable by other organizations, thereby enabling integration of business processes (See for example eCo strategic framework - services and interactions)

▼ Provide an explicitly specified process metamodel that is not merely implied by instantiations or derivations

- ▼ the metamodel SHALL provide set of rules to define the business processes—rules, semantics and syntax
▼ Provide a BPDS that is usable -
  - ▼ globally
  - ▼ cross-industry
  - ▼ by small, medium, and large organizations
  - ▼ by for-profit, government, and non-profit organizations
▼ Provide a BPDS that enables an organization to express its business processes to such an extent that other organizations can discover -
  - ▼ the kind of organization the process belongs to
  - ▼ the business processes belonging to an organization
  - ▼ the interaction points in the organization's business process in order to determine whether and how to engage in business
  - ▼ the kinds of information exchanges required to conduct a particular interaction in the business process
  - ▼ company interactions, and services and categorizations of them
▼ Provide for BPDS compatibility by -
  - ▼ allowing for forward migration from existing frameworks to the degree possible
  - ▼ carrying forward accumulated best of breed experience such as—OAG, RosettaNet, HL7—into the ebXML "superset"
  - ▼ enabling mapability between content provider defined processes
  - ▼ enabling organizations or industry verticals to be able to compare business processes
▼ Provide for BPDS re-usability/extensibility by -
  - ▼ allowing a company to 're-use' and extend standard, template, or actual business processes as starting points for definition of specific business processes
  - ▼ encouraging industry verticals to base their model on the high level framework
  - ▼ supporting re-usable data components
  - ▼ supporting re-usable process components
▼ Enable business processes to be accessible and readable by -
  - ▼ making BPDS-based processes machine readable
  - ▼ expressing processes defined under BPDS in parsable, navigable XML
  - ▼ making processes defined under BPDS visually (diagrammatically) viewable
  - ▼ identifying at least one industry standard based tool or technique, through which BPDS compliant processes can be defined through diagrammatic drawing

▼ Provide a process to create and maintain a -

Note

> This process SHALL be developed in coordination with the *Core Components Project Team's* developing process for identifying core components.

- ▼ glossary of terms related to business process methodology vocabulary such as—functional, non-functional, vertical, message, segment, data type—using TMWG Unified Modeling Methodology document Annex 1 as a starting point
- ▼ glossary of terms specific to each business process to be modeled
- ▼ glossary of XML tags
- ▼ library of documents based on identified services and interactions
- ▼ web site for ready access to glossaries

▼ Be developed in conjunction with the *Registry and Repository Project Team* to incorporate technical specifications, models, and required glossaries into the ebXML repository

6.4 Technical Architecture

The *Technical Architecture Project Team* detailed requirements and deliverables SHALL:

▼ Provide a view for integration of business processes among ad-hoc or established independent business partners by electronic means

▼ Reduce the need for collaborative business partners to have individual and expensive prior agreement on how to integrate business processes

▼ Provide a high-level business-centric view of distributed e-business processes

▼ Specify the roles, interactions, and interfaces among the various ebXML specification components such as—the business process metamodel, core components, registry and repository, message handling, and collaboration profiles and agreements.

▼ Allow for both business processes and enabling technologies to evolve independently while retaining long-term investments in both

▼ Integrate with new and legacy systems throughout the enterprise

▼ Leverage existing technologies and standards

▼ In coordination with BP process specification and core components identification, provide for naming conventions for technical and business content in the technical architecture

▼ Provide design guidelines for ebXML compliant messages

6.5   Core Components

The *Core Components Project Team* detailed requirements and deliverables SHALL:

▼ Be developed in conjunction with the *Business Process Project Team*

▼ Identify a methodology for describing core components within the framework of the Business Process metamodel

▼ Define core component content and structure

▼ Support "re-use" and extensibility

▼ Provide methodology and examples for XML and EDI instantiation

▼ Enable creation of XML business standards

The *Core Components Project Team* SHALL develop core components that SHALL:

▼ Be syntax independent

> **Core components SHALL not be specifically aligned with any existing syntax based semantics such as ANSI ASC X12 or UN/EDIFACT.**   **Note**

▼ Be defined to ensure separation of common core components versus new extensions

▼ Incorporate where appropriate ISO/IEC 11179 rules[14] [15] [16] [17] [18] [19]

---

[14]*Information Technology — Specification and standardization of data elements — Part 1: Framework for the specification and standardization of data elements*, International Standardization Organization, ISO 11179-1, 1999 http://www.iso.ch

[15]*Information Technology — Specification and standardization of data elements — Part 2: Classification for data elements*, International Standardization Organization, ISO 11179-2, 2000 http://www.iso.ch

[16]*Information Technology — Specification and standardization of data elements — Part 3: Basic attributes of data elements*, International Standardization Organization, ISO 11179-3, 1994 http://www.iso.ch

[17]*Information Technology — Specification and standardization of data elements — Part 4: Rules and guidelines for the formulation of data definitions*, International Standardization Organization, ISO 11179-4, 1995 http://www.iso.ch

[18]*Information Technology — Specification and standardization of data elements — Part 5: Naming and identification principles for data elements*, International Standardization Organization, ISO 11179-5, 1995 http://www.iso.ch

[19]*Information Technology — Specification and standardization of data elements — Part 6: Registration of data elements*, International Standardization Organization, ISO 11179-6, 1997 http://www.iso.ch

▼ Use semantics solutions that accommodate currently defined accredited EDI semantics where they add value

▼ Use a single consistent set of terminology

▼ Support context sensitive core components

6.6 Transport/Routing and Packaging

The *Transport/Routing and Packaging Project Team* detailed requirements and deliverables SHALL:

▼ Specify how to envelope business documents in regard to -

    ▼ related messages in a collection
    ▼ physical and/or logical addressing of destination for messages

▼ Specify exchange at the application level

▼ Provide for flexible transaction boundaries

▼ Provide for reliable messaging and error handling

▼ Identify messaging routing

▼ Meet security requirements

▼ Provide for audit trails

▼ Define and meet acceptable levels of quality of service

▼ Support platform independent interoperability

▼ Support restart and recovery

Note   For additional technical details, see the Transport, Routing, and Packaging detail requirements specification.

6.7 Registry and Repository

The Registry and Repository Project Team detailed requirements and deliverables SHALL develop detailed blueprints for an ebXML Registry that:

▼ Uses an open management processes

▼ Has open and perpetually free access

▼ Supports technical specification submission and management

▼ Supports required system services

6.7.1 *Technical Specification Submission and Management*

The registry and repository specifications SHALL address:

▼ Technical specification storage and retrieval for development and run-time views

▼ Object Storage - the ability to store objects in their original form, not limited to -

   ▼ ebXML CPP/CPA/Business Process Schema
   ▼ classification schemes
   ▼ code lists
   ▼ related data, example instances of document definitions, executable code, style sheets
   ▼ relationships between objects, e.g., storage of semantically equivalent objects

▼ A flexible life cycle management, e.g., deprecation and removal

▼ Support for a role-based security model

▼ Support for work request submissions to store associated supporting materials in any electronic format, e.g., PowerPoint documents, audio files, images

▼ Indexing of metadata across all entries in Registry

6.7.2 *Required System Services*

The Registry and Repository specifications SHALL address the following required services.

▼ Query services the ability to send a request and retrieve results from a physical storage mechanism, e.g., exact or similar matches and navigation

▼ Logging services the ability to store transactional events, query events, and metrics

6.8 Trading Partner

The *Trading Partner Project Team* detailed requirements and deliverables SHALL:

▼ Define a collaboration-protocol profile (CPP) by which a party can be found through a discovery process. The profile indicates what kind of electronic business-to-business interactions the party is capable of conducting. The CPP defines the technical components of the interactions, such as supported communication profiles, security information, general messaging specifications, and the definition of the collaborative processes that the party supports in interactions with other parties. Multiple profiles for specific processes, locations, individuals, and systems can exist within a single organization.

Note

The discovery process itself as a business process that is not within the scope of the Trading-Partner team.

▼ Define a collaboration-protocol agreement (CPA), which records agreement between two parties on how to do electronic business with each other. The CPA can be viewed as the intersection of the two parties' CPPs. It defines the common technical capabilities and the particular services that each provides to the other.

Note

It is a long-term goal to extend the CPA to define multiparty interactions.

▼ Define the content of the CPP such that a software process can compose a CPA from the CPPs of the two parties.

▼ Define the CPA such that it serves the purpose of a configuration document that can be used to configure the two parties' run-time systems to perform the desired business.

▼ Work with the Transport-Routing-Packaging team to ensure that the CPP/CPA provides the needed support for message exchanges and that the message header provides the fields needed to support electronic business under control of a CPA.

▼ Define the collaborative processes that the party can engage in with another party based on the ebXML model for the business process. Elements of the definition include:

   ▼ The requests that can be sent to the party
   ▼ The business document schema for each request
   ▼ The response messages that can be sent as a result of each request
   ▼ The choreography of the message exchanges

6.9   Proof of Concept

The *Proof of Concept Project Team* detailed requirements and deliverables SHALL facilitate developing prototype demonstrations for ebXML technical specifications. These prototype demonstrations SHALL:

▼ Demonstrate feasibility and interoperability of each of the ebXML technical specifications within a business domain

▼ Demonstrate viability of overall ebXML technical framework

7 ebXML Organizational and Procedural Requirements

The ebXML Executive Committee MUST put in place organizational and procedural processes as soon as possible. These organizational and procedural processes are critical to enable the various ebXML project teams to make sound decisions in developing their requirements and deliverables. These organizational and procedural processes MUST:

▼ Facilitate the efforts of the *Requirements Project Team* and the various Executive Committee support teams identified in Section Seven.

▼ Support each of the functional project teams to meet their requirements

In developing these organizational and procedural processes, the Executive Committee SHALL:

▼ Follow the purpose, scope, and guiding principles identified in Section Five

▼ Meet the business needs articulated in Section Six

▼ Facilitate the general requirements in Section Seven

▼ Support the requirements of each project team as identified in Section Seven

These organizational and procedural processes MUST provide for

▼ An open and consensus driven ebXML management process

▼ An open, timely, and consensus driven ebXML products development process that

  ▼ is responsive to business needs
  ▼ has sufficient controls to prevent creation of equivalent components

▼ An open, timely, and consensus-driven ebXML technical specifications approval process that is responsive to business needs

Additionally, the Executive and Steering Committees, in conjunction with the full ebXML Working Group MUST determine:

▼ The requirements for short- and long-term ebXML relationships with UN/CEFACT, W3C, ANSI, ISO and other standards bodies

▼ The requirements for short- and long-term ebXML relationships with OASIS, BizTalk, RosettaNet, OAG, and other XML business standards bodies

▼ A common ebXML technical specification template to be utilized by each of the project teams in developing their technical specifications

▼ The appropriateness of moving ebXML technical specifications to recognized international standards under the cognizance of an international standards body

▼ The single body that is responsible for long term maintenance of the ebXML technical specifications, repository, and supporting mechanisms - OASIS, UN/CEFACT, or ebXML

▼ The process for long term maintenance of the ebXML technical specifications

▼ ebXML funding methodology

▼ The need for and definition of measures of success

7.1 Executive Committee Support

To help meet the requirements identified above, the Executive Committee has established three Executive Committee support teams. The requirements for these support teams are contained in the following subsections.

7.1.1 Quality Review

The *Quality Review Team* SHALL review all candidate technical specifications prior to each public review period and final vote and SHALL identify via clear, concise written documentation:

▼ Deviations from the overall requirements specifications

▼ Deviations from the ebXML traceability matrix

▼ Completeness

▼ Technical consistency within the overall ebXML technical framework.

▼ Proposed solutions to identified problems or gaps where deemed appropriate by the QR team

▼ The *Quality Review Team* SHALL consider the following features of the candidate material:

▼ Scope and alignment with ebXML vision

▼ Completeness

▼ Satisfies ebXML requirements

▼ Consistency with Technical Architecture

▼ Consistency with component naming rules

▼ Addresses Security Risk Assessment document

▼ Editorial quality, that is…

  ▼ uses ebXML template
  ▼ adheres to the ebXML documentation style guidelines
  ▼ uses consistent language (glossary)
  ▼ uses correct grammar
  ▼ uses correct spelling
  ▼ avoids unsubstantiated rhetoric
  ▼ contains no logical inconsistencies
  ▼ contains no 'placeholders' for future content
  ▼ provides adequate exposition and clarity of meaning
  ▼ uses appropriate diagrams, examples and sample source code
  ▼ maintains a structural integrity
  ▼ avoids ambiguity

▼ In addition, the Quality Review Team SHALL be responsible for project management support to include:

▼ Capturing the deliverables from the project teams

▼ Using the deliverable information to create and maintain a project plan that identifies the critical milestones and deliverables of the ebXML initiative

▼ Facilitating visibility to all ebXML project teams of the relationships between the critical ebXML deliverables

▼ Providing risk assessment analysis for the Executive Committee on any critical area that may impact meeting the ebXML timeline

7.1.2 Marketing Awareness

The true measure of success for ebXML will be in its adoption by the business community. To help facilitate that adoption, the *Marketing Awareness Support Team* SHALL:

▼ Create an ebXML awareness program

▼ Define general ebXML web site content and management approaches

▼ Define allowable content of ebXML Project Team public pages

▼ Define and execute ebXML marketing communications

▼ Promote and support regional ebXML promotion efforts

8 ebXML Project Team Deliverables

This section identifies the major specifications that SHALL be delivered by each of the ebXML project teams. It also describes in general terms the expected nature of the various ebXML project team deliverables to guide each team in developing those deliverables and ensure a single consistent approach.

8.1 Major ebXML Technical Specifications

The major ebXML technical specifications to be delivered SHALL consist of the:

▼ Technical Architecture Specification - contains an overview of the technical infrastructure that comprises ebXML and itemize the design rules and guidelines

▼ Repository and Registry Specification - includes functional specification and technical design, interfaces, services

▼ Transport, Routing and Packaging Specification - addresses transport of ebXML messages, the means of security employed, and the physical construction of the messaging used within the scope of the ebXML system. Specific deliverables SHALL include -

  ▼ message structure specification
  ▼ message header specification
  ▼ a textual API example
  ▼ choreographic of messages
  ▼ security specification

▼ Business Process Modeling Specification - the business process metamodel and the recommended methodology for using it

▼ Core Components Specification - The set of ebXML core components and the prescribed methodology for deriving them

▼ Trading Partner Specification - A collaboration profile template that supports manual and electronic discovery and agreement

To assist in visualizing the above, Figure 8-1 is a conceptual model of overall ebXML stack interactions.

Business Applications and Delivery Systems (external to ebXML)
Business Process Methodology
Core Components
Registry and Repository
Collaboration Protocol Profile and Agreement
Transport/Routing and Packaging
Technical Architecture
Technology Base (external to ebXML)

Executive Committee
Steering Committee
Proof of Concept
Quality Review
Requirements
Project Management
Marketing Awareness

FIGURE 8-1   ebXML Stack Interactions

9   Disclaimer

The views and specification expressed in this document are those of the authors and are not necessarily those of their employers. The authors and their employers specifically disclaim responsibility for any problems arising from correct or incorrect implementation or use of this design.

10   Contact Information

Team Leader

   Michael C. Rawlins

   Rawlins EC Consulting

PMB 29

14 Canyon Creek Village

Richardson, TX 75080-1602

USA

Phone: 972-783-8573

EMail: rawlins@metronet.com

Editor

Mark Crawford

Logistics Management Institute

2000 Corporate Ridge

McLean, Virginia 22026

USA

Phone: 703-917-7177

Email: *mcrawford@lmi.org*

CHAPTER
2

Technical Architecture Specification

v1.0.4
Technical Architecture Team
16 February 2001

TABLE OF CONTENTS

1   Status of this Document

This document specifies an ebXML Technical Specification for the eBusiness community.

Distribution of this document is unlimited.

The document formatting is based on the Internet Society's Standard RFC format.

This version:
www.ebxml.org/specs/ebTA.pdf

Latest version:
www.ebxml.org/specs/ebTA.pdf

2   ebXML Technical Architecture Participants

We would like to recognize the following for their significant participation in the development of this document.

Team Lead:

    Brian Eisenberg   DataChannel

Editors:

    Brian Eisenberg   DataChannel

    Duane Nickull   XML Global Technologies

Participants:

    Colin Barham   TIE

    Al Boseman   ATPCO

    Christian Barret   GIP-MDS

    Dick Brooks   Group 8760

    Cory Casanave   DataAccess Technologies

    Robert Cunningham   Military Traffic Management Command, US Army

Christopher Ferris	Sun Microsystems
Anders Grangard	EDI France
Peter Kacandes	Sun Microsystems
Kris Ketels	SWIFT
Piming Kuo	Worldspan
Kyu-Chul Lee	Chungnam National University
Henry Lowe	OMG
Matt MacKenzie	XML Global Technologies
Melanie McCarthy	General Motors
Stefano Pagliani	Sun Microsystems
Bruce Peat	eProcessSolutions
John Petit	KPMG Consulting
Mark Heller	MITRE
Scott Hinkelman	IBM
Lynne Rosenthal	NIST
Nikola Stojanovic	Encoda Systems, Inc.
Jeff Sutor	Sun Microsystems
David RR Webber	XML Global Technologies

3   Introduction

3.1   Summary of Contents of Document

The keywords MUST, MUST NOT, REQUIRED, SHALL, SHALL NOT, SHOULD, SHOULD NOT, RECOMMENDED, MAY, and OPTIONAL, when they appear in this document, are to be interpreted as described in RFC 2119 [Bra97].

The following conventions are used throughout this document:

Capitalized Italics words are defined in the ebXML Glossary.

Notes are used to further clarify the discussion or to offer additional suggestions and/or resources   Note

3.2 Audience and Scope

This document is intended primarily for the ebXML project teams to help guide their work. Secondary audiences include, but are not limited to: software implementers, international standards bodies, and other industry organizations.

This document describes the underlying architecture for ebXML. It provides a high level overview of ebXML and describes the relationships, interactions, and basic functionality of ebXML. It SHOULD be used as a roadmap to learn: (1) what ebXML is, (2) what problems ebXML solves, and (3) core ebXML functionality and architecture.

3.3 Related Documents

As mentioned above, other documents provide detailed definitions of the components of ebXML and of their inter-relationship. They include ebXML specifications on the following topics:

1. Requirements
2. Business Process and Information Meta Model
3. Core Components
4. Registry and Repository
5. Trading Partner Information
6. Messaging Services

These specifications are available for download at

http://www.ebxml.org/specs

3.4 Normative References

The following standards contain provisions that, through reference in this text, constitute provisions of this specification. At the time of publication, the editions indicated below were valid. All standards are subject to revision, and parties to agreements based on this specification are encouraged to investigate the possibility of applying the most recent editions of the standards indicated below.

ISO/IEC 14662: Open-edi Reference Model

ISO 11179/3 Metadata Repository

ISO 10646: Character Encoding

ISO 8601:2000 Date/Time/Number Data typing

OASIS Registry/Repository Technical Specification

RFC 2119: Keywords for use in RFC's to Indicate Requirement Levels

UN/CEFACT Modeling Methodology (UMM)

W3C XML v1.0 Second Edition Specification

4 Design Objectives

4.1 Problem Description and Goals for ebXML

For over 25 years *Electronic Data Interchange (EDI)* has given companies the prospect of eliminating paper documents, reducing costs, and improving efficiency by exchanging business information in electronic form. Ideally, companies of all sizes could conduct *eBusiness* in a completely ad hoc fashion, without prior agreement of any kind. But this vision has not been realized with *EDI*; only large companies are able to afford to implement it, and much *EDI*-enabled *eBusiness* is centered around a dominant enterprise that imposes proprietary integration approaches on its *Trading Partners.*

In the last few years, the *Extensible Markup Language (XML)* has rapidly become the first choice for defining data interchange formats in new *eBusiness* applications on the Internet. Many people have interpreted the *XML* groundswell as evidence that *"EDI* is dead" – made completely obsolete by the *XML* upstart — but this view is naïve from both business and technical standpoints.

EDI implementations encode substantial experience in *Business Processes,* and companies with large investments in *EDI* integration will not abandon them without good reason. *XML* enables more open, more flexible business transactions than *EDI. XML* might enable more flexible and innovative "eMarketplace" business models than *EDI.* But the challenges of designing M*essages* that meet *Business Process* requirements and standardizing their semantics are independent of the syntax in which the M*essages* are encoded.

The ebXML specifications provide a framework in which *EDI's* substantial investments in *Business Processes* can be preserved in an architecture that exploits *XML's* new technical capabilities.

4.2   Caveats and Assumptions

This specification is designed to provide a high level overview of ebXML, and as such, does not provide the level of detail required to build *ebXML Applications*, components, and related services. Please refer to each of the respective ebXML specifications to get the level of detail.

4.3   Design Conventions for ebXML Specifications

In order to enforce a consistent capitalization and naming convention across all ebXML specifications "Upper Camel Case" (*UCC*) and "Lower Camel Case" (*LCC*) Capitalization styles SHALL be used. *UCC* style capitalizes the first character of each word and compounds the name. *LCC* style capitalizes the first character of each word except the first word.

1. ebXML DTD, XML Schema and *XML* instance documents SHALL have the effect of producing ebXML *XML* instance documents such that:
   ▼ Element names SHALL be in *UCC* convention (example:
   ▼ <UpperCamelCaseElement/>).
   ▼ Attribute names SHALL be in *LCC* convention (example: <UpperCamelCaseElement lowerCamelCaseAttribute="Whatever"/>).

2. When *UML* and *Object Constrained Language (OCL)* are used to specify ebXML artifacts Capitalization naming SHALL follow the following rules:
   ▼ Class, *Interface*, Association, Package, State, Use Case, Actor names SHALL use UCC convention (examples: ClassificationNode, Versionable, Active, InsertOrder, Buyer).
   ▼ Attribute, Operation, Role, Stereotype, Instance, Event, Action names SHALL use LCC convention (examples: name, notifySender, resident, orderArrived).

3. General rules for all names are:
   ▼ Acronyms SHOULD be avoided, but in cases where they are used, the capitalization SHALL remain (example: XMLSignature).
   ▼ Underscore (_), periods (.) and dashes (-) MUST NOT be used (don't use: header.manifest, stock_quote_5, commercial-transaction, use HeaderManifest, stockQuote5, CommercialTransaction instead).

5 ebXML System Overview

Figure 1 below shows a high-level use case scenario for two *Trading Partners*, first configuring and then engaging in a simple business transaction and interchange. This model is provided as an example of the process and steps that may be required to configure and deploy *ebXML Applications* and related architecture components. These components can be implemented in an incremental manner. The ebXML specifications are not limited to this simple model, provided here as quick introduction to the concepts. Specific ebXML implementation examples are described in Appendix A.

The conceptual overview described below introduces the following concepts and underlying architecture:

1. A standard mechanism for describing a *Business Process* and its associated information model.

2. A mechanism for registering and storing *Business Process and Information Meta Models* so they can be shared and reused.

3. Discovery of information about each participant including:
   ▼ The *Business Processes* they support.
   ▼ The *Business Service Interfaces* they offer in support of the *Business Process.*
   ▼ The *Business Messages* that are exchanged between their respective *Business Service Interfaces.*
   ▼ The technical configuration of the supported transport, security and encoding protocols.

4. A mechanism for registering the aforementioned information so that it may be discovered and retrieved.

5. A mechanism for describing the execution of a mutually agreed upon business arrangement which can be derived from information provided by each participant from item 3 above. (*Collaboration Protocol Agreement – CPA*)

6. A standardized business *Messaging Service* framework that enables interoperable, secure and reliable exchange of M*essages* between *Trading Partners.*

7. A mechanism for configuration of the respective *Messaging Services* to engage in the agreed upon *Business Process* in accordance with the constraints defined in the business arrangement.

In Figure 1, Company A has become aware of an ebXML *Registry* that is accessible on the Internet (Figure 1, step 1). Company A, after reviewing the contents of the ebXML *Registry*, decides to build and deploy its own ebXML compliant

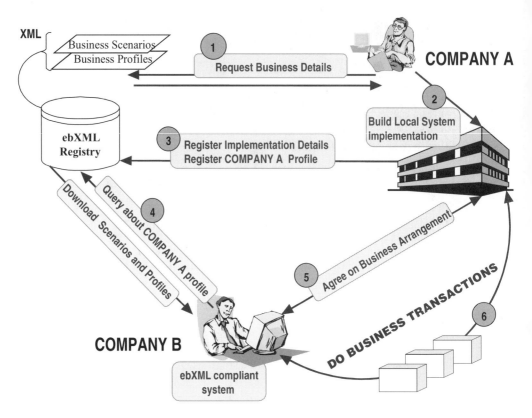

FIGURE 1   A High Level Overview of the Interaction of Two Companies Conducting eBusiness Using ebXML.

application (Figure 1, step 2). Custom software development is not a necessary prerequisite for ebXML participation. ebXML compliant applications and components may also be commercially available as shrink-wrapped solutions.

Company A then submits its own *Business Profile* information (including implementation details and reference links) to the ebXML *Registry* (Figure 1, step 3). The business profile submitted to the ebXML *Registry* describes the company's ebXML capabilities and constraints, as well as its supported business scenarios. These business scenarios are *XML* versions of the *Business Processes* and associated information bundles (e.g. a sales tax calculation) in which the company is able to engage. After receiving verification that the format and usage of a business scenario is correct, an acknowledgment is sent to Company A (Figure 1, step 3).

Company B discovers the business scenarios supported by Company A in the ebXML *Registry* (Figure 1, step 4). Company B sends a request to Company A stating that they would like to engage in a business scenario using ebXML (Figure 1, step 5). Company B acquires an ebXML compliant shrink-wrapped application.

Before engaging in the scenario Company B submits a proposed business arrangement directly to Company A's ebXML compliant software *Interface*. The proposed business arrangement outlines the mutually agreed upon business scenarios and specific agreements. The business arrangement also contains information pertaining to the messaging requirements for transactions to take place, contingency plans, and security-related requirements (Figure 1, step 5). Company A then accepts the business agreement. Company A and B are now ready to engage in *eBusiness* using ebXML (Figure 1, step 6).

6 ebXML Recommended Modeling Methodology

Business Process and Information Modeling is not mandatory. However, if implementers and users select to model *Business Processes and Information*, then they SHALL use the *UN/CEFACT Modeling Methodology (UMM)* that utilizes *UML*.

6.1 Overview

While business practices from one organization to another are highly variable, most activities can be decomposed into *Business Processes* which are more generic to a specific type of business. This analysis through the modeling process will identify *Business Process and Information Meta Models* that are likely candidates for standardization. The ebXML approach looks for standard reusable components from which to construct interoperable and components.

The *UN/CEFACT Modeling Methodology (UMM)* uses the following two views to describe the relevant aspects of *eBusiness* transactions. This model is based upon the Open-edi Reference Model, ISO/IEC 14662.

The *UN/CEFACT Modeling Methodology (UMM)* is broken down into the *Business Operational View (BOV)* and the supporting *Functional Service View (FSV)* described above. The assumption for ebXML is that the *FSV* serves as a reference model that MAY be used by commercial software vendors to help guide them during the development process. The underlying goal of the *UN/CEFACT Modeling Methodology (UMM)* is to provide a clear distinction between the operational and functional views, so as to ensure the maximum level of system interoperabil-

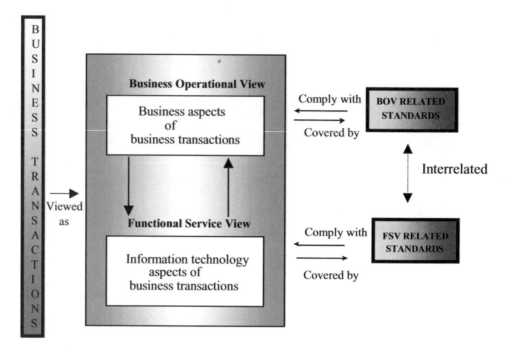

FIGURE 2   ebXML Recommended Modeling Methodology

ity and backwards compatibility with legacy systems (when applicable). As such, the resultant *BOV*-related standards provide the *UN/CEFACT Modeling Methodology (UMM)* for constructing *Business Process and Information Meta Models* for ebXML compliant applications and components.

The *BOV* addresses:

  a.) The semantics of business data in transactions and associated data interchanges

  b.) The architecture for business transactions, including:
     ▼ operational conventions;
     ▼ agreements and arrangements;
     ▼ mutual obligations and requirements.

These specifically apply to the business needs of ebXML *Trading Partners.*

The *FSV* addresses the supporting services meeting the mechanistic needs of ebXML. It focuses on the information technology aspects of:

  ▼ Functional capabilities;

  ▼ *Business Service Interfaces;*

  ▼ Protocols and *Messaging Services.*

This includes, but is not limited to:

▼ Capabilities for implementation, discovery, deployment and run time scenarios;

▼ User *Interfaces;*

▼ Data transfer infrastructure *Interfaces;*

▼ *Protocols* for enabling interoperability of *XML* vocabulary deployments from different organizations.

6.2 ebXML Business Operational View

The modeling techniques described in this section are not mandatory requirements for participation in ebXML compliant business transactions.

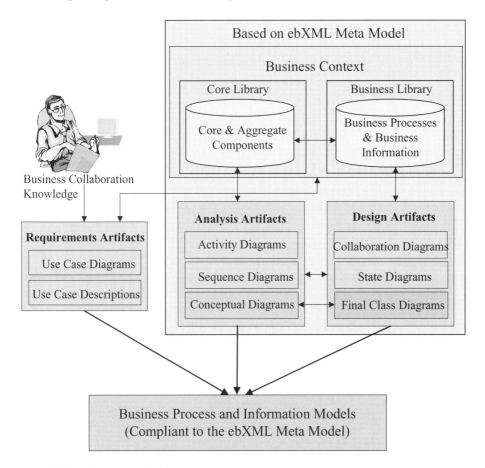

FIGURE 3 Detailed Representation of the Business Operational View

In Figure 3 above, *Business Collaboration Knowledge* is captured in a *Core Library*. The *Core Library* contains data and process definitions, including relationships and cross-references, as expressed in business terminology that MAY be tied to an accepted industry classification scheme or taxonomy. The *Core Library* is the bridge between the specific business or industry language and the knowledge expressed by the models in a more generalized context neutral language.

The first phase defines the requirements artifacts that describe the problem using *Use Case Diagrams and Descriptions.* If *Core Library* entries are available from an ebXML compliant *Registry* they will be utilized, otherwise new *Core Library* entries will be created and registered in an ebXML compliant *Registry.*

The second phase (analysis) will create activity and sequence diagrams (as defined in the *UN/CEFACT Modeling Methodology* specification) describing the *Business Processes. Class Diagrams* will capture the associated information parcels (business documents). The analysis phase reflects the business knowledge contained in the *Core Library.* No effort is made to force the application of object-oriented principles. The class diagram is a free structured data diagram. Common *Business Processes* in the Business Library MAY be referenced during the process of creating analysis and design artifacts.

The design phase is the last step of standardization, which MAY be accomplished by applying object-oriented principles based on the *UN/CEFACT Modeling Methodology.* In addition to generating collaboration diagrams, a state diagram MAY also be created. The class view diagram from the analysis phase will undergo harmonization to align it with other models in the same industry and across others.

In ebXML, interoperability is achieved by applying *Business Information Objects* across all class models. *Business Processes* are created by applying the *UN/CEFACT Modeling Metholodogy (UMM)* which utilizes a common set of *Business Information Objects* and *Core Components.*

6.3   ebXML Functional Service View

As illustrated in Figure 4 above, the ebXML *Registry Service* serves as the storage facility for the *Business Process and Information Models,* the *XML*-based representations of those models, *Core Components,* and *Collaboration Protocol Profiles.* The *Business Process and Information Meta Models* MAY be stored in modeling syntax, however they MAY be also stored as *XML* syntax in the *Registry.* This *XML*-based business information SHALL be expressed in a manner that allows discovery down to the atomic data level via a consistent methodology.

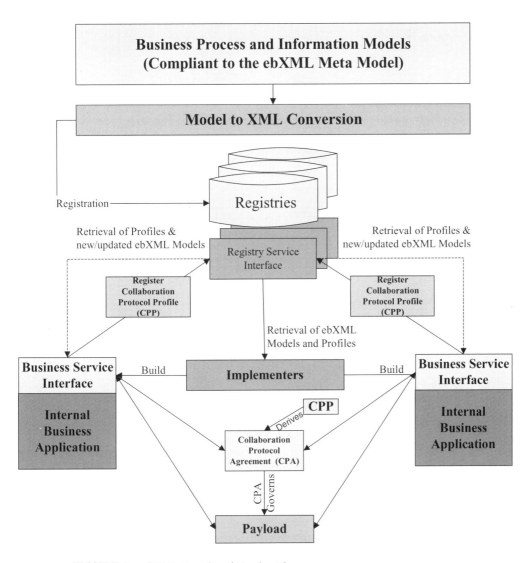

FIGURE 4 ebXML Functional Service View

The underlying ebXML Architecture is distributed in such a manner to minimize the potential for a single point of failure within the ebXML infrastructure. This specifically refers to *Registry Services* (see Registry Functionality, Section 8.4 for details of this architecture).

7 ebXML Functional Phases

7.1 Implementation Phase

The implementation phase deals specifically with the procedures for creating an application of the ebXML infrastructure. A *Trading Partner* wishing to engage in an ebXML compliant transaction SHOULD first acquire copies of the ebXML Specifications. The *Trading Partner* studies these specifications and subsequently downloads the *Core Library* and the *Business Library*. The *Trading Partner* MAY also request other *Trading Partners' Business Process* information (stored in their business profile) for analysis and review. Alternatively, the Trading Partner MAY implement ebXML by utilizing 3rd party applications. The *Trading Partner* can also submit its own *Business Process* information to an ebXML compliant *Registry Service*.

Figure 5 below, illustrates a basic interaction between an ebXML *Registry Service* and a *Trading Partner*.

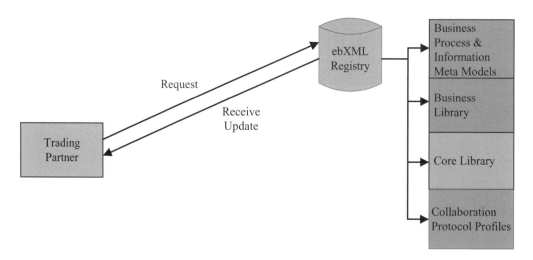

FIGURE 5   Functional Service View: Implementation Phase

7.2 Discovery and Retrieval Phase

The Discovery and Retrieval Phase covers all aspects of the discovery of ebXML related resources. A *Trading Partner* who has implemented an ebXML *Business Service Interface* can now begin the process of discovery and retrieval (Figure 6 below). One possible discovery method may be to request the *Collaboration Proto-col Profile* of another *Trading Partner.* Requests for updates to *Core Libraries, Busi-ness Libraries* and updated or new *Business Process and Information Meta Models* SHOULD be supported by an ebXML *Business Service Interface.* This is the phase where *Trading Partners* discover the meaning of business information being re-quested by other *Trading Partners.*

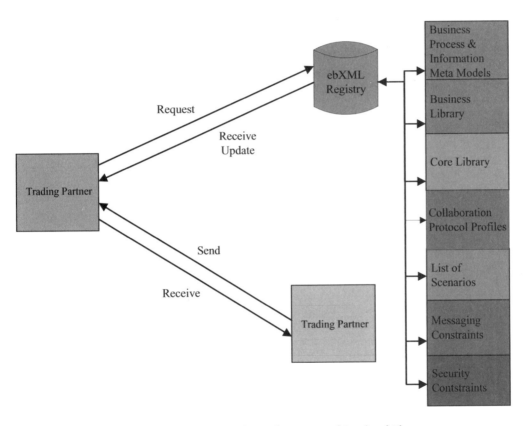

FIGURE 6   Functional Service View: Discovery and Retrieval Phase

7.3   Run Time Phase

The run time phase covers the execution of an ebXML scenario with the ac-tual associated ebXML transactions. In the Run Time Phase, ebXML *Messages* are being exchanged between *Trading Partners* utilizing the ebXML *Messaging Service.*

For example, an ebXML *CPA* is a choreographed set of business *Message* exchanges linked together by a well-defined choreography using the ebXML *Messaging Service*.

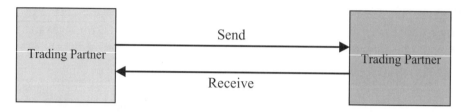

FIGURE 7   Functional Service View: Run Time Phase

Note

> There is no run time access to the *Registry*. If it becomes necessary to make calls to the *Registry* during the run time, this SHOULD be considered as a reversion to the Discovery and Retrieval Phase.]

8   ebXML Infrastructure

8.1   Trading Partner Information [CPP and CPA's]

8.1.1   Introduction

To facilitate the process of conducting *eBusiness*, potential *Trading Partners* need a mechanism to publish information about the *Business Processes* they support along with specific technology implementation details about their capabilities for exchanging business information. This is accomplished through the use of a *Collaboration Protocol Profile (CPP)*. The *CPP* is a document which allows a *Trading Partner* to express their supported *Business Processes* and *Business Service Interface* requirements in a manner where they can be universally understood by other ebXML compliant *Trading Partners*.

A special business agreement called a *CPA* is derived from the intersection of two or more *CPP's*. The *CPA* serves as a formal handshake between two or more *Trading Partners* wishing to conduct business transactions using ebXML.

8.1.2   CPP Formal Functionality

The *CPP* describes the specific capabilities that a *Trading Partner* supports as well as the *Service Interface* requirements that need to be met in order to exchange business documents with that *Trading Partner*. The *CPP* contains essential information about the *Trading Partner* including, but not limited to: contact information, industry classification, supported *Business Processes, Interface* requirements and *Messaging Service* requirements. *CPP's* MAY also contain security and other implementation specific details. Each ebXML compliant *Trading Partner* SHOULD register their *CPP(s)* in an ebXML compliant *Registry Service,* thus providing a discovery mechanism that allows *Trading Partners* to (1) find one another, (2) discover the *Business Process* that other *Trading Partners* support.

The *CPP* definition SHALL provide for unambiguous selection of choices in all instances where there may be multiple selections (e.g. HTTP or SMTP transport).

8.1.3   CPA Formal Functionality

A *Collaboration Protocol Agreement (CPA)* is a document that represents the intersection of two *CPP's* and is mutually agreed upon by both Trading Partners who wish to conduct *eBusiness* using ebXML.

A *CPA* describes: (1) the *Messaging Service* and (2) the *Business Process* requirements that are agreed upon by two or more *Trading Partners.* Conceptually, ebXML supports a three level view of narrowing subsets to arrive at *CPA's* for transacting *eBusiness.* The outer-most scope relates to all of the capabilities that a *Trading Partner* can support, with a subset of what a *Trading Partner* "will" actually support.

A *CPA* contains the *Messaging Service Interface* requirements as well as the implementation details pertaining to the mutually agreed upon *Business Processes* that both *Trading Partners* agree to use to conduct *eBusiness. Trading Partners* may decide to register their *CPA's* in an ebXML compliant *Registry Service,* but this is not a mandatory part of the *CPA* creation process.

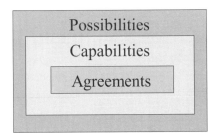

FIGURE 8   Three Level View of CPA's

Business Collaborations are the first order of support that can be claimed by ebXML *Trading Partners.* This "claiming of support" for specific *Business Collaborations* is facilitated by a distinct profile defined specifically for publishing, or advertising in a directory service, such as an ebXML *Registry* or other available service. Figure 9 below outlines the scope for *Collaboration Protocol Agreements* within ebXML.

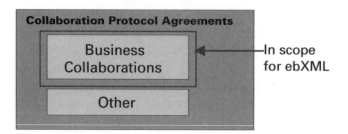

FIGURE 9 Scope for CPA's

The *CPA-CPP* specification includes a non-normative appendix that discusses *CPA* composition and negotiation and includes advice as to composition and negotiation procedures.

8.1.4 CPP Interfaces

8.1.4.1 Interface to Business Processes

A *CPP* SHALL be capable of referencing one or more *Business Processes* supported by the *Trading Partner* owning the *CPP* instance. The *CPP* SHALL reference the Roles within a *Business Process* that the user is capable of assuming. An example of a Role could be the notion of a "Seller" and "Buyer" within a "Purchasing" *Business Process*.

The *CPP* SHALL be capable of being stored and retrieved from an ebXML *Registry* Mechanism

A *CPP* SHOULD also describe binding details that are used to build an ebXML *Message Header*.

8.1.5 CPA Interfaces

A *CPA* governs the *Business Service Interface* used by a *Trading* Partner to constrain the *Business Service Interface* to a set of parameters agreed to by all *Trading Partners* who will execute such an agreement.

CPA's have *Interfaces* to *CPP's* in that the *CPA* is derived through a process of mutual negotiation narrowing the *Trading Partners* capabilities (*CPP*) into what the *Trading Partner* "will" do (*CPA*).

A *CPA* must reference to a specific *Business Process* and the interaction requirements needed to execute that *Business Process*.

A *CPA* MAY be stored in a *Registry* mechanism, hence an implied ability to be stored and retrieved is present.

8.1.6 Non-Normative Implementation Details [CPP and CPA's]

A *CPA* is negotiated after the Discovery and Retrieval Phase and is essentially a snapshot of the *Messaging Services* and *Business Process* related information that two or more *Trading Partners* agree to use to exchange business information. If any parameters contained within an accepted *CPA* change after the agreement has been executed, a new *CPA* SHOULD be negotiated between *Trading Partners*.

In some circumstances there may be a need or desire to describe casual, informal or implied *CPA's*.

An eventual goal of ebXML is to facilitate fully automated *CPA* generation. In order to meet this goal, a formal methodology SHOULD be specified for the *CPA* negotiation process.

8.2 Business Process and Information Modeling

8.2.1 Introduction

The ebXML *Business Process and Information Meta Model* is a mechanism that allows *Trading Partners* to capture the details for a specific business scenario using a consistent modeling methodology. A *Business Process* describes in detail how *Trading Partners* take on roles, relationships and responsibilities to facilitate interaction with other *Trading Partners* in shared collaborations. The interaction between roles takes place as a choreographed set of business transactions. Each business transaction is expressed as an exchange of electronic *Business Documents*. *Business Documents* MAY be composed from re-useable *Business Information Objects* (see "Relationships to Core Components" under 8.2.3 "*Interfaces*" below). At a lower level, *Business Processes* can be composed of re-useable *Core Processes*, and *Business Information Objects* can be composed of re-useable *Core Components*.

The ebXML *Business Process and Information Meta Model* supports requirements, analysis and design viewpoints that provide a set of semantics (vocabulary) for each viewpoint and forms the basis of specification of the artifacts that are required to facilitate *Business Process* and information integration and interoperability.

An additional view of the *Meta Model*, the *Specification Schema*, is also provided to support the direct specification of the set of elements required to configure a run-time system in order to execute a set of ebXML business transactions. By drawing out modeling elements from several of the other views, the *Specification Schema* forms a semantic subset of the ebXML *Business Process and Information Meta Model*. The *Specification Schema* is available in two stand-alone representations, a *UML* profile, and a DTD.

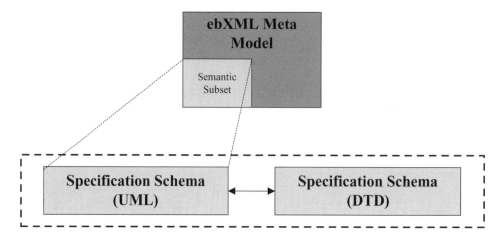

FIGURE 10   ebXML Meta Model - Semantic Subset

The relationship between the ebXML *Business Process and Information Meta Model* and the ebXML *Specification Schema* can be shown as follows:

The *Specification Schema* supports the specification of business transactions and the choreography of business transactions into *Business Collaborations.* Each *Business Transaction* can be implemented using one of many available standard patterns. These patterns determine the actual exchange of M*essages* and signals between *Trading Partners* to achieve the required electronic transaction. To help specify the patterns *the Specification Schema* is accompanied by a set of standard patterns, and a set of modeling elements common to those patterns. The full specification of a *Business Process* consists of a *Business Process and Information Meta Model* specified against the *Specification Schema* and an identification of the desired pattern(s). This information serves as the primary input for the formation of *Collaboration Protocol Profiles* (*CPP's*) and *CPA's.* This can be shown as follows:

There are no formal requirements to mandate the use of a modeling language to compose new *Business Processes,* however, if a modeling language is used to develop *Business Processes,* it SHALL be the *Unified Modeling Language (UML).* This mandate ensures that a single, consistent modeling methodology is used to create new *Business Processes.* One of the key benefits of using a single consistent modeling methodology is that it is possible to compare models to avoid duplication of existing *Business Processes.*

To further facilitate the creation of consistent *Business Processes* and information models, ebXML will define a common set of *Business Processes* in parallel with a *Core Library.* It is possible that users of the ebXML infrastructure may wish to extend this set or use their own *Business Processes.*

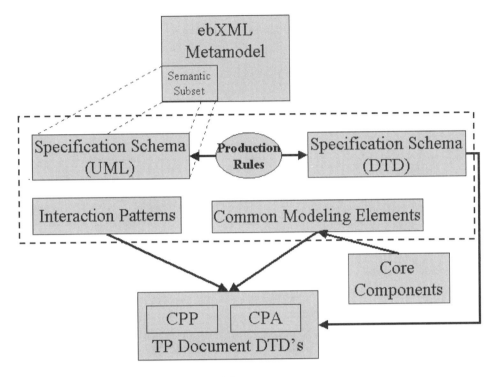

FIGURE 11   ebXML Meta Model

8.2.2 Formal Functionality

The representation of a *Business Process* document instance SHALL be in a form that will allow both humans and applications to read the information. This is necessary to facilitate a gradual transition to full automation of business interactions.

The *Business Process* SHALL be storable and retrievable in a *Registry* mechanism. *Business Processes* MAY be registered in an ebXML *Registry* in order to facilitate discovery and retrieval.

To be understood by an application, a *Business Process* SHALL be expressible in *XML* syntax. A *Business Process* MAY be constructed as an *Business Process and Information Meta Model* or an *XML* representation of that model. *Business Processes* are capable of expressing the following types of information:

▼ Choreography for the exchange of document instances. (e.g. the choreography of necessary *Message* exchanges between two Trading Partners executing a "Purchasing" ebXML transaction.)

▼ References to *Business Process and Information Meta Model* or *Business Documents* (possibly *DTD's* or *Schemas*) that add structure to business data.

▼ Definition of the roles for each participant in a *Business Process.*

A *Business Process:*

▼ Provides the contextual constraints for using *Core Components*

▼ Provides the framework for establishing *CPAs*

▼ Specifies the domain owner of a *Business Process,* along with relevant contact information.

Note | **The above lists are not inclusive.**

8.2.3   *Interfaces*

8.2.3.1   Relationship to CPP and CPA

The *CPP* instance of a *Trading Partner* defines that partner's functional and technical capability to support zero, one, or more *Business Processes* and one or more roles in each process.

The agreement between two *Trading Partners* defines the actual conditions under which the two partners will conduct business transactions together. The *Interface* between the *Business Process,* its *Information Meta Model,* and the *CPA* is the part of the *Business Process* document. This MAY be instantiated as an *XML* document representing the business transactional and collaboration layers of the *Business Process and Information Meta Model.* The expression of the sequence of commercial transactions in *XML* is shared between the *Business Process* and *Trading Partner Information* models.

8.2.3.2   Relationship to Core Components

A *Business Process* instance SHOULD specify the constraints for exchanging business data with other *Trading Partners.* The business information MAY be comprised of components of the ebXML *Core Library.* A *Business Process* document SHALL reference the *Core Components* directly or indirectly using a *XML* document that references the appropriate Business and Information Models and/or Business Documents (possibly *DTD's* or Schemas). The mechanism for interfacing with the *Core Components* and *Core Library* SHALL be by way of a unique identifier for each component.

8.2.3.3   Relationship to ebXML Messaging

A *Business Process* instance SHALL be capable of being transported from a *Registry Service* to another *Registry Service* via an ebXML *Message.* It SHALL also be capable of being transported between a *Registry* and a users application via the ebXML *Messaging Service.*

8.2.3.4   Relationship to a Registry System

A *Business Process* instance intended for use within the ebXML infrastructure SHALL be retrievable through a *Registry* query, and therefore, each *Business Process* SHALL contain a unique identifier.

8.2.4   *Non-Normative Implementation Details*

The exact composition of *Business Information Objects* or a *Business Document* is guided by a set of contexts derived from the *Business Process.* The modeling layer of the architecture is highlighted in green in Figure 12 below.

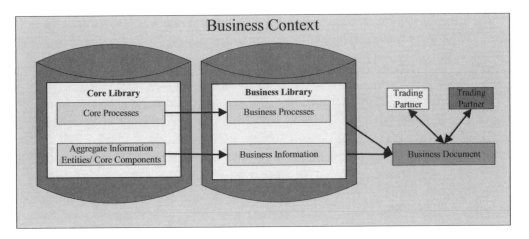

FIGURE 12   ebXML Business Process and Information Modeling Layer

ebXML *Business Process and Information Meta Model* MAY be created following the recommended UN/CEFACT *Modeling Methodology* (*UMM*), or MAY be arrived at in any other way, as long as they comply with the ebXML *Business Process and Information Meta Model.*

8.3   Core Components and Core Library Functionality

8.3.1   *Introduction*

A *Core Component* captures information about a real world business concept, and the relationships between that concept, other *Business Information Objects,* and a contextual description that describes how a *Core* or *Aggregate Information Entity* may be used in a particular ebXML *eBusiness* scenario.

A *Core Component* can be either an individual piece of business information, or a natural "go-together" family of *Business Information Objects* that may be assembled into *Aggregate Information Entities.*

The ebXML Core Components project team SHALL define an initial set of *Core Components.* ebXML users may adopt and/or extend components from the ebXML *Core Library.*

8.3.2   Formal Functionality

As a minimum set of requirements, *Core Components* SHALL facilitate the following functionality:

> *Core Components* SHALL be storable and retrievable using an ebXML *Registry* Mechanism.

> *Core Components* SHALL capture and hold a minimal set of information to satisfy *eBusiness* needs.

> *Core Components* SHALL be capable of being expressed in *XML* syntax.

> A *Core Component* SHALL be capable of containing:
> - ▼ Another *Core Component* in combination with one or more individual pieces of *Business Information Objects.*
> - ▼ Other *Core Components* in combination with zero or more individual pieces of *Business Information Objects.*

A *Core Component* SHALL be able to be uniquely identified.

8.3.3   Interfaces

A *Core Component* MAY be referenced indirectly or directly from a *Business Document* instance. The *Business Process* MAY specify a single or group of *Core Components* as required or optional information as part of a *Business Document* instance.

A *Core Component* SHALL interface with a *Registry* mechanism by way of being storable and retrievable in such a mechanism.

A *Core Component* MAY interface with an *XML* Element from another *XML* vocabulary by the fact it is bilaterally or unilaterally referenced as a semantic equivalent.

8.3.4   Non-normative Implementation Details

A *Core Component* MAY contain attribute(s) or be part of another *Core Component,* thus specifying the precise context or combination of contexts in which it is used.

The process of aggregating *Core Components* for a specific business context, shall include a means to identify the placement of a *Core Component* within another *Core Component.* It MAY also be a combination of structural contexts to facilitate

Core Component re-use at different layers within another *Core Component* or *Aggregate Information Entity.* This is referred to as *Business Context.*

Context MAY also be defined using the *Business Process and Information Meta Model,* which defines the instances of *Business Information Objects* in which the *Core Component* occurs.

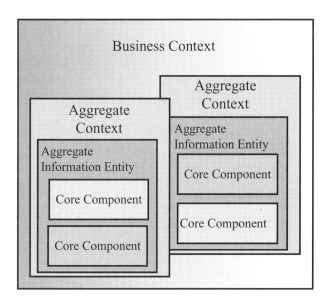

FIGURE 13 Business Context Defined in Terms of Aggregate Context, Aggregate Information Entities, and Core Components

The pieces of *Business Information Objects,* or *Core Components,* within a generic *Core Component* may be either mandatory, or optional. A *Core Component* in a specific context or combination of contexts (aggregate or business context) may alter the fundamental mandatory/optional cardinality.

8.4 Registry Functionality

8.4.1 Introduction

An ebXML *Registry* provides a set of services that enable the sharing of information between *Trading Partners.* A *Registry* is a component that maintains an interface to metadata for a registered item. Access to an ebXML *Registry* is provided through *Interfaces* (APIs) exposed by *Registry Services.*

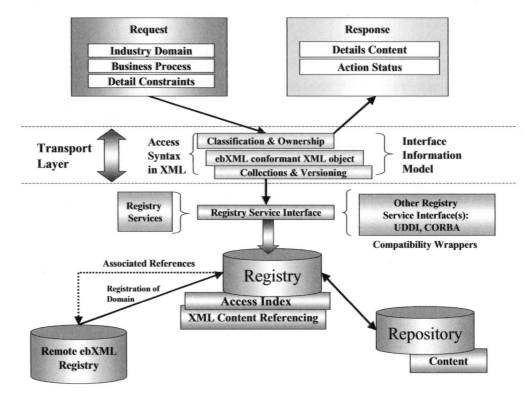

FIGURE 14   Overall Registry Architecture

8.4.2   *Formal Functionality*

A *Registry* SHALL accommodate the storage of items expressed in syntax using multi-byte character sets.

Each *Registry Item*, at each level of granularity as defined by the *Submitting Organization*, MUST be uniquely identifiable. This is essential to facilitate application-to-Registry queries.

A *Registry* SHALL return either zero or one positive matches in response to a contextual query for a unique identifier. In such cases where two or more positive results are displayed for such queries, an error message SHOULD be reported to the *Registry Authority*.

A *Registry Item* SHALL be structured to allow information associations that identify, name, describe it, give its administrative and access status, define its persistence and mutability, classify it according to pre-defined classification schemes, declare its file representation type, and identify the submitting and responsible organizations.

The *Registry Interface* serves as an application-to-registry access mechanism. Human-to-registry interactions SHALL be built as a layer over a *Registry Interface* (e.g. a Web browser) and not as a separate *Interface*.

The *Registry Interface* SHALL be designed to be independent of the underlying network protocol stack (e.g. HTTP/SMTP over TCP/IP). Specific instructions on how to interact with the *Registry Interface* MAY be contained in the payload of the ebXML *Message*.

The processes supported by the *Registry* MAY also include:

▼ A special *CPA* between the *Registry* and *Registry Clients*.

▼ A set of functional processes involving the *Registry* and *Registry Clients*.

▼ A set of *Business Messages* exchanged between a *Registry Client* and the *Registry* as part of a specific *Business Process*.

▼ A set of primitive *Interface* mechanisms to support the *Business Messages* and associated query and response mechanisms.

▼ A special *CPA* for orchestrating the interaction between ebXML compliant Registries.

▼ A set of functional processes for *Registry-to-Registry* interactions.

▼ A set of error responses and conditions with remedial actions.

To facilitate the discovery process, browse and drill down queries MAY be used for human interactions with a *Registry* (e.g. via a Web browser). A user SHOULD be able to browse and traverse the content based on the available *Registry* classification schemes.

Registry Services exist to create, modify, and delete *Registry Items* and their metadata.

Appropriate security protocols MAY be deployed to offer authentication and protection for the *Repository* when accessed by the *Registry.*

Unique Identifiers (*UIDs*) SHALL be assigned to all items within an ebXML *Registry System. UID* keys are REQUIRED references for all ebXML content. *Universally Unique Identifiers (UUIDs)* MAY be used to ensure that *Registry* entries are truly globally unique, and thus when systems query a *Registry* for a *UUID*, one and only one result SHALL be retrieved.

To facilitate semantic recognition of *Business Process and Information Meta Models*, the *Registry Service* SHALL provide a mechanism for incorporating human readable descriptions of *Registry* items. Existing *Business Process and Information Meta Models* (e.g. RosettaNet PIPs) and *Core Components* SHALL be assigned *UID* keys when they are registered in an ebXML compliant *Registry Service*. These *UID* keys MAY be implemented in physical *XML* syntax in a variety of ways. These mechanisms MAY include, but are not limited to:

▼ A pure explicit reference mechanism (example: URN:*UID* method),

▼ A referential method (example: URI:*UID* / namespace:*UID*),

▼ An object-based reference compatible with W3C Schema (*example* URN:complextype name), and

▼ A datatype based reference (example: ISO 8601:2000 Date/Time/Number datatyping and then legacy datatyping).

Components in ebXML MUST facilitate multilingual support. A *UID* reference is particularly important here as it provides a language neutral reference mechanism. To enable multilingual support, the ebXML specification SHALL be compliant with Unicode and ISO/IEC 10646 for character set and UTF-8 or UTF-16 for character encoding.

8.4.3 Interfaces

ebXML Messaging:

The query syntax used by the *Registry* access mechanisms is independent of the physical implementation of the backend system.

The ebXML *Messaging Service* MAY serve as the transport mechanism for all communication into and out of the *Registry*.

Business Process:

Business Processes are published and retrieved via ebXML *Registry Services.*

Core Components:

Core Components are published and retrieved via ebXML *Registry Services.*

Any Item with Metadata:

XML elements provide standard metadata about the item being managed through ebXML *Registry Services*. Since ebXML Registries are distributed each *Registry* MAY interact with and cross-reference another ebXML *Registry.*

8.4.4 Non-normative Implementation Details

The *Business Process and Information Meta Models* within a *Registry* MAY be stored according to various classification schemes.

The existing ISO11179/3 work on *Registry* implementations MAY be used to provide a model for the ebXML *Registry* implementation.

Registry Items and their metadata MAY also be addressable as *XML* based URI references using only HTTP for direct access.

Examples of extended *Registry Services* functionality may be deferred to a subsequent phase of the ebXML initiative. This includes, but is not limited to transformation services, workflow services, quality assurance services and extended security mechanisms.

A *Registry Service* MAY have multiple deployment models as long as the *Registry Interfaces* are ebXML compliant.

The *Business Process and Information Meta Model* for an ebXML *Registry Service* may be an extension of the existing OASIS Registry/Repository Technical Specification, specifically tailored for the storage and retrieval of business information, whereas the OASIS model is a superset designed for handling extended and generic information content.

8.5   Messaging Service Functionality

8.5.1   Introduction

The ebXML *Message Service* mechanism provides a standard way to exchange business *Messages* among ebXML *Trading Partners.* The ebXML *Messaging Service* provides a reliable means to exchange business *Messages* without relying on proprietary technologies and solutions. An ebXML *Message* contains structures for a *Message Header* (necessary for routing and delivery) and a *Payload* section.

The ebXML *Messaging Service* is conceptually broken down into three parts: (1) an abstract *Service Interface,* (2) functions provided by the *Messaging Service Layer,* and (3) the mapping to underlying transport service(s). The relation of the abstract *Interface, Messaging Service Layer,* and transport service(s) are shown in Figure 15 below.

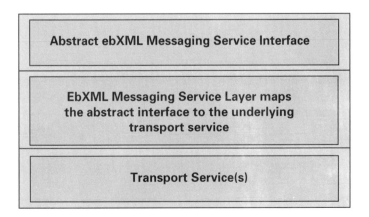

FIGURE 15   ebXML Messaging Service

The following diagram depicts a logical arrangement of the functional modules that exist within the ebXML *Messaging Services* architecture. These modules are arranged in a manner to indicate their inter-relationships and dependencies. This architecture diagram illustrates the flexibility of the ebXML *Messaging Service,* reflecting the broad spectrum of services and functionality that may be implemented in an ebXML system.

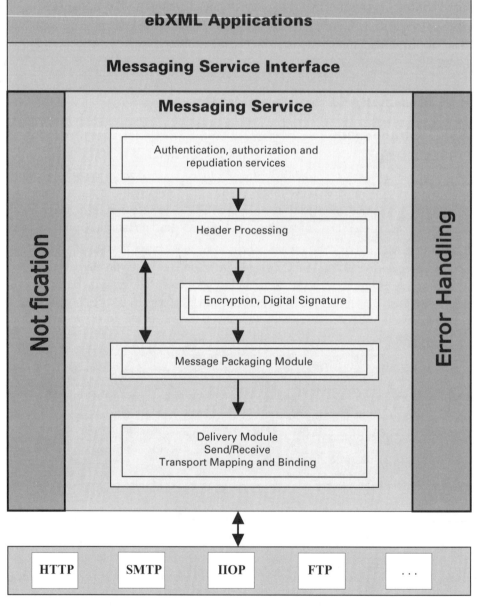

FIGURE 16 The Messaging Service Architecture

8.5.2   Formal Functionality

The ebXML *Messaging Service* provides a secure, consistent and reliable mechanism to exchange ebXML *Messages* between users of the ebXML infrastructure over various transport *Protocols* (possible examples include SMTP, HTTP/S, FTP, etc.).

The ebXML *Messaging Service* prescribes formats for all *Messages* between distributed ebXML *Components* including *Registry* mechanisms and compliant user *Applications*.

The ebXML *Messaging Service* does not place any restrictions on the content of the payload.

The ebXML *Messaging Service* supports simplex (one-way) and request/response (either synchronous or asynchronous) *Message* exchanges.

The ebXML *Messaging Service* supports sequencing of payloads in instances where multiple payloads or multiple *Messages* are exchanged between *Trading Partners*.

The ebXML *Messaging Service Layer* enforces the "rules of engagement" as defined by two *Trading Partners* in a *Collaboration Protocol Agreement* (including, but not limited to security and *Business Process* functions related to *Message* delivery). The *Collaboration Protocol Agreement* defines the acceptable behavior by which each *Trading Partner* agrees to abide. The definition of these ground rules can take many forms including formal *Collaboration Protocol Agreements*, interactive agreements established at the time a business transaction occurs (e.g. buying a book online), or other forms of agreement. There are *Messaging Service Layer* functions that enforce these ground rules. Any violation of the ground rules result in an error condition, which is reported using the appropriate means.

The ebXML *Messaging Service* performs all security related functions including:

▼ Identification

▼ Authentication (verification of identity)

▼ Authorization (access controls)

▼ Privacy (encryption)

▼ Integrity (message signing)

▼ Non-repudiation

▼ Logging

8.5.3   Interfaces

The ebXML *Messaging Service* provides ebXML with an abstract *Interface* whose functions, at an abstract level, include:

▼ <u>Send</u> – send an ebXML *Message* – values for the parameters are derived from the ebXML *Message Headers*.

▼ <u>Receive</u> – indicates willingness to receive an ebXML *Message*.

▼ <u>Notify</u> – provides notification of expected and unexpected events.

▼ <u>Inquire</u> – provides a method of querying the status of the particular ebXML *Message* interchange.

The ebXML *Messaging Service* SHALL interface with internal systems including:

▼ Routing of received *Messages* to internal systems

▼ Error notification

The ebXML *Messaging Service* SHALL help facilitate the *Interface* to an ebXML *Registry*.

8.5.4   *Non-normative Implementation Details*

8.5.4.1   ebXML Message Structure and Packaging

Figure 17 below illustrates the logical structure of an ebXML *Message*.

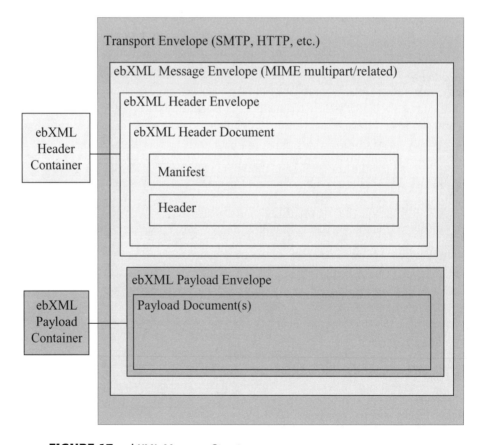

FIGURE 17   ebXML Message Structure

An ebXML *Message* consists of an optional transport *Protocol* specific outer *Communication Protocol Envelope* and a *Protocol* independent ebXML *Message Envelope*. The ebXML *Message Envelope* is packaged using the MIME multi-part/related content type. MIME is used as a packaging solution because of the diverse nature of information exchanged between *Partners* in *eBusiness* environments. For example, a complex *Business Transaction* between two or more *Trading Partners* might require a payload that contains an array of business documents (*XML* or other document formats), binary images, or other related Business Information.

9 Conformance

9.1 Introduction

This clause specifies the general framework, concepts and criteria for *Conformance* to ebXML, including an overview of the conformance strategy for ebXML, guidance for addressing conformance in each ebXML technical specification, and the conformance clause specific to the Technical Architecture specification. Except for the Technical Architecture Specification, this clause does not define the conformance requirements for each of the ebXML technical specifications – the latter is the purview of the technical specifications.

The objectives of this section are to:

a.) Ensure a common understanding of conformance and what is required to claim conformance to this family of specifications;

b.) Ensure that conformance is consistently addressed in each of the component specifications;

c.) Promote interoperability and open interchange of *Business Processes* and *Messages*;

d.) Encourage the use of applicable conformance test suites as well as promote uniformity in the development of conformance test suites.

Conformance to ebXML is defined in terms of conformance to the ebXML infrastructure and conformance to each of the technical specifications for ebXML. The primary purpose of conformance to ebXML is to increase the probability of successful interoperability between implementations and the open interchange of *XML* business documents and *Messages*. Successful inter-operability and open interchange is more likely to be achieved if implementations conform to the requirements in the ebXML specifications.

9.2   Conformance to ebXML

ebXML Conformance is defined as conformance to an ebXML system that is comprised of all the architectural components of the ebXML infrastructure and satisfies at least the minimum conformance requirements for each of the ebXML technical specifications, including the functional and *Interface* requirements in this Technical Architecture specification.

In the context of ebXML, an implementation is said to exhibit conformance if it complies with the requirements of each applicable ebXML technical specification. The conformance requirements are stated in the conformance clause of each technical specification of ebXML. The conformance clause specifies explicitly all the requirements that have to be satisfied to claim conformance to that specification. These requirements MAY be applied and grouped at varying levels within each specification.

9.3   Conformance to the Technical Architecture Specification

This section details the conformance requirements for claiming conformance to the Technical Architecture specification.

In order to conform to this specification, each ebXML technical specification:

a.) SHALL support all the functional and *Interface* requirements defined in this specification that are applicable to that technical specification;

b.) SHALL NOT specify any requirements that would contradict or cause non-conformance to ebXML or any of its components;

c.) MAY contain a conformance clause that adds requirements that are more specific and limited in scope than the requirements in this specification;

d.) SHALL only contain requirements that are testable.

A conforming implementation SHALL satisfy the conformance requirements of the applicable parts of this specification and the appropriate technical specification(s).

9.4   General Framework of Conformance Testing

The objective of conformance testing is to determine whether an implementation being tested conforms to the requirements stated in the relative ebXML specification. Conformance testing enables vendors to implement compatible and interoperable systems built on the ebXML foundations. ebXML *Implementations* and *Applications* SHOULD be tested to available test suites to verify their conformance to ebXML Specifications as soon as test suites are available.

Publicly available test suites from vendor neutral organizations such as OASIS and NIST SHOULD be used to verify the conformance of ebXML *Implementations*, *Applications*, and *Components* claiming conformance to ebXML. Open source reference implementations MAY be available to allow vendors to test their products for *Interface* compatibility, conformance, and interoperability.

10   Security Considerations

10.1   Introduction

A comprehensive *Security Model* for ebXML will be expressed in a separate document. The *Security Model* will be applied to the entire *ebXML Infrastructure,* with the underlying goal of best meeting the needs of users of ebXML.

The Security Model will comply with security needs specified in the ebXML Requirements Document.

11   Disclaimer

The views and specification expressed in this document are those of the authors and are not necessarily those of their employers. The authors and their employers specifically disclaim responsibility for any problems arising from correct or incorrect implementation or use of this design.

Appendix A   Example ebXML Business Scenarios

Definition

This set of scenarios defines how ebXML compliant software could be used to implement popular, well-known *eBusiness* models.

Scope

These scenarios are oriented to properly position the ebXML specifications as a convenient mean for companies to properly run electronic business over the Internet using open standards. They bridge the specifications to real life uses.

Audience

Companies planning to use ebXML compliant software will benefit from these scenarios because they will show how these companies may be able to implement popular business scenarios onto the ebXML specifications.

List

a.) Two *Trading Partners* set-up an agreement and run the associated electronic exchange.

b.) Three or more *Trading Partners* set-up a *Business Process* implementing a supply-chain and run the associated exchanges

c.) A Company sets up a Portal that defines a *Business Process* involving the use of external business services.

d.) Three or more *Trading Partners* conduct business using shared *Business Processes* and run the associated exchanges.

Scenario 1 : Two Trading Partners Set-Up an Agreement and Run the Associated Exchange

In this scenario:

▼ Each *Trading Partner* defines its own Profile (*CPP*).

Each Profile references:
  ▼ One or more existing *Business Process* found in the ebXML *Registry*
  ▼ One of more *Message* Definitions. Each *Message* definition is built from reusable components (*Core Components*) found in the ebXML *Registry*

Each Profile (*CPP*) defines:

▼ The business transactions that the *Trading Partner* is able to engage into
▼ The Technical protocol (like HTPP, SMTP etc) and the technical properties (such as special encryption, validation, authentication) that the *Trading Partner* supports in the engagement
▼ The *Trading Partners* acknowledge each other profile and create a *CPA*.

▼ The *Trading Partners* implement the respective part of the Profile. This is done:
   ▼ Either by creating/configuring a *Business Service Interface*.
   ▼ Or properly upgrading the legacy software running at their side

In both cases, this step is about :
▼ Plugging the Legacy into the ebXML technical infrastructure as specified by the *Messaging Service*.
▼ Granting that the software is able to properly engage the stated conversations
▼ Granting that the exchanges semantically conform to the agreed upon *Message* Definitions
▼ Granting that the exchanges technically conform with the underlying ebXML *Messaging Service*.

▼ The *Trading Partners* start exchanging *Messages* and performing the agreed upon commercial transactions.

Scenario 2: Three or More Parties Set-Up a Business Process Implementing a Supply-Chain and Run the Associated Exchanges

The simple case of a supply-chain involving two *Trading Partners* can be redefined in terms of the Scenario 1.

Here we are dealing with situations where more *Trading Partners* are involved. We consider a supply chain of the following type:

What fundamentally differs from Scenario 1 is that *"Trading Partner* 2" is engaged at the same time with two different *Trading Partners*. The assumption is that the "state" of the local portion of the *Business Process* is managed by each *Trading Partner*, i.e. that each *Trading Partner* is fully responsible of the Business Transaction involving it (*"Trading Partner* 3" only knows about *"Trading Partner* 2",

"Trading Partner 2" knows about *"Trading Partner 3"* and *"Trading Partner 1"*, *"Trading Partner 1"* knows about *"Trading Partner 2"*).

In this scenario:

▼ Each *Trading Partner* defines its own Profile (*CPP*). Each Profile (*CPP*) references:

   ▼ One or more existing *Business Process* found in the ebXML *Registry*

   ▼ One of more *Message* Definitions. Each *Message* definition is built from reusable components (*Core Components*) found in the ebXML *Registry*

   Each Profile (*CPP*) defines:

   ▼ The Commercial Transactions that the *Trading Partner* is able to engage into. *"Trading Partner 2"* must be able to support at least 2 Commercial Transactions.

   ▼ The Technical protocol (like HTPP, SMTP etc) and the technical properties (such as special encryption, validation, authentication) that the *Trading Partner* supports in the engagement. As to *"Trading Partner 2"*, the technical requirements for the exchanges with *"Trading Partner 1"* and *"Trading Partner 3"* may be different. In such case, *"Trading Partner 2"* must be able to support different protocols and/or properties.

   ▼ The *Trading Partners* acknowledge each other profile and create the relevant *CPA*. (at least 2 in this Scenario).

   ▼ *"Trading Partner 2"* is engaged in 2 *CPA's*

▼ The *Trading Partners* implement the respective part of the Profile. This is done:

   ▼ Either by creating/configuring a *Business Service Interface*.

   ▼ Or properly upgrading the legacy software running at their side.

   In both cases, this step is about:

   ▼ Plugging the Legacy into the ebXML technical infrastructure as specified by the *Messaging Service*

   ▼ Granting that the software is able to properly engage the stated conversations

   ▼ Granting that the exchanges semantically conform to the agreed upon ebXML *Message* definitions

   ▼ Granting that the exchanges technically conform with the underlying ebXML *Messaging Service*.

   ▼ *"Trading Partner 2"* may need to implement a complex *Business Service Interface* in order to be able to engage with different *Trading Partners*.

▼ The *Trading Partners* start exchanging *Messages* and performing the agreed upon commercial transactions.

▼ *"Trading Partner* 3*"* places an order at *"Trading Partner* 2*"*
▼ *"Trading Partner* 2*"* (eventually) places an order with *"Trading Partner* 1*"*
▼ *"Trading Partner* 1*"* fulfills the order
▼ *"Trading Partner* 2*"* fulfill the order

Scenario 3 : A Company Sets Up a Portal Which Defines a Business Process Involving the Use of External Business Services

This is the Scenario describing a Service Provider. A "client" asks the Service Provider for a Service. The Service Provider fulfills the request by properly managing the exchanges with other *Trading Partners* that provide information to build the final answer.

In the simplest case, this Scenario could be modeled as follows :

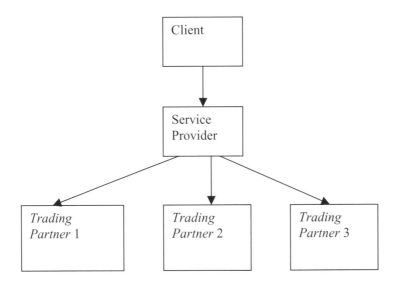

This is an evolution of Scenario 2. The Description of this scenario is omitted.

Scenario 4: Three or More Trading Partners Conduct Business Using Shared Business Processes and Run the Associated Exchanges

This Scenario is about 3 or more *Trading Partners* having complex relationships. An example of this is the use of an external delivery service for delivering goods.

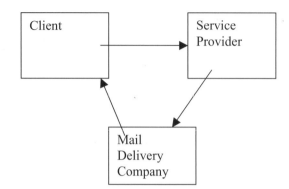

In this Scenario, each *Trading Partner* is involved with more than one other *Trading Partner* but the relationship is not linear. The product or good that is ordered by the *Client* with a Service Provider is delivered by a 3rd party.

In this scenario:

▼ Each *Trading Partner* defines its own Profile (*CPP*). Each Profile (*CPP*) references:
  ▼ One or more existing *Business Process* found in the ebXML *Registry*
  ▼ One of more *Registry* Definitions. Each *Registry* definition is built from reusable components (*Core Components*) found in the ebXML *Registry*

  Each Profile (*CPP*) defines:
  ▼ The Commercial Transactions that the *Trading Partner* is able to engage into. In this case, each *Trading Partner* must be able to support at least 2 Commercial Transactions.
  ▼ The Technical protocol (like HTPP, SMTP etc) and the technical properties (such as special encryption, validation, authentication) that the *Trading Partner* supports in the engagement.
    In case the technical infrastructure underlying the different exchanges differes, each *Trading Partner* must be able to support different protocols and/or properties. (an example is that the order is done through a Web Site and the delivery is under the form of an email).
  ▼ The *Trading Partners* acknowledge each other profile and create a *CPA*. Each *Trading Partner*, in this Scenario, must be able to negotiate at least 2 Agreements.
    Each *Trading Partner* is enagaged in 2 Agreements (*CPA*).

▼ The *Trading Partners* implement the respective part of the Profile. This is done:
  ▼ Either by creating/configuring a *Business Service Interface*.
  ▼ Or properly upgrading the legacy software running at their side

In both cases, this step is about:

▼ Plugging the Legacy into the ebXML technical infrastructure as specified by the *Messaging Service.*

▼ Granting that the software is able to properly engage the stated conversations

▼ Granting that the exchanges semantically conform to the agreed upon *Message* definitions.

▼ Granting that the exchanges technical conform with the underlying ebXML *Messaging Service.*

▼ All *Trading Partners* may need to implement complex *Business Service Interfaces* to accommodate the differences in the *CPA*'s with different *Trading Partners.*

▼ The *Trading Partners* start exchanging *Messages* and performing the agreed upon commercial transactions.

▼ The *Client* places an Order at the Service Provider.

▼ The Service Provider Acknowledges the Order with The *Client.*

▼ The Service Provider informs the Mail Delivery Service about a good to be delivered at the *Client*

▼ The Mail Delivery Service delivers the good at the *Client*

▼ The *Clients* notifies the Service Provider that the good is received.

CHAPTER 3

Business Process Specification Schema

v1.01
Business Process Team
11 May 2001

TABLE OF CONTENTS

1   Status of this Document

This document specifies an ebXML Technical Specification for the eBusiness community.

Distribution of this document is unlimited.

The document formatting is based on the Internet Society's Standard RFC format.

This version:
www.ebxml.org/specs/ebBPSS.pdf

Latest version:
www.ebxml.org/specs/ebBPSS.pdf

2   ebXML BP/CoreComponents Metamodel Participants

We would like to recognize the following for their significant participation to the development of this document.

Team Lead:

Paul Levine	Telcordia

Editors:

Jim Clark	E2Open - previously Edifecs: (Transaction Semantics)
Cory Casanave	Data Access Technologies: (UML model)
Kurt Kanaskie	Lucent Technologies: (DTD and Examples)
Betty Harvey	Electronic Commerce Connection: (DTD documentation)
Jamie Clark	McLure-Moynihan, Inc.: (Legal aspects)
Neal Smith	Chevron: (Issues Lists, and W3C schema)
John Yunker	Edifecs: (Signal structures)
Karsten Riemer	Sun Microsystems: (Overall Document)

Participants:

Antoine Lonjon	Mega
J.J. Dubray	Excelon
Bob Haugen	Logistical Software
Bill McCarthy	Michigan State University
Paul Levine	Telcordia
Brian Hayes	CommerceOne
Nita Sharma	Netfish
David Welsh	Nordstrom
Christopher Ferris	Sun Microsystems
Antonio Carrasco	Data Access Technologies

3   Introduction

3.1   Executive Summary

The ebXML Specification Schema provides a standard framework by which business systems may be configured to support execution of business collaborations consisting of business transactions. It is based upon prior UN/CEFACT work, specifically the metamodel behind the UN/CEFACT Modeling Methodology (UMM) defined in the N090R9.1 specification.

The Specification Schema supports the specification of Business Transactions and the choreography of Business Transactions into Business Collaborations. Each Business Transaction can be implemented using one of many available standard patterns. These patterns determine the actual exchange of Business Documents and business signals between the partners to achieve the required electronic commerce transaction.

The current version of the specification schema addresses collaborations between two parties (Binary Collaborations).

It is anticipated that a subsequent version will address additional features such as the semantics of economic exchanges and contracts, more complex multi-party choreography, and context based content.

3.2   Summary of Contents of Document

This document describes the ebXML Specification Schema

This document describes the Specification Schema, both in its UML form and in its DTD form.

The document first introduces general concepts and semantics, then applies these semantics in a detail discussion of each part of the model. The document then specifies all elements in the UML form, and then in the XML form.

The keywords MUST, MUST NOT, REQUIRED, SHALL, SHALL NOT, SHOULD, SHOULD NOT, RECOMMENDED, MAY, and OPTIONAL, when they appear in this document, are to be interpreted as described in RFC 2119 [Bra97].

3.3   Audience

The primary audience is business process analysts. We define a business process analyst as someone who interviews business people and as a result documents business processes in unambiguous syntax.

An additional audience is designers of business process definition tools who need to specify the conversion of user input in the tool into the XML representation of the Specification Schema.

The audience is not business application developers.

3.4   Related Documents

As mentioned above, other documents provide detailed definitions of some of the components of the ebXML Specification Schema and of their inter-relationship. They include ebXML Specifications on the following topics:

[ebTA] ebXML Technical Architecture Specification, version 1.04

[ccDICT] ebXML Core Components Dictionary, version 1.04

[ebCCNAM] ebXML Naming Convention for Core Components, version 1.04

[ebCPP] ebXML Collaboration-Protocol Profile and Agreement Specification V1.0

[bpOVER] ebXML Business Process and Business Information Analysis Overview, version 1.0

[bpWS] ebXML Business Process Analysis Worksheets & Guidelines, version 1.0

[bpPATT] ebXML E-Commerce Patterns, version 1.0

[bpPROC] ebXML Catalog of Common Business Processes, version 1.0

[ebMS] ebXML Message Service Specification version 1.0

UN/CEFACT Modeling Methodology (UMM) as defined in the N090R9.1
    specification

3.5 Prerequisites

It is assumed that the audience will be familiar with or have knowledge of the
following technologies and techniques:

▼ Business process modeling techniques and principles

▼ The UML syntax and semantics

▼ The Extensible Markup Language (XML)

4 Design Objectives

4.1 Goals/Objectives/Requirements/Problem Description

Business process models describe interoperable business processes that allow
business partners to collaborate. Business process models for e-business must
be turned into software components that collaborate on behalf of the business
partners.

The goal of the ebXML Specification Schema is to provide the bridge between
e-business process modeling and specification of e-business software
components.

The ebXML Specification Schema provides for the nominal set of specification elements necessary to specify a collaboration between business partners,
and to provide configuration parameters for the partners' runtime systems in
order to execute that collaboration between a set of e-business software
components.

A specification created against the ebXML Business Process Specification Schema
is referred to as an ebXML Business Process Specification.

The *ebXML Business Process Specification Schema* is available in two stand-alone
representations, a UML version, and an XML version.

The UML version of the *ebXML Business Process Specification Sch*ema is merely a
UML Class Diagram. It is not intended for the direct creation of ebXML Business

Process Specifications. Rather, it is a self-contained statement of all the specification elements and relationships required to be able to create an ebXML compliant Business Process Specification. Any methodologies and/or metamodels used for the creation of ebXML compliant Business Process Specifications must at minimum support these elements and relationships.

The XML version of the *ebXML Business Process Specification Schema* provides the specification for XML based instances of ebXML Business Process Specifications, and as a target for production rules from other representations. Both a DTD and a W3C Schema are provided.

The UML and XML based versions of the *ebXML Business Process Specification Schema* are unambiguously mapped to each other.

4.2 Caveats and Assumptions

This specification is designed to specify the run time aspects of a business collaboration.

It is not intended to incorporate a methodology, and does not directly prescribe the use of a methodology. However, if a methodology is to be used, it is recommended that it be UN/CEFACT Modeling Methodology (UMM).

The *ebXML Business Process Specification Schema* does not by itself define Business Documents Structures. It is intended to work in conjunction with already existing Business Document definitions, and/or the document metamodel defined by the ebXML Core Components specifications.

4.2.1 Relationship Between ebXML Business Process Specification Schema and UMM

The UN/CEFACT Modeling Methodology (UMM) is a methodology for business process and information modeling.

This section describes the relationship between UMM and the ebXML *Business Process Specification Schema*.

The UMM Meta Model is a description of business semantics that allows Trading Partners to capture the details for a specific business scenario (a Business Process) using a consistent modeling methodology. A Business Process describes in detail how Trading Partners take on shared roles, relationships and responsibilities to facilitate interaction with other Trading Partners. The interaction between roles takes place as a choreographed set of Business Transactions. Each Business Transaction is expressed as an exchange of electronic Business Documents. The sequence of the exchange is determined by the Business Process, and by messaging and security considerations. Business Documents are composed from re-useable Business Information Objects. At a lower level, Business Processes can be composed of re-useable Common Business Processes, and Business Information Objects can be composed of re-useable Core Components. Common Business Processes and Business Information Objects reside in a UMM Business Library.

The UMM Meta Model supports a set of Business Process viewpoints that provide a set of semantics (vocabulary) for each viewpoint and forms the basis of specification of the semantics and artifacts that are required to facilitate business process and information integration and interoperability. Using the UMM methodology and the UMM metamodel, the user may thus create a complete Business Process and Information Model. This model contains more information than what is required for configuring ebXML compliant software. Also the model is syntax independent and not directly interpretable by ebXML compliant software.

The *ebXML Business Process Specification Schema* provides an additional view of the UMM metamodel. This subset is provided to support the direct specification of the nominal set of elements necessary to configure a runtime system in order to execute a set of ebXML business transactions. By drawing out modeling elements from several of the other views, the *ebXML Business Process Specification Schema* forms a semantic subset of the UMM Meta Model. Using the *ebXML Business Process Specification Schema* the user may thus create a Business Process Specification that contains only the information required to configure ebXML compliant software.

The *ebXML Business Process Specification Schema* is available in two stand-alone representations, a UML version , and an XML version. The XML version is intended to be interpretable by ebXML compliant software.

The relationship between the UMM Meta Model and the *ebXML Business Process Specification Schema* is shown in Figure 1.

Using the UMM methodology, and drawing on content from the UMM Business Library a user may create complete Business Process and Information Model conforming to the UMM metamodel.

Since the ebXML *Business Process Specification Schema* is a semantic subset of the UMM metamodel, the user may then in an automated fashion extract from the Business Process and Information Model the required set of elements and relationships, and transform them into an ebXML Business Process Specification conforming to the *ebXML Business Process Specification Schema.*

Likewise, since the ebXML CC document metamodel is aligned with the UMM Metamodel, the user may then in an automated fashion extract from the Business

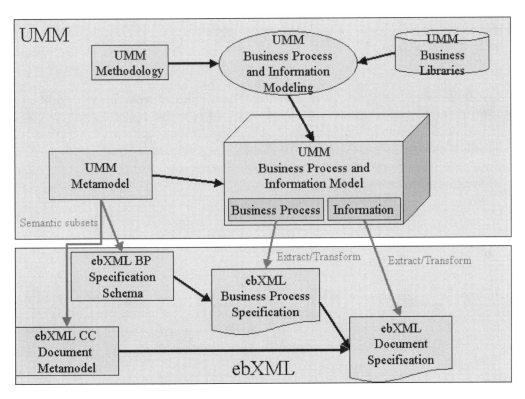

FIGURE 1   UMM Metamodel and *ebXML Business Process Specification Schema*

Process and Information Model the required set of elements and relationships, and transform them into an ebXML document model conforming to ebXML Core Component specifications.

The UMM methodology is not part of the formal set of ebXML specifications.

Likewise, the UMM metamodel in its entirety is not part of the formal set of ebXML specifications. Only the semantic subset represented by the *ebXML Business Process Specification Schema* and CC are part of the formal set of ebXML specifications.

The remainder of this document focuses on the *ebXML Business Process Specification Schema* and Business Process Specifications created against it. It is understood that proper Business Process and Information Modeling may have taken place prior to beginning the activity of creating a Business Process Specification.

5 System Overview

The ebXML *Business Process Specification Schema* provides a standard framework for business process specification. As such, it works with the ebXML Collaboration Protocol Profile (CPP) and Collaboration Protocol Agreement (CPA) specifications to bridge the gap between Business Process Modeling and the configuration of ebXML compliant e-commerce software, e.g. an ebXML Business Service Interface, as depicted in Figure 2.

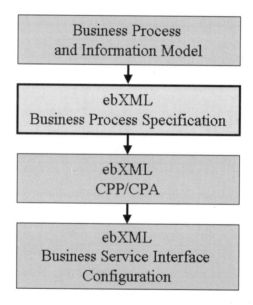

FIGURE 2   Business Process Specification and Business Service Interface Configuration

Using Business Process Modeling, a user may create a complete Business Process and Information Model.

Based on this Business Process and Information Model and using the ebXML *Business Process Specification Schema* the user will then extract and format the nominal set of elements necessary to configure an ebXML runtime system in order to execute a set of ebXML business transactions. The result is an ebXML *Business Process Specification.*

Alternatively the ebXML *Business Process Specification* may be created directly, without prior explicit business process modeling.

An ebXML *Business Process Specification* contains the specification of Business Transactions and the choreography of Business Transactions into Business Collaborations.

This ebXML *Business Process Specification* is then the input to the formation of ebXML trading partner Collaboration Protocol Profiles and Collaboration Protocol Agreements (CPP and CPA).

These ebXML trading partner Collaboration Protocol Profiles and Collaboration Protocol Agreements in turn serve as configuration files for ebXML Business Service Interface software.

The architecture of the ebXML *Business Process Specification Schema* consists of the following functional components:

▼ UML version of the *Business Process Specification Schema*

▼ XML version of the *Business Process Specification Schema*

▼ Production Rules defining the mapping from the UML version of the *Business Process Specification Schema* to the XML version

▼ Business Signal Definitions

Together these components allow you to fully specify all the run time aspects of a business process model.

These components are shown (inside the dotted box) in figure 3 below.

The following provides a description of each of the components in the ebXML *Business Process Specification Schema* and their relationship to UMM, and ebXML CC and CPP/CPA:

UML Version of Business Process Specification Schema

The UML version of the *ebXML Business Process Specification Schema* is a semantic subset of the metamodel behind UMM as specified in UN/CEFACT TMWG's N090R9.1

N090R9.1 is as of this writing not yet approved by UN/CEFACT. It is the intent to keep the *ebXML Business Process Specification Schema and the* UN/CEFACT TMWG's N090 semantically aligned.

The UML version of the ebXML *Business Process Specification Schema* is merely a UML Class Diagram. It is not intended for the direct creation of ebXML Business Process Specifications. Rather, it is a self-contained statement of all the specifica-

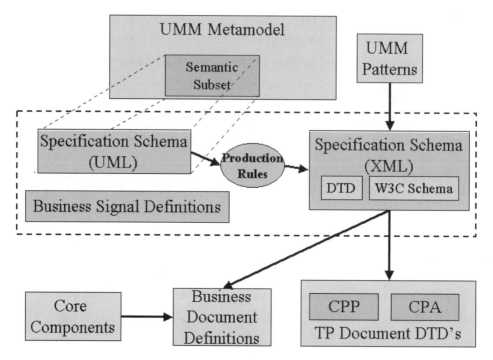

FIGURE 3 Relationship of ebXML *Business Process Specification Schema* to UMM, CPP/CPA and Core Components

tion elements and relationships required to be able to create an ebXML compliant Business Process Specification.

XML Version of Business Process Specification Schema

The XML version of the ebXML *Business Process Specification Schema* provides the specification for XML based instances of ebXML Business Process Specifications, and serves as a target for production rules from other representations. Thus, a user may either create a *Business Process Specification* directly as an XML document, or may chose to use some other means of specification first and then apply production rules to arrive at the XML document version.

Any methodologies and/or metamodels used for the creation of ebXML compliant Business Process Specifications must at minimum support the production of the elements and relationships contained in the XML version of the ebXML *Business Process Specification Schema*.

Both a DTD and a W3C Schema is provided. Each is an isomorphic definition of the UML version of the ebXML *Business Process Specification Schema*.

UMM Business Process Interaction Patterns

ebXML Business Service Interfaces are configured to execute the business processes specified in a *Business Process Specification.* They do so by exchanging ebXML messages and business signals.

Each Business Transaction can be implemented using one of many available standard patterns. These patterns determine the actual exchange of messages and business signals between the partners to achieve the required electronic commerce transaction.

The Business Transaction Interaction Patterns set forth in Chapter 8 of the UMM N090R9.1 document illustrate recommended permutations of message sequences as determined by the type of business transaction defined and the timing policies specified in the transactions.

While the UMM patterns themselves are not part of the ebXML specifications, all the security and timing parameters required to express the pattern properties are provided as attributes of elements in the ebXML *Business Process Specification Schema.*

Business Signal Definitions

Business signals are application level documents that 'signal' the current state of the business transaction. These business signals have specific business purpose and are separate from lower protocol and transport signals.

However, the structures of ebXML business signals are 'universal' and do not vary from transaction to transaction. Thus, they can be defined once and for all as part of the ebXML *Business Process Specification Schema* itself.

The Business Process Specification Schema provides both the choreography of business signals, and the structure definition of the business payload of a business signal. The ebXML Message Service Specification signal structures provide business service state alignment infrastructure, including unique message identifiers and digests used to meet the basic process alignment requirements. The business signal payload structures provided herein are optional and normative and are intended to provide business and legal semantics to the business signals.

A DTD is provided for each of the possible business signals.

Production Rules

A set of production rules are provided, defining the mapping from the UML version of the ebXML *Business Process Specification Schema* to the XML version.

The primary purpose for these production rules is to govern the one-time generation of the DTD version of the ebXML *Business Process Specification Schema* from the UML Class Diagram version of the ebXML *Business Process Specification Schema.*

The Class Diagram version of *Business Process Specification Schema* is not intended for the direct creation of ebXML Business Process Specifications. However, if a *Business Process Specification* was in fact (programmatically) created as an instance of this class diagram, the production rules would also apply for its conversion into a DTD conformant XML document.

Separately, it is expected that a set of production rules will be constructed for the production of an XML version of an ebXML *Business Process Specification* from a set of UML diagrams constructed through the use of UMM.

An instance of the UML Class Diagram version of the ebXML *Business Process Specification Schema* will through the application of its production rules produce an XML Specification Document that is analytically, semantically and functionally equivalent to one arrived at by modeling the same subset through the use of UMM and its associated production rules.

Relationship to CPP/CPA

A *Business Process Specification* is in essence the machine interpretable run time business process specification needed for an ebXML Business Service Interface. The *Business Process Specification* is therefore incorporated with or referenced by ebXML trading partner Collaboration Protocol Profiles (CPP) and Collaboration Protocol Agreements (CPA). Each CPP declares its support for one or more Roles within the *Business Process Specification.* Within these CPP profiles and CPA agreements are then added further technical parameters resulting in a full specification of the run-time software at each trading partner.

Relationship to ebXML Core Components

The *Business Process Specification Schema* does not by itself support the definiton of Business Documents. Rather, a *Business Process Specification* merely points to the definition of Business Documents. Such definitions may either be XML based, or – as attachments – may be any other structure, or completely unstructured. XML based Business Document Specifications may be based on the ebXML Core Components specifications.

Relationship to ebXML Message Service Specification

The Business Process Specification Schema will provide choreography of business messages and signals. The ebXML Message Service Specification provides the infrastructure for message / signal identification, typing, and integrity; as well as placing any one message in sequence with respect to other messages in the choreography.

5.1   Key Concepts of the ebXML Business Process Specification Schema

The ebXML *Business Process Specification Schema* provides the semantics, elements, and properties necessary to define business collaborations.

A business collaboration consists of a set of roles collaborating through a set of choreographed transactions by exchanging business documents.

These basic semantics of a business collaboration are shown in Figure 4.

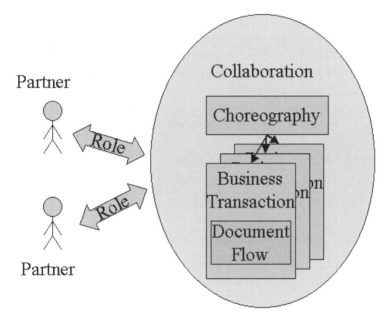

FIGURE 4   Basic Semantics of a Business Collaboration

Two or more business partners participate in the business collaboration through roles. The roles interact with each other through Business Transactions. The business transactions are sequenced relative to each other in a Choreography. Each Business Transaction consists of one or two predefined Business document flows. A Business Transaction may be additionally supported by one or more Business Signals.

The following section describes the concepts of a Business Collaboration, a Business Transaction, a Business document flow, and a Choreography

1. Business Collaborations

   A business collaboration is a set of Business Transactions between business partners. Each partner plays one or more roles in the collaboration.

The ebXML *Business Process Specification Schema* supports two levels of business collaborations, Binary Collaborations and Multiparty Collaborations.

Binary Collaborations are between two roles only.

Multiparty Collaborations are among more than two roles, but such Multiparty Collaborations are always synthesized from two or more Binary Collaborations. For instance if Roles A, B, and C collaborate and all parties interact with each other, there will be a separate Binary Collaboration between A and B, one between B and C, and one between A and C. The Multiparty Collaboration will be the synthesis of these three Binary Collaborations.

Binary Collaborations are expressed as a set of Business Activities between the two roles. Each Business Activity reflects a state in the collaboration. The Business Activity can be a Business Transaction Activity, i.e. the activity of conducting a single Business Transaction, or a Collaboration Activity, i.e. the activity of conducting another Binary Collaboration. An example of the former is the activity of placing a purchase order. An example of the latter is the activity of negotiating a contract. In either case the activities can be choreographed relative to other activities as per below.

The ability of a Binary Collaboration to have activities that in effect are executing other Binary Collaborations, is the key to recursive compositions of Binary Collaboration, and to the re-use of Binary Collaborations.

In essence each Binary Collaboration is a re-useable protocol between two roles.

2. Business Transactions

   A Business Transaction is the atomic unit of work in a trading arrangement between two business partners. A Business Transaction is conducted between two parties playing opposite roles in the transaction. The roles are always a requesting role and a responding role.

   Like a Binary Collaboration, a Business Transaction is a re-useable protocol between two roles. The way it is re-used is by referencing it from a Binary Collaboration through the use of a Business Transaction Activity as per above. In a Business Transaction Activity the roles of the Binary Collaboration are assigned to the execution of the Business Transaction.

   Unlike a Binary Collaboration, however, the Business Transaction is atomic, it cannot be decomposed into lower level Business Transactions.

   A Business Transaction is a very specialized and very constrained protocol, in order to achieve very precise and enforceable transaction semantics. These semantics are expected to be enforced by the software managing the transaction, i.e. an ebXML Business Service Interface (BSI).

A Business Transaction will always either succeed or fail. If it succeeds it may be designated as legally binding between the two partners, or otherwise govern their collaborative activity. If it fails it is null and void, and each partner must relinquish any mutual claim established by the transaction. This can be thought of as 'rolling back' the Business Transaction upon failure.

3. Business Document flows

A business transaction is realized as Business Document flows between the requesting and responding roles. There is always a requesting Business Document, and optionally a responding Business Document, depending on the desired transaction semantics, e.g. one-way notification vs. two-way conversation.

Actual document definition is achieved using the ebXML core component specifications, or by some methodology external to ebXML but resulting in a DTD or Schema that an ebXML *Business Process Specification* can point to.

4. Choreography

The Business Transaction Choreography describes the ordering and transitions between business transactions or sub collaborations within a binary collaboration. In a UML tool this can be done using a UML activity diagram. The choreography is described in the ebXML *Business Process Specification Schema* using activity diagram concepts such as start state, completion state, activities, synchronizations, transitions between activities, and guards on the transitions.

5. Patterns

The ebXML *Business Process Specification Schema* provides a set of unambiguous semantics within which to specify transactions and collaborations. Within these semantics the user community has flexibility to specify an infinite number of specific transactions and collaborations. The use of predefined patterns combines this flexibility with a consistency that facilitates faster design, faster implementation, and enables generic processing.

A set of predefined transaction interaction patterns, defining common combinations of transaction interaction parameter settings can be found in UMM.

While the UMM transaction interaction patterns themselves are not part of the ebXML specifications, all the security and timing parameters required to express the pattern properties are provided as attributes of elements in the *Business Process Specification Schema*.

It is also anticipated that patterns for collaboration choreographies will emerge. An example of such a pattern is in the ebXML E-Commerce Patterns.

Re-use, recursion, and patterns are among the key concepts of the ebXML *Business Process Specification Schema*. The following section will illustrate these key concepts.

5.2 How to Use the ebXML Business Process Specification Schema

The ebXML *Business Process Specification Schema* should be used wherever ebXML compliant software is being specified to execute Business Collaborations. The generic term for such software is a Business Service Interface (BSI).

The ebXML *Business Process Specification Schema* is used to specify the business process related configuration parameters for configuring a BSI to execute these collaborations.

This section discusses

▼ How the ebXML *Business Process Specification Schema* fits in with other ebXML specifications.

▼ How to use the ebXML *Business Process Specification Schema* at design time, either for specifying brand new collaborations and transactions, or for re-using existing ones.

▼ How to specify core transaction semantics and parameters needed for a Collaboration-Protocol Profile and Agreement (CPP/CPA).

▼ Run-time transaction and collaboration semantics that the ebXML *Business Process Specification Schema* specifies and the Business Service Interface (BSI) is expected to manage.

5.3 How ebXML Business Process Specification Schema Is Used with Other ebXML Specifications

The ebXML *Business Process Specification Schema* provides the semantics, elements, and properties necessary to define Business Collaborations.

A collaboration consists of a set of roles collaborating through a set of choreographed transactions by exchanging Business Documents.

As shown in Figure 5, Business Documents are defined at the intersection between the Business Process Specification and the ebXML Core Component specifications. A Business Process Specification will reference, but not define, a set of required Business Documents. At ebXML Business Documents are either defined by some external document specification, or assembled directly or indirectly from lower level information structures called core components. The assembly is based on a set of contexts, many of which are provided by the business processes, i.e. collaborations that use the documents in their document flows.

The combination of the business process specification and the document specification become the basis against which partners can make agreements on conducting electronic business with each other.

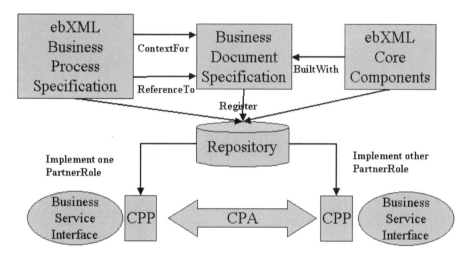

FIGURE 5   ebXML *Business Process Specification Schema* and Other ebXML Specifications

The user will extract and transform the necessary information from an existing Business Process and Information Model. Associated production rules could aid in creating an XML version of a *Business Process Specification.*

Alternatively a user would use an XML based tool to produce the XML version directly. Production rules could then aid in converting into XMI, so that it could be loaded into a UML tool, if required.

In either case, the XML version of the *Business Process Specification* gets stored in the ebXML repository and registered in the ebXML registry for future retrieval. The *Business Process Specification* would be registered using classifiers derived during its design.

When implementers want to establish trading partner Collaboration Protocol Profile and Agreement the *Business Process Specification* XML document, or the relevant parts of it, are simply imbedded in or referenced by the CPP and CPA

XML documents. ebXML CPP and CPA documents can only reference ebXML *Business Process Specifications* and only XML versions thereof.

Guided by the CPP and CPA specifications the resulting XML document then becomes the configuration file for one or more Business Service Interfaces (BSI), i.e. the software that will actually manage either partner's participation in the collaboration.

5.4   How to Design Collaborations and Transactions, Re-using at Design Time

This section describes the ebXML *Business Process Specification Schema* modeling relationships by building a complete Multiparty Collaboration from the bottom up, as follows:

1. Specify a Business Transaction
2. Specify the Business Document flow for a Business Transaction
3. Specify a Binary Collaboration re-using the Business Transaction
4. Specify a Choreography for the Binary Collaboration
5. Specify a higher level Binary Collaboration re-using the lower level Binary Collaboration
6. Specify a Multiparty Collaboration re-using Binary Collaborations

Although this section, for purposes of introduction, discusses the specification of a collaboration from the bottom up, the ebXML *Business Process Specification Schema* very much is intended for specifying collaborations from the top down, re-using existing lower level content as much as possible.

The constructs listed above support the specification of fairly complex multi party collaborations. However, an ebXML compliant Business Process Specificaton may be as simple as a single Binary Collaboration referencing a single Business Transaction. This involves only numbers 1 through 3 above. In other words, Higher-level Binary Collaborations, Multi-party Collaborations and choreography expressions are not required for ebXML Business Process Specification compliance.

5.4.1   *Specify a Business Transaction and Its Business Document Flow*

Figure 6 illustrates a business transaction.

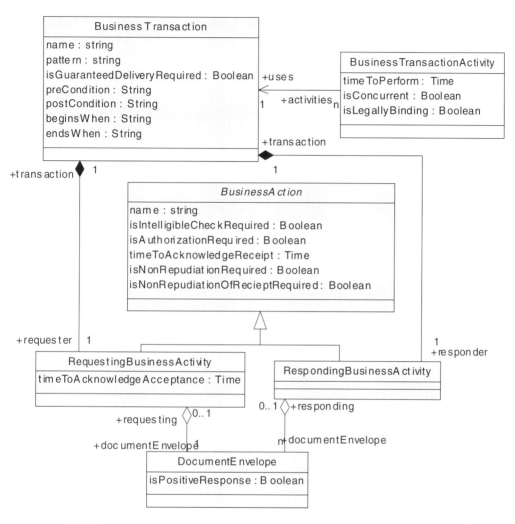

FIGURE 6 UML Diagram of a Business Transaction

5.4.1.1 Key Semantics of a Business Transaction

A Business Transaction is the atomic unit of work in a trading arrangement between two business partners.

A business transaction consists of a Requesting Business Activity, a Responding Business Activity, and one or two document flows between them. A Business Transaction may be additionally supported by one or more Business Signals that govern the use and meaning of acknowledgements and related matters in the transaction.

Implicitly there is a requesting role performing the Requesting Business Activity and a responding role performing the Responding Business Activity. These roles become explicit when the transaction is used within a Business Transaction Activity within a Binary Collaboration.

There is always a Request document flow.

Whether a Response document is required is part of the definition of the Business Transaction. Some Business Transactions need this type of request and response, typically for the formation of a contract or agreement. Other Business Transactions are more like notifications, and have only a Request document flow.

An abstract superclass, Business Action, is the holder of attributes that are common to both Requesting Business Activity and Responding Business Activity.

5.4.1.2 Sample Syntax

Here is a simple notification transaction with just one document flow:

```
<BusinessTransaction name="Notify of advanceshipment">
    <RequestingBusinessActivity name="">
        <DocumentEnvelope
            businessDocument name="ASN"/>
    </RequestingBusinessActivity>
    <RespondingBusinessActivity name="">
    </RespondingBusinessActivity>
</BusinessTransaction>
```

Associated with each document flow can be one or more business signals acknowledging the document flow. These acknowledgment signals are not modeled explicitly but parameters associated with the transaction specify whether the signals are required or not.

The possible Document Flows and business signals within a Business Transaction are shown in Figure 7.

These acknowledgment signals (a.k.a. Business Signals) are application level documents that 'signal' the current state of the business transaction.

Whether a receiptAcknowledgement and/or acceptanceAcknowledgement signal are required is part of the pattern specified for the Business Transaction. These business signals have specific business purposes, relating to the processing and management of documents and document envelopes *prior* to evaluation of their business terms, and are separate from lower protocol and transport signals.

The Receipt acknowledgement business signal, if used, signals that a message has been properly received. The property **isIntelligibleCheckRequired** allows partners to agree that a message should be confirmed by a Receipt acknowledge-

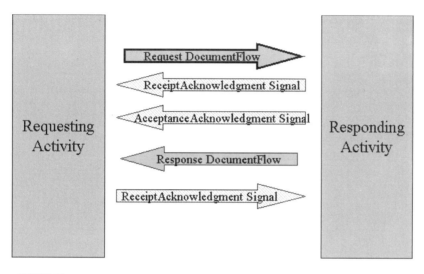

FIGURE 7   Possible Document Flows and Signals and Their Sequence

ment only if it also is legible. Legible means that it has been passed a structure/ schema validity check. Both the proper receipt and, if evaluated, the legibility of a message are reviewed (and if present acknowledged) *prior* to the application of any business rules or evaluation of the terms or guard expressions in the message's business documents or document envelope.

The Acceptance Acknowledgement business signal, if used, signals that the message received has been accepted for business processing. This is the case if the contents of the message's business documents and document envelope have passed a business rule validity check.

Failure to send either signal, when required (by specifying a timeout value in timeToAcknowledgeReceipt or timeToAcknowledgeAcceptance), will result in the transaction being null and void, and therefore will prevent any "success" end state that would have depended on receipt of a business document satisfying the associated timeToPerform.

5.4.1.3   Sample Syntax

Here is a slightly more complex transaction with two document flows and three business signals.

The request requires both receipt and acceptance acknowledgement, the response requires only receipt acknowledgement. "P2D" is a W3C Schema syntax adopted from the ISO 8601 standard and means Period=2 Days. P3D means Period= 3 Days, P5D means Period=5 Days. These periods are all measured from original sending of request.

```
<BusinessTransaction name="Create Order">
    <RequestingBusinessActivity name=""
                isNonRepudiationRequired="true"
                timeToAcknowledgeReceipt="P2D"
                timeToAcknowledgeAcceptance="P3D">
        <DocumentEnvelope
                businessDocument="Purchase Order"/>
    </RequestingBusinessActivity>
    <RespondingBusinessActivity name=""
            isNonRepudiationRequired="true"
            timeToAcknowledgeReceipt="P5D">
            <DocumentEnvelope isPositiveResponse="true"
                businessDocument="PO Acknowledgement"/>

    </RespondingBusinessActivity>
</BusinessTransaction>
```

5.4.1.4   Specifying Business Document Flows

Request document flows and response document flows contain Business Documents that pertain to the Business Transaction. The model for this is shown in Figure 8. Business Documents have varying structures. Business signals, however always have the same structure, defined once and for all as part of the ebXML *Business Process Specification Schema*.

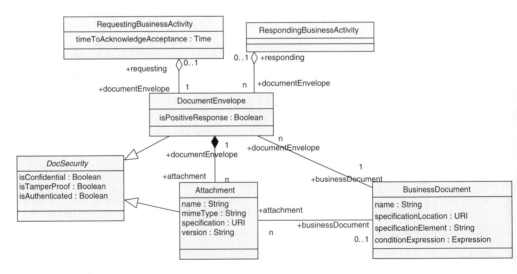

FIGURE 8   UML Diagram of Document Flow

A document flow is not modeled directly. Rather it is modeled indirectly as a Document Envelope sent by one role and received by the other. The Document Envelope is always associated with one Requesting Business Activity and one Responding Business Activity to model the flow.

Document Envelopes are named. There is always only one named Document Envelope for a Requesting Activity. There may be zero, one, or many mutually exclusive, named Document Envelopes for a Responding Activity. For example, the Response Document Envelopes for a purchase order transaction might be named PurchaseOrderAcceptance, PurchaseOrderDenial, and PartialPurchaseOrder-Acceptance. In the actual execution of the purchase order transaction, however, only one of the defined possible responses will be sent.

The Document Envelope represents the flow of documents between the activities. Each Document Envelope carries exactly one primary Business Document.

A Document Envelope can optionally have one or more attachments, all related to the primary Business Document. The document and its attachments in essence form one transaction in the payload in the ebXML Message Service message structure.

5.4.1.5   Sample Syntax

This example shows a business transaction with one request and two possible responses, a success and a failure. The request has an attachment. All the the Business Documents are fully qualified with the schema name.

```
<BusinessDocument name=" Purchase Order "
specificationLocation="someplace"/>
<BusinessDocument name=" PO Acknowledgement "
specificationLocation="someplace"/>
<BusinessDocument name=" PO Rejection "
specificationLocation="someplace"/>
<BusinessDocument name="Delivery Instructions"
specificationLocation="someplace"/>
<BusinessTransaction name="Create Order">
                <RequestingBusinessActivity name="">
  <DocumentEnvelope
                businessDocument="ebXML1.0/PO Acknowledgement">
<Attachment
     name="DeliveryNotes"
     mimeType="XML"
     businessDocument=
     "ebXML1.0/Delivery Instructions"
     specification=""
     isConfidential="true"
     isTamperProof="true"
     isAuthenticated="true">
```

```
                </Attachment>
              </DocumentEnvelope>
</RequestingBusinessActivity>
<RespondingBusinessActivity name="">
   <DocumentEnvelope
        businessDocument="ebXML1.0/PO  Acknowledgement">
                  </DocumentEnvelope>
   <DocumentEnvelope isPositiveResponse="false"
              businessDocument=" ebXML1.0/PO Rejection">
                  </DocumentEnvelope>
                </RespondingBusinessActivity>
              </BusinessTransaction>
```

5.4.2   *Specify a Binary Collaboration*

Figure 9 illustrates a binary collaboration.

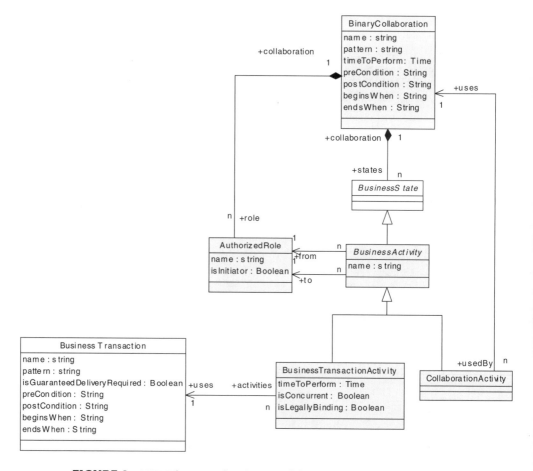

FIGURE 9   UML Diagram of a Binary Collaboration

5.4.2.1 Key Semantics of a Binary Collaboration

A Binary Collaboration is always between two roles. These two roles are called Authorized Roles, because they represent the actors that are authorized to participate in the collaboration.

A Binary Collaboration consists of one or more Business Activities. These Business Activities are always conducted **between** the two Authorized Roles of the Binary Collaboration. For each activity one of two roles is assigned to be the InitiatingRole (from) and the other to be the RespondingRole (to).

A Business Activity can be either a Business Transaction Activity or a Collaboration Activity.

A Business Transaction Activity is the performance of a Business Transaction. Business Transactions are re-useable relative to Business Transaction Activity. The same Business Transaction can be performed by multiple Business Transaction Activities in different Binary Collaborations, or even by multiple Business Transaction Activities in the same Binary Collaboration.

A Collaboration Activity is the performance of a Binary Collaboration, possibly within another Binary Collaboration. Binary Collaborations are re-useable relative to Collaboration Activity. The same Binary Collaboration can be performed by multiple Collaboration Activities in different Binary Collaborations, or even by multiple Collaboration Activities in the same Binary Collaboration.

When performing a Binary Collaboration within a Binary Collaboration there is an implicit relationship between the roles at the two levels. Assume that Binary Collaboration X is performing Binary Collaboration Y through Collaboration Activity Q. Binary Collaboration X has Authorized roles Customer and Vendor. In Collaboration Activity Q we assign Customer to be the initiator, and Vendor to be the responder. Binary Collaboration X has Authorized roles Buyer and Seller and a Business Transaction Activity where Buyer is the initiator and Seller the responder. We have now established a role relationship between the roles Customer and Buyer because they are both initiators in activities in the related performing and performed Binary Collaborations.

Since a Business Transaction is atomic in nature, the performing of a single Business Transaction through a Business Transaction Activity is also atomic in nature. If the desired semantic is not atomic, then the task should be split over multiple transactions. For instance if it is desired to model several partial acceptances of a request, then the request should be modeled as one transaction within a binary collaboration and the partial acceptance(s) as separate transactions.

The CPA/CPP Specification requires that parties agree upon a Collaboration Protocol Agreement (CPA) in order to transact business. A CPA associates itself with a specific Binary Collaboration. Thus, all Business Transactions performed between two parties should be referenced through Business Transaction Activities contained within a Binary Collaboration.

5.4.2.2 Sample Syntax

Here is a simple Binary Collaboration using one of the Business Transactions defined above:

```
<BinaryCollaboration name="Firm Order" timeToPerform="P2D">
    <Documentation>
        timeToPerform =
        Period: 2 days from start of transaction
    </Documentation>
    <InitiatingRole name="buyer"/>
    <RespondingRole name="seller"/>
    <BusinessTransactionActivity name="Create Order"
    businessTransaction="Create Order"
fromAuthorizedRole="buyer"
        toAuthorizedRole="seller"/>
</BinaryCollaboration>
```

Here is a slightly more complex Binary Collaboration re-using the same Business Transaction as the previous Binary Collaboration, and adding the use of another of the Business Transactions defined above:

```
<BinaryCollaboration name="Product Fulfillment"
timeToPerform="P5D">
    <Documentation>
        timeToPerform =
        Period: 5 days from start of transaction
    </Documentation>
    <InitiatingRole name="buyer"/>
    <RespondingRole name="seller"/>
    <BusinessTransactionActivity name="Create Order"
    businessTransaction="Create Order"
fromAuthorizedRole="buyer"
            toAuthorizedRole="seller"
            isLegallyBinding="true" />
    <BusinessTransactionActivity
        name="Notify shipment" businessTransaction=
        "Notify of advance shipment"
        fromAuthorizedRole="buyer"
        toAuthorizedRole="seller"/>
</BinaryCollaboration>
```

5.4.3 Specify a Multiparty Collaboration

Figure 10 illustrates a multiparty collaboration

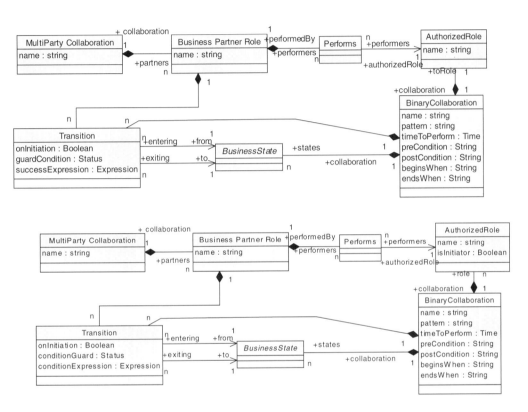

FIGURE 10 UML Diagram of a MultiParty Collaboration

5.4.3.1 Key Semantics of a Multiparty Collaboration

A Multiparty Collaboration is a synthesis of Binary Collaborations.

A Multiparty Collaboration consists of a number of Business Partner Roles.

Each Business Partner Role performs one Authorized Role in one of the binary collaborations, or perhaps one Authorized Role in each of several binary collaborations. This is modeled by use of the Performs element.

This 'Performs' linkage between a Business Partner Role and an Authorized Role is the synthesis of Binary Collaborations into Multiparty Collaborations. Implicitly the Multiparty Collaboration consists of all the Binary Collaborations in which its Business Partner Roles play Authorized Roles.

Each binary pair of trading partners will be subject to one or more distinct CPAs.

Within a Multiparty Collaboration, you may choreograph transitions between Business Transaction Activities in different Binary Collaborations, as described below.

5.4.3.2   Sample Syntax

Here is a simple Multiparty Collaboration using the Binary Collaborations defined above.

```
        <MultiPartyCollaboration name="DropShip">
        <BusinessPartnerRole name="Customer">
            <Performs
            initiatingRole=
            '//binaryCollaboration[@name="Firm Order"]
            /InitiatingRole[@name="buyer"]'/>
        </BusinessPartnerRole>
        <BusinessPartnerRole name="Retailer">
            <Performs
            respondingRole=
            '//binaryCollaboration[@name="Firm Order"]
            /RespondingRole[@name="seller"]'/>
            <Performs
            initiatingRole=
            '//binaryCollaboration[@name=" Product Fulfillment"
            /InitiatingRole[@name="buyer"]'/>
        </BusinessPartnerRole>
        <BusinessPartnerRole name="DropShip Vendor">
            <Performs
                respondingRole=
              '//binaryCollaboration[@name=" Product
            Fulfillment" /RespondingRole[@name="seller"]'/>
        </BusinessPartnerRole>
</MultiPartyCollaboration>
```

5.4.4   *Specify a Choreography*

Figure 11 illustrates a choreography.

5.4.4.1   Key Semantics of a Choreography

A Choreography is an ordering and sequencing of Business Activities within a Binary Collaboration.

The choreography is specified in terms of Business States, and transitions between those Business States.

A Business Activity is an abstract kind of Business State. Its two subtypes Business Transaction Activity and Collaboration Activity are concrete Business States. The purpose of a Choreography is to order and sequence Business Transaction

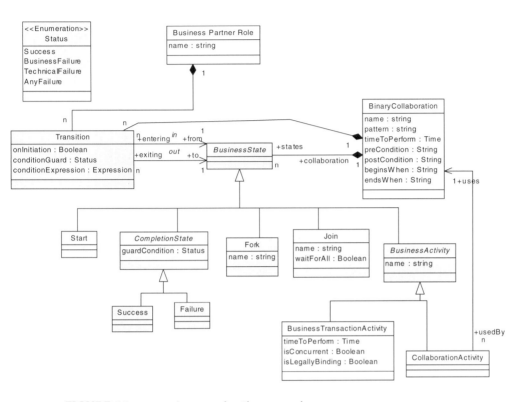

FIGURE 11　UML Diagram of a Choreography

Activity and/or Collaboration Activity within a Binary Collaboration, or across Binary Collaborations within a Multiparty Collaboration.

There are a number of auxiliary kinds of Business States that facilitate the choreographing of Business Activities. These include a Start state, a Completion state (which comes in a Success and Failure flavor), a Fork state and a Synchronization state. These are all equivalent to diagramming artifacts on a UML activity chart.

Transitions are between Business States. Transitions can be gated by Guards. Guards can refer to the status of the Document Envelope that caused the transition, the type of Document sent, the content of the document, or postconditions on the prior state.

A Transition can also be used to create nested BusinessTransactionActivities. A nested BusinessTransactionActivity is one where a first transition happens after the receipt of the request in the first transaction, and then the entire second transaction is performed before returning to the first transaction to send the response back to the original requestor. The flag 'onInitiation' in Transition is used for this purpose. Nested BusinessTransactionActivity are typically within a multiparty collaboration. In essence an Authorized Role in one Binary Collaboration receives a request, then turns around and becomes the requestor in an other Binary Collaboration before coming back and sending the response in the first Binary Collaboration.

isConcurrent is a parameter that governs the flow of transactions. Unlike the security and timing parameters it does not govern the internal flow of a transaction, rather it determines whether multiple instances of that transaction type can be 'open' at the same time as part of the same business transaction activity. IsConcurrent is the parameter that governs this. It is at the business transaction activity level.

5.4.4.2   Sample Syntax

Here is the same Binary Collaboration as used before, with choreography added at the end. There is a transition between the two, a start and two possible outcomes of this collaboration, success and failure:

```
<BinaryCollaboration name="Product Fulfillment"
timeToPerform="P5D">
      <Documentation>
           timeToPerform =
           Period: 5 days from start of transaction
      </Documentation>
      <InitiatingRole name="buyer"/>
      <RespondingRole name="seller"/>
      <BusinessTransactionActivity name="Create Order"
      businessTransaction="Create Order"
fromAuthorizedRole="buyer"
           toAuthorizedRole="seller"/>
      <BusinessTransactionActivity
           name="Notify shipment" businessTransaction=
           "Notify of advance shipment"
           fromAuthorizedRole="buyer"
           toAuthorizedRole="seller"/>
      <Start toBusinessState="Create Order"/>
      <Transition
           fromBusinessState="Create Order"
           toBusinessState="Notify shipment"/>
      <Success fromBusinessState="Notify shipment"
conditionGuard="Success"/>
      <Failure fromBusinessState="Notify shipment"
conditionGuard="BusinessFailure"/>
      </BinaryCollaboration>
```

Here is the same Multiparty Collaboration as defined before, but with a simple choreography (transition) across two Binary Collaborations.

```
<MultiPartyCollaboration name="DropShip">
          <BusinessPartnerRole name="Customer">
              <Performs
              initiatingRole=
              '//binaryCollaboration[@name="Firm Order"]
              /InitiatingRole[@name="buyer"]'/>
          </BusinessPartnerRole>
          <BusinessPartnerRole name="Retailer">
              <Performs
              respondingRole=
              '//binaryCollaboration[@name="Firm Order"]
              /RespondingRole[@name="seller"]'/>
              <Performs
              initiatingRole=
              '//binaryCollaboration[@name=" Product Fulfillment"
              /initiatingRole[@name="buyer"]'/>
              <Transition

              fromBusinessState=
              '//binaryCollaboration[@name="Firm Order"]
              /[@name="Create Order"]'
              toBusinessState=
              '//binaryCollaboration[@name="Product Fulfillment"]
              /[@name="Create Order"]'
              />
          </BusinessPartnerRole>
          <BusinessPartnerRole name="DropShip Vendor">
              <Performs
                  respondingRole=
                '//binaryCollaboration[@name=" Product
              Fulfillment" /RespondingRole[@name="seller"]'/>
          </BusinessPartnerRole>
      </MultiPartyCollaboration>
```

5.4.5   The Whole Model

Figure 12 shows the above semantics collectively as a UML class diagram. This diagram contains the whole UML version of the ebXML *Business Process Specification Schema*

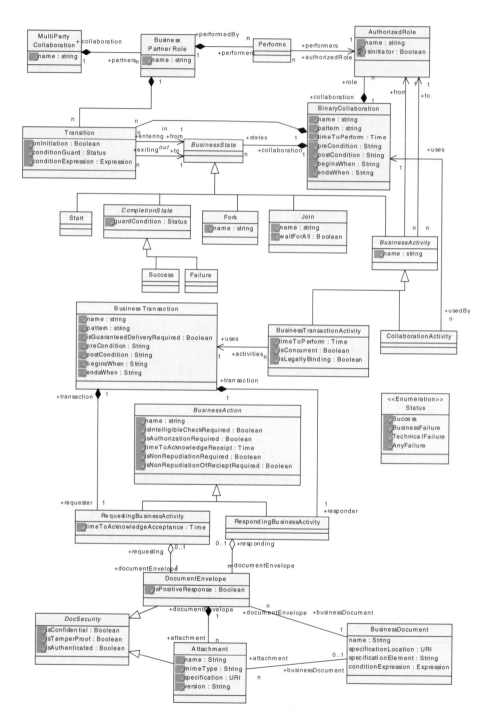

FIGURE 12   Overall ebXML *Business Process Specification Schema* as UML Class Diagram

5.5   Core Business Transaction Semantics

The ebXML concept of a business transaction and the semantics behind it are central to predictable, enforceable commerce. It is expected that any Business Service Interface (BSI) will be capable of managing a transaction according to these semantics.

The ebXML Business Transaction semantics allows you to specify electronic commerce transactions that provide

- ▼ Interaction Predictability, i.e. have clear roles, clear transaction scope, clear time bounds, clear business information semantics, clear determination of success or failure.

- ▼ Ability to create Legally Binding Contracts, i.e. the ability to specify that Business Transactions may be agreed to bind the parties.

- ▼ Nonrepudiation, i.e. may specify the keeping of artifacts to aid in legal enforceability.

- ▼ Authorization Security, i.e. may be specified to require athorization of parties performing roles.

- ▼ Document Security, i.e. may be specified to be authorized, authenticated, confidential, tamperproof.

- ▼ Reliability, i.e. the ability to specify reliable delivery of Business Documents and signals.

- ▼ Run time Business Transaction Semantics, i.e. the rules and configuration parameters required for Business Service Interface software to predictably and deterministically execute ebXML Business Transactions.

Each of the above characteristics of ebXML Business Transaction semantics is discussed in detail below.

5.5.1   Interaction Predictability

All Business Transactions follow a very precisely prescribed flow, or a precisely defined subset there-of. The following is an overall illustration of this flow. It can be thought of as the state machine across the two business partners. The N090R9.1 chapter on the UMM metamodel has a detail state chart for each of the business partners.

In the ebXML model the business transaction always has the following semantics.

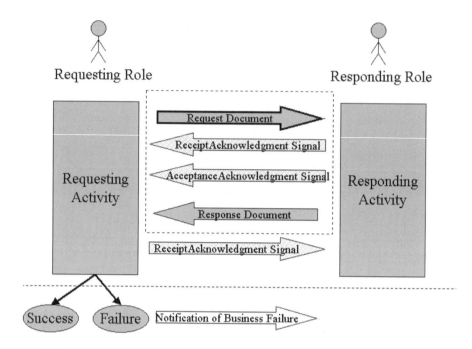

FIGURE 13   Schematic of Core Business Transaction Semantics

1. The Business Transaction is a unit of work. All of the interactions in a business transaction must succeed or the transaction must be rolled back to a defined state before the transaction was initiated.

2. A Business Transaction is conducted between two business partners playing opposite roles in the transaction. These roles are always the Requesting Role and the Responding Role.

3. A Business Transaction definition specifies exactly when the Requesting Activity is in control, when the Responding Activity is in control, and when control transitions from one to the other. In all Business Transactions control starts at the Requesting Activity, then transitions to the Responding Activity, and then returns to the Requesting Activity.

4. A Business Transaction always starts with a request sent out by the requesting activity.

5. The request serves to transition control to the responding role.

6. After the receipt of the Request document flow, the responding activity may send a receiptAcknowledgement signal and/or an acceptanceAcknowledgement signal to the requesting role.

7. The responding role then enters a responding activity. During or upon completion of the responding activity zero or one response is sent.

8. Control will be returned back to the requesting activity if either a receiptAcknowledgement and/or acceptanceAcknowledgement and/or a response is specified as required. A receiptAcknowledgement (if required) must always occur before an acceptanceAcknowledgement (if required), and an acceptanceAcknowledgement must always occur before a response (if required). Control is returned to the requesting activity based on the last required of these three (if any). If none required, control stays with the responding activity.

9. All business transactions succeed or fail. Success or failure depends on:

    a.) The receipt or non-receipt of the request, the response and/or business signals

    b.) The occurrence of time-outs

    c.) The occurrence of a business exception

    d.) The occurrence of a control exception

    e.) The interpretation of the received response and guard expressions on transitions to success or failure

10. The determination of Business Transaction success or failure is established by the requesting party based on the above success or failure factors. Once success or failure is thus established, the Business Transaction is considered closed with respect to both parties.

11. Upon receipt of a response the requesting activity may send a receiptAcknowledgement signal back to the responding role. This is merely a signal and does not pass control back to the responding activity, nor does it alter the successful or failed completion of the Business Transaction that was based on the receipt of the Response.

12. Upon identifying a time-out or exception in the processing of a Business Transaction, and closing the transaction accordingly, the requesting party may send a notification of failure to the responding party. This is considered a new Business Transaction and does not alter the already established conclusion of the Business Transaction.

5.5.1.1 Transaction Interaction Patterns

The business transaction specification will specify whether a requesting document requires a responding substantive document in order to achieve a "success" end state. In addition, the transaction may specify a proper nonzero time duration for timeToPerform, imposing a deadline for the substantive response.

Furthermore, the specification of a business transaction may indicate, for the request whether receiptAcknowledgement and/or acceptanceAcknowledgement are required, and for the response whether receiptAcknowledgement is required.

The way to specify that a receiptAcknowledgement is required is to set the parameter timeToAcknowledgeReceipt to any proper time duration other than zero. If this parameter has been set to a proper nonzero time duration, optionally either or both of the isIntelligibleCheckRequired and isNonrepudiationOfReceiptRequired parameters may also be set to 'Yes'.

The way to specify that a acceptanceAcknowledgement is required is to set the parameter timeToAcknowledgeAcceptance to any proper time duration other than zero.

So these two acknowledgement related parameters double as Boolean flags for whether the signal is required as part of the transaction, and as values for timeout of the transaction if the signal is not received.

The specification of a business transaction may require each one of these signals independently of whether the other is required. If one is not required, it is actually not allowed. Therefore there is a finite set of combinations. The UMM supplies an illustrative set of patterns representing those combinations, for potential re-use.

5.5.2   Creating Legally Binding Contracts

Trading partners may wish to indicate that a Business Transaction performed as part of an ebXML arrangement is, or is not, intended to be binding. A declaration of intent to be bound is a key element in establishing the legal equivalence of an electronic message to an enforceable signed physical writing. Parties may create explicit evidence of that intent by (1) adopting the ebXML Business Process Specification Schema standard and (2) manipulating the parameter ("isLegallyBinding") designated by the standard to indicate that intent.

In some early electronic applications, trading partners have simply used the presence, or absence, of an electronic signature (such as under the XML-DSIG standard) to indicate that intent. However, documents which rely solely on the presence of a signature may or may not be correctly interpreted, if there is semantic content indicating that a so-called contract is a draft, or nonbinding, or the like.

In ebXML, the presence or absence of an electronic signature cannot indicate by itself determine legally binding assent, because XML-DSIG signatures are reserved for other uses as an assurance of sender identity and message integrity.

isLegallyBinding is a parameter at the BusinessTransactionActivity level, which means that the performing of a BusinessTransaction within a Binary Collaboration is either specified as legally binding or not.

When operating under this standard, parties form binding agreements by exchanging binding messages that agree to terms (e.g., offer and acceptance). The "isLegallyBinding" parameter is Boolean, and its default value is "true." Under this standard, the exclusive manner for indicating that a Business Activity is not intended to be binding is to include a "false" value for the "isLegallyBinding" parameter for the transaction activity. As in EDI, the ebXML standard assumes that Business Transactions are intended by the trading parties to be binding unless otherwise indicated.

As a non-normative matter, parties may wish to conduct nonbinding transactions for a variety of reasons, including testing, and the exchange of proposed offers and counteroffers on a non-committal basis so as to discover a possible agreed set of terms. When using tangible signed documents, parties often do so by withholding a manual signature, or using a "DRAFT" stamp. In ebXML, trading partners may indicate that result by use of the "isLegallyBinding" parameter. See the illustrative Simple Negotiation Pattern set forth in the ebXML E-Commerce Patterns.

5.5.3 Non-repudiation

Trading partners may wish to conduct legally enforceable business transactions over ebXML. A party may elect to use non-repudiation protocols in order to generate documentation that would assist in the enforcement of the contractual obligation in court, in the case that the counterparty later attempts to repudiate its ebXML Business Documents and messages.

Repudiation generally refers to the ability of a trading partner to argue at a later time, based on the persistent artifacts of a transaction, that it did not agree to the transaction. That argument might be based on assertions that a replying document was not sent, or was not sent by the proper party, or was incorrectly interpreted (under the applicable standard or the trading partners' business rules) as forming agreement.

There are two kinds of non-repudiation protocol available under this document. Each protocol provides the user with some degree of additional evidentiary assurance by creating or requesting additional artifacts that would assist in a later dispute over repudiation issues. Neither is a dispositive absolute assurance. As in the paper world, trading partners are always free to invent colorful new arguments than an apparently-enforceable statement should be ignored. These parameters simply offer some opportunities to make that more difficult.

One imposes a duty on each party to save copies of all Business Documents and Document Envelopes comprising the transaction, each on their own side, i.e., requestor saves his request, responder saves his response. This is the isNonRepudiationRequired parameter in the requesting or responding activity. It is logically equivalent to a request that the other trading partner maintain an audit trail. However, failure to comply with that request is not necessarily computationally detectable at run time, nor would it override the determination of a "success" or "failure" end state.

The other requires the responder to send a signed copy of the receipt, which the requestor then saves. This is the isNonRepudiationOfReceiptRequired parameter in the requesting business activity.

NonRepudiationOfReceipt is tied to the ReceiptAcknowledgement, in that it requires the latter to be digitally signed. So NonRepudiationOfReceipt is meaningless if ReceiptAcknowledgement is not required. Failure to comply with NonRepudiation of Receipt would be computationally detectable at run time, and would override the determination of a "failure" end state. If a timeTo-AcknowledgeReceipt is imposed on a requesting message, and NonRepudiationOfReceipt is true, only a digitally signed receipt will satisfy the imposed timeout deadline. Thus, a failure to send a *signed* receipt within timeToAcknowledgeReceipt, would make the transaction null and void.

Parameter	BSI Requirement
isNonRepudiationRequired	Must save audit trail of messages it sends
isNonRepudiationOfReceiptRequired	Must digitally sign receiptAcknowledgements

5.5.4 Authorization Security

Each request or response may be sent by a variety of individuals, representatives or automated systems associated with a business partner. There may be cases where trading partners have more than one ebXML-capable business service interface, representing different levels of authority. In such a case, the parties may establish rules regarding which interfaces or authors may be confidently relied upon as speaking for the enterprise.

In order to invoke those rules, a party may specify IsAuthorizationRequired on a requesting or and responding activity accordingly, with the result that [the activity] will only be processed as valid if the party interpreting it successfully matches the stated identity of the activity's [Authorized Role] to a list of allowed values previously supplied by that party.

Parameter	BSI Requirement
IsAuthorizationRequired	Must validate identity of originator against a list of authorized originators

IsAuthorizationRequired is specified on the requesting and responding activity accordingly.

5.5.5 Document Security

The following security characteristics of each Business Document being transported, even if many are collected in the same message, can be specified individually, or collectively within a Document Envelope:

Parameter	Delivery Channel Requirement
isConfidential.	The information entity is encrypted so that unauthorized parties cannot view the information
isTamperProof.	The information entity has an encrypted message digest that can be used to check if the message has been tampered with. This requires a digital signature (sender's digital certificate and encrypted message digest) associated with the document entity.
isAuthenticated.	There is a digital certificate associated with the document entity. This provides proof of the signer's identity.

The value of *isConfidential, isTamperProof, isAuthenticated* at the Document Envelope always applies to the primary Business Document. It also applies to each of the attachments unless specifically overridden at the Attachment level.

When set to YES (or TRUE) these parameters assume that the corresponding security characteristic is provided in a manner providing persistence. Compliance requires that the specified character of the document survive its reception at a business service interface, and persist as the document is archived or forwarded.

5.5.6 Reliability

This parameter at the Business Transaction level states whether guaranteed delivery of the transaction's Business Documents is required.

Parameter	Delivery Channel Requirement
IsGuaranteedDeliveryRequired	This means that Business Documents transferred are guaranteed (by some delivery channel or other party other than the trading partners) to be delivered

This is a declaration that trading partners must employ only a delivery channel that provides a third-party delivery guarantee, to send Business Documents in the relevant transaction.

5.5.7 Parameters Required for CPP/CPA

The ebXML *Business Process Specification Schema* provides parameters that can be used to specify certain levels of security and reliability. The ebXML *Business Process Specification Schema* provides these parameters in general business terms.

These parameters are generic requirements for the business process, but for ebXML implementations, these parameters are specifically used to instruct the CPP and CPA to require BSI and/or delivery channel capabilities to achieve the specified service levels.

The CPP and CPA translate these into parameters of two kinds.

One kind of parameter determines the selection of certain security and reliability parameters applicable to the transport method and techniques used by the delivery channel. Document security, and Reliability above, are determinators of delivery channel selection.

The other kind of parameter determines the selection of certain service levels or capabilities of the BSI itself, in order for it to support the run time Business Transaction semantics as listed below.

5.6 Run Time Business Transaction Semantics

The ebXML concept of a business transaction and the semantics behind it are central to predictable, enforceable commerce. It is expected that any Business Service Interface (BSI) will be capable of managing a transaction according to these semantics.

Therefore, the Business Service Interface (BSI), or any software that implements one role in an ebXML collaboration needs at minimum to be able to support the following transaction semantics:

1. Detection of the opening of a transaction
2. Detection of transfer of control
3. Detection of successful completion of a transaction
   a.) Application of business rules expressed as isPositiveResponse and transition conditionGuard for determination of success
4. Detection of failed completion of a transaction
   a.) Detection of time-outs
   b.) Detection of exceptions
   c.) Application of business rules expressed as isPositiveResponse and transition conditionGuard for determination of failure

5. Notification of failure

6. Receipt of notification of failure

7. Rollback upon failure (note this is the independent responsibility of each role, it is not a co-coordinated roll-back, there are no 2-phase commits in ebXML)

ebXML does not specify how these transaction semantics are implemented but it is assumed that any Business Service Interface (BSI) will be able to support these basic transaction semantics at runtime. If either party cannot provide full support, then the requirements may be relaxed as overrides in the CPP/CPA.

The following sections discuss the two causes of failure: Time-outs and Exceptions. When either one happens, it is the responsibility of the two roles to do the necessary roll-back, and to exit the transaction. The responsibilities of the two roles differ slightly and are described in each of the sections below. Generally, if a failure happens at the responding role, the responding role will send an exception signal to the requesting role, and both parties will exit the current transaction. If a failure happens at the requesting role, the requesting role will exit the current transaction and in a separate transaction notify the responding role about the failure. This way the flow of control within a transaction is always unambiguous and finite.

5.6.1 Timeouts

Since all business transactions must have a distinct time boundary, there are time-out parameters associated with the response, and each of the acknowledgement signals. If the time-out occurs before the corresponding response or signal arrives, the transaction is null and void.

Here are the time-out parameters relative to the three response types:

Response Required	Parameter Name	Meaning of Timeout
Receipt acknowledgement	timeToAcknowledgeReceipt	The time a responding role has to acknowledge receipt of a business document.
Acceptance Acknowledgement (Non-substantive)	timeToAcknowledge Acceptance	The time a responding role has to non-substantively acknowledge business acceptance of a business document.
Substantive Response	TimeToPerform	The time a responding role has to substantively acknowledge business acceptance of a business document.

A time-out parameter must be specified whenever a requesting partner expects one or more responses to a business document request. A requesting partner must not remain in an infinite wait state.

The time-out value for each of the time-out parameters is absolute i.e. not relative to each other. All timers start when the initial requesting business document is sent. The timer values must comply with the well-formedness rules for timer values.

A BSI needs to comply with the above parameters to detect the appropriate time outs. To preserve the atomic semantics of the Business Transaction, the requesting and responding roles take different action based on time outs.

A responding partner simply terminates if a timeout is thrown. This prevents responding business transactions from hanging indefinitely.

A requesting partner terminates if a timeout is thrown and then sends a notification of failure to the responder as part of a separate transaction.

When the time to perform an activity equals the time to acknowledge receipt or the time to acknowledge business acceptance then the highest priority time out exception must be used when the originator provides a reason for revoking their original business document offer. The time to perform exception is lower priority than both the time to acknowledge receipt and the time to acknowledge business acceptance.

5.6.2 Exceptions

Under all normal circumstances the response message and/or the time-outs determine the success or failure of a business transaction. However the business processing of the transaction can go wrong at either the responding or the requesting role.

5.6.2.1 ControlException

A *ControlException* signals an error condition in the management of a business transaction. This business signal is asynchronously returned to the initiating activity that originated the request. This exception must terminate the business transaction. These errors deal with the mechanisms of message exchange such as verification, validation, authentication and authorization and will occur up to message acceptance. Typically the rules and constraints applied to the message will have only dealt with structure, syntax and message element values.

5.6.2.2 Business Protocol Exceptions

A Business Protocol Exception (or *ProcessException)* signals an error condition in a business activity. This business signal is asynchronously returned to the initiating role that originated the request. This exception must terminate the *business transaction*. These errors deal with the mechanisms that process the *business transaction* and will occur after message verification and validation. Typically the rules and constraints applied to the message will deal with the semantics of message elements and the validity of the request itself.The content is not valid with respect to a responding role's business rules. This type of exception is usually generated after an *AcceptanceAcknowledgement* has been returned.

A business protocol exception terminates the business transaction. The following are business protocol exceptions.

▼ Negative acknowledgement of receipt. The structure/schema of a message is invalid.

▼ Negative acknowledgement of acceptance. The business rules are violated.

▼ Performance exceptions. The requested business action cannot be performed.

▼ Sequence exceptions. The order or type of a business document or business signal is incorrect.

▼ Syntax exceptions. There is invalid punctuation, vocabulary or grammar in the business document or business signal.

▼ Authorization exceptions. Roles are not authorized to participate in the business transaction.

▼ Business process control exceptions. Business documents are not signed for non-repudiation when required.

A Business Transaction is defined in very atomic and deterministic terms. It always is initiated by the requesting role, and will always conclude at the requesting role. Upon receipt of the required response and/or signals, or time-out of same, the requesting role can unambiguously determine the success or failure of the Business Transaction. To preserve this semantics, control failures and business failures are treated differently by the requesting and responding roles as follows:

A responding role that encounters a business protocol exception signals the exception back to the requesting role and then terminates the business transaction. If any business exceptions (includes negative receipt and acceptance acknowledgements) are signaled then the business transaction must terminate.

A requesting role that encounters a business protocol exception terminates the transaction but does NOT send a business exception signal to the responding role. Rather, the requesting role then sends as a separate Business Transaction a notification revoking the offending business document request. This new transaction may be defined as a continuation of the current Binary Collaboration, or it may start a new Binary Collaboration specifically defined to handle this notification of failure.

A BSI needs to comply specifically with the following parameters to produce the associated special exceptions. The requesting and responding roles take different action as per below.

IsAuthorizationRequired

If a partner role needs authorization to request a business action or to respond to a business action then the sending partner role must sign the business document exchanged and the receiving partner role must validate this business control and approve the authorizer. A responding partner must signal an authorization exception if the requesting partner role is not authorized to perform the business activity. A sending partner must send notification of failed authorization if a requesting partner is not authorized to perform the responding business activity.

IsNonRepudiationRequired

If non-repudiation of origin and content is required then the business activity must store the business document in its original form for the duration mutually agreed to in a trading partner agreement. A responding partner must signal a business control exception if the sending partner role has not properly delivered their business document. A requesting partner must send notification of failed business control if a responding partner has not properly delivered their business document.

isNonRepudiationOfReceiptRequired.

Both partners agree to mutually verify receipt of a requesting business document and that the receipt must be non-repudiatable. A requesting partner must send notification of failed business control (possibly revoking a contractual offer) if a responding partner has not properly delivered their business document. For a further discussion of nonrepudiation of receipt, see also the ebXML E-Commerce and Simple Negotiation Patterns.

Non-repudiation of receipt provides the data for the following audit controls.

> **Verify responding role identity** (authenticate) – Verify the identity of the responding role (individual or organization) that received the requesting business document.

> **Verify content integrity** – Verify the integrity of the original content of the business document request.

isPositiveResponse

An expression whose evaluation results in TRUE or FALSE. If TRUE this DocumentEnvelope is intended as a positive response to the request. The value for this parameter supplied for a DocumentEnvelope is an assertion by the sender of the

DocumentEnvelope regarding its intent for the transaction to which it relates, but does not bind the recipient, or override the computation of transactional success or failure using the transaction's guard expressions.

If a requesting role, upon evaluation of these expressions, determines a failure, then the requesting role will "roll back" the Business Transaction and send a notification of failure.

5.7 Runtime Collaboration Semantics

The ebXML collaboration semantics contain a number of relationships between multiparty collaborations and binary collaborations, between recursive layers of binary collaborations, and choreographies among transactions in binary collaborations. It is anticipated that over time BSI software will evolve to the point of monitoring and managing the state of a collaboration, similar to the way a BSI today is expected to manage the state of a transaction. For the immediate future, such capabilities are not expected and not required.

5.8 Where the ebXML Business Process Specification Schema May be Implemented

The ebXML *Business Process Specification Schema* should be used wherever software is being specified to perform a role in an ebXML business collaboration. Specifically, the ebXML *Business Process Specification Schema* is intended to provide the business process and document specification for the formation of ebXML trading partner Collaboration Protocol Profiles and Agreements.

However, the ebXML *Business Process Specification Schema* may be used to specify any electronic commerce collaboration. It may also be used for non-commerce collaborations, for instance in defining transactional collaborations among nonprofit organizations or internally in enterprises.

6 UML Element Specification

In the following we will review all the specification elements in the UML version of the ebXML *Business Process Specification Schema,* grouped as follows:

▼ Business Collaborations
    ▼ Multiparty
    ▼ Binary

▼ Business Transactions

▼ Document flow

▼ Choreography

6.1 Business Collaborations

6.1.1 MultipartyCollaboration

A Multiparty Collaboration is a synthesis of Binary Collaborations. A Multiparty Collaboration consists of a number of Business Partner Roles each playing roles in binary collaborations with each other.

Tagged Values:

name.   Defines the name of the MultiPartyCollaboration

Associations:

partners   A multiparty collaboration has two or more BusinessPartnerRoles

Wellformedness Rules:

All multiparty collaborations must be synthesized from binary collaborations

6.1.2 BusinessPartnerRole

A BusinessPartnerRole is the role played by a business partner in a MultiParty-Collaboration. A BusinessPartnerRole performs at most one Authorized Role in each of the Binary Collaborations that make up the Multiparty Collaboration.

Tagged Values:

name.   Defines the name of the role played by partner in the overall multiparty business collaboration, e.g. customer or supplier.

Associations:

performers.   The Authorized Roles performed by a partner in the binary business collaboration.

transitions   The transitions (managed by this Business-PartnerRole) between activities across binary collaborations

collaboration	The Business Partner Role participates in one multi party collaboration

Wellformedness Rules:

A partner must not perform both roles in a given business activity.

6.1.3 Performs

Performs is an explicit modeling of the relationship between a BusinessPartner-Role and the Roles it plays. This specifies the use of an Authorized Role within a multiparty collaboration.

Tagged Values:

NONE

Associations:

performedBy	An instance of Performs is performed by only one BusinessPartnerRole
authorizedRole	The AuthorizedRole that will be performed by the Business PartnerRole

Wellformedness Rules:

For every Performs performing an AuthorizedRole there must be a Performs that performs the opposing AuthorizedRole, otherwise the Multi-Party Collaboration is not complete.

6.1.4 AuthorizedRole

An Authorized Role is a role that is authorized to send the request or response, e.g. the buyer is authorized to send the request for purchase order, the seller is authorized to send the acceptance of purchase order.

Tagged Values:

name	Defines the name of the AuthorizedRole uniquely within the Binary Collaboration
isInitiator	Boolean, determining whether this authorized role is the initiator of its associated binary collaboration

Associations:

performers	An AuthorizedRole may be used by one or more performers, i.e. Business Partner Roles in a multiparty collaboration
from	An AuthorizedRole may be the initiator in a business activity

to	An AuthorizedRole may be the responder in a business activity
collaboration	An AuthorizedRole may be in only one BinaryCollaboration

Wellformedness Rules:

An AuthorizedRole may not be both the requestor and the responder in a business transaction

An AuthorizedRole may not be both the initiator and the responder in a binary business collaboration

6.1.5   BinaryCollaboration

A Binary Collaboration defines a protocol of interaction between two authorized roles.

A Binary Collaboration is a choreographed set of states among collaboration roles. The activities of performing business transactions or other collaborations are a kind of state.

A Binary Collaboration choreographs one or more business transaction activities between two roles.

A Binary Collaboration is not an atomic transaction and should not be used in cases where Business Transaction rollback is required.

Tagged Values:

name	Defines the name of the BinaryCollaboration
timeToPerform	The period of time, starting upon initiation of the first activity, within which this entire collaboration must conclude.
preCondition	A description of a state external to this collaboration that is required before this collaboration can commence.
postCondition	A description of a state that does not exist before the execution of this collaboration but will exist as a result of the execution of this collaboration.
beginsWhen	A description of an event external to the collaboration that normally causes this collaboration to commence.
endsWhen	A description of an event external to this collaboration that normally causes this collaboration to conclude.

pattern	The optional reference to a pattern that this binary collaboration is based on

Associations:

role	A binary collaboration consists of two authorized roles. One must be designated the Initiating Role, and one the Responding Role.
states	A binary collaboration consists of one or more states, some of which are 'static', and some of which are action states
usedBy	A binary collaboration may be used within another binary collaboration via a collaboration activity
transitions	The transitions between activities in this binary collaboration

Wellformedness Rules:

NONE

6.1.6 BusinessActivity

A business activity is an action state within a binary collaboration. It is the super type for BusinessTransactionActivity and CollaborationActivity, specifying the activity of performing a transaction or another binary collaboration respectively.

Supertype of:

BusinessTransactionActivity, CollaborationActivity

Subtype of:

BusinessState

Tagged Values:

name	Defines the name of the activity uniquely within the binary collaboration

Associations:

from	This must match one of the Authorized-Roles in the parent binary collaboration and will become the initiator in the Binary-Collaboration or BusinessTransaction performed by this activity
to	This must match one of the Authorized-Roles in the parent binary collaboration and will become the responder in the

BinaryCollaboration or BusinessTransaction performed by this activity

Wellformedness Rules:

NONE

6.1.7 BusinessTransactionActivity

A business transaction activity defines the use of a business transaction within a binary collaboration.

A business transaction activity is a business activity that executes a specified business transaction. More than one instance of the same business transaction activity can be open at one time if the **isConcurrent** property is **true.**

Subtype of:

BusinessActivity

Tagged Values:

timeToPerform	The period of time, starting upon the sending of the request, within which both partners agree to conclude the business transaction executed by this Business Transaction Activity.
isConcurrent.	If the BusinessTransactionActivity is concurrent then more than one instance of the associated BusinessTransaction can be performed as part of the execution of this BusinesTransactionActivity
isLegallyBinding	Defines whether the Business Transaction performed by this activity is intended by the trading parties to be binding. Default value is True.

Associations:

uses.	The business transaction activity performs (uses) exactly one business transaction.

Wellformedness Rules:

NONE

6.1.8 CollaborationActivity

A collaboration activity is the activity of performing a binary collaboration within another binary collaboration.

Subtype of:

> BusinessActivity

Tagged Values:

> NONE (*other than inherited*)

Associations:

> *uses*   A collaboration activity uses exactly one bi-
>   nary collaboration

Wellformedness Rules:

> A binary collaboration may not re-use itself

6.2   Business Transactions

6.2.1   BusinessTransaction

A business transaction is a set of business information and business signal exchanges amongst two commercial partners that must occur in an agreed format,
sequence and time period. If any of the agreements are violated then the transaction is terminated and all business information and business signal exchanges
must be discarded. Business Transactions can be formal as in the formation of online offer/acceptance commercial contracts and informal as in the distribution of
product announcements.

Tagged Values:

name	Defines the name of the Business Transaction.
isGuaranteedDeliveryRequired.	Both partners must agree to use a transport that guarantees delivery
preCondition	A description of a state external to this transaction that is required before this transaction can commence.
postCondition	A description of a state that does not exist before the execution of this transaction but will exist as a result of the execution of this transaction.
beginsWhen	A description of an event external to the transaction that normally causes this transaction to commence.
endsWhen	A description of an event external to this transaction that normally causes this transaction to conclude.

pattern	The optional reference to a pattern that this transaction is based on.

Associations:

activities	A BusinessTransaction can be performed by many BusinessTransactionActivites
requester	A BusinessTransaction has exactly one RequestingBusinessActivity
responder	A BusinessTransaction has exactly one RespondingBusinessActivity

Wellformedness Rules:

NONE

6.2.2   Business Action

A Business Action is an abstract super class. Business Action, is the holder of attributes that are common to both Requesting Business Activity and Responding Business Activity.

Supertype of:

RequestingBusinessActivity, RespondingBusinessActivity

Tagged Values:

name	Defines the name of the RequestingBusinessTransaction or RespondingBusinessTransaction depending on the subtype
IsAuthorizationRequired	Receiving party must validate identity of originator against a list of authorized originators. This parameter is specified on the sending side. (See also section on action security)
IsNonRepudiationRequired	Receiving party must check that a requesting document is not garbled (unreadable, unintelligible) before sending acknowledgement of receipt. This parameter is specified on the sending side. (See also section on core transaction semantics)
isNonRepudiationOfReceipt Required.	Requires the receiving party to return a signed receipt, and the original sender to save copy of the receipt. This parameter is

	specified on the sending side. (See also section on nonrepuditation)
timeToAcknowledgeReceipt	The time a receiving role has to acknowledge receipt of a business document. This parameter is specified on the sending side. (See also section on core transaction semantics)
isIntelligibleCheckRequired	Receiving party must check that a requesting document is not garbled (unreadable, unintelligible) before sending acknowledgement of receipt. This parameter is specified on the sending side. (See also section on core transaction semantics)

Associations:

NONE

Wellformedness Rules:

NONE

6.2.3 RequestingBusinessActivity

A RequestingBusinessActivity is a Business Action that is performed by the requesting role within a Business Transaction. It specifies the Document Envelope which will carry the request.

Subtype of:

BusinessAction

Tagged Values:

| *timeToAcknowledgeAcceptance* | The time a responding role has to non-substantively acknowledge business acceptance of a business document. This parameter is specified on the requesting side. (See also section on core transaction semantics) |

Associations:

| *transaction* | A requesting activity is performed in exactly one business transaction |
| *documentEnvelope* | A requesting activity sends exactly one Document Envelope |

Wellformedness Rules:

NONE

6.2.4   *RespondingBusinessActivity*

A RespondingBusinessActivity is a Business Action that is performed by the responding role within a Business Transaction. It specifies the Document Envelope which will carry the response.

There may be multiple possible response Document Envelopes defined, but only one of them will be sent during an actual transaction instance.

Subtype of:

BusinessAction

Tagged Values:

NONE, except as inherited from Business Action

Associations:

transaction	A responding activity is performed in exactly one business transaction
DocumentEnvelope	A responding activity may specify zero or more but sends at most one Document Envelope

Wellformedness Rules:

NONE

6.3   Document Flow

6.3.1   *Document Security*

DocumentSecurity is an abstract super class holding the security related attributes for DocumentEnvelope and Attachment.

Supertype of:

DocumentEnvelope and Attachment

Tagged Values:

IsAuthenticated	There is a digital certificate associated with the document entity. This provides proof of the signer's identity. (See also section on Document Security)
IsConfidential	The information entity is encrypted so that unauthorized parties cannot view the information. (See also section on Document Security)

| *isTamperProof* | The information entity has an encrypted message digest that can be used to check if the message has been tampered with. This requires a digital signature (sender's digital certificate and encrypted message digest) associated with the document entity. (See also section on Document Security) |

Associations:

> NONE

Wellformedness Rules:

> NONE

6.3.2 Document Envelope

A Document Envelope is what conveys business information between the two roles in a business transaction. One Document Envelope conveys the request from the requesting role to the responding role, and another Document Envelope conveys the response (if any) from the responding role back to the requesting role.

Subtype of:

> DocumentSecurity

Tagged Values:

| *isPositiveResponse* | TRUE or FALSE. If TRUE this DocumentEnvelope is intended as a positive response to the request. This parameter is only relevant on the response envelope. Its value does not bind the recipient, or override the computation of transactional success or failure using the transaction's guard expressions. |

Associations:

| *requesting* | This is a reference to the requesting activity associated with this DocumentEnvelope. This requesting activity may be the sender, or the receiver depending on whether the DocumentEnvelope represents a request or a response. |

responding	This is a reference to the requesting activity associated with this DocumentEnvelope. This responding activity may be the sender, or the receiver depending on whether the DocumentEnvelope represents a request or a response.
BusinessDocument	This identifies the primary Business Document in the envelope. A Document Envelope contains exactly one primary Business Document.
attachment	A Document Envelope contains an optional set of attachments related to the primary document

Wellformedness Rules:

A Document Envelope is associated with exactly one requesting and one responding activity.

IsPositiveResponse is not a relevant parameter on a DocumentEnvelope sent by a requesting activity.

6.3.3   BusinessDocument

BusinessDocument is a generic name of a document.

Tagged Values:

name	Defines the generic name of the Business Document as it is known within this Business Process Specification
conditionExpression	A Business Document may have one Condition Expression. This determines whether this is a valid business document for its envelope

Associations:

documentEnvelope	A Business Document can be in multiple Document Envelopes
attachment	A Business Document can serve to specify the type of many attachments

Wellformedness Rules:

NONE

6.3.4 Attachment

Attachment is an optional attachment to a BusinessDocument in a Document Envelope

Subtype of:

> DocumentSecurity

Tagged Values:

name	Defines the name of the attachment
mimeType	Defines the valid MIME (Multipurpose Internet Mail Extensions) type of this Attachment
specification	A reference to an external source of description of this attachment.
version	The version of the Attachment

Associations:

documentEnvelope	An Attachment is in exactly one Document Envelope
businessDocument	An Attachment can be defined by a BusinessDocument. If it is not of a defined Business Document, the mime type and spec will be the only indication of its type.

Wellformedness Rules:

> NONE

6.4 Choreography within Collaborations.

6.4.1 BusinessState

A business state is any state that a binary collaboration can be in. Start and CompletionState are a snapshot right before or right after an activity, BusinessActivity is an action states that denote the state of being in an activity. Fork and Join reflect the activity of forking to multiple activities or joining back from them.

Supertype of:

> Start, CompletionState, Fork, Join, BusinessActivity

Tagged Values:

> *none*

Associations:

collaboration	A business state belongs to only one binary collaboration
entering	A transition that reflects entry into this state
exiting	A transition that reflects exiting from this state

Wellformedness Rules:

NONE

6.4.2 Transition

A transition is a transition between two business states in a binary collaboration.

Choreography is expressed as transitions between business states

Tagged Values:

onInitiation	This specifies this is a nested BusinessTransactionActivity and that upon receipt of the request in the associated transaction a second activity is performed before returning to the transaction to send the response back to the original requestor.
conditionGuard	A reference to the status of the previous transaction. A fixed value of Success, BusinessFailure, TechnicalFailure, or AnyFailure
conditionExpression	A transition may have one Condition Expression. For a transition, this determines whether this transition should happen or not.

Associations:

in	The business state this transition is entering
out	The business state this transition is exiting

Wellformedness Rules:

A transition cannot enter and exit the same state

6.4.3 Start

The starting state for a Binary Collaboration. A Binary Collaboration should have at least one starting activity. If none defined, then all activities are considered allowable entry points.

Subtype of:

> BusinessState

Tagged Values:

> *NONE*

Associations:

> *NONE*

Wellformedness Rules:

> NONE

6.4.4 CompletionState

The ending state of an binary collaboration, sub classed by success and failure

Supertype of:

> Success, Failure

Subtype of:

> BusinessState

Tagged Values:

> *NONE*

Associations:

> *NONE*

Wellformedness Rules:

> *NONE*

6.4.5 Success

Defines the successful conclusion of a binary collaboration as a transition from an activity.

Subtype of:

> CompletionState

Tagged Values:

> *conditionExpression*   A success state may have one Condition Expression for the transition. This determines whether this transition should happen or not.

Associations:

> *NONE*, except as inherited

Wellformedness Rules:

Every activity Binary Collaboration should have at least one success

6.4.6   Failure

A subtype of CompletionState which defines the unsuccessful conclusion of a binary collaboration as a transition from an activity.

Subtype of:

CompletionState

Tagged Values:

conditionExpression	A failure state may have one Condition Expression for the transition. This determines whether this transition should happen or not.

Associations:

NONE, except as inherited

Wellformedness Rules:

Every Binary Collaboration should have at least one failure

6.4.7   Fork

A Fork is a state with one inbound transition and multiple outbound transitions. All activities pointed to by the outbound transitions are assumed to happen in parallel.

Subtype of:

BusinessState

Tagged Values:

Name	Defines the name of the Fork state

Associations:

None

Wellformedness Rules:

None

6.4.8   Join

A business state where an activity is waiting for the completion of one or more other activities. Defines the point where previously forked activities join up again.

Subtype of:

> BusinessState

Tagged Values:

Name	Defines the name of the Join state
waitForAll	Boolean value indicating if this Join state should wait for all incoming transitions to complete. If TRUE, wait for all, if False proceed on first incoming transition.

Associations:

> *None*

Wellformedness Rules:

> *None*

6.5   Definition and Scope

The ebXML *Business Process Specification Schema* should be used wherever software is being specified to perform a role in an ebXML binary collaboration. Specifically, the ebXML *Business Process Specification Schema* is intended to provide the business process and document specification for the formation of a trading partner Collaboration Protocol Profile and Agreement. A set of specification rules have been established to properly constrain the expression of a business process and information model in a way that can be directly incorporated into a trading partner Collaboration Protocol Profile and Agreement.

6.6   Collaboration and Transaction Well-formedness Rules

The following rules should be used in addition to standard parsing to properly constrain the values of the attributes of the elements in an ebXML Business Process Specification.

> *Business Transaction*

[0] If non-repudiation is required then the input or returned business document must be a tamper-proofed entity.

[1] If authorization is required then the input business document and business signal must be an authenticated or a tamper proofed secure entity.

[2] The time to acknowledge receipt must be less than the time to acknowledge acceptance if both properties have values.
timeToAcknowledgeReceipt < timeToAcknowledgeAcceptance

[3] If the time to acknowledge acceptance is null then the time to perform an activity must either be equal to or greater than the time to acknowledge receipt.

[4] The time to perform a transaction cannot be null if either the time to acknowledge receipt or the time to acknowledge acceptance is not null.

[5] If non-repudiation of receipt is required then the time to acknowledge receipt cannot be null.

[6] The time to acknowledge receipt, time to acknowledge acceptance and time to perform cannot all be zero.

[7] If non-repudiation is required at the requesting business activity, then there must be a responding business document.

RequestingBusinessActivity

[8] There must be one input transition whose source state vertex is an initial pseudo state.

[9] There must be one output transition whose target state vertex is a final state specifying the state of the machine when the activity is successfully performed.

[10] There must be one output transition whose target state vertex is a final state specifying the state of the machine when the activity is NOT successfully performed due to a process control exception.

[11] There must be one output transition whose target state vertex is a final state specifying the state of the machine when the activity is NOT successfully performed due to a business process exception.

[12] There must be one output document flow from a requesting business activity that in turn is the input to a responding business activity.

[13] There must be zero or one output document flow from a responding business activity that in turn is the input to the requesting business activity.

RespondingBusinessActivity

[14] There must be one input transition from a document flow that in turn has one input transition from a requesting business activity.

[15] There must be zero or one output transition to an document flow that in turn has an output transition to a requesting business activity.

Business Collaboration

[16] A Business Partner Role cannot provide both the initiating and responding roles of the same business transaction activity.

7   ebXML Business Process Specification Schema – (DTD)

In this section we describe the DTD and XML Schema version of the Specification Schema. There are minimal differences between the DTD and the XML Schema, therefore the elements will only be described once, noting differences when needed. This discussion includes

  ▼ An example XML Business Process Specification listed in Appendix A.

  ▼ A listing of the DTD in Appendix B and the XML Schema in Appendix C

  ▼ A table listing all the elements with definitions and parent/child relationships

  ▼ A table listing all the attributes with definitions and parent element relationships

  ▼ A table listing all the elements, each with a cross reference to the corresponding class in the UML version of the specification schema

  ▼ Rules about namespaces and element references

7.1   Documentation for the DTD

This section will document the DTD. The DTD has been derived from the UML model. The correlation between the UML classes and DTD elements will be shown separately later in this document.

Overall Structure excluding attribute definitions:

ProcessSpecification (Documentation*, SubstitutionSet*, (Include | Business-Document |

ProcessSpecification | Package | BinaryCollaboration | BusinessTransaction | MultiPartyCollaboration)*)

  Documentation ( )

  SubstitutionSet (DocumentSubstitution | AttributeSubstitution | Documentation)*

    DocumentSubstitution (Documentation*)

AttributeSubstitution (Documentation*)

Include (Documentation*)

BusinessDocument (ConditionExpression? | Documentation*)

ConditionExpression (Documentation*)

Package (Documentation*, (Package | BinaryCollaboration |

BusinessTransaction | MultiPartyCollaboration)*)

BinaryCollaboration (Documentation*, InitiatingRole, RespondingRole,

(Documentation | Start | Transition | Success | Failure |

BusinessTransactionActivity | CollaborationActivity | Fork | Join)*)

InitiatingRole (Documentation*)

RespondingRole (Documentation*)

Start (Documentation*)

Transition (ConditionExpression | Documentation)*

Success (ConditionExpression | Documentation)*

Failure (ConditionExpression | Documentation)*

Fork (Documentation*)

Join (Documentation*)

BusinessTransactionActivity (Documentation*)

CollaborationActivity (Documentation*)

BusinessTransaction (Documentation*, RequestingBusinessActivity,

RespondingBusinessActivity)

RequestingBusinessActivity (Documentation*, DocumentEnvelope)

RespondingBusinessActivity (Documentation*, DocumentEnvelope*)

MultiPartyCollaboration (Documentation*, BusinessPartnerRole*)

BusinessPartnerRole (Documentation*, Performs*, Transition*)

Performs (Documentation*)

Transition (Documentation*)

a.) Attachment

XML Element Name: Attachment

DTD Declaration:

```
<!ELEMENT Attachment (Documentation*)>
<!ATTLIST Attachment
     name                   CDATA #REQUIRED
     nameID                 ID    #IMPLIED
     BusinessDocument       CDATA #IMPLIED
     BusinessDocumentIDRef  IDREF #IMPLIED
     mimeType               CDATA #IMPLIED
     specification          CDATA #IMPLIED
     version                CDATA #IMPLIED
     isConfidential         (true | false) "false"
     isTamperProof          (true | false) "false"
     isAuthenticated        (true | false) "false">
```

Definition:

An optional attachment to a BusinessDocument in a DocumentEnvelope.

Parent Elements:

▼ DocumentEnvelope

Attributes:

Attribute Name	Definition	Default Value
name	Defines the name of the attachment.	Required input
nameID	XML ID version of name	Optional input
businessDocument	An Attachment's type can be defined by a BusinessDocument. If it is not of a defined Business Document, the mime type and spec will be the only indication of its type.	Required input
businessDocumentIDRef	The XML IDREF version of businessDocument	Optional input
isAuthenticated	There is a digital certificate associated with the document entity. This provides proof of the signer's identity. (See also section on Document Security)	**false** {true, false}

Attribute Name	Definition	Default Value
isConfidential	The information entity is encrypted so that unauthorized parties cannot view the information (See also section on Document Security)	**false** {true, false}
isTamperProof	The information entity has an encrypted message digest that can be used to check if the message has been tampered with. This requires a digital signature (sender's digital certificate and encrypted message digest) associated with the document entity. (See also section on Document Security)	**false** Valid values {true, false}
mimeType	Defines the valid MIME (Multipurpose Internet Mail Extensions) type of this Attachment	Optional input. Example: 'application/pdf'
specification	A reference to an external source of description of this attachment.	Optional Input
version	The version of the Attachment	Optional Input

b.) AttributeSubstitution

Element Name: AttributeSubstitution

DTD Declaration:

```
<!ELEMENT AttributeSubstitution (Documentation*)>
<!ATTLIST AttributeSubstitution
attributeName CDATA #IMPLED
     value CDATA #IMPLIED>
```

Definition:

Attribute Substitution specifies that an attribute value should be used in place of some attribute value in an existing process specification.

Parents:

▼ SubstitutionSet

Attributes:

Attribute Name	Definition	Default Value
attributeName	The name of an attribute of any element within the scope of the substitution set.	Required Input
value	The value which shall replace the current value of the attribute.	Required Input

c.) Binary Collaboration

XML Element Name: BinaryCollaboration

DTD Declaration:

```
<!ELEMENT BinaryCollaboration (Documentation*, InitiatingRole,
RespondingRole, (Documentation | Start | Transition | Success |
Failure | BusinessTransactionActivity | CollaborationActivity |
Fork | Join)*)>
<!ATTLIST BinaryCollaboration
         name          CDATA #REQUIRED
         nameID        ID    #IMPLIED
         pattern       CDATA #IMPLIED
         beginsWhen    CDATA #IMPLIED
         endsWhen      CDATA #IMPLIED
         precondition  CDATA #IMPLIED
         postCondition CDATA #IMPLIED
         timeToPerform CDATA #IMPLIED
>
```

Definition:

A Binary Collaboration defines a protocol of interaction between two authorized roles.

A Binary Collaboration is a choreographed set of states among collaboration roles. The activities of performing business transactions or other collaborations are a kind of state.

A Binary Collaboration choreographs one or more business transaction activities between two roles.

A Binary Collaboration is not an atomic transaction and should not be used in cases where Business Transaction rollback is required.

Parents:

▼ ProcessSpecification

▼ Package

Hierarchical Model:

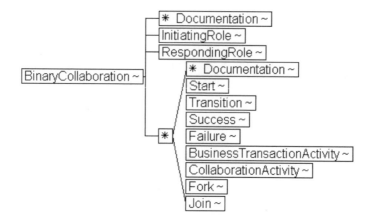

Attributes:

Attribute Name	Definition	Default Value
name	Defines the name of the Binary Collaboration.	Required Input.
nameID	The XML ID version of name	Optional
beginsWhen	A description of an event external to the collaboration that normally causes this collaboration to commence.	Optional Input.
endsWhen	A description of an event external to this collaboration that normally causes this collaboration to conclude.	Optional Input.
pattern	The optional reference to a pattern that this binary collaboration is based on. In the XML Schema version the data type is xsd:anyURI	
preCondition	A description of a state external to this collaboration that is required before this collaboration can commence.	Optional Input.
postCondition	A description of a state that does not exist before the execution of this collaboration but will exist as a result of the execution of this collaboration.	Optional Input..
timeToPerform	The period of time, starting upon initiation of the first activity, within which this entire collaboration must conclude.	Optional Input.

d.) BusinessDocument

Element Name: BusinessDocument

DTD Declaration:
```
<!ELEMENT BusinessDocument (ConditionExpression?,
Documentation*) >
<!ATTLIST BusinessDocument
      name    CDATA #REQUIRED
      nameID ID    #IMPLIED
      specificationLocation CDATA #IMPLIED
      specificationElement CDATA #IMPLIED>
```

Definition:

BusinessDocument is a generic name of a document.

Parents:

▼ ProcessSpecification

▼ Attachment

Attributes:

Attribute Name	Definition	Default Value
name	Defines the generic name of the Business Document as it is known within this Business Process Specification	Required Input
nameID	XML ID version of name	Optional
specificationLocation	Reference to an external source of the schema definition. In the XML Schema version the data type is xsd:anyURI	Optional
specificationElement	Reference to the element within the schema definition that defines this document.	Optional

e.) Business Partner Role

Element Name: BusinessPartnerRole

DTD Declaration:
```
<!ELEMENT BusinessPartnerRole (Documentation*, Performs*,
                          Transition*)>
<!ATTLIST BusinessPartnerRole
        name   CDATA #REQUIRED
        nameID ID    #IMPLIED>
```

Definition:

A BusinessPartnerRole is the role played by a business partner in a Multi-PartyCollaboration. A BusinessPartnerRole performs at most one Authorized Role in each of the Binary Collaborations that make up the Multiparty Collaboration.

Parents:

▼ MultiPartyCollaboration

Hierarchical Model:

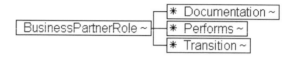

Attributes:

Attribute Name	Definition	Default Value
Name	Defines the name of the role played by a partner in the overall multiparty business collaboration, e.g. customer or supplier.	Required Input.
nameID	The XML ID version of name	Optional

f.) Business Transaction

Element Name: BusinessTransaction

Content Model:

```
<!ELEMENT BusinessTransaction (Documentation*,
RequestingBusinessActivity, RespondingBusinessActivity)>
<!ATTLIST BusinessTransaction
        name                       CDATA #REQUIRED
        nameID                     ID    #IMPLIED
        pattern                    CDATA #IMPLIED
        beginsWhen                 CDATA #IMPLIED
        endsWhen                   CDATA #IMPLIED
        isGuaranteedDeliveryRequired (true | false) false
        precondition               CDATA #IMPLIED
        postCondition              CDATA #IMPLIED>
```

Definition:

A business transaction is a set of business information and business signal exchanges amongst two commercial partners that must occur in an agreed format, sequence and time period. If any of the agreements are violated then the transaction is terminated and all business information and business signal exchanges must be discarded. Business Transactions can be formal as in the formation of online offer/acceptance commercial contracts and informal as in the distribution of product announcements.

Parents:

▼ ProcessSpecification

▼ Package

Hierarchical Model:

Attributes:

Attribute Name	Definition	Default Value
name	Defines the name of the Business Transaction.	Required Input.
nameID	The XML ID version of name	Optional
pattern	The optional reference to a pattern that this transaction is based on.In the XML Schema version the data type is xsd:anyURI	Optional
beginsWhen	A description of an event external to the transaction that normally causes this transaction to commence.	Optional Input..
endsWhen	A description of an event external to this transaction that normally causes this transaction to conclude.	Optional Input.
isGuaranteedDeliveryRequired	Both partners must agree to use a transport that guarantees delivery	**false** Valid Values: {true, false}
preCondition	A description of a state external to this transaction that is required before this transaction can commence.	Optional Input.
postCondition	A description of a state that does not exist before the execution of this transaction but will exist as a result of the execution of this transaction.	Optional Input.

g.) Business Transaction Activity

Element Name: BusinessTransactionActivity

Content Model:

```
<!ELEMENT BusinessTransactionActivity (Documentation*)>
<!ATTLIST BusinessTransactionActivity
          name                     CDATA #REQUIRED
          nameID                   ID    #IMPLIED
          businessTransaction      CDATA #REQUIRED
          businessTransactionIDRef IDREF #IMPLIED
          fromAuthorizedRole       CDATA #REQUIRED
          fromAuthorizedRoleIDRef  IDREF #IMPLIED
          toAuthorizedRole         CDATA #REQUIRED
          toAuthorizedRoleIDRef    IDREF #IMPLIED
          isConcurrent (true | false) "true"
          isLegallyBinding (true | false) "true"
          timeToPerform CDATA #IMPLIED>
```

Definition:

A business transaction activity defines the use of a business transaction within a binary collaboration.

A business transaction activity is a business activity that executes a specified business transaction. More than one instance of the same business transaction activity can be open at one time if the `isConcurrent` property is `true`.

Parents:

▼ BinaryCollaboration

Attributes:

Attribute Name	Definition	Default Value
name	Defines the name of the activity uniquely within the binary collaboration	Required Input.
nameID	The XML ID version of name	Optional Input
businessTransaction	A reference, by name to the Business Transaction performed by this Business Transaction Activity	Required Input.
businessTransactionIDRef	The XML IDREF version of businessTransaction	Optional Input.
fromAuthorizedRole	The name of the initiating role in Business Transaction Activity. This must match one of the AuthorizedRoles in the binary collaboration and will become	Required Input.

Attribute Name	Definition	Default Value
	the requestor in the BusinessTransaction performed by this activity	
fromAuthorizedRoleIDRef	The XML IDREF version of fromAuthorizedRole	OptionalInput.
toAuthorizedRole	The name of the responding role in Business Transaction Activity. This must match one of the AuthorizedRoles in the binary collaboration and will become the responder in the BusinessTransaction performed by this activity	Required Input.
toAuthorizedRoleIDRef	The XML IDREF version of toAuthorizedRole	Optional Input.
timeToPerform	The period of time, starting upon the sending of the request, within which both partners agree to conclude the business transaction executed by this Business Transaction Activity.	Optional Input.
isLegallyBinding	Defines whether the Business Transaction performed by this activity is intended by the trading parties to be binding. Default value is True.	**true** Valid Values: {true, false}
isConcurrent	If the BusinessTransactionActivity is concurrent then more than one instance of the associated BusinessTransaction can be open the same time as part of the execution of this BusinesTransactionActivity	**true** Valid Values: {true, false}

h.) Collaboration Activity

Element Name: CollaborationActivity

DTD Declaration:

```
<!ELEMENT CollaborationActivity (Documentation*)>
<!ATTLIST CollaborationActivity
    name                      CDATA #REQUIRED
    nameID                    ID    #IMPLIED
    fromAuthorizedRole        CDATA #REQUIRED
    fromAuthorizedRoleIDRef   CDATA #IMPLIED
    toAuthorizedRole          CDATA #REQUIRED
    toAuthorizedRoleIDRef     CDATA #IMPLIED
    binaryCollaboration       CDATA #REQUIRED>
    binaryCollaborationIDRef  CDATA #IMPLIED>
```

Definition:

A collaboration activity is the activity of performing a binary collaboration within another binary collaboration.

Parents:

▼ BinaryCollaboration

Attributes:

Attribute Name	Definition	Default Value
Name	Defines the name of the activity uniquely within the binary collaboration	Required Input.
nameID	The XML ID version of name	Optional Input
fromAuthorizedRole	The name of the initiating role in the Collaboration Activity. This must match one of the AuthorizedRoles in the parent binary collaboration and will become the initiator in the BinaryCollaboration performed by this activity	Required Input
FromAuthorizedRoleIDRef	The XML IDREF version of fromAuthorizedRole	OptionalInput.
toAuthorizedRole	The name of the responding role in the Collaboration Activity. This must match one of the AuthorizedRoles in the parent binary collaboration and will become the responder in the BinaryCollaboration performed by this activity	Required Input.
toAuthorizedRoleIDRef	The XML IDREF version of toAuthorizedRole	Optional Input.
binaryCollaboration	A reference, by name, to the Binary Collaboration performed by this Collaboration Activity	Required Input.
BinaryCollaborationIDRef	The XML IDREF version of binaryCollaboration	Optional Input.

i.) ConditionExpression

Element Name: ConditionExpression

DTD Declaration:
```
<!ELEMENT ConditionExpression (Documentation*)>
<!ATTLIST ConditionExpression
```

```
expressionLanguage CDATA #IMPLIED
expression CDATA #IMPLIED
```

Definition:

Condition Expression is an expression that can be evaluated to TRUE or FALSE.

Parents:

▼ BusinessDocument

▼ Transition

▼ Failure

▼ Success

Attributes:

Attribute Name	Definition	Default Value
expressionLanguage	The language of the expression, e.g. Java.	Required Input
expression	An expression whose evaluation results in TRUE or FALSE. For a transition, this determines whether this transition should happen or not. For a business document, this determines whether this is a valid business document for its envelope. The expression can refer to the name or content of the most recent DocumentEnvelope or content of documents within it.	Optional

j.) Documentation

Element Name: Documentation

DTD Declaration:
```
<!ELEMENT Documentation (#PCDATA)>
<!ATTLIST Documentation
    uri CDATA #IMPLIED>
```

Definition:

Defines user documentation for any element. Must be the first element of its container. Documentation can be either inline PCDATA and/or a URI to where more complete documentation is to be found

Parents:

▼ AuthorizedRole

▼ BinaryCollaboration

▼ BusinessPartnerRole

▼ BusinessTransaction

▼ BusinessTransactionActivity

▼ CollaborationActivity

▼ DocumentEnvelope

▼ BusinessDocument

▼ ProcessSpecification

▼ MultiPartyCollaboration

▼ Package

▼ Performs

▼ RequestingBusinessActivity

▼ RespondingBusinessActivity

▼ Transition

Attributes:

Attribute Name	Definition	Default Value
uri	Defines the URI (Uniform Resource Identifier) where external documentation is located. In the XML Schema version the data type is xsd:anyURI	No Default Value. Valid URI is required.

k.) DocumentEnvelope

Element Name: DocumentEnvelope

Content Model:

```
<!ELEMENT DocumentEnvelope (Documentation*,
                     Attachment*)>
<!ATTLIST DocumentEnvelope
    businessDocument CDATA #REQUIRED
    businessDocumentIDRef IDREF #IMPLIED
    isPositiveResponse (true | false) "false"
    isAuthenticated  (true | false) "false"
    isConfidential   (true | false) "false"
    isTamperProof    (true | false) "false">
```

Definition:

A DocumentEnvelope is what conveys business information between the two roles in a business transaction. One DocumentEnvelope conveys the request from the requesting role to the responding role, and another DocumentEnvelope conveys the response (if any) from the responding role back to the requesting role.

Parents:

▼ RequestingBusinessActivity

▼ RespondingBusinessActivity

Hierarchical Model:

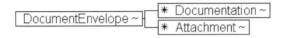

Attributes:

Attribute Name	Definition	Default Value
businessDocument	The name of the business document.	Required Input.
businessDocument IDRef	The XML IDREF version of businessDocument	Optional Input.
isPositiveResponse	TRUE or FALSE. If TRUE this DocumentEnvelope is intended as a positive response to the request. The value for this parameter supplied for a DocumentEnvelope is an assertion by the sender of the DocumentEnvelope regarding its intent for the transaction to which it relates, but does not bind the recipient, or override the computation of transactional success or failure using the transaction's guard expressions. In some situations this could be an XPath expression that interrogates the BusinessDocument in the envelope. IsPositiveResponse is only relevant for responses, and is ignored in requests.	Optional Input.
isAuthenticated	There is a digital certificate associated with the document entity. This provides proof of the signer's identity. (See also section on Document Security)	**false** Valid Values: {true, false}
isConfidential	The information entity is encrypted so that unauthorized parties cannot view the information. (See also section on Document Security)	**false** Valid Values: {true, false}

Attribute Name	Definition	Default Value
isTamperProof	The information entity has an encrypted message digest that can be used to check if the message has been tampered with. This requires a digital signature (sender's digital certificate and encrypted message digest) associated with the document entity. (See also section on Document Security)	**false** Valid Values: {true, false}

l.) DocumentSubstitution

Element Name: DocumentSubstitution

DTD Declaration:

```
<!ELEMENT BusinessDocument (Documentation*) >
<!ATTLIST DocumentSubstitution
     originalBusinessDocument CDATA #IMPLIED
     originalBusinessDocumentID IDREF #IMPLIED
     substituteBusinessDocument CDATA #IMPLIED
     substituteBusinessDocumentId IDREF #IMPLIED
```

Definition:

DocumentSubstitution specifies a document that should be used in place of a document in an existing process specification.

Parents:

▼ SubstitutionSet

Attributes:

Attribute Name	Definition	Default Value
originalBusinessDocument	The name of a business document within the scope of the substitution set.	Required Input
originalBusinessDocument ID	The ID of the business document.	Optional
substitueBusinessDocument	The document which shall replace the current document.	Required Input
substitueBusinessDocumentID	The ID of the replacement document.	Optional

m.) Failure

Element Name: Failure

DTD Declaration:

```
<!ELEMENT Failure (ConditionExpression?, Documentation*) >
<!ATTLIST Failure
        fromBusinessState      CDATA #REQUIRED
        fromBusinessStateIDRef IDREF #IMPLIED
        conditionGuard (Success | BusinessFailure |
                TechnicalFailure | AnyFailure) #IMPLIED
```

Definition:

Defines the unsuccessful conclusion of a binary collaboration as a transition from
an activity.

Parents:

▼ BinaryCollaboration

Attributes:

Attribute Name	Definition	Default Value
fromBusinessState	The name of the activity from which this indicates a transition to unsuccessful conclusion of the BusinessTransaction or BinaryCollaboration	Required Input.
fromBusinessStateIDRef	The XML IDREF version of fromBusinessState	Optional
conditionGuard	The condition that guards this transition	Optional Valid Values: {Success, BusinessFailure, TechnicalFailure, AnyFailure}

n.) Fork

Element Name: Fork

DTD Declaration:

```
<!ELEMENT Fork (Documentation*) >
<!ATTLIST Fork
        name   CDATA  #REQUIRED
        nameID ID     #IMPLIED >
```

Definition:

A Fork is a state with one inbound transition and multiple outbound transitions.
All activities pointed to by the outbound transitions are assumed to happen in
parallel.

Parents:

▼ BinaryCollaboration

Attributes:

Attribute Name	Definition	Default Value
name	Defines the name of the Fork state	Required Input
nameID	The XML ID version of name	Optional

o.) Include

Element Name: Include

DTD Declaration:

```
<!ELEMENT Include (Documentation*) >
<!ATTLIST Include
          name    CDATA #REQUIRED
          version CDATA #REQUIRED
          uuid    CDATA #REQUIRED
          uri     CDATA #REQUIRED >
```

Definition:

Includes another process specification document and merges that specification with the current specification. Any elements of the same name and in the same name scope must have exactly the same specification except that packages may have additional content.

Documents are merged based on name scope. A name in an included package will be indistinguishable from a name in the base document.

Parents:

▼ ProcessSpecification

Hierarchical Model:

```
┌─────────────┐ ┌───────────────────┐
│ * Include ~ │─│ * Documentation ~ │
└─────────────┘ └───────────────────┘
```

Attributes:

Attribute Name	Definition	Default Value
name	Defines the name of a model element. This name must be unique within the context of the model element and will be used to reference the element from other points in the model.	Required

Attribute Name	Definition	Default Value
uri	Uniform Resource Indicator. In the XML Schema data type is xsd:anyURI	Required
uuid	Universally unique identifier.	Required
version	Version of the included specification.	Required

p.) Initiating Role

XML Element Name: InitiatingRole

DTD Declaration:

```
<!ELEMENT InitiatingRole (Documentation*)>
<!ATTLIST InitiatingRole
          name    CDATA #REQUIRED
          nameID ID    #IMPLIED>
```

Definition:

An Initiating Role is a role that is authorized to send the first request, e.g. the buyer is authorized to send the request for purchase order. The Initiating Role initiates the binary collaboration.

Parents:

▼ BinaryCollaboration

Attributes:

Attribute Name	Definition	Default Value
Name	Defines the name of the Initiating Role	**Required input.**
nameID	XML ID version of name	Optional

q.) Join

Element Name: Join

DTD Declaration:

```
<!ELEMENT Join (Documentation*) >
<!ATTLIST Join
          name      CDATA #REQUIRED
          nameID    ID    #IMPLIED
          waitForAll (true | false) "true">
```

Definition:

A business state where an activity is waiting for the completion of one or more other activities. Defines the point where previously forked activities join up again.

Parents:

▼ BinaryCollaboration

Attributes:

Attribute Name	Definition	Default Value
name	Defines the name of the Join state.	Required Input
nameID	The XML ID version of name	Optional
waitForAll	Boolean value indicating if this Join state should wait for all incoming transitions to complete. If TRUE, wait for all, if False proceed on first incoming transition.	**true** Valid Values: {true, false}

r.) MultiParty Collaboration

Element Name: MultiPartyCollaboration

DTD Declaration:

```
<!ELEMENT MultiPartyCollaboration (Documentation*,
                                   BusinessPartnerRole+) >
<!ATTLIST MultiPartyCollaboration
          name    CDATA #REQUIRED
          nameID ID     #IMPLIED >
```

Definition:

A Multiparty Collaboration is a synthesis of Binary Collaborations. A Multiparty Collaboration consists of a number of Business Partner Roles each playing roles in binary collaborations with each other.

Parents:

▼ ProcessSpecification

▼ Package

Hierarchical Model:

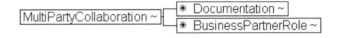

Attributes:

Attribute Name	Definition	Default Value
name	Defines the name of the MultiPartyCollaboration	Required Input
nameID	The XML ID version of name	Optional Input

s.) Package

Element Name: Package

DTD Declaration:
```
<!ELEMENT Package (Documentation*, (Package |
                   BinaryCollaboration |
                   MultiPartyCollaboration |
                   BusinessTransaction)*) >
<!ATTLIST Package
     name   CDATA #REQUIRED
     nameID ID    #IMPLIED >
```

Definition:
Defines a hierarchical name scope containing reusable elements.

Parents:

▼ ProcessSpecification

▼ Package

Hierarchical Model:

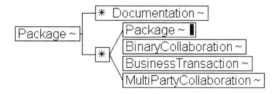

Attributes:

Attribute Name	Definition	Default Value
name	Defines the name of a model element. This name must be unique within the context of the model element and will be used to reference the element from other points in the model.	Required Input
nameID	XML ID version of name	Optional

t.) Performs

Element Name: Performs

DTD Declaration:
```
<!ELEMENT Performs (Documentation*) >
<!ATTLIST Performs
        initiatingRole      CDATA #IMPLIED
        initiatingRoleIDRef IDREF #IMPLIED
```

```
            respondingRole      CDATA #IMPLIED
            respondingRoleIDRef IDREF #IMPLIED >
```

Definition:

Performs is an explicit modeling of the relationship between a BusinessPartner-Role and the Roles it plays. This specifies the use of an authorized role within a multiparty collaboration. The authorized role must be stated as either an initiatingRole *or* a respondingRole. One and only one authorized role must be specified in a given Performs element.

Parents:

▼ BusinessPartnerRole

Attributes:

Attribute Name	Definition	Default Value
initiatingRole	The InitiatingRole that will be performed by the Business PartnerRole, qualified with the name of the BinaryCollaboration	Optional Input
initiatingRoleIDRef	The XML IDREF version of InitiatingRole	Optional Input
respondingRole	The RespondingRole that will be performed by the Business PartnerRole, qualified with the name of the BinaryCollaboration	Optional Input
respondingRoleIDRef	The XML IDREF version of RespondingRole	Optional Input

u.) ProcessSpecification

Element Name: ProcessSpecification

DTD Declaration:
```
<!ELEMENT ProcessSpecification (Documentation*, SubstitutionSet*,
(Include | BusinessDocument | ProcessSpecification | Package |
BinaryCollaboration | BusinessTransaction |
MultiPartyCollaboration)*)>
<!ATTLIST ProcessSpecification
        name    ID    #REQUIRED
        version CDATA #REQUIRED
        uuid    CDATA #REQUIRED >
```

Definition:

Root element of a process specification document that has a globally unique identity.

Hierarchical Model:

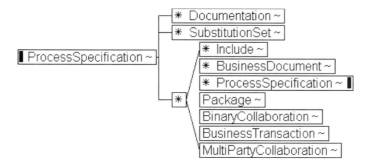

Attributes:

Attribute Name	Definition	Default Value
name	Defines the name of a model element. This name must be unique within the context of the model element and will be used to reference the element from other points in the model. It is defined as an XML ID.	Required
uuid	Universally unique identifier.	Required
version	Version of the specification.	Required

v.) Requesting Business Activity

Element Name: RequestingBusinessActivity

DTD Declaration:
```
<!ELEMENT RequestingBusinessActivity (Documentation*,
                                  DocumentEnvelope) >
<!ATTLIST RequestingBusinessActivity
    name                            CDATA        #IMPLIED
    nameID                          ID           #IMPLIED
    isAuthorizationRequired         (true | false) "false"
    isIntelligibleCheckRequired     (true | false) "false"
    isNonRepudiationReceiptRequired (true | false) "false"
    isNonRepudiationRequired        (true | false) "false"
    timeToAcknowledgeAcceptance     CDATA        #IMPLIED
    timeToAcknowledgeReceipt        CDATA        #IMPLIED>
```

Definition:

A RequestingBusinessActivity is a Business Action that is performed by the requesting role within a Business Transaction. It specifies the Document Envelope which will carry the request.

Parents:

▼ BusinessTransaction

Hierarchical Model:

Attributes:

Attribute Name	Definition	Default Value
name	Defines the name of the RequestingBusinessTransaction	Optional Input
nameID	The XML ID version of name	Optional Input
isAuthorizationRequired	Receiving party must validate identity of originator against a list of authorized originators. This parameter is specified on the sending side. (See also section on action security)	**false** Valid Values: {true, false}
isIntelligibleCheckRequired	Receiving party must check that a requesting document is not garbled (unreadable, unintelligible) before sending acknowledgement of receipt This parameter is specified on the sending side. (See also section on core transaction semantics)	**false** Valid Values: {true, false}
isNonRepudiationReceiptRequired	Requires the receiving party to return a signed receipt, and the original sender to save copy of the receipt. This parameter is specified on the sending side. (See also section on nonrepudiation)	**false** Valid Values: {true, false}

Attribute Name	Definition	Default Value
isNonRepudiationRequired	Requires the sending parties to save copies of the transacted documents before sending them (See also section on nonrepudiation)	**false** Valid Values: {true, false}
timeToAcknowledgeAcceptance	The time a responding role has to non-substantively acknowledge business acceptance of a business document. This parameter is specified on the requesting side. (See also section on core transaction semantics)	No default value.
timeToAcknowledgeReceipt	The time the receiving party has to acknowledge receipt of a business document. This parameter is specified on the sending side. (See also section on core transaction semantics)	No default value.

w.) Responding Business Activity

Element Name: RespondingBusinessActivity

DTD Declaration:

```
<!ELEMENT RespondingBusinessActivity (Documentation*,
                                  DocumentEnvelope*) >
<!ATTLIST RespondingBusinessActivity
    name                          CDATA           #IMPLIED
    nameID                        ID              #IMPLIED
    isAuthorizationRequired       (true | false)  "false"
    isIntelligibleCheckRequired   (true | false)  "false"
    isNonRepudiationReceiptRequired (true | false)  "false"
    isNonRepudiationRequired      (true | false)  "false"
    timeToAcknowledgeReceipt      CDATA           #IMPLIED>
```

Definition:

A RespondingBusinessActivity is a Business Action that is performed by the responding role within a Business Transaction. It specifies the Document Envelope which will carry the response.

There may be multiple possible response Document Envelopes defined, but only one of them will be sent during an actual transaction instance.

Parents:

▼ BusinessTransaction

Hierarchical Model:

Attributes:

Attribute Name	Definition	Default Value
name	Defines the name of the RespondingBusinessTransaction	Optional Input
nameID	The XML ID version of name	Optional Input
isAuthorizationRequired	Receiving party must validate identity of originator against a list of authorized originators.	**false** Valid Values: {true, false}
	This parameter is specified on the sending side.	
	(See also section on action security)	
isIntelligibleCheckRequired	Receiving party must check that a requesting document is not garbled (unreadable, unintelligible) before sending acknowledgement of receipt	**false** Valid Values: {true, false}
	This parameter is specified on the sending side.	
	(See also section on core transaction semantics)	
isNonRepudiationReceiptRequired	Requires the receiving party to return a signed receipt, and the original sender to save copy of the receipt.	**false** Valid Values: {true, false}
	This parameter is specified on the sending side.	
	(See also section on nonrepudiation)	

Attribute Name	Definition	Default Value
isNonRepudiationRequired	Requires the sending parties to save copies of the transacted documents before sending them (See also section on nonrepudiation)	**false** Valid Values: {true, false}
timeToAcknowledgeReceipt	The time the receiving party has to acknowledge receipt of a business document. This parameter is specified on the sending side. (See also section on core transaction semantics)	No default value.

x.) Responding Role

XML Element Name: RespondingRole

DTD Declaration:

```
<!ELEMENT RespondingRole (Documentation*)>
<!ATTLIST RespondingRole
          name    CDATA #REQUIRED
          nameID  ID    #IMPLIED>
```

Definition:

A Responding Role is a role that is authorized to send the first response, e.g. the seller is authorized to send the acceptance of purchase order. This role is the responder in a binary collaboration.

Parents:

▼ BinaryCollaboration

Attributes:

Attribute Name	Definition	Default Value
Name	Defines the name of the Responding Role	**Required input.**
nameID	XML ID version of name	Optional

y.) Start

Element Name: Start

DTD Declaration:

```
<!ELEMENT Start (Documentation*) >
<!ATTLIST Start
        toBusinessState    CDATA #REQUIRED
        toBusinessStateIDRef IDREF #IMPLIED >
```

Definition:

The starting state for an Binary Collaboration. A Binary Collaboration should have at least one starting activity. If none defined, then all activities are considered allowable entry points.

Parents:

▼ BinaryCollaboration

Attributes:

Attribute Name	Definition	Default Value
toBusinessState	The name of an activity which is an allowable starting point for this for BinaryCollaboration	Required Input
toBusinessStateIDRef	The XML IDREF version of toBusinessState	Optional

z.) SubstitutionSet

Element Name: SubstitutionSet

DTD Declaration:

```
    <!ELEMENT SubstitutionSet (DocumentSubstitution |
AttributeSubstitution, Documentation)*>
    <!ATTLIST SubstitutionSet
        name        CDATA #IMPLIED
        nameID      ID    #IMPLIED
        applyToScope CDATA #IMPLIED
    >
```

Definition:

A Substitution Set is a container for one or more AttributeSubstitution and/or DocumentSubstitution elements. The entire SubstitutionSet specifies document or attribute values that should be used in place of some documents and attribute values in an existing process specification.

Parents:

▼ ProcessSpecification

Attributes:

Attribute Name	Definition	Default Value
name	Name of the substitution set.	Optional Input
nameID	The ID of the substitution set.	Optional Input
applyToScope	Specifies the path to attributes or documents that are to be substituted for.	Optional Input

aa.) Success

Element Name: Success

DTD Declaration:

```
<!ELEMENT Success (ConditionExpression?, Documentation*) >
<!ATTLIST Success
          fromBusinessState CDATA #REQUIRED
          conditionGuard (Success | BusinessFailure |
                TechnicalFailure | AnyFailure) #IMPLIED
```

Definition:

Defines the successful conclusion of a binary collaboration as a transition from an activity.

Parents:

▼ BinaryCollaboration

Attributes:

Attribute Name	Definition	Default Value
fromBusinessState	The name of the activity from which this indicates a transition to successful conclusion of the BusinessTransaction or BinaryCollaboration	Required Input.
conditionGuard	The condition that guards this transition	Optional Valid Values: {Success, BusinessFailure, TechnicalFailure, AnyFailure}

bb.) Transition

ELEMENT Name: Transition

DTD Declaration:

```
<!ELEMENT Transition (ConditionExpression?, Documentation*) >
<!ATTLIST Transition
         onInitiation (true | false)  "false"
         fromBusinessState      CDATA #IMPLIED
         fromBusinessStateIDRef IDREF #IMPLIED
         toBusinessState        CDATA #IMPLIED
         toBusinessStateIDRef   IDREF #IMPLIED
         conditionGuard (Success | BusinessFailure |
              TechnicalFailure | AnyFailure) #IMPLIED
```

Definition:

A transition is a transition between two business states in a binary collaboration.
Choreography is expressed as transitions between business states.

Parents:

▼ BinaryCollaboration

▼ BusinessPartnerRole

Attributes:

Attribute Name	Definition	Default Value
onInitiation	This specifies this is a nested BusinessTransactionActivity and that upon receipt of the request in the associated transaction a second activity is performed before returning to the transaction to send the response back to the original requestor	**false** Valid Values: {true, false}
fromBusinessState	The name of the state transitioned from	No default value.
fromBusinessStateIDRef	The XML IDREF version of fromBusinessState	Optional
toBusinessState	The name of the state transitioned to	No default value.
toBusinessStateIDRef	The XML IDREF version of toBusinessState	Optional
conditionGuard	A reference to the status of the previous transaction. A fixed value of Success, BusinessFailure, TechnicalFailure, or AnyFailure	Optional Valid Values: {Success, Business-Failure, Technical-Failure, AnyFailure}

7.2 XML to UML Cross-Reference

The following is a table that references the XML element names in the DTD to their counterpart classes in the UML specification schema.

XML Element	UML Class
Attachment	Attachment
InitiatingRole	AuthorizedRole
RespondingRole	AuthorizedRole
Binary Collaboration	Binary Collaboration
BusinessPartner Role	BusinessPartner Role
Business Transaction Activity	Business Transaction Activity
Business Transaction	Business Transaction
Responding BusinessActivity	Responding BusinessActivity
Requesting BusinessActivity	Requesting BusinessActivity
Collaboration Activity	Collaboration Activity
DocumentEnvelope	DocumentEnvelope
Documentation	None (Should be added)
ebXML Process Specification	(From Package model: ebXML Process Specification)
Failure	Failure
Include	(From Package model: Include)
MultiParty Collaboration	MultiParty Collaboration
Package	(From Package model: Package)
Performs	Performs
Schema	Schema
Fork	Fork
Start	Start
Success	Success
Join	Join
Transition	Transition

The following classes in the UML specification schema are abstract, and do not have an element equivalent in the DTD. Only their concrete subtypes are in the DTD:

▼ BusinessState

▼ CompletionState

▼ BusinessActivity

▼ BusinessAction

▼ DocumentSecurity

7.3 Scoped Name Reference

The structure of ebXML business process specifications encourages re-use. An ProcessSpecification can include another ProcessSpecification by reference.

In addition the contents of a ProcessSpecification can be arranged in a recursive package structure. The ProcessSpecification is a package container, so it can contain packages within it. Package in itself is also a package container, so it can contain further packages within it.

Packages function as namespaces as per below.

Finally a Package, at any level can have PackageContent. Types of PackageContent are BusinessTransaction, BinaryCollaboration, MultiPartyCollaboration.

PackageContent are always uniquely named within a package. Lower level elements a uniquely named within their parent PackageContent.

Each PackageContent type is a built-in context provider for the core components Logical Model for the Business Document definitions referenced by this ProcessSpecification.

Within a ProcessSpecification the following applies to naming:

Specification elements reference other specification elements by name through the use of attributes. The design pattern is that elements have a name attribute and other elements that reference the named elements do so through an attribute defined as the lowerCamelCase version of the referenced element (e.g. InitiatingRole has attribute name while Performs, which references InitiatingRole, has attribute initiatingRole). Two types of attributes are provided for names and references, XML ID/IDREF based and plain text. Each named element has a required name attribute and an optional nameID attribute. Referencing elements have lowerCamelCase and lowerCamelCaseIDRef attributes for the referenced element. XML ID/IDREF functionality requires all IDs to be unique within a document and that all IDREFs point to a defined ID value. Plain text attributes do not have this capability and may result in duplicate names. To unambiguously identify a referenced element using plain text attribute in the referencing attribute it is strongly recommended that XPath syntax be used. However, this is not enforced in the DTD or Schema.

The purpose of providing both solutions is to facilitate creation of Process Specification Documents directly in XML and to support future development tools that can automatically assign machine readable nameIDs and references. Both styles can be used simultaneously, in which case the ID and IDREF versions provide the unambiguous referencing and the plain text versions are used to provide meaningful names. Examples of named elements and references:

```
<Package name="ebXMLOrdering">
    <BinaryCollaboration name="OrderCollaboration" nameID="b112">
        <InitiatingRole name="buyer" nameID="r224"/>
        <RespondingRole name="seller" nameID="r225"/>
    </BinaryCollaboration>
</Package>

<!-the XPath approach -->
<Performs
initiatingRole='//Package[@name="ebXMLOrdering"]/BinaryCollabora-
tion[@name="OrderCollaboration"]/InitiatingRole[@name="buyer"]'/>

<!-Combination approach -->
<Performs initiatingRole="buyer" initiatingRoleIDRef="r224"/>
```

It is not required to use the full path specification as shown above, other forms of XPath expressions could be used as long as they resolve to a single reference. For example if buyer was unique to the document then the Xpath could have been:

```
<Performs initiatingRole='//InitiatingRole[@name="buyer"]'/>
Relative paths are also allowed for example:
<BusinessTransactionActivity
fromAuthorizedRole='../InitiatingRole[@name="buyer"]' ... />
```

7.4 Substitution Sets

Generic ebXML Business Process Specifications are not tightly coupled to technology and business details, such as specific document formats and structures and timing parameters. Substitution sets support the capability to take a generic business process and specialize it for a specific use. For example, an ordering process may be very generic but a specific use of that process may require specific document capabilities that go beyond the generic.

A substitution set is placed in a copy of the more specific process specification and replaces or makes more explicit document definition references and attribute values.

A Substitution Set is a container for one or more AttributeSubstitution and/or DocumentSubstitution elements. The entire SubstitutionSet specifies document or attribute values that should be used in place of some documents and attribute values in an existing process specification.

7.5 Sample XML Document Against above DTD

Provided in Appendix A

8 Business Signal Structures

The ebXML Message Service Specification signal structures provide business service state alignment infrastructure, including unique message identifiers and digests used to meet the basic process alignment requirements. The business signal payload structures provided herein are optional and normative and are intended to provide business and legal semantic to the business signals. Since signals do not differ in structure from business transaction to business transaction, they are defined once and for all, and their definition is implied by the conjunction of the Business Process Specification Schema and Message Service Specification. Here are the DTD's for business signal payload for receiptAcknowledgment (from the RosettaNet website, courtesy of RosettaNet, and Edifecs) and for acceptanceAcknowledgement and exception.

8.1.1 ReceiptAcknowledgment DTD

```
<!--
   RosettaNet XML Message Schema.
   http://www.rosettanet.org
   RosettaNet XML Message Schema
   Receipt Acknowledgement
   Version 1.1
-->
<!ENTITY % common-attributes "id CDATA #IMPLIED">
<!ELEMENT ReceiptAcknowledgement (
        fromRole ,
        NonRepudiationInformation? ,
        receivedDocumentDateTime ,
        receivedDocumentIdentifier ,
        thisMessageDateTime ,
        thisMessageIdentifier ,
        toRole ) >
<!ELEMENT fromRole
         ( PartnerRoleDescription ) >
<!ELEMENT PartnerRoleDescription (
        ContactInformation? ,
```

```
          GlobalPartnerRoleClassificationCode ,
          PartnerDescription ) >
<!ELEMENT ContactInformation (
          contactName ,
          EmailAddress ,
          telephoneNumber ) >
<!ELEMENT contactName
          ( FreeFormText ) >
<!ELEMENT FreeFormText
          ( #PCDATA ) >
<!ATTLIST FreeFormText
          xml:lang CDATA #IMPLIED >
<!ELEMENT EmailAddress
          ( #PCDATA ) >
<!ELEMENT telephoneNumber
          ( CommunicationsNumber ) >
<!ELEMENT CommunicationsNumber
          ( #PCDATA ) >
<!ELEMENT GlobalPartnerRoleClassificationCode
          ( #PCDATA ) >
<!ELEMENT PartnerDescription (
          BusinessDescription ,
          GlobalPartnerClassificationCode ) >
<!ELEMENT BusinessDescription (
          GlobalBusinessIdentifier ,
          GlobalSupplyChainCode ) >
<!ELEMENT GlobalBusinessIdentifier
          ( #PCDATA ) >
<!ELEMENT GlobalSupplyChainCode
          ( #PCDATA ) >
<!ELEMENT GlobalPartnerClassificationCode
          ( #PCDATA ) >
<!ELEMENT NonRepudiationInformation (
          GlobalDigestAlgorithmCode ,
          OriginalMessageDigest ) >
<!ELEMENT GlobalDigestAlgorithmCode
          ( #PCDATA ) >
<!ELEMENT OriginalMessageDigest
          ( #PCDATA ) >
<!ELEMENT receivedDocumentDateTime
          ( DateTimeStamp ) >
<!ELEMENT DateTimeStamp
          ( #PCDATA ) >
<!ELEMENT receivedDocumentIdentifier
          ( ProprietaryDocumentIdentifier ) >
<!ELEMENT ProprietaryDocumentIdentifier
          ( #PCDATA ) >
```

```
<!ELEMENT thisMessageDateTime
          ( DateTimeStamp ) >
<!ELEMENT thisMessageIdentifier
          ( ProprietaryMessageIdentifier ) >
<!ELEMENT ProprietaryMessageIdentifier
          ( #PCDATA ) >
<!ELEMENT toRole
          ( PartnerRoleDescription ) >
```

8.1.2   AcceptanceAcknowledgement DTD

```
<!--
   RosettaNet XML Message Schema.
   http://www.rosettanet.org
   RosettaNet XML Message Schema.
   Acceptance Acknowledgement Exception
   Version 1.1
-->
<!ENTITY % common-attributes "id CDATA #IMPLIED">
<!ELEMENT AcceptanceAcknowledgementException (
          fromRole ,
          reason ,
          theMessageDatetime ,
          theOffendingDocumentDateTime ,
          theOffendingDocumentIdentifier ,
          thisMessageIdentifier ,
          toRole ) >
<!ELEMENT fromRole
           ( PartnerRoleDescription ) >
<!ELEMENT PartnerRoleDescription (
          ContactInformation? ,
          GlobalPartnerRoleClassificationCode ,
          PartnerDescription ) >
<!ELEMENT ContactInformation (
          contactName ,
          EmailAddress ,
          telephoneNumber ) >
<!ELEMENT contactName
          ( FreeFormText ) >
<!ELEMENT FreeFormText
          ( #PCDATA ) >
<!ATTLIST FreeFormText
          xml:lang CDATA #IMPLIED >
<!ELEMENT EmailAddress
          ( #PCDATA ) >
<!ELEMENT telephoneNumber
          ( CommunicationsNumber ) >
```

```
<!ELEMENT CommunicationsNumber
          ( #PCDATA ) >
<!ELEMENT GlobalPartnerRoleClassificationCode
          ( #PCDATA ) >
<!ELEMENT PartnerDescription (
          BusinessDescription ,
          GlobalPartnerClassificationCode ) >
<!ELEMENT BusinessDescription (
          GlobalBusinessIdentifier ,
          GlobalSupplyChainCode ) >
<!ELEMENT GlobalBusinessIdentifier
          ( #PCDATA ) >
<!ELEMENT GlobalSupplyChainCode
          ( #PCDATA ) >
<!ELEMENT GlobalPartnerClassificationCode
          ( #PCDATA ) >
<!ELEMENT reason
          ( FreeFormText ) >
<!ELEMENT theMessageDatetime
          ( DateTimeStamp ) >
<!ELEMENT DateTimeStamp
          ( #PCDATA ) >
<!ELEMENT theOffendingDocumentDateTime
          ( DateTimeStamp ) >
<!ELEMENT theOffendingDocumentIdentifier
          ( ProprietaryDocumentIdentifier ) >
<!ELEMENT ProprietaryDocumentIdentifier
          ( #PCDATA ) >
<!ELEMENT thisMessageIdentifier
          ( ProprietaryMessageIdentifier ) >
<!ELEMENT ProprietaryMessageIdentifier
          ( #PCDATA ) >
<!ELEMENT toRole
          ( PartnerRoleDescription ) >
```

8.1.3 Exception Signal DTD

```
<!--
   RosettaNet XML Message Schema.
   http://www.rosettanet.org
   RosettaNet XML Message Schema.
   Exception
   Version 1.1
-->
<!ENTITY % common-attributes "id CDATA #IMPLIED">
<!ELEMENT Exception (
          fromRole? ,
```

```
                   reason ,
                   theMessageDatetime ,
                   theOffendingDocumentDateTime? ,
                   theOffendingDocumentIdentifier? ,
                   thisMessageIdentifier ,
                   toRole? ) >
<!ELEMENT fromRole
          ( PartnerRoleDescription ) >
<!ELEMENT PartnerRoleDescription (
          ContactInformation? ,
          GlobalPartnerRoleClassificationCode? ,
          PartnerDescription? ) >
<!ELEMENT ContactInformation (
          contactName? ,
          EmailAddress? ,
          telephoneNumber? ) >
<!ELEMENT contactName
          ( FreeFormText ) >
<!ELEMENT FreeFormText
          ( #PCDATA ) >
<!ATTLIST FreeFormText
           xml:lang CDATA #IMPLIED >
<!ELEMENT EmailAddress
          ( #PCDATA ) >
<!ELEMENT telephoneNumber
          ( CommunicationsNumber ) >
<!ELEMENT CommunicationsNumber
          ( #PCDATA ) >
<!ELEMENT GlobalPartnerRoleClassificationCode
          ( #PCDATA ) >
<!ELEMENT PartnerDescription (
          BusinessDescription? ,
          GlobalPartnerClassificationCode? ) >
<!ELEMENT BusinessDescription (
          GlobalBusinessIdentifier? ,
          GlobalSupplyChainCode? ) >
<!ELEMENT GlobalBusinessIdentifier
          ( #PCDATA ) >
<!ELEMENT GlobalSupplyChainCode
          ( #PCDATA ) >
<!ELEMENT GlobalPartnerClassificationCode
          ( #PCDATA ) >
<!ELEMENT reason
          ( FreeFormText ) >
<!ELEMENT theMessageDatetime
          ( DateTimeStamp ) >
<!ELEMENT DateTimeStamp
```

```
            ( #PCDATA ) >
<!ELEMENT theOffendingDocumentDateTime
            ( DateTimeStamp ) >
<!ELEMENT theOffendingDocumentIdentifier
            ( ProprietaryDocumentIdentifier ) >
<!ELEMENT ProprietaryDocumentIdentifier
            ( #PCDATA ) >
<!ELEMENT thisMessageIdentifier
            ( ProprietaryMessageIdentifier ) >
<!ELEMENT ProprietaryMessageIdentifier
            ( #PCDATA ) >
<!ELEMENT toRole
            ( PartnerRoleDescription ) >
```

9 Production Rules

This section provides a set of production rules, defining the mapping from the UML version of the *Business Process Specification Schema* to the XML version.

The primary purpose for these production rules is to govern the one-time generation of the DTD version of the *Business Process Specification Schema* from the UML Class Diagram version of *Business Process Specification Schema*.

The Class Diagram version of *Business Process Specification Schema* is not intended for the direct creation of ebXML Business Process Specifications. However, if a *Business Process Specification* was in fact (programmatically) created as an instance of this class diagram, the production rules would also provide the prescriptive definition necessary to translate a such an instance into a XML Specification Document conformant with the DTD. The production rules are defined for concrete classes, abstract classes, aggregate associations, specialization associations and unidirectional associations.

1. Classes are rendered as XML elements.

2. Class attributes are rendered as XML attributes. NOTE: occurrence requirements (required vs optional) and default values for attributes are not modeled.

3. Specialization classes (classes that inherit from another class) are rendered as XML elements including all attributes and aggregate associations from the base class. Repeated attributes are normalized to a single occurrence.

4. Abstract classes are not rendered in the XML DTD. Abstract classes are inherited from and represent a form of collection. A class that aggregates an

abstract class, essentially aggregates "any of each" of the specialization classes.

5. An aggregate association renders the aggregated class as an XML child element with appropriate cardinality.

6. A unidirectional association defines an attribute in the originating class of the same name as the class the association points to. This type of attribute is called a "reference attribute" and contains the name of the class it points to. The referenced class must have a "name" attribute.

7. A class attribute data type, that has a class of the same name with stereotype <<Enumeration>> is rendered as an XML attribute enumeration. The Enumeration class does not have an explicit association.

8. A class attribute data type (e.g. Time, URI, Boolean) that has no corresponding class definition is rendered as a string in the DTD. In the XML Schema version these data types are mapped as:

Time - xsd:duration

URI - xsd:anyURI

Boolean - xsd:boolean

9. Each class is given an optional "Documentation*" element which is intended for annotation of the specification instances. This is not modeled.

10   References

UN/CEFACT Modelling Methodology (CEFACT/TMWG/N090R9.1)

RosettaNet Implementation Framework: Core Specification, Version: Release 2.00.00, 3 January 2001

11   Disclaimer

The views and specification expressed in this document are those of the authors and are not necessarily those of their employers. The authors and their employers specifically disclaim responsibility for any problems arising from correct or incorrect implementation or use of this design.

12   Contact Information

Team Leader (Of the BP team):

   Paul Levine

   Telcordia Technologies, Inc.

   45 Knightsbridge Road

   Piscataway, N.J. 08854

   US

   Phone: 732-699-3042

   EMail: plevine@telcordia.com

Sub Team Lead (Of the context/MetamodelGroup) :

   Karsten Riemer

   Sun Microsystems

   1 Network Drive

   Burlington, MA 01803

   USA

   Phone: 781-442-2679

   EMail: karsten.riemer@sun.com

Editor (of this document):

   Karsten Riemer

   Sun Microsystems

   1 Network Drive

   Burlington, MA 01803

   USA

   Phone: 781-442-2679

   EMail: karsten.riemer@sun.com

Appendix A   Sample XML Business Process Specification

```
<!-- edited by Kurt Kanaskie (Lucent Technologies) -->
<!DOCTYPE ProcessSpecification SYSTEM "ebBPSS-v1.01.dtd">
<ProcessSpecification name="Simple" version="1.1" uuid="[1234-
5678-901234]">
        <!-- Business Documents -->
                <BusinessDocument name="Catalog Request"/>
                <BusinessDocument name="Catalog"/>
                <BusinessDocument name="Purchase Order"/>
                <BusinessDocument name="PO Acknowledgement"/>
                <BusinessDocument name="Credit Request"/>
                <BusinessDocument name="Credit Confirm"/>
                <BusinessDocument name="ASN"/>
                <BusinessDocument name="CreditAdvice"/>
                <BusinessDocument name="DebitAdvice"/>
                <BusinessDocument name="Invoice"/>
                <BusinessDocument name="Payment"/>
                <BusinessDocument name="Inventory Report Request"/>
                <BusinessDocument name="Inventory Report"/>
                <BusinessDocument name="Inventory Report"/>
        <Package name="Ordering">
                <!-- First the overall MultiParty Collaboration -->
                <MultiPartyCollaboration name="DropShip">
                        <BusinessPartnerRole name="Customer">
                                <Performs initiatingRole="requestor"/>
                                <Performs initiatingRole="buyer"/>
                                <Transition fromBusinessState="Catalog
Request" toBusinessState="Create Order"/>
                        </BusinessPartnerRole>
                        <BusinessPartnerRole name="Retailer">
                                <Performs respondingRole="provider"/>
                                <Performs respondingRole="seller"/>
                                <Performs initiatingRole="Creditor"/>
                                <Performs initiatingRole="buyer"/>
                                <Performs initiatingRole="Payee"/>
                                <Performs respondingRole="Payor"/>
                                <Performs initiatingRole="requestor"/>
                                <Transition fromBusinessState="Create
```

```
Order" toBusinessState="Check Credit"/>
                        <Transition fromBusinessState="Check Credit"
toBusinessState="Create Order"/>
                </BusinessPartnerRole>
                <BusinessPartnerRole name="DropShip Vendor">
                        <Performs respondingRole="seller"/>
                        <Performs initiatingRole="payee"/>
                        <Performs respondingRole="provider"/>
                </BusinessPartnerRole>
                <BusinessPartnerRole name="Credit Authority">
                        <Performs respondingRole="credit service"/>
                        <Performs respondingRole="payor"/>
                </BusinessPartnerRole>
        </MultiPartyCollaboration>
        <!-- Now the Binary Collaborations -->
        <BinaryCollaboration name="Request Catalog">
                <InitiatingRole name="requestor"/>
                <RespondingRole name="provider"/>
                <BusinessTransactionActivity name="Catalog
Request" businessTransaction="Catalog Request" fromAuthorized-
Role="requestor"
toAuthorizedRole="provider"/>
        </BinaryCollaboration>
        <BinaryCollaboration name="Firm Order" timeToPerform=
"P2D">
                <Documentation>timeToPerform = Period: 2 days
from start of transaction</Documentation>
                <InitiatingRole name="buyer"/>
                <RespondingRole name="seller"/>
                <BusinessTransactionActivity name="Create Order"
businessTransaction="Create Order" fromAuthorizedRole="buyer"
toAuthorizedRole="seller"/>
        </BinaryCollaboration>
        <BinaryCollaboration name="Product Fulfillment"
timeToPerform="P5D">
                <Documentation>timeToPerform = Period: 5 days
from start of transaction</Documentation>
                <InitiatingRole name="buyer"/>
                <RespondingRole name="seller"/>
                <BusinessTransactionActivity name="Create Order"
businessTransaction="Create Order" fromAuthorizedRole="buyer"
toAuthorizedRole="seller"/>
                <BusinessTransactionActivity name="Notify ship-
```

```
ment" businessTransaction="Notify of advance shipment" from-
AuthorizedRole="buyer"
toAuthorizedRole="seller"/>
                <Start toBusinessState="Create Order"/>
                <Transition fromBusinessState="Create Order"
toBusinessState="Notify shipment"/>
                <Success fromBusinessState="Notify shipment"
conditionGuard="Success"/>
                <Failure fromBusinessState="Notify shipment"
conditionGuard="BusinessFailure"/>
            </BinaryCollaboration>
            <BinaryCollaboration name="Inventory Status">
                <InitiatingRole name="requestor"/>
                <RespondingRole name="provider"/>
                <BusinessTransactionActivity name="Inventory
Report Request" businessTransaction="Inventory Report Request"
fromAuthorizedRole="requestor" toAuthorizedRole="provider"/>
                <BusinessTransactionActivity name="Inventory
Report" businessTransaction="Inventory Report" fromAuthorized-
Role="provider"
toAuthorizedRole="requestor"/>
            </BinaryCollaboration>
            <BinaryCollaboration name="Credit Inquiry">
                <InitiatingRole name="creditor"/>
                <RespondingRole name="credit service"/>
                <BusinessTransactionActivity name="Check Credit"
businessTransaction="Check Credit" fromAuthorizedRole="creditor"
toAuthorizedRole="credit service"/>
            </BinaryCollaboration>
            <BinaryCollaboration name="Credit Payment">
                <InitiatingRole name="payee"/>
                <RespondingRole name="payor"/>
                <BusinessTransactionActivity name="Process
Credit Payment" businessTransaction="Process Credit Payment"
fromAuthorizedRole="payee" toAuthorizedRole="payor"/>
            </BinaryCollaboration>
            <!-- A compound BinaryCollaboration for illustration
purposes-->
            <BinaryCollaboration name="Credit Charge">
                <InitiatingRole name="charger"/>
                <RespondingRole name="credit service"/>
                <CollaborationActivity name="Credit Inquiry"
binaryCollaboration="Credit Inquiry" fromAuthorizedRole="charger"
```

```
toAuthorizedRole="credit service"/>
                <CollaborationActivity name="Credit Payment"
binaryCollaboration="Credit Payment" fromAuthorizedRole="charger"
toAuthorizedRole="credit service"/>
                <Transition fromBusinessState="Credit Inquiry"
toBusinessState="Credit Payment"/>
            </BinaryCollaboration>
            <BinaryCollaboration name="Fulfillment Payment">
                <InitiatingRole name="payee"/>
                <RespondingRole name="payor"/>
                <BusinessTransactionActivity name="Process
Payment" businessTransaction="Process Payment" fromAuthorized-
Role="payee"
toAuthorizedRole="payor"/>
            </BinaryCollaboration>
            <!-- Here are all the Business Transactions needed -->
            <BusinessTransaction name="Catalog Request">
                <RequestingBusinessActivity name="">
                    <DocumentEnvelope isPositiveResponse="true"
businessDocument="Catalog Request"/>
                </RequestingBusinessActivity>
                <RespondingBusinessActivity name="">
                    <DocumentEnvelope isPositiveResponse="true"
businessDocument="Catalog"/>
                </RespondingBusinessActivity>
            </BusinessTransaction>
            <BusinessTransaction name="Create Order">
                <RequestingBusinessActivity name=""
isNonRepudiationRequired="true" timeToAcknowledgeReceipt="P2D"
timeToAcknowledgeAcceptance="P3D">
                    <DocumentEnvelope isPositiveResponse="true"
businessDocument="Purchase Order"/>
                </RequestingBusinessActivity>
                <RespondingBusinessActivity name=""
isNonRepudiationRequired="true" timeToAcknowledgeReceipt="P5D">
                    <DocumentEnvelope isPositiveResponse="true"
businessDocument="PO Acknowledgement"/>
                </RespondingBusinessActivity>
            </BusinessTransaction>
            <BusinessTransaction name="Check Credit ">
                <RequestingBusinessActivity name="">
                    <DocumentEnvelope isPositiveResponse="true"
businessDocument="Credit Request"/>
                </RequestingBusinessActivity>
```

```
                <RespondingBusinessActivity name="">
                        <DocumentEnvelope isPositiveResponse="true"
businessDocument="Credit Confirm"/>
                </RespondingBusinessActivity>
        </BusinessTransaction>
        <BusinessTransaction name="Notify of advance shipment">
                <RequestingBusinessActivity name="">
                        <DocumentEnvelope isPositiveResponse="true"
businessDocument="ASN"/>
                </RequestingBusinessActivity>
                <RespondingBusinessActivity name=""
timeToAcknowledgeReceipt="P2D"/>
        </BusinessTransaction>
        <BusinessTransaction name="Process Credit Payment">
                <RequestingBusinessActivity name="">
                        <DocumentEnvelope isPositiveResponse="true"
businessDocument="CreditAdvice"/>
                </RequestingBusinessActivity>
                <RespondingBusinessActivity name="">
                        <DocumentEnvelope isPositiveResponse="true"
businessDocument="DebitAdvice"/>
                </RespondingBusinessActivity>
        </BusinessTransaction>
        <BusinessTransaction name="Process Payment">
                <RequestingBusinessActivity name="">
                        <DocumentEnvelope isPositiveResponse="true"
businessDocument="Invoice"/>
                </RequestingBusinessActivity>
                <RespondingBusinessActivity name="">
                        <DocumentEnvelope isPositiveResponse="true"
businessDocument="Payment"/>
                </RespondingBusinessActivity>
        </BusinessTransaction>
        <BusinessTransaction name="Request Inventory Report">
                <RequestingBusinessActivity name="">
                        <DocumentEnvelope isPositiveResponse="true"
businessDocument="Inventory Report Request"/>
                </RequestingBusinessActivity>
                <RespondingBusinessActivity name="">
                        <DocumentEnvelope isPositiveResponse="true"
businessDocument="Inventory Report"/>
                </RespondingBusinessActivity>
        </BusinessTransaction>
        <BusinessTransaction name="Inventory Report">
                <RequestingBusinessActivity name="">
```

```
                    <DocumentEnvelope isPositiveResponse="true"
businessDocument="Inventory Report"/>
                </RequestingBusinessActivity>
                <RespondingBusinessActivity name=""/>
            </BusinessTransaction>
        </Package>
</ProcessSpecification>
```

Appendix B Business Process Specification Schema DTD

```
<!--
================================================================ -->
<!-- Editor: Kurt Kanaskie (Lucent Technologies)         -->
<!-- Version: Version 1.01                               -->
<!-- Updated: 2001-05-24                                 -->
<!--                                                     -->
<!-- Public Identifier:                                  -->
<!-- "-//ebXML//DTD BusinessProcessSpecificationSchema v1.01//EN"
-->
<!--                                                     -->
<!-- Purpose:                                            -->
<!--   The ebXML Specification DTD provides a standard   -->
<!--   framework by which business systems may be        -->
<!--   configured to support execution of business       -->
<!--   transactions. It is based upon prior UN/CEFACT    -->
<!--   work, specifically the metamodel behind the       -->
<!--   UN/CEFACT Unified Modeling Methodology (UMM) defined -->
<!--   in the N090R9.1 specification.                    -->
<!--                                                     -->
<!--   The Specification Schema supports the specification -->
<!--   of Business Transactions and the choreography of  -->
<!--   Business Transactions into Business Collaborations. -->
<!--                                                     -->
<!-- Notes:                                              -->
<!--   time periods are represented using ISO 8601 format -->
<!--   (e.g. P2D for 2 Days, P2H30M for 2 Hours 30 Minutes -->
<!--                                                     -->
```

```
<!--  Naming and reference is based on convention that an      -->
<!--  Element with a name attribute (e.g. AuthorizedRole)      -->
<!--  is refernced by an attribute in another element with     -->
<!--  the name in lowerCamelCase (e.g. authorizedRole).        -->
<!--                                                           -->
<!--  fromBusinessState and toBusinessState refer to the       -->
<!--  the names of a BusinessTransactionActivity,              -->
<!--  CollaborationActivity, Fork, and Join, all are targets for
-->
<!--  from/to in Transition. This deviates from the normal     -->
<!--  convention of lowerCamelCase attribute name              -->
<!--  BusinessState is used as a generic term for:             -->
<!--  Fork, Join, Success, Failure                             -->
<!--                                                           -->
<!-- Constraints:                                              -->
<!--  - attributes specificationLocation, pattern, specification
-->
<!--  uri, are of type xsd:anyURI                              -->
<!--  - attributes timeTo* are of type xsd:duration            -->
<!--                                                           -->
<!--
=============================================================== -->
<!ELEMENT ProcessSpecification (Documentation*, SubstitutionSet*,
(Include | BusinessDocument | ProcessSpecification | Package |
BinaryCollaboration | BusinessTransaction |
MultiPartyCollaboration)*)>
<!ATTLIST ProcessSpecification
     name ID #REQUIRED
     uuid CDATA #REQUIRED
     version CDATA #REQUIRED
>
<!ELEMENT Documentation (#PCDATA)>
<!ATTLIST Documentation
     uri CDATA #IMPLIED
>
<!ELEMENT Include (Documentation*)>
<!ATTLIST Include
     name CDATA #REQUIRED
     uuid CDATA #REQUIRED
     uri CDATA #REQUIRED
     version CDATA #REQUIRED
>
<!ELEMENT BusinessDocument (ConditionExpression?, Documentation*)>
<!ATTLIST BusinessDocument
     name CDATA #REQUIRED
```

```
      nameID ID #IMPLIED
      specificationLocation CDATA #IMPLIED
      specificationElement CDATA #IMPLIED
>
<!ELEMENT ConditionExpression (Documentation*)>
<!ATTLIST ConditionExpression
      expressionLanguage CDATA #IMPLIED
      expression CDATA #IMPLIED
>
<!ELEMENT SubstitutionSet (DocumentSubstitution | Attribute-
Substitution |
Documentation)*>
<!ATTLIST SubstitutionSet
      name CDATA #IMPLIED
      nameId IDREF #IMPLIED
      applyToScope CDATA #IMPLIED
>
<!ELEMENT DocumentSubstitution (Documentation*)>
<!ATTLIST DocumentSubstitution
      originalBusinessDocument CDATA #IMPLIED
      originalBusinessDocumentID IDREF #IMPLIED
      substituteBusinessDocument CDATA #IMPLIED
      substituteBusinessDocumentId IDREF #IMPLIED
>
<!ELEMENT AttributeSubstitution (Documentation*)>
<!ATTLIST AttributeSubstitution
      attributeName CDATA #IMPLIED
      value CDATA #IMPLIED
>
<!ELEMENT Package (Documentation*, (Package | BinaryCollaboration
|
BusinessTransaction | MultiPartyCollaboration)*)>
<!ATTLIST Package
      name CDATA #REQUIRED
      nameID ID #IMPLIED
>
<!ELEMENT BinaryCollaboration (Documentation*, InitiatingRole,
RespondingRole, (Documentation | Start | Transition | Success |
Failure | BusinessTransactionActivity | CollaborationActivity |
Fork | Join)*)>
<!ATTLIST BinaryCollaboration
      name CDATA #REQUIRED
      nameID ID #IMPLIED
      pattern CDATA #IMPLIED
      beginsWhen CDATA #IMPLIED
```

```
       endsWhen CDATA #IMPLIED
       preCondition CDATA #IMPLIED
       postCondition CDATA #IMPLIED
       timeToPerform CDATA #IMPLIED
>
<!ELEMENT MultiPartyCollaboration (Documentation*, Business-
PartnerRole*)>
<!ATTLIST MultiPartyCollaboration
       name CDATA #REQUIRED
       nameID ID #IMPLIED
>
<!ELEMENT InitiatingRole (Documentation*)>
<!ATTLIST InitiatingRole
       name CDATA #REQUIRED
       nameID ID #IMPLIED
>
<!ELEMENT RespondingRole (Documentation*)>
<!ATTLIST RespondingRole
       name CDATA #REQUIRED
       nameID ID #IMPLIED
>
<!-- A BusinessState is one of Start, Success, Failure, Fork,
Join, BusinessTransactionActivity or CollaborationActivity -->
<!-- fromBusinessState and toBusinessState are fully qualified
using XPath -->
<!ELEMENT Transition (ConditionExpression?, Documentation*)>
<!ATTLIST Transition
       onInitiation (true | false) "false"
       fromBusinessState CDATA #IMPLIED
       fromBusinessStateIDRef IDREF #IMPLIED
       toBusinessState CDATA #IMPLIED
       toBusinessStateIDRef IDREF #IMPLIED
       conditionGuard (Success | BusinessFailure | TechnicalFailure |
AnyFailure) #IMPLIED
>
<!-- Start is a special type of Transition in that it only has a
destination -->
<!ELEMENT Start (Documentation*)>
<!ATTLIST Start
       toBusinessState CDATA #REQUIRED
       toBusinessStateIDRef IDREF #IMPLIED
>
<!-- Success is a special type of Transition in that it only has a
origination -->
<!ELEMENT Success (ConditionExpression?, Documentation*)>
<!ATTLIST Success
```

```
      fromBusinessState CDATA #REQUIRED
      fromBusinessStateIDRef IDREF #IMPLIED
      conditionGuard (Success | BusinessFailure | TechnicalFailure |
AnyFailure) #IMPLIED
>
<!-- Failure is a special type of Transition in that it only has a
origination -->
<!ELEMENT Failure (ConditionExpression?, Documentation*)>
<!ATTLIST Failure
      fromBusinessState CDATA #REQUIRED
      fromBusinessStateIDRef IDREF #IMPLIED
      conditionGuard (Success | BusinessFailure | TechnicalFailure |
AnyFailure) #IMPLIED
>
<!-- Fork is a special type of BusinessState that can be transi-
tioned to -->
<!ELEMENT Fork (Documentation*)>
<!ATTLIST Fork
      name CDATA #REQUIRED
      nameID ID #IMPLIED
>
<!-- Join is a special type of BusinessState that can be transi-
tioned to -->
<!ELEMENT Join (Documentation*)>
<!ATTLIST Join
      name CDATA #REQUIRED
      nameID ID #IMPLIED
      waitForAll (true | false) "true"
>
<!-- fromAuthorizedRole and toAuthorizedRole are fully qualified
using XPath -->
<!-- BusinessTransactionActivity is a BusinessState that can be
transitioned
to -->
<!ELEMENT BusinessTransactionActivity (Documentation*)>
<!ATTLIST BusinessTransactionActivity
      name CDATA #REQUIRED
      nameID ID #IMPLIED
      businessTransaction CDATA #REQUIRED
      businessTransactionIDRef IDREF #IMPLIED
      fromAuthorizedRole CDATA #REQUIRED
      fromAuthorizedRoleIDRef IDREF #IMPLIED
      toAuthorizedRole CDATA #REQUIRED
      toAuthorizedRoleIDRef IDREF #IMPLIED
      isConcurrent (true | false) "true"
      isLegallyBinding (true | false) "true"
```

```
               timeToPerform CDATA #IMPLIED
>
<!-- fromAuthorizedRole and toAuthorizedRole are fully qualified
using XPath -->
<!-- CollaborationActivity is a BusinessState that can be transi-
tioned to -->
<!ELEMENT CollaborationActivity (Documentation*)>
<!ATTLIST CollaborationActivity
       name CDATA #REQUIRED
       nameID ID #IMPLIED
       fromAuthorizedRole CDATA #REQUIRED
       fromAuthorizedRoleIDRef IDREF #IMPLIED
       toAuthorizedRole CDATA #REQUIRED
       toAuthorizedRoleIDRef IDREF #IMPLIED
       binaryCollaboration CDATA #REQUIRED
       binaryCollaborationIDRef IDREF #IMPLIED
>
<!ELEMENT BusinessTransaction (Documentation*, RequestingBusiness-
Activity, RespondingBusinessActivity)>
<!ATTLIST BusinessTransaction
       name CDATA #REQUIRED
       nameID ID #IMPLIED
       pattern CDATA #IMPLIED
       beginsWhen CDATA #IMPLIED
       endsWhen CDATA #IMPLIED
       isGuaranteedDeliveryRequired (true | false) "false"
       preCondition CDATA #IMPLIED
       postCondition CDATA #IMPLIED
>
<!ELEMENT RequestingBusinessActivity (Documentation*, Document-
Envelope)>
<!ATTLIST RequestingBusinessActivity
       name CDATA #IMPLIED
       nameID ID #IMPLIED
       isAuthorizationRequired (true | false) "false"
       isIntelligibleCheckRequired (true | false) "false"
       isNonRepudiationReceiptRequired (true | false) "false"
       isNonRepudiationRequired (true | false) "false"
       timeToAcknowledgeAcceptance CDATA #IMPLIED
       timeToAcknowledgeReceipt CDATA #IMPLIED
>
<!ELEMENT RespondingBusinessActivity (Documentation*, Document-
Envelope*)>
<!ATTLIST RespondingBusinessActivity
       name CDATA #IMPLIED
       nameID ID #IMPLIED
```

```
         isAuthorizationRequired (true | false) "false"
         isIntelligibleCheckRequired (true | false) "false"
         isNonRepudiationReceiptRequired (true | false) "false"
         isNonRepudiationRequired (true | false) "false"
         timeToAcknowledgeReceipt CDATA #IMPLIED
>
<!ELEMENT DocumentEnvelope (Documentation*, Attachment*)>
<!ATTLIST DocumentEnvelope
         businessDocument CDATA #REQUIRED
         businessDocumentIDRef IDREF #IMPLIED
         isPositiveResponse (true | false) "false"
         isAuthenticated (true | false) "false"
         isConfidential (true | false) "false"
         isTamperProof (true | false) "false"
>
<!ELEMENT Attachment (Documentation*)>
<!ATTLIST Attachment
         name CDATA #REQUIRED
         nameID ID #IMPLIED
         businessDocument CDATA #IMPLIED
         businessDocumentIDRef IDREF #IMPLIED
         mimeType CDATA #REQUIRED
         specification CDATA #IMPLIED
         version CDATA #IMPLIED
         isAuthenticated (true | false) "false"
         isConfidential (true | false) "false"
         isTamperProof (true | false) "false"
>
<!ELEMENT BusinessPartnerRole (Documentation*, Performs*,
Transition*)>
<!ATTLIST BusinessPartnerRole
         name CDATA #REQUIRED
         nameID ID #IMPLIED
>
<!-- initiatingRole/respondingRole is fully qualified using XPath
-->
<!ELEMENT Performs (Documentation*)>
<!ATTLIST Performs
         initiatingRole CDATA #IMPLIED
         inititiatingRoleIDRef IDREF #IMPLIED
         respondingRole CDATA #IMPLIED
         respondingRoleIDRef IDREF #IMPLIED
>
```

Appendix C   Business Process Specification Schema XML Schema

```
<?xml version="1.0" encoding="UTF-8"?>
<!-- edited by Kurt Kanaskie (Lucent Technologies) -->
<!-- Updated 2001-05-24
     Differences from DTD version:
     <xsd:attribute name="pattern" type="xsd:anyURI"/>
     <xsd:attribute name="uri" type="xsd:anyURI" use="required"/>
     <xsd:attribute name="location" type="xsd:anyURI"/>
     <xsd:attribute name="logicalModel" type="xsd:anyURI"/>
     <xsd:attribute name="specification" type="xsd:anyURI"/>
     <xsd:attribute name="timeToPerform" type="xsd:duration"/>
     <xsd:attribute name="timeToPerform" type="xsd:duration"/>
     <xsd:attribute name="timeToAcknowledgeAcceptance" type=
"xsd:duration"/>
     <xsd:attribute name="timeToAcknowledgeReceipt" type="xsd:
duration"/>
     <xsd:attribute name="timeToAcknowledgeAcceptance" type="xsd:
duration"/>
     <xsd:attribute name="timeToAcknowledgeReceipt" type="xsd:
duration"/>
     <xsd:attribute name="isAuthenticated" type="xsd:boolean"
value="false"/>
     <xsd:attribute name="isConfidential" type="xsd:boolean"
value="false"/>
     <xsd:attribute name="isTamperProof" type="xsd:boolean"
value="false"/>
     <xsd:attribute name="isGuaranteedDeliveryRequired" type="xsd:
boolean" value="false"/>
     <xsd:attribute name="isConcurrent" type="xsd:boolean"
value="true"/>
     <xsd:attribute name="isLegallyBinding" type="xsd:boolean"
value="true"/>
     <xsd:attribute name="isAuthenticated" type="xsd:boolean"
value="false"/>
     <xsd:attribute name="isConfidential" type="xsd:boolean"
value="false"/>
     <xsd:attribute name="isTamperProof" type="xsd:boolean"
value="false"/>
```

```
      <xsd:attribute name="waitForAll" type="xsd:boolean"
value="true"/>
      <xsd:attribute name="isAuthorizationRequired"
type="xsd:boolean" value="false"/>
      <xsd:attribute name="isIntelligibleCheckRequired"
type="xsd:boolean" value="false"/>
      <xsd:attribute name="isNonRepudiationReceiptRequired"
type="xsd:boolean" value="false"/>
      <xsd:attribute name="isNonRepudiationRequired"
type="xsd:boolean" value="false"/>
      <xsd:attribute name="isAuthorizationRequired"
type="xsd:boolean" value="false"/>
      <xsd:attribute name="isIntelligibleCheckRequired" type="xsd:
boolean" value="false"/>
      <xsd:attribute name="isNonRepudiationReceiptRequired"
type="xsd:boolean" value="false"/>
      <xsd:attribute name="isNonRepudiationRequired"
type="xsd:boolean" value="false"/>
      <xsd:attribute name="onInitiation" type="xsd:boolean"
value="false"/>
      <xsd:attribute name="isPositiveResponse" type="xsd:boolean"/>
-->
<xsd:schema targetNamespace="http://www.ebxml.org/BusinessProcess"
xmlns:xsd="http://www.w3.org/2000/10/XMLSchema"
xmlns="http://www.ebxml.org/BusinessProcess"
elementFormDefault="qualified">
      <xsd:element name="Attachment">
            <xsd:complexType>
                  <xsd:sequence>
                        <xsd:element ref="Documentation" min-
Occurs="0"
maxOccurs="unbounded"/>
                  </xsd:sequence>
                  <xsd:attribute name="name" type="xsd:string"
use="required"/>
                  <xsd:attribute name="nameID" type="xsd:ID"/>
                  <xsd:attribute name="businessDocument"
type="xsd:string"/>
                  <xsd:attribute name="businessDocumentIDRef"
type="xsd:IDREF"/>
                  <xsd:attribute name="specification" type="xsd:
anyURI"/>
                  <xsd:attribute name="mimeType" type="xsd:string"
use="required"/>
                  <xsd:attribute name="version" type="xsd:string"/>
                  <xsd:attribute name="isAuthenticated" type="xsd:
boolean" value="false"/>
```

```
                    <xsd:attribute name="isConfidential" type="xsd:
boolean" value="false"/>
                    <xsd:attribute name="isTamperProof" type="xsd:
boolean" value="false"/>
            </xsd:complexType>
    </xsd:element>
    <xsd:element name="InitiatingRole">
            <xsd:complexType>
                    <xsd:sequence>
                            <xsd:element ref="Documentation" min-
Occurs="0" maxOccurs="unbounded"/>
                    </xsd:sequence>
                    <xsd:attribute name="name" type="xsd:string"
use="required"/>
                    <xsd:attribute name="nameID" type="xsd:ID"/>
            </xsd:complexType>
    </xsd:element>
    <xsd:element name="RespondingRole">
            <xsd:complexType>
                    <xsd:sequence>
                            <xsd:element ref="Documentation" min-
Occurs="0" maxOccurs="unbounded"/>
                    </xsd:sequence>
                    <xsd:attribute name="name" type="xsd:string"
use="required"/>
                    <xsd:attribute name="nameID" type="xsd:ID"/>
            </xsd:complexType>
    </xsd:element>
    <xsd:element name="BinaryCollaboration">
            <xsd:complexType>
                    <xsd:sequence>
                            <xsd:element ref="Documentation" min-
Occurs="0" maxOccurs="unbounded"/>
                            <xsd:element ref="InitiatingRole"/>
                            <xsd:element ref="RespondingRole"/>
                            <xsd:choice minOccurs="0" maxOccurs=
"unbounded">
                                    <xsd:element ref="Documentation"/>
                                    <xsd:element ref="Start"/>
                                    <xsd:element ref="Transition"/>
                                    <xsd:element ref="Success"/>
                                    <xsd:element ref="Failure"/>
                                    <xsd:element
ref="BusinessTransactionActivity"/>
                                    <xsd:element ref="Collaboration-
Activity"/>
```

```
                              <xsd:element ref="Fork"/>
                              <xsd:element ref="Join"/>
                       </xsd:choice>
               </xsd:sequence>
               <xsd:attribute name="name" type="xsd:string"
use="required"/>
               <xsd:attribute name="nameID" type="xsd:ID"/>
               <xsd:attribute name="pattern" type="xsd:anyURI"/>
               <xsd:attribute name="beginsWhen" type="xsd:
string"/>
               <xsd:attribute name="endsWhen" type="xsd:string"/>
               <xsd:attribute name="preCondition" type="xsd:
string"/>
               <xsd:attribute name="postCondition" type="xsd:
string"/>
               <xsd:attribute name="timeToPerform" type="xsd:
duration"/>
       </xsd:complexType>
   </xsd:element>
   <xsd:element name="BusinessDocument">
       <xsd:complexType>
           <xsd:sequence>
               <xsd:element ref="Documentation" min-
Occurs="0" maxOccurs="unbounded"/>
               <xsd:element ref="ConditionExpression"
minOccurs="0" maxOccurs="1"/>
           </xsd:sequence>
           <xsd:attribute name="name" type="xsd:string"
use="required"/>
           <xsd:attribute name="nameID" type="xsd:ID"/>
           <xsd:attribute name="specificationLocation"
type="xsd:string"/>
           <xsd:attribute name="specificationElement"
type="xsd:string"/>
       </xsd:complexType>
   </xsd:element>
   <xsd:element name="SubstitutionSet">
       <xsd:complexType>
           <xsd:sequence>
               <xsd:element ref="DocumentSubstitution"
minOccurs="0" maxOccurs="unbounded"/>
               <xsd:element ref="AttributeSubstitution"
minOccurs="0" maxOccurs="unbounded"/>
               <xsd:element ref="Documentation" min-
Occurs="0" maxOccurs="unbounded"/>
           </xsd:sequence>
```

```
                    <xsd:attribute name="name" type="xsd:string"/>
                    <xsd:attribute name="nameId" type="xsd:ID"/>
                    <xsd:attribute name="applyToScope"
type="xsd:string"/>
            </xsd:complexType>
      </xsd:element>
      <xsd:element name="DocumentSubstitution">
            <xsd:complexType>
                  <xsd:sequence>
                        <xsd:element ref="Documentation" min-
Occurs="0" maxOccurs="unbounded"/>
                  </xsd:sequence>
                  <xsd:attribute name="originalBusinessDocument"
type="xsd:string"/>
                        <xsd:attribute name="originalBusinessDocumentID"
type="xsd:ID"/>
                  <xsd:attribute name="substituteBusinessDocument"
type="xsd:string"/>
                        <xsd:attribute name="substituteBusinessDocumentId"
type="xsd:ID"/>
            </xsd:complexType>
      </xsd:element>
      <xsd:element name="AttributeSubstitution">
            <xsd:complexType>
                  <xsd:sequence>
                        <xsd:element ref="Documentation" min-
Occurs="0" maxOccurs="unbounded"/>
                  </xsd:sequence>
                  <xsd:attribute name="attributeName" type="xsd:
string"/>
                  <xsd:attribute name="value" type="xsd:string"/>
            </xsd:complexType>
      </xsd:element>
      <xsd:element name="ConditionExpression">
            <xsd:complexType>
                  <xsd:sequence>
                        <xsd:element ref="Documentation" min-
Occurs="0" maxOccurs="unbounded"/>
                  </xsd:sequence>
                  <xsd:attribute name="expressionLanguage"
type="xsd:string"/>
                  <xsd:attribute name="expression" type="xsd:
string"/>
            </xsd:complexType>
      </xsd:element>
      <xsd:element name="BusinessPartnerRole">
```

```
                <xsd:complexType>
                    <xsd:sequence>
                        <xsd:element ref="Documentation" min-
Occurs="0" maxOccurs="unbounded"/>
                        <xsd:element ref="Performs" minOccurs="0"
maxOccurs="unbounded"/>
                        <xsd:element ref="Transition" minOccurs="0"
maxOccurs="unbounded"/>
                    </xsd:sequence>
                    <xsd:attribute name="name" type="xsd:string"
use="required"/>
                    <xsd:attribute name="nameID" type="xsd:ID"/>
                </xsd:complexType>
        </xsd:element>
        <xsd:element name="BusinessTransaction">
                <xsd:complexType>
                    <xsd:sequence>
                        <xsd:element ref="Documentation" min-
Occurs="0" maxOccurs="unbounded"/>
                        <xsd:element ref="RequestingBusiness-
Activity"/>
                        <xsd:element ref="RespondingBusiness-
Activity"/>
                    </xsd:sequence>
                    <xsd:attribute name="name" type="xsd:string"
use="required"/>
                    <xsd:attribute name="nameID" type="xsd:ID"/>
                    <xsd:attribute name="pattern" type="xsd:anyURI"/>
                    <xsd:attribute name="beginsWhen" type="xsd:
string"/>
                    <xsd:attribute name="endsWhen" type="xsd:string"/>
                    <xsd:attribute name="isGuaranteedDeliveryRequired"
type="xsd:boolean" value="false"/>
                    <xsd:attribute name="preCondition" type="xsd:
string"/>
                    <xsd:attribute name="postCondition" type="xsd:
string"/>
                </xsd:complexType>
        </xsd:element>
        <xsd:element name="BusinessTransactionActivity">
                <xsd:complexType>
                    <xsd:sequence>
                        <xsd:element ref="Documentation" min-
Occurs="0" maxOccurs="unbounded"/>
                    </xsd:sequence>
                    <xsd:attribute name="name" type="xsd:string"
```

```
                     use="required"/>
                        <xsd:attribute name="nameID" type="xsd:ID"/>
                        <xsd:attribute name="businessTransaction"
type="xsd:string"
use="required"/>
                        <xsd:attribute name="businessTransactionIDRef"
type="xsd:IDREF"/>
                        <xsd:attribute name="fromAuthorizedRole"
type="xsd:string" use="required"/>
                        <xsd:attribute name="fromAuthorizedRoleIDRef"
type="xsd:IDREF"/>
                        <xsd:attribute name="toAuthorizedRole" type="xsd:
string" use="required"/>
                        <xsd:attribute name="toAuthorizedRoleIDRef"
type="xsd:IDREF"/>
                        <xsd:attribute name="isConcurrent" type="xsd:
boolean" value="true"/>
                        <xsd:attribute name="isLegallyBinding" type="xsd:
boolean" value="true"/>
                        <xsd:attribute name="timeToPerform" type="xsd:
duration"/>
                </xsd:complexType>
        </xsd:element>
        <xsd:element name="CollaborationActivity">
                <xsd:complexType>
                        <xsd:sequence>
                                <xsd:element ref="Documentation" min-
Occurs="0" maxOccurs="unbounded"/>
                        </xsd:sequence>
                        <xsd:attribute name="nameID" type="xsd:ID"/>
                        <xsd:attribute name="name" type="xsd:string"
use="required"/>
                        <xsd:attribute name="fromAuthorizedRole"
type="xsd:string" use="required"/>
                        <xsd:attribute name="fromAuthorizedRoleIDRef"
type="xsd:IDREF"/>
                        <xsd:attribute name="toAuthorizedRole"
type="xsd:string" use="required"/>
                        <xsd:attribute name="toAuthorizedRoleIDRef"
type="xsd:IDREF"/>
                        <xsd:attribute name="binaryCollaboration"
type="xsd:string" use="required"/>
                        <xsd:attribute name="binaryCollaborationIDRef"
type="xsd:IDREF"/>
                </xsd:complexType>
        </xsd:element>
        <xsd:element name="DocumentEnvelope">
```

```
            <xsd:complexType>
                <xsd:sequence>
                    <xsd:element ref="Documentation" min-
Occurs="0" maxOccurs="unbounded"/>
                    <xsd:element ref="Attachment" min-
Occurs="0" maxOccurs="unbounded"/>
                </xsd:sequence>
                <xsd:attribute name="businessDocument"
type="xsd:string"
use="required"/>
                <xsd:attribute name="businessDocumentIDRef"
type="xsd:IDREF"/>
                <xsd:attribute name="isPositiveResponse"
type="xsd:boolean"/>
                <xsd:attribute name="isAuthenticated"
type="xsd:boolean" value="false"/>
                <xsd:attribute name="isConfidential"
type="xsd:boolean" value="false"/>
                <xsd:attribute name="isTamperProof"
type="xsd:boolean" value="false"/>
            </xsd:complexType>
        </xsd:element>
        <xsd:element name="Documentation">
            <xsd:complexType>
                <xsd:simpleContent>
                    <xsd:restriction base="xsd:string">
                        <xsd:attribute name="uri"
type="xsd:anyURI"/>
                    </xsd:restriction>
                </xsd:simpleContent>
            </xsd:complexType>
        </xsd:element>
        <xsd:element name="Failure">
            <xsd:complexType>
                <xsd:sequence>
                    <xsd:element ref="Documentation" min-
Occurs="0" maxOccurs="unbounded"/>
                    <xsd:element ref="ConditionExpression"
minOccurs="0" maxOccurs="1"/>
                </xsd:sequence>
                <xsd:attribute name="fromBusinessState"
type="xsd:string" use="required"/>
                <xsd:attribute name="fromBusinessStateIDRef"
type="xsd:IDREF"/>
                <xsd:attribute name="conditionGuard">
                    <xsd:simpleType>
                        <xsd:restriction base="xsd:NMTOKEN">
```

```
                                        <xsd:enumeration value=
"Success"/>
                                        <xsd:enumeration value=
"BusinessFailure"/>
                                        <xsd:enumeration value=
"TechnicalFailure"/>
                                        <xsd:enumeration value="Any-
Failure"/>
                              </xsd:restriction>
                      </xsd:simpleType>
                  </xsd:attribute>
            </xsd:complexType>
      </xsd:element>
      <xsd:element name="Fork">
            <xsd:complexType>
                  <xsd:sequence>
                        <xsd:element ref="Documentation" min-
Occurs="0" maxOccurs="unbounded"/>
                  </xsd:sequence>
                  <xsd:attribute name="name" type="xsd:string"
use="required"/>
                  <xsd:attribute name="nameID" type="xsd:ID"/>
            </xsd:complexType>
      </xsd:element>
      <xsd:element name="Include">
            <xsd:complexType>
                  <xsd:sequence>
                        <xsd:element ref="Documentation" min-
Occurs="0" maxOccurs="unbounded"/>
                  </xsd:sequence>
                  <xsd:attribute name="name" type="xsd:string"
use="required"/>
                  <xsd:attribute name="uuid" type="xsd:string"
use="required"/>
                  <xsd:attribute name="uri" type="xsd:anyURI"
use="required"/>
                  <xsd:attribute name="version" type="xsd:string"
use="required"/>
            </xsd:complexType>
      </xsd:element>
      <xsd:element name="Join">
            <xsd:complexType>
                  <xsd:sequence>
                        <xsd:element ref="Documentation" min-
Occurs="0" maxOccurs="unbounded"/>
                  </xsd:sequence>
                  <xsd:attribute name="name" type="xsd:string"
```

```
use="required"/>
                    <xsd:attribute name="nameID" type="xsd:ID"/>
                    <xsd:attribute name="waitForAll" type="xsd:
boolean"
value="true"/>
             </xsd:complexType>
      </xsd:element>
      <xsd:element name="MultiPartyCollaboration">
             <xsd:complexType>
                    <xsd:sequence>
                           <xsd:element ref="Documentation" min-
Occurs="0" maxOccurs="unbounded"/>
                           <xsd:element ref="BusinessPartnerRole"
minOccurs="0" maxOccurs="unbounded"/>
                    </xsd:sequence>
                    <xsd:attribute name="name" type="xsd:string"
use="required"/>
                    <xsd:attribute name="nameID" type="xsd:ID"/>
             </xsd:complexType>
      </xsd:element>
      <xsd:element name="Package">
             <xsd:complexType>
                    <xsd:sequence>
                           <xsd:element ref="Documentation" min-
Occurs="0" maxOccurs="unbounded"/>
                           <xsd:choice minOccurs="0" maxOccurs="un-
bounded">
                                  <xsd:element ref="Package"/>
                                  <xsd:element ref="Binary-
Collaboration"/>
                                  <xsd:element ref="Business-
Transaction"/>
                                  <xsd:element ref="MultiParty-
Collaboration"/>
                           </xsd:choice>
                    </xsd:sequence>
                    <xsd:attribute name="name" type="xsd:string"
use="required"/>
                    <xsd:attribute name="nameID" type="xsd:ID"/>
             </xsd:complexType>
      </xsd:element>
      <xsd:element name="Performs">
             <xsd:complexType>
                    <xsd:sequence>
                           <xsd:element ref="Documentation" min-
Occurs="0" maxOccurs="unbounded"/>
                    </xsd:sequence>
```

```
                    <xsd:attribute name="initiatingRole" type="xsd:
string" use="optional"/>
                    <xsd:attribute name="initiatingRoleIDRef"
type="xsd:IDREF"/>
                    <xsd:attribute name="respondingRole"
type="xsd:string"
use="optional"/>
                    <xsd:attribute name="respondingRoleIDRef"
type="xsd:IDREF"/>
            </xsd:complexType>
    </xsd:element>
    <xsd:element name="ProcessSpecification">
            <xsd:complexType>
                    <xsd:sequence>
                            <xsd:element ref="Documentation" min-
Occurs="0" maxOccurs="unbounded"/>
                            <xsd:element ref="SubstitutionSet" min-
Occurs="0" maxOccurs="unbounded"/>
                            <xsd:choice minOccurs="0" maxOccurs=
"unbounded">
                                    <xsd:element ref="Include"/>
                                    <xsd:element ref="BusinessDocument"/>
                                    <xsd:element ref="Process-
Specification"/>
                                    <xsd:element ref="Package"/>
                                    <xsd:element ref="Binary-
Collaboration"/>
                                    <xsd:element ref="Business-
Transaction"/>
                                    <xsd:element ref="MultiParty-
Collaboration"/>
                            </xsd:choice>
                    </xsd:sequence>
                    <xsd:attribute name="name" type="xsd:ID" use=
"required"/>
                    <xsd:attribute name="uuid" type="xsd:string"
use="required"/>
                    <xsd:attribute name="version" type="xsd:string"
use="required"/>
            </xsd:complexType>
    </xsd:element>
    <xsd:element name="RequestingBusinessActivity">
            <xsd:complexType>
                    <xsd:sequence>
                            <xsd:element ref="Documentation" min-
Occurs="0" maxOccurs="unbounded"/>
```

```
                        <xsd:element ref="DocumentEnvelope"/>
                </xsd:sequence>
                <xsd:attribute name="name" type="xsd:string"
use="required"/>
                <xsd:attribute name="nameID" type="xsd:ID"/>
                <xsd:attribute name="isAuthorizationRequired"
type="xsd:boolean" value="false"/>
                <xsd:attribute name="isIntelligibleCheckRequired"
type="xsd:boolean" value="false"/>
                <xsd:attribute name="isNonRepudiationReceipt-
Required" type="xsd:boolean" value="false"/>
                <xsd:attribute name="isNonRepudiationRequired"
type="xsd:boolean" value="false"/>
                <xsd:attribute name="timeToAcknowledgeAcceptance"
type="xsd:duration"/>
                <xsd:attribute name="timeToAcknowledgeReceipt"
type="xsd:duration"/>
            </xsd:complexType>
        </xsd:element>
        <xsd:element name="RespondingBusinessActivity">
            <xsd:complexType>
                <xsd:sequence>
                        <xsd:element ref="Documentation" min-
Occurs="0" maxOccurs="unbounded"/>
                        <xsd:element ref="DocumentEnvelope" min-
Occurs="0" maxOccurs="unbounded"/>
                </xsd:sequence>
                <xsd:attribute name="name" type="xsd:string"
use="required"/>
                <xsd:attribute name="nameID" type="xsd:ID"/>
                <xsd:attribute name="isAuthorizationRequired"
type="xsd:boolean" value="false"/>
                <xsd:attribute name="isIntelligibleCheckRequired"
type="xsd:boolean" value="false"/>
                <xsd:attribute name="isNonRepudiationReceipt-
Required" type="xsd:boolean" value="false"/>
                <xsd:attribute name="isNonRepudiationRequired"
type="xsd:boolean" value="false"/>
                <xsd:attribute name="timeToAcknowledgeReceipt"
type="xsd:duration"/>
            </xsd:complexType>
        </xsd:element>
        <xsd:element name="Start">
            <xsd:complexType>
                <xsd:sequence>
```

```
                                  <xsd:element ref="Documentation" min-
Occurs="0" maxOccurs="unbounded"/>
                        </xsd:sequence>
                        <xsd:attribute name="toBusinessState" type="xsd:
string" use="required"/>
                        <xsd:attribute name="toBusinessStateIDRef"
type="xsd:IDREF"/>
                </xsd:complexType>
        </xsd:element>
        <xsd:element name="Success">
                <xsd:complexType>
                        <xsd:sequence>
                                <xsd:element ref="Documentation" min-
Occurs="0" maxOccurs="unbounded"/>
                                <xsd:element ref="ConditionExpression"
minOccurs="0" maxOccurs="1"/>
                        </xsd:sequence>
                        <xsd:attribute name="fromBusinessState"
type="xsd:string" use="required"/>
                        <xsd:attribute name="fromBusinessStateIDRef"
type="xsd:IDREF"/>
                        <xsd:attribute name="conditionGuard">
                                <xsd:simpleType>
                                        <xsd:restriction base="xsd:NMTOKEN">
                                                <xsd:enumeration value=
"Success"/>
                                                <xsd:enumeration value=
"BusinessFailure"/>
                                                <xsd:enumeration value=
"TechnicalFailure"/>
                                                <xsd:enumeration value="Any-
Failure"/>
                                        </xsd:restriction>
                                </xsd:simpleType>
                        </xsd:attribute>
                </xsd:complexType>
        </xsd:element>
        <xsd:element name="Transition">
                <xsd:complexType>
                        <xsd:sequence>
                                <xsd:element ref="Documentation" min-
Occurs="0" maxOccurs="unbounded"/>
                                <xsd:element ref="ConditionExpression"
minOccurs="0" maxOccurs="1"/>
                        </xsd:sequence>
                        <xsd:attribute name="onInitiation" type="xsd:
boolean" value="false"/>
```

```
                    <xsd:attribute name="fromBusinessState"
type="xsd:string"/>
                    <xsd:attribute name="fromBusinessStateIDRef"
type="xsd:IDREF"/>
                    <xsd:attribute name="toBusinessState"
type="xsd:string"/>
                    <xsd:attribute name="toBusinessStateIDRef"
type="xsd:IDREF"/>
                    <xsd:attribute name="conditionGuard">
                        <xsd:simpleType>
                            <xsd:restriction base="xsd:NMTOKEN">
                                <xsd:enumeration value=
"Success"/>
                                <xsd:enumeration value=
"BusinessFailure"/>
                                <xsd:enumeration value=
"TechnicalFailure"/>
                                <xsd:enumeration value="Any-
Failure"/>
                            </xsd:restriction>
                        </xsd:simpleType>
                    </xsd:attribute>
                </xsd:complexType>
            </xsd:element>
</xsd:schema>
```

CHAPTER
4

Registry Information Model
v1.0
Registry Team
11 May 2001

TABLE OF CONTENTS

1 Status of this Document

This document specifies an ebXML Technical Specification for the eBusiness community.

Distribution of this document is unlimited.

The document formatting is based on the Internet Society's Standard RFC format.

This version:
http://www.ebxml.org/specs/ebRIM.pdf

Latest version:
http://www.ebxml.org/specdrafts/RegistryInfoModelv1.0.pdf

2 ebXML Participants

We would like to recognize the following for their significant participation to the development of this document.

Lisa Carnahan	NIST
Joe Dalman	Tie
Philippe DeSmedt	Viquity
Sally Fuger,	AIAG
Len Gallagher	NIST
Steve Hanna	Sun Microsystems
Scott Hinkelman	IBM
Michael Kass	NIST
Jong.L Kim	Innodigital
Kyu-Chul Lee	Chungnam National University
Sangwon Lim	Korea Institute for Electronic Commerce
Bob Miller	GXS
Kunio Mizoguchi	Electronic Commerce Promotion Council of Japan
Dale Moberg	Sterling Commerce

Ron Monzillo	Sun Microsystems
JP Morgenthal	eThink Systems, Inc.
Joel Munter	Intel
Farrukh Najmi	Sun Microsystems
Scott Nieman	Norstan Consulting
Frank Olken	Lawrence Berkeley National Laboratory
Michael Park	eSum Technologies
Bruce Peat	eProcess Solutions
Mike Rowley	Excelon Corporation
Waqar Sadiq	Vitria
Krishna Sankar	Cisco Systems Inc.
Kim Tae Soo	Government of Korea
Nikola Stojanovic	Encoda Systems Inc.
David Webber	XML Global
Yutaka Yoshida	Sun Microsystems
Prasad Yendluri	webmethods
Peter Z. Zhoo	Knowledge For the new Millennium

3 Introduction

3.1 Summary of Contents of Document

This document specifies the information model for the ebXML *Registry*.

A separate document, ebXML Registry Services Specification [ebRS], describes how to build *Registry Services* that provide access to the information content in the ebXML *Registry*.

3.2 General Conventions

▼ UML diagrams are used as a way to concisely describe concepts. They are not intended to convey any specific Implementation or methodology requirements.

▼ Interfaces are often used in UML diagrams. They are used instead of Classes with attributes to provide an abstract definition without implying any specific Implementation. Specifically, they do not imply that objects in the Registry will be accessed directly via these interfaces. Objects in the Registry are accessed via interfaces described in the ebXML Registry Services Specification. Each get method in every interface has an explicit indication of the attribute name that the get method maps to. For example getName method maps to an attribute named name.

▼ The term "repository item" is used to refer to an object that has been submitted to a Registry for storage and safekeeping (e.g. an XML document or a DTD). Every repository item is described by a RegistryEntry instance.

▼ The term "RegistryEntry" is used to refer to an object that provides metadata about a repository item.

▼ The term "RegistryObject" is used to refer to the base interface in the information model to avoid the confusion with the common term "object". However, when the term "object" is used to refer to a class or an interface in the information model, it may also mean RegistryObject because almost all classes are descendants of RegistryObject.

The information model does not deal with the actual content of the repository. All *Elements* of the information model represent metadata about the content and not the content itself.

Software practitioners MAY use this document in combination with other ebXML specification documents when creating ebXML compliant software.

The keywords MUST, MUST NOT, REQUIRED, SHALL, SHALL NOT, SHOULD, SHOULD NOT, RECOMMENDED, MAY, and OPTIONAL, when they appear in this document, are to be interpreted as described in RFC 2119 [Bra97].

3.2.1 Naming Conventions

In order to enforce a consistent capitalization and naming convention in this document, "Upper Camel Case" *(UCC)* and "Lower Camel Case" *(LCC)* Capitalization styles are used in the following conventions

▼ Element name is in *UCC* convention

(example: <UpperCamelCaseElement/>).

▼ Attribute name is in *LCC* convention

(example: <UpperCamelCaseElement lowerCamelCaseAttribute="Whatever"/>).

▼ *Class*, Interface names use UCC convention

(examples: ClassificationNode, Versionable).

▼ Method name uses LCC convention

(example: getName(), setName())

Also, *Capitalized Italics* words are defined in the ebXML Glossary [ebGLOSS].

3.3 Audience

The target audience for this specification is the community of software developers who are:

▼ Implementers of ebXML *Registry Services*

▼ Implementers of ebXML *Registry Clients*

3.4 Related Documents

The following specifications provide some background and related information to the reader:

▼ [ebRS] ebXML Registry Services Specification v1.0 - defines the actual *Registry Services* based on this information model

▼ [ebCPP] ebXML Collaboration-Protocol Profile and Agreement Specification v1.0 - defines how profiles can be defined for a *Party* and how two *Parties'* profiles may be used to define a *Party* agreement

▼ [ebBPSS] ebXML Business Process Specification Schema v1.01

▼ [ebTA] ebXML Technical Architecture Specification v1.04

4 Design Objectives

4.1 Goals

The goals of this version of the specification are to:

▼ Communicate what information is in the *Registry* and how that information is organized

▼ Leverage as much as possible the work done in the *OASIS* [OAS] and the *ISO* 11179 [ISO] Registry models

▼ Align with relevant works within other ebXML working groups

▼ Be able to evolve to support future ebXML *Registry* requirements

▼ Be compatible with other ebXML specifications

5 System Overview

5.1 Role of ebXML Registry

The *Registry* provides a stable store where information submitted by a *Submitting Organization* is made persistent. Such information is used to facilitate ebXML-based *Business* to *Business* (B2B) partnerships and transactions. Submitted content may be *XML* schema and documents, process descriptions, *Core Components*, context descriptions, *UML* models, information about parties and even software components.

5.2 Registry Services

A set of *Registry Services* that provide access to *Registry* content to clients of the *Registry* is defined in the ebXML Registry Services Specification [ebRS]. This document does not provide details on these services but may occasionally refer to them.

5.3 What the Registry Information Model Does

The Registry Information Model provides a blueprint or high-level schema for the ebXML *Registry*. Its primary value is for implementers of ebXML *Registries*. It provides these implementers with information on the type of metadata that is stored in the *Registry* as well as the relationships among metadata *Classes*.

The Registry information model:

▼ Defines what types of objects are stored in the *Registry*

▼ Defines how stored objects are organized in the *Registry*

▼ Is based on ebXML metamodels from various working groups

5.4   How the Registry Information Model Works

Implementers of the ebXML *Registry* MAY use the information model to determine which *Classes* to include in their *Registry Implementation* and what attributes and methods these *Classes* may have. They MAY also use it to determine what sort of database schema their *Registry Implementation* may need.

Note

> **The information model is meant to be illustrative and does not prescribe any specific *Implementation* choices.**

5.5   Where the Registry Information Model May Be Implemented

The Registry Information Model MAY be implemented within an ebXML *Registry* in the form of a relational database schema, object database schema or some other physical schema. It MAY also be implemented as interfaces and *Classes* within a *Registry Implementation*.

5.6   Conformance to an ebXML Registry

If an *Implementation* claims *Conformance* to this specification then it supports all required information model *Classes* and interfaces, their attributes and their semantic definitions that are visible through the ebXML *Registry Services*.

6   Registry Information Model: High Level Public View

This section provides a high level public view of the most visible objects in the *Registry*.

Figure 1 shows the high level public view of the objects in the *Registry* and their relationships as a *UML Class Diagram*. It does not show *Inheritance*, *Class* attributes or *Class* methods.

The reader is again reminded that the information model is not modeling actual repository items.

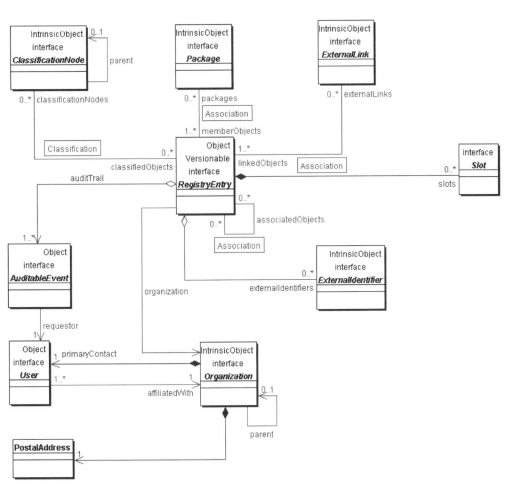

FIGURE 1 Information Model High Level Public View

6.1 RegistryEntry

The central object in the information model is a RegistryEntry. An *Instance* of RegistryEntry exists for each content *Instance* submitted to the *Registry*. *Instances* of the RegistryEntry *Class* provide metadata about a repository item. The actual repository item (e.g. a *DTD*) is not contained in an *Instance* of the RegistryEntry *Class*. Note that most *Classes* in the information model are specialized sub-classes of RegistryEntry. Each RegistryEntry is related to exactly one repository item.

6.2 Slot

Slot *Instances* provide a dynamic way to add arbitrary attributes to RegistryEntry *Instances*. This ability to add attributes dynamically to RegistryEntry *Instances* enables extensibility within the Registry Information Model.

6.3 Association

Association *Instances* are RegistryEntries that are used to define many-to-many associations between objects in the information model. Associations are described in detail in section 10.

6.4 ExternalIdentifier

ExternalIdentifier *Instances* provide additional identifier information to RegistryEntry such as DUNS number, Social Security Number, or an alias name of the organization.

6.5 ExternalLink

ExternalLink *Instances* are RegistryEntries that model a named URI to content that is not managed by the *Registry*. Unlike managed content, such external content may change or be deleted at any time without the knowledge of the *Registry*. RegistryEntry may be associated with any number of ExternalLinks.

Consider the case where a *Submitting Organization* submits a repository item (e.g. a *DTD*) and wants to associate some external content to that object (e.g. the *Submitting Organization*'s home page). The ExternalLink enables this capability. A potential use of the ExternalLink capability may be in a GUI tool that displays the ExternalLinks to a RegistryEntry. The user may click on such links and navigate to an external web page referenced by the link.

6.6 ClassificationNode

ClassificationNode *Instances* are RegistryEntries that are used to define tree structures where each node in the tree is a ClassificationNode. *Classification* trees constructed with ClassificationNodes are used to define *Classification* schemes or ontologies. ClassificationNode is described in detail in section 11.

6.7 Classification

Classification *Instances* are RegistryEntries that are used to classify repository items by associating their RegistryEntry *Instance* with a ClassificationNode within a *Classification* scheme. Classification is described in detail in section 11.

6.8 Package

Package *Instances* are RegistryEntries that group logically related RegistryEntries together. One use of a Package is to allow operations to be performed on an entire *Package* of objects. For example all objects belonging to a Package may be deleted in a single request.

6.9 AuditableEvent

AuditableEvent *Instances* are Objects that are used to provide an audit trail for RegistryEntries. AuditableEvent is described in detail in section 8.

6.10 User

User *Instances* are Objects that are used to provide information about registered users within the *Registry*. User objects are used in audit trail for RegistryEntries. User is described in detail in section 8.

6.11 PostalAddress

PostalAddress is a simple reusable *Entity Class* that defines attributes of a postal address.

6.12 Organization

Organization *Instances* are RegistryEntries that provide information on organizations such as a *Submitting Organization*. Each Organization *Instance* may have a reference to a parent Organization.

7 Registry Information Model: Detail View

This section covers the information model *Classes* in more detail than the Public View. The detail view introduces some additional *Classes* within the model that were not described in the public view of the information model.

Figure 2 shows the *Inheritance* or "is a" relationships between the *Classes* in the information model. Note that it does not show the other types of relationships, such as "has a" relationships, since they have already been shown in a previous figure. *Class* attributes and *class* methods are also not shown. Detailed description of methods and attributes of most interfaces and *Classes* will be displayed in tabular form following the description of each *Class* in the model.

The interface Association will be covered in detail separately in section 10. The interfaces Classification and ClassificationNode will be covered in detail separately in section 11.

The reader is again reminded that the information model is not modeling actual repository items.

7.1   Interface RegistryObject

All Known Subinterfaces:

Association, Classification, ClassificationNode, ExternalLink, ExtrinsicObject, IntrinsicObject, RegistryEntry, Organization, Package, User, AuditableEvent, ExternalIdentifier

RegistryObject provides a common base interface for almost all objects in the information model. Information model *Classes* whose *Instances* have a unique identity and an independent life cycle are descendants of the RegistryObject *Class*.

Note   Slot and PostalAddress are not descendants of the RegistryObject *Class* because their *Instances* do not have an independent existence and unique identity. They are always a part of some other *Class*'s *Instance* (e.g. Organization has a PostalAddress).

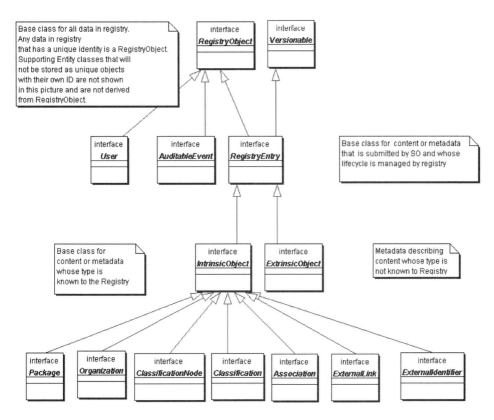

FIGURE 2 Information Model *Inheritance* View

Method Summary of RegistryObject

<u>AccessControlPolicy</u>	**getAccessControlPolicy** ( ) Gets the AccessControlPolicy object associated with this RegistryObject. An AccessControlPolicy defines the *Security Model* associated with the RegistryObject in terms of "who is permitted to do what" with that RegistryObject. Maps to attribute named `accessControlPolicy`.
String	**getDescription** ( ) Gets the context independent textual description for this RegistryObject. Maps to attribute named `description`.
String	**getName** ( ) Gets user friendly, context independent name for this RegistryObject. Maps to attribute named `name`.

Method Summary of RegistryObject	
`String`	**getID**`()`
	Gets the universally unique ID, as defined by [UUID], for this RegistryObject. Maps to attribute named `id`.
`void`	**setDescription**`(String description)`
	Sets the context, independent textual description for this RegistryObject.
`void`	**setName**`(String name)`
	Sets user friendly, context independent name for this Registry-Object.
`void`	**setID**`(String id)`
	Sets the universally unique ID, as defined by [UUID], for this RegistryObject.

7.2 Interface Versionable

All Known Subinterfaces:

<u>Association</u>, <u>Classification</u>, <u>ClassificationNode</u>, <u>ExternalLink</u>, <u>ExtrinsicObject</u>, <u>IntrinsicObject</u>, <u>RegistryEntry</u>, <u>Organization</u>, <u>Package</u>, <u>ExternalIdentifier</u>

The Versionable interface defines the behavior common to *Classes* that are capable of creating versions of their *Instances*. At present all RegistryEntry *Classes* are REQUIRED to implement the Versionable interface.

Method Summary of Versionable	
`int`	**getMajorVersion**`()`
	Gets the major revision number for this version of the Versionable object. Maps to attribute named `majorVersion`.
`int`	**getMinorVersion**`()`
	Gets the minor revision number for this version of the Versionable object. Maps to attribute named `minorVersion`.
`void`	**setMajorVersion**`(int majorVersion)`
	Sets the major revision number for this version of the Versionable object.
`void`	**setMinorVersion**`(int minorVersion)`
	Sets the minor revision number for this version of the Versionable object.

7.3   Interface RegistryEntry

All Superinterfaces:

RegistryObject, Versionable

All Known Subinterfaces:

Association, Classification, ClassificationNode, ExternalLink, ExtrinsicObject, IntrinsicObject, Organization, Package, ExternalIdentifier

RegistryEntry is a common base *Class* for all metadata describing submitted content whose life cycle is managed by the *Registry*. Metadata describing content submitted to the *Registry* is further specialized by the ExtrinsicObject and IntrinsicObject subclasses of RegistryEntry.

	Method Summary of RegistryEntry
Collection	**getAssociatedObjects**()
	Returns the collection of RegistryObjects associated with this RegistryObject. Maps to attribute named `associatedObjects`.
Collection	**getAuditTrail**()
	Returns the complete audit trail of all requests that effected a state change in this RegistryObject as an ordered Collection of AuditableEvent objects. Maps to attribute named `auditTrail`.
Collection	**getClassificationNodes**()
	Returns the collection of ClassificationNodes associated with this RegistryObject. Maps to attribute named `classificationNodes`.
Collection	**getExternalLinks**()
	Returns the collection of ExternalLinks associated with this RegistryObject. Maps to attribute named `externalLinks`.
Collection	**getExternalIdentifiers**()
	Returns the collection of ExternalIdentifiers associated with this RegistryObject. Maps to attribute named `externalIdentifiers`.
String	**getObjectType**()
	Gets the pre-defined object type associated with this RegistryEntry. This SHOULD be the name of a object type as described in 7.3.2. Maps to attribute named `objectType`.
Collection	**getOrganizations**()
	Returns the collection of Organizations associated with this RegistryObject. Maps to attribute named `organizations`.
Collection	**getPackages**()
	Returns the collection of Packages associated with this RegistryObject. Maps to attribute named `packages`.

Method Summary of RegistryEntry

String	**getStatus**()
	Gets the life cycle status of the RegistryEntry within the *Registry*. This SHOULD be the name of a RegistryEntry status type as described in 7.3.1. Maps to attribute named `status`.
String	**getUserVersion**()
	Gets the userVersion attribute of the RegistryEntry within the *Registry*. The userVersion is the version for the RegistryEntry as assigned by the user.
void	**setUserVersion**(`String` UserVersion)
	Sets the userVersion attribute of the RegistryEntry within the *Registry*.
String	**getStability**()
	Gets the stability indicator for the RegistryEntry within the *Registry*. The stability indicator is provided by the submitter as a guarentee of the level of stability for the content. This SHOULD be the name of a stability type as described in 7.3.3. Maps to attribute named `stability`.
Date	**getExpirationDate**()
	Gets expirationDate attribute of the RegistryEntry within the *Registry*. This attribute defines a time limit upon the stability guarentee provided by the stability attribute. Once the expirationDate has been reached the stability attribute in effect becomes STABILITY_DYNAMIC implying that content can change at any time and in any manner. A null value implies that there is no expiration on stability attribute. Maps to attribute named `expirationDate`.
void	**setExpirationDate**(`Date` ExpirationDate)
	Sets expirationDate attribute of the RegistryEntry within the *Registry*.
Collection	**getSlots**()
	Gets the collection of slots that have been dynamically added to this RegistryObject. Maps to attribute named `slots`.
void	**addSlots**(`Collection` newSlots)
	Adds one or more slots to this RegistryObject. Slot names MUST be locally unique within this RegistryObject. Any existing slots are not effected.
void	**removeSlots**(`Collection` slotNames)
	Removes one or more slots from this RegistryObject. Slots to be removed are identified by their name.

Methods Inherited from Interface RegistryObject

getAccessControlPolicy, getDescription, getName, getID, setDescription, setName, setID

Methods Inherited from Interface Versionable
getMajorVersion, getMinorVersion, setMajorVersion, setMinorVersion

7.3.1 Pre-defined RegistryEntry Status Types

The following table lists pre-defined choices for RegistryEntry status attribute.

These pre-defined status types are defined as a *Classification* scheme. While the scheme may easily be extended, a *Registry* MUST support the status types listed below.

Name	Description
Submitted	Status of a RegistryEntry that catalogues content that has been submitted to the *Registry*.
Approved	Status of a RegistryEntry that catalogues content that has been submitted to the *Registry* and has been subsequently approved.
Deprecated	Status of a RegistryEntry that catalogues content that has been submitted to the *Registry* and has been subsequently deprecated.
Withdrawn	Status of a RegistryEntry that catalogues content that has been withdrawn from the *Registry*.

7.3.2 Pre-defined Object Types

The following table lists pre-defined object types. Note that for an ExtrinsicObject there are many types defined based on the type of repository item the ExtrinsicObject catalogs. In addition there there are object types defined for IntrinsicObject sub-classes that may have concrete *Instances*.

These pre-defined object types are defined as a *Classification* scheme. While the scheme may easily be extended a *Registry* MUST support the object types listed below.

Name	Description
Unknown	An ExtrinsicObject that catalogues content whose type is unspecified or unknown.
CPA	An ExtrinsicObject of this type catalogues an *XML* document
	Collaboration Protocol Agreement (*CPA*) representing a technical agreement between two parties on how they plan to communicate with each other using a specific protocol.

Name	Description
CPP	An ExtrinsicObject of this type catalogues an document called *Collaboration Protocol Profile* (*CPP*) that provides information about a *Party* participating in a *Business* transaction.
Process	An ExtrinsicObject of this type catalogues a process description document.
Role	An ExtrinsicObject of this type catalogues an *XML* description of a *Role* in a *Collaboration Protocol Profile* (*CPP*).
ServiceInterface	An ExtrinsicObject of this type catalogues an *XML* description of a service interface as defined by [ebCPP].
SoftwareComponent	An ExtrinsicObject of this type catalogues a software component (e.g., an EJB or *Class* library).
Transport	An ExtrinsicObject of this type catalogues an *XML* description of a transport configuration as defined by [ebCPP].
UMLModel	An ExtrinsicObject of this type catalogues a *UML* model.
XMLSchema	An ExtrinsicObject of this type catalogues an *XML* schema (*DTD*, *XML* Schema, RELAX grammar, etc.).
Package	A Package object
ExternalLink	An ExternalLink object
ExternalIdentifier	An ExternalIdentifier object
Association	An Association object
Classification	A Classification object
ClassificationNode	A ClassificationNode object
AuditableEvent	An AuditableEvent object
User	A User object
Organization	An Organization object

7.3.3 Pre-defined RegistryEntry Stability Enumerations

The following table lists pre-defined choices for RegistryEntry stability attribute.

These pre-defined stability types are defined as a *Classification* scheme. While the scheme may easily be extended, a *Registry* MAY support the stability types listed below.

Name	Description
Dynamic	Stability of a RegistryEntry that indicates that the content is dynamic and may be changed arbitrarily by submitter at any time.

Name	Description
DynamicCompatible	Stability of a RegistryEntry that indicates that the content is dynamic and may be changed in a backward compatible way by submitter at any time.
Static	Stability of a RegistryEntry that indicates that the content is static and will not be changed by submitter.

7.4 Interface Slot

Slot *Instances* provide a dynamic way to add arbitrary attributes to RegistryEntry *Instances*. This ability to add attributes dynamically to RegistryEntry *Instances* enables extensibility within the Registry Information Model.

In this model, a RegistryEntry may have 0 or more Slots. A slot is composed of a name, a slotType and a collection of values. The name of slot is locally unique within the RegistryEntry *Instance*. Similarly, the value of a Slot is locally unique within a slot *Instance*. Since a Slot represent an extensible attribute whose value may be a collection, therefore a Slot is allowed to have a collection of values rather than a single value. The slotType attribute may optionally specify a type or category for the slot.

	Method Summary of Slot
String	**getName**()
	Gets the name of this RegistryObject. Maps to attribute named `name`.
void	**setName**(`String name`)
	Sets the name of this RegistryObject. Slot names are locally unique within a RegistryEntry *Instance*.
String	**getSlotType**()
	Gets the slotType or category for this slot. Maps to attribute named `slotType`.
void	**setSlotType**(`String slotType`)
	Sets the slotType or category for this slot.
Collection	**getValues**()
	Gets the collection of values for this RegistryObject. The type for each value is String. Maps to attribute named `values`.
void	**setValues**(`Collection values`)
	Sets the collection of values for this RegistryObject.

7.5   Interface ExtrinsicObject

All Superinterfaces:

RegistryEntry, RegistryObject, Versionable

ExtrinsicObjects provide metadata that describes submitted content whose type is not intrinsically known to the *Registry* and therefore MUST be described by means of additional attributes (e.g., mime type).

Examples of content described by ExtrinsicObject include *Collaboration Protocol Profiles* (CPP), *Business Process* descriptions, and schemas.

Method Summary of Extrinsic Object

String	**getContentURI**()
	Gets the URI to the content catalogued by this ExtrinsicObject. A *Registry* MUST guarantee that this URI is resolvable. Maps to attribute named `contentURI`.
String	**getMimeType**()
	Gets the mime type associated with the content catalogued by this ExtrinsicObject. Maps to attribute named `mimeType`.
boolean	**isOpaque**()
	Determines whether the content catalogued by this ExtrinsicObject is opaque to (not readable by) the *Registry*. In some situations, a *Submitting Organization* may submit content that is encrypted and not even readable by the *Registry*. Maps to attribute named `opaque`.
void	**setContentURI**(`String uri`
	Sets the URI to the content catalogued by this ExtrinsicObject.
void	**setMimeType**(`String mimeType`)
	Sets the mime type associated with the content catalogued by this ExtrinsicObject.
void	**setOpaque**(`boolean isOpaque`)
	Sets whether the content catalogued by this ExtrinsicObject is opaque to (not readable by) the *Registry*.

Note   **Methods inherited from the base interfaces of this interface are not shown.**

7.6   Interface IntrinsicObject

All Superinterfaces:

RegistryEntry, RegistryObject, Versionable

All Known Subinterfaces:

Association, Classification, ClassificationNode, ExternalLink, Organization, Package, ExternalIdentifier

IntrinsicObject serve as a common base *Class* for derived *Classes* that catalogue submitted content whose type is known to the *Registry* and defined by the ebXML *Registry* specifications.

This interface currently does not define any attributes or methods. Note that methods inherited from the base interfaces of this interface are not shown.

7.7   Interface Package

All Superinterfaces:

IntrinsicObject, RegistryEntry, RegistryObject, Versionable

Logically related RegistryEntries may be grouped into a Package. It is anticipated that *Registry Services* will allow operations to be performed on an entire *Package* of objects in the future.

	Method Summary of Package
Collection	**getMemberObjects**() Get the collection of RegistryEntries that are members of this Package. Maps to attribute named `memberObjects`.

7.8   Interface ExternalIdentifier

All Superinterfaces:

IntrinsicObject, RegistryEntry, RegistryObject, Versionable

ExternalIdentifier *Instances* provide the additional identifier information to RegistryEntry such as DUNS number, Social Security Number, or an alias name of the organization. The attribute *name* inherited from RegistryObject is used to contain the identification scheme (Social Security Number, etc), and the attribute *value* contains the actual information. Each RegistryEntry may have 0 or more association(s) with ExternalIdentifier.

See Also:

Method Summary of ExternalIdentifier

String   **getValue**()
            Gets the value of this ExternalIdentifier. Maps to attribute named `value`.
void   **setValue**(`String value`)
            Sets the value of this ExternalIdentifier.

Note   Methods inherited from the base interfaces of this interface are not shown.

7.9   Interface ExternalLink

All Superinterfaces:

IntrinsicObject, RegistryEntry, RegistryObject, Versionable

ExternalLinks use URIs to associate content in the *Registry* with content that may reside outside the *Registry*. For example, an organization submitting a *DTD* could use an ExternalLink to associate the *DTD* with the organization's home page.

Method Summary of ExternalLink

Collection   getLinkedObjects()
             Gets the collection of RegistryObjects that use this external link. Maps to attribute named `linkedObjects`.
URI   **getExternalURI**()
             Gets URI to the external content. Maps to attribute named `externalURI`.
void   **setExternalURI**(`URI uri`)
             Sets URI to the external content.

Note   Methods inherited from the base interfaces of this interface are not shown.

8   Registry Audit Trail

This section describes the information model *Elements* that support the audit trail capability of the *Registry*. Several *Classes* in this section are *Entity Classes* that are used as wrappers to model a set of related attributes. These *Entity Classes* do not have any associated behavior. They are analogous to the "struct" construct in the C programming language.

The getAuditTrail() method of a RegistryEntry returns an ordered Collection of AuditableEvents. These AuditableEvents constitute the audit trail for the RegistryEntry. AuditableEvents include a timestamp for the *Event*. Each AuditableEvent has a reference to a User identifying the specific user that performed an action that resulted in an AuditableEvent. Each User is affiliated with an Organization, which is usually the *Submitting Organization*.

8.1   Interface AuditableEvent

All Superinterfaces:

RegistryObject

AuditableEvent *Instances* provide a long-term record of *Events* that effect a change of state in a RegistryEntry. A RegistryEntry is associated with an ordered Collection of AuditableEvent *Instances* that provide a complete audit trail for that RegistryObject.

AuditableEvents are usually a result of a client-initiated request. AuditableEvent *Instances* are generated by the *Registry Service* to log such *Events*.

Often such *Events* effect a change in the life cycle of a RegistryEntry. For example a client request could Create, Update, Deprecate or Delete a RegistryEntry. No AuditableEvent is created for requests that do not alter the state of a Registry-Entry. Specifically, read-only requests do not generate an AuditableEvent. No AuditableEvent is generated for a RegistryEntry when it is classified, assigned to a Package or associated with another RegistryObject.

8.1.1   *Pre-defined AuditableEvent Types*

The following table lists pre-defined auditable event types. These pre-defined event types are defined as a *Classification* scheme. While the scheme may easily be extended, a *Registry* MUST support the event types listed below.

Name	Description
Created	An *Event* that created a RegistryEntry.
Deleted	An *Event* that deleted a RegistryEntry.
Deprecated	An *Event* that deprecated a RegistryEntry.
Updated	An *Event* that updated the state of a RegistryEntry.
Versioned	An *Event* that versioned a RegistryEntry.

Method Summary of AuditableEvent	
<u>User</u>	**getUser**() Gets the User that sent the request that generated this *Event*. Maps to attribute named `user`.
`String`	**getEventType**() The type of this *Event* as defined by the name attribute of an event type as defined in section 8.1.1. Maps to attribute named `eventType`.
<u>RegistryEntry</u>	**getRegistryEntry**() Gets the RegistryEntry associated with this AuditableEvent. Maps to attribute named `registryEntry`.
`Timestamp`	**getTimestamp**() Gets the Timestamp for when this *Event* occured. Maps to attribute named `timestamp`.

Note

Methods inherited from the base interfaces of this interface are not shown.

8.2   Interface User

All Superinterfaces:

<u>RegistryObject</u>

User *Instances* are used in an AuditableEvent to keep track of the identity of the requestor that sent the request that generated the AuditableEvent.

Method Summary of User	
<u>Organization</u>	**getOrganization**() Gets the *Submitting Organization* that sent the request that effected this change. Maps to attribute named `organization`.

	Method Summary of User
PostalAddress	**getAddress**() Gets the postal address for this user. Maps to attribute named `address`.
String	**getEmail**() Gets the email address for this user. Maps to attribute named `email`.
TelephoneNumber	**getFax**() The FAX number for this user. Maps to attribute named `fax`.
TelephoneNumber	**getMobilePhone**() The mobile telephone number for this user. Maps to attribute named `mobilePhone`.
PersonName	**getPersonName**() Name of contact person. Maps to attribute named `personName`.
TelephoneNumber	**getPager**() The pager telephone number for this user. Maps to attribute named `pager`.
TelephoneNumber	**getTelephone**() The default (land line) telephone number for this user. Maps to attribute named `telephone`.
URL	**getUrl**() The *URL* to the web page for this contact. Maps to attribute named `url`.

8.3 Interface Organization

All Superinterfaces:

IntrinsicObject, RegistryEntry, RegistryObject, Versionable

Organization *Instances* provide information on organizations such as a *Submitting Organization*. Each Organization *Instance* may have a reference to a parent Organization. In addition it may have a contact attribute defining the primary contact within the organization. An Organization also has an address attribute.

	Method Summary of Organization
PostalAddress	**getAddress**() Gets the PostalAddress for this Organization. Maps to attribute named `address`.

Method Summary of Organization

<u>User</u>	**getPrimaryContact**()
	Gets the primary Contact for this Organization. The primary contact is a reference to a User object. Maps to attribute named `primaryContact`.
`TelephoneNumber`	**getFax**()
	Gets the FAX number for this Organization. Maps to attribute named `fax`.
<u>Organization</u>	**getParent**()
	Gets the parent Organization for this Organization. Maps to attribute named `parent`.
`TelephoneNumber`	**getTelephone**()
	Gets the main telephone number for this Organization. Maps to attribute named `telephone`.

Note **Methods inherited from the base interfaces of this interface are not shown.**

8.4   Class PostalAddress

PostalAddress is a simple reusable *Entity Class* that defines attributes of a postal address.

Field Summary

`String`	**city**
	The city.
`String`	**country**
	The country.
`String`	**postalCode**
	The postal or zip code.
`String`	**state**
	The state or province.
`String`	**street**
	The street.

8.5   Class TelephoneNumber

A simple reusable *Entity Class* that defines attributes of a telephone number.

	Field Summary
String	**areaCode** Area code.
String	**countryCode** country code.
String	**extension** internal extension if any.
String	**number** The telephone number suffix not including the country or area code.
String	**url** A *URL* that can dial this number electronically.

8.6   Class PersonName

A simple *Entity Class* for a person's name.

	Field Summary
String	**firstName** The first name for this person.
String	**lastName** The last name (surname) for this person.
String	**middleName** The middle name for this person.

9   RegistryEntry Naming

A RegistryEntry has a name that may or may not be unique within the *Registry*.

In addition a RegistryEntry may have any number of context sensitive alternate names that are valid only in the context of a particular *Classification* scheme. Alternate contextual naming will be addressed in a later version of the Registry Information Model.

10   Association of RegistryEntry

A RegistryEntry may be associated with 0 or more RegistryObjects. The information model defines an Association *Class*. An *Instance* of the Association *Class* represents an association between a RegistryEntry and another RegistryObject. An example of such an association is between ExtrinsicObjects that catalogue a new *Collaboration Protocol Profile* (CPP) and an older *Collaboration Protocol Profile* where the newer *CPP* supersedes the older *CPP* as shown in **Figure 3.**

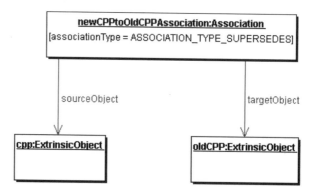

FIGURE 3   Example of RegistryEntry Association

10.1   Interface Association

All Superinterfaces:

IntrinsicObject, RegistryEntry, RegistryObject, Versionable

Association *Instances* are used to define many-to-many associations between RegistryObjects in the information model.

An *Instance* of the Association *Class* represents an association between two RegistryObjects.

	Method Summary of Association
String	**getAssociationType**() Gets the association type for this Association. This MUST be the name attribute of an association type as defined by 10.1.1. Maps to attribute named `associationType`.
Object	**getSourceObject**() Gets the RegistryObject that is the source of this Association. Maps to attribute named `sourceObject`.
String	**getSourceRole**() Gets the name of the *Role* played by the source RegistryObject in this Association. Maps to attribute named `sourceRole`.
Object	**getTargetObject**() Gets the RegistryObject that is the target of this Association. Maps to attribute named `targetObject`.
String	**getTargetRole**() Gets the name of the *Role* played by the target RegistryObject in this Association. Maps to attribute named `targetRole`.
boolean	**isBidirectional**() Determine whether this Association is bi-directional. Maps to attribute named `bidirectional`.
void	**setBidirectional**(`boolean bidirectional`) Set whether this Association is bi-directional.
void	**setSourceRole**(`String sourceRole`) Sets the name of the *Role* played by the source RegistryObject in this Association.
void	**setTargetRole**(`String targetRole`) Sets the name of the *Role* played by the destination RegistryObject in this Association.

10.1.1 Pre-defined Association Types

The following table lists pre-defined association types. These pre-defined association types are defined as a *Classification* scheme. While the scheme may easily be extended a *Registry* MUST support the association types listed below.

Name	Description
RelatedTo	Defines that source RegistryObject is related to target RegistryObject.
HasMember	Defines that the source Package object has the target RegistryEntry object as a member. Reserved for use in Packaging of RegistryEntries.
ExternallyLinks	Defines that the source ExternalLink object externally links the target RegistryEntry object. Reserved for use in associating ExternalLinks with RegistryEntries.
ExternallyIdentifies	Defines that the source ExternalIdentifier object identifies the target RegistryEntry object. Reserved for use in associating ExternalIdentifiers with RegistryEntries.
ContainedBy	Defines that source RegistryObject is contained by the target RegistryObject.
Contains	Defines that source RegistryObject contains the target RegistryObject.
Extends	Defines that source RegistryObject inherits from or specializes the target RegistryObject.
Implements	Defines that source RegistryObject implements the functionality defined by the target RegistryObject.
InstanceOf	Defines that source RegistryObject is an *Instance* of target RegistryObject.
SupersededBy	Defines that the source RegistryObject is superseded by the target RegistryObject.
Supersedes	Defines that the source RegistryObject supersedes the target RegistryObject.
UsedBy	Defines that the source RegistryObject is used by the target RegistryObject in some manner.
Uses	Defines that the source RegistryObject uses the target RegistryObject in some manner.
ReplacedBy	Defines that the source RegistryObject is replaced by the target RegistryObject in some manner.
Replaces	Defines that the source RegistryObject replaces the target RegistryObject in some manner.

Note

In some association types, such as Extends and Implements, although the association is between RegistryObjects, the actual relationship specified by that type is between repository items pointed by RegistryObjects.

11 Classification of RegistryEntry

This section describes the how the information model supports *Classification* of RegistryEntry. It is a simplified version of the *OASIS* classification model [OAS].

A RegistryEntry may be classified in many ways. For example the RegistryEntry for the same *Collaboration Protocol Profile* (*CPP*) may be classified by its industry, by the products it sells and by its geographical location.

A general *Classification* scheme can be viewed as a *Classification* tree. In the example shown in **Figure 4**, RegistryEntries representing *Collaboration Protocol Profiles*

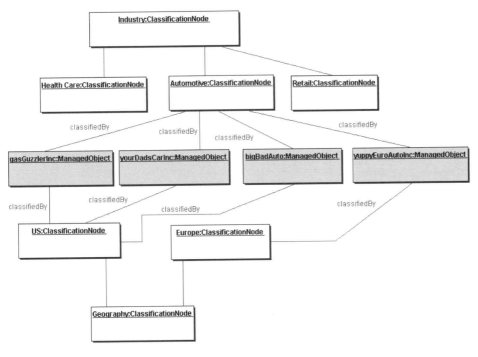

FIGURE 4   Example Showing a *Classification* Tree

It is important to point out that the dark nodes (gasGuzzlerInc, yourDadsCarInc etc.) are not part of the *Classification* tree. The leaf nodes of the *Classification* tree are Health Care, Automotive, Retail, US and Europe. The dark nodes are associated with the *Classification* tree via a *Classification Instance* that is not shown in the picture.

Note

are shown as shaded boxes. Each *Collaboration Protocol Profile* represents an automobile manufacturer. Each *Collaboration Protocol Profile* is classified by the ClassificationNode named Automotive under the root ClassificationNode named Industry. Furthermore, the US Automobile manufacturers are classified by the US ClassificationNode under the Geography ClassificationNode. Similarly, a European automobile manufacturer is classified by the Europe ClassificationNode under the Geography ClassificationNode.

The example shows how a RegistryEntry may be classified by multiple *Classification* schemes. A *Classification* scheme is defined by a ClassificationNode that is the root of a *Classification* tree (e.g. Industry, Geography).

In order to support a general *Classification* scheme that can support single level as well as multi-level *Classifications*, the information model defines the *Classes* and relationships shown in **Figure 5.**

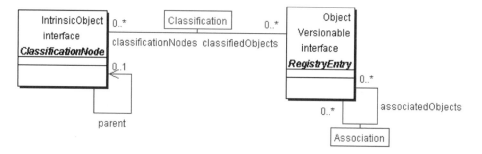

FIGURE 5   Information Model *Classification* View

A Classification is a specialized form of an Association. **Figure 6** shows an example of an ExtrinsicObject *Instance* for a *Collaboration Protocol Profile* (*CPP*) object that is classified by a ClassificationNode representing the Industry that it belongs to.

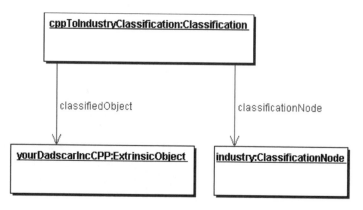

FIGURE 6   Classification *Instance* Diagram

11.1 Interface ClassificationNode

All Superinterfaces:

IntrinsicObject, RegistryEntry, RegistryObject, Versionable

ClassificationNode *Instances* are used to define tree structures where each node in the tree is a ClassificationNode. Such *Classification* trees constructed with ClassificationNodes are used to define *Classification* schemes or ontologies.

See Also:

Classification

	Method Summary of ClassificationNode
`Collection`	**getClassifiedObjects**()
	Get the collection of RegistryObjects classified by this ClassificationNode. Maps to attribute named `classifiedObjects`.
ClassificationNode	**getParent**()
	Gets the parent ClassificationNode for this ClassificationNode. Maps to attribute named `parent`.
`String`	**getPath**()
	Gets the path from the root ancestor of this ClassificationNode. The path conforms to the [XPATH] expression syntax (e.g "/Geography/Asia/Japan"). Maps to attribute named `path`.
`void`	**setParent**(ClassificationNode parent)
	Sets the parent ClassificationNode for this ClassificationNode.
`String`	**getCode**()
	Gets the code for this ClassificationNode. See section 11.4 for details. Maps to attribute named `code`.
`void`	**setCode**(String code)
	Sets the code for this ClassificationNode. See section 11.4 for details.

Methods inherited from the base interfaces of this interface are not shown.

Note

In **Figure 4,** several *Instances* of ClassificationNode are defined (all light colored boxes). A ClassificationNode has zero or one ClassificationNodes for its parent and zero or more ClassificationNodes for its immediate children. If a ClassificationNode has no parent then it is the root of a *Classification* tree. Note that the entire *Classification* tree is recursively defined by a single information model *Element* ClassificationNode.

11.2   Interface Classification

All Superinterfaces:

IntrinsicObject, RegistryEntry, RegistryObject, Versionable

Classification *Instances* are used to classify repository item by associating their RegistryEntry *Instance* with a ClassificationNode *Instance* within a *Classification* scheme.

In **Figure 4,** Classification *Instances* are not explicitly shown but are implied as associations between the RegistryEntries (shaded leaf node) and the associated ClassificationNode

---

	Method Summary of Classification
RegistryObject	**getClassifiedObject**()
	Gets the RegistryObject that is classified by this Classification. Maps to attribute named `classifiedObject`.
RegistryObject	**getClassificationNode**()
	Gets the ClassificationNode that classifies the RegistryObject in this Classification. Maps to attribute named `classificationNode`.

Note   **Methods inherited from the base interfaces of this interface are not shown.**

11.2.1   *Context-sensitive Classification*

Consider the case depicted in **Figure 7** where a *Collaboration Protocol Profile* for ACME Inc. is classified by the Japan ClassificationNode under the Geography *Classification* scheme. In the absence of the context for this *Classification* its meaning is ambiguous. Does it mean that ACME is located in Japan, or does it mean that ACME ships products to Japan, or does it have some other meaning? To address this ambiguity a Classification may optionally be associated with another ClassificationNode (in this example named isLocatedIn) that provides the missing context for the Classification. Another *Collaboration Protocol Profile* for MyParcelService may be classified by the Japan ClassificationNode where this Classification is associated with a different ClassificationNode (e.g. named shipsTo) to indicate a different context than the one used by ACME Inc.

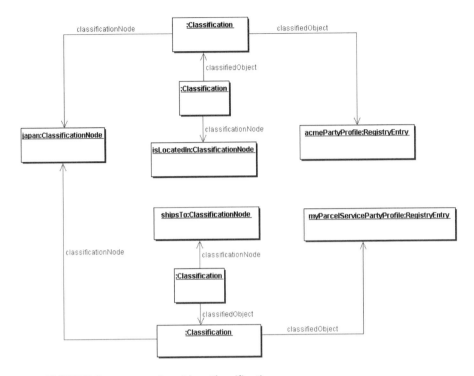

FIGURE 7   Context Sensitive *Classification*

Thus, in order to support the possibility of Classification within multiple contexts, a Classification is itself classified by any number of Classifications that
bind the first Classification to ClassificationNodes that provide the missing
contexts.

In summary, the generalized support for *Classification* schemes in the information
model allows:

▼ A RegistryEntry to be classified by defining a Classification that associates
it with a ClassificationNode in a *Classification* tree.

▼ A RegistryEntry to be classified along multiple facets by having multiple
Classifications that associate it with multiple ClassificationNodes.

▼ A *Classification* defined for a RegistryEntry to be qualified by the contexts in
which it is being classified.

11.3   Example of Classification Schemes

The following table lists some examples of possible *Classification* schemes enabled by the information model. These schemes are based on a subset of contextual concepts identified by the ebXML Business Process and Core Components Project Teams. This list is meant to be illustrative not prescriptive.

TABLE 1   Sample *Classification* Schemes

Classification Scheme (Context)	Usage Example
Industry	Find all Parties in Automotive industry
Process	Find a ServiceInterface that implements a Process
Product	Find a *Business* that sells a product
Locale	Find a Supplier located in Japan
Temporal	Find Supplier that can ship with 24 hours
Role	Find All Suppliers that have a *Role* of "Seller"

11.4   Standardized Taxonomy Support

Standardized taxonomies also referred to as ontologies or coding schemes exist in various industries to provide a structured coded vocabulary. The ebXML *Registry* does not define support for specific taxonomies. Instead it provides a general capability to link RegistryEntries to codes defined by various taxonomies.

The information model provides two alternatives for using standardized taxonomies for *Classification* of RegistryEntries.

11.4.1   Full-Featured Taxonomy-Based Classification

The information model provides a full-featured taxonomy based *Classification* alternative based Classification and ClassificationNode *Instances*. This alternative requires that a standard taxonomy be imported into the *Registry* as a *Classification* tree consisting of ClassificationNode *Instances*. This specification does not prescribe the transformation tools necessary to convert standard taxonomies into ebXML *Registry Classification* trees. However, the transformation MUST ensure that:

1. The name attribute of the root ClassificationNode is the *name* of the standard taxonomy (e.g. NAICS, ICD-9, SNOMED).

2. All codes in the standard taxonomy are preserved in the *code* attribute of a ClassificationNode.

3. The intended structure of the standard taxonomy is preserved in the ClassificationNode tree, thus allowing polymorphic browse and drill down discovery. This means that is searching for entries classified by Asia will find entries classified by descendants of Asia (e.g. Japan and Korea).

11.4.2   *Light-Weight Taxonomy-Based Classification*

The information model also provides a lightweight alternative for classifying RegistryEntry *Instances* by codes defined by standard taxonomies, where the submitter does not wish to import an entire taxonomy as a native *Classification* scheme.

In this alternative the submitter adds one or more taxonomy related Slots to the RegistryEntry for a submitted repository item. Each Slot's name identifies a standardized taxonomy while the Slot's value is the code within the specified taxonomy. Such taxonomy related Slots MUST be defined with a slotType of `Classification`.

For example if a RegistryEntry has a Slot with name "NAICS", a slotType of "Classification" and a value "51113" it implies that the RegistryEntry is classified by the code for "Book Publishers" in the NAICS taxonomy. Note that in this example, there is no need to import the entire NAICS taxonomy, nor is there any need to create *Instances* of ClassificationNode or Classification.

The following points are noteworthy in this light weight *Classification* alternative:

▼ Validation of the name and the value of the Classification" is responsibility of the SO and not of the ebXML *Registry* itself.

▼ Discovery is based on exact match on slot name and slot value rather than the flexible "browse and drill down discovery" available to the heavy weight *Classification* alternative.

12   Information Model: Security View

This section describes the aspects of the information model that relate to the security features of the *Registry*.

Figure 8 shows the view of the objects in the *Registry* from a security perspective. It shows object relationships as a *UML Class* diagram. It does not show *Class* attributes or *Class* methods that will be described in subsequent sections. It is meant to be illustrative not prescriptive.

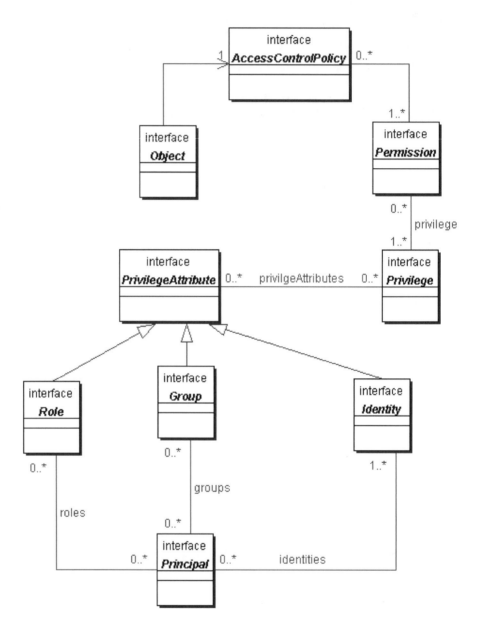

FIGURE 8   Information Model: Security View

12.1   Interface AccessControlPolicy

Every RegistryObject is associated with exactly one AccessControlPolicy which defines the policy rules that govern access to operations or methods performed on that RegistryObject. Such policy rules are defined as a collection of Permissions.

Method Summary of AccessControlPolicy	
Collection	**getPermissions**() Gets the Permissions defined for this AccessControlPolicy. Maps to attribute named `permissions`.

12.2 Interface Permission

The Permission object is used for authorization and access control to Registry-Objects in the *Registry*. The Permissions for a RegistryObject are defined in an AccessControlPolicy object.

A Permission object authorizes access to a method in a RegistryObject if the requesting Principal has any of the Privileges defined in the Permission.

See Also:

<u>Privilege</u>, <u>AccessControlPolicy</u>

Method Summary of Permission	
String	**getMethodName**() Gets the method name that is accessible to a Principal with specified Privilege by this Permission. Maps to attribute named `methodName`.
Collection	**getPrivileges**() Gets the Privileges associated with this Permission. Maps to attribute named `privileges`.

12.3 Interface Privilege

A Privilege object contains zero or more PrivilegeAttributes. A PrivilegeAttribute can be a Group, a Role, or an Identity.

A requesting Principal MUST have all of the PrivilegeAttributes specified in a Privilege in order to gain access to a method in a protected RegistryObject. Permissions defined in the RegistryObject's AccessControlPolicy define the Privileges that can authorize access to specific methods.

This mechanism enables the flexibility to have object access control policies that are based on any combination of Roles, Identities or Groups.

See Also:

<u>PrivilegeAttribute</u>, <u>Permission</u>

Method Summary of Privilege	
Collection	**getPrivilegeAttributes**() Gets the PrivilegeAttributes associated with this Privilege. Maps to attribute named `privilegeAttributes`.

12.4   Interface PrivilegeAttribute

All Known Subinterfaces:

Group, Identity, Role

PrivilegeAttribute is a common base *Class* for all types of security attributes that are used to grant specific access control privileges to a Principal. A Principal may have several different types of PrivilegeAttributes. Specific combination of PrivilegeAttributes may be defined as a Privilege object.

See Also:

Principal, Privilege

12.5   Interface Role

All Superinterfaces:

PrivilegeAttribute

A security Role PrivilegeAttribute. For example a hospital may have *Roles* such as Nurse, Doctor, Administrator etc. Roles are used to grant Privileges to Principals. For example a Doctor *Role* may be allowed to write a prescription but a Nurse *Role* may not.

12.6   Interface Group

All Superinterfaces:

PrivilegeAttribute

A security Group PrivilegeAttribute. A Group is an aggregation of users that may have different Roles. For example a hospital may have a Group defined for Nurses and Doctors that are participating in a specific clinical trial (e.g. AspirinTrial group). Groups are used to grant Privileges to Principals. For example the members of the AspirinTrial group may be allowed to write a prescription for Aspirin (even though Nurse Role as a rule may not be allowed to write prescriptions).

12.7   Interface Identity

All Superinterfaces:

PrivilegeAttribute

A security Identity PrivilegeAttribute. This is typically used to identify a person, an organization, or software service. Identity attribute may be in the form of a digital certificate.

12.8   Interface Principal

Principal is a completely generic term used by the security community to include both people and software systems. The Principal object is an entity that has a set of PrivilegeAttributes. These PrivilegeAttributes include at least one identity, and optionally a set of role memberships, group memberships or security clearances. A principal is used to authenticate a requestor and to authorize the requested action based on the PrivilegeAttributes associated with the Principal.

See Also:

`PrivilegeAttributes`, Privilege, Permission

	Method Summary of Principal
Collection	**getGroups**() Gets the Groups associated with this Principal. Maps to attribute named `groups`.
Collection	**getIdentities**() Gets the Identities associated with this Principal. Maps to attribute named `identities`.
Collection	**getRoles**() Gets the Roles associated with this Principal. Maps to attribute named `roles`.

13   References

[ebGLOSS] ebXML Glossary,

http://www.ebxml.org/specs/ebGLOSS.pdf

[ebTA] ebXML Technical Architecture Specification

http://www.ebxml.org/specs/ebTA.pdf

[OAS] OASIS Information Model

http://xsun.sdct.itl.nist.gov/regrep/OasisRegrepSpec.pdf

[ISO] ISO 11179 Information Model

http://208.226.167.205/SC32/jtc1sc32.nsf/576871ad2f11bba785256621005419d7/
    b83fc7816a6064c68525690e0065f913?OpenDocument

[BRA97] IETF (Internet Engineering Task Force). RFC 2119: Key words for use in
    RFCs to Indicate Requirement Levels

http://www.cis.ohio-state.edu/cgi-bin/rfc/rfc2119.html

[ebRS] ebXML Registry Services Specification

http://www.ebxml.org/specs/ebRS.pdf

[ebBPSS] ebXML Business Process Specification Schema

http://www.ebxml.org/specs/ebBPSS.pdf

[ebCPP] ebXML Collaboration-Protocol Profile and Agreement Specification

http://www.ebxml.org/specs/ebCPP.pdf

[UUID] DCE 128 bit Universal Unique Identifier

http://www.opengroup.org/onlinepubs/009629399/apdxa.htm#tagcjh_20

http://www.opengroup.org/publications/catalog/c706.htmhttp://www.w3.org/
    TR/REC-xml

[XPATH] XML Path Language (XPath) Version 1.0

http://www.w3.org/TR/xpath

14 Disclaimer

The views and specification expressed in this document are those of the authors
and are not necessarily those of their employers. The authors and their employers specifically disclaim responsibility for any problems arising from correct or
incorrect implementation or use of this design.

15   Contact Information

Team Leader

Name:	Scott Nieman
Company:	Norstan Consulting
Street:	5101 Shady Oak Road
City, State, Postal Code	Minnetonka, MN 55343
Country:	USA
Phone:	952.352.5889
Email:	Scott.Nieman@Norstan

Vice Team Lead

Name:	Yutaka Yoshida
Company:	Sun Microsystems
Street:	901 San Antonio Road, MS UMPK17-102
City, State, Postal Code	Palo Alto, CA 94303
Country:	USA
Phone:	650.786.5488
Email:	Yutaka.Yoshida@eng.sun.com

Editor

Name:	Farrukh S. Najmi
Company:	Sun Microsystems
Street:	1 Network Dr., MS BUR02-302
City, State, Postal Code	Burlington, MA, 01803-0902
Country:	USA
Phone:	781.442.0703
Email:	najmi@east.sun.com

CHAPTER
5

Registry Services Specification
v1.0
Registry Team
10 May 2001

TABLE OF CONTENTS

1   Status of this Document

This document specifies an ebXML Technical Specification for the eBusiness community.

Distribution of this document is unlimited.

The document formatting is based on the Internet Society's Standard RFC format.

This version:
http://www.ebxml.org/specs/ebRS.pdf

Latest version:
http://www.ebxml.org/specs/ebRS.pdf

2   ebXML Participants

ebXML Registry Services, v1.0 was developed by the ebXML Registry Project Team. At the time this specification was approved, the membership of the ebXML Registry Project Team was as follows:

Lisa Carnahan	NIST
Joe Dalman	Tie
Philippe DeSmedt	Viquity
Sally Fuger	AIAG
Len Gallagher	NIST
Steve Hanna	Sun Microsystems
Scott Hinkelman	IBM
Michael Kass	NIST
Jong.L Kim	Innodigital
Kyu-Chul Lee	Chungnam National University
Sangwon Lim	Korea Institute for Electronic Commerce
Bob Miller	GXS
Kunio Mizoguchi	Electronic Commerce Promotion Council of Japan
Dale Moberg	Sterling Commerce

Ron Monzillo	Sun Microsystems
JP Morgenthal	eThink Systems Inc.
Joel Munter	Intel
Farrukh Najmi	Sun Microsystems
Scott Nieman	Norstan Consulting
Frank Olken	Lawrence Berkeley National Laboratory
Michael Park	eSum Technologies
Bruce Peat	eProcess Solutions
Mike Rowley	Excelon Corporation
Waqar Sadiq	Vitria
Krishna Sankar	Cisco Systems Inc.
Kim Tae Soo	Government of Korea
Nikola Stojanovic	Encoda Systems Inc.
David Webber	XML Global
Yutaka Yoshida	Sun Microsystems
Prasad Yendluri	webmethods
Peter Z. Zhoo	Knowledge For the new Millennium

3 Introduction

3.1 Summary of Contents of Document

This document defines the interface to the ebXML *Registry* Services as well as interaction protocols, message definitions and XML schema.

A separate document, *ebXML Registry Information Model* [ebRIM], provides information on the types of metadata that are stored in the Registry as well as the relationships among the various metadata classes.

3.2 General Conventions

The following conventions are used throughout this document:

▼ UML diagrams are used as a way to concisely describe concepts. They are not intended to convey any specific *Implementation* or methodology requirements.

▼ The term *"repository item"* is used to refer to an object that has been submitted to a Registry for storage and safekeeping (e.g. an XML document or a DTD). Every repository item is described by a RegistryEntry instance.

▼ The term *"RegistryEntry"* is used to refer to an object that provides meta-data about a *repository item*.

▼ *Capitalized Italic* words are defined in the ebXML Glossary.

The keywords MUST, MUST NOT, REQUIRED, SHALL, SHALL NOT, SHOULD, SHOULD NOT, RECOMMENDED, MAY, and OPTIONAL, when they appear in this document, are to be interpreted as described in RFC 2119 [Bra97].

3.3   Audience

The target audience for this specification is the community of software developers who are:

▼ Implementers of ebXML Registry Services

▼ Implementers of ebXML Registry Clients

3.4   Related Documents

The following specifications provide some background and related information to the reader:

▼ [ebRIM] ebXML Registry Information Model v1.0

▼ [ebMS] ebXML Message Service Specification v1.0

▼ [ebBPM] ebXML Business Process Specification Schema v1.01

▼ [ebCPP] ebXML Collaboration-Protocol Profile and Agreement Specification v1.0

4   Design Objectives

4.1   Goals

The goals of this version of the specification are to:

▼ Communicate functionality of Registry services to software developers

▼ Specify the interface for Registry clients and the Registry

▼ Provide a basis for future support of more complete ebXML Registry requirements

▼ Be compatible with other ebXML specifications

4.2 Caveats and Assumptions

The Registry Services specification is first in a series of phased deliverables. Later versions of the document will include additional functionality planned for future development.

It is assumed that:

1. Interoperability requirements dictate that the ebXML Message Services Specification is used between an ebXML Registry and an ebXML Registry Client. The use of other communication means is not precluded; however, in those cases interoperability cannot be assumed. Other communication means are outside the scope of this specification.

2. All access to the Registry content is exposed via the interfaces defined for the Registry Services.

3. The Registry makes use of a Repository for storing and retrieving persistent information required by the Registry Services. This is an implementation detail that will not be discussed further in this specification.

5 System Overview

5.1 What the ebXML Registry Does

The ebXML Registry provides a set of services that enable sharing of information between interested parties for the purpose of enabling *business process* integration between such parties based on the ebXML specifications. The shared information is maintained as objects in a repository and managed by the ebXML Registry Services defined in this document.

5.2 How the ebXML Registry Works

This section describes at a high level some use cases illustrating how Registry clients may make use of Registry Services to conduct B2B exchanges. It is meant to be illustrative and not prescriptive.

The following scenario provides a high level textual example of those use cases in terms of interaction between Registry clients and the Registry. It is not a complete listing of the use cases that could be envisioned. It assumes for purposes of example, a buyer and a seller who wish to conduct B2B exchanges using the RosettaNet PIP3A4 Purchase Order business protocol. It is assumed that both buyer and seller use the same Registry service provided by a third party. Note that the architecture supports other possibilities (e.g. each party uses its own private Registry).

5.2.1 Schema Documents Are Submitted

A third party such as an industry consortium or standards group submits the necessary schema documents required by the RosettaNet PIP3A4 Purchase Order business protocol with the Registry using the ObjectManager service of the Registry described in Section 7.3.

5.2.2 Business Process Documents Are Submitted

A third party, such as an industry consortium or standards group, submits the necessary business process documents required by the RosettaNet PIP3A4 Purchase Order business protocol with the Registry using the ObjectManager service of the Registry described in Section 7.3.

5.2.3 Seller's Collaboration Protocol Profile Is Submitted

The seller publishes its *Collaboration Protocol* Profile or CPP as defined by [ebCPP] to the Registry. The CPP describes the seller, the role it plays, the services it offers and the technical details on how those services may be accessed. The seller classifies their Collaboration Protocol Profile using the Registry's flexible *Classification* capabilities.

5.2.4 Buyer Discovers the Seller

The buyer browses the Registry using *Classification* schemes defined within the Registry using a Registry Browser GUI tool to discover a suitable seller. For example the buyer may look for all parties that are in the Automotive Industry, play a seller role, support the RosettaNet PIP3A4 process and sell Car Stereos.

The buyer discovers the seller's CPP and decides to engage in a partnership with the seller.

5.2.5   CPA Is Established

The buyer unilaterally creates a *Collaboration Protocol Agreement* or CPA as defined by [ebCPP] with the seller using the seller's CPP and their own CPP as input. The buyer proposes a trading relationship to the seller using the unilateral CPA. The seller accepts the proposed CPA and the trading relationship is established.

Once the seller accepts the CPA, the parties may begin to conduct B2B transactions as defined by [ebMS].

5.3   Where the Registry Services May Be Implemented

The Registry Services may be implemented in several ways including, as a public web site, as a private web site, hosted by an ASP or hosted by a VPN provider.

5.4   Implementation Conformance

An implementation is a *conforming* ebXML Registry if the implementation meets the conditions in Section 5.4.1. An implementation is a conforming ebXML Registry Client if the implementation meets the conditions in Section 5.4.2. An implementation is a conforming ebXML Registry and a conforming ebXML Registry Client if the implementation conforms to the conditions of Section 5.4.1 and Section 5.4.2. An implementation shall be a conforming ebXML Registry, a conforming ebXML Registry Client, or a conforming ebXML Registry and Registry Client.

5.4.1   Conformance as an ebXML Registry

An implementation conforms to this specification as an ebXML registry if it meets the following conditions:

1. Conforms to the ebXML Registry Information Model [ebRIM].
2. Supports the syntax and semantics of the Registry Interfaces and Security Model.
3. Supports the defined ebXML Registry DTD (Appendix A)
4. Optionally supports the syntax and semantics of Section 8.3, SQL Query Support.

5.4.2   Conformance as an ebXML Registry Client

An implementation conforms to this specification, as an ebXML Registry Client if it meets the following conditions:

1. Supports the ebXML CPA and bootstrapping process.
2. Supports the syntax and the semantics of the Registry Client Interfaces.

3. Supports the defined ebXML Error Message DTD.

4. Supports the defined ebXML Registry DTD.

6 Registry Architecture

The ebXML Registry architecture consists of an ebXML Registry and ebXML Registry Clients. The Registry Client interfaces may be local to the registry or local to the user. **Figure 1** depicts the two possible topologies supported by the registry architecture with respect to the Registry and Registry Clients.

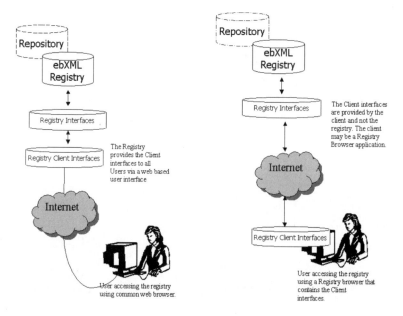

FIGURE 1   Registry Architecture Supports Flexible Topologies

The picture on the left side shows the scenario where the Registry provides a web based "thin client" application for accessing the Registry that is available to the user using a common web browser. In this scenario the Registry Client interfaces reside across the internet and are local to the Registry from the user's view.

The picture on the right side shows the scenario where the user is using a "fat client" Registry Browser application to access the registry. In this scenario the

Registry Client interfaces reside within the Registry Browser tool and are local to the Registry from the user's view. The Registry Client interfaces communicate with the Registry over the internet in this scenario.

A third topology made possible by the registry architecture is where the Registry Client interfaces reside in a server side business component such as a Purchasing business component. In this topology there may be no direct user interface or user intervention involved. Instead the Purchasing business component may access the Registry in an automated manner to select possible sellers or service providers based current business needs.

Clients communicate with the Registry using the ebXML Messaging Service in the same manner as any two ebXML applications communicating with each other.

Future versions of this specification may provide additional services to explicitly extend the Registry architecture to support distributed registries. However this current version of the specification does not preclude ebXML Registries from co-operating with each other to share information, nor does it preclude owners of ebXML Registries from registering their ebXML registries with other registry systems, catalogs, or directories.

Examples include:

▼ an ebXML Registry of Registries that serves as a centralized registration point;

▼ cooperative ebXML Registries, where registries register with each other in a federation;

▼ registration of ebXML Registries with other Registry systems that act as white pages or yellow pages. The document [ebXML-UDDI] provides an example of ebXML Registries being discovered through a system of emerging white/yellow pages known as UDDI.

6.1   ebXML Registry Profiles and Agreements

The ebXML CPP specification [ebCPP] defines a Collaboration-Protocol Profile (CPP) and a Collaboration-Protocol Agreement (CPA) as mechanisms for two parties to share information regarding their respective business processes. That specification assumes that a CPA has been agreed to by both parties in order for them to engage in B2B interactions.

This specification does not mandate the use of a CPA between the Registry and the Registry Client. However if the Registry does not use a CPP, the Registry shall provide an alternate mechanism for the Registry Client to discover the services and other information provided by a CPP. This alternate mechanism could be simple URL.

The CPA between clients and the Registry should describe the interfaces that the Registry and the client expose to each other for Registry-specific interactions. These interfaces are described in Figure 2 and subsequent sections. The definition of the Registry CPP template and a Registry Client CPP template are beyond the scope of this document.

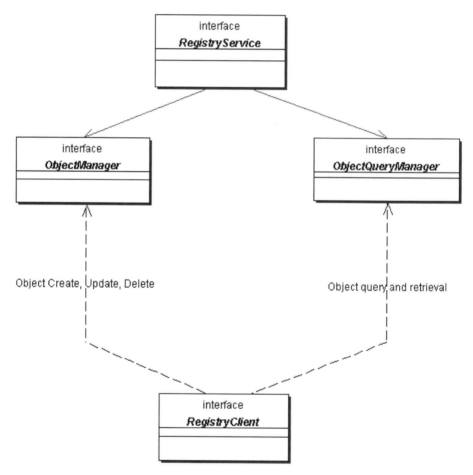

FIGURE 2   ebXML Registry Interfaces

6.2   Client-to-Registry Communication Bootstrapping

Since there is no previously established CPA between the Registry and the RegistryClient, the client must know at least one Transport-specific communication address for the Registry. This communication address is typically a URL to the Registry, although it could be some other type of address such as an email address.

For example, if the communication used by the Registry is HTTP, then the communication address is a URL. In this example, the client uses the Registry's public URL to create an implicit CPA with the Registry. When the client sends a request to the Registry, it provides a URL to itself. The Registry uses the client's URL to form its version of an implicit CPA with the client. At this point a session is established within the Registry.

For the duration of the client's session with the Registry, messages may be exchanged bidirectionally as required by the interaction protocols defined in this specification.

6.3 Interfaces

This specification defines the interfaces exposed by both the Registy (Section 6.4) and the Registry Client (Section 6.5). Figure 2 shows the relationship between the interfaces and the mapping of specific Registy interfaces with specific Registry Client interfaces.

6.4 Interfaces Exposed by the Registry

When using the ebXML Messaging Services Specification, ebXML Registry Services elements correspond to Messaging Services elements as follows:

▼ The value of the Service element in the MessageHeader is an ebXML Registry Service interface name (e.g., "ObjectManager"). The type attribute of the Service element should have a value of "ebXMLRegistry".

▼ The value of the Action element in the MessageHeader is an ebXML Registry Service method name (e.g., "submitObjects").

The above allows the Registry Client only one interface/method pair per message. This implies that a Registry Client can only invoke one method on a specified interface for a given request to a registry. **Note**

6.4.1 Synchronous and Asynchronous Responses

All methods on interfaces exposed by the registry return a response message.

▼ Asynchronous response
  ▼ MessageHeader only;
  ▼ No registry response element (e.g., AdHocQueryResponse and Get-ContentResponse).

▼ Synchronous response
  ▼ MessageHeader;
  ▼ Registry response element including
    ▼ a status attribute (success or failure)
    ▼ an optional ebXML Error.

The ebXML Registry implements the following interfaces as its services (Registry Services).

6.4.2   Interface RegistryService

This is the principal interface implemented by the Registry. It provides the methods that are used by the client to discover service-specific interfaces implemented by the Registry.

Method Summary of RegistryService

ObjectManager	**getObjectManager** ( ) Returns the ObjectManager interface implemented by the Registry service.
ObjectQueryManager	**getObjectQueryManager** ( ) Returns the ObjectQueryManager interface implemented by the Registry service.

6.4.3   Interface ObjectManager

This is the interface exposed by the Registry Service that implements the Object life cycle management functionality of the Registry. Its methods are invoked by the Registry Client. For example, the client may use this interface to submit objects, to classify and associate objects and to deprecate and remove objects. For this specification the semantic meaning of submit, classify, associate, deprecate and remove is found in [ebRIM].

Method Summary of ObjectManager

RegistryResponse	**approveObjects** (ApproveObjectsRequest req) Approves one or more previously submitted objects.
RegistryResponse	**deprecateObjects** (DeprecateObjectsRequest req) Deprecates one or more previously submitted objects.
RegistryResponse	**removeObjects** (RemoveObjectsRequest req) Removes one or more previously submitted objects from the Registry.

	Method Summary of ObjectManager
RegistryResponse	**submitObjects** (<u>SubmitObjectsRequest</u> `req`)
	Submits one or more objects and possibly related metadata such as Associations and Classifications.
RegistryResponse	**addSlots** (<u>AddSlotsRequest</u> `req`)
	Add slots to one or more registry entries.
RegistryResponse	**removeSlots** (<u>RemoveSlotsRequest</u> `req`)
	Remove specified slots from one or more registry entries.

6.4.4 Interface ObjectQueryManager

This is the interface exposed by the Registry that implements the Object Query management service of the Registry. Its methods are invoked by the Registry Client. For example, the client may use this interface to perform browse and drill down queries or ad hoc queries on registry content.

	Method Summary of ObjectQueryManager
<u>RegistryResponse</u>	**getClassificationTree** (
	<u>GetClassificationTreeRequest</u> `req`)
	Returns the ClassificationNode Tree under the ClassificationNode specified in GetClassificationTreeRequest.
<u>RegistryResponse</u>	**getClassifiedObjects** (
	<u>GetClassifiedObjectsRequest</u> `req`)
	Returns a collection of references to RegistryEntries classified under specified ClassificationItem.
<u>RegistryResponse</u>	**getContent** ( )
	Returns the content of the specified Repository Item. The response includes all the content specified in the request as additional payloads within the response message.
<u>RegistryResponse</u>	**getRootClassificationNodes** (
	<u>GetRootClassificationNodesRequest</u> `req`)
	Returns all root ClassificationNodes that match the namePattern attribute in GetRootClassificationNodesRequest request.
<u>RegistryResponse</u>	**submitAdhocQuery** (<u>AdhocQueryRequest</u> `req`)
	Submit an ad hoc query request.

6.5 Interfaces Exposed by Registry Clients

An ebXML Registry client implements the following interface.

6.5.1   *Interface RegistryClient*

This is the principal interface implemented by a Registry client. The client provides this interface when creating a connection to the Registry. It provides the methods that are used by the Registry to deliver asynchronous responses to the client. Note that a client need not provide a RegistryClient interface if the [CPA] between the client and the registry does not support asynchronous responses.

The registry sends all asynchronous responses to operations to the onResponse method.

Method Summary of RegistryClient

---

void   **onResponse** (<u>RegistryResponse</u> `resp`)

             Notifies client of the response sent by registry to previously submitted request.

6.6   Registry Response Class Hierarchy

Since many of the responses from the registry have common attributes they are arranged in the following class hierarchy. This hierarchy is reflected in the registry DTD.

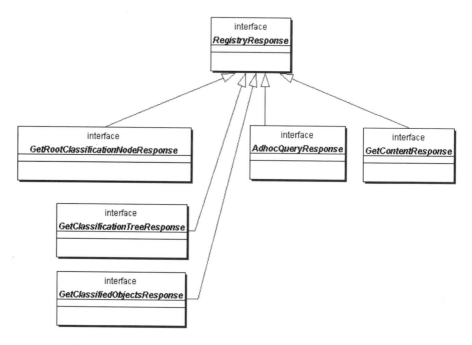

FIGURE 3   Registry Reponse Class Hierarchy

7 Object Management Service

This section defines the ObjectManagement service of the Registry. The Object Management Service is a sub-service of the Registry service. It provides the functionality required by RegistryClients to manage the life cycle of repository items (e.g. XML documents required for ebXML business processes). The Object Management Service can be used with all types of repository items as well as the metadata objects specified in [ebRIM] such as Classification and Association.

The minimum *security policy* for an ebXML registry is to accept content from any client if the content is digitally signed by a certificate issued by a Certificate Authority recognized by the ebXML registry. Submitting Organizations do not have to register prior to submitting content.

7.1 Life Cycle of a Repository Item

The main purpose of the ObjectManagement service is to manage the life cycle of repository items.

Figure 4 shows the typical life cycle of a repository item. Note that the current version of this specification does not support Object versioning. Object versioning will be added in a future version of this specification.

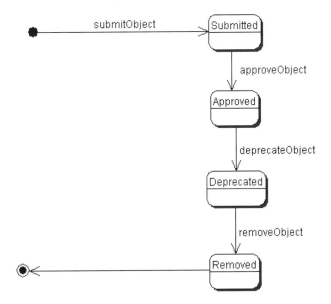

FIGURE 4   Life Cycle of a Repository Item

7.2   RegistryObject Attributes

A repository item is associated with a set of standard metadata defined as attributes of the RegistryObject class and its sub-classes as described in [ebRIM]. These attributes reside outside of the actual repository item and catalog descriptive information about the repository item. XML elements called ExtrinsicObject and IntrinsicObject (See 10 for details) encapsulate all object metadata attributes defined in [ebRIM] as XML attributes.

7.3   The Submit Objects Protocol

This section describes the protocol of the Registry Service that allows a RegistryClient to submit one or more repository items to the repository using the *ObjectManager* on behalf of a Submitting Organization. It is expressed in UML notation as described in Appendix B.

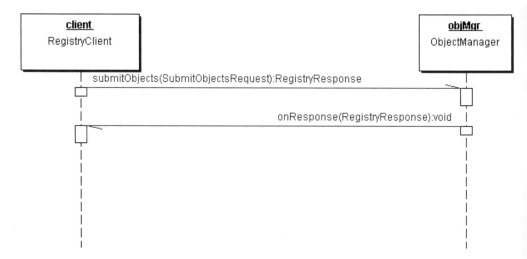

FIGURE 5   Submit Objects Sequence Diagram

For details on the schema for the *Business documents* shown in this process refer to 10.

The SubmitObjectRequest message includes a RegistrEntryList element.

The RegistryEntryList element specifies one or more ExtrinsicObjects or other RegistryEntries such as Classifications, Associations, ExternalLinks, or Packages.

An ExtrinsicObject element provides required metadata about the content being submitted to the Registry as defined by [ebRIM]. Note that these standard ExtrinsicObject attributes are separate from the repository item itself, thus allowing the ebXML Registry to catalog objects of any object type.

In the event of success, the registry sends a RegistryResponse with a status of "success" back to the client. In the event of failure, the registry sends a RegistryResponse with a status of "failure" back to the client.

7.3.1 Universally Unique ID Generation

As specified by [ebRIM], all objects in the registry have a unique id. The id must be a *Universally Unique Identifier (UUID)* and must conform to the to the format of a URN that specifies a DCE 128 bit UUID as specified in [UUID].

(e.g. urn:uuid:a2345678-1234-1234-123456789012)

This id is usually generated by the registry. The id attribute for submitted objects may optionally be supplied by the client. If the client supplies the id and it conforms to the format of a URN that specifies a DCE 128 bit UUID then the registry assumes that the client wishes to specify the id for the object. In this case, the registry must honor a client-supplied id and use it as the id attribute of the object in the registry. If the id is found by the registry to not be globally unique, the registry must raise the error condition: InvalidIdError.

If the client does not supply an id for a submitted object then the registry must generate a universally unique id. Whether the id is generated by the client or whether it is generated by the registry, it must be generated using the DCE 128 bit UUID generation algorithm as specified in [UUID].

7.3.2 ID Attribute and Object References

The id attribute of an object may be used by other objects to reference the first object. Such references are common both within the SubmitObjects-Request as well as within the registry. Within a SubmitObjectsRequest, the id attribute may be used to refer to an object within the SubmitObjects-Request as well as to refer to an object within the registry. An object in the SubmitObjectsRequest that needs to be referred to within the request document may be assigned an id by the submitter so that it can be referenced within the request. The submitter may give the object a proper uuid URN, in which case the id is permanently assigned to the object within the registry. Alternatively, the submitter may assign an arbitrary id (not a proper uuid URN) as long as the id is unique within the request document. In this case the id serves as a linkage mechanism within the request document but must be ignored by the registry and replaced with a registry generated id upon submission.

When an object in a SubmitObjectsRequest needs to reference an object that is already in the registry, the request must contain an ObjectRef element whose id attribute is the id of the object in the registry. This id is by definition a proper uuid URN. An ObjectRef may be viewed as a proxy within the request for an object that is in the registry.

7.3.3   Sample SubmitObjectsRequest

The following example shows several different use cases in a single SubmitObjectsRequest. It does not show the complete ebXML Message with the message header and additional payloads in the message for the repository items.

A SubmitObjectsRequest includes a RegistryEntryList which contains any number of objects that are being submitted. It may also contain any number of ObjectRefs to link objects being submitted to objects already within the registry.

```
<?xml version = "1.0" encoding = "UTF-8"?>
<!DOCTYPE SubmitObjectsRequest SYSTEM "file:////home/najmi/Registry.dtd">
<SubmitObjectsRequest>
  <RegistryEntryList>
    <!--
    The following 3 objects package specified ExtrinsicObject in
    specified Package, where both the Package and the Extrinsic-
    Object are being submitted
      -->
    <Package id = "acmePackage1" name = "Package #1" description =
      "ACME's package #1"/>
    <ExtrinsicObject id = "acmeCPP1" contentURI = "CPP1"
      objectType = "CPP" name = "Widget Profile" description =
      "ACME's profile for selling widgets"/>
    <Association id = "acmePackage1-acmeCPP1-Assoc" association-
      Type = "Packages" sourceObject = "acmePackage1" targetObject
      = "acmeCPP1"/>

    <!--
    The following 3 objects package specified ExtrinsicObject in
    specified Package, Where the Package is being submitted and
    the ExtrinsicObject is already in registry
      -->
```

```
<Package id = "acmePackage2" name = "Package #2" description =
  "ACME's package #2"/>
<ObjectRef id = "urn:uuid:a2345678-1234-1234-123456789012"/>
<Association id = "acmePackage2-alreadySubmittedCPP-Assoc"
  associationType = "Packages" sourceObject = "acmePackage2"
  targetObject = "urn:uuid:a2345678-1234-1234-123456789012"/>
<!--
The following 3 objects package specified ExtrinsicObject in
specified Package, where the Package and the ExtrinsicObject
are already in registry
-->
<ObjectRef id = "urn:uuid:b2345678-1234-1234-123456789012"/>
<ObjectRef id = "urn:uuid:c2345678-1234-1234-123456789012"/>
<!-- id is unspecified implying that registry must create a
  uuid for this object -->
<Association associationType = "Packages" sourceObject =
  "urn:uuid:b2345678-1234-1234-123456789012" targetObject =
  "urn:uuid:c2345678-1234-1234-123456789012"/>
<!--
The following 3 objects externally link specified Extrinsic-
Object using specified ExternalLink, where both the External-
Link and the ExtrinsicObject are being submitted
-->
<ExternalLink id = "acmeLink1" name = "Link #1" description =
  "ACME's Link #1"/>
<ExtrinsicObject id = "acmeCPP2" contentURI = "CPP2" object-
  Type = "CPP" name = "Sprockets Profile" description =
  "ACME's profile for selling sprockets"/>
<Association id = "acmeLink1-acmeCPP2-Assoc" associationType =
  "ExternallyLinks" sourceObject = "acmeLink1" targetObject =
  "acmeCPP2"/>
<!--
The following 2 objects externally link specified Extrinsic-
Object using specified ExternalLink, where the ExternalLink
is being submitted and the ExtrinsicObject is already in reg-
istry. Note that the targetObject points to an ObjectRef in a
previous line
-->
<ExternalLink id = "acmeLink2" name = "Link #2" description =
  "ACME's Link #2"/>
<Association id = "acmeLink2-alreadySubmittedCPP-Assoc" asso-
  ciationType = "ExternallyLinks" sourceObject = "acmeLink2"
  targetObject = "urn:uuid:a2345678-1234-1234-123456789012"/>
<!--
```

```
The following 2 objects externally identify specified Extrin-
sicObject using specified ExternalIdentifier, where the Exter-
nalIdentifier is being submitted and the ExtrinsicObject is
already in registry. Note that the targetObject points to an
ObjectRef in a previous line
-->
<ExternalIdentifier id = "acmeDUNSId" name = "DUNS" descrip-
  tion = "DUNS ID for ACME" value = "13456789012"/>
<Association id = "acmeDUNSId-alreadySubmittedCPP-Assoc"
  associationType = "ExternallyIdentifies" sourceObject =
  "acmeDUNSId" targetObject = "urn:uuid:a2345678-1234-1234-
  123456789012"/>
<!--
The following show submission of a brand new classification
scheme in its entirety
-->
<ClassificationNode id = "geographyNode" name = "Geography"
  description = "The Geography scheme example from Registry
  Services Spec" />
<ClassificationNode id = "asiaNode" name = "Asia"
  description = "The Asia node under the Geography node"
  parent="geographyNode" />
<ClassificationNode id = "japanNode" name = "Japan"
  description ="The Japan node under the Asia node"
  parent="asiaNode" />
<ClassificationNode id = "koreaNode" name = "Korea"
  description ="The Korea node under the Asia node"
  parent="asiaNode" />
<ClassificationNode id = "europeNode" name = "Europe"
  description = "The Europe node under the Geography node"
  parent="geographyNode" />
<ClassificationNode id = "germanyNode" name = "Germany"
  description ="The Germany node under the Asia node"
  parent="europeNode" />
<ClassificationNode id = "northAmericaNode" name = "North
  America" description = "The North America node under the
  Geography node" parent="geographyNode" />
<ClassificationNode id = "usNode" name = "US"
  description ="The US node under the Asia node"
  parent="northAmericaNode" />

<!--
The following show submission of a Automotive sub-tree of
ClassificationNodes that gets added to an existing classifica-
tion scheme named 'Industry' that is already in the registry
```

```
-->
<ObjectRef id="urn:uuid:d2345678-1234-1234-123456789012" />
<ClassificationNode id = "automotiveNode" name = "Automotive"
  description = "The Automotive sub-tree under Industry scheme"
  parent = "urn:uuid:d2345678-1234-1234-123456789012"/>
<ClassificationNode id = "partSuppliersNode" name = "Parts
  Supplier" description = "The Parts Supplier node under the
  Automotive node" parent="automotiveNode" />
<ClassificationNode id = "engineSuppliersNode" name = "Engine
  Supplier" description = "The Engine Supplier node under the
  Automotive node" parent="automotiveNode" />
<!--
The following show submission of 2 Classifications of an ob-
ject that is already in the registry using 2 Classification-
Nodes. One ClassificationNode is being submitted in this
request (Japan) while the other is already in the registry.
-->
<Classification id = "japanClassification"
  description = "Classifies object by /Geography/Asia/Japan
  node"
  classifiedObject="urn:uuid:a2345678-1234-1234-123456789012"
  classificationNode="japanNode" />
<Classification id = "classificationUsingExistingNode"
  description = "Classifies object using a node in the reg-
  istry"
  classifiedObject="urn:uuid:a2345678-1234-1234-123456789012"
  classificationNode="urn:uuid:e2345678-1234-1234-
  123456789012" />
  <ObjectRef id="urn:uuid:e2345678-1234-1234-123456789012" />
</RegistryEntryList>
</SubmitObjectsRequest>
```

7.4 The Add Slots Protocol

This section describes the protocol of the Registry Service that allows a client to add slots to a previously submitted registry entry using the ObjectManager. Slots provide a dynamic mechanism for extending registry entries as defined by [ebRIM].

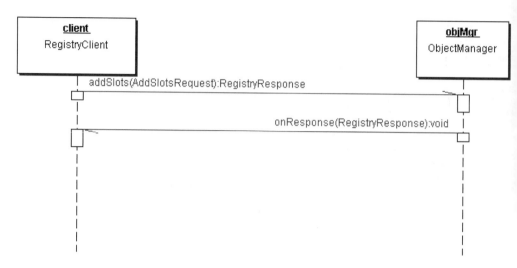

FIGURE 7   Add Slots Sequence Diagram

In the event of success, the registry sends a RegistryResponse with a status of "success" back to the client. In the event of failure, the registry sends a RegistryResponse with a status of "failure" back to the client.

7.5   The Remove Slots Protocol

This section describes the protocol of the Registry Service that allows a client to remove slots to a previously submitted registry entry using the ObjectManager.

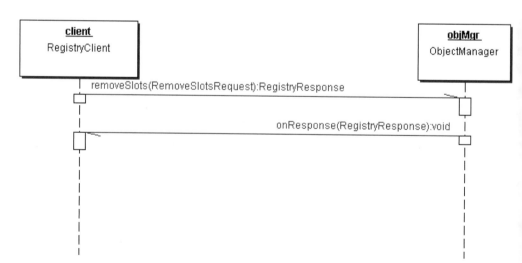

FIGURE 8   Remove Slots Sequence Diagram

In the event of success, the registry sends a RegistryResponse with a status of "success" back to the client. In the event of failure, the registry sends a RegistryResponse with a status of "failure" back to the client.

7.6 The Approve Objects Protocol

This section describes the protocol of the Registry Service that allows a client to approve one or more previously submitted repository items using the Object-Manager. Once a repository item is approved it will become available for use by business parties (e.g. during the assembly of new CPAs and Collaboration Protocol Profiles).

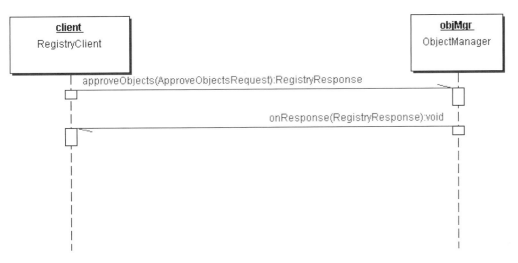

FIGURE 9 Approve Objects Sequence Diagram

In the event of success, the registry sends a RegistryResponse with a status of "success" back to the client. In the event of failure, the registry sends a Registry-Response with a status of "failure" back to the client.

For details on the schema for the business documents shown in this process refer to 10.

7.7 The Deprecate Objects Protocol

This section describes the protocol of the Registry Service that allows a client to deprecate one or more previously submitted repository items using the ObjectManager. Once an object is deprecated, no new references (e.g. *new* Associations, Classifications and ExternalLinks) to that object can be submit-

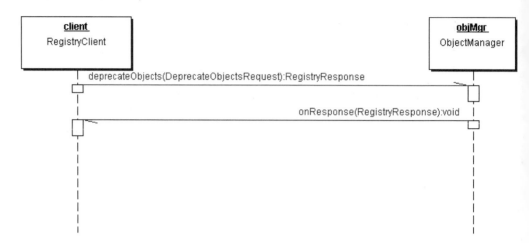

FIGURE 10   Deprecate Objects Sequence Diagram

ted. However, existing references to a deprecated object continue to function normally.

In the event of success, the registry sends a RegistryResponse with a status of "success" back to the client. In the event of failure, the registry sends a Registry-Response with a status of "failure" back to the client.

For details on the schema for the business documents shown in this process refer to 10.

7.8   The Remove Objects Protocol

This section describes the protocol of the Registry Service that allows a client to remove one or more RegistryEntry instances and/or repository items using the ObjectManager.

The RemoveObjectsRequest message is sent by a client to remove RegistryEntry instances and/or repository items. The RemoveObjectsRequest element includes an XML attribute called *deletionScope* which is an enumeration that can have the values as defined by the following sections.

7.8.1   Deletion Scope DeleteRepositoryItemOnly

This deletionScope specifies that the request should delete the repository items for the specified registry entries but not delete the specified registry entries. This is useful in keeping references to the registry entries valid.

7.8.2 Deletion Scope DeleteAll

This deletionScope specifies that the request should delete both the Registry-Entry and the repository item for the specified registry entries. Only if all references (e.g. Associations, Classifications, ExternalLinks) to a Registry-Entry have been removed, can that RegistryEntry then be removed using a RemoveObjectsRequest with deletionScope DeleteAll. Attempts to remove a RegistryEntry while it still has references raises an error condition: InvalidRequestError.

The remove object protocol is expressed in UML notation as described in Appendix B.

FIGURE 11   Remove Objects Sequence Diagram

In the event of success, the registry sends a RegistryResponse with a status of "success" back to the client. In the event of failure, the registry sends a Registry-Response with a status of "failure" back to the client.

For details on the schema for the business documents shown in this process refer to Appendix A.

8 Object Query Management Service

This section describes the capabilities of the Registry Service that allow a client (ObjectQueryManagerClient) to search for or query RegistryEntries in the ebXML Registry using the ObjectQueryManager interface of the Registry.

The Registry supports multiple query capabilities. These include the following:

1. Browse and Drill Down Query

2. Filtered Query

3. SQL Query

The browse and drill down query in Section 8.1 and the filtered query mechanism in Section 8.2 SHALL be supported by every Registry implementation. The SQL query mechanism is an optional feature and MAY be provided by a registry implementation. However, if a vendor provides an SQL query capability to an ebXML Registry it SHALL conform to this document. As such this capability is a normative yet optional capability.

In a future version of this specification, the W3C XQuery syntax may be considered as another query syntax.

Any errors in the query request messages are indicated in the corresponding query response message.

8.1 Browse and Drill-down Query Support

The browse and drill drown query style is supported by a set of interaction protocols between the ObjectQueryManagerClient and the ObjectQueryManager. Sections 8.1.1, 8.1.2 and 8.1.3 describe these protocols.

8.1.1 Get Root Classification Nodes Request

An ObjectQueryManagerClient sends this request to get a list of root ClassificationNodes defined in the repository. Root classification nodes are defined as nodes that have no parent. Note that it is possible to specify a namePattern attribute that can filter on the name attribute of the root ClassificationNodes. The namePattern must be specified using a wildcard pattern defined by SQL-92 LIKE clause as defined by [SQL].

FIGURE 12   Get Root Classification Nodes Sequence Diagram

In the event of success, the registry sends a GetRootClassificationNodeResponse with a status of "success" back to the client. In the event of failure, the registry sends a GetRootClassificationNodeResponse with a status of "failure" back to the client.

For details on the schema for the business documents shown in this process refer to 10.

8.1.2   Get Classification Tree Request

An ObjectQueryManagerClient sends this request to get the ClassificationNode sub-tree defined in the repository under the ClassificationNodes specified in the request. Note that a GetClassificationTreeRequest can specify an integer attribute called *depth* to get the sub-tree up to the specified depth. If *depth* is the default value of 1, then only the immediate children of the specified ClassificationNodeList are returned. If *depth* is 0 or a negative number then the entire sub-tree is retrieved.

FIGURE 14   Get Classification Tree Sequence Diagram

In the event of success, the registry sends a GetClassificationTreeResponse with a status of "success" back to the client. In the event of failure, the registry sends a GetClassificationTreeResponse with a status of "failure" back to the client.

For details on the schema for the business documents shown in this process refer to 10.

8.1.3 Get Classified Objects Request

An ObjectQueryManagerClient sends this request to get a list of RegistryEntries that are classified by all of the specified ClassificationNodes (or any of their descendants), as specified by the ObjectRefList in the request.

It is possible to get RegistryEntries based on matches with multiple classifications. Note that specifying a ClassificationNode is implicitly specifying a logical OR with all descendants of the specified ClassificationNode.

When a GetClassifiedObjectsRequest is sent to the ObjectQueryManager it should return Objects that are:

1. Either directly classified by the specified ClassificationNode

2. Or are directly classified by a descendant of the specified ClassificationNode

8.1.3.1   Get Classified Objects Request Example

FIGURE 16   A Sample Geography Classification

Let us say a classification tree has the structure shown in **Figure 16**:

▼ If the Geography node is specified in the GetClassifiedObjectsRequest then the GetClassifiedObjectsResponse should include all RegistryEntries that are directly classified by Geography *or* North America *or* US *or* Asia *or* Japan *or* Korea *or* Europe *or* Germany.

▼ If the Asia node is specified in the GetClassifiedObjectsRequest then the GetClassifiedObjectsResponse should include all RegistryEntries that are directly classified by Asia *or* Japan *or* Korea.

▼ If the Japan *and* Korea nodes are specified in the GetClassifiedObjectsRequest then the GetClassifiedObjectsResponse should include all RegistryEntries that are directly classified by both Japan *and* Korea.

▼ If the North America *and* Asia node is specified in the GetClassifiedObjects-Request then the GetClassifiedObjectsResponse should include all RegistryEntries that are directly classified by (North America *or* US) *and* (Asia *or* Japan *or* Korea).

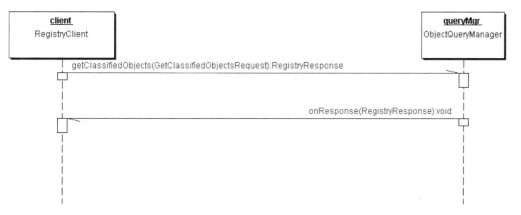

FIGURE 17   Get Classified Objects Sequence Diagram

In the event of success, the registry sends a GetClassifiedObjectsResponse with a status of "success" back to the client. In the event of failure, the registry sends a GetClassifiedObjectsResponse with a status of "failure" back to the client.

8.2   Filter Query Support

FilterQuery is an XML syntax that provides simple query capabilities for any ebXML conforming Registry implementation. Each query alternative is directed against a single class defined by the ebXML Registry Information Model (ebRIM). The result of such a query is a set of identifiers for instances of that class. A FilterQuery may be a stand-alone query or it may be the initial action of a ReturnRegistryEntry query or a ReturnRepositoryItem query.

A client submits a FilterQuery, a ReturnRegistryEntry query, or a Return-RepositoryItem query to the ObjectQueryManager as part of an AdhocQuery-Request. The ObjectQueryManager sends an AdhocQueryResponse back to the client, enclosing the appropriate FilterQueryResponse, ReturnRegistryEntry-Response, or ReturnRepositoryItemResponse specified herein. The sequence diagrams for AdhocQueryRequest and AdhocQueryResponse are specified in Section 8.4.

Each FilterQuery alternative is associated with an ebRIM Binding that identifies a hierarchy of classes derived from a single class and its associations with other classes as defined by ebRIM. Each choice of a class pre-determines a virtual XML document that can be queried as a tree. For example, let C be a class, let Y and Z be classes that have direct associations to C, and let V be a class that is associated with Z. The ebRIM Binding for C might be as in **Figure 19**.

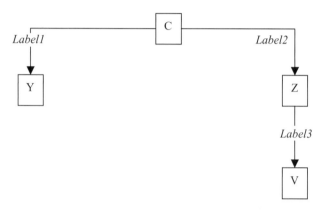

FIGURE 19   Example ebRIM Binding

Label1 identifies an association from C to Y, Label2 identifies an association from C to Z, and Label3 identifies an association from Z to V. Labels can be omitted if there is no ambiguity as to which ebRIM association is intended. The name of the query is determined by the root class, i.e. this is an ebRIM Binding for a CQuery. The Y node in the tree is limited to the set of Y instances that are linked to C by the association identified by Label1. Similarly, the Z and V nodes are limited to instances that are linked to their parent node by the identified association.

Each FilterQuery alternative depends upon one or more *class filters*, where a class filter is a restricted *predicate clause* over the attributes of a single class. The supported class filters are specified in Section 8.2.9 and the supported predicate clauses are defined in Section 8.2.10. A FilterQuery will be composed of elements that traverse the tree to determine which branches satisfy the designated class filters, and the query result will be the set of root node instances that support such a branch.

In the above example, the CQuery element will have three subelements, one a CFilter on the C class to eliminate C instances that do not satisfy the predicate of the CFilter, another a YFilter on the Y class to eliminate branches from C to Y where the target of the association does not satisfy the YFilter, and a third to eliminate branches along a path from C through Z to V. The third element is called a *branch* element because it allows class filters on each class along the path from X to V. In general, a branch element will have subelements that are themselves class filters, other branch elements, or a full-blown query on the terminal class in the path.

If an association from a class C to a class Y is one-to-zero or one-to-one, then at most one branch or filter element on Y is allowed. However, if the association is one-to-many, then multiple filter or branch elements are allowed. This allows one to specify that an instance of C must have associations with multiple instances of Y before the instance of C is said to satisfy the branch element.

The FilterQuery syntax is tied to the structures defined in ebRIM. Since ebRIM is intended to be stable, the FilterQuery syntax is stable. However, if new structures are added to the ebRIM, then the FilterQuery syntax and semantics can be extended at the same time.

Support for FilterQuery is required of every conforming ebXML Registry implementation, but other query options are possible. The Registry will hold a self-describing CPP that identifies all supported AdhocQuery options. This profile is described in Section 6.1.

The ebRIM Binding paragraphs in Sections 8.2.2 through 8.2.6 below identify the virtual hierarchy for each FilterQuery alternative. The Semantic Rules for each query alternative specify the effect of that binding on query semantics.

The ReturnRegistryEntry and ReturnRepositoryItem services defined below provide a way to structure an XML document as an expansion of the result of a RegistryEntryQuery. The ReturnRegistryEntry element specified in Section 8.2.7 allows one to specify what metadata one wants returned with each registry entry identified in the result of a RegistryEntryQuery. The ReturnRepositoryItem specified in Section 8.2.8 allows one to specify what repository items one wants returned based on their relationships to the registry entries identified by the result of a RegistryEntryQuery.

8.2.1 FilterQuery

8.2.1.1 Purpose

To identify a set of registry instances from a specific registry class. Each alternative assumes a specific binding to ebRIM. The query result for each query alternative is a set of references to instances of the root class specified by the binding. The status is a success indication or a collection of warnings and/or exceptions.

8.2.1.2 Definition

```
<!ELEMENT FilterQuery
  (    RegistryEntryQuery
    |  AuditableEventQuery
```

```
            |   ClassificationNodeQuery
            |   RegistryPackageQuery
            |   OrganizationQuery   )>
<!ELEMENT FilterQueryResult
    (   RegistryEntryQueryResult
        |   AuditableEventQueryResult
        |   ClassificationNodeQueryResult
        |   RegistryPackageQueryResult
        |   OrganizationQueryResult )>
<!ELEMENT RegistryEntryQueryResult ( RegistryEntryView* )>
<!ELEMENT RegistryEntryView EMPTY >
<!ATTLIST RegistryEntryView
    objectURN  CDATA  #REQUIRED
    contentURI CDATA  #IMPLIED
    objectID   CDATA  #IMPLIED >
<!ELEMENT AuditableEventQueryResult ( AuditableEventView* )>
<!ELEMENT AuditableEventView EMPTY >
<!ATTLIST AuditableEventView
    objectID   CDATA  #REQUIRED
    timestamp  CDATA  #REQUIRED >
<!ELEMENT ClassificationNodeQueryResult
                (ClassificationNodeView*)>
<!ELEMENT ClassificationNodeView EMPTY >
<!ATTLIST ClassificationNodeView
    objectURN  CDATA  #REQUIRED
    contentURI CDATA  #IMPLIED
    objectID   CDATA  #IMPLIED >
<!ELEMENT RegistryPackageQueryResult ( RegistryPackageView* )>
<!ELEMENT RegistryPackageView EMPTY >
<!ATTLIST RegistryPackageView
    objectURN  CDATA  #REQUIRED
    contentURI CDATA  #IMPLIED
    objectID   CDATA  #IMPLIED >
<!ELEMENT OrganizationQueryResult ( OrganizationView* )>
<!ELEMENT OrganizationView EMPTY >
<!ATTLIST OrganizationView
    orgURN     CDATA  #REQUIRED
    objectID   CDATA  #IMPLIED >
```

8.2.1.3   Semantic Rules

The semantic rules for each FilterQuery alternative are specified in subsequent subsections.

1. Each FilterQueryResult is a set of XML reference elements to identify each instance of the result set. Each XML attribute carries a value derived from the value of an attribute specified in the Registry Information Model as follows:

a.) objectID is the value of the ID attribute of the RegistryObject class,

b.) objectURN and orgURN are URN values derived from the object ID,

c.) contentURI is a URL value derived from the contentURI attribute of the RegistryEntry class,

d.) timestamp is a literal value to represent the value of the timestamp attribute of the AuditableEvent class.

2. If an error condition is raised during any part of the execution of a FilterQuery, then the status attribute of the XML RegistryResult is set to "failure" and no query result element is returned; instead, a RegistryErrorList element must be returned with its highestSeverity element set to "error". At least one of the RegistryError elements in the RegistryErrorList will have its severity attribute set to "error".

3. If no error conditions are raised during execution of a FilterQuery, then the status attribute of the XML RegistryResult is set to "success" and an appropriate query result element must be included. If a RegistryErrorList is also returned, then the highestSeverity attribute of the RegistryErrorList is set to "warning" and the serverity attribute of each RegistryError is set to "warning".

8.2.2 RegistryEntryQuery

8.2.2.1 Purpose

To identify a set of registry entry instances as the result of a query over selected registry metadata.

8.2.2.2 ebRIM Binding

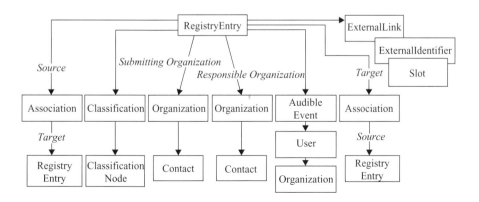

8.2.2.3   Definition

```
<!ELEMENT RegistryEntryQuery
    (   RegistryEntryFilter?,
        SourceAssociationBranch*,
        TargetAssociationBranch*,
        HasClassificationBranch*,
        SubmittingOrganizationBranch?,
        ResponsibleOrganizationBranch?,
        ExternalIdentifierFilter*,
        ExternalLinkFilter*,
        SlotFilter*,
        HasAuditableEventBranch*          )>
<!ELEMENT SourceAssociationBranch
    (   AssociationFilter?,
        RegistryEntryFilter?              )>
<!ELEMENT TargetAssociationBranch
    (   AssociationFilter?,
        RegistryEntryFilter?              )>
<!ELEMENT HasClassificationBranch
    (   ClassificationFilter?,
        ClassificationNodeFilter?         )>
<!ELEMENT SubmittingOrganizationBranch
    (   OrganizationFilter?,
        ContactFilter?                    )>
<!ELEMENT ResponsibleOrganizationBranch
    (   OrganizationFilter?,
        ContactFilter?                    )>
<!ELEMENT HasAuditableEventBranch
    (   AuditableEventFilter?,
        UserFilter?,
        OrganizationFilter?               )>
```

8.2.2.4   Semantic Rules

1. Let RE denote the set of all persistent RegistryEntry instances in the Registry. The following steps will eliminate instances in RE that do not satisfy the conditions of the specified filters.

   a.) If a RegistryEntryFilter is not specified, or if RE is empty, then continue below; otherwise, let x be a registry entry in RE. If x does not satisfy the RegistryEntryFilter as defined in Section 8.2.9, then remove x from RE.

   b.) If a SourceAssociationBranch element is not specified, or if RE is empty, then continue below; otherwise, let x be a remaining registry entry in RE. If x is not the source object of some Association instance, then remove x from RE; otherwise, treat each SourceAssociationBranch element separately as follows:

If no AssociationFilter is specified within SourceAssociationBranch, then let AF be the set of all Association instances that have x as a source object; otherwise, let AF be the set of Association instances that satisfy the AssociationFilter and have x as the source object. If AF is empty, then remove x from RE. If no RegistryEntryFilter is specified within SourceAssociationBranch, then let RET be the set of all RegistryEntry instances that are the target object of some element of AF; otherwise, let RET be the set of RegistryEntry instances that satisfy the RegistryEntryFilter and are the target object of some element of AF. If RET is empty, then remove x from RE.

c.) If a TargetAssociationBranch element is not specified, or if RE is empty, then continue below; otherwise, let x be a remaining registry entry in RE. If x is not the target object of some Association instance, then remove x from RE; otherwise, treat each TargetAssociationBranch element separately as follows:

If no AssociationFilter is specified within TargetAssociationBranch, then let AF be the set of all Association instances that have x as a target object; otherwise, let AF be the set of Association instances that satisfy the AssociationFilter and have x as the target object. If AF is empty, then remove x from RE. If no RegistryEntryFilter is specified within Target-AssociationBranch, then let RES be the set of all RegistryEntry instances that are the source object of some element of AF; otherwise, let RES be the set of RegistryEntry instances that satisfy the RegistryEntryFilter and are the source object of some element of AF. If RES is empty, then remove x from RE.

d.) If a HasClassificationBranch element is not specified, or if RE is empty, then continue below; otherwise, let x be a remaining registry entry in RE. If x is not the source object of some Classification instance, then remove x from RE; otherwise, treat each HasClassificationBranch element separately as follows:

If no ClassificationFilter is specified within the HasClassificationBranch, then let CL be the set of all Classification instances that have x as a source object; otherwise, let CL be the set of Classification instances that satisfy the ClassificationFilter and have x as the source object. If CL is empty, then remove x from RE. If no ClassificationNodeFilter is specified within HasClassificationBranch, then let CN be the set of all ClassificationNode instances that are the target object of some element of CL; otherwise, let CN be the set of RegistryEntry instances that satisfy the ClassificationNodeFilter and are the target object of some element of CL. If CN is empty, then remove x from RE.

e.) If a SubmittingOrganizationBranch element is not specified, or if RE is empty, then continue below; otherwise, let x be a remaining registry entry in RE. If x does not have a submitting organization, then remove x from RE. If no OrganizationFilter is specified within Submitting-OrganizationBranch, then let SO be the set of all Organization instances that are the submitting organization for x; otherwise, let SO be the set of Organization instances that satisfy the OrganizationFilter and are the submitting organization for x. If SO is empty, then remove x from RE. If no ContactFilter is specified within SubmittingOrganizationBranch, then let CT be the set of all Contact instances that are the contacts for some element of SO; otherwise, let CT be the set of Contact instances that satisfy the ContactFilter and are the contacts for some element of SO. If CT is empty, then remove x from RE.

f.) If a ResponsibleOrganizationBranch element is not specified, or if RE is empty, then continue below; otherwise, let x be a remaining registry entry in RE. If x does not have a responsible organization, then remove x from RE. If no OrganizationFilter is specified within Responsible-OrganizationBranch, then let RO be the set of all Organization instances that are the responsible organization for x; otherwise, let RO be the set of Organization instances that satisfy the OrganizationFilter and are the responsible organization for x. If RO is empty, then remove x from RE. If no ContactFilter is specified within SubmittingOrganizationBranch, then let CT be the set of all Contact instances that are the contacts for some element of RO; otherwise, let CT be the set of Contact instances that satisfy the ContactFilter and are the contacts for some element of RO. If CT is empty, then remove x from RE.

g.) If an ExternalLinkFilter element is not specified, or if RE is empty, then continue below; otherwise, let x be a remaining registry entry in RE. If x is not linked to some ExternalLink instance, then remove x from RE; otherwise, treat each ExternalLinkFilter element separately as follows:

Let EL be the set of ExternalLink instances that satisfy the ExternalLink-Filter and are linked to x. If EL is empty, then remove x from RE.

h.) If an ExternalIdentifierFilter element is not specified, or if RE is empty, then continue below; otherwise, let x be a remaining registry entry in RE. If x is not linked to some ExternalIdentifier instance, then remove x from RE; otherwise, treat each ExternalIdentifierFilter element separately as follows:

Let EI be the set of ExternalIdentifier instances that satisfy the External-IdentifierFilter and are linked to x. If EI is empty, then remove x from RE.

i.) If a SlotFilter element is not specified, or if RE is empty, then continue below; otherwise, let x be a remaining registry entry in RE. If x is not linked to some Slot instance, then remove x from RE; otherwise, treat each SlotFilter element separately as follows:

Let SL be the set of Slot instances that satisfy the SlotFilter and are linked to x. If SL is empty, then remove x from RE.

j.) If a HasAuditableEventBranch element is not specified, or if RE is empty, then continue below; otherwise, let x be a remaining registry entry in RE. If x is not linked to some AuditableEvent instance, then remove x from RE; otherwise, treat each HasAuditableEventBranch element separately as follows:

If an AuditableEventFilter is not specified within HasAuditableEventBranch, then let AE be the set of all AuditableEvent instances for x; otherwise, let AE be the set of AuditableEvent instances that satisfy the AuditableEventFilter and are auditable events for x. If AE is empty, then remove x from RE. If a UserFilter is not specified within HasAuditableEventBranch, then let AI be the set of all User instances linked to an element of AE; otherwise, let AI be the set of User instances that satisfy the UserFilter and are linked to an element of AE.

If AI is empty, then remove x from RE. If an OrganizationFilter is not specified within HasAuditableEventBranch, then let OG be the set of all Organization instances that are linked to an element of AI; otherwise, let OG be the set of Organization instances that satisfy the OrganizationFilter and are linked to an element of AI. If OG is empty, then remove x from RE.

2. If RE is empty, then raise the warning: *registry entry query result is empty*.

3. Return RE as the result of the RegistryEntryQuery.

8.2.2.5 Examples

A client wants to establish a trading relationship with XYZ Corporation and wants to know if they have registered any of their business documents in the Registry. The following query returns a set of registry entry identifiers for currently registered items submitted by any organization whose name includes the string "XYZ". It does not return any registry entry identifiers for superceded, replaced, deprecated, or withdrawn items.

```
<RegistryEntryQuery>
   <RegistryEntryFilter>
        status EQUAL "Approved"          -- code by Clause, Section 8.2.10
```

```
    </RegistryEntryFilter>
    <SubmittingOrganizationBranch>
        <OrganizationFilter>
            name CONTAINS "XYZ"                    -- code by Clause, Section 8.2.10
        </OrganizationFilter>
    </SubmittingOrganizationBranch>
</RegistryEntryquery>
```

A client is using the United Nations Standard Product and Services Classification (UNSPSC) scheme and wants to identify all companies that deal with products classified as "Integrated circuit components", i.e. UNSPSC code "321118". The client knows that companies have registered their party profile documents in the Registry, and that each profile has been classified by the products the company deals with. The following query returns a set of registry entry identifiers for profiles of companies that deal with integrated circuit components.

```
<RegistryEntryQuery>
    <RegistryEntryFilter>
        objectType EQUAL "CPP" AND               -- code by Clause, Section 8.2.10
        status EQUAL "Approved"
    </RegistryEntryFilter>
    <HasClassificationBranch>
        <ClassificationNodeFilter>
            id STARTSWITH "urn:un:spsc:321118"-- code by Clause, Section 8.2.10
        </ClassificationNodeFilter>
    <HasClassificationBranch>
</RegistryEntryQuery>
```

A client application needs all items that are classified by two different classification schemes, one based on "Industry" and another based on "Geography". Both schemes have been defined by ebXML and are registered. The root nodes of each scheme are identified by "urn:ebxml:cs:industry" and "urn:ebxml:cs:geography", respectively. The following query identifies registry entries for all registered items that are classified by "Industry/Automotive" and by "Geography/Asia/Japan".

```
<RegistryEntryQuery>
    <HasClassificationBranch>
        <ClassificationNodeFilter>
            id STARTSWITH "urn:ebxml:cs:industry" AND
            path EQUAL "Industry/Automotive"      -- code by Clause, Section 8.2.10
        </ClassificationNodeFilter>
        <ClassificationNodeFilter>
            id STARTSWITH "urn:ebxml:cs:geography" AND
```

```
              path EQUAL "Geography/Asia/Japan" -- code by Clause, Section 8.2.10
         </ClassificationNodeFilter>
      </HasClassificationBranch>
</RegistryEntryQuery>
```

A client application wishes to identify all registry Package instances that have a
given registry entry as a member of the package. The following query identifies
all registry packages that contain the registry entry identified by URN
"urn:path:myitem" as a member:

```
<RegistryEntryQuery>
   <RegistryEntryFilter>
      objectType EQUAL "RegistryPackage"    -- code by Clause, Section 8.2.10
   </RegistryEntryFilter>
   <SourceAssociationBranch>
      <AssociationFilter>                        -- code by Clause, Section 8.2.10
         associationType EQUAL "HasMember" AND
         targetObject EQUAL "urn:path:myitem"
      </AssociationFilter>
   </SourceAssociationBranch>
</RegistryEntryQuery>
```

A client application wishes to identify all ClassificationNode instances that have
some given keyword as part of their name or description. The following query
identifies all registry classification nodes that contain the keyword "transistor" as
part of their name or as part of their description.

```
<RegistryEntryQuery>
   <RegistryEntryFilter>
      ObjectType="ClassificationNode" AND
      (name CONTAINS "transistor" OR        -- code by Clause, Section 8.2.10
      description CONTAINS "transistor")
   </RegistryEntryFilter>
</RegistryEntryQuery>
```

8.2.3 *AuditableEventQuery*

8.2.3.1 Purpose

To identify a set of auditable event instances as the result of a query over selected
registry metadata.

ebRIM Binding

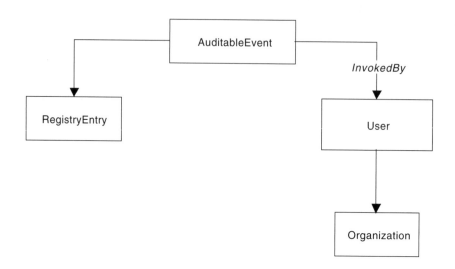

8.2.3.2 Definition

```
<!ELEMENT AuditableEventQuery
   (   AuditableEventFilter?,
       RegistryEntryQuery*,
       InvokedByBranch?      )>
<!ELEMENT InvokedByBranch
   (   UserFilter?,
       OrganizationQuery?    )>
```

8.2.3.3 Semantic Rules

Let AE denote the set of all persistent AuditableEvent instances in the Registry. The following steps will eliminate instances in AE that do not satisfy the conditions of the specified filters.

a.) If an AuditableEventFilter is not specified, or if AE is empty, then continue below; otherwise, let x be an auditable event in AE. If x does not satisfy the AuditableEventFilter as defined in Section 8.2.9, then remove x from AE.

b.) If a RegistryEntryQuery element is not specified, or if AE is empty, then continue below; otherwise, let x be a remaining auditable event in AE. Treat each RegistryEntryQuery element separately as follows:

c.) Let RE be the result set of the RegistryEntryQuery as defined in Section 8.2.2. If x is not an auditable event for some registry entry in RE, then remove x from AE.

d.) If an InvokedByBranch element is not specified, or if AE is empty, then continue below; otherwise, let x be a remaining auditable event in AE.

Let u be the user instance that invokes x. If a UserFilter element is specified within the InvokedByBranch, and if u does not satisfy that filter, then remove x from AE; otherwise, continue below.

If an OrganizationQuery element is not specified within the InvokedBy-Branch, then continue below; otherwise, let OG be the set of Organization instances that are identified by the organization attribute of u and are in the result set of the OrganizationQuery. If OG is empty, then remove x from AE.

1. If AE is empty, then raise the warning: auditable event query result is empty.

2. Return AE as the result of the AuditableEventQuery.

8.2.3.4 Examples

A Registry client has registered an item and it has been assigned a URN identifier "urn:path:myitem". The client is now interested in all events since the beginning of the year that have impacted that item. The following query will return a set of AuditableEvent identifiers for all such events.

```
<AuditableEventquery>
   <AuditableEventFilter>
      timestamp GE "2001-01-01" AND          -- code by Clause, Section 8.2.10
      registryEntry EQUAL "urn:path:myitem"
   </AuditableEventFilter>
</AuditableEventQuery>
```

A client company has many registered objects in the Registry. The Registry allows events submitted by other organizations to have an impact on your registered items, e.g. new classifications and new associations. The following query will return a set of identifiers for all auditable events, invoked by some other party, that had an impact on an item submitted by "myorg" and for which "myorg" is the responsible organization.

```
<AuditableEventQuery>
   <RegistryEntryQuery>
      <SubmittingOrganizationBranch>
         <OrganizationFilter>
            id EQUAL "urn:somepath:myorg"   -- code by Clause, Section 8.2.10
         </OrganizationFilter>
      </SubmittingOrganizationBranch>
      <ResponsibleOrganizationBranch>
         <OrganizationFilter>
            id EQUAL "urn:somepath:myorg"   -- code by Clause, Section 8.2.10
         </OrganizationFilter>
      </ResponsibleOrganizationBranch>
```

```
    </RegistryEntryQuery>
    <InvokedByBranch>
      <OrganizationQuery>
        <OrganizationFilter>
            id -EQUAL "urn:somepath:myorg"  -- code by Clause, Section 8.2.10
        </OrganizationFilter>
      </OrganizationQuery>
    </InvokedByBranch>
</AuditableEventQuery>
```

8.2.4   *ClassificationNodeQuery*

8.2.4.1   Purpose

To identify a set of classification node instances as the result of a query over selected registry metadata.

8.2.4.2   ebRIM Binding

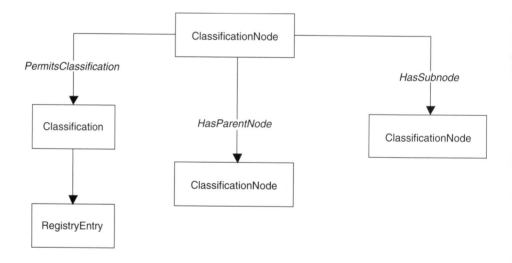

8.2.4.3   Definition

```
<!ELEMENT ClassificationNodeQuery
    ( ClassificationNodeFilter?,
      PermitsClassificationBranch*,
      HasParentNode?,
      HasSubnode*              )>
<!ELEMENT PermitsClassificationBranch
    ( ClassificationFilter?,
      RegistryEntryQuery?      )>
<!ELEMENT HasParentNode
    ( ClassificationNodeFilter?,
```

```
    HasParentNode?              )>
<!ELEMENT HasSubnode
   ( ClassificationNodeFilter?,
     HasSubnode*                )>
```

8.2.4.4 Semantic Rules

1. Let CN denote the set of all persistent ClassificationNode instances in the Registry. The following steps will eliminate instances in CN that do not satisfy the conditions of the specified filters.

   a.) If a ClassificationNodeFilter is not specified, or if CN is empty, then continue below; otherwise, let x be a classification node in CN. If x does not satisfy the ClassificationNodeFilter as defined in Section 8.2.9, then remove x from AE.

   b.) If a PermitsClassificationBranch element is not specified, or if CN is empty, then continue below; otherwise, let x be a remaining classification node in CN. If x is not the target object of some Classification instance, then remove x from CN; otherwise, treat each PermitsClassificationBranch element separately as follows:

   If no ClassificationFilter is specified within the PermitsClassification-Branch element, then let CL be the set of all Classification instances that have x as the target object; otherwise, let CL be the set of Classification instances that satisfy the ClassificationFilter and have x as the target object. If CL is empty, then remove x from CN. If no RegistryEntryQuery is specified within the PermitsClassificationBranch element, then let RES be the set of all RegistryEntry instances that are the source object of some classification instance in CL; otherwise, let RE be the result set of the RegistryEntryQuery as defined in Section 8.2.2 and let RES be the set of all instances in RE that are the source object of some classification in CL. If RES is empty, then remove x from CN.

   c.) If a HasParentNode element is not specified, or if CN is empty, then continue below; otherwise, let x be a remaining classification node in CN and execute the following paragraph with n=x.

   Let n be a classification node instance. If n does not have a parent node (i.e. if n is a root node), then remove x from CN. Let p be the parent node of n. If a ClassificationNodeFilter element is directly contained in HasParentNode and if p does not satisfy the ClassificationNodeFilter, then remove x from CN.

   If another HasParentNode element is directly contained within this HasParentNode element, then repeat the previous paragraph with n=p.

d.) If a HasSubnode element is not specified, or if CN is empty, then continue below; otherwise, let x be a remaining classification node in CN. If x is not the parent node of some ClassificationNode instance, then remove x from CN; otherwise, treat each HasSubnode element separately and execute the following paragraph with n = x.

Let n be a classification node instance. If a ClassificationNodeFilter is not specified within the HasSubnode element then let CNC be the set of all classification nodes that have n as their parent node; otherwise, let CNC be the set of all classification nodes that satisfy the ClassificationNodeFilter and have n as their parent node. If CNC is empty then remove x from CN; otherwise, let y be an element of CNC and continue with the next paragraph.

If the HasSubnode element is terminal, i.e. if it does not directly contain another HasSubnode element, then continue below; otherwise, repeat the previous paragraph with the new HasSubnode element and with n = y.

2. If CN is empty, then raise the warning: *classification node query result is empty.*

3. Return CN as the result of the ClassificationNodeQuery.

8.2.4.5   Examples

A client application wishes to identify all classification nodes defined in the Registry that are root nodes and have a name that contains the phrase "product code" or the phrase "product type".

Note

> **By convention, if a classification node has no parent (i.e. is a root node), then the parent attribute of that instance is set to null and is represented as a literal by a zero length string.**

```
<ClassificationNodeQuery>
   <ClassificationNodeFilter>
      (name CONTAINS "product code" OR      -- code by Clause, Section 8.2.10
       name CONTAINS "product type") AND
       parent EQUAL ""
   </ClassificationNodeFilter>
</ClassificationNodeQuery>
```

A client application wishes to identify all of the classification nodes at the third level of a classification scheme hierarchy. The client knows that the URN identifier for the root node is "urn:ebxml:cs:myroot". The following query identifies all nodes at the second level under "myroot" (i.e. third level overall).

```
<ClassificationNodeQuery>
   <HasParentNode>
      <HasParentNode>
         <ClassificationNodeFilter>
             id EQ "urn:ebxml:cs:myroot"      -- code by Clause, Section 8.2.10
         </ClassificationNodeFilter>
      </HasParentNode>
   </HasParentNode>
</ClassificationNodeQuery>
```

8.2.5   RegistryPackageQuery

8.2.5.1   Purpose

To identify a set of registry package instances as the result of a query over selected registry metadata.

8.2.5.2   ebRIM Binding

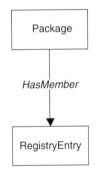

8.2.5.3   Definition

```
<!ELEMENT RegistryPackageQuery
   (   PackageFilter?,
       HasMemberBranch*     )>
<!ELEMENT HasMemberBranch
   (   RegistryEntryQuery?  )>
```

8.2.5.4   Semantic Rules

1. Let RP denote the set of all persistent Package instances in the Registry. The following steps will eliminate instances in RP that do not satisfy the conditions of the specified filters.

   a.) If a PackageFilter is not specified, or if RP is empty, then continue below; otherwise, let x be a package instance in RP. If x does not satisfy the PackageFilter as defined in Section 8.2.9, then remove x from RP.

b.) If a HasMemberBranch element is not directly contained in the RegistryPackageQuery, or if RP is empty, then continue below; otherwise, let x be a remaining package instance in RP. If x is an empty package, then remove x from RP; otherwise, treat each HasMemberBranch element separately as follows:

If a RegistryEntryQuery element is not directly contained in the HasMemberBranch element, then let PM be the set of all RegistryEntry instances that are members of the package x; otherwise, let RE be the set of RegistryEntry instances returned by the RegistryEntryQuery as defined in Section 8.2.2 and let PM be the subset of RE that are members of the package x. If PM is empty, then remove x from RP.

2. If RP is empty, then raise the warning: *registry package query result is empty.*

3. Return RP as the result of the RegistryPackageQuery.

8.2.5.5 Examples

A client application wishes to identify all package instances in the Registry that contain an Invoice extrinsic object as a member of the package.

```
<RegistryPackageQuery>
   <HasMemberBranch>
      <RegistryEntryQuery>
         <RegistryEntryFilter>
            objectType EQ "Invoice"          -- code by Clause, Section 8.2.10
         </RegistryEntryFilter>
      </RegistryEntryQuery>
   </HasMemberBranch>
</RegistryPackageQuery>
```

A client application wishes to identify all package instances in the Registry that are not empty.

```
<RegistryEntryQuery>
   <HasMemberBranch/>
</RegistryEntryQuery>
```

A client application wishes to identify all package instances in the Registry that are empty. Since the RegistryPackageQuery is not set up to do negations, clients will have to do two separate RegistryPackageQuery requests, one to find all packages and another to find all non-empty packages, and then do the set difference themselves. Alternatively, they could do a more complex RegistryEntryQuery and check that the packaging association between the package and its members is non-existent.

A registry package is an intrinsic RegistryEntry instance that is completely determined by its associations with its members. Thus a RegistryPackageQuery can always be re-specified as an equivalent RegistryEntryQuery using appropriate "Source" and "Target" associations. However, the equivalent RegistryEntryQuery is often more complicated to write.

Note

8.2.6 *OrganizationQuery*

8.2.6.1 Purpose

To identify a set of organization instances as the result of a query over selected registry metadata.

8.2.6.2 ebRIM Binding

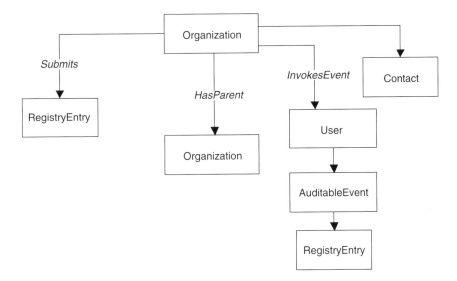

8.2.6.3 Definition

```
<!ELEMENT OrganizationQuery
  (   OrganizationFilter?,
      SubmitsRegistryEntry*,
      HasParentOrganization?,
      InvokesEventBranch*,
      ContactFilter          )>
<!ELEMENT SubmitsRegistryEntry ( RegistryEntryQuery? )>
<!ELEMENT HasParentOrganization
  (   OrganizationFilter?,
      HasParentOrganization?   )>
<!ELEMENT InvokesEventBranch
```

```
(   UserFilter?,
    AuditableEventFilter?,
    RegistryEntryQuery?  )>
```

8.2.6.4 Semantic Rules

1. Let ORG denote the set of all persistent Organization instances in the Registry. The following steps will eliminate instances in ORG that do not satisfy the conditions of the specified filters.

   a.) If an OrganizationFilter element is not directly contained in the OrganizationQuery element, or if ORG is empty, then continue below; otherwise, let x be an organization instance in ORG. If x does not satisfy the OrganizationFilter as defined in Section 8.2.9, then remove x from RP.

   b.) If a SubmitsRegistryEntry element is not specified within the OrganizationQuery, or if ORG is empty, then continue below; otherwise, consider each SubmitsRegistryEntry element separately as follows:

   If no RegistryEntryQuery is specified within the SubmitsRegistryEntry element, then let RES be the set of all RegistryEntry instances that have been submitted to the Registry by organization x; otherwise, let RE be the result of the RegistryEntryQuery as defined in Section 8.2.2 and let RES be the set of all instances in RE that have been submitted to the Registry by organization x. If RES is empty, then remove x from ORG.

   c.) If a HasParentOrganization element is not specified within the OrganizationQuery, or if ORG is empty, then continue below; otherwise, execute the following paragraph with o = x:

   Let o be an organization instance. If an OrganizationFilter is not specified within the HasParentOrganization and if o has no parent (i.e. if o is a root organization in the Organization hierarchy), then remove x from ORG; otherwise, let p be the parent organization of o. If p does not satisfy the OrganizationFilter, then remove x from ORG.

   If another HasParentOrganization element is directly contained within this HasParentOrganization element, then repeat the previous paragraph with o = p.

   d.) If an InvokesEventBranch element is not specified within the OrganizationQuery, or if ORG is empty, then continue below; otherwise, consider each InvokesEventBranch element separately as follows:

   If an UserFilter is not specified, and if x is not the submitting organization of some AuditableEvent instance, then remove x from ORG. If an AuditableEventFilter is not specified, then let AE be the set of all AuditableEvent instances that have x as the submitting organization;

otherwise, let AE be the set of AuditableEvent instances that satisfy the AuditableEventFilter and have x as the submitting organization. If AE is empty, then remove x from ORG. If a RegistryEntryQuery is not specified in the InvokesEventBranch element, then let RES be the set of all RegistryEntry instances associated with an event in AE; otherwise, let RE be the result set of the RegistryEntryQuery, as specified in Section 8.2.2, and let RES be the subset of RE of entries submitted by x. If RES is empty, then remove x from ORG.

e.) If a ContactFilter is not specified within the OrganizationQuery, or if ORG is empty, then continue below; otherwise, consider each Contact-Filter separately as follows:

Let CT be the set of Contact instances that satisfy the ContactFilter and are the contacts for organization x. If CT is empty, then remove x from ORG.

2. If ORG is empty, then raise the warning: *organization query result is empty*.

3. Return ORG as the result of the OrganizationQuery.

8.2.6.5 Examples

A client application wishes to identify a set of organizations, based in France, that have submitted a PartyProfile extrinsic object this year.

```
<OrganizationQuery>
   <OrganizationFilter>
      country EQUAL "France"              -- code by Clause, Section 8.2.10
   </OrganizationFilter>
   <SubmitsRegistryEntry>
      <RegistryEntryQuery>
         <RegistryEntryFilter>
            objectType EQUAL "CPP"        -- code by Clause, Section 8.2.10
         </RegistryEntryFilter>
         <HasAuditableEventBranch>
            <AuditableEventFilter>
               timestamp GE "2001-01-01"  -- code by Clause, Section 8.2.10
            </AuditablcEvcntFilter>
         </HasAuditableEventBranch>
      </RegistryEntryQuery>
   </SubmitsRegistryEntry>
</OrganizationQuery>
```

A client application wishes to identify all organizations that have XYZ, Corporation as a parent. The client knows that the URN for XYZ, Corp. is urn:ebxml: org:xyz, but there is no guarantee that subsidiaries of XYZ have a URN that uses the same format, so a full query is required.

```
<OrganizationQuery>
  <HasParentOrganization>
    <OrganizationFilter>
        id EQUAL "urn:ebxml:org:xyz"          -- code by Clause, Section 8.2.10
    </OrganizationFilter>
  </HasParentOrganization>
</OrganizationQuery>
```

8.2.7 ReturnRegistryEntry

8.2.7.1 Purpose

To construct an XML document that contains selected registry metadata associated with the registry entries identified by a RegistryEntryQuery

Note   Initially, the RegistryEntryQuery could be the URN identifier for a single registry entry.

8.2.7.2 Definition

```
<!ELEMENT ReturnRegistryEntry
   (   RegistryEntryQuery,
       WithClassifications?,
       WithSourceAssociations?,
       WithTargetAssociations?,
       WithAuditableEvents?,
       WithExternalLinks?                   )>
<!ELEMENT WithClassifications ( ClassificationFilter? )>
<!ELEMENT WithSourceAssociations ( AssociationFilter? )>
<!ELEMENT WithTargetAssociations ( AssociationFilter? )>
<!ELEMENT WithAuditableEvents ( AuditableEventFilter? )>
<!ELEMENT WithExternalLinks ( ExternalLinkFilter? )>
<!ELEMENT ReturnRegistryEntryResult
   (   RegistryEntryMetadata*)>
<!ELEMENT RegistryEntryMetadata
    ( RegistryEntry,
      Classification*,
      SourceAssociations?,
      TargetAssociations?,
      AuditableEvent*,
      ExternalLink*                         )>
<!ELEMENT SourceAssociations ( Association* )>
<!ELEMENT TargetAssociations ( Association* )>
```

8.2.7.3 Semantic Rules

1. The RegistryEntry, Classification, Association, AuditableEvent, and ExternalLink elements contained in the ReturnRegistryEntryResult are defined by the ebXML Registry DTD specified in Appendix A.

2. Execute the RegistryEntryQuery according to the Semantic Rules specified in Section 8.2.2, and let R be the result set of identifiers for registry entry instances. Let S be the set of warnings and errors returned. If any element in S is an error condition, then stop execution and return the same set of warnings and errors along with the ReturnRegistryEntryResult.

3. If the set R is empty, then do not return a RegistryEntryMetadata subelement in the ReturnRegistryEntryResult. Instead, raise the warning: *no resulting registry entry*. Add this warning to the error list returned by the RegistryEntryQuery and return this enhanced error list with the ReturnRegistryEntryResult.

4. For each registry entry E referenced by an element of R, use the attributes of E to create a new RegistryEntry element as defined in Appendix A. Then create a new RegistryEntryMetadata element as defined above to be the parent element of that RegistryEntry element.

5. If no With option is specified, then the resulting RegistryEntryMetadata element has no Classification, SourceAssociations, TargetAssociations, AuditableEvent, or ExternalData subelements. The set of RegistryEntryMetadata elements, with the Error list from the RegistryEntryQuery, is returned as the ReturnRegistryEntryResult.

6. If WithClassifications is specified, then for each E in R do the following: If a ClassificationFilter is not present, then let C be any classification instance linked to E; otherwise, let C be a classification instance linked to E that satisfies the ClassificationFilter (Section 8.2.9). For each such C, create a new Classification element as defined in Appendix A. Add these Classification elements to their parent RegistryEntryMetadata element.

7. If WithSourceAssociations is specified, then for each E in R do the following: If an AssociationFilter is not present, then let A be any association instance whose source object is E; otherwise, let A be an association instance that satisfies the AssociationFilter (Section 8.2.9) and whose source object is E. For each such A, create a new Association element as defined in Appendix A. Add these Association elements as subelements of the WithSourceAssociations and add that element to its parent RegistryEntryMetadata element.

8. If WithTargetAssociations is specified, then for each E in R do the following: If an AssociationFilter is not present, then let A be any association instance whose target object is E; otherwise, let A be an association instance that satisfies the AssociationFilter (Section 8.2.9) and whose target object is E. For each such A, create a new Association element as defined in Appendix A. Add these Association elements as subelements of the WithTargetAssociations and add that element to its parent RegistryEntryMetadata element.

9. If WithAuditableEvents is specified, then for each E in R do the following: If an AuditableEventFilter is not present, then let A be any auditable event instance linked to E; otherwise, let A be any auditable event instance linked to E that satisfies the AuditableEventFilter (Section 8.2.9). For each such A, create a new AuditableEvent element as defined in Appendix A. Add these AuditableEvent elements to their parent RegistryEntryMetadata element.

10. If WithExternalLinks is specified, then for each E in R do the following: If an ExternalLinkFilter is not present, then let L be any external link instance linked to E; otherwise, let L be any external link instance linked to E that satisfies the ExternalLinkFilter (Section 8.2.9). For each such D, create a new ExternalLink element as defined in Appendix A. Add these ExternalLink elements to their parent RegistryEntryMetadata element.

11. If any warning or error condition results, then add the code and the message to the RegistryResponse element that includes the RegistryEntryQueryResult.

12. Return the set of RegistryEntryMetadata elements as the content of the ReturnRegistryEntryResult.

8.2.7.4   Examples

A customer of XYZ Corporation has been using a PurchaseOrder DTD registered by XYZ some time ago. Its URN identifier is "urn:com:xyz:po:325". The customer wishes to check on the current status of that DTD, especially if it has been superceded or replaced, and get all of its current classifications. The following query request will return an XML document with the registry entry for the existing DTD as the root, with all of its classifications, and with associations to registry entries for any items that have superceded or replaced it.

```
<ReturnRegistryEntry>
   <RegistryEntryQuery>
      <RegistryEntryFilter>
         id EQUAL "urn:com:xyz:po:325"      -- code by Clause, Section 8.2.10
      </RegistryEntryFilter>
   </RegistryEntryQuery>
   <WithClassifications/>
   <WithSourceAssociations>
      <AssociationFilter>                   -- code by Clause, Section 8.2.10
         associationType EQUAL "SupercededBy" OR
         associationType EQUAL "ReplacedBy"
      </AssociationFilter>
   </WithSourceAssociations>
</ReturnRegistryEntry>
```

A client of the Registry registered an XML DTD several years ago and is now thinking of replacing it with a revised version. The identifier for the existing DTD is "urn:xyz:dtd:po97". The proposed revision is not completely upward compatible with the existing DTD. The client desires a list of all registered items that use the existing DTD so they can assess the impact of an incompatible change. The following query returns an XML document that is a list of all RegistryEntry elements that represent registered items that use, contain, or extend the given DTD. The document also links each RegistryEntry element in the list to an element for the identified association.

```
<ReturnRegistryEntry>
   <RegistryEntryQuery>
      <SourceAssociationBranch>
         <AssociationFilter>                    -- code by Clause, Section 8.2.10
            associationType EQUAL "Contains" OR
            associationType EQUAL "Uses" OR
            associationType EQUAL "Extends"
         </AssociationFilter>
         <RegistryEntryFilter>                  -- code by Clause, Section 8.2.10
            id EQUAL "urn:xyz:dtd:po97"
         </RegistryEntryFilter>
      </SourceAssociationBranch>
   </RegistryEntryQuery>
   <WithSourceAssociations>
      <AssociationFilter>                       -- code by Clause, Section 8.2.10
         associationType EQUAL "Contains" OR
         associationType EQUAL "Uses" OR
         associationType EQUAL "Extends"
      </AssociationFilter>
   </WithSourceAssociations>
</ReturnRegistryEntry>
```

A user has been browsing the registry and has found a registry entry that describes a package of core-components that should solve the user's problem. The package URN identifier is "urn:com:cc:pkg:ccstuff". Now the user wants to know what's in the package. The following query returns an XML document with a registry entry for each member of the package along with that member's Uses and HasMemberBranch associations.

```
<ReturnRegistryEntry>
   <RegistryEntryQuery>
      <TargetAssociationBranch>
         <AssociationFilter>                    -- code by Clause, Section 8.2.10
            associationType EQUAL "HasMember"
         </AssociationFilter>
```

```
        <RegistryEntryFilter>              -- code by Clause, Section 8.2.10
            id EQUAL " urn:com:cc:pkg:ccstuff "
        </RegistryEntryFilter>
      </TargetAssociationBranch>
    </RegistryEntryQuery>
    <WithSourceAssociations>
      <AssociationFilter>                  -- code by Clause, Section 8.2.10
          associationType EQUAL "HasMember" OR
          associationType EQUAL "Uses"
      </AssociationFilter>
    </WithSourceAssociations>
</ReturnRegistryEntry>
```

8.2.8   *ReturnRepositoryItem*

8.2.8.1   Purpose

To construct an XML document that contains one or more repository items, and
some associated metadata, by submitting a RegistryEntryQuery to the
registry/repository that holds the desired objects.

Note

> Initially, the RegistryEntryQuery could be the URN identifier for a single registry entry.

8.2.8.2   Definition

```
<!ELEMENT ReturnRepositoryItem
(  RegistryEntryQuery,
   RecursiveAssociationOption?,
   WithDescription?            )>
<!ELEMENT RecursiveAssociationOption ( AssociationType+ )>
<!ATTLIST RecursiveAssociationOption
     depthLimit CDATA #IMPLIED        >
<!ELEMENT AssociationType EMPTY >
<!ATTLIST AssociationType
     role CDATA #REQUIRED >
<!ELEMENT WithDescription EMPTY >
<!ELEMENT ReturnRepositoryItemResult
   ( RepositoryItem*)>
<!ELEMENT RepositoryItem
     (    ClassificationScheme
      | RegistryPackage
      | ExtrinsicObject
      | WithdrawnObject
      | ExternalLinkItem        )>
<!ATTLIST RepositoryItem
   identifier      CDATA  #REQUIRED
```

```
   name            CDATA   #REQUIRED
   contentURI      CDATA   #REQUIRED
   objectType      CDATA   #REQUIRED
   status          CDATA   #REQUIRED
   stability       CDATA   #REQUIRED
   description     CDATA   #IMPLIED >
<!ELEMENT ExtrinsicObject (#PCDATA) >
<!ATTLIST ExtrinsicObject
   byteEncoding CDATA "Base64" >
<!ELEMENT WithdrawnObject EMPTY >
<!ELEMENT ExternalLinkItem EMPTY >
```

8.2.8.3 Semantic Rules

1. If the RecursiveOption element is not present , then set Limit=0. If the Re-
    cursiveOption element is present, interpret its depthLimit attribute as an in-
    teger literal. If the depthLimit attribute is not present, then set Limit = -1. A
    Limit of 0 means that no recursion occurs. A Limit of -1 means that recur-
    sion occurs indefinitely. If a depthLimit value is present, but it cannot be in-
    terpreted as a positive integer, then stop execution and raise the exception:
    invalid depth limit; otherwise, set Limit=N, where N is that positive integer.
    A Limit of N means that exactly N recursive steps will be executed unless
    the process terminates prior to that limit.

2. Set Depth=0. Let Result denote the set of RepositoryItem elements to be re-
    turned as part of the ReturnRepositoryItemResult. Initially Result is empty.
    Semantic rules 4 through 10 determine the content of Result.

3. If the WithDescription element is present, then set WSD="yes"; otherwise,
    set WSD="no".

4. Execute the RegistryEntryQuery according to the Semantic Rules specified
    in Section 8.2.2, and let R be the result set of identifiers for registry entry in-
    stances. Let S be the set of warnings and errors returned. If any element in S
    is an error condition, then stop execution and return the same set of warn-
    ings and errors along with the ReturnRepositoryItemResult.

5. Execute Semantic Rules 6 and 7 with X as a set of registry references derived
    from R. After execution of these rules, if Depth is now equal to Limit, then re-
    turn the content of Result as the set of RepositoryItem elements in the Return-
    RepositoryItemResult element; otherwise, continue with Semantic Rule 8.

6. Let X be a set of RegistryEntry instances. For each registry entry E in X, do
    the following:

    a.) If E.contentURI references a repository item in this registry/repository,
        then create a new RepositoryItem element, with values for its attributes
        derived as specified in Semantic Rule 7.

    i) If E.objectType="ClassificationScheme", then put the referenced ClassificationScheme DTD as the subelement of this RepositoryItem. [NOTE: Requires DTD specification!]

    ii) If E.objectType="RegistryPackage", then put the referenced RegistryPackage DTD as the subelement of this RepositoryItem. [NOTE: Requires DTD specification!]

    iii) Otherwise, i.e., if the object referenced by E has an unknown internal structure, then put the content of the repository item as the #PCDATA of a new ExtrinsicObject subelement of this RepositoryItem.

b.) If E.objectURL references a registered object in some other registry/repository, then create a new RepositoryItem element, with values for its attributes derived as specified in Semantic Rule 7, and create a new ExternalLink element as the subelement of this RepositoryItem.

c.) If E.objectURL is void, i.e. the object it would have referenced has been withdrawn, then create a new RepositoryItem element, with values for its attributes derived as specified in Semantic Rule 7, and create a new WithdrawnObject element as the subelement of this RepositoryItem.

7. Let E be a registry entry and let RO be the RepositoryItem element created in Semantic Rule 6. Set the attributes of RO to the values derived from the corresponding attributes of E. If WSD="yes", include the value of the description attribute; otherwise, do not include it. Insert this new RepositoryItem element into the Result set.

8. Let R be defined as in Semantic Rule 3. Execute Semantic Rule 9 with Y as the set of RegistryEntry instances referenced by R. Then continue with Semantic rule 10.

9. Let Y be a set of references to RegistryEntry instances. Let NextLevel be an empty set of RegistryEntry instances. For each registry entry E in Y, and for each AssociationType A of the RecursiveAssociationOption, do the following:

a.) Let Z be the set of target items E' linked to E under association instances having E as the source object, E' as the target object, and A as the AssociationType.

b.) Add the elements of Z to NextLevel.

10. Let X be the set of new registry entries that are in NextLevel but are not yet represented in the Result set.

Case:

a.) If X is empty, then return the content of Result as the set of RepositoryItem elements in the ReturnRepositoryItemResult element.

b.) If X is not empty, then execute Semantic Rules 6 and 7 with X as the input set. When finished, add the elements of X to Y and set Depth= Depth+1. If Depth is now equal to Limit, then return the content of Result as the set of RepositoryItem elements in the ReturnRepositoryItem-Result element; otherwise, repeat Semantic Rules 9 and 10 with the new set Y of registry entries.

11. If any exception, warning, or other status condition results during the execution of the above, then return appropriate RegistryError elements in the RegistryResult associated with the ReturnRepositoryItemResult element created in Semantic Rule 5 or Semantic Rule 10.

8.2.8.4 Examples

A registry client has found a registry entry for a core-component item. The item's URN identity is "urn:ebxml:cc:goodthing". But "goodthing" is a composite item that uses many other registered items. The client desires the collection of all items needed for a complete implementation of "goodthing". The following query returns an XML document that is a collection of all needed items.

```
<ReturnRepositoryItem>
   <RegistryEntryQuery>
      <RegistryEntryFilter>                  -- code by Clause, Section 8.2.10
         id EQUAL "urn:ebxml:cc:goodthing"
      </RegistryEntryFilter>
   </RegistryEntryQuery>
   <RecursiveAssociationOption>
      <AssociationType role="Uses" />
      <AssociationType role="ValidatesTo" />
   </RecursiveAssociationOption>
</ReturnRepositoryItem>
```

A registry client has found a reference to a core-component routine ("urn: ebxml:cc:rtn:nice87") that implements a given business process. The client knows that all routines have a required association to its defining UML specification. The following query returns both the routine and its UML specification as a collection of two items in a single XML document.

```
<ReturnRepositoryItem>
   <RegistryEntryQuery>
      <RegistryEntryFilter>                  -- code by Clause, Section 8.2.10
         id EQUAL "urn:ebxml:cc:rtn:nice87"
      </RegistryEntryFilter>
   </RegistryEntryQuery>
   <RecursiveAssociationOption depthLimit="1" >
      <AssociationType role="ValidatesTo" />
```

```
    </RecursiveAssociationOption>
</ReturnRepositoryItem>
```

A user has been told that the 1997 version of the North American Industry Classification System (NAICS) is stored in a registry with URN identifier "urn:nist:cs:naics-1997". The following query would retrieve the complete classification scheme, with all 1810 nodes, as an XML document that validates to a classification scheme DTD.

```
<ReturnRepositoryItem>
  <RegistryEntryQuery>
    <RegistryEntryFilter>                -- code by Clause, Section 8.2.10
        id EQUAL "urn:nist:cs:naics-1997"
    </RegistryEntryFilter>
  </RegistryEntryQuery>
</ReturnRepositoryItem>
```

Note

The ReturnRepositoryItemResult would include a single RepositoryItem that consists of a ClassificationScheme document whose content is determined by the URL ftp://xsun.sdct.itl.nist.gov/regrep/scheme/naics.txt.

8.2.9 *Registry Filters*

8.2.9.1 Purpose

To identify a subset of the set of all persistent instances of a given registry class.

8.2.9.2 Definition

```
<!ELEMENT ObjectFilter ( Clause )>
<!ELEMENT RegistryEntryFilter ( Clause )>
<!ELEMENT IntrinsicObjectFilter ( Clause )>
<!ELEMENT ExtrinsicObjectFilter ( Clause )>
<!ELEMENT PackageFilter ( Clause )>
<!ELEMENT OrganizationFilter ( Clause )>
<!ELEMENT ContactFilter ( Clause )>
<!ELEMENT ClassificationNodeFilter ( Clause )>
<!ELEMENT AssociationFilter ( Clause )>
<!ELEMENT ClassificationFilter ( Clause )>
<!ELEMENT ExternalLinkFilter ( Clause )>
<!ELEMENT ExternalIdentifierFilter ( Clause )>
<!ELEMENT SlotFilter ( Clause )>
<!ELEMENT AuditableEventFilter ( Clause )>
<!ELEMENT UserFilter ( Clause )>
```

8.2.9.3 Semantic Rules

1. The Clause element is defined in Section 8.2.10, Clause.

2. For every ObjectFilter XML element, the leftArgument attribute of any containing SimpleClause shall identify a public attribute of the RegistryObject UML class defined in [ebRIM]. If not, raise exception: *object attribute error*. The ObjectFilter returns a set of identifiers for RegistryObject instances whose attribute values evaluate to *True* for the Clause predicate.

3. For every RegistryEntryFilter XML element, the leftArgument attribute of any containing SimpleClause shall identify a public attribute of the RegistryEntry UML class defined in [ebRIM].

   If not, raise exception: *registry entry attribute error*. The RegistryEntryFilter returns a set of identifiers for RegistryEntry instances whose attribute values evaluate to *True* for the Clause predicate.

4. For every IntrinsicObjectFilter XML element, the leftArgument attribute of any containing SimpleClause shall identify a public attribute of the IntrinsicObject UML class defined in [ebRIM]. If not, raise exception: *intrinsic object attribute error*. The IntrinsicObjectFilter returns a set of identifiers for IntrinsicObject instances whose attribute values evaluate to *True* for the Clause predicate.

5. For every ExtrinsicObjectFilter XML element, the leftArgument attribute of any containing SimpleClause shall identify a public attribute of the ExtrinsicObject UML class defined in [ebRIM]. If not, raise exception: *extrinsic object attribute error*. The ExtrinsicObjectFilter returns a set of identifiers for ExtrinsicObject instances whose attribute values evaluate to *True* for the Clause predicate.

6. For every PackageFilter XML element, the leftArgument attribute of any containing SimpleClause shall identify a public attribute of the Package UML class defined in [ebRIM]. If not, raise exception: *package attribute error*. The PackageFilter returns a set of identifiers for Package instances whose attribute values evaluate to *True* for the Clause predicate.

7. For every OrganizationFilter XML element, the leftArgument attribute of any containing SimpleClause shall identify a public attribute of the Organization or PostalAddress UML classes defined in [ebRIM]. If not, raise exception: *organization attribute error*. The OrganizationFilter returns a set of identifiers for Organization instances whose attribute values evaluate to *True* for the Clause predicate.

8. For every ContactFilter XML element, the leftArgument attribute of any containing SimpleClause shall identify a public attribute of the Contact or PostalAddress UML class defined in [ebRIM]. If not, raise exception: *contact attribute error*. The ContactFilter returns a set of identifiers for Contact instances whose attribute values evaluate to *True* for the Clause predicate.

9. For every ClassificationNodeFilter XML element, the leftArgument attribute of any containing SimpleClause shall identify a public attribute of the ClassificationNode UML class defined in [ebRIM]. If not, raise exception: *classification node attribute error*. The ClassificationNodeFilter returns a set of identifiers for ClassificationNode instances whose attribute values evaluate to *True* for the Clause predicate.

10. For every AssociationFilter XML element, the leftArgument attribute of any containing SimpleClause shall identify a public attribute of the Association UML class defined in [ebRIM]. If not, raise exception: *association attribute error*. The AssociationFilter returns a set of identifiers for Association instances whose attribute values evaluate to *True* for the Clause predicate.

11. For every ClassificationFilter XML element, the leftArgument attribute of any containing SimpleClause shall identify a public attribute of the Classification UML class defined in [ebRIM]. If not, raise exception: *classification attribute error*. The ClassificationFilter returns a set of identifiers for Classification instances whose attribute values evaluate to *True* for the Clause predicate.

12. For every ExternalLinkFilter XML element, the leftArgument attribute of any containing SimpleClause shall identify a public attribute of the ExternalLink UML class defined in [ebRIM]. If not, raise exception: *external link attribute error*. The ExternalLinkFilter returns a set of identifiers for ExternalLink instances whose attribute values evaluate to *True* for the Clause predicate.

13. For every ExternalIdentiferFilter XML element, the leftArgument attribute of any containing SimpleClause shall identify a public attribute of the ExternalIdentifier UML class defined in [ebRIM]. If not, raise exception: *external identifier attribute error*. The ExternalIdentifierFilter returns a set of identifiers for ExternalIdentifier instances whose attribute values evaluate to *True* for the Clause predicate.

14. For every SlotFilter XML element, the leftArgument attribute of any containing SimpleClause shall identify a public attribute of the Slot UML class defined in [ebRIM]. If not, raise exception: *slot attribute error*. The SlotFilter returns a set of identifiers for Slot instances whose attribute values evaluate to *True* for the Clause predicate.

15. For every AuditableEventFilter XML element, the leftArgument attribute of any containing SimpleClause shall identify a public attribute of the AuditableEvent UML class defined in [ebRIM]. If not, raise exception: *auditable event attribute error*. The AuditableEventFilter returns a set of

identifiers for AuditableEvent instances whose attribute values evaluate to *True* for the Clause predicate.

16. For every UserFilter XML element, the leftArgument attribute of any containing SimpleClause shall identify a public attribute of the User UML class defined in [ebRIM]. If not, raise exception: *auditable identity attribute error*. The UserFilter returns a set of identifiers for User instances whose attribute values evaluate to *True* for the Clause predicate.

8.2.9.4 Example

The following is a complete example of RegistryEntryQuery combined with Clause expansion of RegistryEntryFilter to return a set of RegistryEntry instances whose objectType attribute is "CPP" and whose status attribute is "Approved".

```
<RegistryEntryQuery>
    <RegistryEntryFilter>
        <Clause>
            <CompoundClause    connectivePredicate="And" >
                <Clause>
                    <SimpleClause leftArgument="objectType" >
            <StringClause stringPredicate="equal" >CPP</StringClause>
                    </SimpleClause>
                </Clause>
                <Clause>
                    <SimpleClause leftArgument="status" >
            <StringClause  stringPredicate="equal" >Approved</String-
Clause>
                    </SimpleClause>
                </Clause>
            </CompoundClause>
        </Clause>
    </RegistryEntryFilter>
</RegistryEntryQuery>
```

8.2.10 XML Clause Constraint Representation

8.2.10.1 Purpose

The simple XML FilterQuery utilizes a formal XML structure based on *Predicate Clauses*. Predicate Clauses are utilized to formally define the constraint mechanism, and are referred to simply as **Clauses** in this specification.

8.2.10.2 Conceptual UML Diagram

The following is a conceptual diagram outlining the Clause base structure. It is expressed in UML for visual depiction.

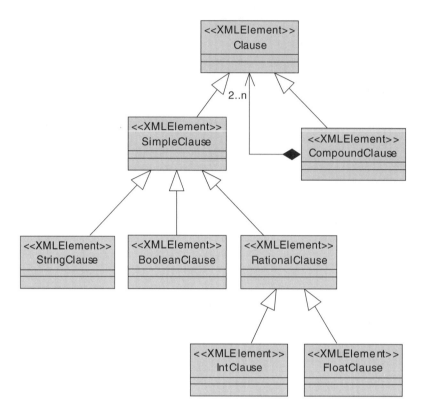

FIGURE 20   The Clause Base Structure

8.2.10.3 Semantic Rules

Predicates and *Arguments* are combined into a "LeftArgument - Predicate - RightArgument" format to form a *Clause*. There are two types of Clauses: *SimpleClauses* and *CompoundClauses*.

SimpleClauses

A SimpleClause always defines the leftArgument as a text string, sometimes referred to as the *Subject* of the Clause. SimpleClause itself is incomplete (abstract) and must be extended. SimpleClause is extended to support BooleanClause, StringClause, and RationalClause (abstract).

BooleanClause implicitly defines the predicate as 'equal to', with the right argument as a boolean. StringClause defines the predicate as an enumerated attribute of appropriate string-compare operations and a right argument as the element's text data. Rational number support is provided through a common RationalClause providing an enumeration of appropriate rational number compare operations, which is further extended to IntClause and FloatClause, each with appropriate signatures for the right argument.

CompoundClauses

A CompoundClause contains two or more Clauses (Simple or Compound) and a connective predicate. This provides for arbitrarily complex Clauses to be formed.

8.2.10.4 Definition

```
<!ELEMENT Clause ( SimpleClause | CompoundClause )>
<!ELEMENT SimpleClause
   ( BooleanClause | RationalClause | StringClause )>
<!ATTLIST SimpleClause
   leftArgument CDATA #REQUIRED >
<!ELEMENT CompoundClause ( Clause, Clause+ )>
<!ATTLIST CompoundClause
   connectivePredicate ( And | Or ) #REQUIRED>
<!ELEMENT BooleanClause EMPTY >
<!ATTLIST BooleanClause
   booleanPredicate ( True | False ) #REQUIRED>
<!ELEMENT RationalClause ( IntClause | FloatClause )>
<!ATTLIST RationalClause
   logicalPredicate ( LE | LT | GE | GT | EQ | NE ) #REQUIRED >
<!ELEMENT IntClause ( #PCDATA )
<!ATTLIST IntClause
   e-dtype NMTOKEN #FIXED 'int' >
<!ELEMENT FloatClause ( #PCDATA )>
<!ATTLIST FloatClause
   e-dtype NMTOKEN #FIXED 'float' >
<!ELEMENT StringClause ( #PCDATA )>
<!ATTLIST StringClause
   stringPredicate
      ( contains | -contains |
        startswith | -startswith |
        equal | -equal
        endswith | -endswith ) #REQUIRED >
```

8.2.10.5 Examples

Simple BooleanClause: "Smoker" = True

```
<?xml version="1.0" encoding="UTF-8"?>
<!DOCTYPE Clause SYSTEM "Clause.dtd" >
<Clause>
  <SimpleClause leftArgument="Smoker">
    <BooleanClause booleanPredicate="True"/>
  </SimpleClause>
</Clause>
```

Simple StringClause: "Smoker" contains "mo"

```xml
<?xml version="1.0" encoding="UTF-8"?>
<!DOCTYPE Clause SYSTEM "Clause.dtd" >
<Clause>
  <SimpleClause leftArgument="Smoker">
    <StringClause stringcomparepredicate="contains">
      mo
  </StringClause>
 </SimpleClause>
</Clause>
```

Simple IntClause: "Age" >= 7

```xml
<?xml version="1.0" encoding="UTF-8"?>
<!DOCTYPE Clause SYSTEM "Clause.dtd" >
<Clause>
  <SimpleClause leftArgument="Age">
    <RationalClause logicalPredicate="GE">
      <IntClause e-dtype="int">7</IntClause>
    </RationalClause>
  </SimpleClause>
</Clause>
```

Simple FloatClause: "Size" = 4.3

```xml
<?xml version="1.0" encoding="UTF-8"?>
<!DOCTYPE Clause SYSTEM "Clause.dtd" >
<Clause>
  <SimpleClause leftArgument="Size">
    <RationalClause logicalPredicate="E">
      <FloatClause e-dtype="float">4.3</FloatClause>
    </RationalClause>
  </SimpleClause>
</Clause>
```

Compound with two Simples (("Smoker" = False)AND("Age" =< 45))

```xml
<?xml version="1.0" encoding="UTF-8"?>
<!DOCTYPE Clause SYSTEM "Clause.dtd" >
<Clause>
  <CompoundClause connectivePredicate="And">
    <Clause>
      <SimpleClause leftArgument="Smoker">
        <BooleanClause booleanPredicate="False"/>
      </SimpleClause>
    </Clause>
```

```
      <Clause>
        <SimpleClause leftArgument="Age">
          <RationalClause logicalPredicate="EL">
            <IntClause e-dtype="int">45</IntClause>
          </RationalClause>
        </SimpleClause>
      </Clause>
    </CompoundClause>
</Clause>
```

Coumpound with one Simple and one Compound

(("Smoker" = False)And(("Age" =< 45)Or("American"=True)))

```
<?xml version="1.0" encoding="UTF-8"?>
<!DOCTYPE Clause SYSTEM "Clause.dtd" >
<Clause>
  <CompoundClause connectivePredicate="And">
    <Clause>
      <SimpleClause leftArgument="Smoker">
        <BooleanClause booleanPredicate="False"/>
      </SimpleClause>
    </Clause>
    <Clause>
      <CompoundClause connectivePredicate="Or">
        <Clause>
          <SimpleClause leftArgument="Age">
            <RationalClause logicalPredicate="EL">
              <IntClause e-dtype="int">45</IntClause>
            </RationalClause>
          </SimpleClause>
        </Clause>
          <Clause>
            <SimpleClause leftArgument="American">
              <BooleanClause booleanPredicate="True"/>
            </SimpleClause>
          </Clause>
      </CompoundClause>
    </Clause>
  </CompoundClause>
</Clause>
```

8.3 SQL Query Support

The Registry may optionally support an SQL based query capability that is designed for Registry clients that demand more complex query capability. The optional SQLQuery element in the AdhocQueryRequest allows a client to submit complex SQL queries using a declarative query language.

The syntax for the SQLQuery of the Registry is defined by a stylized use of a proper subset of the "SELECT" statement of Entry level SQL defined by ISO/IEC 9075:1992, Database Language SQL [SQL], extended to include <sql invoked routines> (also known as stored procedures) as specified in ISO/IEC 9075-4 [SQL-PSM] and pre-defined routines defined in template form in Appendix C. The exact syntax of the Registry query language is defined by the BNF grammar in "SQL query syntax specification."

Note

> **The use of a subset of SQL syntax for SQLQuery does not imply a requirement to use relational databases in a Registry implementation.**

8.3.1   SQL Query Syntax Binding To [ebRIM]

SQL Queries are defined based upon the query syntax in in Appendix C and a fixed relational schema defined in "Relational schema for SQL queries." The relational schema is an algorithmic binding to [ebRIM] as described in the following sections.

8.3.1.1   Interface and Class Binding

A subset of the Interface and class names defined in [ebRIM] map to table names that may be queried by an SQL query. Appendix C, "Relational schema for SQL queries," defines the names of the ebRIM interfaces and classes that may be queried by an SQL query.

The algorithm used to define the binding of [ebRIM] classes to table definitions in Appendix C, "Relational schema for SQL queries," is as follows:

▼ Only those classes and interfaces that have concrete instances are mapped to relational tables. This results in intermediate interfaces in the inheritance hierarchy, such as RegistryObject and IntrinsicObject, to not map to SQL tables. An exception to this rule is RegistryEntry, which is defined next.

▼ A special view called RegistryEntry is defined to allow SQL queries to be made against RegistryEntry instances. This is the only interface defined in [ebRIM] that does not have concrete instances but is queryable by SQL queries.

▼ The names of relational tables are the same as the corresponding [ebRIM] class or interface name. However, the name binding is case insensitive.

▼ Each [ebRIM] class or interface that maps to a table in Appendix C includes column definitions in : Relational schema for SQL queries," where the column definitions are based on a subset of attributes defined for that class or interface in [ebRIM]. The attributes that map to columns include the inherited attributes for the [ebRIM] class or interface. Comments indicate which ancestor class or interface contributed which column definitions.

An SQLQuery against a table not defined in Appendix C, "Relational schema for SQL queries," may raise an error condition: InvalidQueryException.

The following sections describe the algorithm for mapping attributes of [ebRIM] to SQLcolumn definitions.

8.3.1.2 Accessor Method to Attribute Binding

Most of the [ebRIM] interfaces methods are simple get methods that map directly to attributes. For example the getName method on RegistryObject maps to a name attribute of type String. Each get method in [ebRIM] defines the exact attribute name that it maps to in the interface definitions in [ebRIM].

8.3.1.3 Primitive Attributes Binding

Attributes defined by [ebRIM] that are of primitive types (e.g. String) may be used in the same way as column names in SQL. Again the exact attribute names are defined in the interface definitions in [ebRIM]. Note that while names are in mixed case, SQL-92 is case insensitive. It is therefore valid for a query to contain attribute names that do not exactly match the case defined in [ebRIM].

8.3.1.4 Reference Attribute Binding

A few of the [ebRIM] interface methods return references to instances of interfaces or classes defined by [ebRIM]. For example, the getAccessControlPolicy method of the RegistryObject class returns a reference to an instance of an AccessControlPolicy object.

In such cases the reference maps to the id attribute for the referenced object. The name of the resulting column is the same as the attribute name in [ebRIM] as defined by 8.3.1.3. The data type for the column is UUID as defined in Appendix C, Relational schema for SQL queries."

When a reference attribute value holds a null reference, it maps to a null value in the SQL binding and may be tested with the <null specification> as defined by [SQL].

Reference attribute binding is a special case of a primitive attribute mapping.

8.3.1.5 Complex Attribute Binding

A few of the [ebRIM] interfaces define attributes that are not primitive types. Instead they are of a complex type as defined by an entity class in [ebRIM]. Examples include attributes of type TelephoneNumber, Contact, PersonName etc. in interface Organization and class Contact.

The SQL query schema algorithmically maps such complex attributes as multiple primitive attributes within the parent table. The mapping simply flattens out the entity class attributes within the parent table. The attribute name for the flattened attributes are composed of a concatenation of attribute names in the refernce chain. For example Organization has a contact attribute of type Contact. Contact has an address attribute of type PostalAddress. PostalAddress has a String attribute named city. This city attribute will be named contact_address_city.

8.3.1.6   Collection Attribute Binding

A few of the [ebRIM] interface methods return a collection of references to instances of interfaces or classes defined by [ebRIM]. For example, the getPackages method of the ManagedObject class returns a Collection of references to instances of Packages that the object is a member of.

Such collection attributes in [ebRIM] classes have been mapped to stored procedures in Appendix C such that these stored procedures return a collection of id attribute values. The returned value of these stored procedures can be treated as the result of a table sub-query in SQL.

These stored procedures may be used as the right-hand-side of an SQL IN clause to test for membership of an object in such collections of references.

8.3.2   *Semantic Constraints on Query Syntax*

This section defines simplifying constraints on the query syntax that cannot be expressed in the BNF for the query syntax. These constraints must be applied in the semantic analysis of the query.

1. Class names and attribute names must be processed in a case insensitive manner.

2. The syntax used for stored procedure invocation must be consistent with the syntax of an SQL procedure invocation as specified by ISO/IEC 9075-4 [SQL/PSM].

3. For this version of the specification, the SQL select column list consists of exactly one column, and must always be t.id, where t is a table reference in the FROM clause.

8.3.3   *SQL Query Results*

The results of an SQL query is always an ObjectRefList as defined by the AdHoc-QueryResponse in 8.4. This means the result of an SQL query is always a collection of references to instances of a sub-class of the RegistryObject interface in [ebRIM]. This is reflected in a semantic constraint that requires that the SQL select column specified must always be an id column in a table in Appendix C, "Relational schema for SQL queries," for this version of the specification.

8.3.4 Simple Metadata Based Queries

The simplest form of an SQL query is based upon metadata attributes specified for a single class within [ebRIM]. This section gives some examples of simple metadata based queries.

For example, to get the collection of ExtrinsicObjects whose name contains the word 'Acme' and that have a version greater than 1.3, the following query predicates must be supported:

```
SELECT id FROM ExtrinsicObject WHERE name LIKE '%Acme%' AND
      majorVersion >= 1 AND
      (majorVersion >= 2 OR minorVersion > 3);
```

The query syntax allows for conjugation of simpler predicates into more complex queries as shown in the simple example above.

8.3.5 RegistryEntry Queries

Given the central role played by the RegistryEntry interface in ebRIM, the schema for the SQL query defines a special view called RegistryEntry that allows doing a polymorphic query against all RegistryEntry instances regardless of their actual concrete type or table name.

The following example is the same as Section 8.3.4 except that it is applied against all RegistryEntry instances rather than just ExtrinsicObject instances. The result set will include id for all qualifying RegistryEntry instances whose name contains the word 'Acme' and that have a version greater than 1.3.

```
SELECT id FROM RegistryEntry WHERE name LIKE '%Acme%' AND
      objectType = 'ExtrinsicObject' AND
      majorVersion >= 1 AND
      (majorVersion >= 2 OR minorVersion > 3);
```

8.3.6 Classification Queries

This section describes the various classification related queries that must be supported.

8.3.6.1 Identifying ClassificationNodes

Like all objects in [ebRIM], ClassificationNodes are identified by their ID. However, they may also be identified as a path attribute that specifies an XPATH expression [XPT] from a root classification node to the specified classification node in the XML document that would represent the ClassificationNode tree including the said ClassificationNode.

8.3.6.2   Getting Root ClassificationNodes

To get the collection of root ClassificationNodes the following query predicate must be supported:

```
SELECT cn.id FROM ClassificationNode cn WHERE parent IS NULL
```

The above query returns all ClassificationNodes that have their parent attribute set to null. Note that the above query may also specify a predicate on the name if a specific root ClassificationNode is desired.

8.3.6.3   Getting Children of Specified ClassificationNode

To get the children of a ClassificationNode given the ID of that node the following style of query must be supported:

```
SELECT cn.id FROM ClassificationNode cn WHERE parent = <id>
```

The above query returns all ClassificationNodes that have the node specified by <id> as their parent attribute.

8.3.6.4   Getting Objects Classified by a ClassificationNode

To get the collection of ExtrinsicObjects classified by specified Classification-Nodes the following style of query must be supported:

```
SELECT id FROM ExtrinsicObject
WHERE
    id IN (SELECT classifiedObject FROM Classification
           WHERE
                 classificationNode IN (SELECT id FROM
ClassificationNode
                 WHERE path = '/Geography/Asia/Japan'))
  AND
    id IN (SELECT classifiedObject FROM Classification
           WHERE
                 classificationNode IN (SELECT id FROM
ClassificationNode
                 WHERE path = '/Industry/Automotive'))
```

The above query gets the collection of ExtrinsicObjects that are classified by the Automotive Industry and the Japan Geography. Note that according to the semantics defined for GetClassifiedObjectsRequest, the query will also contain any objects that are classified by descendents of the specified ClassificationNodes.

8.3.6.5   Getting ClassificationNodes that Classify an Object

To get the collection of ClassificationNodes that classify a specified Object the following style of query must be supported:

```
SELECT id FROM ClassificationNode
      WHERE id IN (RegistryEntry_classificationNodes(<id>))
```

8.3.7   Association Queries

This section describes the various Association related queries that must be supported.

8.3.7.1   Getting All Association with Specified Object As Its Source

To get the collection of Associations that have the specified Object as its source, the following query must be supported:

```
SELECT id FROM Association WHERE sourceObject = <id>
```

8.3.7.2   Getting All Association with Specified Object As Its Target

To get the collection of Associations that have the specified Object as its target, the following query must be supported:

```
SELECT id FROM Association WHERE targetObject = <id>
```

8.3.7.3   Getting Associated Objects Based on Association Attributes

To get the collection of Associations that have specified Association attributes, the following queries must be supported:

Select Associations that have the specified name.

```
SELECT id FROM Association WHERE name = <name>
```

Select Associations that have the specified source role name.

```
SELECT id FROM Association WHERE sourceRole = <roleName>
```

Select Associations that have the specified target role name.

```
SELECT id FROM Association WHERE targetRole = <roleName>
```

Select Associations that have the specified association type, where association type is a string containing the corresponding field name described in [ebRIM].

```
SELECT id FROM Association WHERE
      associationType = <associationType>
```

8.3.7.4   Complex Association Queries

The various forms of Association queries may be combined into complex predicates. The following query selects Associations from an object with a specified id, that have the sourceRole "buysFrom" and targetRole "sellsTo":

```
SELECT id FROM Association WHERE
       sourceObject = <id> AND
       sourceRole = 'buysFrom' AND
       targetRole = 'sellsTo'
```

8.3.8 Package Queries

To find all Packages that a specified ExtrinsicObject belongs to, the following query is specified:

```
SELECT id FROM Package WHERE id IN (RegistryEntry_packages(<id>))
```

8.3.8.1   Complex Package Queries

The following query gets all Packages that a specified object belongs to, that are not deprecated and where name contains "RosettaNet."

```
SELECT id FROM Package WHERE
       id IN (RegistryEntry_packages(<id>)) AND
       name LIKE '%RosettaNet%' AND
       status <> 'Deprecated'
```

8.3.9 ExternalLink Queries

To find all ExternalLinks that a specified ExtrinsicObject is linked to, the following query is specified:

```
SELECT id From ExternalLink WHERE id IN (RegistryEntry_
externalLinks(<id>))
```

To find all ExtrinsicObjects that are linked by a specified ExternalLink, the following query is specified:

```
SELECT id From ExtrinsicObject WHERE id IN (RegistryEntry_
linkedObjects(<id>))
```

8.3.9.1   Complex ExternalLink Queries

The following query gets all ExternalLinks that a specified ExtrinsicObject belongs to, that contain the word 'legal' in their description and have a URL for their externalURI.

```
SELECT id FROM ExternalLink WHERE
       id IN (RegistryEntry_externalLinks(<id>)) AND
       description LIKE '%legal%' AND
       externalURI LIKE '%http://%'
```

8.3.10   Audit Trail Queries

To get the complete collection of AuditableEvent objects for a specified Managed-Object, the following query is specified:

```
SELECT id FROM AuditableEvent WHERE registryEntry = <id>
```

8.4   Ad hoc Query Request/Response

A client submits an ad hoc query to the ObjectQueryManager by sending an Ad-hocQueryRequest. The AdhocQueryRequest contains a sub-element that defines a query in one of the supported Registry query mechanisms.

The ObjectQueryManager sends an AdhocQueryResponse either synchronously or asynchronously back to the client. The AdhocQueryResponse returns a collection of objects whose element type is in the set of element types represented by the leaf nodes of the RegistryEntry hierarchy in [ebRIM].

FIGURE 21   Submit Ad Hoc Query Sequence Diagram

For details on the schema for the business documents shown in this process refer to 10.

8.5   Content Retrieval

A client retrieves content via the Registry by sending the GetContentRequest to the ObjectQueryManager. The GetContentRequest specifies a list of Object references for Objects that need to be retrieved. The ObjectQueryManager returns the specified content by sending a GetContentResponse message to the Object-QueryManagerClient interface of the client. If there are no errors encountered, the GetContentResponse message includes the specified content as additional payloads within the message. In addition to the GetContentResponse payload, there is one additional payload for each content that was requested. If there are errors encountered, the RegistryResponse payload includes an error and there are no additional content specific payloads.

8.5.1 Identification of Content Payloads

Since the GetContentResponse message may include several repository items as additional payloads, it is necessary to have a way to identify each payload in the message. To facilitate this identification, the Registry must do the following:

▼ Use the ID for each RegistryEntry instance that describes the repository item as the DocumentLabel element in the DocumentReference for that object in the Manifest element of the ebXMLHeader.

8.5.2 GetContentResponse Message Structure

The following message fragment illustrates the structure of the GetContent-Response Message that is returning a Collection of CPPs as a result of a Get-ContentRequest that specified the IDs for the requested objects. Note that the ID for each object retrieved in the message as additional payloads is used as its DocumentLabel in the Manifest of the ebXMLHeader.

```
...
--PartBoundary
...
<eb:MessageHeader SOAP-ENV:mustUnderstand="1" eb:version="1.0">
...
   <eb:Service eb:type="ebXMLRegistry">ObjectManager</eb:Service>
   <eb:Action>submitObjects</eb:Action>
...
</eb:MessageHeader>
...
<eb:Manifest SOAP-ENV:mustUnderstand="1" eb:version="1.0">
  <eb:Reference xlink:href="cid:registryentries@example.com" ...>
    <eb:Description xml:lang="en-us">XML instances that are para-
meters   for the particular Registry Interface / Method. These are
RIM structures that don't include repository items, just a refer-
ence - contentURI to them.</eb:Description>
  </eb:Reference>
```

```
  <eb:Reference xlink:href="cid:cpp1@example.com" …>
    <eb:Description xml:lang="en-us">XML instance of CPP 1. This
is a repository item.</eb:Description>
  </eb:Reference>
  <eb:Reference xlink:href="cid:cpp2@example.com" …>
    <eb:Description xml:lang="en-us">XML instance of CPP 2. This
is a repository item.</eb:Description>
  </eb:Reference>
</eb:Manifest>
--PartBoundary
Content-ID: registryentries@example.com
Content-Type: text/xml

…
<?xml version="1.0" encoding="UTF-8"?>
<RootElement>
<SubmitObjectsRequest>
  <RegistryEntryList>
    <ExtrinsicObject … contentURI="cid:cpp1@example.com" …/>
    <ExtrinsicObject … contentURI="cid:cpp2@example.com" …/>
  </RegistryEntryList>
</SubmitObjectsRequest>
</RootElement>
--PartBoundary
Content-ID: cpp1@example.com
Content-Type: text/xml

…
<CPP>

…
</CPP>
--PartBoundary
Content-ID: cpp2@example.com
Content-Type: text/xml

…
<CPP>

…
</CPP>
--PartBoundary--
```

8.6   Query and Retrieval: Typical Sequence

The following diagram illustrates the use of both browse/drilldown and ad hoc
queries followed by a retrieval of content that was selected by the queries.

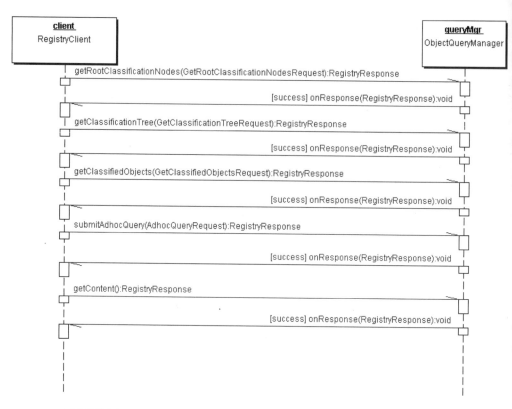

FIGURE 23   Typical Query and Retrieval Sequence

9   Registry Security

This chapter describes the security features of the ebXML Registry. It is assumed that the reader is familiar with the security related classes in the Registry information model as described in [ebRIM].

In the current version of this specification, a minimalist approach has been specified for Registry security. The philosophy is that "Any *known* entity can publish content and *anyone* can view published content." The Registry information model has been designed to allow more sophisticated security policies in future versions of this specification.

9.1   Integrity of Registry Content

It is assumed that most business registries do not have the resources to validate the veracity of the content submitted to them. The minimal integrity that the Registry must provide is to ensure that content submitted by a Submitting Organization (SO) is maintained in the Registry without any tampering either *en-route* or *within* the Registry. Furthermore, the Registry must make it possible to identify the SO for any Registry content unambiguously.

9.1.1   Message Payload Signature

Integrity of Registry content requires that all submitted content must be signed by the Registry client as defined by [SEC]. The signature on the submitted content ensures that:

▼ The content has not been tampered with en-route or within the Registry.

▼ The content's veracity can be ascertained by its association with a specific submitting organization

9.2   Authentication

The Registry must be able to authenticate the identity of the Principal associated with client requests. *Authentication* is required to identify the ownership of content as well as to identify what "privileges" a Principal can be assigned with respect to the specific objects in the Registry.

The Registry must perform Authentication on a per request basis. From a security point of view, all messages are independent and there is no concept of a session encompassing multiple messages or conversations. Session support may be added as an optimization feature in future versions of this specification.

The Registry must implement a credential-based authentication mechanism based on digital certificates and signatures. The Registry uses the certificate DN from the signature to authenticate the user.

9.2.1   Message Header Signature

Message headers may be signed by the sending ebXML Messaging Service as defined by [SEC]. Since this specification is not yet finalized, this version does not require that the message header be signed. In the absence of a message header signature, the payload signature is used to authenticate the identity of the requesting client.

9.3 Confidentiality

9.3.1 On-the-wire Message Confidentiality

It is suggested but not required that message payloads exchanged between clients and the Registry be encrypted during transmission. Payload encryption must abide by any restrictions set forth in [SEC].

9.3.2 Confidentiality of Registry Content

In the current version of this specification, there are no provisions for confidentiality of Registry content. All content submitted to the Registry may be discovered and read by *any* client. Therefore, the Registry must be able to decrypt any submitted content after it has been received and prior to storing it in its repository. This implies that the Registry and the client have an a priori agreement regarding encryption algorithm, key exchange agreements, etc. This service is not addressed in this specification.

9.4 Authorization

The Registry must provide an authorization mechanism based on the information model defined in [ebRIM]. In this version of the specification the authorization mechanism is based on a default Access Control Policy defined for a pre-defined set of roles for Registry users. Future versions of this specification will allow for custom Access Control Policies to be defined by the Submitting Organization.

9.4.1 Pre-defined Roles for Registry Users

The following roles must be pre-defined in the Registry:

Role	Description
ContentOwner	The submitter or owner of a Registry content. Submitting Organization (SO) in ISO 11179
RegistryAdministrator	A "super" user that is an administrator of the Registry. Registration Authority (RA) in ISO 11179
RegistryGuest	Any unauthenticated user of the Registry. Clients that browse the Registry do not need to be authenticated.

9.4.2 Default Access Control Policies

The Registry must create a default AccessControlPolicy object that grants the default permissions to Registry users based upon their assigned role.

The following table defines the Permissions granted by the Registry to the various pre-defined roles for Registry users based upon the default AccessControlPolicy.

Role	Permissions
ContentOwner	Access to *all* methods on Registry Objects that are owned by the ContentOwner.
RegistryAdministrator	Access to *all* methods on *all* Registry Objects
RegistryGuest	Access to *all* read-only (getXXX) methods on *all* Registry Objects (read-only access to all content).

The following list summarizes the default role-based AccessControlPolicy:

▼ The Registry must implement the default AccessControlPolicy and associate it with all Objects in the Registry

▼ Anyone can publish content, but needs to be authenticated

▼ Anyone can access the content without requiring authentication

▼ The ContentOwner has access to all methods for Registry Objects owned by them

▼ The RegistryAdministrator has access to all methods on all Registry Objects

▼ Unauthenticated clients can access all read-only (getXXX) methods

▼ At the time of content submission, the Registry must assign the default ContentOwner role to the Submitting Organization (SO) as authenticated by the credentials in the submission message. In the current version of this specification, it will be the DN as identified by the certificate

▼ Clients that browse the Registry need not use certificates. The Registry must assign the default RegistryGuest role to such clients.

10   References

[Bra97] Keywords for use in RFCs to Indicate Requirement Levels.

[ebGLOSS] ebXML Glossary

http://www.ebxml.org/specs/ebGLOSS.pdf

[TA] ebXML Technical Architecture

http://www.ebxml.org/specs/ebTA.pdf

[OAS] OASIS Information Model

http://www.nist.gov/itl/div897/ctg/regrep/oasis-work.html

[ISO] ISO 11179 Information Model

http://208.226.167.205/SC32/jtc1sc32.nsf/576871ad2f11bba785256621005419d7/
     b83fc7816a6064c68525690e0065f913?OpenDocument

[ebRIM] ebXML Registry Information Model

http://www.ebxml.org/specs/ebRIM.pdf

[ebBPSS] ebXML Business Process Specification Schema

http://www.ebxml.org/specs/ebBPSS.pdf

[ebCPP] ebXML Collaboration-Protocol Profile and Agreement Specification

http://www.ebxml.org/specs/ebCPP.pdf

[rrUDDI] Using UDDI to Find ebXML Reg/Reps

http://www.ebxml.org/specs/rrUDDI.pdf

[CTB] Context table informal document from Core Components

[ebMS] ebXML Messaging Service Specification, Version 0.21

http://www.ebxml.org/specs/ebMS.pdf

[secRISK] ebXML Risk Assessment Technical Report, Version 1.0

http://www.ebxml.org/specs/secRISK.pdf

[XPT] XML Path Language (XPath) Version 1.0

http://www.w3.org/TR/xpath

[SQL] Structured Query Language (FIPS PUB 127-2)

http://www.itl.nist.gov/fipspubs/fip127-2.htm

[SQL/PSM] Database Language SQL — Part 4: Persistent Stored Modules
     (SQL/PSM) [ISO/IEC 9075-4:1996]

[IANA] IANA (Internet Assigned Numbers Authority).

Official Names for Character Sets, ed. Keld Simonsen et al.

ftp://ftp.isi.edu/in-notes/iana/assignments/character-sets

[RFC 1766] IETF (Internet Engineering Task Force). RFC 1766:

Tags for the Identification of Languages, ed. H. Alvestrand. 1995.

http://www.cis.ohio-state.edu/htbin/rfc/rfc1766.html

[RFC 2277] IETF (Internet Engineering Task Force). RFC 2277:

IETF policy on character sets and languages, ed. H. Alvestrand. 1998.

http://www.cis.ohio-state.edu/htbin/rfc/rfc2277.html

[RFC 2278] IETF (Internet Engineering Task Force). RFC 2278:

IANA Charset Registration Procedures, ed. N. Freed and J. Postel. 1998.

http://www.cis.ohio-state.edu/htbin/rfc/rfc2278.html

[RFC 3023] IETF (Internet Engineering Task Force). RFC 3023:

XML Media Types, ed. M. Murata. 2001.

ftp://ftp.isi.edu/in-notes/rfc3023.txt

[REC-XML] W3C Recommendation. Extensible Markup language(XML)1.0
(Second Edition)

http://www.w3.org/TR/REC-xml

[UUID] DCE 128 bit Universal Unique Identifier

http://www.opengroup.org/onlinepubs/009629399/apdxa.htm#tagcjh_20

http://www.opengroup.org/publications/catalog/c706.htmttp://www.w3.org/
TR/REC-xml

11   Disclaimer

The views and specification expressed in this document are those of the authors
and are not necessarily those of their employers. The authors and their employers specifically disclaim responsibility for any problems arising from correct or
incorrect implementation or use of this design.

12   Contact Information

Team Leader
    Name: Scott Nieman
    Company: Norstan Consulting
    Street: 5101 Shady Oak Road

City, State, Postal Code:	Minnetonka, MN 55343
Country:	USA
Phone:	952.352.5889
Email:	Scott.Nieman@Norstan

Vice Team Lead

Name:	Yutaka Yoshida
Company:	Sun Microsystems
Street:	901 San Antonio Road, MS UMPK17-102
City, State, Postal Code:	Palo Alto, CA 94303
Country:	USA
Phone:	650.786.5488
Email:	Yutaka.Yoshida@eng.sun.com

Editor

Name:	Farrukh S. Najmi
Company:	Sun Microsystems
Street:	1 Network Dr., MS BUR02-302
City, State, Postal Code:	Burlington, MA, 01803-0902
Country:	USA
Phone:	781.442.0703
Email:	najmi@east.sun.com

Appendix A   ebXML Registry DTD Definition

The following is the definition for the various ebXML Message payloads described in this document.

```
<?xml version="1.0" encoding="UTF-8"?>
<!-- Begin information model mapping. -->
<!--
```

ObjectAttributes are attributes from the RegistryObject interface in ebRIM. id may be empty. If specified it may be in
urn:uuid format or be in some arbitrary format. If id is empty
registry must generate globally unique id. If id is provided
and in proper UUID syntax (starts with urn:uuid:) registry will
honour it.
If id is provided and is not in proper UUID syntax then it is
used for linkage within document and is ignored by the registry. In this case the registry generates a UUID for id attribute.
id must not be null when object is being retrieved from the
registry.
-->
<!ENTITY % ObjectAttributes "
   id   ID   #IMPLIED
   name   CDATA   #IMPLIED
   description CDATA   #IMPLIED
">
<!--
Use as a proxy for an Object that is in the registry already.
Specifies the id attribute of the object in the registry as its id
attribute. id attribute in ObjectAttributes is exactly the same
syntax and semantics as id attribute in RegistryObject.
-->
<!ELEMENT ObjectRef EMPTY>
<!ATTLIST ObjectRef
    id ID #IMPLIED
>
<!ELEMENT ObjectRefList (ObjectRef)*>
<!--
RegistryEntryAttributes are attributes from the RegistryEntry
interface in ebRIM.
It inherits ObjectAttributes
-->
<!ENTITY % RegistryEntryAttributes " %ObjectAttributes;
   majorVersion   CDATA   '1'
   minorVersion   CDATA   '0'
   status   CDATA   #IMPLIED
   userVersion   CDATA   #IMPLIED
   stability   CDATA   'Dynamic'
   expirationDate CDATA   #IMPLIED">
<!ELEMENT RegistryEntry (SlotList?)>
<!ATTLIST RegistryEntry
       %RegistryEntryAttributes; >
<!ELEMENT Value (#PCDATA)>
<!ELEMENT ValueList (Value*)>

```
<!ELEMENT Slot (ValueList?)>
<!ATTLIST Slot
        name CDATA #REQUIRED
        slotType CDATA #IMPLIED
>
<!ELEMENT SlotList (Slot*)>
<!--
ExtrinsicObject are attributes from the ExtrinsicObject interface
in ebRIM.
It inherits RegistryEntryAttributes
-->
<!ELEMENT ExtrinsicObject EMPTY >
<!ATTLIST ExtrinsicObject
        %RegistryEntryAttributes;
        contentURI CDATA #REQUIRED
        mimeType CDATA #IMPLIED
        objectType CDATA #REQUIRED
        opaque (true | false) "false"
>
<!ENTITY % IntrinsicObjectAttributes " %RegistryEntryAttributes;">
<!-- Leaf classes that reflect the concrete classes in ebRIM -->
<!ELEMENT RegistryEntryList
(Association | Classification | ClassificationNode | Package |
 ExternalLink | ExternalIdentifier | Organization |
 ExtrinsicObject | ObjectRef)*>
<!--
An ExternalLink specifies a link from a RegistryEntry and an
external URI
-->
<!ELEMENT ExternalLink EMPTY>
<!ATTLIST ExternalLink
        %IntrinsicObjectAttributes;
        externalURI CDATA #IMPLIED
>
<!--
An ExternalIdentifier provides an identifier for a RegistryEntry
The value is the value of the identifier (e.g. the social security
number)
-->
<!ELEMENT ExternalIdentifier EMPTY>
<!ATTLIST ExternalIdentifier
        %IntrinsicObjectAttributes;
        value CDATA #REQUIRED
>
<!--
An Association specifies references to two previously submitted
```

```
registry entrys.
The sourceObject is id of the sourceObject in association
The targetObject is id of the targetObject in association
-->
<!ELEMENT Association EMPTY>
<!ATTLIST Association
        %IntrinsicObjectAttributes;
        sourceRole CDATA #IMPLIED
        targetRole CDATA #IMPLIED
        associationType CDATA #REQUIRED
        bidirection (true | false) "false"
        sourceObject IDREF #REQUIRED
        targetObject IDREF #REQUIRED
>
<!--
A Classification specifies references to two registry entrys.
The classifiedObject is id of the Object being classified.
The classificationNode is id of the ClassificationNode classying
the object
-->
<!ELEMENT Classification EMPTY>
<!ATTLIST Classification
        %IntrinsicObjectAttributes;
        classifiedObject IDREF #REQUIRED
        classificationNode IDREF #REQUIRED
>
<!--
A Package is a named collection of objects.
-->
<!ELEMENT Package EMPTY>
<!ATTLIST Package
        %IntrinsicObjectAttributes;
>
<!-- Attributes inherited by various types of telephone number
elements -->
<!ENTITY % TelephoneNumberAttributes " areaCode CDATA #REQUIRED
   contryCode CDATA  #REQUIRED
   extension  CDATA  #IMPLIED
   number     CDATA  #REQUIRED
   url        CDATA  #IMPLIED">
<!ELEMENT TelephoneNumber EMPTY>
<!ATTLIST TelephoneNumber
        %TelephoneNumberAttributes;
>
<!ELEMENT FaxNumber EMPTY>
<!ATTLIST FaxNumber
```

```
            %TelephoneNumberAttributes;
>
<!ELEMENT PagerNumber EMPTY>
<!ATTLIST PagerNumber
            %TelephoneNumberAttributes;
>
<!ELEMENT MobileTelephoneNumber EMPTY>
<!ATTLIST MobileTelephoneNumber
            %TelephoneNumberAttributes;
>
<!-- PostalAddress -->
<!ELEMENT PostalAddress EMPTY>
<!ATTLIST PostalAddress
            city CDATA #REQUIRED
            country CDATA #REQUIRED
            postalCode CDATA #REQUIRED
            state CDATA #IMPLIED
            street CDATA #REQUIRED
>
<!-- PersonName -->
<!ELEMENT PersonName EMPTY>
<!ATTLIST PersonName
            firstName CDATA #REQUIRED
            middleName CDATA #IMPLIED
            lastName CDATA #REQUIRED
>
<!-- Organization -->
<!ELEMENT Organization (PostalAddress, FaxNumber?, Telephone-
Number)>
<!ATTLIST Organization
            %IntrinsicObjectAttributes;
            parent IDREF #IMPLIED
            primaryContact IDREF #REQUIRED
>
<!ELEMENT User (PersonName, PostalAddress, TelephoneNumber,
                                            MobileTelephoneNumber?,
                                            FaxNumber?, PagerNumber?)>
<!ATTLIST User
            %ObjectAttributes;
            organization IDREF #IMPLIED
            email CDATA #IMPLIED
            url CDATA #IMPLIED
>
<!ELEMENT AuditableEvent EMPTY>
<!ATTLIST AuditableEvent
            %ObjectAttributes;
            eventType CDATA #REQUIRED
```

```
        registryEntry IDREF #REQUIRED
        timestamp CDATA #REQUIRED
        user IDREF #REQUIRED
>
<!--
ClassificationNode is used to submit a Classification tree to the
Registry.
parent is the id to the parent node. code is an optional code
value for a ClassificationNode
often defined by an external taxonomy (e.g. NAICS)
-->
<!ELEMENT ClassificationNode EMPTY>
<!ATTLIST ClassificationNode
        %IntrinsicObjectAttributes;
        parent IDREF #IMPLIED
        code CDATA #IMPLIED
>
<!--
End information model mapping.
Begin Registry Services Interface
<!ELEMENT RequestAcceptedResponse EMPTY>
<!ATTLIST RequestAcceptedResponse
        xml:lang NMTOKEN #REQUIRED
>
<!--
The SubmitObjectsRequest allows one to submit a list of Registry-
Entry elements. Each RegistryEntry element provides metadata for a
single submitted object. Note that the repository item being sub-
mitted is in a separate document that is not in this DTD. The
ebXML Messaging Services Specfication defines packaging, for sub-
mission, of the metadata of a repository item with the repository
item itself. The value of the contentURI attribute of the
ExtrinsicObject element must be the same as the xlink:href at-
tribute within the Reference element within the Manifest element
of the MessageHeader.
-->
<!ELEMENT SubmitObjectsRequest (RegistryEntryList)>
<!ELEMENT AddSlotsRequest (ObjectRef, SlotList)+>
<!-- Only need name in Slot within SlotList -->
<!ELEMENT RemoveSlotsRequest (ObjectRef, SlotList)+>
<!--
The ObjectRefList is the list of
refs to the registry entrys being approved.
-->
<!ELEMENT ApproveObjectsRequest (ObjectRefList)>
<!--
The ObjectRefList is the list of
```

```
refs to the registry entrys being deprecated.
-->
<!ELEMENT DeprecateObjectsRequest (ObjectRefList)>
<!--
The ObjectRefList is the list of
refs to the registry entrys being removed
-->
<!ELEMENT RemoveObjectsRequest (ObjectRefList)>
<!ATTLIST RemoveObjectsRequest
        deletionScope (DeleteAll | DeleteRepositoryItemOnly)
"DeleteAll"
>
<!ELEMENT GetRootClassificationNodesRequest EMPTY>
<!--
The namePattern follows SQL-92 syntax for the pattern specified in
LIKE clause. It allows for selecting only those root nodes that
match the namePattern. The default value of '*' matches all root
nodes.
-->
<!ATTLIST GetRootClassificationNodesRequest
        namePattern CDATA "*"
>
<!--
The response includes one or more ClassificationNodes
-->
<!ELEMENT GetRootClassificationNodesResponse ( Classification-
Node+ )>
<!--
Get the classification tree under the ClassificationNode specified
parentRef.
If depth is 1 just fetch immediate child nodes, otherwise fetch
the descendant tree upto the specified depth level.
If depth is 0 that implies fetch entire sub-tree
-->
<!ELEMENT GetClassificationTreeRequest EMPTY>
<!ATTLIST GetClassificationTreeRequest
        parent CDATA #REQUIRED
        depth CDATA "1"
>
<!--
The response includes one or more ClassificationNodes which in-
cludes only immediate ClassificationNode children nodes if depth
attribute in GetClassificationTreeRequest was 1, otherwise the
decendent nodes upto specified depth level are returned.
-->
<!ELEMENT GetClassificationTreeResponse ( ClassificationNode+ )>
```

```
<!--
Get refs to all registry entrys that are classified by all the
ClassificationNodes specified by ObjectRefList.
Note this is an implicit logical AND operation
-->
<!ELEMENT GetClassifiedObjectsRequest (ObjectRefList)>
<!--
objectType attribute can specify the type of objects that the reg-
istry client is interested in, that is classified by this Classi-
ficationNode.
It is a String that matches a choice in the type attribute of
ExtrinsicObject.
The default value of '*' implies that client is interested in all
types of registry entrys that are classified by the specified
ClassificationNode.
-->
<!--
The response includes a RegistryEntryList which has zero or more
RegistryEntrys that are classified by the ClassificationNodes
specified in the ObjectRefList in GetClassifiedObjectsRequest.
-->
<!ELEMENT GetClassifiedObjectsResponse ( RegistryEntryList )>
<!--
An Ad hoc query request specifies a query string as defined by
[RS] in the queryString attribute
-->
<!ELEMENT AdhocQueryRequest (FilterQuery | ReturnRegistryEntry |
ReturnRepositoryItem | SQLQuery)>
<!ELEMENT SQLQuery (#PCDATA)>
<!--
The response includes a RegistryEntryList which has zero or more
RegistryEntrys that match the query specified in AdhocQuery-
Request.
-->
<!ELEMENT AdhocQueryResponse
  ( RegistryEntryList |
    FilterQueryResult |
    ReturnRegistryEntryResult |
    ReturnRepositoryItemResult )>
<!--
Gets the actual content (not metadata) specified by the ObjectRefList
-->
<!ELEMENT GetContentRequest (ObjectRefList)>
<!--
The GetObjectsResponse will have no sub-elements if there were no
errors.
```

```
The actual contents will be in the other payloads of the message.
-->
<!ELEMENT GetContentResponse EMPTY >
<!--
Describes the capability profile for the registry and what op-
tional features are supported
-->
<!ELEMENT RegistryProfile (OptionalFeaturesSupported)>
<!ATTLIST RegistryProfile
        version CDATA #REQUIRED
>
<!ELEMENT OptionalFeaturesSupported EMPTY>
<!ATTLIST OptionalFeaturesSupported
        sqlQuery (true | false) "false"
        xQuery (true | false) "false"
>
<!-- Begin FilterQuery DTD -->
<!ELEMENT FilterQuery (RegistryEntryQuery | AuditableEventQuery |
ClassificationNodeQuery | RegistryPackageQuery | Organization-
Query)>
<!ELEMENT FilterQueryResult (RegistryEntryQueryResult | Au-
ditableEventQueryResult | ClassificationNodeQueryResult | Reg-
istryPackageQueryResult | OrganizationQueryResult)>
<!ELEMENT RegistryEntryQueryResult (RegistryEntryView*)>
<!ELEMENT RegistryEntryView EMPTY>
<!ATTLIST RegistryEntryView
        objectURN CDATA #REQUIRED
        contentURI CDATA #IMPLIED
        objectID CDATA #IMPLIED
>
<!ELEMENT AuditableEventQueryResult (AuditableEventView*)>
<!ELEMENT AuditableEventView EMPTY>
<!ATTLIST AuditableEventView
        objectID CDATA #REQUIRED
        timestamp CDATA #REQUIRED
>
<!ELEMENT ClassificationNodeQueryResult (ClassificationNodeView*)>
<!ELEMENT ClassificationNodeView EMPTY>
<!ATTLIST ClassificationNodeView
        objectURN CDATA #REQUIRED
        contentURI CDATA #IMPLIED
        objectID CDATA #IMPLIED
>
<!ELEMENT RegistryPackageQueryResult (RegistryPackageView*)>
<!ELEMENT RegistryPackageView EMPTY>
<!ATTLIST RegistryPackageView
```

```
         objectURN CDATA #REQUIRED
         contentURI CDATA #IMPLIED
         objectID CDATA #IMPLIED
>
<!ELEMENT OrganizationQueryResult (OrganizationView*)>
<!ELEMENT OrganizationView EMPTY>
<!ATTLIST OrganizationView
         orgURN CDATA #REQUIRED
         objectID CDATA #IMPLIED
>
<!ELEMENT RegistryEntryQuery
   ( RegistryEntryFilter?,
     SourceAssociationBranch*,
     TargetAssociationBranch*,
     HasClassificationBranch*,
     SubmittingOrganizationBranch?,
     ResponsibleOrganizationBranch?,
     ExternalIdentifierFilter*,
     ExternalLinkFilter*,
     SlotFilter*,
     HasAuditableEventBranch*          )>
<!ELEMENT SourceAssociationBranch (AssociationFilter?, Registry-
EntryFilter?)>
<!ELEMENT TargetAssociationBranch (AssociationFilter?, Registry-
EntryFilter?)>
<!ELEMENT HasClassificationBranch (ClassificationFilter?, Classi-
ficationNodeFilter?)>
<!ELEMENT SubmittingOrganizationBranch (OrganizationFilter?, Con-
tactFilter?)>
<!ELEMENT ResponsibleOrganizationBranch (OrganizationFilter?, Con-
tactFilter?)>
<!ELEMENT HasAuditableEventBranch (AuditableEventFilter?, User-
Filter?, OrganizationFilter?)>
<!ELEMENT AuditableEventQuery
   (AuditableEventFilter?, RegistryEntryQuery*, InvokedByBranch? )>
<!ELEMENT InvokedByBranch
   ( UserFilter?, OrganizationQuery? )>
<!ELEMENT ClassificationNodeQuery (ClassificationNodeFilter?,
PermitsClassificationBranch*, HasParentNode?, HasSubnode*)>
<!ELEMENT PermitsClassificationBranch (ClassificationFilter?,
RegistryEntryQuery?)>
<!ELEMENT HasParentNode (ClassificationNodeFilter?, HasParent-
Node?)>
<!ELEMENT HasSubnode (ClassificationNodeFilter?, HasSubnode*)>
<!ELEMENT RegistryPackageQuery (PackageFilter?, HasMemberBranch*)>
<!ELEMENT HasMemberBranch (RegistryEntryQuery?)>
```

```
<!ELEMENT OrganizationQuery (OrganizationFilter?, SubmitsReg-
istryEntry*, HasParentOrganization?, InvokesEventBranch*, Contact-
Filter*)>
<!ELEMENT SubmitsRegistryEntry (RegistryEntryQuery?)>
<!ELEMENT HasParentOrganization (OrganizationFilter?, HasParent-
Organization?)>
<!ELEMENT InvokesEventBranch (UserFilter?, AuditableEventFilter?,
RegistryEntryQuery?)>
<!ELEMENT ReturnRegistryEntry (RegistryEntryQuery, WithClassifica-
tions?, WithSourceAssociations?, WithTargetAssociations?, With-
AuditableEvents?, WithExternalLinks?)>
<!ELEMENT WithClassifications (ClassificationFilter?)>
<!ELEMENT WithSourceAssociations (AssociationFilter?)>
<!ELEMENT WithTargetAssociations (AssociationFilter?)>
<!ELEMENT WithAuditableEvents (AuditableEventFilter?)>
<!ELEMENT WithExternalLinks (ExternalLinkFilter?)>
<!ELEMENT ReturnRegistryEntryResult (RegistryEntryMetadata*)>
<!ELEMENT RegistryEntryMetadata (RegistryEntry, Classification*,
SourceAssociations?, TargetAssociations?, AuditableEvent*, Exter-
nalLink*)>
<!ELEMENT SourceAssociations (Association*)>
<!ELEMENT TargetAssociations (Association*)>
<!ELEMENT ReturnRepositoryItem (RegistryEntryQuery, Recursive-
AssociationOption?, WithDescription?)>
<!ELEMENT RecursiveAssociationOption (AssociationType+)>
<!ATTLIST RecursiveAssociationOption
        depthLimit CDATA #IMPLIED
>
<!ELEMENT AssociationType EMPTY>
<!ATTLIST AssociationType
        role CDATA #REQUIRED
>
<!ELEMENT WithDescription EMPTY>
<!ELEMENT ReturnRepositoryItemResult (RepositoryItem*)>
<!ELEMENT RepositoryItem (RegistryPackage | ExtrinsicObject |
WithdrawnObject | ExternalLink)>
<!ATTLIST RepositoryItem
        identifier CDATA #REQUIRED
        name CDATA #REQUIRED
        contentURI CDATA #REQUIRED
        objectType CDATA #REQUIRED
        status CDATA #REQUIRED
        stability CDATA #REQUIRED
        description CDATA #IMPLIED
>
<!ELEMENT RegistryPackage EMPTY>
```

```
<!ELEMENT WithdrawnObject EMPTY>
<!ELEMENT ExternalLinkItem EMPTY>
<!ELEMENT ObjectFilter (Clause)>
<!ELEMENT RegistryEntryFilter (Clause)>
<!ELEMENT IntrinsicObjectFilter (Clause)>
<!ELEMENT ExtrinsicObjectFilter (Clause)>
<!ELEMENT PackageFilter (Clause)>
<!ELEMENT OrganizationFilter (Clause)>
<!ELEMENT ContactFilter (Clause)>
<!ELEMENT ClassificationNodeFilter (Clause)>
<!ELEMENT AssociationFilter (Clause)>
<!ELEMENT ClassificationFilter (Clause)>
<!ELEMENT ExternalLinkFilter (Clause)>
<!ELEMENT SlotFilter (Clause)>
<!ELEMENT ExternalIdentifierFilter (Clause)>
<!ELEMENT AuditableEventFilter (Clause)>
<!ELEMENT UserFilter (Clause)>
<!--
The following lines define the XML syntax for Clause.
-->
<!ELEMENT Clause (SimpleClause | CompoundClause)>
<!ELEMENT SimpleClause (BooleanClause | RationalClause | String-
Clause)>
<!ATTLIST SimpleClause
        leftArgument CDATA #REQUIRED
>
<!ELEMENT CompoundClause (Clause, Clause+)>
<!ATTLIST CompoundClause
        connectivePredicate (And | Or) #REQUIRED
>
<!ELEMENT BooleanClause EMPTY>
<!ATTLIST BooleanClause
        booleanPredicate (true | false) #REQUIRED
>
<!ELEMENT RationalClause (IntClause | FloatClause)>
<!ATTLIST RationalClause
        logicalPredicate (LE | LT | GE | GT | EQ | NE) #REQUIRED
>
<!ELEMENT IntClause (#PCDATA)>
<!ATTLIST IntClause
        e-dtype NMTOKEN #FIXED "int"
>
<!ELEMENT FloatClause (#PCDATA)>
<!ATTLIST FloatClause
        e-dtype NMTOKEN #FIXED "float"
>
```

```
<!ELEMENT StringClause (#PCDATA)>
<!ATTLIST StringClause
        stringPredicate
        (contains | -contains |
            startswith | -startswith |
            equal | -equal |
            endswith | -endswith) #REQUIRED
>
<!-- End FilterQuery DTD -->
<!-- Begin RegistryError definition -->
<!-- The RegistryErrorList is derived from the ErrorList element
    from the ebXML Message Service Specification -->
<!ELEMENT RegistryErrorList ( RegistryError+ )>
<!ATTLIST RegistryErrorList
    highestSeverity ( Warning | Error ) 'Warning' >

<!ELEMENT RegistryError (#PCDATA) >
<!ATTLIST RegistryError
    codeContext   CDATA   #REQUIRED
    errorCode     CDATA   #REQUIRED
    severity   ( Warning | Error ) 'Warning'
    location      CDATA   #IMPLIED
    xml:lang      NMTOKEN  #IMPLIED>
<!ELEMENT RegistryResponse
  (( AdhocQueryResponse |
    GetContentResponse |
    GetClassificationTreeResponse |
    GetClassifiedObjectsResponse |
    GetRootClassificationNodesResponse )?,
    RegistryErrorList? )>
<!ATTLIST RegistryResponse
    status (success | failure ) #REQUIRED >
<!-- The contrived root node -->
<!ELEMENT RootElement
  ( SubmitObjectsRequest |
    ApproveObjectsRequest |
    DeprecateObjectsRequest |
    RemoveObjectsRequest |
    GetRootClassificationNodesRequest |
    GetClassificationTreeRequest |
    GetClassifiedObjectsRequest |
    AdhocQueryRequest |
    GetContentRequest |
    AddSlotsRequest |
    RemoveSlotsRequest |
    RegistryResponse |
    RegistryProfile) >
```

```
<!ELEMENT Href (#PCDATA )>
<!ELEMENT XMLDocumentErrorLocn (DocumentId , Xpath )>
<!ELEMENT DocumentId (#PCDATA )>
<!ELEMENT Xpath (#PCDATA)>
```

Appendix B   Interpretation of UML Diagrams

This section describes in *abstract terms* the conventions used to define ebXML business process description in UML.

UML Class Diagram

A UML class diagram is used to describe the Service Interfaces (as defined by [ebCPP]) required to implement an ebXML Registry Services and clients. See **Figure 2** on page 272 for an example. The UML class diagram contains:

1. A collection of UML interfaces where each interface represents a Service Interface for a Registry service.

2. Tabular description of methods on each interface where each method represents an Action (as defined by [ebCPP]) within the Service Interface representing the UML interface.

3. Each method within a UML interface specifies one or more parameters, where the type of each method argument represents the ebXML message type that is exchanged as part of the Action corresponding to the method. Multiple arguments imply multiple payload documents within the body of the corresponding ebXML message.

UML Sequence Diagram

A UML sequence diagram is used to specify the business protocol representing the interactions between the UML interfaces for a Registry specific ebXML business process. A UML sequence diagram provides the necessary information to determine the sequencing of messages, request to response association as well as request to error response association as described by [ebCPP].

Each sequence diagram shows the sequence for a specific conversation protocol as method calls from the requestor to the responder. Method invocation may be synchronous or asynchronous based on the UML notation used on the arrow-head for the link. A half arrow-head represents asynchronous communication. A full arrow-head represents synchronous communication.

Each method invocation may be followed by a response method invocation from the responder to the requestor to indicate the ResponseName for the previous Request. Possible error response is indicated by a conditional response method invocation from the responder to the requestor. See on page 278 for an example.

Appendix C SQL Query

SQL Query Syntax Specification

This section specifies the rules that define the SQL Query syntax as a subset of SQL-92. The terms enclosed in angle brackets are defined in [SQL] or in [SQL/PSM]. The SQL query syntax conforms to the <query specification>, modulo the restrictions identified below:

1. A <select list> may contain at most one <select sublist>.

2. In a <select list> must be is a single column whose data type is UUID, from the table in the <from clause>.

3. A <derived column> may not have an <as clause>.

4. <table expression> does not contain the optional <group by clause> and <having clause> clauses.

5. A <table reference> can only consist of <table name> and <correlation name>.

6. A <table reference> does not have the optional AS between <table name> and <correlation name>.

7. There can only be one <table reference> in the <from clause>.

8. Restricted use of sub-queries is allowed by the syntax as follows. The <in predicate> allows for the right hand side of the <in predicate> to be limited to a restricted <query specification> as defined above.

9. A <search condition> within the <where clause> may not include a <query expression>.

10. The SQL query syntax allows for the use of `<sql invoked routines>` invocation from [SQL/PSM] as the RHS of the `<in predicate>`.

Non-normative BNF for Query Syntax Grammar

The following BNF exemplifies the grammar for the registry query syntax. It is provided here as an aid to implementors. Since this BNF is not based on [SQL] it is provided as non-normative syntax. For the normative syntax rules see the previous section.

```
/*****************************************************************
**
 * The Registry Query (Subset of SQL-92) grammar starts here

*****************************************************************
*/
RegistryQuery = SQLSelect [";"]
SQLSelect = "SELECT" SQLSelectCols "FROM" SQLTableList [ SQLWhere ]
SQLSelectCols = ID
SQLTableList = SQLTableRef
SQLTableRef = ID
SQLWhere = "WHERE" SQLOrExpr
SQLOrExpr = SQLAndExpr ( "OR" SQLAndExpr)*
SQLAndExpr = SQLNotExpr ("AND" SQLNotExpr)*
SQLNotExpr = [ "NOT" ] SQLCompareExpr

SQLCompareExpr =
    (SQLColRef "IS") SQLIsClause
  | SQLSumExpr [ SQLCompareExprRight ]
SQLCompareExprRight =
    SQLLikeClause
  | SQLInClause
  | SQLCompareOp SQLSumExpr

SQLCompareOp =
    "="
  | "<>"
  | ">"
  | ">="
  | "<"
  | "<="
SQLInClause = [ "NOT" ] "IN" "(" SQLLValueList ")"
SQLLValueList = SQLLValueElement ( "," SQLLValueElement )*
SQLLValueElement = "NULL" | SQLSelect
SQLIsClause = SQLColRef "IS" [ "NOT" ] "NULL"
```

```
SQLLikeClause = [ "NOT" ] "LIKE" SQLPattern
SQLPattern = STRING_LITERAL
SQLLiteral =
      STRING_LITERAL
   |  INTEGER_LITERAL
   |  FLOATING_POINT_LITERAL
SQLColRef = SQLLvalue
SQLLvalue = SQLLvalueTerm
SQLLvalueTerm = ID ( "." ID )*
SQLSumExpr = SQLProductExpr (( "+" | "-" ) SQLProductExpr )*

SQLProductExpr = SQLUnaryExpr (( "*" | "/" ) SQLUnaryExpr )*
SQLUnaryExpr = [ ( "+" | "-") ] SQLTerm
SQLTerm = "(" SQLOrExpr ")"
   |  SQLColRef
   |  SQLLiteral
INTEGER_LITERAL = (["0"-"9"])+
FLOATING_POINT_LITERAL =
           (["0"-"9"])+ "." (["0"-"9"])+ (EXPONENT)?
        |  "." (["0"-"9"])+ (EXPONENT)?
        |  (["0"-"9"])+ EXPONENT
        |  (["0"-"9"])+ (EXPONENT)?
EXPONENT = ["e","E"] (["+","-"])? (["0"-"9"])+
STRING_LITERAL: "'" (~["'"])* ( "'" (~["'"])* )* "'"
ID = ( <LETTER> )+ ( "_" | "$" | "#" | <DIGIT> | <LETTER> )*
LETTER = ["A"-"Z", "a"-"z"]
DIGIT = ["0"-"9"]
```

Relational Schema for SQL Queries

```
--SQL Load file for creating the ebXML Registry tables
--Minimal use of SQL-99 features in DDL is illustrative and may be
easily mapped to SQL-92
CREATE TYPE ShortName AS VARCHAR(64) NOT FINAL;
CREATE TYPE LongName AS VARCHAR(128) NOT FINAL;
CREATE TYPE FreeFormText AS VARCHAR(256) NOT FINAL;
CREATE TYPE UUID UNDER ShortName FINAL;
CREATE TYPE URI UNDER LongName FINAL;
CREATE TABLE ExtrinsicObject (
--RegistryObject Attributes
  id                              UUID PRIMARY KEY NOT NULL,
  name                            LongName,
  description             FreeFormText,
  accessControlPolicy   UUID NOT NULL,
--Versionable attributes
  majorVersion                 INT DEFAULT 0 NOT NULL,
```

```
  minorVersion                   INT DEFAULT 1 NOT NULL,
--RegistryEntry attributes
  status                            INT DEFAULT 0 NOT NULL,
  userVersion                  ShortName,
  stability                         INT    DEFAULT 0 NOT NULL,
  expirationDate             TIMESTAMP,
--ExtrinsicObject attributes
  contentURI                 URI,
  mimeType                               ShortName,
  objectType                 INT DEFAULT 0 NOT NULL,
  opaque                                 BOOLEAN DEFAULT false
NOT NULL
);
CREATE PROCEDURE RegistryEntry_associatedObjects(registryEntryId) {
--Must return a collection of UUIDs for related RegistryEntry in-
stances
}
CREATE PROCEDURE RegistryEntry_auditTrail(registryEntryId) {
--Must return an collection of UUIDs for AuditableEvents related
to the RegistryEntry.
--Collection must be in ascending order by timestamp
}
CREATE PROCEDURE RegistryEntry_externalLinks(registryEntryId) {
--Must return a collection of UUIDs for ExternalLinks annotating
this RegistryEntry.
}
CREATE PROCEDURE RegistryEntry_externalIdentifiers(registryEntryId) {
--Must return a collection of UUIDs for ExternalIdentifiers for
this RegistryEntry.
}
CREATE PROCEDURE RegistryEntry_classificationNodes(registryEntryId) {
--Must return a collection of UUIDs for ClassificationNodes clas-
sifying this RegistryEntry.
}
CREATE PROCEDURE RegistryEntry_packages(registryEntryId) {
--Must return a collection of UUIDs for Packages that this Reg-
istryEntry belongs to.
}
CREATE TABLE Package (
--RegistryObject Attributes
  id                               UUID PRIMARY KEY NOT NULL,
  name                             LongName,
  description                FreeFormText,
  accessControlPolicy  UUID NOT NULL,
--Versionable attributes
  majorVersion                   INT DEFAULT 0 NOT NULL,
  minorVersion                   INT DEFAULT 1 NOT NULL,
```

```
--RegistryEntry attributes
  status                              INT DEFAULT 0 NOT NULL,
  userVersion                 ShortName,
  stability                           INT    DEFAULT 0 NOT NULL,
  expirationDate              TIMESTAMP,
--Package attributes
);
CREATE PROCEDURE Package_memberbjects(packageId) {
--Must return a collection of UUIDs for RegistryEntrys that are
memebers of this Package.
}
CREATE TABLE ExternalLink (
--RegistryObject Attributes
  id                                  UUID PRIMARY KEY NOT NULL,
  name                                LongName,
  description             FreeFormText,
  accessControlPolicy  UUID NOT NULL,
--Versionable attributes
  majorVersion            INT DEFAULT 0 NOT NULL,
  minorVersion            INT DEFAULT 1 NOT NULL,
--RegistryEntry attributes
  status                              INT DEFAULT 0 NOT NULL,
  userVersion                 ShortName,
  stability                           INT    DEFAULT 0 NOT NULL,
  expirationDate              TIMESTAMP,
--ExternalLink attributes
  externalURI             URI NOT NULL
);
CREATE PROCEDURE ExternalLink_linkedObjects(registryEntryId) {
--Must return a collection of UUIDs for objects in this relationship
}
CREATE TABLE ExternalIdentifier (
--RegistryObject Attributes
  id                                  UUID PRIMARY KEY NOT NULL,
  name                                LongName,
  description             FreeFormText,
  accessControlPolicy  UUID NOT NULL,
--Versionable attributes
  majorVersion            INT DEFAULT 0 NOT NULL,
  minorVersion            INT DEFAULT 1 NOT NULL,
--RegistryEntry attributes
  status                              INT DEFAULT 0 NOT NULL,
  userVersion                 ShortName,
  stability                           INT    DEFAULT 0 NOT NULL,
  expirationDate              TIMESTAMP,
--ExternalIdentifier attributes
  value                               ShortName NOT NULL
```

```
);
--A SlotValue row represents one value of one slot in some
--RegistryEntry
CREATE TABLE SlotValue (
--RegistryObject Attributes
  registryEntry                UUID  PRIMARY KEY NOT NULL,
--Slot attributes
  name                         LongName NOT NULL PRIMARY KEY NOT
NULL,
  value                        ShortName NOT NULL
);
CREATE TABLE Association (
--RegistryObject Attributes
  id                                 UUID PRIMARY KEY NOT NULL,
  name                               LongName,
  description                  FreeFormText,
  accessControlPolicy  UUID NOT NULL,
--Versionable attributes
  majorVersion                 INT DEFAULT 0 NOT NULL,
  minorVersion                 INT DEFAULT 1 NOT NULL,
--RegistryEntry attributes
  status                             INT DEFAULT 0 NOT NULL,
  userVersion                  ShortName,
  stability                          INT    DEFAULT 0 NOT NULL,
  expirationDate               TIMESTAMP,
--Association attributes
  associationType              INT NOT NULL,
  bidirectional                      BOOLEAN DEFAULT false NOT
NULL,
  sourceObject                 UUID NOT NULL,
  sourceRole                   ShortName,
  label                              ShortName,
  targetObject                 UUID NOT NULL,
  targetRole                   ShortName
);
--Classification is currently identical to Association
CREATE TABLE Classification (
--RegistryObject Attributes
  id                                 UUID PRIMARY KEY NOT NULL,
  name                               LongName,
  description                  FreeFormText,
  accessControlPolicy  UUID NOT NULL,
--Versionable attributes
  majorVersion                 INT DEFAULT 0 NOT NULL,
  minorVersion                 INT DEFAULT 1 NOT NULL,
--RegistryEntry attributes
  status                             INT DEFAULT 0 NOT NULL,
```

```
    userVersion                    ShortName,
    stability                           INT    DEFAULT 0 NOT NULL,
    expirationDate                 TIMESTAMP,
--Classification attributes. Assumes not derived from Association
    sourceObject                   UUID NOT NULL,
    targetObject                   UUID NOT NULL,
);
CREATE TABLE ClassificationNode (
--RegistryObject Attributes
    id                                    UUID PRIMARY KEY NOT NULL,
    name                                  LongName,
    description                    FreeFormText,
    accessControlPolicy  UUID NOT NULL,
--Versionable attributes
    majorVersion                   INT DEFAULT 0 NOT NULL,
    minorVersion                   INT DEFAULT 1 NOT NULL,
--RegistryEntry attributes
    status                             INT DEFAULT 0 NOT NULL,
    userVersion                    ShortName,
    stability                           INT    DEFAULT 0 NOT NULL,
    expirationDate                 TIMESTAMP,
--ClassificationNode attributes
    parent                             UUID,
    path                               VARCHAR(512) NOT NULL,
    code                               ShortName
);
CREATE PROCEDURE ClassificationNode_classifiedObjects(classifica-
tionNodeId) {
--Must return a collection of UUIDs for RegistryEntries classified
by this ClassificationNode
}
--Begin Registry Audit Trail tables
CREATE TABLE AuditableEvent (
--RegistryObject Attributes
    id                                    UUID PRIMARY KEY NOT NULL,
    name                                  LongName,
    description                    FreeFormText,
    accessControlPolicy  UUID NOT NULL,
--AuditableEvent attributes
    user          UUID,
    eventType                      INT DEFAULT 0 NOT NULL,
    registryEntry                  UUID NOT NULL,
    timestamp                      TIMESTAMP NOT NULL,
);
CREATE TABLE User (
--RegistryObject Attributes
    id                                    UUID PRIMARY KEY NOT NULL,
```

```
  name                             LongName,
  description                      FreeFormText,
  accessControlPolicy  UUID NOT NULL,
--User attributes
  organization         UUID NOT NULL
--address attributes flattened
  address_city         ShortName,
  address_country      ShortName,
  address_postalCode   ShortName,
  address_state                ShortName,
  address_street       ShortName,
  email                        ShortName,
--fax attribute flattened
  fax_areaCode         VARCHAR(4) NOT NULL,
  fax_countryCode      VARCHAR(4),
  fax_extension                VARCHAR(8),
  fax_umber                    VARCHAR(8) NOT NULL,
  fax_url                      URI

 --mobilePhone attribute flattened
  mobilePhone_areaCode         VARCHAR(4) NOT NULL,
  mobilePhone_countryCode      VARCHAR(4),
  mobilePhone_extension              VARCHAR(8),
  mobilePhone_umber                  VARCHAR(8) NOT NULL,
  mobilePhone_url                    URI

--name attribute flattened
  name_firstName       ShortName,
  name_middleName      ShortName,
  name_lastName                ShortName,
--pager attribute flattened
  pager_areaCode       VARCHAR(4) NOT NULL,
  pager_countryCode    VARCHAR(4),
  pager_extension      VARCHAR(8),
  pager_umber          VARCHAR(8) NOT NULL,
  pager_url                    URI

--telephone attribute flattened
  telephone_areaCode           VARCHAR(4) NOT NULL,
  telephone_countryCode              VARCHAR(4),
  telephone_extension          VARCHAR(8),
  telephone_umber                    VARCHAR(8) NOT NULL,
  telephone_url                      URI,

 url                                 URI,

);
```

```
CREATE TABLE Organization (
--RegistryObject Attributes
  id                      UUID PRIMARY KEY NOT NULL,
  name                    LongName,
  description       FreeFormText,
  accessControlPolicy  UUID NOT NULL,
--Versionable attributes
  majorVersion        INT DEFAULT 0 NOT NULL,
  minorVersion        INT DEFAULT 1 NOT NULL,
--RegistryEntry attributes
  status                  INT DEFAULT 0 NOT NULL,
  userVersion         ShortName,
  stability               INT    DEFAULT 0 NOT NULL,
  expirationDate      TIMESTAMP,
--Organization attributes
--Organization.address attribute flattened
  address_city        ShortName,
  address_country     ShortName,
  address_postalCode  ShortName,
  address_state                   ShortName,
  address_street      ShortName,
--primary contact for Organization, points to a User.
--Note many Users may belong to the same Organization
  contact                         UUID NOT NULL,
--Organization.fax attribute falttened
  fax_areaCode        VARCHAR(4) NOT NULL,
  fax_countryCode     VARCHAR(4),
  fax_extension        VARCHAR(8),
  fax_umber            VARCHAR(8) NOT NULL,
  fax_url              URI,
--Organization.parent attribute
  parent              UUID,
--Organization.telephone attribute falttened
  telephone_areaCode    VARCHAR(4) NOT NULL,
  telephone_countryCode     VARCHAR(4),
  telephone_extension   VARCHAR(8),
  telephone_umber           VARCHAR(8) NOT NULL,
  telephone_url                 URI
);
--Note that the ebRIM security view is not visible through the
public query mechanism
--in the current release
--The RegistryEntry View allows polymorphic queries over all ebRIM
classes derived
--from RegistryEntry
CREATE VIEW RegistryEntry (
--RegistryObject Attributes
```

```
  id,
  name,
  description,
  accessControlPolicy,
--Versionable attributes
  majorVersion,
  minorVersion,
--RegistryEntry attributes
  status,
  userVersion,
  stability,
  expirationDate
) AS
  SELECT
--RegistryObject Attributes
  id,
  name,
  description,
  accessControlPolicy,
--Versionable attributes
  majorVersion,
  minorVersion,
--RegistryEntry attributes
  status,
  userVersion,
  stability,
  expirationDate

  FROM ExtrinsicObject
  UNION
  SELECT
--RegistryObject Attributes
  id,
  name,
  description,
  accessControlPolicy,
--Versionable attributes
  majorVersion,
  minorVersion,
--RegistryEntry attributes
  status,
  userVersion,
  stability,
  expirationDate
  FROM (Registry)Package
  UNION
  SELECT
```

```
--RegistryObject Attributes
  id,
  name,
  description,
  accessControlPolicy,
--Versionable attributes
  majorVersion,
  minorVersion,
--RegistryEntry attributes
  status,
  userVersion,
  stability,
  expirationDate
FROM ClassificationNode;
```

Appendix D   Non-normative Content Based Ad Hoc Queries

The Registry SQL query capability supports the ability to search for content based not only on metadata that catalogs the content but also the data contained within the content itself. For example it is possible for a client to submit a query that searches for all Collaboration Party Profiles that define a role named "seller" within a RoleName element in the CPP document itself. Currently content-based query capability is restricted to XML content.

Automatic Classification of XML Content

Content-based queries are indirectly supported through the existing classification mechanism supported by the Registry.

A submitting organization may define logical indexes on any XML schema or DTD when it is submitted. An instance of such a logical index defines a link between a specific attribute or element node in an XML document tree and a ClassificationNode in a classification scheme within the registry.

The registry utilizes this index to automatically classify documents that are instances of the schema at the time the document instance is submitted. Such documents are classified according to the data contained within the document itself.

Such automatically classified content may subsequently be discovered by clients using the existing classification-based discovery mechanism of the Registry and the query facilities of the ObjectQueryManager.

> This approach is conceptually similar to the way databases support indexed retrieval. DBAs define indexes on tables in the schema. When data is added to the table, the data gets automatically indexed.

Note

Index Definition

This section describes how the logical indexes are defined in the SubmittedObject element defined in the Registry DTD. The complete Registry DTD is specified in Appendix A.

A SubmittedObject element for a schema or DTD may define a collection of ClassificationIndexes in a ClassificationIndexList optional element. The ClassificationIndexList is ignored if the content being submitted is not of the SCHEMA objectType.

The ClassificationIndex element inherits the attributes of the base class Registry-Object in [ebRIM]. It then defines specialized attributes as follows:

1. classificationNode: This attribute references a specific ClassificationNode by its ID.

2. contentIdentifier: This attribute identifies a specific data element within the document instances of the schema using an XPATH expression as defined by [XPT].

Example of Index Definition

To define an index that automatically classifies a CPP based upon the roles defined within its RoleName elements, the following index must be defined on the CPP schema or DTD:

```
<ClassificationIndex
        classificationNode='id-for-role-classification-scheme'
        contentIdentifier='/Role//RoleName'
/>
```

Proposed XML Definition

```
<!--
A ClassificationIndexList is specified on ExtrinsicObjects of
```

```
objectType 'Schema' to define an automatic Classification of in-
stance objects of the schema using the specified classification-
Node as parent and a ClassificationNode created or selected by
the object content as selected by the contentIdentifier
-->
<!ELEMENT ClassificationIndex EMPTY>
<!ATTLIST ClassificationIndex
        %ObjectAttributes;
        classificationNode IDREF #REQUIRED
        contentIdentifier CDATA #REQUIRED
>
<!-- ClassificationIndexList contains new ClassificationIndexes -->
<!ELEMENT ClassificationIndexList (ClassificationIndex)*>
```

Example of Automatic Classification

Assume that a CPP is submitted that defines two roles as "seller" and "buyer." When the CPP is submitted it will automatically be classified by two ClassificationNodes named "buyer" and "seller" that are both children of the ClassificationNode (e.g. a node named Role) specified in the classificationNode attribute of the ClassificationIndex. Note that if either of the two ClassificationNodes named "buyer" and "seller" did not previously exist, the ObjectManager would automatically create these ClassificationNodes.

Appendix E   Security Implementation Guideline

This section provides a suggested blueprint for how security processing may be implemented in the Registry. It is meant to be illustrative not prescriptive. Registries may choose to have different implementations as long as they support the default security roles and authorization rules described in this document.

Authentication

1. As soon as a message is received, the first work is the authentication. A principal object is created.

2. If the message is signed, it is verified (including the validity of the certificate) and the DN of the certificate becomes the identity of the principal. Then the Registry is searched for the principal and if found, the roles and groups are filled in.

3. If the message is not signed, an empty principal is created with the role RegistryGuest. This step is for symmetry and to decouple the rest of the processing.

4. Then the message is processed for the command and the objects it will act on.

Authorization

For every object, the access controller will iterate through all the AccessControl-Policy objects with the object and see if there is a chain through the permission objects to verify that the requested method is permitted for the Principal. If any of the permission objects which the object is associated with has a common role, or identity, or group with the principal, the action is permitted.

Registry Bootstrap

When a Registry is newly created, a default Principal object should be created with the identity of the Registry Admin's certificate DN with a role RegistryAdmin. This way, any message signed by the Registry Admin will get all the privileges.

When a Registry is newly created, a singleton instance of AccessControlPolicy is created as the default AccessControlPolicy. This includes the creation of the necessary Permission instances as well as the Privilges and Privilege attributes.

Content Submission – Client Responsibility

The Registry client has to sign the contents before submission – otherwise the content will be rejected.

Content Submission – Registry Responsibility

1. Like any other request, the client will be first authenticated. In this case, the Principal object will get the DN from the certificate.

2. As per the request in the message, the RegistryEntry will be created.

3. The RegistryEntry is assigned the singleton default AccessControlPolicy.

4. If a principal with the identity of the SO is not available, an identity object with the SO's DN is created

5. A principal with this identity is created

Content Delete/Deprecate – Client Responsibility

The Registry client has to sign the payload (not entire message) before submission, for authentication purposes; otherwise, the request will be rejected

Content Delete/Deprecate – Registry Responsibility

1. Like any other request, the client will be first authenticated. In this case, the Principal object will get the DN from the certificate. As there will be a principal with this identity in the Registry, the Principal object will get all the roles from that object

2. As per the request in the message (delete or deprecate), the appropriate method in the RegistryObject class will be accessed.

3. The access controller performs the authorization by iterating through the Permission objects associated with this object via the singleton default AccessControlPolicy.

4. If authorization succeeds then the action will be permitted. Otherwise an error response is sent back with a suitable AuthorizationException error message.

Appendix F   Native language support (NLS)

Definitions

Although this section discusses only character set and language, the following terms have to be defined clearly.

Coded Character Set (CCS):

CCS is a mapping from a set of abstract characters to a set of integers. [RFC 2130]. Examples of CCS are ISO-10646, US-ASCII, ISO-8859-1, and so on.

Character Encoding Scheme (CES):

CES is a mapping from a CCS (or several) to a set of octets. [RFC 2130]. Examples of CES are ISO-2022, UTF-8.

Character Set (charset):

charset is a set of rules for mapping from a sequence of octets to a sequence of characters.[RFC 2277],[RFC 2278]. Examples of character set are ISO-2022-JP, EUC-KR.

A list of registered character sets can be found at [IANA].

NLS and Request/Response Messages

For the accurate processing of data in both registry client and registry services, it is essential to know which character set is used. Although the body part of the transaction may contain the charset in xml encoding declaration, registry client and registry services shall specify charset parameter in MIME header when they use text/xml. Because as defined in [RFC 3023], if a text/xml entity is received with the charset parameter omitted, MIME processors and XML processors MUST use the default charset value of "us-ascii".

Ex. Content-Type: text/xml; charset=ISO-2022-JP

Also, when an application/xml entity is used, the charset parameter is optional, and registry client and registry services must follow the requirements in Section 4.3.3 of [REC-XML] which directly address this contingency.

If another Content-Type is chosen to be used, usage of charset must follow [RFC 3023].

NLS and Storing of RegistryEntry

This section provides NLS guidelines on how a registry should store **RegistryEntry** instances.

Character Set of RegistryEntry

This is basically an implementation issue because the actual character set that the RegistryEntry is stored with, does not affect the interface. However, it is highly recommended to use UTF-16 or UTF-8 for covering various languages.

Language Information of RegistryEntry

The language may be specified in xml:lang attribute (Section 2.12 [REC-XML]). If the xml:lang attribute is specified, then the registry may use that language code as the value of a special Slot with name language and sloType of nls in the RegistryEntry. The value must be compliant to [RFC 1766]. Slots are defined in [ebRIM].

NLS and Storing of Repository Items

This section provides NLS guidelines on how a registry should store repository items.

Character Set of Repository Items

Unlike the character set of **RegistryEntry**, the charset of a repository item must be preserved as it is originally specified in the transaction. The registry may use a special Slot with name **repositoryItemCharset,** and sloType of **nls** for the **RegistryEntry** for storing the charset of the corresponding repository item. Value must be the one defined in [RFC 2277], [RFC 2278]. The **repositoryItemCharset** is optional because not all repository items require it.

Language Information of Repository Item

Specifying only character set is not enough to tell which language is used in the repository item. A registry may use a special Slot with name **repositoryItemLang,** and sloType of **nls** to store that information. This attribute is optional because not all repository items require it. Value must be compliant to [RFC 1766]

This document currently specifies only the method of sending the information of character set and language, and how it is stored in a registry. However, the language information may be used as one of the query criteria, such as retrieving only DTD written in French. Furthermore, a language negotiation procedure, like registry client is asking a favorite language for messages from registry services, could be another functionality for the future revision of this document.

Appendix G   Terminology Mapping

While every attempt has been made to use the same terminology used in other works there are some terminology differences.

The following table shows the terminology mapping between this specification and that used in other specifications and working groups.

TABLE 1   Terminology Mapping Table

This Document	OASIS	ISO 11179
"repository item"	RegisteredObject	
RegistryEntry	RegistryEntry	Administered Component
ExternalLink	RelatedData	N/A
Object.id	regEntryId, orgId, etc.	
ExtrinsicObject.uri	objectURL	
ExtrinsicObject.objectType	defnSource, objectType	
RegistryEntry.name	commonName	
Object.description	shortDescription, Description	
ExtrinsicObject.mimeType	objectType="mime" fileType="<mime type>"	
Versionable.majorVersion	userVersion only	
Versionable.minorVersion	userVersion only	
RegistryEntry.status	registrationStatus	

Collaboration-Protocol Profile and Agreement Specification

v1.0
Trading Partners Team
10 May 2001

Table of Contents

1   Status of this Document

This document specifies an ebXML Technical Specification for the eBusiness community.

Distribution of this document is unlimited.

The document formatting is based on the Internet Society's Standard RFC format.

This version:
http://www.ebxml.org/specs/ebCPP.pdf

Latest version:
http://www.ebxml.org/specs/ebCPP.pdf

2   ebXML Participants

The authors wish to recognize the following for their significant participation to the development of this document.

David Burdett	CommerceOne
Tim Chiou	United World Chinese Commercial Bank
Chris Ferris	Sun
Scott Hinkelman	IBM
Maryann Hondo	IBM
Sam Hunting	ECOM XML
John Ibbotson	IBM
Kenji Itoh	JASTPRO
Ravi Kacker	eXcelon Corp.
Thomas Limanek	iPlanet
Daniel Ling	VCHEQ
Henry Lowe	OMG
Dale Moberg	Cyclone Commerce

Duane Nickull	XMLGlobal Technologies
Stefano Pogliani	Sun
Rebecca Reed	Mercator
Karsten Riemer	Sun
Marty Sachs	IBM
Yukinori Saito	ECOM
Tony Weida	Edifecs

3 Introduction

3.1 Summary of Contents of Document

As defined in the ebXML Business Process Specification Schema[ebBPSS], a *Business Partner* is an entity that engages in *Business Transactions* with another *Business Partner(s)*. Each *Partner's* capabilities (both commercial/*Business* and technical) to engage in electronic *Message* exchanges with other *Partners* MAY be described by a document called a *Trading-Partner Profile* (*TPP*). The agreed interactions between two *Partners* MAY be documented in a document called a *Trading-Partner Agreement (TPA)*. A *TPA* MAY be created by computing the intersection of the two *Partners' TPPs*.

The *Message*-exchange capabilities of a *Party* MAY be described by a *Collaboration-Protocol Profile (CPP)* within the TPP. The Message-exchange agreement between two Parties MAY be described by a *Collaboration-Protocol Agreement (CPA)* within the TPA. Included in the CPP and CPA are details of transport, messaging, security constraints, and bindings to a *Business-Process-Specification* (or, for short, *Process-Specification*) document that contains the definition of the interactions between the two Parties while engaging in a specified electronic *Business Collaboration*.

This specification contains the detailed definitions of the *Collaboration-Protocol Profile (CPP)* and the *Collaboration-Protocol Agreement (CPA)*.

This specification is a component of the suite of ebXML specifications. An overview of the ebXML specifications and their interrelations can be found in the ebXML Technical Architecture Specification[ebTA].

This specification is organized as follows:

▼ Section 4 defines the objectives of this specification.

▼ Section 5 provides a system overview.

▼ Section 6 contains the definition of the *CPP*, identifying the structure and all necessary fields.

▼ Section 7 contains the definition of the *CPA*.

▼ The appendices include examples of XML *CPP* and *CPA* documents (non-normative), the DTD (normative), an XML Schema document equivalent to the DTD (normative), formats of information in the *CPP* and *CPA* (normative), and composing a *CPA* from two *CPPs* (non-normative).

3.2 Document Conventions

Terms in *Italics* are defined in the ebXML Glossary of Terms[ebGLOSS]. Terms listed in **Bold Italics** represent the element and/or attribute content of the XML *CPP or CPA* definitions.

In this specification, indented paragraphs beginning with "NOTE:" provide non-normative explanations or suggestions that are not required by the specification.

References to external documents are represented with BLOCK text enclosed in brackets, e.g. [RFC2396]. The references are listed in Section 8, "References".

The keywords MUST, MUST NOT, REQUIRED, SHALL, SHALL NOT, SHOULD, SHOULD NOT, RECOMMENDED, MAY, and OPTIONAL, when they appear in this document, are to be interpreted as described in [RFC 2119].

> **Vendors should carefully consider support of elements with cardinalities (0 or 1) or (0 or more). Support of such an element means that the element is processed appropriately for its defined function and not just recognized and ignored. A given *Party* might use these elements in some *CPPs* or *CPAs* and not in others. Some of these elements define parameters or operating modes and should be implemented by all vendors. It might be appropriate to implement optional elements that represent major run-time functions, such as various alternative communication protocols or security functions, by means of plug-ins so that a given *Party* MAY acquire only the needed functions rather than having to install all of them.**

Note

3.3 Use of XML Schema

The schema of the *CPP* and *CPA* is based on the Candidate-Recommendation version of the XML Schema specification[XMLSCHEMA-1,XMLSCHEMA-2]. When XML Schema advances to Recommendation status, some changes will be needed in this specification and its schema. The changes are indicated by XML comments in the current schema document in Appendix D

3.4   Version of the Specification

Whenever this specification is modified, it SHALL be given a new version number. The value of the **version** attribute of the **Schema** element of the XML Schema document SHALL be equal to the version of the specification.

3.5   Definitions

Technical terms in this specification are defined in the ebXML Glossary [ebGLOSS].

3.6   Audience

One target audience for this specification is implementers of ebXML services and other designers and developers of middleware and application software that is to be used for conducting electronic *Business*. Another target audience is the people in each enterprise who are responsible for creating *CPPs* and *CPAs*.

3.7   Assumptions

It is expected that the reader has an understanding of [XML] and is familiar with the concepts of electronic *Business* (eBusiness).

3.8   Related Documents

Related documents include ebXML Specifications on the following topics:

> [ebTA] ebXML Technical Architecture Specification v1.04
>
> [ebMS] ebXML *Message* Service Specification v1.0
>
> [ebBPSS] ebXML Business Process Specification Schema v1.01
>
> [ebGLOSS] ebXML Glossary
>
> [ccOVER] ebXML Core Component and Business Document Overview v1.05
>
> [ebRS] ebXML Registry Services Specification v1.0

See Section 8 for the complete list of references.

4 Design Objectives

The objective of this specification is to ensure interoperability between two *Parties* even though they MAY procure application software and run-time support software from different vendors. The *CPP* defines a *Party's Message*-exchange capabilities and the *Business Collaborations* that it supports. The *CPA* defines the way two *Parties* will interact in performing the chosen *Business Collaboration*. Both *Parties* SHALL use identical copies of the *CPA* to configure their run-time systems. This assures that they are compatibly configured to exchange *Messages* whether or not they have obtained their run-time systems from the same vendor. The configuration process MAY be automated by means of a suitable tool that reads the *CPA* and performs the configuration process.

In addition to supporting direct interaction between two *Parties*, this specification MAY also be used to support interaction between two *Parties* through an intermediary such as a portal or broker. In this initial version of this specification, this MAY be accomplished by creating a *CPA* between each *Party* and the intermediary in addition to the *CPA* between the two *Parties*. The functionality needed for the interaction between a *Party* and the intermediary is described in the *CPA* between the *Party* and the intermediary. The functionality needed for the interaction between the two *Parties* is described in the *CPA* between the two *Parties*.

It is an objective of this specification that a *CPA* SHALL be capable of being composed by intersecting the respective *CPPs* of the *Parties* involved. The resulting *CPA* SHALL contain only those elements that are in common, or compatible, between the two *Parties*. Variable quantities, such as number of retries of errors, are then negotiated between the two *Parties*. The design of the *CPP* and *CPA* schemata facilitates this composition/negotiation process. However, the composition and negotiation processes themselves are outside the scope of this specification. Appendix Fcontains a non-normative discussion of this subject.

It is a further objective of this specification to facilitate migration of both traditional EDI-based applications and other legacy applications to platforms based on the ebXML specifications. In particular, the *CPP* and *CPA* are components of the migration of applications based on the X12 838 Trading-Partner Profile to more automated means of setting up *Business* relationships and doing *Business* under them.

5   System Overview

5.1   What this Specification Does

The exchange of information between two *Parties* requires each *Party* to know the other *Party's* supported *Business Collaborations,* the other *Party's* role in the *Business Collaboration,* and the technology details about how the other *Party* sends and receives *Messages.* In some cases, it is necessary for the two *Parties* to reach agreement on some of the details.

The way each *Party* can exchange information, in the context of a *Business Collaboration,* can be described by a *Collaboration-Protocol Profile (CPP).* The agreement between the *Parties* can be expressed as *a Collaboration-Protocol Agreement (CPA).*

A *Party* MAY describe itself in a single *CPP.* A *Party* MAY create multiple *CPPs* that describe, for example, different *Business Collaborations* that it supports, its operations in different regions of the world, or different parts of its organization.

To enable *Parties* wishing to do *Business* to find other *Parties* that are suitable *Business Partners, CPPs* MAY be stored in a repository such as is provided by the ebXML Registry[ebRS]. Using a discovery process provided as part of the specifications of a repository, a *Party* MAY then use the facilities of the repository to find *Business Partners.*

The document that defines the interactions between two *Parties* is a *Process-Specification* document that MAY conform to the ebXML Business Process Specification Schema[ebBPSS]. The *CPP* and *CPA* include references to this *Process-Specification* document. The *Process-Specification* document MAY be stored in a repository such as the ebXML Registry. See NOTE about alternative *Business-Collaboration* descriptions in section 6.5.4.

Figure 1 illustrates the relationships between a *CPP* and two *Process-Specification* documents, A1 and A2, in an ebXML Registry. On the left is a *CPP,* A, which includes information about two parts of an enterprise that are represented as different *Parties.* On the right are shown two *Process-Specification* documents. Each of the **PartyInfo** elements in the *CPP* contains a reference to one of the *Process-Specification* documents. This identifies the *Business Collaboration* that the *Party* can perform.

This specification defines the markup language vocabulary for creating electronic *CPPs* and *CPAs. CPPs* and *CPAs* are [XML] documents. In the appendices of this specification are a sample *CPP,* a sample *CPA,* the DTD, and the corresponding XML Schema document.

Repository

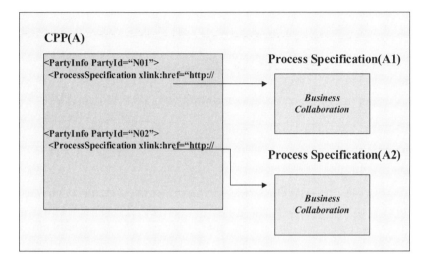

FIGURE 1 Structure of CPP & Business Process Specification in an ebXML Registry

The *CPP* describes the capabilities of an individual *Party*. A *CPA* describes the capabilites that two *Parties* have agreed to use to perform a particular *Business Collaboration*. These *CPAs* define the "information technology terms and conditions" that enable *Business* documents to be electronically interchanged between *Parties.* The information content of a *CPA* is similar to the information-technology specifications sometimes included in Electronic Data Interchange (EDI) *Trading Partner Agreements (TPAs).* However, these *CPAs* are not paper documents. Rather, they are electronic documents that can be processed by computers at the *Parties'* sites in order to set up and then execute the desired *Business* information exchanges. The "legal" terms and conditions of a *Business* agreement are outside the scope of this specification and therefore are not included in the *CPP* and *CPA.*

An enterprise MAY choose to represent itself as multiple *Parties.* For example, it might represent a central office supply procurement organization and a manufacturing supplies procurement organization as separate *Parties.* The enterprise MAY then construct a *CPP* that includes all of its units that are represented as separate *Parties.* In the *CPP*, each of those units would be represented by a separate **PartyInfo** element.

In general, the *Parties* to a *CPA* can have both client and server characteristics. A client requests services and a server provides services to the *Party* requesting services. In some applications, one *Party* only requests services and one *Party* only provides services. These applications have some resemblance to traditional client-server applications. In other applications, each *Party* MAY request services of the other. In that case, the relationship between the two *Parties* can be described as a peer-peer relationship rather than a client-server relationship.

5.2   Forming a CPA from Two CPPs

This section summarizes the process of discovering a *Party* to do *Business* with and forming a *CPA* from the two *Parties' CPPs*. In general, this section is an overview of a possible procedure and is not to be considered a normative specification. See Appendix F "Composing a CPA from Two CPPs (Non-Normative)" for more information.

Figure 2 illustrates forming a *CPP. Party* A tabulates the information to be placed in a repository for the discovery process, constructs a *CPP* that contains this information, and enters it into an ebXML Registry or similar repository along with additional information about the *Party*. The additional information might include a description of the *Businesses* that the *Party* engages in. Once *Party* A's information is in the repository, other *Parties* can discover *Party* A by using the repository's discovery services.

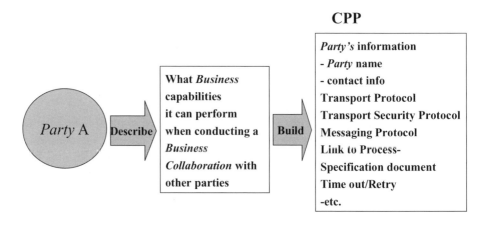

FIGURE 2   Overview of Collaboration-Protocol Profiles (CPP)

In figure 3, *Party* A and *Party* B use their *CPPs* to jointly construct a single copy of a *CPA* by calculating the intersection of the information in their *CPPs*. The resulting *CPA* defines how the two *Parties* will behave in performing their *Business Collaboration*.

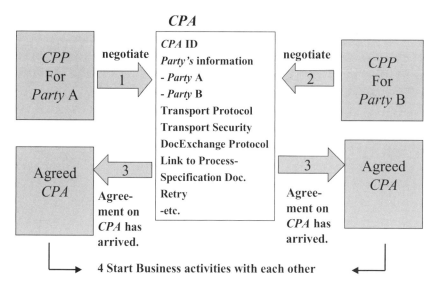

FIGURE 3   Overview of *Collaboration-Protocol Agreements (CPA)*

Figure 4 illustrates the entire process. The steps are listed at the left. The end of the process is that the two *Parties* configure their systems from identical copies of the agreed *CPA* and they are then ready to do *Business*.

1. Any *Party* may register its CPPs to an ebXML Registry.

2. *Party* B discovers trading partner A (Seller) by searching in the Registry and downloads *CPP*(A) to *Party* B's server.

3. *Party* B creates *CPA*(A,B) and sends *CPA*(A,B) to *Party* A.

4. *Parties* A and B negotiate and store identical copies of the completed *CPA* as a document in both servers. This process is done manually or automatically.

5. *Parties* A and B configure their run-time systems with the information in the *CPA*.

6. *Parties* A and B do business under the new *CPA*.

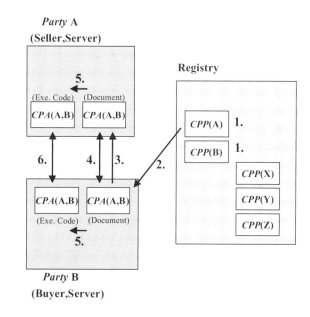

FIGURE 4   Overview of Working Architecture of CPP/CPA with ebXML Registry

> This specification makes the assumption that a *CPP* that has been registered in an ebXML or other Registry will be referenced by some Registry-assigned globally-unique identifier that MAY be used to distinguish among multiple *CPPs* belonging to the same *Party*. See section 6.1 for more information.

5.3 How the CPA Works

A *CPA* describes all the valid visible, and hence enforceable, interactions between the *Parties* and the way these interactions are carried out. It is independent of the internal processes executed at each *Party*. Each *Party* executes its own internal processes and interfaces them with the *Business Collaboration* described by the *CPA* and *Process-Specification* document. The *CPA* does not expose details of a *Party's* internal processes to the other *Party*. The intent of the *CPA* is to provide a high-level specification that can be easily comprehended by humans and yet is precise enough for enforcement by computers.

The information in the *CPA* is used to configure the *Parties'* systems to enable exchange of *Messages* in the course of performing the selected *Business Collaboration*. Typically, the software that performs the *Messages* exchanges and otherwise supports the interactions between the *Parties* is middleware that can support any selected *Business Collaboration*. One component of this middleware MAY be the ebXML *Message* Service Handler[ebMS]. In this specification, the term "run-time system" or "run-time software" is used to denote such middleware.

The *CPA* and the *Process-Specification* document that it references define a conversation between the two *Parties*. The conversation represents a single unit of *Business* as defined by the *Binary-Collaboration* component of the *Process-Specification* document. The conversation consists of one or more *Business Transactions*, each of which is a request *Message* from one *Party* and zero or one response *Message* from the other *Party*. The *Process-Specification* document defines, among other things, the request and response *Messages* for each *Business Transaction* and the order in which the *Business Transactions* are REQUIRED to occur. See [ebBPSS] for a detailed explanation.

The *CPA* MAY actually reference more than one *Process-Specification* document. When a *CPA* references more than one *Process-Specification* document, each *Process-Specification* document defines a distinct type of conversation. Any one conversation involves only a single *Process-Specification* document.

A new conversation is started each time a new unit of *Business* is started. The *Business Collaboration* also determines when the conversation ends. From the viewpoint of a *CPA* between *Party* A and *Party* B, the conversation starts at *Party* A when *Party* A sends the first request *Message* to *Party* B. At *Party* B, the conversation starts when it receives the first request of the unit of *Business* from *Party* A. A conversation ends when the *Parties* have completed the unit of *Business*.

> The run-time system SHOULD provide an interface by which the *Business* application can request initiation and ending of conversations.

Note

5.4 Where the CPA May Be Implemented

Conceptually, a *Business*-to-*Business* (B2B) server at each *Party's* site implements the CPA and Process-Specification document. The B2B server includes the run-time software, i.e. the middleware that supports communication with the other *Party,* execution of the functions specified in the *CPA*, interfacing to each *Party's* back-end processes, and logging the interactions between the *Parties* for purposes such as audit and recovery. The middleware might support the concept of a long-running conversation as the embodiment of a single unit of *Business* between the *Parties*. To configure the two *Parties'* systems for *Business* to *Business* operations, the information in the copy of the *CPA* and *Process-Specification* documents at each *Party's* site is installed in the run-time system. The static information MAY be recorded in a local database and other information in the *CPA* and *Process-Specification* document MAY be used in generating or customizing the necessary code to support the *CPA*.

> It is possible to provide a graphic *CPP/CPA*-authoring tool that understands both the semantics of the *CPP/CPA* and the XML syntax. Equally important, the definitions in this specification make it feasible to automatically generate, at each *Party's* site, the code needed to execute the *CPA*, enforce its rules, and interface with the *Party's* back-end processes.

Note

5.5 Definition and Scope

This specification defines and explains the contents of the *CPP* and *CPA* XML documents. Its scope is limited to these definitions. It does not define how to compose a *CPA* from two *CPPs* nor does it define anything related to run-time support for the *CPP* and *CPA*. It does include some non-normative suggestions and recommendations regarding run-time support where these notes serve to clarify the *CPP* and *CPA* definitions. See section 9 for a discussion of conformance to this specification.

> This specification is limited to defining the contents of the *CPP* and *CPA*, and it is possible to be conformant with it merely by producing a *CPP* or *CPA* document that conforms to the DTD and XML Schema documents defined herein. It is, however, important to understand that the value of this specification lies in its enabling a run-time system that supports electronic commerce between two *Parties* under the guidance of the information in the *CPA*.

Note

6 CPP Definition

A *CPP* defines the capabilities of a *Party* to engage in electronic *Business* with other *Parties.* These capabilities include both technology capabilities, such as supported communication and messaging protocols, and *Business* capabilities in terms of what *Business Collaborations* it supports.

This section defines and discusses the details in the *CPP* in terms of the individual XML elements. The discussion is illustrated with some XML fragments. See Appendix Cand Appendix Dfor the DTD and XML Schema, respectively, and Appendix Afor a sample *CPP* document.

The **ProcessSpecification, DeliveryChannel, DocExchange,** and **Transport** elements of the *CPP* describe the processing of a unit of *Business* (conversation). These elements form a layered structure somewhat analogous to a layered communication model. The remainder of this section describes both the above-mentioned elements and the corresponding run-time processing.

Process-Specification layer - The *Process-Specification* layer defines the heart of the *Business* agreement between the *Parties:* the services (*Business Transactions*) which *Parties* to the *CPA* can request of each other and transition rules that determine the order of requests. This layer is defined by the separate *Process-Specification* document that is referenced by the *CPP* and *CPA.*

Delivery Channels - A delivery channel describes a *Party's Message*-receiving characteristics. It consists of one document-exchange definition and one transport definition. Several delivery channels MAY be defined in one *CPP.*

Document-Exchange layer - The document-exchange layer accepts a *Business* document from the *Process-Specification* layer at one *Party,* encrypts it if specified, adds a digital signature for nonrepudiation if specified, and passes it to the transport layer for transmission to the other *Party.* It performs the inverse steps for received *Messages.* The options selected for the document-exchange layer are complementary to those selected for the transport layer. For example, if *Message* security is desired and the selected transport protocol does not provide *Message* encryption, then it must be specified at the document-exchange layer. The protocol for exchanging *Messages* between two *Parties* is defined by the ebXML *Message* Service Specification[ebMS] or other similar messaging service.

Transport layer - The transport layer is responsible for *Message* delivery using the selected transport protocol. The selected protocol affects the choices selected for the document-exchange layer. For example, some transport-layer protocols might provide encryption and authentication while others have no such facility.

It should be understood that the functional layers encompassed by the *CPP* have no understanding of the contents of the payload of the *Business* documents.

6.1   Globally-Unique Identifier of CPP Instance Document

When a *CPP* is placed in an ebXML or other Registry, the Registry assigns it a globally-unique identifier (GUID) that is part of its metadata. That GUID MAY be used to distinguish among *CPPs* belonging to the same *Party*.

> **A Registry cannot insert the GUID into the *CPP*. In general, a Registry does not alter the content of documents submitted to it. Furthermore, a *CPP* MAY be signed and alteration of a signed *CPP* would invalidate the signature.**

 Note

6.2   SchemaLocation Attribute

The W3C XML Schema specification[XMLSCHEMA-1,XMLSCHEMA-2] that went to Candidate Recommendation status, effective October 24, 2000, has recently gone to Proposed Recommendation effective March 30, 2001. Many, if not most, tools providing support for schema validation and validating XML parsers available at the time that this specification was written have been designed to support the Candidate Recommendation draft of the XML Schema specification.

In order to enable validating parsers and various schema-validating tools to correctly process and parse ebXML CPP and CPA documents, it has been necessary that the ebXML TP team produce a schema that conforms to the W3C Candidate Recommendation draft of the XML Schema specification. Implementations of CPP and CPA authoring tools are STRONGLY RECOMMENDED to include the XMLSchema-instance namespace-qualified schemaLocation attribute in the document's root element to indicate to validating parsers the location URI of the schema document that should be used to validate the document. Failure to include the schemaLocation attribute MAY result in interoperability issues with other tools that need to be able to validate these documents.

At such time as the XML Schema specification is adopted as a W3C Recommendation, a revised CPP/CPA schema SHALL be produced that SHALL contain any updates as necessary to conform to that Recommendation.

An example of the use of the schemaLocation attribute follows:

```
<CollaborationProtocolAgreement
    xmlns="http://www.ebxml.org/namespaces/tradePartner"
    xmlns:xsi="http://www.w3.org/2000/10/XMLSchema-instance"
```

```
        xsi:schemaLocation="http://www.ebxml.org/namespaces/trade-
Partner
               http://ebxml.org/project_teams/trade_partner/cpp-
cpa-10.xsd"
        ...
        >
        ...
   </CollaborationProtocolAgreement>
```

6.3   CPP Structure

Following is the overall structure of the *CPP*. Unless otherwise noted, *CPP* elements MUST be in the order shown here. Subsequent sections describe each of the elements in greater detail.

```
<CollaborationProtocolProfile
      xmlns="http://www.ebxml.org/namespaces/tradePartner"
      xmlns:ds="http://www.w3.org/2000/09/xmldsig#"
      xmlns:xlink="http://www.w3.org/1999/xlink"
      version="1.1">
      <PartyInfo> <!--one or more-->
      ...
      </PartyInfo>
      <Packaging id="ID"> <!--one or more-->
          ...
      <Packaging>
      <ds:Signature> <!--zero or one-->
      ...
      </ds:Signature>
      <Comment>text</Comment> <!--zero or more-->
      </CollaborationProtocolProfile>
```

6.4   CollaborationProtocolProfile Element

The **CollaborationProtocolProfile** element is the root element of the *CPP* XML document.

The REQUIRED [XML] Namespace[XMLNS] declarations for the basic document are as follows:

▼ The default namespace:
   xmlns="http://www.ebxml.org/namespaces/tradePartner",

▼ XML Digital Signature namespace:
xmlns:ds="http://www.w3.org/2000/09/xmldsig#",

▼ and the XLINK namespace:
xmlns:xlink="http://www.w3.org/1999/xlink".

In addition, the **CollaborationProtocolProfile** element contains an IMPLIED **version** attribute that indicates the version of the *CPP*. Its purpose is to provide versioning capabilities for instances of an enterprise's *CPP*. The value of the version attribute SHOULD be a string representation of a numeric value such as "1.0" or "2.3". The value of the version string SHOULD be changed with each change made to the *CPP* document after it has been published.

> The method of assigning the version-identifier value is left to the implementation.   **Note**

The **CollaborationProtocolProfile** element SHALL consist of the following child elements:

▼ One or more REQUIRED **PartyInfo** elements that identify the organization (or parts of the organization) whose capabilities are described by the *CPP*,

▼ One REQUIRED **Packaging** element,

▼ Zero or one **ds:Signature** elements that contain the digital signature that signs the *CPP* document,

▼ Zero or more **Comment** elements.

A *CPP* document MAY be digitally signed so as to provide for a means of ensuring that the document has not been altered (integrity) and to provide for a means of authenticating the author of the document. A digitally signed *CPP* SHALL be signed using technology that conforms to the joint W3C/IETF XML Digital Signature specification[XMLDSIG].

6.5   PartyInfo Element

The **PartyInfo** element identifies the organization whose capabilities are described in this *CPP* and includes all the details about this *Party*. More than one **PartyInfo** element MAY be provided in a *CPP* if the organization chooses to represent itself as subdivisions with different characteristics. Each of the subelements of **PartyInfo** is discussed later. The overall structure of the **PartyInfo** element is as follows:

```
<PartyInfo>
      <PartyId type="..."> <!--one or more-->
            . . .
      </PartyId>
      <PartyRef xlink:type="...", xlink:href="..."/>
      <CollaborationRole> <!--one or more-->
            . . .
      </CollaborationRole>
      <Certificate> <!--one or more-->
            . . .
      </Certificate>
      <DeliveryChannel> <!--one or more-->
      . . .
      </DeliveryChannel>
      <Transport> <!--one or more-->
      . . .
      </Transport>
      <DocExchange> <!--one or more-->
      . . .
      </DocExchange>
</PartyInfo>
```

The **PartyInfo** element consists of the following child elements:

▼ One or more REQUIRED **PartyId** elements that provide a logical identifier for the organization.

▼ A REQUIRED **PartyRef** element that provides a pointer to more information about the *Party*.

▼ One or more REQUIRED **CollaborationRole** elements that identify the roles that this *Party* can play in the context of a *Process Specification*.

▼ One or more REQUIRED **Certificate** elements that identify the certificates used by this *Party* in security functions.

▼ One or more REQUIRED **DeliveryChannel** elements that define the characteristics of each delivery channel that the *Party* can use to receive *Messages*. It includes both the transport level (e.g. HTTP) and the messaging protocol (e.g. ebXML *Message* Service).

▼ One or more REQUIRED **Transport** elements that define the characteristics of the transport protocol(s) that the *Party* can support to receive *Messages*.

▼ One or more REQUIRED **DocExchange** elements that define the *Message*-exchange characteristics, such as the *Message*-exchange protocol, that the *Party* can support.

6.5.1 PartyId Element

The REQUIRED **PartyId** element provides a logical identifier that MAY be used to logically identify the *Party*. Additional **PartyId** elements MAY be present under the same **PartyInfo** element so as to provide for alternative logical identifiers for the *Party*. If the *Party* has preferences as to which logical identifier is used, the **PartyId** elements SHOULD be listed in order of preference starting with the most-preferred identifier.

In a *CPP* that contains multiple **PartyInfo** elements, different **PartyInfo** elements MAY contain **PartyId** elements that define different logical identifiers. This permits a large organization, for example, to have different identifiers for different purposes.

The value of the **PartyId** element is any string that provides a unique identifier. The identifier MAY be any identifier that is understood by both *Parties* to a *CPA*. Typically, the identifier would be listed in a well-known directory such as DUNS or in any naming system specified by [ISO6523].

The **PartyId** element has a single IMPLIED attribute: **type** that has a string value.

If the **type** attribute is present, then it provides a scope or namespace for the content of the **PartyId** element.

If the **type** attribute is not present, the content of the **PartyId** element MUST be a URI that conforms to [RFC2396]. It is RECOMMENDED that the value of the **type** attribute be a URN that defines a namespace for the value of the **PartyId** element. Typically, the URN would be registered as a well-known directory of organization identifiers.

The following example illustrates two URI references.

```
<PartyId type = "uriReference">urn:duns:123456789</PartyId>
<PartyId type = "uriReference">urn:www.example.com</PartyId>
```

The first example is the URN for the *Party's* DUNS number, assuming that Dun and Bradstreet has registered a URN for DUNS numbers with the Internet Assigned Numbers Authority (IANA). The last field is the DUNS number of the organization.

The second example shows an arbitrary URN. This might be a URN that the *Party* has registered with IANA to identify itself directly.

6.5.2 PartyRef Element

The **PartyRef** element provides a link, in the form of a URI, to additional information about the *Party*. Typically, this would be the URL from which the information can be obtained. The information might be at the *Party's* web site or in a publicly accessible repository such as an ebXML Registry, a UDDI repository, or an LDAP directory. Information available at that URI MAY include contact names, addresses, and phone numbers, and perhaps more information about the *Business Collaborations* that the *Party* supports. This information MAY be in the form of an ebXML Core Component[ccOVER]. It is not within the scope of this specification to define the content or format of the information at that URI.

The **PartyRef** element is an [XLINK] simple link. It has the following attributes:

▼ a REQUIRED **xlink:type** attribute,

▼ a REQUIRED **xlink:href** attribute,

▼ an IMPLIED **type** attribute.

6.5.2.1   xlink:type Attribute

The REQUIRED **xlink:type** attribute SHALL have a FIXED value of "simple". This identifies the element as being an [XLINK] simple link.

6.5.2.2   xlink:href Attribute

The REQUIRED **xlink:href** attribute SHALL have a value that is a URI that conforms to [RFC2396] and identifies the location of the external information about the *Party*.

6.5.2.3   type Attribute

The value of the IMPLIED **type** attribute identifies the document type of the external information about the *Party*. It MUST be a URI that defines the namespace associated with the information about the *Party*. If the **type** attribute is omitted, the external information about the *Party* MUST be an HTML web page.

An example of the **PartyRef** element is:

```
<PartyRef xlink:type="simple"
    xlink:href="http://example2.com/ourInfo.xml"
    type="uri-reference"/>
```

6.5.3   CollaborationRole Element

The **CollaborationRole** element associates a *Party* with a specific role in the *Business Collaboration* that is defined in the *Process-Specification* document[ebBPSS]. Generally, the *Process Specification* is defined in terms of roles such as "buyer" and "seller". The association between a specific *Party* and the role(s) it is capable of fulfilling within the context of a *Process Specification* is defined in both the *CPP* and *CPA* documents. In a *CPP*, the **Collaboration-Role** element identifies which role the *Party* is capable of playing in each *Process Specification* documents referenced by the *CPP*. An example of the **CollaborationRole** element is:

```
<CollaborationRole id="N11" >
    <ProcessSpecification name="BuySell" version="1.0">
    ...
    </ProcessSpecification>
    <Role name="buyer" xlink:href="..."/>
    <CertificateRef certId = "N03"/>
      <!-- primary binding with "preferred" DeliveryChannel -->
    <ServiceBinding name="some process" channelId="N02" package-
Id="N06">
        <!-- override "default" deliveryChannel for selected
message(s)-->
        <Override action="OrderAck" channelId="N05" packageId="N09"
            xlink:type="simple"
            xlink:href="..."/>
    </ServiceBinding>
    <!-- the first alternate binding -->
    <ServiceBinding channelId="N04" packageId="N06">
        <Override action="OrderAck" channelId="N05" packageId="N09"
      xlink:type="simple"
            xlink:href="..."/>
    </ServiceBinding>
</CollaborationRole>
```

To indicate that the *Party* can play roles in more than one *Business Collaboration* or more than one role in a given *Business Collaboration*, the **PartyInfo** element SHALL contain more than one **CollaborationRole** element. Each **Collaboration-Role** element SHALL contain the appropriate combination of **Process-Specification** element and **Role** element.

The **CollaborationRole** element SHALL consist of the following child elements: a REQUIRED **ProcessSpecification** element, a REQUIRED **Role** element, zero or one **CertificateRef** element, and one or more **ServiceBinding** elements. The **ProcessSpecification** element identifies the *Process-Specification* document that defines such role. The **Role** element identifies which role the *Party* is capable of supporting. The **CertificateRef** element identifies the certificate to be used. Each **ServiceBinding** element provides a binding of the role to a default **Delivery-Channel.** The default **DeliveryChannel** describes the receive properties of all *Message* traffic that is to be received by the *Party* within the context of the role in the identified *Process-Specification* document. Alternative **DeliveryChannels** MAY be specified for specific purposes, using **Override** elements as described below.

When there are more than one **ServiceBinding** child elements of a **Collabora-tionRole**, then the order of the **ServiceBinding** elements SHALL be treated as signifying the *Party's* preference starting with highest and working towards lowest. The default delivery channel for a given *Process-Specification* document is the delivery channel identified by the highest-preference **ServiceBinding** element that references the particular *Process-Specification* document.

Note

> When a *CPA* is composed, the ServiceBinding **preferences are applied in choosing the highest-preference delivery channels that are compatible between the two *Parties*.**

When a *CPA* is composed, only **ServiceBinding** elements that are compatible between the two *Parties* SHALL be retained. Each *Party* SHALL have a default delivery channel for each *Process-Specification* document referenced in the *CPA*. For each *Process-Specification* document, the default delivery channel for each *Party* is the delivery channel that is indicated by the **channelId** attribute in the highest-preference **ServiceBinding** element that references that *Process-Specification* document.

Note

> **An implementation MAY provide the capability of dynamically assigning delivery channels on a per *Message* basis during performance of the *Business Collaboration*. The delivery channel selected would be chosen, based on present conditions, from those identified by** ServiceBinding **elements that refer to the *Business Collaboration* that is sending the *Message*. If more than one delivery channel is applicable, the one referred to by the highest-preference** ServiceBinding **element is used.**

The **CollaborationRole** element has the following attribute:

▼ a REQUIRED **id** attribute.

6.5.3.1   id Attribute

The REQUIRED **id** attribute is an [XML] ID attribute by which this **CollaborationRole** element can be referenced from elsewhere in the *CPP* document.

6.5.3.2   CertificateRef Element

The EMPTY **CertificateRef** element contains an IMPLIED IDREF attribute, **certId,** which identifies the certificate to be used by referring to the **Certificate** element (under **PartyInfo**) that has the matching ID attribute value.

6.5.3.3   certId Attribute

The IMPLIED **certId** attribute is an [XML] IDREF that associates the **CollaborationRole** with a **Certificate** with a matching ID attribute**.**

Note

> **This** certId **attribute relates to the authorizing role in the *Process Specification* while the certificates identified in the delivery-channel description relate to *Message* exchanges.**

6.5.4 ProcessSpecification Element

The **ProcessSpecification** element provides the link to the *Process-Specification* document that defines the interactions between the two *Parties*. It is RECOMMENDED that this *Business-Collaboration* description be prepared in accord with the ebXML Business Process Specification Schema[ebBPSS]. The *Process-Specification* document MAY be kept in an ebXML Registry.

> A *Party* MAY describe the *Business Collaboration* using any desired alternative to the ebXML Business Process Specification Schema. When an alternative *Business-Collaboration* description is used, the *Parties* to a *CPA* MUST agree on how to interpret the *Business-Collaboration* description and how to interpret the elements in the *CPA* that reference information in the *Business-Collaboration* description. The affected elements in the *CPA* are the Role element, the Override element, and some attributes of the Characteristics element.

The syntax of the **ProcessSpecification** element is:

```
<ProcessSpecification
      name="BuySell"
      version="1.0"
      xlink:type="simple"
      xlink:href="http://www.ebxml.org/services/purchasing.xml"
      <ds:Reference ds:URI="http://www.ebxml.org/services/
purchasing.xml">
            <ds:Transforms>
                  <ds:Transform
            ds:Algorithm="http://www.w3.org/TR/2000/CR-xml-c14n-
20001026"/>
            </ds:Transforms>
            <ds:DigestMethod
                  ds:Algorithm="http://www.w3.org/2000/09/
xmldsig#dsa-sha1">
                  String
            </ds:DigestMethod>
            <ds:DigestValue>j6lwx3rvEPO0vKtMup4NbeVu8nk=</ds:
DigestValue>
      </ds:Reference>
</ProcessSpecification>
```

The **ProcessSpecification** element has a single REQUIRED child element, **ds: Reference,** and the following attributes:

▼ a REQUIRED **name** attribute, with type ID,

▼ a REQUIRED **version** attribute,

▼ a FIXED **xlink:type** attribute,

▼ a REQUIRED **xlink:href** attribute.

The **ds:Reference** element relates to the **xlink:type** and **xlink:href** attributes as follows. Each **ProcessSpecification** element SHALL contain one **xlink:href** attribute and one **xlink:type** attribute with a value of "simple", and MAY contain one **ds:Reference** element formulated according to the XML Digital Signature specification[XMLDSIG]. In case the document is signed, it MUST use the **ds: Reference** element. When the **ds:Reference** element is present, it MUST include a **ds:URI** attribute whose value is identical to that of the **xlink:href** attribute in the enclosing **ProcessSpecification** element.

6.5.4.1   name Attribute

The **ProcessSpecification** element MUST include a REQUIRED **name** attribute: an [XML] ID that MAY be used to refer to this element from elsewhere within the *CPP* document.

6.5.4.2   version Attribute

The **ProcessSpecification** element includes a REQUIRED **version** attribute to identify the version of the *Process-Specification* document identified by the **xlink:href** attribute (and also identified by the **ds:Reference** element, if any).

6.5.4.3   xlink:type Attribute

The **xlink:type** attribute has a FIXED value of "simple". This identifies the element as being an [XLINK] simple link.

6.5.4.4   xlink:href Attribute

The REQUIRED **xlink:href** attribute SHALL have a value that identifies the *Process-Specification* document and is a URI that conforms to [RFC2396].

6.5.4.5   ds:Reference Element

The **ds:Reference** element identifies the same *Process-Specification* document as the enclosing **ProcessSpecification** element's **xlink:href** attribute and additionally provides for verification that the *Process-Specification* document has not changed since the *CPP* was created.

Note

> *Parties* **MAY test the validity of the *CPP* or *CPA* at any time. The following validity tests MAY be of particular interest:**

▼ test of the validity of a *CPP* and the referenced *Process-Specification* documents at the time composition of a *CPA* begins in case they have changed since they were created,

▼ test of the validity of a *CPA* and the referenced *Process-Specification* documents at the time a *CPA* is installed into a *Party's* system,

▼ test of the validity of a *CPA* at intervals after the *CPA* has been installed into a *Party's* system. The *CPA* and the referenced *Process-Specification* documents MAY be processed by an installation tool into a form suited to the particular middleware. Therefore, alterations to the *CPA* and the referenced *Process-Specification* documents do not necessarily affect ongoing run-time operations. Such alterations might not be detected until it becomes necessary to reinstall the *CPA* and the referenced *Process-Specification* documents.

The syntax and semantics of the **ds:Reference** element and its child elements are defined in the XML Digital Signature specification[XMLDSIG]. As an alternative to the string value of the **ds:DigestMethod,** shown in the above example, the child element, **ds:HMACOutputLength,** with a string value, MAY be used.

According to [XMLDSIG], a **ds:Reference** element can have a **ds:Transforms** child element, which in turn has an ordered list of one or more **ds:Transform** child elements to specify a sequence of transforms. However, this specification currently REQUIRES the Canonical XML[XMLC14N] transform and forbids other transforms. Therefore, the following additional requirements apply to a **ds:Reference** element within a **ProcessSpecification** element:

▼ The **ds:Reference** element MUST have a **ds:Transforms** child element.

▼ That **ds:Transforms** element MUST have exactly one **ds:Transform** child element.

▼ That **ds:Transform** element MUST specify the Canonical XML[XMLC14N] transform via the following REQUIRED value for its REQUIRED **ds: Algorithm** attribute: *http://www.w3.org/TR/2000/CR-xml-c14n-20001026*

Note that implementation of Canonical XML is REQUIRED by the XML Digital Signature specification[XMLDSIG].

A **ds:Reference** element in a **ProcessSpecification** element has implications for *CPP* validity:

▼ A CPP MUST be considered invalid if any **ds:Reference** element within a **ProcessSpecification** element fails reference validation as defined by the XML Digital Signature specification[XMLDSIG].

▼ A CPP MUST be considered invalid if any **ds:Reference** within it cannot be dereferenced.

Other validity implications of such **ds:Reference** elements are specified in the description of the **ds:Signature** element.

Note

The XML Digital Signature specification[XMLDSIG] states "The signature application MAY rely upon the identification (URI) and Transforms provided by the signer in the Reference element, or it MAY obtain the content through other means such as a local cache" (emphases on MAY added). However, it is RECOMMENDED that ebXML *CPP/CPA* implementations not make use such cached results when signing or validating.

Note

It is recognized that the XML Digital Signature specification[XMLDSIG] provides for signing an XML document together with externally referenced documents. In cases where a *CPP* or *CPA* document is in fact suitably signed, that facility could also be used to ensure that the referenced *Process-Specification* documents are unchanged. However, this specification does not currently mandate that a *CPP* or *CPA* be signed.

Note

If the *Parties* to a *CPA* wish to customize a previously existing *Process-Specification* document, they MAY copy the existing document, modify it, and cause their *CPA* to reference the modified copy. It is recognized that for reasons of clarity, brevity, or historical record, the parties might prefer to reference a previously existing *Process-Specification* document in its original form and accompany that reference with a specification of the agreed modifications. Therefore, *CPP* usage of the ds:Reference element's ds:Transforms subelement within a ProcessSpecification element might be expanded in the future to allow other transforms as specified in the XML Digital Signature specification[XMLDSIG]. For example, modifications to the original document could then be expressed as XSLT transforms. After applying any transforms, it would be necessary to validate the transformed document against the ebXML Business Process Specification Schema[ebBPSS].

6.5.5 Role Element

The REQUIRED **Role** element identifies which role in the *Process Specification* the *Party* is capable of supporting via the **ServiceBinding** element(s) siblings within this **CollaborationRole** element.

The **Role** element has the following attributes:

▼ a REQUIRED **name** attribute,

▼ a FIXED **xlink:type** attribute,

▼ a REQUIRED **xlink:href** attribute.

6.5.5.1   name Attribute

The REQUIRED **name** attribute is a string that gives a name to the **Role.** Its value is taken from one of the following sources in the *Process Specification*[ebBPSS] that is referenced by the **ProcessSpecification** element depending upon which element is the "root" (highest order) of the process referenced:

▼ name attribute of a BinaryCollaboration/initiatingRole element,

▼ **name** attribute of a **BinaryCollaboration/respondingRole** element,

▼ **fromAuthorizedRole** attribute of a **BusinessTransactionActivity** element,

▼ **toAuthorizedRole** attribute of a **BusinessTransactionActivity** element,

▼ **fromAuthorizedRole** attribute of a **CollaborationActivity** element,

▼ **toAuthorizedRole** attribute of a **CollaborationActivity** element,

▼ **name** attribute of the **business-partner-role** element.

See NOTE in section 6.5.4 regarding alternative *Business-Collaboration* descriptions.

6.5.5.2 xlink:type Attribute

The **xlink:type** attribute has a FIXED value of "simple". This identifies the element as being an [XLINK] simple link.

6.5.5.3 xlink:href Attribute

The REQUIRED **xlink:href** attribute SHALL have a value that is a URI that conforms to [RFC2396]. It identifies the location of the element or attribute within the *Process-Specification* document that defines the role in the context of the *Business Collaboration*. An example is:

> Xlink:href="http://www.ebxml.org/processes/purchasing#N05

Where "N05" is the value of the ID attribute of the element in the Process-Specification document that defines the role name.

6.5.6 *ServiceBinding Element*

The **ServiceBinding** element identifies a default **DeliveryChannel** element for all of the *Message* traffic that is to be sent to the *Party* within the context of the identified *Process-Specification* document. An example of the **ServiceBinding** element is:

```
<ServiceBinding channelId="X03" packageId="N06">
        <Service type="string">serviceName</Service>
        <Override action="OrderAck"
            channelId="X04"
            packageId="N09"
            xlink:type="simple"
            xlink"href="..."/> <!--zero or more-->
    </ServiceBinding>
```

The **ServiceBinding** element SHALL have one child **Service** element and zero or more **Override** child elements.

The **ServiceBinding** element has the following attributes:

▼ a REQUIRED **channelId** attribute,

▼ a REQUIRED **packageId** attribute.

6.5.6.1   channelId Attribute

The REQUIRED **channelId** attribute is an [XML] IDREF that identifies the **DeliveryChannel** that SHALL provide a default technical binding for all of the *Message* traffic that is received for the *Process Specification* that is referenced by the **ProcessSpecification** element.

6.5.6.2   packageId Attribute

The REQUIRED **packageId** attribute is an [XML] IDREF that identifies the **Packaging** element that SHALL be used with the **ServiceBinding** element.

6.5.7   Service Element

The value of the **Service** element is a string that SHALL be used as the value of the **Service** element in the ebXML *Message Header*[ebMS] or a similar element in the *Message Header* of an alternative *message* service. The **Service** element has an IMPLIED **type** attribute.

If the *Process-Specification* document is defined by the ebXML Business Process Specification Schema[ebBPSS], then the value of the **Service** element is an overall identifier for the set of *Business Transactions* associated with the authorized role corresponding to the role identified in the parent **CollaborationRole** element.

Note

> The purpose of the Service **element is only to provide routing information for the** ebXML *Message Header.* **The** CollaborationRole **element and its child elements identify the information in the** ProcessSpecification **document that is relevant to the *CPP* or *CPA.***

6.5.7.1   type Attribute

If the **type** attribute is present, it indicates that the *Parties* sending and receiving the *Message* know, by some other means, how to interpret the value of the **Service** element. The two *Parties* MAY use the value of the **type** attribute to assist the interpretation.

If the **type** attribute is not present, the value of the **Service** element MUST be a URI[RFC2396].

6.5.8   Override Element

The **Override** element provides a *Party* with the ability to map, or bind, a different **DeliveryChannel** to *Messages* of a selected *Business Transaction* that are to be received by the *Party* within the context of the parent **ServiceBinding** element.

Each **Override** element SHALL specify a different **DeliveryChannel** for selected *Messages* that are to be received by the *Party* in the context of the *Process Specification* that is associated with the parent **ServiceBinding** element. The **Override** element has the following attributes:

▼ a REQUIRED **action** attribute,

▼ a REQUIRED **channelId** attribute,

▼ a REQUIRED **packageId** attribute,

▼ an IMPLIED **xlink:href** attribute,

▼ a FIXED **xlink:type** attribute.

Under a given **ServiceBinding** element, there SHALL be only one **Override** element whose **action** attribute has a given value.

> It is possible that when a *CPA* is composed from two *CPPs*, a delivery channel in one *CPP* might have an Override element that will not be compatible with the other *Party*. This incompatibility MUST be resolved either by negotiation or by reverting to a compatible default delivery channel.

Note

6.5.8.1 action Attribute

The value of the REQUIRED **action** attribute is a string that identifies the *Business Transaction* that is to be associated with the **DeliveryChannel** that is identified by the **channelId** attribute. If the *Process-Specification* document is defined by the ebXML Business Process Specification Schema[ebBPSS], the value of the **action** attribute MUST match the value of the **name** attribute of the desired BusinessTransaction **element in the** *Process-Specification* **document that is referenced by the ProcessSpecification** element.

See NOTE in section 6.5.4 regarding alternative *Business-Collaboration* descriptions.

6.5.8.2 channelId Attribute

The REQUIRED **channelId** attribute is an [XML] IDREF that identifies the **DeliveryChannel** element that is to be associated with the *Message* that is identified by the **action** attribute.

6.5.8.3 packageId Attribute

The REQUIRED **packageId** attribute is an [XML] IDREF that identifies the **Packaging** element that is to be associated with the *Message* that is identified by the **action** attribute.

6.5.8.4 xlink:href Attribute

The IMPLIED **xlink:href** attribute MAY be present. If present, it SHALL provide an absolute [XPOINTER] URI expression that specifically identifies the **BusinessTransaction** element within the associated *Process-Specification* document[ebBPSS] that is identified by the **ProcessSpecification** element.

6.5.8.5 xlink:type Attribute

The IMPLIED **xlink:type** attribute has a FIXED value of "simple". This identifies the element as being an [XLINK] simple link.

6.5.9 Certificate Element

The **Certificate** element defines certificate information for use in this *CPP*. One or more **Certificate** elements MAY be provided for use in the various security functions in the *CPP*. An example of the **Certificate** element is:

```
<Certificate certId = "N03">
    <ds:KeyInfo>. . .</ds:KeyInfo>
</Certificate>
```

The **Certificate** element has a single REQUIRED attribute: **certId.** The **Certificate** element has a single child element: **ds:KeyInfo.**

6.5.9.1 certId Attribute

The REQUIRED **certId** attribute is an ID attribute. Its is referred to in a **CertificateRef** element, using an IDREF attribute, where a certificate is specified elsewhere in the *CPP*. For example:

```
<CertificateRef certId = "N03"/>
```

6.5.9.2 ds:KeyInfo Element

The **ds:KeyInfo** element defines the certificate information. The content of this element and any subelements are defined by the XML Digital Signature specification[XMLDSIG].

Note

Software for creation of *CPPs* and *CPAs* MAY recognize the ds:KeyInfo **element and insert the subelement structure necessary to define the certificate.**

6.5.10 DeliveryChannel Element

A delivery channel is a combination of a **Transport** element and a **DocExchange** element that describes the *Party's Message*-receiving characteristics. The *CPP* SHALL contain one or more **DeliveryChannel** elements, one or more **Transport** elements, and one or more **DocExchange** elements. Each delivery channel MAY refer to any combination of a **DocExchange** element and a **Transport** element. The same **DocExchange** element or the same **Transport** element MAY be referred to by more than one delivery channel. Two delivery channels MAY use the same transport protocol and the same document-exchange protocol and differ only in details such as communication addresses or security definitions. Figure 5 illustrates three delivery channels.

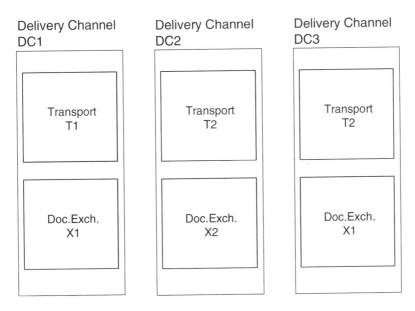

FIGURE 5 Three Delivery Channels

The delivery channels have ID attributes with values "DC1", "DC2", and "DC3". Each delivery channel contains one transport definition and one document-exchange definition. Each transport definition and each document-exchange definition also has a name as shown in the figure. Note that delivery-channel DC3 illustrates that a delivery channel MAY refer to the same transport definition and document-exchange definition used by other delivery channels but a different combination. In this case delivery-channel DC3 is a combination of transport definition T2 (also referred to by delivery-channel DC2) and document-exchange definition X1 (also referred to by delivery-channel DC1).

A specific delivery channel SHALL be associated with each **ServiceBinding** element or **Override** element (**action** attribute). Following is the delivery-channel syntax.

```
<DeliveryChannel channelId="N04" transportId="N05" docExchangeId=
"N06">
```

```
<Characteristics
        syncReplyMode = "responseOnly"
        nonrepudiationOfOrigin = "true"
        nonrepudiationOfReceipt = "true"
        secureTransport = "true"
        confidentiality = "true"
        authenticated = "true"
        authorized = "true"/>
</DeliveryChannel>
```

Each **DeliveryChannel** element identifies one **Transport** element and one **Doc-Exchange** element that make up a single delivery channel definition.

The **DeliveryChannel** element has the following attributes:

▼ a REQUIRED **channelId** attribute,

▼ a REQUIRED **transportId** attribute,

▼ a REQUIRED **docExchangeId** attribute.

The **DeliveryChannel** element has one REQUIRED child element, **Characteristics.**

6.5.10.1   channelId Attribute

The **channelId** attribute is an [XML] ID attribute that uniquely identifies the **DeliveryChannel** element for reference, using IDREF attributes, from other parts of the *CPP* or *CPA*.

6.5.10.2   transportId Attribute

The **transportId** attribute is an [XML] IDREF that identifies the **Transport** element that defines the transport characteristics of the delivery channel. It MUST have a value that is equal to the value of a **transportId** attribute of a **Transport** element elsewhere within the *CPP* document.

6.5.10.3   docExchangeId Attribute

The **docExchangeId** attribute is an [XML] IDREF that identifies the **DocExchange** element that defines the document-exchange characteristics of the delivery channel. It MUST have a value that is equal to the value of a **docExchangeId** attribute of a **DocExchange** element elsewhere within the *CPP* document.

6.5.11   Characteristics Element

The **Characteristics** element describes the security characteristics and other attributes of the delivery channel. The attributes of the **Characteristics** element, except **syncReplyMode,** MAY be used to override the values of the corresponding attributes in the *Process-Specification* document.

See NOTE in section 6.5.4 regarding alternative *Business-Collaboration* descriptions.

The **Characteristics** element has the following attributes:

▼ An IMPLIED **syncReplyMode** attribute,

▼ an IMPLIED **nonrepudiationOfOrigin** attribute,

▼ an IMPLIED **nonrepudiationOfReceipt** attribute,

▼ an IMPLIED **secureTransport** attribute,

▼ an IMPLIED **confidentiality** attribute,

▼ an IMPLIED **authenticated** attribute,

▼ an IMPLIED **authorized** attribute.

6.5.11.1   syncReplyMode Attribute

The **syncReplyMode** attribute is an enumeration comprised of the following possible values:

▼ "signalsOnly"

▼ "responseOnly"

▼ "signalsAndResponse"

▼ "none"

This attribute, when present, indicates what the receiving application expects in a response when bound to a synchronous communication protocol such as HTTP. The value of "signalsOnly" indicates that the response returned (on the HTTP 200 response in the case of HTTP) will only include one or more *Business* signals as defined in the *Process Specification* document[ebBPSS], but not a *Business*-response *Message*. The value of "responseOnly" indicates that only the *Business*-response *Message* will be returned. The value of "signalsAndResponse" indicates that the application will return the *Business*-response *Message* in addition to one or more *Business* signals. The value of "none", which is the implied default value in the absence of the **syncReplyMode** attribute, indicates that neither the *Business*-response *Message* nor any *Business* signals will be returned synchronously. In this case, the *Business*-response *Message* and any *Business* signals will be returned as separate asynchronous responses.

The ebXML *Message* Service's **syncReply** attribute is set to a value of "true" whenever the **syncReplyMode** attribute has a value other than "none".

If the delivery channel identifies a transport protocol that has no synchronous capabilities (such as SMTP) and the **Characteristics** element has a **syncReplyMode** attribute with a value other than "none", a response SHALL contain the same content as if the transport protocol did support synchronous responses.

6.5.11.2   nonrepudiationOfOrigin Attribute

The **nonrepudiationOfOrigin** attribute is a Boolean with possible values of "true" and "false". If the value is "true" then the delivery channel REQUIRES the *Message* to be digitally signed by the certificate of the *Party* that sent the *Message*.

6.5.11.3   nonrepudiationOfReceipt Attribute

The **nonrepudiationOfReceipt** attribute is a Boolean with possible values of "true" and "false". If the value is "true" then the delivery channel REQUIRES that the *Message* be acknowledged by a digitally signed *Message*, signed by the certificate of the *Party* that received the *Message*, that includes the digest of the *Message* being acknowledged.

6.5.11.4   secureTransport Attribute

The **secureTransport** attribute is a Boolean with possible values of "true" and "false". If the value is "true" then it indicates that the delivery channel uses a secure transport protocol such as [SSL] or [IPSEC].

6.5.11.5   confidentiality Attribute

The **confidentiality** attribute is a Boolean with possible values of "true" and "false". If the value is "true" then it indicates that the delivery channel REQUIRES that the *Message* be encrypted in a persistent manner. It MUST be encrypted above the level of the transport and delivered, encrypted, to the application.

6.5.11.6   authenticated Attribute

The **authenticated** attribute is a Boolean with possible values of "true" and "false". If the value is "true" then it indicates that the delivery channel REQUIRES that the sender of the *Message* be authenticated before delivery to the application.

6.5.11.7   authorized Attribute

The **authorized** attribute is a Boolean with possible of values of "true" and "false". If the value is "true" then it indicates that the delivery channel REQUIRES that the sender of the *Message* be authorized before delivery to the application.

6.5.12   Transport Element

The **Transport** element of the *CPP* defines the *Party's* capabilities with regard to communication protocol, encoding, and transport security information.

The overall structure of the **Transport** element is as follows:

```
<Transport transportId = "N05">
      <!--protocols are HTTP, SMTP, and FTP-->
```

```
<SendingProtocol version = "1.1">HTTP</SendingProtocol>
    <!--one or more SendingProtocol elements-->
<ReceivingProtocol version = "1.1">HTTP</ReceivingProtocol>
<!  onc or more endpoints-->
<Endpoint uri="http://example.com/servlet/ebxmlhandler"
    type = "request"/>
<TransportSecurity> <!--0 or 1 times-->
    <Protocol version =·"3.0">SSL</Protocol>
    <CertificateRef certId = "N03"/>
</TransportSecurity>
</Transport>
```

6.5.12.1 transportId Attribute

The **Transport** element has a single REQUIRED **transportId** attribute, of type [XML] ID, that provides a unique identifier for each **Transport** element, which SHALL be referred to by the **transportId** IDREF attribute in a **DeliveryChannel** element elsewhere within the *CPP* or *CPA* document.

6.5.12.2 Synchronous Responses

One distinguishing characteristic of transport protocols is whether a given transport protocol supports synchronous replies. See section 6.5.11.1 for a discussion of synchronous replies.

6.5.13 Transport Protocol

Supported communication protocols are HTTP, SMTP, and FTP. The *CPP* MAY specify as many protocols as the *Party* is capable of supporting.

> **It is the aim of this specification to enable support for any transport capable of carrying MIME content using the vocabulary defined herein.**

Note

6.5.13.1 SendingProtocol Element

The **SendingProtocol** element identifies the protocol that a *Party* can, or will, use to send *Business* data to its intended collaborator. The IMPLIED **version** attribute identifies the specific version of the protocol. For example, suppose that within a *CPP*, a **Transport** element, containing **SendingProtocol** elements whose values are SMTP and HTTP, is referenced within a **DeliveryChannel** element. Suppose, further, that this **DeliveryChannel** element is referenced for the role of Seller within a purchase-ordering process. Then the party is asserting that it can send purchase orders by either SMTP or HTTP. In a *CPP*, the **SendingProtocol** element MAY appear one or more times under each **Transport** element. In a *CPA*, the **SendingProtocol** element SHALL appear once.

6.5.13.2   ReceivingProtocol Element

The **ReceivingProtocol** element identifies the protocol by which a *Party* can receive its *Business* data from the other *Party*. The IMPLIED **version** attribute identifies the specific version of the protocol. For example, suppose that within a *CPP*, a **Transport** element is referenced within a **DeliveryChannel** element containing a **ReceivingProtocol** element whose value is HTTP. Suppose further that this **DeliveryChannel** element is referenced for the role of seller within a purchase ordering *Business Collaboration*. Then the party is asserting that it can receive *Business* responses to purchase orders over HTTP.

Within a *CPA*, the **SendingProtocol** and **ReceivingProtocol** elements serve to indicate the actual agreement upon what transports will be used for the complementary roles of the collaborators. For example, continuing the earlier examples, the seller in a purchase-order *Business Collaboration* could specify its receiving protocol to be SMTP and its sending protocol to be HTTP. These collaborator capabilities would match the buyer capabilities indicated in the *CPP*. These matches support an interoperable transport agreement where the buyer would send purchase orders by SMTP and where the responses to purchase orders (acknowledgements, cancellations, or change requests, for example) would be sent by the seller to the buyer using HTTP.

To fully describe receiving transport capabilities, the receiving-protocol information needs to be combined with URLs that provide the endpoints (see below).

Note

> Though the URL scheme gives information about the protocol used, an explicit ReceivingProtocol **element remains useful for future extensibility to protocols all of whose endpoints are identified by the same URL schemes, such as distinct transport protocols that all make use of HTTP endpoints. Likewise, both URL schemes of HTTP:// and HTTPS:// can be regarded as the same receiving protocol since HTTPS is HTTP with [SSL] for the transport-security protocol. Therefore, the** ReceivingProtocol **element is separated from the endpoints, which are, themselves, needed to provide essential information needed for connections.**

6.5.14   Endpoint Element

The REQUIRED **uri** attribute of the **Endpoint** element specifies the *Party's* communication addressing information associated with the **ReceiveProtocol** element. One or more **Endpoint** elements SHALL be provided for each **Transport** element in order to provide different addresses for different purposes. The value of the **uri** attribute is a URI that contains the electronic address of the *Party* in the form REQUIRED for the selected protocol. The value of the **uri** attribute SHALL conform to the syntax for expressing URIs as defined in [RFC2396].

The **type** attribute identifies the purpose of this endpoint. The value of **type** is an enumeration; permissible values are "login", "request", "response", "error", and "allPurpose". There can be, at most, one of each. The **type** attribute MAY be omitted. If it is omitted, its value defaults to "allPurpose". The "login" endpoint MAY be used for the address for the initial *Message* between the two *Parties*. The "request" and "response" endpoints are used for request and response *Messages*, respectively. The "error" endpoint MAY be used as the address for error *Messages* issued by the messaging service. If no "error" endpoint is defined, these error *Messages* SHALL be sent to the "response" address, if defined, or to the "allPurpose" endpoint. To enable error *Messages* to be received, each **Transport** element SHALL contain at least one endpoint of type "error", "response", or "allPurpose".

6.5.15   Transport Protocols

In the following sections, we discuss the specific details of each supported transport protocol.

6.5.15.1   HTTP

HTTP is Hypertext Transfer Protocol[HTTP]. For HTTP, the address is a URI that SHALL conform to [RFC2396]. Depending on the application, there MAY be one or more endpoints, whose use is determined by the application.

Following is an example of an HTTP endpoint:

```
<Endpoint uri="http://example.com/servlet/ebxmlhandler"
     type = "request"/>
```

The "request" and "response" endpoints MAY be dynamically overridden for a particular request or asynchronous response by application-specified URIs exchanged in *Business* documents exchanged under the *CPA*.

For a synchronous response, the "response" endpoint is ignored if present. A synchronous response is always returned on the existing connection, i.e. to the URI that is identified as the source of the connection.

6.5.15.2   SMTP

SMTP is Simple Mail Transfer Protocol[SMTP]. For use with this standard, Multipurpose Internet Mail Extensions[MIME] MUST be supported. The MIME media type used by the SMTP transport layer is "Application" with a sub-type of "octet-stream".

For SMTP, the communication address is the fully qualified mail address of the destination *Party* as defined by [RFC822]. Following is an example of an SMTP endpoint:

```
<Endpoint uri="mailto:ebxmlhandler@example.com"
         type = "request"/>
```

SMTP with MIME automatically encodes or decodes the document as required, on each link in the path, and presents the decoded document to the destination document-exchange function.

> The SMTP mail transfer agent encodes binary data (i.e. data that are not 7-bit ASCII) unless it is aware that the upper level (mail user agent) has already encoded the data.

> SMTP by itself (without any authentication or encryption) is subject to denial of service and masquerading by unknown *Parties*. It is strongly suggested that those *Parties* who choose SMTP as their transport layer also choose a suitable means of encryption and authentication either in the document-exchange layer or in the transport layer such as [S/MIME].

> SMTP is an asynchronous protocol that does not guarantee a particular quality of service. A transport-layer acknowledgment (i.e. an SMTP acknowledgment) to the receipt of a mail *Message* constitutes an assertion on the part of the SMTP server that it knows how to deliver the mail *Message* and will attempt to do so at some point in the future. However, the *Message* is not hardened and might never be delivered to the recipient. Furthermore, the sender will see a transport-layer acknowledgment only from the nearest node. If the *Message* passes through intermediate nodes, SMTP does not provide an end-to-end acknowledgment. Therefore receipt of an SMTP acknowledgement does not guarantee that the *Message* will be delivered to the application and failure to receive an SMTP acknowledgment is not evidence that the *Message* was not delivered. It is recommended that the reliable-messaging protocol in the ebXML *Message* Service be used with SMTP.

6.5.15.3   FTP

FTP is File Transfer Protocol[RFC959].

Since a delivery channel specifies receive characteristics, each *Party* sends a *Message* using FTP PUT. The endpoint specifies the user id and input directory path (for PUTs to this *Party*). An example of an FTP endpoint is:

```
<Endpoint uri="ftp://userid@server.foo.com"
          type = "request"/>
```

Since FTP must be compatible across all implementations, the FTP for ebXML will use the minimum sets of commands and parameters available for FTP as specified in [RFC959], section 5.1, and modified in [RFC1123], section 4.1.2.13. The mode SHALL be stream only and the type MUST be either ASCII Non-print (AN), Image (I) (binary), or Local 8 (L 8) (binary between 8-bit machines and machines with 36 bit words – for an 8-bit machine Local 8 is the same as Image).

Stream mode closes the data connection upon end of file. The server side FTP MUST set control to "PASV" before each transfer command to obtain a unique port pair if there are multiple third party sessions.

> [RFC 959] states that User-FTP SHOULD send a PORT command to assign a non-default data port before each transfer command is issued to allow multiple transfers during a single FTP because of the long delay after a TCP connection is closed until its socket pair can be reused.

Note

> The format of the 227 reply to a PASV command is not well-standardized and an FTP client may assume that the parentheses indicated in [RFC959] will be present when in some cases they are not. If the User-FTP program doesn't scan the reply for the first digit of host and port numbers, the result will be that the User-FTP might point at the wrong host. In the response, the h1, h2, h3, h4 is the IP address of the server host and the p1, p2 is a non-default data transfer port that PASV has assigned.

Note

> As a recommendation for firewall transparency, [RFC1579] proposes that the client sends a PASV command, allowing the server to do a passive TCP open on some random port, and inform the client of the port number. The client can then do an active open to establish the connection.

Note

> Since STREAM mode closes the data connection upon end of file, the receiving FTP may assume abnormal disconnect if a 226 or 250 control code hasn't been received from the sending machine.

Note

> [RFC1579] also makes the observation that it might be worthwhile to enhance the FTP protocol to have the client send a new command APSV (all passive) at startup that would allow a server that implements this option to always perform a passive open. A new reply code 151 would be issued in response to all file transfer requests not preceded by a PORT or PASV command; this *Message* would contain the port number to use for that transfer. A PORT command could still be sent to a server that had previously received APSV; that would override the default behavior for the next transfer operation, thus permitting third-party transfers.

Note

6.5.16 *Transport Security*

The **TransportSecurity** element provides the *Party's* security specifications, associated with the **ReceivingProtocol** element, for the transport layer of the *CPP*. It MAY be omitted if transport security will not be used for any *CPAs* composed from this *CPP*. Unless otherwise specified below, transport security applies to *Messages* in both directions.

Following is the syntax:

```
<TransportSecurity>
    <Protocol version = "3.0">SSL</Protocol>
    <CertificateRef certId = "N03"/> <!--zero or one-->
</TransportSecurity>
```

The **TransportSecurity** element contains two REQUIRED child elements, **Protocol** and **CertificateRef.**

6.5.16.1 Protocol Element

The value of the **Protocol** element can identify any transport security protocol that the *Party* is prepared to support. The IMPLIED **version** attribute identifies the version of the specified protocol.

The specific security properties depend on the services provided by the identified protocol. For example, SSL performs certificate-based encryption and certificate-based authentication.

Whether authentication is bidirectional or just from *Message* sender to *Message* recipient depends on the selected transport-security protocol.

6.5.16.2 CertificateRef Element

The EMPTY **CertificateRef** element contains an IMPLIED IDREF attribute, **certId** that identifies the certificate to be used by referring to the **Certificate** element (under **PartyInfo**) that has the matching ID attribute value. The **CertificateRef** element MUST be present if the transport-security protocol uses certificates. It MAY be omitted otherwise (e.g. if authentication is by password).

6.5.16.3 Specifics for HTTP

For encryption with HTTP, the protocol is SSL[SSL] (Secure Socket Layer) Version 3.0, which uses public-key encryption.

6.6 DocExchange Element

The **DocExchange** element provides information that the *Parties* must agree on regarding exchange of documents between them. This information includes the messaging service properties (e.g. ebXML *Message* Service[ebMS]).

Following is the structure of the **DocExchange** element of the *CPP*. Subsequent sections describe each child element in greater detail.

```
<DocExchange docExchangeId = "N06">
      <ebXMLBinding version = "0.92">
            <ReliableMessaging> <!--cardinality 0 or 1-->
            ...
            </ReliableMessaging>
            <NonRepudiation> <!--cardinality 0 or 1-->
                  ...
            </NonRepudiation>
            <DigitalEnvelope> <!--cardinality 0 or 1-->
                  ...
            </DigitalEnvelope>
            <NamespaceSupported> <!-- 1 or more -->
                  ...
            </NamespaceSupported>
      </ebXMLBinding>
</DocExchange>
```

The **DocExchange** element of the *CPP* defines the properties of the messaging service to be used with *CPAs* composed from the *CPP*.

The **DocExchange** element is comprised of a single **ebXMLBinding** child element.

> **The document-exchange section can be extended to messaging services other than the ebXML *Message* service by adding additional** xxxBinding **elements and their child elements that describe the other services, where** xxx **is replaced by the name of the additional binding. An example is** XPBinding, **which might define support for the future XML Protocol specification.**

6.6.1 docExchangeId Attribute

The **DocExchange** element has a single IMPLIED **docExchangeId** attribute that is an [XML] ID that provides a unique identifier that MAY be referenced from elsewhere within the *CPP* document.

6.6.2 ebXMLBinding Element

The **ebXMLBinding** element describes properties specific to the ebXML *Message* Service[ebMS]. The **ebXMLBinding** element is comprised of the following child elements:

▼ zero or one **ReliableMessaging** element which specifies the characteristics of reliable messaging,

▼ zero or one **NonRepudiation** element which specifies the requirements for signing the *Message,*

▼ zero or one **DigitalEnvelope** element which specifies the requirements for encryption by the digital-envelope[DIGENV] method,

▼ zero or more **NamespaceSupported** elements that identify any namespace extensions supported by the messaging service implementation.

6.6.3   *version Attribute*

The **ebXMLBinding** element has a single REQUIRED **version** attribute that identifies the version of the ebXML *Message* Service specification being used.

6.6.4   *ReliableMessaging Element*

The **ReliableMessaging** element specifies the properties of reliable ebXML *Message* exchange. The default that applies if the **ReliableMessaging** element is omitted is "BestEffort". See Section 6.6.4.1. The following is the element structure:

```
<ReliableMessaging deliverySemantics="OnceAndOnlyOnce"
          idempotency="false"
          messageOrderSemantics="Guaranteed">
   <!--The triplet of elements Retries, RetryInterval, and
       PersistDuration has cardinality 0 or 1-->
      <Retries>5</Retries>
      <RetryInterval>60</RetryInterval> <!--time in seconds-->
      <PersistDuration>30S</PersistDuration>
</ReliableMessaging>
```

The **ReliableMessaging** element is comprised of the following child elements. These elements have cardinality 0 or 1. They MUST either be all present or all absent.

▼ a **Retries** element,

▼ a **RetryInterval** element,

▼ a PersistDuration element.

The **ReliableMessaging** element has attributes as follows:

▼ a REQUIRED **deliverySemantics** attribute,

▼ a REQUIRED **idempotency** attribute,

▼ an IMPLIED **messageOrderSemantics** attribute.

6.6.4.1   deliverySemantics Attribute

The **deliverySemantics** attribute of the **ReliableMessaging** element specifies the degree of reliability of *Message* delivery. This attribute is an enumeration of possible values that consist of:

▼ "OnceAndOnlyOnce",

▼ "BestEffort".

A value of "OnceAndOnlyOnce" specifies that a *Message* must be delivered exactly once. "BestEffort" specifies that reliable-messaging semantics are not to be used.

6.6.4.2 idempotency Attribute

The **idempotency** attribute of the **ReliableMessaging** element specifies whether the *Party* requires that all *Messages* exchanged be subject to an idempotency test (detection and appropriate processing of duplicate *Messages*) in the document-exchange layer. The attribute is a Boolean with possible values of "true" and "false". If the value of the attribute is "true", all *Messages* are subject to the test. If the value is "false", *Messages* are not subject to an idempotency test in the document-exchange layer. Testing for duplicates is based on the *Message* identifier; other information that is carried in the *Message Header* MAY also be tested, depending on the context.

> **Additional testing for duplicates MAY take place in the *Business* application based on application information in the *Messages* (e.g. purchase order number).**

Note

If a communication protocol always checks for duplicate *Messages,* the check in the communication protocol overrides any idempotency specifications in the *CPA*.

6.6.4.3 messageOrderSemantics Attribute

The **messageOrderSemantics** attribute of the **ReliableMessaging** element controls the order in which *Messages* are received when reliable messaging is in effect (the value of the **deliverySemantics** attribute is "OnceAndOnlyOnce"). This attribute has possible values of:

▼ "Guaranteed": For each conversation, the *Messages* are passed to the receiving application in the order that the sending application specified.

▼ "NotGuaranteed": The *Messages* MAY be passed to the receiving application in different order from the order which sending application specified.

It should be understood that when the value of the **messageOrderSemantics** attribute is "Guaranteed", ordering of *Messages* applies separately to each conversation; the relative order of Messages in different conversations is not specified.

The default value of the **messageOrderSemantics** attribute is "NotGuaranteed". This attribute MUST NOT be present when the value of the **deliverySemantics** attribute is anything other than "OnceAndOnlyOnce".

The sending ebXML *Message* Service[ebMS] sets the value of the **messageOrder-Semantics** attribute of the **QualityOfServiceInfo** element in the *Message* header to the value of the **messageOrderSemantics** attribute specified by the To *Party* in the *CPA*.

6.6.4.4   Retries and RetryInterval Elements

The **Retries** and **RetryInterval** elements specify the permitted number of retries and interval between retries (in seconds) of a request following a timeout. The purpose of the **RetryInterval** element is to improve the likelihood of success on retry by deferring the retry until any temporary conditions that caused the error might be corrected.

The **Retries** and **RetryInterval** elements MUST be included together or MAY be omitted together. If they are omitted, the values of the corresponding quantities (number of retries and retry interval) are a local matter at each *Party*.

6.6.4.5   PersistDuration Element

The value of the **PersistDuration** element is the minimum length of time, expressed as an XML Schema[XMLSCHEMA-2] timeDuration, that data from a *Message* that is sent reliably is kept in *Persistent Storage* by an ebXML *Message*-Service implementation that receives that *Message*.

6.6.5   NonRepudiation Element

Non-repudiation both proves who sent a *Message* and prevents later repudiation of the contents of the *Message*. Non-repudiation is based on signing the *Message* using XML Digital Signature[XMLDSIG]. The element structure is as follows:

```
<NonRepudiation>
      <Protocol version="2000/10/31">http://www.w3.org/2000/09/
xmldsig#
      </Protocol>
      <HashFunction>sha1</HashFunction>
      <SignatureAlgorithm>rsa</SignatureAlgorithm>
      <CertificateRef certId = "N03"/>
</NonRepudiation>
```

If the **NonRepudiation** element is omitted, the *Messages* are not digitally signed.

Security at the document-exchange level applies to all *Messages* in both directions for *Business Transactions* for which security is enabled.

The **NonRepudiation** element is comprised of the following child elements:

▼ a REQUIRED **Protocol** element,

▼ a REQUIRED **HashFunction** (e.g. SHA1, MD5) element,

▼ a REQUIRED **SignatureAlgorithm** element,

▼ a REQUIRED **Certificate** element.

6.6.5.1 Protocol Element

The REQUIRED **Protocol** element identifies the technology that will be used to digitally sign a *Message*. It has a single IMPLIED **version** attribute whose value is is a string that identifies the version of the specified technology. An example of the **Protocol** element follows:

```
<Protocol version="2000/10/31">http://www.w3.org/2000/09/xmldsig#
</Protocol>
```

6.6.5.2 HashFunction Element

The REQUIRED **HashFunction** element identifies the algorithm that is used to compute the digest of the *Message* being signed.

6.6.5.3 SignatureAlgorithm Element

The REQUIRED **SignatureAlgorithm** element identifies the algorithm that is used to compute the value of the digital signature.

6.6.5.4 CertificateRef Element

The REQUIRED **CertificateRef** element refers to one of the **Certificate** elements elsewhere within the *CPP* document, using the IMPLIED **certId** IDREF attribute.

6.6.6 DigitalEnvelope Element

The **DigitalEnvelope** element[DIGENV] is an encryption procedure in which the *Message* is encrypted by symmetric encryption (shared secret key) and the secret key is sent to the *Message* recipient encrypted with the recipient's public key. The element structure is:

```
<DigitalEnvelope>
      <Protocol version = "2.0">S/MIME</Protocol>
      <EncryptionAlgorithm>rsa</EncryptionAlgorithm>
      <CertificateRef certId = "N03"/>
</DigitalEnvelope>
```

Security at the document-exchange level applies to all *Messages* in both directions for *Business Transaction*s for which security is enabled.

6.6.6.1 Protocol Element

The REQUIRED **Protocol** element identifies the security protocol to be used. The FIXED **version** attribute identifies the version of the protocol.

6.6.6.2   EncryptionAlgorithm Element

The REQUIRED **EncryptionAlgorithm** element identifies the encryption algorithm to be used.

6.6.6.3   CertificateRef Element

The REQUIRED **CertificateRef** element identifies the certificate to be used by means of its **certId** attribute. The IMPLIED **certId** attribute is an attribute of type [XML] IDREF, which refers to a matching ID attribute in a **Certificate** element elsewhere in the *CPP* or *CPA*.

6.6.7   *NamespaceSupported Element*

The **NamespaceSupported** element identifies any namespace extensions supported by the messaging service implementation. Examples are Security Services Markup Language[S2ML] and Transaction Authority Markup Language[XAML]. For example, support for the S2ML namespace would be defined as follows:

```
        <NamespaceSupported location = "http://www.s2ml.org/s2ml.xsd"
version = "0.8">http://www.s2ml.org/s2ml</NamespaceSupported>
```

6.7   Packaging Element

The subtree of the **Packaging** element provides specific information about how the *Message Header* and payload constituent(s) are packaged for transmittal over the transport, including the crucial information about what document-level security packaging is used and the way in which security features have been applied. Typically the subtree under the **Packaging** element indicates the specific way in which constituent parts of the *Message* are organized. MIME processing capabilities are typically the capabilities or agreements described in this subtree. The **Packaging** element provides information about MIME content types, XML namespaces, security parameters, and MIME structure of the data that is exchanged between *Parties*.

Following is an example of the **Packaging** element:

```
<Packaging id="id">
<!--The Packaging triple MAY appear one or more times-->
      <ProcessingCapabilities parse="..." generate="..."/>
      <SimplePart
            id="id" mimetype="type"/> <!--one or more-->
            <NamespaceSupported location = "" version="">
             URI
            </NamespaceSupported> <!--zero or more-->
      <!--The child of CompositeList is an enumeration of either
      Composite or Encapsulation. The enumeration MAY appear one
      or more time, with the two elements intermixed-->
```

```
<CompositeList>
    <Composite mimetype="type"
          id="name"
          mimeparameters="parameter">
          <Constituent idref="name"/>
    </Composite>
    <Encapsulation mimetype="type" id="name">
          <Constituent idref="name"/>
    </Encapsulation>
</CompositeList>
</Packaging>
```

See "Matching Packaging" in Appendix F for a more specific example.

The **Packaging** element has one attribute; the REQUIRED **id** attribute, with type ID. It is referred to in the **ServiceBinding** element and in the **Override** element, by using the IDREF attribute, **packageId.**

The child elements of the **Packaging** element are **ProcessingCapabilities, Simple-Part,** and **CompositeList.** This set of elements MAY appear one or more times as a child of each **Packaging** element in a *CPP* and SHALL appear once as a child of each **Packaging** element in a *CPA.*

6.7.1   ProcessingCapabilities Element

The **ProcessingCapabilities** element has two REQUIRED attributes with Boolean values of either "true" or "false". The attributes are **parse** and **generate.** Normally, these attributes will both have values of "true" to indicate that the packaging constructs specified in the other child elements can be both produced as well as processed at the software *Message* service layer.

At least one of the **generate** or **parse** attributes MUST be true.

6.7.2   SimplePart Element

The **SimplePart** element provides a repeatable list of the constituent parts, primarily identified by the MIME content-type value. The **SimplePart** element has two REQUIRED attributes: **id** and **mimetype**. The **id** attribute, type ID, provides the value that will be used later to reference this *Message* part when specifying how the parts are packaged into composites, if composite packaging is present. The **mimetype** attribute provides the actual value of content-type for the simple *Message* part being specified.

6.7.3   SimplePart Element

The **SimplePart** element can have zero or more **NamespaceSupported** elements. Each of these identifies any namespace extensions supported for the XML packaged in the parent simple body part. Examples include Security Services Markup

Language[S2ML] and Transaction Authority Markup Language[XAML]. For example, support for the S2ML namespace would be defined as follows:

```
<NamespaceSupported location = "http://www.s2ml.org/s2ml.xsd"
version = "0.8">http://www.s2ml.org/s2ml</NamespaceSupported>
```

6.7.4   CompositeList Element

The final child element of **Packaging** is **CompositeList,** which is a container for the specific way in which the simple parts are combined into groups (MIME multiparts) or encapsulated within security-related MIME content-types. The **CompositeList** element MAY be omitted from **Packaging** when no security encapsulations or composite multiparts are used. When the **CompositeList** element is present, the content model for the **CompositeList** element is a repeatable sequence of choices of **Composite** or **Encapsulation** elements. The **Composite** and **Encapsulation** elements MAY appear intermixed as desired.

The sequence in which the choices are presented is important because, given the recursive character of MIME packaging, composites or encapsulations MAY include previously mentioned composites (or rarely, encapsulations) in addition to the *Message* parts characterized within the **SimplePart** subtree. Therefore, the "top-level" packaging will be described last in the sequence.

The **Composite** element has the following attributes:

▼ a REQUIRED **mimetype** attribute,

▼ a REQUIRED **id** attribute,

▼ an IMPLIED **mimeparameters** attribute.

The **mimetype** attribute provides the value of the MIME content-type for this *Message* part, and this will be some MIME composite type, such as "multipart/related" or "multipart/signed". The **id** attribute, type ID, provides a way to refer to this composite if it needs to be mentioned as a constituent of some later element in the sequence. The **mimeparameters** attribute provides the values of any significant MIME parameter (such as "type=application/vnd.eb+xml") that is needed to understand the processing demands of the content-type.

The **Composite** element has one child element, **Constituent.**

The **Constituent** element has one REQUIRED attribute, **idref,** type IDREF, and has an EMPTY content model. The **idref** attribute has as its value the value of the **id** attribute of a previous **Composite, Encapsulation,** or **SimplePart** element. The purpose of this sequence of **Constituents** is to indicate both the contents and the order of what is packaged within the current **Composite** or **Encapsulation.**

The **Encapsulation** element is typically used to indicate the use of MIME security mechanisms, such as [S/MIME] or Open-PGP[RFC2015]. A security body part can encapsulate a MIME part that has been previously characaterized. For convenience, all such security structures are under the **Encapsulation** element, even when technically speaking the data is not "inside" the body part. (In other words, the so-called clear-signed or detached signature structures possible with MIME multipart/signed are for simplicity found under the **Encapsulation** element.)

The **Encapsulation** element has the following attributes:

▼ a REQUIRED **mimetype** attribute,

▼ a REQUIRED **id** attribute,

▼ an IMPLIED **mimeparameters** attribute.

The **mimetype** attribute provides the value of the MIME content-type for this *Message* part, such as "application/pkcs7-mime". The **id** attribute, type ID, provides a way to refer to this encapsulation if it needs to be mentioned as a constituent of some later element in the sequence. The **mimeparameters** attribute provides the values of any significant MIME parameter(s) needed to understand the processing demands of the content-type.

Both the **Encapsulation** element and the **Composite** element have child elements consisting of a **Constituent** element or of a repeatable sequence of **Constituent** elements, respectively.

6.8   ds:Signature Element

The *CPP* MAY be digitally signed using technology that conforms with the XML Digital Signature specification[XMLDSIG]. The **ds:Signature** element is the root of a subtree of elements that MAY be used for signing the *CPP*. The syntax is:

```
<ds:Signature>...</ds:Signature>
```

The content of this element and any subelements are defined by the XML Digital Signature specification. See Section 7.7 for a detailed discussion. The following additional constraints on **ds:Signature** are imposed:

▼ A *CPP* MUST be considered invalid if any **ds:Signature** element fails core validation as defined by the XML Digital Signature specification[XMLD-SIG].

▼ Whenever a *CPP* is signed, each **ds:Reference** element within a **ProcessSpecification** element MUST pass reference validation and each **ds:Signature** element MUST pass core validation.

Software for creation of *CPPs* and *CPAs* MAY recognize ds:Signature **and automatically insert the element structure necessary to define signing of the *CPP* and *CPA*. Signature creation itself is a cryptographic process that is outside the scope of this specification.**

See non-normative note in Section 6.5.4.5 for a discussion of times at which validity tests MAY be made.

6.9 Comment Element

The **CollaborationProtocolProfile** element MAY contain zero or more **Comment** elements. The **Comment** element is a textual note that MAY be added to serve any purpose the author desires. The language of the **Comment** is identified by a REQUIRED **xml:lang** attribute. The **xml:lang** attribute MUST comply with the rules for identifying languages specified in [XML]. If multiple **Comment** elements are present, each MAY have a different **xml:lang** attribute value. An example of a **Comment** element follows:

```
<Comment xml:lang="en-gb">yadda yadda, blah blah</Comment>
```

When a *CPA* is composed from two *CPPs,* all **Comment** elements from both *CPPs* SHALL be included in the *CPA* unless the two *Parties* agree otherwise.

7 CPA Definition

A *Collaboration-Protocol Agreement (CPA)* defines the capabilities that two *Parties* must agree upon to enable them to engage in electronic *Business* for the purposes of the particular *CPA*. This section defines and discusses the details of the *CPA*. The discussion is illustrated with some XML fragments.

Most of the XML elements in this section are described in detail in section 6, "CPP Definition". In general, this section does not repeat that information. The discussions in this section are limited to those elements that are not in the *CPP* or for which additional discussion is required in the *CPA* context. See also Appendix Cand Appendix Dfor the DTD and XML Schema, respectively, and Appendix Bfor an example of a *CPA* document.

7.1   CPA Structure

Following is the overall structure of the *CPA*:

```
<CollaborationProtocolAgreement
      xmlns="http://www.ebxml.org/namespaces/tradePartner"
      xmlns:bpm="http://www.ebxml.org/namespaces/businessProcess"
      xmlns:ds = "http://www.w3.org/2000/09/xmldsig#"
      xmlns:xlink = "http://www.w3.org/1999/xlink"
      cpaid="YoursAndMyCPA"
      version="1.2">
      <Status value = "proposed"/>
      <Start>1988-04-07T18:39:09</Start>
      <End>1990-04-07T18:40:00</End>
      <!--ConversationConstraints MAY appear 0 or 1 times-->
      <ConversationConstraints invocationLimit = "100"
            concurrentConversations = "4"/>
      <PartyInfo>
            ...
      </PartyInfo>
      <PartyInfo>
            ...
      </PartyInfo>
      <Packaging id="N20"> <!--one or more-->
            ...
      </Packaging>
      <!--ds:signature MAY appear 0 or more times-->
      <ds:Signature>any combination of text and elements
      </ds:Signature>
      <Comment xml:lang="en-gb">any text</Comment> <!--zero or
more-->
</CollaborationProtocolAgreement>
```

7.2   CollaborationProtocolAgreement Element

The **CollaborationProtocolAgreement** element is the root element of a *CPA*. It has a REQUIRED **cpaid** attribute of type [XML] CDATA that supplies a unique idenfier for the document. The value of the **cpaid** attribute SHALL be assigned by one *Party* and used by both. It is RECOMMENDED that the value of the **cpaid** attribute be a URI. The value of the **cpaid** attribute MAY be used as the value of the **CPAId** element in the ebXML *Message Header*[ebMS] or of a similar element in a *Message Header* of an alternative messaging service.

Note

> Each *Party* MAY associate a local identifier with the cpaid attribute.

In addition, the **CollaborationProtocolAgreement** element has an IMPLIED **version** attribute. This attribute indicates the version of the *CPA*. Its purpose is to provide versioning capabilities for an instance of a *CPA* as it undergoes negotiation between the two parties. The **version** attribute SHOULD also be used to provide versioning capability for a *CPA* that has been deployed and then modified. The value of the **version** attribute SHOULD be a string representation of a numeric value such as "1.0" or "2.3". The value of the version string SHOULD be changed with each change made to the *CPA* document both during negotiation and after it has been deployed.

Note

> The method of assigning version identifiers is left to the implementation.

The **CollaborationProtocolAgreement** element has REQUIRED [XML] Namespace[XMLNS] declarations that are defined in Section 6, "CPP Definition".

The **CollaborationProtocolAgreement** element is comprised of the following child elements, each of which is described in greater detail in subsequent sections:

- ▼ a REQUIRED **Status** element that identifies the state of the process that creates the *CPA*,
- ▼ a REQUIRED **Start** element that records the date and time that the *CPA* goes into effect,
- ▼ a REQUIRED **End** element that records the date and time after which the *CPA* must be renegotiated by the *Parties*,
- ▼ zero or one **ConversationConstraints** element that documents certain agreements about conversation processing,
- ▼ two REQUIRED **PartyInfo** elements, one for each *Party* to the *CPA*,
- ▼ one or more **ds:Signature** elements that provide signing of the *CPA* using the XML Digital Signature[XMLDSIG] standard.

7.3   Status Element

The **Status** element records the state of the composition/negotiation process that creates the *CPA*. An example of the **Status** element follows:

```
<Status value = "proposed"/>
```

The Status element has a REQUIRED **value** attribute that records the current state of composition of the *CPA*. This attribute is an enumeration comprised of the following possible values:

▼ "proposed", meaning that the *CPA* is still being negotiated by the *Parties,*

▼ "agreed", meaning that the contents of the *CPA* have been agreed to by both *Parties,*

▼ "signed", meaning that the *CPA* has been "signed" by the *Parties.* This "signing" MAY take the form of a digital signature that is described in section 7.7 below.

> **The** Status **element MAY be used by a** *CPA* **composition and negotiation tool to assist it in the process of building a** *CPA.*

Note

7.4   CPA Lifetime

The lifetime of the *CPA* is given by the **Start** and **End** elements. The syntax is:

```
<Start>1988-04-07T18:39:09</Start>
<End>1990-04-07T18:40:00</End>
```

7.4.1   Start Element

The **Start** element specifies the starting date and time of the *CPA*. The **Start** element SHALL be a string value that conforms to the content model of a canonical timeInstant as defined in the XML Schema Datatypes Specification[XMLSCHEMA-2]. For example, to indicate 1:20 pm UTC (Coordinated Universal Time) on May 31, 1999, a **Start** element would have the following value:

```
1999-05-31T13:20:00Z
```

The **Start** element SHALL be represented as Coordinated Universal Time (UTC).

7.4.2   End Element

The **End** element specifies the ending date and time of the *CPA*. The **End** element SHALL be a string value that conforms to the content model of a canonical timeInstant as defined in the XML Schema Datatypes Specification[XMLSCHEMA-2]. For example, to indicate 1:20 pm UTC (Coordinated Universal Time) on May 31, 1999, an **End** element would have the following value:

```
1999-05-31T13:20:00Z
```

The **End** element SHALL be represented as Coordinated Universal Time (UTC).

When the end of the *CPA's* lifetime is reached, any *Business Transactions* that are still in progress SHALL be allowed to complete and no new *Business Transactions* SHALL be started. When all in-progress *Business Transactions* on each conversation are completed, the *Conversation* shall be terminated whether or not it was completed.

> It should be understood that if a *Business* application defines a conversation as consisting of multiple *Business Transactions*, such a conversation MAY be terminated with no error indication when the end of the lifetime is reached. The run-time system could provide an error indication to the application.

> It should be understood that it MAY not be feasible to wait for outstanding conversations to terminate before ending the *CPA* since there is no limit on how long a conversation MAY last.

> The run-time system SHOULD return an error indication to both *Parties* when a new *Business Transaction* is started under this *CPA* after the date and time specified in the End element.

7.5   ConversationConstraints Element

The **ConversationConstraints** element places limits on the number of conversations under the *CPA*. An example of this element follows:

```
<ConversationConstraints invocationLimit = "100"
                         concurrentConversations = "4"/>
```

The **ConversationConstraints** element has the following attributes:

▼   an IMPLIED **invocationLimit** attribute,

▼   an IMPLIED **concurrentConversations** attribute.

7.5.1   invocationLimit Attribute

The **invocationLimit** attribute defines the maximum number of conversations that can be processed under the *CPA*. When this number has been reached, the *CPA* is terminated and must be renegotiated. If no value is specified, there is no upper limit on the number of conversations and the lifetime of the *CPA* is controlled solely by the **End** element.

> **The** invocationLimit **attribute sets a limit on the number of units of *Business* that can be performed under the *CPA*. It is a *Business* parameter, not a performance parameter.**

Note

7.5.2 concurrentConversations Attribute

The **concurrentConversations** attribute defines the maximum number of conversations that can be in process under this *CPA* at the same time. If no value is specified, processing of concurrent conversations is strictly a local matter.

> **The** concurrentConversations **attribute provides a parameter for the *Parties* to use when it is necessary to limit the number of conversations that can be concurrently processed under a particular *CPA*. For example, the back-end process might only support a limited number of concurrent conversations. If a request for a new conversation is received when the maximum number of conversations allowed under this *CPA* is already in process, an implementation MAY reject the new conversation or MAY enqueue the request until an existing conversation ends. If no value is given for** concurrentConversations**, how to handle a request for a new conversation for which there is no capacity is a local implementation matter.**

Note

7.6 PartyInfo Element

The general characteristics of the **PartyInfo** element are discussed in section 6.5.

The *CPA* SHALL have one **PartyInfo** element for each *Party* to the *CPA*. The **PartyInfo** element specifies the *Parties'* agreed terms for engaging in the *Business Collaborations* defined by the *Process-Specification* documents referenced by the *CPA*. If a *CPP* has more than one **PartyInfo** element, the appropriate **PartyInfo** element SHALL be selected from each *CPP* when composing a *CPA*.

In the *CPA*, there SHALL be one **PartyId** element under each **PartyInfo** element. The value of this element is the same as the value of the **PartyId** element in the ebXML *Message* Service specification[ebMS] or similar messaging service specification. One **PartyId** element SHALL be used within a **To** or **From** *Header* element of an ebXML *Message*.

7.6.1 ProcessSpecification Element

The **ProcessSpecification** element identifies the *Business Collaboration* that the two *Parties* have agreed to perform. There MAY be one or more **Process-Specification** elements in a *CPA*. Each SHALL be a child element of a separate **CollaborationRole** element. See the discussion in Section 6.5.3.

7.7 ds:Signature Element

A *CPA* document MAY be digitally signed by one or more of the *Parties* as a means of ensuring its integrity as well as a means of expressing the agreement just as a corporate officer's signature would do for a paper document. If signatures are being used to digitally sign an ebXML *CPA* or *CPP* document, then it is strongly RECOMMENDED that [XMLDSIG] be used to digitally sign the document. The **ds:Signature** element is the root of a subtree of elements that MAY be used for signing the *CPP*. The syntax is:

```
<ds:Signature>...</ds:Signature>
```

The content of this element and any subelements are defined by the XML Digital Signature specification[XMLDSIG]. The following additional constraints on **ds:Signature** are imposed:

▼ A *CPA* MUST be considered invalid if any **ds:Signature** fails core validation as defined by the XML Digital Signature specification.

▼ Whenever a *CPA* is signed, each **ds:Reference** within a **Process-Specification** MUST pass reference validation and each **ds:Signature** MUST pass core validation.

In case a *CPA* is unsigned, software MAY nonetheless validate the ds:Reference elements within ProcessSpecification elements and report any exceptions.

Software for creation of *CPPs* and *CPAs* MAY recognize ds:Signature and automatically insert the element structure necessary to define signing of the *CPP* and *CPA*. Signature creation itself is a cryptographic process that is outside the scope of this specification.

See non-normative note in section 6.5.4.5 for a discussion of times at which a *CPA* MAY be validated.

7.7.1 Persistent Digital Signature

If [XMLDSIG] is used to sign an ebXML *CPP* or *CPA*, the process defined in this section of the specification SHALL be used.

7.7.1.1 Signature Generation

Following are the steps to create a digital signature:

1. Create a **SignedInfo** element, a child element of **ds:Signature. SignedInfo** SHALL have child elements **SignatureMethod, CanonicalizationMethod,** and **Reference** as prescribed by [XMLDSIG].

2. Canonicalize and then calculate the **SignatureValue** over **SignedInfo** based on algorithms specified in **SignedInfo** as specified in [XMLDSIG].

3. Construct the **Signature** element that includes the **SignedInfo, KeyInfo** (RECOMMENDED), and **SignatureValue** elements as specified in [XMLD-SIG].

4. Include the namespace qualified **Signature** element in the document just signed, following the last **PartyInfo** element.

7.7.1.2 ds:SignedInfo Element

The **ds:SignedInfo** element SHALL be comprised of zero or one **ds:Canonical-izationMethod** element, the **ds:SignatureMethod** element, and one or more **ds:Reference** elements.

7.7.1.3 ds:CanonicalizationMethod element

The **ds:CanonicalizationMethod** element is defined as OPTIONAL in [XMLD-SIG], meaning that the element need not appear in an instance of a **ds:Signed-Info** element. The default canonicalization method that is applied to the data to be signed is [XMLC14N] in the absence of a **ds:CanonicalizationMethod** element that specifies otherwise. This default SHALL also serve as the default canonical-ization method for the ebXML *CPP* and *CPA* documents.

7.7.1.4 ds:SignatureMethod Element

The **ds:SignatureMethod** element SHALL be present and SHALL have an **Algo-rithm** attribute. The RECOMMENDED value for the **Algorithm** attribute is:

> http://www.w3.org/2000/09/xmldsig#dsa-sha1

This RECOMMENDED value SHALL be supported by all compliant ebXML *CPP* or *CPA* software implementations.

7.7.1.5 ds:Reference Element

The **ds:Reference** element for the *CPP* or *CPA* document SHALL have a RE-QUIRED URI attribute value of "" to provide for the signature to be applied to the document that contains the **ds:Signature** element (the *CPA* or *CPP* docu-ment). The **ds:Reference** element for the *CPP* or *CPA* document MAY include an IMPLIED **type** attribute that has a value of:

> "http://www.w3.org/2000/09/xmldsig#Object"

in accordance with [XMLDSIG]. This attribute is purely informative. It MAY be omitted. Implementations of software designed to author or process an ebXML *CPA* or *CPP* document SHALL be prepared to handle either case. The

ds:Reference element MAY include the **id** attribute, type ID, by which this **ds:Reference** element MAY be referenced from a **ds:Signature** element.

7.7.1.6   ds:Transform Element

The **ds:Reference** element for the *CPA* or *CPP* document SHALL include a descendant **ds:Transform** element that excludes the containing **ds:Signature** element and all its descendants. This exclusion is achieved by means of specifying the **ds:Algorithm** attribute of the **Transform** element as

"http://www.w3.org/2000/09/xmldsig#enveloped-signature".

For example:

```
<ds:Reference ds:URI="">
    <ds:Transforms>
        <ds:Transform
ds:Algorithm="http://www.w3.org/2000/09/xmldsig#enveloped-
signature "/>
    </ds:Transforms>
    <ds:DigestMethod
  ds:Algorithm="http://www.w3.org/2000/09/xmldsig#sha1"/>
    <ds:DigestValue>...</ds:DigestValue>
</ds:Reference>
```

7.7.1.7   ds:Algorithm Element

The **ds:Transform** element SHALL include a ds:**Algorithm** attribute that has a value of:

http://www.w3.org/2000/09/xmldsig#enveloped-signature

Note

> When digitally signing a *CPA*, it is RECOMMENDED that each *Party* sign the document in accordance with the process described above. The first *Party* that signs the *CPA* will sign only the *CPA* contents, excluding their own signature. The second *Party* signs over the contents of the *CPA* as well as the ds:Signature **element that contains the first** *Party's* **signature. It MAY be necessary that a notary sign over both signatures.**

7.8   Comment Element

The **CollaborationProtocolAgreement** element MAY contain zero or more **Comment** elements. See section 6.9 for details of the syntax of the **Comment** element.

7.9   Composing a CPA from Two CPPs

This section discusses normative issues in composing a *CPA* from two *CPPs*. See also Appendix F, "Composing a CPA from Two CPPs (Non-Normative)".

7.9.1   ID Attribute Duplication

In composing a *CPA* from two *CPPs*, there is a hazard that ID attributes from the two *CPPs* might have duplicate values. When a *CPA* is composed from two *CPPs*, duplicate ID attribute values SHALL be tested for. If a duplicate ID attribute value is present, one of the duplicates shall be given a new value and the corresponding IDREF attribute values from the corresponding *CPP* SHALL be corrected.

7.10   Modifying Parameters of the Process-Specification Cocument Based on Information in the CPA

A *Process-Specification* document contains a number of parameters, expressed as XML attributes. An example is the security attributes that are counterparts of the attributes of the *CPA* **Characteristics** element. The values of these attributes can be considered to be default values or recommendations. When a *CPA* is created, the *Parties* MAY decide to accept the recommendations in the *Process-Specification* or they MAY agree on values of these parameters that better reflect their needs.

When a *CPA* is used to configure a run-time system, choices specified in the *CPA* MUST always assume precedence over choices specified in the referenced *Process-Specification* document. In particular, all choices expressed in a *CPA's* **Characteristics** and **Packaging** elements MUST be implemented as agreed to by the *Parties*. These choices SHALL override the default values expressed in the *Process-Specification* document. The process of installing the information from the *CPA* and *Process-Specification* document MUST verify that all of the resulting choices are mutually consistent and MUST signal an error if they are not.

> There are several ways of overriding the information in the *Process-Specification* document by information from the *CPA*. For example: **Note**

  ▼ The CPA composition tool can create a separate copy of the Process-Specification document. The tool can then directly modify the *Process-Specification* document with information from the *CPA*. One advantage of this method is that the override process is performed entirely by the *CPA* composition tool. A second advantage is that with a separate copy of the *Process-Specification* document associated with the particular *CPA*, there is no exposure to modifications of the *Process-Specification* document between the time that the *CPA* is created and the time it is installed in the *Parties'* systems.

  ▼ A *CPA* installation tool can dynamically override parameters in the *Process-Specification* document using information from the corresponding parameters in the *CPA* at the time the *CPA* and *Process-Specification* document are installed in the *Parties'* systems. This eliminates the need to create a separate copy of the *Process-Specification* document.

▼ Other possible methods might be based on XSLT transformations of the parameter information in the *CPA* and/or the *Process-Specification* document.

8   References

Some references listed below specify functions for which specific XML definitions are provided in the *CPP* and *CPA*. Other specifications are referred to in this specification in the sense that they are represented by keywords for which the *Parties* to the *CPA* MAY obtain plug-ins or write custom support software but do not require specific XML element sets in the *CPP* and *CPA*.

In a few cases, the only available specification for a function is a proprietary specification. These are indicated by notes within the citations below.

[ccOVER] ebXML Core Components and Business Process Document Overview, http://www.ebxml.org.

[DIGENV] Digital Envelope, RSA Laboratories, *http://www.rsasecurity.com/rsalabs/*.

Note

At this time, the only available specification for digital envelope appears to be the RSA Laboratories specification.

[ebBPSS] ebXML Business Process Specification Schema, http://www.ebxml.org/specs

[ebGLOSS] ebXML Glossary, http://www.ebxml.org/specs.

[ebMS] ebXML Message Service Specification, http://www.ebxml.org/specs.

[ebRS] ebXML Registry Services Specification, http://www.ebxml.org/specs.

[ebTA] ebXML Technical Architecture Specification, http://www.ebxml.org/specs.

[HTTP] Hypertext Transfer Protocol, Internet Engineering Task Force RFC2616.

[IPSEC] IP Security Document Roadmap, Internet Engineering Task Force RFC 2411.

[ISO6523] Structure for the Identification of Organizations and Organization Parts, International Standards Organization ISO-6523.

[MIME] MIME (Multipurpose Internet Mail Extensions) Part One: Mechanisms for Specifying and Describing the Format of Internet *Message* Bodies. Internet Engineering Task Force RFC 1521.

[RFC822] Standard for the Format of ARPA Internet Text Messages, Internet Engineering Task Force RFC 822.

[RFC959] File Transfer Protocol (FTP), Internet Engineering Task Force RFC 959.

[RFC1123] Requirements for Internet Hosts — Application and Support, R. Braden, Internet Engineering Task Force, October 1989.

[RFC1579] Firewall-Friendly FTP, S. Bellovin, Internet Engineering Task Force, February 1994.

[RFC2015] MIME Security with Pretty Good Privacy, M. Elkins, Internet Engineering Task Force, RFC 2015.

[RFC2119] Key Words for use in RFCs to Indicate Requirement Levels, Internet Engineering Task Force RFC 2119.

[RFC2396] Uniform Resource Identifiers (URI): Generic Syntax; T. Berners-Lee, R. Fielding, L. Masinter - August 1998.

[S/MIME] S/MIME Version 3 Message Specification, Internet Engineering Task Force RFC 2633.

[S2ML] Security Services Markup Language, http://s2ml.org/.

[SMTP] Simple Mail Transfer Protocol, Internet Engineering Task Force RFC 821.

[SSL] Secure Sockets Layer, Netscape Communications Corp. http://developer.netscape.com.

At this time, it appears that the Netscape specification is the only available specification of SSL. Work is in progress in IETF on "Transport Layer Security", which is intended as a replacement for SSL.

Note

[XAML] Transaction Authority Markup Language, http://xaml.org/.

[XLINK] XML Linking Language, http://www.w3.org/TR/xlink/.

[XML] Extensible Markup Language (XML), World Wide Web Consortium, http://www.w3.org.

[XMLC14N] Canonical XML, Ver. 1.0, http://www.w3.org/TR/XML-C14N/.

[XMLDSIG] XML Signature Syntax and Processing, Worldwide Web Consortium, http://www.w3.org/TR/xmldsig-core/.

[XMLNS] Namespaces in XML, T. Bray, D. Hollander, and A. Layman, Jan. 1999, http://www.w3.org/TR/REC-xml-names/.

[XMLSCHEMA-1] XML Schema Part 1: Structures,
     http://www/w3/org/TR/xmlschema-1/.

[XMLSCHEMA-2] XML Schema Part 2: Datatypes,
     http://www.w3.org/TR/xmlschema-2/.

[XPOINTER] XML Pointer Language, ver. 1.0, *http://www.w3.org/TR/xptr.*

9   Conformance

In order to conform to this specification, an implementation:

a.) SHALL support all the functional and interface requirements defined in this specification,

b.) SHALL NOT specify any requirements that would contradict or cause non-conformance to this specification.

A conforming implementation SHALL satisfy the conformance requirements of the applicable parts of this specification.

An implementation of a tool or service that creates or maintains ebXML *CPP* or *CPA* instance documents SHALL be determined to be conformant by validation of the *CPP* or *CPA* instance documents, created or modified by said tool or service, against the XML Schema[XMLSCHEMA-1] definition of the *CPP* or *CPA* in Appendix Dand available from

     http://www.ebxml.org/schemas/cpp-cpa-v1_0.xsd

by using two or more validating XML Schema parsers that conform to the W3C XML Schema specifications[XMLSCHEMA-1,XMLSCHEMA-2].

The objective of conformance testing is to determine whether an implementation being tested conforms to the requirements stated in this specification. Conformance testing enables vendors to implement compatible and interoperable systems. Implementations and applications SHALL be tested using available test suites to verify their conformance to this specification.

Publicly available test suites from vendor neutral organizations such as OASIS and the U.S.A. National Institute of Science and Technology (NIST) SHOULD be used to verify the conformance of implementations, applications, and components claiming conformance to this specification. Open-source reference implementations MAY be available to allow vendors to test their products for interface compatibility, conformance, and interoperability.

10 Disclaimer

The views and specification expressed in this document are those of the authors and are not necessarily those of their employers. The authors and their employers specifically disclaim responsibility for any problems arising from correct or incorrect implementation or use of this design.

11 Contact Information

Martin W. Sachs (Team Leader)

   IBM T. J. Watson Research Center

   P.O.B. 704

   Yorktown Hts, NY 10598

   USA

   Phone: 914-784-7287

   email: mwsachs@us.ibm.com

Chris Ferris

   XML Technology Development

   Sun Microsystems, Inc

   One Network Drive

   Burlington, Ma 01824-0903

   USA

   Phone: 781-442-3063

   email: chris.ferris@east.sun.com

Dale W. Moberg

   Cyclone Commerce

   17767 North Perimeter Dr., Suite 103

   Scottsdale, AZ 85255

USA

Phone: 480-627-1800

email: dmoberg@columbus.rr.com

Tony Weida

Edifecs

2310 130th Ave. NE, Suite 100

Bellevue, WA 98005

USA

Phone: 212-678-5265

email: TonyW@edifecs.com

Appendix A   Example of CPP Document (Non-Normative)

A text version of this schema is available on the ebXML web site at www.ebxml.org/specs/

```
<?xml version="1.0" encoding="UTF-8"?>
<tp:CollaborationProtocolProfile
    xmlns:tp="http://www.ebxml.org/namespaces/tradePartner"
    xmlns:xsi="http://www.w3.org/2000/10/XMLSchema-instance"
    xmlns:xlink="http://www.w3.org/1999/xlink"
    xmlns:ds="http://www.w3.org/2000/09/xmldsig#"
    xsi:schemaLocation="http://www.ebxml.org/namespaces/trade-
Partner http://ebxml.org/project_teams/trade_partner/cpp-cpa-v1
_0.xsd"
    tp:version="1.1">
    <tp:PartyInfo>
        <tp:PartyId tp:type="DUNS">123456789</tp:PartyId>
        <tp:PartyRef tp:href="http://example.com/about.html"/>
        <tp:CollaborationRole tp:id="N00">
            <tp:ProcessSpecification tp:version="1.0"
tp:name="buySell" xlink:type="simple" xlink:href="http://www.ebxml
.org/processes/buySell.xml"/>
            <tp:Role tp:name="buyer" xlink:type="simple"
xlink:href="http://ebxml.org/processes/buySell.xml#buyer"/>
```

```
                    <tp:CertificateRef tp:certId="N03"/>
                    <tp:ServiceBinding tp:channelId="N04" tp:pack-
ageId="N0402">
                         <tp:Service tp:type=
"uriReference">uri:example.com/services/buyerService</tp:Service>
                         <tp:Override tp:action="orderConfirm"
tp:channelId="N07" tp:packageId="N0402"
xlink:href="http://ebxml.org/processes/buySell.xml#orderConfirm"
xlink:type="simple"/>
                    </tp:ServiceBinding>
              </tp:CollaborationRole>
              <tp:Certificate tp:certId="N03">
                    <ds:KeyInfo/>
              </tp:Certificate>
              <tp:DeliveryChannel tp:channelId="N04" tp:transport-
Id="N05" tp:docExchangeId="N06">
                    <tp:Characteristics tp:syncReplyMode="none"
tp:nonrepudiationOfOrigin="true" tp:nonrepudiationOfReceipt=
"false"
tp:secureTransport="true" tp:confidentiality="true" tp:authenti-
cated="true"
tp:authorized="false"/>
              </tp:DeliveryChannel>
              <tp:DeliveryChannel tp:channelId="N07" tp:transport-
Id="N08"
tp:docExchangeId="N06">
                    <tp:Characteristics tp:syncReplyMode="none"
tp:nonrepudiationOfOrigin="true" tp:nonrepudiationOfReceipt=
"false"
tp:secureTransport="false" tp:confidentiality="true" tp:authenti-
cated="true"
tp:authorized="false"/>
              </tp:DeliveryChannel>
              <tp:Transport tp:transportId="N05">
                    <tp:SendingProtocol
tp:version="1.1">HTTP</tp:SendingProtocol>
                    <tp:ReceivingProtocol
tp:version="1.1">HTTP</tp:ReceivingProtocol>
                    <tp:Endpoint
tp:uri="https://www.example.com/servlets/ebxmlhandler" tp:type=
"allPurpose"/>
                    <tp:TransportSecurity>
                         <tp:Protocol tp:version="3.0">SSL</tp:Pro-
tocol>
                         <tp:CertificateRef tp:certId="N03"/>
                    </tp:TransportSecurity>
```

```
            </tp:Transport>
            <tp:Transport tp:transportId="N08">
                    <tp:SendingProtocol
tp:version="1.1">HTTP</tp:SendingProtocol>
                    <tp:ReceivingProtocol
tp:version="1.1">SMTP</tp:ReceivingProtocol>
                    <tp:Endpoint tp:uri="mailto:ebxmlhandler
@example.com"
tp:type="allPurpose"/>
            </tp:Transport>
            <tp:DocExchange tp:docExchangeId="N06">
                    <tp:ebXMLBinding tp:version="0.98b">
                        <tp:ReliableMessaging
tp:deliverySemantics="OnceAndOnlyOnce" tp:idempotency="true"
tp:messageOrderSemantics="Guaranteed">
                                <tp:Retries>5</tp:Retries>
                                <tp:RetryInterval>30</tp:Retry-
Interval>
                                <tp:PersistDuration>P1D</tp:Persist-
Duration>
                        </tp:ReliableMessaging>
                        <tp:NonRepudiation>
    <tp:Protocol>http://www.w3.org/2000/09/xmldsig#</tp:Protocol>
    <tp:HashFunction>http://www.w3.org/2000/09/xmldsig#sha1 </tp:
HashFunction>
    <tp:SignatureAlgorithm>http://www.w3.org/2000/09/xmldsig#dsa-
sha1</tp:SignatureAlgorithm>
                                <tp:CertificateRef tp:certId="N03"/>
                        </tp:NonRepudiation>
                        <tp:DigitalEnvelope>
                                <tp:Protocol
tp:version="2.0">S/MIME</tp:Protocol>
                                <tp:EncryptionAlgorithm>DES-
CBC</tp:EncryptionAlgorithm>
                                <tp:CertificateRef tp:certId="N03"/>
                        </tp:DigitalEnvelope>
                    </tp:ebXMLBinding>
            </tp:DocExchange>
        </tp:PartyInfo>
        <tp:Packaging tp:id="N0402">
            <tp:ProcessingCapabilities tp:parse="true" tp:
generate="true"/>
            <tp:SimplePart tp:id="N40" tp:mimetype="text/xml">
                <tp:NamespaceSupported
tp:location="http://ebxml.org/project_teams/transport/message-
Service.xsd"
```

```
tp:version="0.98b">http://www.ebxml.org/namespaces/messageService
</tp:NamespaceSupported>
                <tp:NamespaceSupported
tp:location="http://ebxml.org/project teams/transport/xmldsig-
core-schema.xsd"
tp:version="1.0">http://www.w3.org/2000/09/xmldsig</tp:Namespace-
Supported>
        </tp:SimplePart>
        <tp:SimplePart tp:id="N41" tp:mimetype="text/xml">
                <tp:NamespaceSupported
tp:location="http://ebxml.org/processes/buysell.xsd"
tp:version="1.0">http://ebxml.org/processes/buysell.xsd</tp:Name-
spaceSupported>
        </tp:SimplePart>
        <tp:CompositeList>
                <tp:Composite tp:id="N42" tp:mimetype="multi-
part/related"
tp:mimeparameters="type=text/xml;">
                        <tp:Constituent tp:idref="N40"/>
                        <tp:Constituent tp:idref="N41"/>
                </tp:Composite>
        </tp:CompositeList>
    </tp:Packaging>
    <tp:Comment tp:xml_lang="en-us">buy/sell agreement between
example.com and contrived-example.com</tp:Comment>
</tp:CollaborationProtocolProfile>
```

Appendix B   Example of CPA Document (Non-Normative)

The example in this appendix is to be parsed with an XML Schema parser.

A text version of this schema is available on the ebXML web site at www.ebxml.org/specs/

Note

Two separate examples of the CPA are needed because at least some existing tools require the DTD to have a `<!DOCTYPE...>` to assign the DTD and not to have a namespace qualifier.

```
<?xml version="1.0"?>
<!-- edited with XML Spy v3.5 (http://www.xmlspy.com) by christo-
pher ferris (sun microsystems, inc) -->
<tp:CollaborationProtocolAgreement
      xmlns:tp="http://www.ebxml.org/namespaces/tradePartner"
      xmlns:xsi="http://www.w3.org/2000/10/XMLSchema-instance"
      xsi:schemaLocation="http://www.ebxml.org/namespaces/trade-
Partner http://ebxml.org/project_teams/trade_partner/cpp-cpa-
v1_0.xsd"
      xmlns:xlink="http://www.w3.org/1999/xlink"
      xmlns:ds="http://www.w3.org/2000/09/xmldsig#"
      tp:cpaid="uri:yoursandmycpa"
      tp:version="1.2">
      <tp:Status tp:value="proposed"/>
      <tp:Start>2001-05-20T07:21:00Z</tp:Start>
      <tp:End>2002-05-20T07:21:00Z</tp:End>
      <tp:ConversationConstraints tp:invocationLimit="100"
tp:concurrentConversations="100"/>
      <tp:PartyInfo>
            <tp:PartyId tp:type="DUNS">123456789</tp:PartyId>
            <tp:PartyRef xlink:href="http://example.com/about
.html"/>
            <tp:CollaborationRole tp:id="N00">
                  <tp:ProcessSpecification tp:version="1.0"
tp:name="buySell" xlink:type="simple" xlink:href="http://www.ebxml
.org/processes/buySell.xml"/>
                  <tp:Role tp:name="buyer" xlink:type="simple"
xlink:href="http://ebxml.org/processes/buySell.xml#buyer"/>
                  <tp:CertificateRef tp:certId="N03"/>
                  <tp:ServiceBinding tp:channelId="N04" tp:
packageId="N0402">
                        <tp:Service
tp:type="uriReference">uri:example.com/services/buyerService</tp:
Service>
                        <tp:Override tp:action="orderConfirm"
tp:channelId="N08" tp:packageId="N0402" xlink:href="http://
ebxml.org/processes/buySell.xml#orderConfirm"
xlink:type="simple"/>
                  </tp:ServiceBinding>
            </tp:CollaborationRole>
            <tp:Certificate tp:certId="N03">
                  <ds:KeyInfo/>
            </tp:Certificate>
```

```
            <tp:DeliveryChannel tp:channelId="N04" tp:transport-
Id="N05" tp:docExchangeId="N06">
                <tp:Characteristics tp:syncReplyMode="none"
tp:nonrepudiationOfOrigin-"true" tp:nonrepudiationOfReceipt="false"
tp:secureTransport="true" tp:confidentiality="true" tp:authenti-
cated="true" tp:authorized="false"/>
            </tp:DeliveryChannel>
            <tp:DeliveryChannel tp:channelId="N07" tp:transport-
Id="N08" tp:docExchangeId="N06">
                <tp:Characteristics tp:syncReplyMode="none"
tp:nonrepudiationOfOrigin="true" tp:nonrepudiationOfReceipt="false"
tp:secureTransport="false" tp:confidentiality="true" tp:authenti-
cated="true" tp:authorized="false"/>
            </tp:DeliveryChannel>
            <tp:Transport tp:transportId="N05">
                <tp:SendingProtocol
tp:version="1.1">HTTP</tp:SendingProtocol>
                <tp:ReceivingProtocol
tp:version="1.1">HTTP</tp:ReceivingProtocol>
                <tp:Endpoint
tp:uri="https://www.example.com/servlets/ebxmlhandler" tp:type=
"allPurpose"/>
                <tp:TransportSecurity>
                    <tp:Protocol tp:version="3.0">SSL</tp:
Protocol>
                    <tp:CertificateRef tp:certId="N03"/>
                </tp:TransportSecurity>
            </tp:Transport>
            <tp:Transport tp:transportId="N18">
                <tp:SendingProtocol
tp:version="1.1">HTTP</tp:SendingProtocol>
                <tp:ReceivingProtocol
tp:version="1.1">SMTP</tp:ReceivingProtocol>
                <tp:Endpoint tp:uri="mailto:ebxmlhandler@
example.com" tp:type="allPurpose"/>
            </tp:Transport>
            <tp:DocExchange tp:docExchangeId="N06">
                <tp:ebXMLBinding tp:version="0.98b">
                    <tp:ReliableMessaging
tp:deliverySemantics="OnceAndOnlyOnce" tp:idempotency="true"
tp:messageOrderSemantics="Guaranteed">
                        <tp:Retries>5</tp:Retries>
```

```
                    <tp:RetryInterval>30</tp:Retry-
Interval>
                    <tp:PersistDuration>P1D</tp:Persist-
Duration>
                </tp:ReliableMessaging>
                <tp:NonRepudiation>
    <tp:Protocol>http://www.w3.org/2000/09/xmldsig#</tp:Protocol>
    <tp:HashFunction>http://www.w3.org/2000/09/xmldsig#sha1
</tp:HashFunction>
    <tp:SignatureAlgorithm>http://www.w3.org/2000/09/
xmldsig#dsa-sha1</tp:SignatureAlgorithm>
                    <tp:CertificateRef tp:certId="N03"/>
                </tp:NonRepudiation>
                <tp:DigitalEnvelope>
                    <tp:Protocol
tp:version="2.0">S/MIME</tp:Protocol>
                    <tp:EncryptionAlgorithm>DES-
CBC</tp:EncryptionAlgorithm>
                    <tp:CertificateRef tp:certId="N03"/>
                </tp:DigitalEnvelope>
            </tp:ebXMLBinding>
        </tp:DocExchange>
    </tp:PartyInfo>
    <tp:PartyInfo>
        <tp:PartyId tp:type="DUNS">987654321</tp:PartyId>
        <tp:PartyRef xlink:type="simple" xlink:href=
"http://contrived-example.com/about.html"/>
        <tp:CollaborationRole tp:id="N30">
            <tp:ProcessSpecification tp:version="1.0"
tp:name="buySell"
xlink:type="simple" xlink:href="http://www.ebxml.org/processes/
buySell.xml"/>
            <tp:Role tp:name="seller" xlink:type="simple"
xlink:href="http://ebxml.org/processes/buySell.xml#seller"/>
            <tp:CertificateRef tp:certId="N33"/>
            <tp:ServiceBinding tp:channelId="N34" tp:
packageId="N0402">
                <tp:Service
tp:type="uriReference">uri:example.com/services/sellerService</tp:
Service>
            </tp:ServiceBinding>
        </tp:CollaborationRole>
        <tp:Certificate tp:certId="N33">
            <ds:KeyInfo/>
```

```
            </tp:Certificate>
            <tp:DeliveryChannel tp:channelId="N34" tp:transport-
Id="N35" tp:docExchangeId="N36">
                  <tp:Characteristics tp:nonrepudiationOfOrigin=
"true" tp:nonrepudiationOfReceipt="false" tp:secureTransport=
"true" tp:confidentiality="true" tp:authenticated="true" tp:
authorized="false"/>
            </tp:DeliveryChannel>
            <tp:Transport tp:transportId="N35">
                  <tp:SendingProtocol
tp:version="1.1">HTTP</tp:SendingProtocol>
                  <tp:ReceivingProtocol
tp:version="1.1">HTTP</tp:ReceivingProtocol>
                  <tp:Endpoint tp:uri="https://www.contrived-
example.com/servlets/ebxmlhandler" tp:type="allPurpose"/>
                  <tp:TransportSecurity>
                        <tp:Protocol tp:version="3.0">SSL</tp:
Protocol>
                        <tp:CertificateRef tp:certId="N33"/>
                  </tp:TransportSecurity>
            </tp:Transport>
            <tp:DocExchange tp:docExchangeId="N36">
                  <tp:ebXMLBinding tp:version="0.98b">
                        <tp:ReliableMessaging
tp:deliverySemantics="OnceAndOnlyOnce" tp:idempotency="true"
tp:messageOrderSemantics="Guaranteed">
                              <tp:Retries>5</tp:Retries>
                              <tp:RetryInterval>30</tp:Retry-
Interval>
                              <tp:PersistDuration>P1D</tp:Persist-
Duration>
                        </tp:ReliableMessaging>
                        <tp:NonRepudiation>
      <tp:Protocol>http://www.w3.org/2000/09/xmldsig#</tp:Protocol>
      <tp:HashFunction>http://www.w3.org/2000/09/xmldsig#sha1 </tp:
HashFunction>
      <tp:SignatureAlgorithm>http://www.w3.org/2000/09/
xmldsig#dsa-sha1</tp:SignatureAlgorithm>
                              <tp:CertificateRef tp:certId="N33"/>
                        </tp:NonRepudiation>
                        <tp:DigitalEnvelope>
                              <tp:Protocol
```

```
tp:version="2.0">S/MIME</tp:Protocol>
                              <tp:EncryptionAlgorithm>DES-
CBC</tp:EncryptionAlgorithm>
                              <tp:CertificateRef tp:certId="N33"/>
                      </tp:DigitalEnvelope>
              </tp:ebXMLBinding>
          </tp:DocExchange>
      </tp:PartyInfo>
      <tp:Packaging tp:id="N0402">
          <tp:ProcessingCapabilities tp:parse="true" tp:
generate="true"/>
          <tp:SimplePart tp:id="N40" tp:mimetype="text/xml">
              <tp:NamespaceSupported
tp:location="http://ebxml.org/project_teams/transport/message-
Service.xsd" tp:version="0.98b">http://www.ebxml.org/namespaces/
messageService</tp:NamespaceSupported>
              <tp:NamespaceSupported
tp:location="http://ebxml.org/project_teams/transport/xmldsig-core-
schema.xsd"
tp:version="1.0">http://www.w3.org/2000/09/xmldsig</tp:Namespace-
Supported>
          </tp:SimplePart>
          <tp:SimplePart tp:id="N41" tp:mimetype="text/xml">
              <tp:NamespaceSupported
tp:location="http://ebxml.org/processes/buysell.xsd"
tp:version="1.0">http://ebxml.org/processes/buysell.xsd</tp:Name-
spaceSupported>
          </tp:SimplePart>
          <tp:CompositeList>
              <tp:Composite tp:id="N42" tp:mimetype="multi-
part/related"
tp:mimeparameters="type=text/xml;">
                      <tp:Constituent tp:idref="N40"/>
                      <tp:Constituent tp:idref="N41"/>
              </tp:Composite>
          </tp:CompositeList>
      </tp:Packaging>
      <tp:Comment xml:lang="en-us">buy/sell agreement between
example.com and contrived-example.com</tp:Comment>
</tp:CollaborationProtocolAgreement>
```

Appendix C DTD Corresponding to Complete CPP/CPA Definition (Normative)

A text version of this schema is available on the ebXML web site at www.ebxml.org/specs/

```
<?xml version="1.0" encoding="UTF-8"?>
<!--Generated by XML Authority-->
<!ELEMENT CollaborationProtocolAgreement (Status, Start, End,
ConversationConstraints?, PartyInfo+, Packaging, ds:Signature*,
Comment*)>
<!ATTLIST CollaborationProtocolAgreement
      cpaid CDATA #IMPLIED
      version CDATA #IMPLIED
>
<!ELEMENT CollaborationProtocolProfile (PartyInfo+, Packaging,
ds:Signature?, Comment*)>
<!ATTLIST CollaborationProtocolProfile
      version CDATA #IMPLIED
>
<!ELEMENT ProcessSpecification (ds:Reference?)>
<!ATTLIST ProcessSpecification
      version CDATA #REQUIRED
      name CDATA #REQUIRED
      xlink:type CDATA #FIXED "simple"
      xlink:href CDATA #IMPLIED
>
<!ELEMENT Protocol (#PCDATA)>
<!ATTLIST Protocol
      version CDATA #IMPLIED
>
<!ELEMENT SendingProtocol (#PCDATA)>
<!ATTLIST SendingProtocol
      version CDATA #IMPLIED
>
<!ELEMENT ReceivingProtocol (#PCDATA)>
<!ATTLIST ReceivingProtocol
      version CDATA #IMPLIED
>
```

```
<!ELEMENT CollaborationRole (ProcessSpecification, Role, Certifi-
cateRef?,
ServiceBinding+)>
<!ATTLIST CollaborationRole
     id ID #IMPLIED
>
<!ELEMENT PartyInfo (PartyId+, PartyRef, CollaborationRole+,
Certificate+, DeliveryChannel+, Transport+, DocExchange+)>
<!ELEMENT PartyId (#PCDATA)>
<!ATTLIST PartyId
     type CDATA #IMPLIED
>
<!ELEMENT PartyRef EMPTY>
<!ATTLIST PartyRef
     xlink:type (simple) #IMPLIED
     xlink:href CDATA #IMPLIED
>
<!ELEMENT DeliveryChannel (Characteristics)>
<!ATTLIST DeliveryChannel
     channelId ID #REQUIRED
     transportId IDREF #REQUIRED
     docExchangeId IDREF #REQUIRED
>
<!ELEMENT Transport (SendingProtocol+, ReceivingProtocol, End-
point+,
TransportSecurity?)>
<!ATTLIST Transport
     transportId ID #REQUIRED
>
<!ELEMENT Endpoint EMPTY>
<!ATTLIST Endpoint
     uri CDATA #REQUIRED
     type (login | request | response | error | allPurpose)
"allPurpose"
>
<!ELEMENT Retries (#PCDATA)>
<!ELEMENT RetryInterval (#PCDATA)>
<!ELEMENT TransportSecurity (Protocol, CertificateRef?)>
<!ELEMENT Certificate (ds:KeyInfo)>
<!ATTLIST Certificate
     certId ID #REQUIRED
>
<!ELEMENT DocExchange (ebXMLBinding)>
<!ATTLIST DocExchange
     docExchangeId ID #REQUIRED
>
```

```
<!ELEMENT PersistDuration (#PCDATA)>
<!ATTLIST PersistDuration
      e-dtype NMTOKEN #FIXED "timeDuration"
>
<!ELEMENT ReliableMessaging (Retries, RetryInterval, Persist-
Duration)?>
<!ATTLIST ReliableMessaging
      deliverySemantics (OnceAndOnlyOnce | BestEffort) #REQUIRED
      messageOrderSemantics (Guaranteed | NotGuaranteed) "Not-
Guaranteed"
      idempotency CDATA #REQUIRED
>
<!ELEMENT NonRepudiation (Protocol, HashFunction, Signature-
Algorithm, CertificateRef)>
<!ELEMENT HashFunction (#PCDATA)>
<!ELEMENT EncryptionAlgorithm (#PCDATA)>
<!ELEMENT SignatureAlgorithm (#PCDATA)>
<!ELEMENT DigitalEnvelope (Protocol, EncryptionAlgorithm, Certifi-
cateRef)>
<!ELEMENT CertificateRef EMPTY>
<!ATTLIST CertificateRef
      certId IDREF #REQUIRED
>
<!ELEMENT ebXMLBinding (ReliableMessaging?, NonRepudiation?,
DigitalEnvelope?, NamespaceSupported*)>
<!ATTLIST ebXMLBinding
      version CDATA #REQUIRED
>
<!ELEMENT NamespaceSupported (#PCDATA)>
<!ATTLIST NamespaceSupported
      location CDATA #REQUIRED
      version CDATA #IMPLIED
>
<!ELEMENT Characteristics EMPTY>
<!ATTLIST Characteristics
      syncReplyMode (responseOnly | signalsAndResponse | signals-
Only | none)
#IMPLIED
      nonrepudiationOfOrigin CDATA #IMPLIED
      nonrepudiationOfReceipt CDATA #IMPLIED
      secureTransport CDATA #IMPLIED
      confidentiality CDATA #IMPLIED
      authenticated CDATA #IMPLIED
      authorized CDATA #IMPLIED
>
<!ELEMENT ServiceBinding (Service, Override*)>
<!ATTLIST ServiceBinding
```

```
               channelId IDREF #REQUIRED
               packageId IDREF #REQUIRED
>
<!ELEMENT Service (#PCDATA)>
<!ATTLIST Service
          type CDATA #IMPLIED>


<!ELEMENT Status EMPTY>
<!ATTLIST Status
          value (agreed | signed | proposed) #REQUIRED
>
<!ELEMENT Start (#PCDATA)>
<!ELEMENT End (#PCDATA)>
<!ELEMENT Type (#PCDATA)>
<!ELEMENT ConversationConstraints EMPTY>
<!ATTLIST ConversationConstraints
          invocationLimit CDATA #IMPLIED
          concurrentConversations CDATA #IMPLIED
>
<!ELEMENT Override EMPTY>
<!ATTLIST Override
          action CDATA #REQUIRED
          channelId ID #REQUIRED
          packageId IDREF #REQUIRED
          xlink:href CDATA #IMPLIED
          xlink:type CDATA #FIXED "simple"
>
<!ELEMENT Role EMPTY>
<!ATTLIST Role
          name CDATA #REQUIRED
          xlink:type CDATA #FIXED "simple"
          xlink:href CDATA #IMPLIED
>
<!ELEMENT Constituent EMPTY>
<!ATTLIST Constituent
          idref CDATA #REQUIRED
>
<!ELEMENT ProcessingCapabilities EMPTY>
<!ATTLIST ProcessingCapabilities
          parse CDATA #REQUIRED
          generate CDATA #REQUIRED
>
<!ELEMENT SimplePart (NamespaceSupported*)>
<!ATTLIST SimplePart
          id ID #IMPLIED
          mimetype CDATA #REQUIRED
>
```

```
<!ELEMENT Encapsulation (Constituent)>
<!ATTLIST Encapsulation
      id ID #IMPLIED
      mimetype CDATA #REQUIRED
      mimeparameters CDATA #IMPLIED
>
<!ELEMENT Composite (Constituent+)>
<!ATTLIST Composite
      id ID #IMPLIED
      mimetype CDATA #REQUIRED
      mimeparameters CDATA #IMPLIED
>
<!ELEMENT CompositeList (Encapsulation | Composite)+>
<!ELEMENT Packaging (ProcessingCapabilities, SimplePart+, Compos-
iteList?)>
<!ATTLIST Packaging
      id ID #REQUIRED
>
<!ELEMENT Comment (#PCDATA)>
<!ATTLIST Comment
      xml:lang CDATA #REQUIRED
>
<!ELEMENT ds:Signature ANY>
<!ELEMENT ds:Reference ANY>
<!ELEMENT ds:KeyInfo ANY>
```

Appendix D XML Schema Document Corresponding to Complete CPP and CPA Definition (Normative)

A text version of this schema is available on the ebXML web site at www.ebxml.org/specs/

```
<?xml version="1.0" encoding="UTF-8"?>
<schema targetNamespace="http://www.ebxml.org/namespaces/trade-
Partner"
xmlns:xml="http://www.w3.org/XML/1998/namespace"
```

```
xmlns="http://www.w3.org/2000/10/XMLSchema"
xmlns:tns="http://www.ebxml.org/namespaces/tradePartner"
xmlns:xlink="http://www.w3.org/1999/xlink"
xmlns:xsi="http://www.w3.org/2000/10/XMLSchema-instance"
xmlns:ds="http://www.w3.org/2000/09/xmldsig#" elementForm-
Default="qualified"
attributeFormDefault="unqualified" version="1.0">
        <import namespace="http://www.w3.org/1999/xlink"
schemaLocation="http://ebxml.org/project_teams/transport/xlink.xsd"/>
        <import namespace="http://www.w3.org/2000/09/xmldsig#"
schemaLocation="http://ebxml.org/project_teams/transport/xmldsig-
core-schema.xsd"/>
        <import namespace="http://www.w3.org/XML/1998/namespace"
schemaLocation="http://ebxml.org/project_teams/transport/xml_lang.
xsd"/>
        <attributeGroup name="pkg.grp">
            <attribute ref="tns:id"/>
            <attribute name="mimetype" type="tns:non-empty-string"
use="required"/>
            <attribute name="mimeparameters" type="tns:non-empty-
string"/>
        </attributeGroup>
        <attributeGroup name="xlink.grp">
            <attribute ref="xlink:type"/>
            <attribute ref="xlink:href"/>
        </attributeGroup>
        <element name="CollaborationProtocolAgreement">
            <complexType>
                <sequence>
                    <element ref="tns:Status"/>
                    <element ref="tns:Start"/>
                    <element ref="tns:End"/>
                    <element ref="tns:ConversationConstraints"
minOccurs="0"/>
                    <element ref="tns:PartyInfo" maxOccurs=
"unbounded"/>
                    <element ref="tns:Packaging"/>
                    <element ref="ds:Signature" minOccurs="0"
maxOccurs="unbounded"/>
                    <element ref="tns:Comment" minOccurs="0"
maxOccurs="unbounded"/>
                </sequence>
                <attribute name="cpaid" type="tns:non-empty-
string"/>
                <attribute ref="tns:version"/>
```

```
                    <anyAttribute namespace="##targetNamespace
http://www.w3.org/2000/10/XMLSchema-instance" processContents="lax"/>
          </complexType>
     </element>
     <element name="CollaborationProtocolProfile">
          <complexType>
               <sequence>
                    <element ref="tns:PartyInfo" maxOccurs=
"unbounded"/>
                    <element ref="tns:Packaging"/>
                    <element ref="ds:Signature" minOccurs="0"/>
                    <element ref="tns:Comment" minOccurs="0"
maxOccurs="unbounded"/>
               </sequence>
               <attribute ref="tns:version"/>
               <anyAttribute namespace="##targetNamespace
http://www.w3.org/2000/10/XMLSchema-instance" processContents="lax"/>
          </complexType>
     </element>
     <element name="ProcessSpecification">
          <complexType>
               <sequence>
                    <element ref="ds:Reference" minOccurs="0"/>
               </sequence>
               <attribute ref="tns:version"/>
               <attribute name="name" type="tns:non-empty-string"
use="required"/>
               <attributeGroup ref="tns:xlink.grp"/>
          </complexType>
     </element>
     <element name="Service" type="tns:service.type"/>
     <element name="Protocol" type="tns:protocol.type"/>
     <element name="SendingProtocol" type="tns:protocol.type"/>
     <element name="ReceivingProtocol" type="tns:protocol.type"/>
     <element name="CollaborationRole">
          <complexType>
               <sequence>
                    <element ref="tns:ProcessSpecification"/>
                    <element ref="tns:Role"/>
                    <element ref="tns:CertificateRef" min-
Occurs="0"/>
                    <element ref="tns:ServiceBinding"
maxOccurs="unbounded"/>
               </sequence>
               <attribute ref="tns:id"/>
          </complexType>
```

```
            </element>
            <element name="PartyInfo">
                  <complexType>
                        <sequence>
                              <element ref="tns:PartyId" maxOccurs=
"unbounded"/>
                              <element ref="tns:PartyRef"/>
                              <element ref="tns:CollaborationRole"
maxOccurs="unbounded"/>
                              <element ref="tns:Certificate"
maxOccurs="unbounded"/>
                              <element ref="tns:DeliveryChannel"
maxOccurs="unbounded"/>
                              <element ref="tns:Transport"
maxOccurs="unbounded"/>
                              <element ref="tns:DocExchange"
maxOccurs="unbounded"/>
                        </sequence>
                  </complexType>
            </element>
            <element name="PartyId">
                  <complexType>
                        <simpleContent>
                              <extension base="tns:non-empty-string">
                                    <attribute name="type" type="tns:
non-empty-string"/>
                              </extension>
                        </simpleContent>
                  </complexType>
            </element>
            <element name="PartyRef">
                  <complexType>
                        <attributeGroup ref="tns:xlink.grp"/>
                        <attribute name="type" type="tns:non-empty-
string"/>
                  </complexType>
            </element>
            <element name="DeliveryChannel">
                  <complexType>
                        <sequence>
                              <element ref="tns:Characteristics"/>
                        </sequence>
                        <attribute name="channelId" type="ID" use=
"required"/>
                        <attribute name="transportId" type="IDREF"
use="required"/>
```

```
                <attribute name="docExchangeId" type="IDREF"
use="required"/>
            </complexType>
    </clement>
    <element name="Transport">
            <complexType>
                <sequence>
                    <element ref="tns:SendingProtocol"
maxOccurs="unbounded"/>
                    <element ref="tns:ReceivingProtocol"/>
                    <element ref="tns:Endpoint" maxOccurs=
"unbounded"/>
                    <element ref="tns:TransportSecurity"
minOccurs="0"/>
                </sequence>
                <attribute name="transportId" type="ID" use=
"required"/>
            </complexType>
    </element>
    <element name="Endpoint">
            <complexType>
                <attribute name="uri" type="uriReference" use=
"required"/>
                <attribute name="type" type="tns:endpoint-
Type.type" use="default" value="allPurpose"/>
            </complexType>
    </element>
    <element name="Retries" type="string"/>
    <element name="RetryInterval" type="string"/>
    <element name="TransportSecurity">
            <complexType>
                <sequence>
                    <element ref="tns:Protocol"/>
                    <element ref="tns:CertificateRef" min-
Occurs="0"/>
                </sequence>
            </complexType>
    </element>
    <element name="Certificate">
            <complexType>
                <sequence>
                    <element ref="ds:KeyInfo"/>
                </sequence>
                <attribute name="certId" type="ID" use=
"required"/>
```

```
                    </complexType>
            </element>
            <element name="DocExchange">
                    <complexType>
                            <sequence>
                                    <element ref="tns:ebXMLBinding"/>
                            </sequence>
                            <attribute name="docExchangeId" type="ID"
use="required"/>
                    </complexType>
            </element>
            <element name="ReliableMessaging">
                    <complexType>
                            <sequence minOccurs="0">
                                    <element ref="tns:Retries"/>
                                    <element ref="tns:RetryInterval"/>
                                    <element name="PersistDuration"
type="timeDuration"/>
                            </sequence>
                            <attribute name="deliverySemantics" type="tns:
ds.type" use="required"/>
                            <attribute name="idempotency" type="boolean"
use="required"/>
                            <attribute name="messageOrderSemantics"
type="tns:mos.type" use="optional" value="NotGuaranteed"/>
                    </complexType>
                    <!-- <element name="PersistDuration" type="duration"/>
-->
            </element>
            <element name="NonRepudiation">
                    <complexType>
                            <sequence>
                                    <element ref-"tns:Protocol"/>
                                    <element ref="tns:HashFunction"/>
                                    <element ref="tns:SignatureAlgorithm"/>
                                    <element ref="tns:CertificateRef"/>
                            </sequence>
                    </complexType>
            </element>
            <element name="HashFunction" type="string"/>
            <element name="EncryptionAlgorithm" type="string"/>
            <element name="SignatureAlgorithm" type="string"/>
            <element name="DigitalEnvelope">
                    <complexType>
                            <sequence>
                                    <element ref="tns:Protocol"/>
```

```
                        <element ref="tns:EncryptionAlgorithm"/>
                        <element ref="tns:CertificateRef"/>
                </sequence>
        </complexType>
    </element>
    <element name="CertificateRef">
        <complexType>
                <attribute name="certId" type="IDREF" use=
"required"/>
        </complexType>
    </element>
    <element name="ebXMLBinding">
        <complexType>
                <sequence>
                        <element ref="tns:ReliableMessaging"
minOccurs="0"/>
                        <element ref="tns:NonRepudiation" min-
Occurs="0"/>
                        <element ref="tns:DigitalEnvelope" min-
Occurs="0"/>
                        <element ref="tns:NamespaceSupported"
minOccurs="0"
maxOccurs="unbounded"/>
                </sequence>
                <attribute ref="tns:version"/>
        </complexType>
    </element>
    <element name="NamespaceSupported">
        <complexType>
                <simpleContent>
                        <extension base="uriReference">
                                <attribute name="location" type=
"uriReference" use="required"/>
                                <attribute ref="tns:version"/>
                        </extension>
                </simpleContent>
        </complexType>
    </element>
    <element name="Characteristics">
        <complexType>
                <attribute ref="tns:syncReplyMode"/>
                <attribute name="nonrepudiationOfOrigin" type=
"boolean"/>
                <attribute name="nonrepudiationOfReceipt" type=
"boolean"/>
                <attribute name="secureTransport" type="boolean"/>
```

```
                    <attribute name="confidentiality" type="boolean"/>
                    <attribute name="authenticated" type="boolean"/>
                    <attribute name="authorized" type="boolean"/>
            </complexType>
        </element>
        <element name="ServiceBinding">
            <complexType>
                <sequence>
                    <element ref="tns:Service"/>
                    <element ref="tns:Override" minOccurs="0"
maxOccurs="unbounded"/>
                </sequence>
                <attribute name="channelId" type="IDREF" use=
"required"/>
                <attribute name="packageId" type="IDREF" use=
"required"/>
            </complexType>
            <unique name="action.const">
                <selector xpath=".//Override"/>
                <field xpath="@action"/>
            </unique>
        </element>
        <element name="Status">
            <complexType>
                <attribute name="value" type="tns:
statusValue.type" use="required"/>
            </complexType>
        </element>
        <element name="Start" type="timeInstant"/>
        <element name="End" type="timeInstant"/>
        <!--
        <element name="Start" type="dateTime"/>
        <element name="End" type="datcTime"/>
        -->
        <element name="Type" type="string"/>
        <element name="ConversationConstraints">
            <complexType>
                <attribute name="invocationLimit" type="int"/>
                <attribute name="concurrentConversations"
type="int"/>
            </complexType>
        </element>
        <element name="Override">
            <complexType>
                <attribute name="action" type="tns:non-empty-
string" use="required"/>
```

```
                    <attribute name="channelId" type="ID" use=
"required"/>
                    <attribute name="packageId" type="IDREF" use=
"required"/>
                    <attributeGroup ref="tns:xlink.grp"/>
            </complexType>
      </element>
      <element name="Role">
            <complexType>
                    <attribute name="name" type="tns:non-empty-
string" use="required"/>
                    <attributeGroup ref="tns:xlink.grp"/>
            </complexType>
      </element>
      <element name="Constituent">
            <complexType>
                    <attribute ref="tns:idref"/>
            </complexType>
      </element>
      <element name="Packaging">
            <complexType>
                    <sequence>
                        <element name="ProcessingCapabilities">
                            <complexType>
                                    <attribute name="parse" type=
"boolean" use="required"/>
                                    <attribute name="generate"
type="boolean" use="required"/>
                            </complexType>
                        </element>
                        <element name="SimplePart" maxOccurs="un-
bounded">
                            <complexType>
                                <sequence>
                                        <element
ref="tns:NamespaceSupported" minOccurs="0" maxOccurs="unbounded"/>
                                </sequence>
                                <attributeGroup
ref="tns:pkg.grp"/>
                            </complexType>
                        </element>
                        <element name="CompositeList" minOccurs="0">
                            <complexType>
                                <choice maxOccurs="unbounded">
                                    <element name="Encapsu-
lation">
```

```
                                                <complexType>
                                                    <sequence>
                                                        <ele-
ment ref="tns:Constituent"/>
                                                    </sequence>
                                                    <attribute-
Group ref="tns:pkg.grp"/>
                                                </complexType>
                                            </element>
                                            <element name=
"Composite">
                                                <complexType>
                                                    <sequence>
                                                        <ele-
ment ref="tns:Constituent" maxOccurs="unbounded"/>
                                                    </sequence>
                                                    <attribute-
Group ref="tns:pkg.grp"/>
                                                </complexType>
                                            </element>
                                    </choice>
                                </complexType>
                            </element>
                    </sequence>
                    <attribute ref="tns:id"/>
            </complexType>
    </element>
    <element name="Comment">
            <complexType>
                    <simpleContent>
                            <extension base="tns:non-empty-string">
                                    <attribute ref="xml:lang"/>
                            </extension>
                    </simpleContent>
            </complexType>
    </element>
    <!-- COMMON -->
    <simpleType name="ds.type">
            <restriction base="NMTOKEN">
                    <enumeration value="OnceAndOnlyOnce"/>
                    <enumeration value="BestEffort"/>
            </restriction>
    </simpleType>
    <simpleType name="mos.type">
            <restriction base="NMTOKEN">
```

```
                    <enumeration value="Guaranteed"/>
                    <enumeration value="NotGuaranteed"/>
            </restriction>
    </simpleType>
    <simpleType name="statusValue.type">
            <restriction base="NMTOKEN">
                    <enumeration value="agreed"/>
                    <enumeration value="signed"/>
                    <enumeration value="proposed"/>
            </restriction>
    </simpleType>
    <simpleType name="endpointType.type">
            <restriction base="NMTOKEN">
                    <enumeration value="login"/>
                    <enumeration value="request"/>
                    <enumeration value="response"/>
                    <enumeration value="error"/>
                    <enumeration value="allPurpose"/>
            </restriction>
    </simpleType>
    <simpleType name="non-empty-string">
            <restriction base="string">
                    <minLength value="1"/>
            </restriction>
    </simpleType>
    <simpleType name="syncReplyMode.type">
            <restriction base="NMTOKEN">
                    <enumeration value="responseOnly"/>
                    <enumeration value="signalsAndResponse"/>
                    <enumeration value="signalsOnly"/>
                    <enumeration value="none"/>
            </restriction>
    </simpleType>
    <complexType name="service.type">
            <simpleContent>
                    <extension base="tns:non-empty-string">
                            <attribute name="type" type="tns:non-
empty-string"/>
                    </extension>
            </simpleContent>
    </complexType>
    <complexType name="protocol.type">
            <simpleContent>
                    <extension base="tns:non-empty-string">
                            <attribute ref="tns:version"/>
```

```
            </extension>
          </simpleContent>
      </complexType>
      <attribute name="idref" type="IDREF" form="unqualified"/>
      <attribute name="id" type="ID" form="unqualified"/>
      <attribute name="version" type="tns:non-empty-string"/>
      <attribute name="syncReplyMode" type="tns:syncReplyMode
.type"/>
</schema>
```

Appendix E Formats of Information in the CPP and CPA (Normative)

This section defines format information that is not defined by the [XML] specification and is not defined in the descriptions of specific elements.

Formats of Character Strings

Protocol and Version Elements

Values of **Protocol, Version,** and similar elements are flexible. In general, any protocol and version for which the support software is available to both *Parties* to a *CPA* MAY be selected as long as the choice does not require changes to the DTD or schema and therefore a change to this specification.

Note

> A possible implementation MAY be based on the use of plug-ins or exits to support the values of these elements.

Alphanumeric Strings

Alphanumeric strings not further defined in this section follow these rules unless otherwise stated in the description of an individual element:

Values of elements are case insensitive unless otherwise stated.

Strings which represent file or directory names are case sensitive to ensure that they are acceptable to both UNIX and Windows systems.

Numeric Strings

A numeric string is a signed or unsigned decimal integer in the range imposed by a 32-bit binary number, i.e. -2,147,483,648 to +2,417,483,647. Negative numbers MAY or MAY not be permitted in particular elements.

Appendix F Composing a CPA from Two CPPs (Non-Normative)

Overview and Limitations

In this appendix, we discuss the tasks involved in _CPA_ formation from _CPPs_. The detailed procedures for _CPA_ formation are currently left for implementers. Therefore, no normative specification is provided for algorithms for _CPA_ formation. In this initial section, we provide some background on _CPA_ formation tasks.

There are three basic reasons why we prefer to provide information about the component tasks involved in _CPA_ formation rather than attempt to provide an algorithm for _CPA_ formation:

1. The precise informational inputs to the _CPA_ formation procedure vary.

2. There exist at least two distinct approaches to _CPA_ formation. One useful approach for certain situations involves basing _CPA_ formation from a _CPA_ template; the other approach involves composition from _CPPs_.

3. The conditions for output of a given _CPA_ given two _CPPs_ can involve different levels and extents of interoperability. In other words, when an optimal solution that satisfies every level of requirement and every other additional constraint does not exist, a _Party_ MAY propose a _CPA_ that satisfies enough of the requirements for "a good enough" implementation. User input MAY be solicited to determine what is a good enough implementation, and so MAY be as varied as there are user configuration options to express preferences. In practice, compromises MAY be made on security, reliable messaging, levels of signals and acknowledgements, and other matters in order to find some acceptable means of doing _Business_.

Each of these reasons is elaborated in greater detail in the following sections.

Variability in Inputs

User preferences provide one source of variability in the inputs to the *CPA* formation process. Let us suppose in this section that each of the *Parties* has made its *CPP* available to potential collaborators. Normally one *Party* will have a desired *Business Collaboration* (defined in a *Process-Specification* document*)* to implement with its intended collaborator. So the information inputs will normally involve a user preference about intended *Business Collaboration* in addition to just the *CPPs*.

A *CPA* formation tool MAY have access to local user information not advertised in the *CPP* that MAY contribute to the *CPA* that is formed. A user MAY have chosen to only advertise those system capabilities that reflect nondeprecated capabilities. For example, a user MAY only advertise HTTP and omit FTP, even when capable of using FTP. The reason for omitting FTP might be concerns about the scalability of managing user accounts, directories, and passwords for FTP sessions. Despite not advertising an FTP capability, configuration software MAY use tacit knowledge about its own FTP capability to form a *CPA* with an intended collaborator who happens to have only an FTP capability for implementing a desired *Business Collaboration*. In other words, *Business* interests MAY, in this case, override the deprecation policy. Both tacit knowledge and detailed preference information account for variability in inputs into the *CPA* formation process.

Different Approaches

When a *CPA* is formed from a *CPA* template, it is typically because the capabilities of one of the *Parties* are limited, and already tacitly known. For example, if a *CPA* template were implicitly presented to a Web browser for use in an implementation using browser based forms capabilities, then the template maker can assume that the other *Party* has suitable web capabilities (or is about to download them). Therefore, all that really needs to be done is to supply **PartyRef, Certificate,** and similar items for substitution into a *CPA* template. The *CPA* template will already have all the capabilities of both *Parties* specified at the various levels, and will have placeholders for values to be supplied by one of the *Partners*. A simple form might be adequate to gather the needed information and produce a *CPA*.

Variable Output "Satisficing" Policies

A *CPA* can support a fully interoperable configuration in which agreement has been reached on all technical levels needed for *Business Collaboration*. In such a case, matches in capabilities will have been found in all relevant technical levels.

However, there can be interoperable configurations agreed to in a *CPA* in which not all aspects of a *Business Collaboration* match. Gaps MAY exist in packaging, security, signaling, reliable messaging and other areas and yet the systems can still transport the *Business* data, and special means can be employed to handle the exceptions. In such situations, a *CPA* MAY reflect configured policies or expressly solicited user permission to ignore some shortcomings in configurations. A system might not be capable of responding in a *Business Collaboration* so as to support a recommended ability to supply nonrepudiation of receipt, but might still be acceptable for *Business* reasons. A system might not be able to handle all the processing required to support, for example, SOAP with Attachments and yet still be able to treat the multipart according to "multipart/mixed" handling and allow *Business Collaboration* to take place. In fact, short of a failure to be able to transport data and a failure to be able to provide data relevant to the *Business Collaboration*, there are few features that might not be temporarily or indefinitely compromised about, given overriding *Business* interests. This situation of "partial interoperability" is to be expected to persist for some time, and so interferes with formulating a "clean" algorithm for deciding on what is sufficient for interoperability.

In summary, the previous considerations indicate that at the present it is at best premature to seek a simple algorithm for *CPA* formation from *CPPs*. It is to be expected that as capability characterization and exchange becomes a more refined subject, that advances will be made in characterizing *CPA* formation and negotiation.

Despite it being too soon to propose a simple algorithm for *CPA* formation that covers all the above variations, it is currently possible to enumerate the basic tasks involved in matching capabilities within *CPPs*. This information might assist the software implementer in designing a partially automated and partially interactive software system useful for configuring *Business Collaboration* so as to arrive at satisfactorily complete levels of interoperability. To understand the context for characterizing the constituent tasks, the general perspective on *CPPs* and *CPAs* needs to be briefly recalled.

CPA Formation Component Tasks

Technically viewed, a *CPA* provides "bindings" between *Business-Collaboration* specifications (as defined in the *Process-Specification* document) and those services and protocols that are used to implement these specifications. The implementation takes place at several levels and involves varied services at these levels. A *CPA* that arrives at a fully interoperable binding of a *Business Collaboration* to its implementing services and protocols can be thought of as arriving at interoperable, application-to-application integration. *CPAs* MAY fall short of this goal and still be useful and acceptable to the collaborating *Parties*. Certainly, if no matching data-transport capabilities can be discovered, a *CPA* would not provide much in the way of interoperable *Business-to-Business* integration. Likewise, partial *CPAs* will leave significant system work to be done before a completely satisfactory application-to-application integration is realized. Even so, partial integration MAY be sufficient to allow collaboration, and to enjoy payoffs from increased levels of automation.

In practice, the *CPA* formation process MAY produce a complete *CPA*, a failure result, a gap list that drives a dialog with the user, or perhaps even a *CPA* that implements partial interoperability "good enough" for the *Business* collaborators. Because both matching capabilities and interoperability can be matters of degree, the constituent tasks are finding the matches in capabilities at different levels and for different services. We next proceed to characterize many of these constituent tasks.

CPA Formation from CPPs: Enumeration of Tasks

To simplify discussion, assume in the following that we are viewing the tasks faced by a software agent when:

1. an intended collaborator is known and the collaborator's *CPP* has been retrieved,

2. the *Business Collaboration* between us and our intended collaborator has been selected,

3. the specific role that our software agent is to play in the *Business Collaboration* is known, and

4. the capabilities that are to be advertised in our *CPP* are known.

For vividness, we will suppose that our example agent wishes to play the role of supplier and seeks to find one of its current customers to begin a Purchase Order *Business Collaboration* in which the intended player plays a complementary role. For simplicity, we assume that the information about capabilities is restricted to what is available in our agent's *CPP* and in the *CPP* of its intended collaborator.

In general, the constituent tasks consist of finding "matches" between our capabilities and our intended collaborator's at the various levels of the protocol stacks and with respect to the services supplied at these various levels.

Figure 6 illustrates the basic tasks informing a *CPA* from two *CPPs*: matching roles, matching packaging, and matching transport.

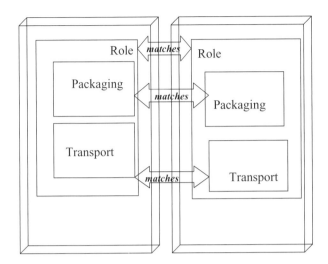

FIGURE 6   Basic Tasks in Forming a CPA

The first task to be considered is certainly the most basic: finding that our intended collaborator and ourselves have complementary role capabilities.

Matching Roles

Our agent has its role already selected in the *Business Collaboration*. So it now begins to check the **Role** elements in its collaborator's *CPP*. The first element to examine is the **PartyInfo** element that contains a subtree of elements called **CollaborationRole.** This set is searched to discover a role that complements the role of our agent within the *Business Collaboration* that we have chosen. For simple binary collaboration cases, it is typically sufficient to find that our intended collaborator's **CollaborationRole** set contains **ProcessSpecification** elements that we intend to implement and where the role is not identical to our role. For more general collaborations, we would need to know the list of roles available within the process, and keep track that for each of the collaborators, the roles chosen instantiate those that have been specified within the *Process-Specification* document. Collaborations involving more than two roles are not discussed further.

Matching Transport

We now have available a list of candidate **CollaborationRole** elements with the desired **ProcessSpecification** element (Purchase Ordering) and where our intended collaborator plays the buyer role. For simplicity, we shall suppose just one **CollaborationRole** element meets these conditions within each of the relevant *CPPs* and not discuss iterating over lists. (Within these remarks, where repetition is possible, we will frame the discussion by assuming that just one element is present.)

Matching transport first means matching the **SendingProtocol** capabilities of our intended collaborator with the **ReceivingProtocol** capabilities found on our side. Perusal of the *CPP* DTD or Schema will reveal that the **ServiceBinding** element provides the doorway to the relevant information from each side's **CollaborationRole** element with the **channelId** attribute. This **channelId** attribute's value allows us to find **DeliveryChannels** within each *CPP*. The **DeliveryChannel** has a **transportId** attribute that allows us to find the relevant **Transport** subtrees.

For example, suppose that our intended buyer has a **Tranport** entry:

```
<Transport transportId = "buyerid001">
      <SendingProtocol>HTTP</SendingProtocol>
      <ReceivingProtocol>
      HTTP
      </ReceivingProtocol>
      <Endpoint uri = "https://www.buyername.com/po-response"
                type = "allPurpose"/>
      <TransportSecurity>
            <Protocol version = "1.0">TLS</Protocol>
            <CertificateRef certId = certid001">BuyerName</
CertificateRef>
      </TransportSecurity>
</Transport>
and our seller has a Transport entry:
<Transport transportId = "sellid001">
      <SendingProtocol>HTTP</SendingProtocol>
      <ReceivingProtocol>
      HTTP
      </ReceivingProtocol>
      <Endpoint uri = "https://www.sellername.com/pos_here"
                type = "allPurpose"/>
      <TransportSecurity>
            <Protocol version = "1.0">TLS</Protocol>
            <CertificateRef certId ="certid002">Sellername</
CertificateRef>
      </TransportSecurity>
</Transport>
```

A transport match for requests involves finding the initiator role or buyer has a **SendingProtocol** that matches one of our **ReceivingProtocol**s. So here, "HTTP" provides a match. A transport match for responses involves finding the responder role or seller has a **SendingProtocol** that matches one of the buyer's **ReceivingProtocol**s. So in the above example, "HTTP" again provides a match. When such matches exist, we then have discovered an interoperable solution at the transport level. If not, no *CPA* will be available, and a high-priority gap has been identified that will need to be remedied by whatever exception handling procedures are in place.

Matching Transport Security

Matches in transport security, such as in the above, will reflect agreement in versions and values of protocols. Software can supply some knowledge here so that if one side has SSL-3 and the other TLS-1, it can guess that security is available by means of a fallback of TLS to SSL.

Matching Document Packaging

Probably one of the most complex matching problems arises when it comes to finding whether there are matches in document-packaging capabilities. Here both security and other MIME handling capabilities can combine to create complexity for appraising whether full interoperability can be attained.

Access to the information needed for undertaking this task is found under the **ServiceBinding** elements, and again we suppose that each side has just one **ServiceBinding** element. However, we will initially suppose that two **Packaging** elements are available to consider under each role. Several quite different ways of thinking about the matching task are available, and several methods for the tasks MAY be performed when assessing whether a good enough match exists.

To continue our previous purchase-ordering example, we recall that the packaging is the particular combination of body parts, XML instances (*Headers* and payloads), and security encapsulations used in assembling the *Message* from its data sources. Both requests and responses will have packaging. The most complete specification of packaging, which MAY not always be needed, would consist of:

1. The buyer asserting what packaging it can generate for its purchase order, and what packaging it can parse for its purchase order response *Messages*.

2. The seller asserting what packaging it can generate for its purchase order responses and what packaging it can parse for received purchase orders.

Matching by structural comparison would then involve comparing the packaging details of the purchase orders generated by the seller with the purchase orders parsable by the buyer. The comparison would seek to establish that the MIME types of the **SimplePart** elements of corresponding subtrees match and would then proceed to check that the **CompositeList** matched in MIME types and in sequence of composition.

For example, if each *CPP* contained the packaging subtrees below, and under the appropriate **ServiceBindings,** then there would be a straightforward match by structural comparison:

```
<Packaging id="I1001">
      <ProcessingCapabilities parse = "true" generate = "true"/>
      <SimplePart id = "P1" mimetype = "text/xml"/>
        <NamespaceSupported location
            = "http://schemas.xmlsoap.org/soap/envelope/"
version = "1.1">
              http://schemas.xmlsoap.org/soap/envelope
        </NamespaceSupported>
        <NamespaceSupported location =
            "http://www.ebxml.org/namespaces/messageHeader"
            version = "1.0">
            http://www.ebxml.org/namespaces/messageHeader
        </NamespaceSupported>   <NamespaceSupported location =
            "http://www.w3.org/2000/09/xmldsig#"
            version = "1.0">
            http://www.w3.org/2000/09/xmldsig#
        </NamespaceSupported>
      <SimplePart id = "P2" mimetype = "application/xml"/>
      <CompositeList>
          <Composite mimetype = "multipart/related" id = "P3"
              mimeparameters = "type=text/xml">
              <Constituent idref = "P1"/>
              <Constituent idref = "P2"/>
          </Composite>
      </CompositeList>
</Packaging>
<Packaging id="I2001">
      <ProcessingCapabilities parse = "true" generate = "true"/>
      <SimplePart id = "P11" mimetype = "text/xml"/>
      <SimplePart id = "P12" mimetype = "application/xml"/>
      <CompositeList>
          <Composite mimetype = "multipart/related" id = "P13"
              mimeparameters = "type=text/xml">
              <Constituent idref = "P11"/>
              <Constituent idref = "P12"/>
          </Composite>
      </CompositeList>
</Packaging>
```

However, it is to be expected that over time it will become possible only to assert what packaging is *generated* within each **ServiceBinding** for the requester and responder roles. This simplification assumes that each side has knowledge of what MIME types it handles correctly, what encapsulations it handles correctly, and what composition modes it handles correctly. By scanning the packaging specifications against its lists of internal capabilities, it can then look up whether other side's generated packaging scheme is one it can process and accept it under those conditions. Knowing what generated packaging style was produced by the other side could enable the software agent to propose a packaging scheme using only the MIME types and packaging styles used in the incoming *Message*. Such a packaging scheme would be likely to be acceptable to the other side when included within a proposed *CPA*. Over time, and as proposal and negotiation conventions get established, it is to be expected that the methods used for determining a match in packaging capabilities will move away from structural comparison to simpler methods, using more economical representations. For example, parsing capabilities may eventually be captured by using a compact description of the accepting grammar for the packaging and content labelling schemes that can be parsed and for which semantic handlers are available.

Matching Document-Level Security

Although the matching task for document-level security is a subtask of the Packaging-matching task, it is useful to discuss some specifics tied to the three major document-level security approaches found in [S/MIME], OpenPGP [RFC2015], and XMLDsig[XMLDSIG].

XMLDsig matching capability can be inferred from document-matching capabilities when the use of ebXML *Message* Service[ebMS] packaging is present. However, there are other sources that should be checked to confirm this match. A **SimplePart** element can have a **NameSpaceSupported** element. XMLDsig capability should be found there. Likewise, a detailed check on this match should examine the information under the **NonRepudiation** element and similar elements under the ebXMLBinding element to check for compatibility in hash functions and algorithms.

The existence of several radically different approaches to document-level security, together with the fact that it is unusual at present for a given *Party* to commit to more than one form of such security, means that there can be basic failures to match security frameworks. Therefore, there might be no match in capabilities that supports full interoperability at all levels. For the moment, we assume that document-level security matches will require both sides able to handle the same security composites (multipart/signed using S/MIME, for example.)

However, suppose that there are matches at the transport and transport layer security levels, but that the two sides have failures at the document-security layer because one side makes use of PGP signatures while the other uses S/MIME. Does this mean that no *CPA* can be proposed? That is not necessarily the case.

Both S/MIME and OpenPGP permit signatures to be packaged within "multipart/signed" composites. In such a case, it MAY be possible to extract the data and arrive at a partial implementation that falls short with respect to nonrepudiation. While neither side could check the other's signatures, it might still be possible to have confidential document transmission and transport-level authentication for the *Business* data. Eventually *CPA*-formation software MAY be created that is able to identify these exceptional situations and "salvage" a proposed *CPA* with downgraded security features. Whether the other side would accept such a proposed *CPA* would, naturally, involve what their preferences are with respect to initiating a *Business Collaboration* and sacrificing some security features. *CPA*-formation software MAY eventually be capable of these adaptations, but it is to be expected that human assistance will be required for such situations in the near term.

Of course, an implementation MAY simply decide to terminate looking for a *CPA* when a match fails in any crucial factor for an interoperable implementation. At the very least, the users should be warned that the only *CPAs* that can be proposed will be missing security or other normally desirable features or features recommended by the *Business Collaboration*.

Other Considerations

Though preferences among multiple capabilities are indicated by the document order in which they are listed, it is possible that ties may occur. At present, these ties are left to be resolved by a negotiation process not discussed here.

CHAPTER
7

Message Service Specification
v1.0
Transport, Routing & Packaging Team
11 May 2001

TABLE OF CONTENTS

1 Status of this Document

This document specifies an ebXML Technical Specification for the eBusiness community.

Distribution of this document is unlimited.

The document formatting is based on the Internet Society's Standard RFC format.

This version
http://www.ebxml.org/specs/ebMS.pdf

Latest version
http://www.ebxml.org/specs/ebMS.pdf

2 ebXML Participants

The authors wish to acknowledge the support of the members of the Transport, Routing and Packaging Project Team who contributed ideas to this specification by the group's discussion eMail list, on conference calls and during face-to-face meeting.

Ralph Berwanger	bTrade.com
Jonathan Borden	Author of XMTP
Jon Bosak	Sun Microsystems
Marc Breissinger	webMethods
Dick Brooks	Group 8760
Doug Bunting	Ariba
David Burdett	Commerce One
David Craft	VerticalNet
Philippe De Smedt	Viquity
Lawrence Ding	WorldSpan
Rik Drummond	Drummond Group
Andrew Eisenberg	Progress Software

Colleen Evans	Progress / Sonic Software
David Fischer	Drummond Group
Christopher Ferris	Sun Microsystems
Robert Fox	Softshare
Brian Gibb	Sterling Commerce
Maryann Hondo	IBM
Jim Hughes	Fujitsu
John Ibbotson	IBM
Ian Jones	British Telecommunications
Ravi Kacker	Kraft Foods
Henry Lowe	OMG
Jim McCarthy	webXI
Bob Miller	GXS
Dale Moberg	Sterling Commerce
Joel Munter	Intel
Shumpei Nakagaki	NEC Corporation
Farrukh Najmi	Sun Microsystems
Akira Ochi	Fujitsu
Martin Sachs	IBM
Saikat Saha	Commerce One
Masayoshi Shimamura	Fujitsu
Prakash Sinha	Netfish Technologies
Rich Salz	Zolera Systems
Tae Joon Song	eSum Technologies, Inc.
Kathy Spector	Extricity
Nikola Stojanovic	Encoda Systems, Inc.
David Turner	Microsoft
Gordon Van Huizen	Progress Software
Martha Warfelt	DaimlerChrysler Corporation
Prasad Yendluri	Web Methods

3 Introduction

This specification is one of a series of specifications that realize the vision of creating a single global electronic marketplace where enterprises of any size and in any geographical location can meet and conduct business with each other through the exchange of XML based messages. The set of specifications enable a modular, yet complete electronic business framework.

This specification focuses on defining a communications-protocol neutral method for exchanging the electronic business messages. It defines specific enveloping constructs that support reliable, secure delivery of business information. Furthermore, the specification defines a flexible enveloping technique that permits ebXML-compliant messages to contain payloads of any format type. This versatility ensures that legacy electronic business systems employing traditional syntaxes (i.e. UN/EDIFACT, ASC X12, or HL7) can leverage the advantages of the ebXML infrastructure along with users of emerging technologies

3.1 Summary of Contents of Document

This specification defines the *ebXML Message Service Protocol* that enables the secure and reliable exchange of messages between two parties. It includes descriptions of:

▼ the ebXML Message structure used to package payload data for transport between parties

▼ the behavior of the Message Service Handler that sends and receives those messages over a data communication protocol.

This specification is independent of both the payload and the communication protocol used, although Appendices to this specification describe how to use this specification with [HTTP] and [SMTP].

This specification is organized around the following topics:

▼ **Packaging Specification** – A description of how to package an ebXML Message and its associated parts into a form that can sent using a communications protocol such as HTTP or SMTP (section 6)

▼ **ebXML SOAP Extensions** – A specification of the structure and composition of the information necessary for an *ebXML Message Service* to successfully generate or process an ebXML Message (section 7)

▼ **Message Service Handler Services** – A description of two services that enable one service to discover the status of another Message Service Handler (MSH) or an individual message

▼ **Reliable Messaging** – The Reliable Messaging function defines an interoperable protocol such that any two Message Service implementations can "reliably" exchange messages that are sent using "reliable messaging" once-and-only-once delivery semantics (section 9)

▼ **Error Handling** – This section describes how one *ebXML Message Service* reports errors it detects to another ebXML Message Service Handler (section 10)

▼ **Security** – This provides a specification of the security semantics for ebXML Messages (section11).

Appendices to this specification cover the following:

▼ **Appendix A Schema** – This normative appendix contains [XMLSchema] for the ebXML SOAP **Header** and **Body.**

▼ **Appendix B Communication Protocol Envelope Mappings** – This normative appendix describes how to transport *ebXML Message Service* compliant messages over [HTTP] and [SMTP]

3.2 Document Conventions

Terms in *Italics* are defined in the ebXML Glossary of Terms [ebGLOSS]. Terms listed in **Bold Italics** represent the element and/or attribute content. Terms listed in `Courier` font relate to MIME components. Notes are listed in Times New Roman font and are informative (non-normative).

The keywords MUST, MUST NOT, REQUIRED, SHALL, SHALL NOT, SHOULD, SHOULD NOT, RECOMMENDED, MAY, and OPTIONAL, when they appear in this document, are to be interpreted as described in [RFC2119] as quoted here:

> **The force of these words is modified by the requirement level of the document in which they are used.**

Note

▼ MUST: This word, or the terms "REQUIRED" or "SHALL", means that the definition is an absolute requirement of the specification.

▼ MUST NOT: This phrase, or the phrase "SHALL NOT", means that the definition is an absolute prohibition of the specification.

▼ SHOULD: This word, or the adjective "RECOMMENDED", means that there may exist valid reasons in particular circumstances to ignore a particular item, but the full implications must be understood and carefully weighed before choosing a different course.

▼ SHOULD NOT: This phrase, or the phrase "NOT RECOMMENDED", means that there may exist valid reasons in particular circumstances when the particular behavior is acceptable or even useful, but the full implications should be understood and the case carefully weighed before implementing any behavior described with this label.

▼ MAY: This word, or the adjective "OPTIONAL", mean that an item is truly optional. One vendor may choose to include the item because a particular marketplace requires it or because the vendor feels that it enhances the product while another vendor may omit the same item. An implementation which does not include a particular option MUST be prepared to interoperate with another implementation which does include the option, though perhaps with reduced functionality. In the same vein an implementation which does include a particular option MUST be prepared to interoperate with another implementation which does not include the option (except, of course, for the feature the option provides.)

3.3 Audience

The target audience for this specification is the community of software developers who will implement the *ebXML Message Service*.

3.4 Caveats and Assumptions

It is assumed that the reader has an understanding of transport protocols, MIME, XML, SOAP, SOAP Messages with Attachments and security technologies.

All examples are to be considered non-normative. If inconsistencies exist between the specification and the examples, the specification supersedes the examples.

3.5 Related Documents

The following set of related specifications are developed independent of this specification as part of the ebXML initiative:

[ebTA] ebXML Technical Architecture Specification v1.04 – defines the overall technical architecture for ebXML

[secRISK] ebXML Technical Architecture Security Risk Assessment v1.0 – identifies the security risks associated with the ebXML technical architecture

[ebCPP] ebXML Collaboration Protocol Profile and Agreement Specification v1.0 - defines how one party can discover and/or agree upon the information that party needs to know about another party prior to sending them a message that complies with this specification

[ebRS] ebXML Registry/Repository Services Specification v1.0 – defines a registry service for the ebXML environment

4 Design Objectives

The design objectives of this specification are to define a wire format and protocol for a Message Service to support XML-based electronic business between small, medium, and large enterprises. While the specification has been primarily designed to support XML-based electronic business, the authors of the specification have made every effort to ensure that the exchange of non-XML business information is fully supported. This specification is intended to enable a low cost solution, while preserving a vendor's ability to add unique value through added robustness and superior performance. It is the intention of the Transport, Routing and Packaging Project Team to keep this specification as straightforward and succinct as possible.

Every effort has been made to ensure that the REQUIRED functionality described in this specification has been prototyped by the ebXML Proof of Concept Team in order to ensure the clarity, accuracy and efficiency of this specification.

5 System Overview

This document defines the *ebXML Message Service* component of the ebXML infrastructure. The *ebXML Message Service* defines the message enveloping and header document schema used to transfer ebXML Messages over a communication protocol such as HTTP, SMTP, etc. This document provides sufficient detail to develop software for the packaging, exchange and processing of ebXML Messages.

The *ebXML Message Service* is defined as a set of layered extensions to the base Simple Object Access Protocol [SOAP] and SOAP Messages with Attachments

[SOAPATTACH] specifications that have a broad industry acceptance, and that serve as the foundation of the work of the W3C XML Protocol Core working group. The *ebXML Message Service* provides the security and reliability features necessary to support international electronic business that are not provided in the SOAP and SOAP Messages with Attachments specifications.

5.1   Message Service Purpose

The *ebXML Message Service* defines robust, yet basic, functionality to transfer messages between trading parties using various existing communication protocols. The *ebXML Message Service* is structured to allow for messaging reliability, persistence, security and extensibility.

The *ebXML Message Service* is provided for environments requiring a robust, yet low cost solution to enable electronic business. It is one of the four "infrastructure" components of ebXML. The other three are: Registry/Repository [ebRS], Collaboration Protocol Profile/Agreement [ebCPP] and ebXML Technical Architecture [ebTA].

5.2   Message Service Overview

The *ebXML Message Service* may be conceptually broken down into following three parts: (1) an abstract *Service Interface*, (2) functions provided by the Message Service Handler (MSH), and (3) the mapping to underlying transport service(s).

The following diagram depicts a logical arrangement of the functional modules that exist within one possible implementation of the *ebXML Message Services* architecture. These modules are arranged in a manner to indicate their interrelationships and dependencies.

▼ **Header Processing** - the creation of the SOAP **Header** elements for the *ebXML Message* uses input from the application, passed through the Message Service Interface, information from the *Collaboration Protocol Agreement* (*CPA* defined in [ebCPP]) that governs the message, and generated information such as digital signature, timestamps and unique identifiers.

▼ **Header Parsing** - extracting or transforming information from a received SOAP **Header** or **Body** element into a form that is suitable for processing by the MSH implementation.

▼ **Security Services** - digital signature creation and verification, authentication and authorization. These services MAY be used by other components of the MSH including the Header Processing and Header Parsing components.

▼ **Reliable Messaging Services** - handles the delivery and acknowledgment of ebXML Messages sent with **deliverySemantics** of **OnceAndOnlyOnce.**

The service includes handling for persistence, retry, error notification and acknowledgment of messages requiring reliable delivery.

▼ **Message Packaging** - the final enveloping of an *ebXML Message* (SOAP **Header** or **Body** elements and payload) into its SOAP Messages with Attachments [SOAPATTACH] container.

▼ **Error Handling** - this component handles the reporting of errors encountered during MSH or Application processing of a message.

▼ **Message Service Interface** - an abstract service interface that applications use to interact with the MSH to send and receive messages and which the MSH uses to interface with applications that handle received messages.

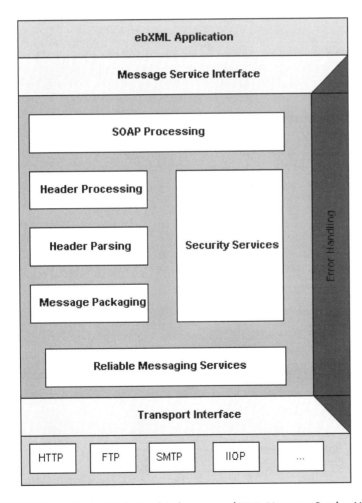

FIGURE 5-1 Typical Relationship between ebXML Message Service Handler Components

5.3   Use of Version Attribute

Each ebXML SOAP extension element has its own version attribute, with a value that matches the ebXML Message Service Specification version level, to allow for elements to change in semantic meaning individually without changing the entire specification.

Use of multiple versions of ebXML SOAP extensions elements within the same ebXML SOAP document, while supported, should only be used in extreme cases where it becomes necessary to semantically change an element, which cannot wait for the next ebXML Message Service Specification version release.

6   Packaging Specification

6.1   Introduction

An ebXML Message is a communication protocol independent MIME/Multipart message envelope, structured in compliance with the SOAP Messages with Attachments [SOAPATTACH] specification, referred to as a *Message Package*.

There are two logical MIME parts within the *Message Package*:

▼ A MIME part, referred to as the *Header Container*, containing one SOAP 1.1 compliant message. This XML document is referred to as a *SOAP Message* for the remainder of this specification,

▼ zero or more MIME parts, referred to as *Payload Containers*, containing application level payloads.

The *SOAP Message* is an XML document that consists of the SOAP **Envelope** element. This is the root element of the XML document representing the *SOAP Message*. The SOAP **Envelope** element consists of the following:

▼ One SOAP **Header** element. This is a generic mechanism for adding features to a *SOAP Message*, including ebXML specific header elements.

▼ One SOAP **Body** element. This is a container for message service handler control data and information related to the payload parts of the message.

The general structure and composition of an ebXML Message is described in the following figure.

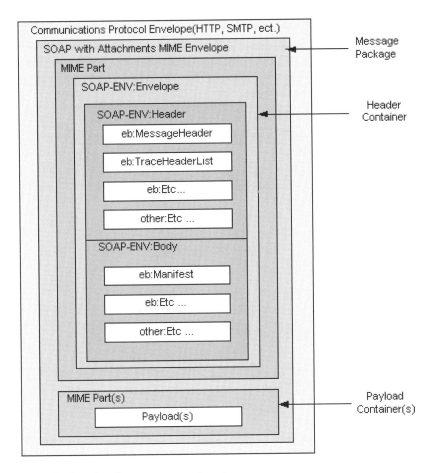

FIGURE 6-1   ebXML Message Structure

6.1.1   SOAP Structural Conformance

ebXML Message packaging SHALL comply with the following specifications:

▼ Simple Object Access Protocol (SOAP) 1.1 [SOAP]

▼ SOAP Messages with Attachments [SOAPATTACH]

Carrying ebXML headers in *SOAP Messages* does not mean that ebXML overrides existing semantics of SOAP, but rather that the semantics of ebXML over SOAP maps directly onto SOAP semantics.

6.2   Message Package

All MIME header elements of the *Message Package* MUST be in conformance with the SOAP Messages with Attachments [SOAPATTACH] specification. In addition, the `Content-Type` MIME header in the *Message Package* MUST contain a `type` attribute that matches the MIME media type of the MIME body part that contains the *SOAP Message* document. In accordance with the [SOAP] specification, the MIME media type of the *SOAP Message* MUST have the value "`text/xml.`"

It is strongly RECOMMENDED that the root part contain a `Content-ID` MIME header structured in accordance with [RFC2045], and that in addition to the required parameters for the Multipart/Related media type, the `start` parameter (OPTIONAL in [RFC2387]) always be present. This permits more robust error detection. For example the following fragment:

```
Content-Type: multipart/related; type="text/xml"; boundary=
"boundaryValue";
start=messagepackage-123@example.com

--boundaryValue
Content-ID: messagepackage-123@example.com
```

6.3   Header Container

The root body part of the *Message Package* is referred to in this specification as the *Header Container*. The *Header Container* is a MIME body part that MUST consist of one *SOAP Message* as defined in the SOAP Messages with Attachments [SOAP-ATTACH] specification.

6.3.1   Content-type

The MIME `Content-Type header` for the *Header Container* MUST have the value "`text/xml`" in accordance with the [SOAP] specification. The `Content-Type` header MAY contain a "`charset`" attribute. For example:

```
Content-Type: text/xml; charset="UTF-8"
```

6.3.1.1   charset Attribute

The MIME `charset` attribute identifies the character set used to create the *SOAP Message*. The semantics of this attribute are described in the "charset parameter / encoding considerations" of `text/xml` as specified in [XMLMedia]. The list of valid values can be found at http://www.iana.org/.

If both are present, the MIME `charset` attribute SHALL be equivalent to the encoding declaration of the *SOAP Message*. If provided, the MIME `charset` attribute MUST NOT contain a value conflicting with the encoding used when creating the *SOAP Message*.

For maximum interoperability it is RECOMMENDED that [UTF-8] be used when encoding this document. Due to the processing rules defined for media types derived from `text/xml` [XMLMedia], this MIME attribute has no default. For example:

```
charset="UTF-8"
```

6.3.2 Header Container Example

The following fragment represents an example of a *Header Container*:

```
Content-ID: messagepackage-123@example.com      ---| Header
Content-Type: text/xml;                             |
            charset="UTF-8"                         |
                                                    |
<SOAP-ENV:Envelope                      --|SOAP Message|
    xmlns:SOAP-ENV="http://schemas.       |         |
    xmlsoap.org/soap/envelope/">          |         |
  <SOAP-ENV:Header>                       |         |
                                          |         |
  ...                                     |         |
  </SOAP-ENV:Header>                      |         |
  <SOAP-ENV:Body>                         |         |
                                          |         |
  ...                                     |         |
  </SOAP-ENV:Body>                        |         |
</SOAP-ENV:Envelope>                    --|         |
---boundaryValue                              ---|
```

6.4 Payload Container

Zero or more *Payload Containers* MAY be present within a *Message Package* in conformance with the SOAP Messages with Attachments [SOAPATTACH] specification.

If the *Message Package* contains an application payload, it MUST be enclosed within a *Payload Container.*

If there is no application payload within the *Message Package* then a *Payload Container* MUST NOT be present.

The contents of each *Payload Container* MUST be identified by the ebXML Message **Manifest** element within the SOAP **Body** (see section 7.11).

The ebXML Message Service Specification makes no provision, nor limits in any way, the structure or content of application payloads. Payloads MAY be a simple-plain-text object or complex nested multipart objects. The specification of the structure and composition of payload objects is the prerogative of the organization that defines the business process or information exchange that uses the *ebXML Message Service*.

6.4.1 Example of a Payload Container

The following fragment represents an example of a *Payload Container* and a payload:

```
Content-ID: <domainname.example.com> -------| ebXML MIME|
Content-Type: application/xml  ------------|          |
                                                       | Payload
<Invoice>                          ------------|       | Container
  <Invoicedata>                               | Payload |
     ...                                      |         |
  </Invoicedata>                              |         |
</Invoice>                         ------------|         |
```

6.5   Additional MIME Parameters

Any MIME part described by this specification MAY contain additional MIME headers in conformance with the [RFC2045] specification. Implementations MAY ignore any MIME header not defined in this specification. Implementations MUST ignore any MIME header that they do not recognize.

For example, an implementation could include `content-length` in a message. However, a recipient of a message with `content-length` could ignore it.

6.6   Reporting MIME Errors

If a MIME error is detected in the *Message Package* then it MUST be reported as specified in [SOAP].

7   ebXML SOAP Extensions

The ebXML Message Service Specification defines a set of namespace-qualified SOAP **Header** and **Body** element extensions within the SOAP **Envelope.** In general, separate ebXML SOAP extension elements are used where:

▼ different software components are likely to be used to generate ebXML SOAP extension elements,

▼ an ebXML SOAP extension element is not always present or,

▼ the data contained in the ebXML SOAP extension element MAY be digitally signed separately from the other ebXML SOAP extension elements.

7.1 XML Prolog

The SOAP *Message's* XML Prolog, if present, MAY contain an XML declaration. This specification has defined no additional comments or processing instructions that may appear in the XML prolog. For example:

```
Content-Type: text/xml; charset="UTF-8"

<?xml version="1.0" encoding="UTF-8"?>
```

7.1.1 XML Declaration

The XML declaration MAY be present in a SOAP *Message*. If present, it MUST contain the version specification required by the XML Recommendation [XML]: version='1.0' and MAY contain an encoding declaration. The semantics described below MUST be implemented by a compliant *ebXML Message Service*.

7.1.2 Encoding Declaration

If both the encoding declaration and the *Header Container* MIME charset are present, the XML prolog for the SOAP *Message* SHALL contain the encoding declaration that SHALL be equivalent to the `charset` attribute of the MIME `Content-Type` of the *Header Container* (see section 6.3).

If provided, the encoding declaration MUST NOT contain a value conflicting with the encoding used when creating the SOAP *Message*. It is RECOMMENDED that UTF-8 be used when encoding the SOAP *Message*.

If the character encoding cannot be determined by an XML processor using the rules specified in section 4.3.3 of [XML], the XML declaration and its contained encoding declaration SHALL be provided in the ebXML SOAP **Header** Document.

> **The encoding declaration is not required in an XML document according to XML v1.0 specification [XML].** **Note**

7.2 ebXML SOAP Envelope Extensions

In conformance with the [SOAP] specification, all extension element content MUST be namespace qualified. All of the ebXML SOAP extension element content defined in this specification MUST be namespace qualified to the ebXML SOAP **Envelope** extensions namespace as defined in section 7.2.1.

Namespace declarations (xmlns psuedo attribute) for the ebXML SOAP extensions MAY be included in the SOAP **Envelope, Header** or **Body** elements, or directly in each of the ebXML SOAP extension elements.

7.2.1 Namespace Pseudo Attribute

The namespace declaration for the ebXML SOAP **Envelope** extensions (**xmlns** pseudo attribute) (see [XML Namespace]) has a REQUIRED value of "http://www.ebxml.org/namespaces/messageHeader".

7.2.2 xsi:schemaLocation Attribute

The SOAP namespace:

```
http://schemas.xmlsoap.org/soap/envelope/
```

resolves to a schema that conforms to an early Working Draft version of the W3C XML Schema specification, specifically identified by the following URI:

```
http://www.w3.org/1999/XMLSchema
```

The W3C XML Schema specification[XMLSchema] has since gone to Candidate Recommendation status, effective October 24, 2000 and more recently to Proposed Recommendation effective March 30, 2001. Many, if not most, tool support for schema validation and validating XML parsers available at the time that this specification was written have been designed to support the Candidate Recommendation draft of the XML Schema specification[XMLSchema]. In addition, the ebXML SOAP extension element schema has been defined using the Candidate Recommendation draft of the XML Schema specification[XMLSchema] (see Appendix A).

In order to enable validating parsers and various schema validating tools to correctly process and parse ebXML SOAP *Messages*, it has been necessary that the ebXML TR&P team adopt an equivalent, but updated version of the SOAP schema that conforms to the W3C Candidate Recommendation draft of the XML Schema specification[XMLSchema]. ebXML MSH implementations are strongly RECOMMENDED to include the XMLSchema-instance namespace qualified **schemaLocation** attribute in the SOAP **Envelope** element to indicate to validating parsers the location of the schema document that should be used to validate the document. Failure to include the **schemaLocation** attribute will possibly preclude *Receiving MSH* implementations from being able to validate messages received.

For example:

```
<SOAP-ENV:Envelope xmlns:SOAP-ENV="http://schemas.xmlsoap.org/
soap/envelope/"
  xmlns:xsi="http://www.w3.org/2000/10/XMLSchema-instance"
  xsi:schemaLocation="http://schemas.xmlsoap.org/soap/envelope/
     http://ebxml.org/project_teams/transport/envelope.xsd" ...>
```

In addition, ebXML SOAP **Header** and **Body** extension element content must be similarly qualified so as to identify the location that validating parsers can find the schema document that contains the ebXML namespace qualified SOAP extension element definitions. Thus, the XMLSchema-instance namespace qualified **schemaLocation** attribute should include a mapping of the ebXML SOAP **Envelope** extensions namespace to its schema document in the same element that declares the ebXML SOAP **Envelope** extensions namespace.

It is RECOMMENDED that use of a separate **schemaLocation** attribute be used so that tools that may not correctly use the **schemaLocation** attribute to resolve schema for more than one namespace will still be capable of validating an ebXML SOAP *message*. For example:

```
<SOAP-ENV:Envelope xmlns:SOAP-ENV="http://schemas.xmlsoap.org/
soap/envelope/"
  xmlns:xsi="http://www.w3.org/2000/10/XMLSchema-instance"
  xsi:schemaLocation="http://schemas.xmlsoap.org/soap/envelope/
     http://ebxml.org/project_teams/transport/envelope.xsd" ...>
  <SOAP-ENV:Header xmlns:eb="http://www.ebxml.org/namespaces/
messageHeader"
    xsi:schemaLocation="http://www.ebxml.org/namespaces/message-
Header
      http://ebxml.org/project_teams/transport/messageHeaderv0_99
.xsd" ...>
    <eb:MessageHeader ...> ...
    </eb:MessageHeader>
  </SOAP-ENV:Header>
  <SOAP-ENV:Body xmlns:eb="http://www.ebxml.org/namespaces/
messageHeader"
    xsi:schemaLocation="http://www.ebxml.org/namespaces/message-
Header
      http://ebxml.org/project_teams/transport/messageHeaderv0_99
.xsd" ...>
    <eb:Manifest ...> ...
    </eb:Manifest>
  </SOAP-ENV:Body>
</SOAP-ENV:Envelope>
```

7.2.3 ebXML SOAP Extensions

An ebXML Message extends the SOAP *Message* with the following principal extension elements:

- ▼ SOAP **Header** extensions:
  - ▼ **MessageHeader** – a REQUIRED element that contains routing information for the message (To/From, etc.) as well as other context information about the message.
  - ▼ **TraceHeaderList** – an element that contains entries that identifies the Message Service Handler(s) that sent and should receive the message. This element MAY be omitted.
  - ▼ **ErrorList** – an element that contains a list of the errors that are being reported against a previous message. The **ErrorList** element is only used if reporting an error on a previous message. This element MAY be omitted.
  - ▼ **Signature** – an element that contains a digital signature that conforms to [XMLDSIG] that signs data associated with the message. This element MAY be omitted.
  - ▼ **Acknowledgment**– an element that is used by a *Receiving MSH* to acknowledge to the *Sending MSH* that a previous message has been received. This element MAY be omitted.
  - ▼ **Via**– an element that is used to convey information to the next ebXML Message Service Handler that receives the message. This element MAY be omitted.

- ▼ SOAP **Body** extensions:
  - ▼ **Manifest** – an element that points to any data present either in the *Payload Container* or elsewhere, e.g. on the web. This element MAY be omitted.
  - ▼ **StatusRequest** – an element that is used to identify a message whose status is being requested. This element MAY be omitted.
  - ▼ **StatusResponse** – an element that is used by a MSH when responding to a request on the status of a message that was previously received. This element MAY be omitted.
  - ▼ **DeliveryReceipt** – an element used by the *To Party* that received a message, to let the *From Party* that sent the message know the message was received. This element MAY be omitted.

7.2.4 #wildcard Element Content

Some ebXML SOAP extension elements allow for foreign namespace-qualified element content to be added to provide for extensibility. The extension element content MUST be namespace-qualified in accordance with [XMLNamespaces] and MUST belong to a foreign namespace. A foreign namespace is one that is NOT http://www.ebxml.org/namespaces/messageHeader.

Any foreign namespace-qualified element added SHOULD include the SOAP **mustUnderstand** attribute. If the SOAP **mustUnderstand** attribute is NOT present, the default value implied is '0' (false). If an implementation of the MSH does not recognize the namespace of the element and the value of the SOAP **mustUnderstand** attribute is '1' (true), the MSH SHALL report an error (see section 10) with **errorCode** set to **NotSupported** and **severity** set to **error.** If the value of the **mustUnderstand** attribute is '0' or if the **mustUnderstand** attribute is not present, then an implementation of the MSH MAY ignore the namespace-qualified element and its content.

7.2.5   id Attributes

Each of the ebXML SOAP extension elements listed above has an optional **id** attribute which is an XML ID that MAY be added to provide for the ability to uniquely identify the element within the SOAP *Message*. This MAY be used when applying a digital signature to the ebXML SOAP *Message* as individual ebXML SOAP extension elements can be targeted for inclusion or exclusion by specifying a URI of "#<idvalue>" in the **Reference** element.

7.3   SOAP Header Element

The SOAP **Header** element is the first child element of the SOAP **Envelope** element. It MUST have a namespace qualifier that matches the SOAP **Envelope** namespace declaration for the namespace "http://schemas.xmlsoap.org/soap/envelope/". For example:

```
<SOAP-ENV:Envelope xmlns:SOAP-ENV="http://schemas.xmlsoap.org/
soap/envelope/" …>
  <SOAP-ENV:Header>…</SOAP-ENV:Header>
  <SOAP-ENV:Body>…</SOAP-ENV:Body>
</SOAP-ENV:Envelope>
```

The SOAP **Header** element contains the ebXML SOAP **Header** extension element content identified above and described in the following sections.

7.4   MessageHeader Element

The **MessageHeader** element is REQUIRED in all ebXML Messages. It MUST be present as a child element of the SOAP **Header** element.

The **MessageHeader** element is a composite element comprised of the following ten subordinate elements:

▼ From

▼ To

▼ CPAId

▼ ConversationId

▼ Service

▼ Action

▼ MessageData

▼ QualityOfServiceInfo

▼ SequenceNumber

▼ Description

The **MessageHeader** element has two REQUIRED attributes as follows:

▼ SOAP **mustUnderstand**

▼ Version

In addition, the **MessageHeader** element MAY include an **id** attribute. See section 7.2.5 for details.

7.4.1   From and To Elements

The REQUIRED **From** element identifies the *Party* that originated the message. The REQUIRED **To** element identifies the *Party* that is the intended recipient of the message. Both **To** and **From** can contain logical identifiers such as a DUNS number, or identifiers that also imply a physical location such as an eMail address.

The **From** and the **To** elements each contain one or more **PartyId** child elements.

If either the **From** or **To** elements contain multiple **PartyId** elements, all members of the list must identify the same organisation. Unless a single **type** value refers to multiple identification systems, a **type** attribute value must not appear more than once in a single list of **PartyId** elements.

Note

This mechanism is particularly useful when transport of a message between the parties may involve multiple intermediaries (see Sections 7.5.4, Multi-hop TraceHeader Sample and 9.3, ebXML Reliable Messaging Protocol). More generally, the *From Party* should provide identification in all domains it knows in support of intermediaries and destinations that may give preference to particular identification systems.

7.4.1.1   PartyID Element

The **PartyId** element has a single attribute, **type** and content that is a string value. The **type** attribute indicates the domain of names to which the string in the content of the **PartyId** element belongs. The value of the **type** attribute MUST be mutually agreed and understood by each of the *Parties*. It is RECOMMENDED that the value of the **type** attribute be a URI. It is further recommended that these values be taken from the EDIRA (ISO 6523), EDIFACT ISO 9735 or ANSI ASC X12 I05 registries.

If the **PartyId type** attribute is not present, the content of the **PartyId** element MUST be a URI [RFC2396], otherwise the *Receiving MSH* SHOULD report an error (see section 10) with **errorCode** set to **Inconsistent** and **severity** set to **Error**. It is strongly RECOMMENDED that the content of the **PartyID** element be a URI.

The following fragment demonstrates usage of the **From** and **To** elements.

```
<eb:From>
   <eb:PartyId eb:type="urn:duns">123456789</eb:PartyId>
   <eb:PartyId eb:type="SCAC">RDWY</PartyId>
</eb:From>
<eb:To>
   <eb:PartyId>mailto:joe@example.com</eb:PartyId>
</eb:To>
```

7.4.2   CPAId Element

The REQUIRED **CPAId** element is a string that identifies the parameters governing the exchange of messages between the parties. The recipient of a message MUST be able to resolve the **CPAId** to an individual set of parameters, taking into account the sender of the message.

The value of a **CPAId** element MUST be unique within a namespace that is mutually agreed by the two parties. This could be a concatenation of the **From** and **To PartyId** values, a URI that is prefixed with the Internet domain name of one of the parties, or a namespace offered and managed by some other naming or registry service. It is RECOMMENDED that the **CPAId** be a URI.

The **CPAId** MAY reference an instance of a *CPA* as defined in the ebXML Collaboration Protocol Profile and Agreement Specification [ebCPP]. An example of the **CPAId** element follows:

```
<eb:CPAId>http://example.com/cpas/ourcpawithyou.xml</eb:CPAId>
```

If the parties are operating under a *CPA*, then the reliable messaging parameters are determined by the appropriate elements from that *CPA*, as identified by the **CPAId** element.

If a receiver determines that a message is in conflict with the *CPA*, the appropriate handling of this conflict is undefined by this specification. Therefore, senders SHOULD NOT generate such messages unless they have prior knowledge of the receiver's capability to deal with this conflict.

If a receiver chooses to generate an error as a result of a detected inconsistency, then it MUST report it with an **errorCode** of **Inconsistent** and a **severity** of **Error**. If it chooses to generate an error because the **CPAId** is not recognized, then it MUST report it with an **errorCode** of **NotRecognized** and a **severity** of **Error**.

7.4.3   *ConversationId Element*

The REQUIRED **ConversationId** element is a string identifying the set of related messages that make up a conversation between two *Parties*. It MUST be unique within the **From** and **To** party pair. The *Party* initiating a conversation determines the value of the **ConversationId** element that SHALL be reflected in all messages pertaining to that conversation.

The **ConversationId** enables the recipient of a message to identify the instance of an application or process that generated or handled earlier messages within a conversation. It remains constant for all messages within a conversation.

The value used for a **ConversationId** is implementation dependent. An example of the **ConversationId** element follows:

```
<eb:ConversationId>20001209-133003-28572</eb:ConversationId>
```

Note

> Implementations are free to choose how they will identify and store conversational state related to a specific conversation. Implementations SHOULD provide a facility for mapping between their identification schema and a *ConversationId* generated by another implementation.

7.4.4   *Service Element*

The REQUIRED **Service** element identifies the *service* that acts on the message and it is specified by the designer of the *service*. The designer of the *service* may be:

▼ a standards organization, or

▼ an individual or enterprise

Note

> In the context of an ebXML business process model, an *action* equates to the lowest possible role based activity in the [ebBPSS] (requesting or responding role) and a *service* is a set of related actions for an authorized role within a party.

An example of the **Service** element follows:

```
<eb:Service>urn:services:SupplierOrderProcessing</eb:Service>
```

The **Service** element has a single **type** attribute.

7.4.4.1 type Attribute

If the **type** attribute is present, it indicates the parties sending and receiving the message know, by some other means, how to interpret the content of the **Service** element. The two parties MAY use the value of the **type** attribute to assist in the interpretation.

If the **type** attribute is not present, the content of the **Service** element MUST be a URI [RFC2396]. If it is not a URI then report an error with an **errorCode** of **Inconsistent** and a **severity** of **Error** (see section 10).

7.4.5 Action Element

The REQUIRED **Action** element identifies a process within a **Service** that processes the Message. **Action** SHALL be unique within the **Service** in which it is defined. An example of the **Action** element follows:

```
<eb:Action>NewOrder</eb:Action>
```

7.4.6 MessageData Element

The REQUIRED **MessageData** element provides a means of uniquely identifying an ebXML Message. It contains the following four subordinate elements:

▼ **MessageId**

▼ **Timestamp**

▼ **RefToMessageId**

▼ **TimeToLive**

The following fragment demonstrates the structure of the **MessageData** element:

```
<eb:MessageData>
   <eb:MessageId>20001209-133003-28572@example.com</eb:MessageId>
   <eb:Timestamp>2001-02-15T11:12:12Z</eb:Timestamp>
   <eb:RefToMessageId>20001209-133003-28571@example.com</eb:Ref-
ToMessageId>
</eb:MessageData>
```

7.4.6.1   MessageId Element

The REQUIRED element **MessageId** is a unique identifier for the message conforming to [RFC2392]. The "local part" of the identifier as defined in [RFC2392] is implementation dependent.

7.4.6.2   Timestamp Element

The REQUIRED **Timestamp** is a value representing the time that the message header was created conforming to an [XMLSchema] timeInstant.

7.4.6.3   RefToMessageId Element

The **RefToMessageId** element has a cardinality of zero or one. When present, it MUST contain the **MessageId** value of an earlier ebXML Message to which this message relates. If there is no earlier related message, the element MUST NOT be present.

For Error messages, the **RefToMessageId** element is REQUIRED and its value MUST be the **MessageId** value of the message in error (as defined in section 10).

For Acknowledgment Messages, the **RefToMessageId** element is REQUIRED, and its value MUST be the **MessageId** value of the ebXML Message being acknowledged. See also sections 7.13.4 and 9.

When **RefToMessageId** is contained inside either a **StatusRequest** or a **Status-Response** element then it identifies a Message whose current status is being queried (see section 8.1)

7.4.6.4   TimeToLive Element

The **TimeToLive** element indicates the time by which a message should be delivered to and processed by the *To Party*. The **TimeToLive** element is discussed under Reliable Messaging in section 9.

7.4.7   QualityOfServiceInfo Element

The **QualityOfServiceInfo** element identifies the quality of service with which the message is delivered. This element has three attributes:

▼ **deliverySemantics**

▼ **messageOrderSemantics**

▼ **deliveryReceiptRequested**

The **QualityOfServiceInfo** element SHALL be present if any of the attributes within the element need to be set to their non-default value. The **delivery-Semantics** attribute supports Reliable Messaging and is discussed in detail in section 9. The **deliverySemantics** attribute indicates whether or not a message is sent reliably.

7.4.7.1   deliveryReceiptRequested Attribute

The **deliveryReceiptRequested** attribute is used by a *From Party* to indicate whether a message received by the *To Party* should result in the *To Party* returning an acknowledgment message containing a **DeliveryReceipt** element.

> To clarify the distinction between an acknowledgement message containing a DeliveryReceipt **and a Reliable Messaging Acknowledgement: (1) An acknowledgement message containing a** Delivery Receipt **indicates the *To Party* has received the message. (2) The Reliable Messaging Acknowledgment indicates a MSH, possibly only an intermediate MSH, has received the message.**

Note

Before setting the value of **deliveryReceiptRequested**, the *From Party* SHOULD check if the *To Party* supports Delivery Receipts of the type requested (see also [ebCPP]).

Valid values for **deliveryReceiptRequested** are:

▼ **Unsigned** - requests that an unsigned Delivery Receipt is requested

▼ **Signed** - requests that a signed Delivery Receipt is requested, or

▼ **None** - indicates that no Delivery Receipt is requested.

The default value for **deliveryReceiptRequested** is **None.**

When a *To Party* receives a message with **deliveryReceiptRequested** attribute set to **Signed** or **Unsigned** then it should verify that it is able to support the type of Delivery Receipt requested.

If the *To Party* can produce the Delivery Receipt of the type requested, then it MUST return to the *From Party* a message containing a **DeliveryReceipt** element.

If the *To Party* cannot return a Delivery Receipt of the type requested then it MUST report the error to the *From Party* using an **errorCode** of **NotSupported** and a **severity** of **Error.**

If there are no errors in the message received and a **DeliveryReceipt** is being sent on its own, not as part of message containing payload data, then the **Service** and **Action** MUST be set as follows:

▼ the **Service** element MUST be set to **uri:www.ebXML.org/messageService/**

▼ the **Action** element MUST be set to **DeliveryReceipt**

An example of **deliveryReceiptRequested** follows:

```
<eb:QualityOfServiceInfo eb:deliverySemantics="OnceAndOnlyOnce"
          eb:messageOrderSemantics="Guaranteed"
          eb:deliveryReceiptRequested="Unsigned"/>
```

7.4.7.2 messageOrderSemantics Attribute

The **messageOrderSemantics** attribute is used to indicate whether the message is passed to the receiving application in the order the sending application specified. Valid Values are:

▼ **Guaranteed** - The messages are passed to the receiving application in the order that the sending application specified.

▼ **NotGuaranteed** - The messages may be passed to the receiving application in different order from the order the sending application specified.

The default value for **messageOrderSemantics** is specified in the *CPA* or in **MessageHeader**. If a value is not specified, the default value is **NotGuaranteed.**

If **messageOrderSemantics** is set to **Guaranteed,** the *To Party* MSH MUST correct invalid order of messages using the value of **SequenceNumber** in the conversation specified by the **ConversationId**. The **Guaranteed** semantics can be set only when **deliverySemantics** is **OnceAndOnlyOnce**. If **messageOrderSemantics** is set to **Guaranteed** the **SequenceNumber** element MUST be present.

If **deliverySemantics** is not **OnceAndOnlyOnce** and **messageOrderSemantics** is set to **Guaranteed** then report the error to the *From Party* with an **errorCode** of **Inconsistent** and a **severity** of **Error** (see sections 9 and 10).

All messages sent within the same conversation, as identified by the **ConversationId** element, that have a **deliverySemantics** attribute with a value of **OnceandOnlyOnce** SHALL each have the same value **messageOrderSemantics** (either **Guaranteed** or **NotGuaranteed**).

If **messageOrderSemantics** is set to **NotGuaranteed,** then the *To Party* MSH does not need to correct invalid order of messages.

If the *To Party* is unable to support the type of **messageOrderSemantics** requested, then the *To Party* MUST report the error to the *From Party* using an **errorCode** of **NotSupported** and a **severity** of **Error**. A sample of **messageOrderSemantics** follows.

```
<eb:QualityOfServiceInfo eb:deliverySemantics="OnceAndOnlyOnce"
    eb:messageOrderSemantics="Guaranteed"/>
```

7.4.8 SequenceNumber Element

The **SequenceNumber** element indicates the sequence in which messages MUST be processed by a *Receiving MSH*. The **SequenceNumber** is unique within the **ConversationId** and MSH. The *From Party* MSH and the *To Party* MSH each set an independent **SequenceNumber** as the *Sending MSH* within the **ConversationID.** It is set to zero on the first message from that MSH for a conversation and then incremented by one for each subsequent message sent.

The **SequenceNumber** element MUST appear only when **deliverySemantics** has a value of **OnceAndOnlyOnce** and **messageOrderSemantics** has a value of **Guaranteed.** If this criterion is not met, an error MUST be reported to the From Party MSH with an **errorCode** of **Inconsistent** and a **severity** of **Error.**

A MSH that receives a message with a **SequenceNumber** element MUST NOT pass the message to an application as long as the storage required to save out-of-sequence messages is within the implementation defined limits and until all the messages with lower **SequenceNumbers** have been received and passed to the application.

If the implementation defined limit for saved out-of-sequence messages is reached, then the *Receiving MSH* MUST indicate a delivery failure to the *Sending MSH* with **errorCode** set to **DeliveryFailure** and **severity** set to **Error** (see section 10).

The **SequenceNumber** element is an integer value that is incremented by the *Sending MSH* (e.g. 0, 1, 2, 3, 4...) for each application-prepared message sent by that MSH within the **ConversationId**. The next value of 99999999 in the increment is "0". The value of **SequenceNumber** consists of ASCII numerals in the range 0-99999999. In following cases, **SequenceNumber** takes the value "0":

1. First message from the *Sending MSH* within the conversation

2. First message after resetting **SequenceNumber** information by the *Sending MSH*

3. First message after wraparound (next value after 99999999)

The **SequenceNumber** element has a single attribute, **status**. This attribute is an enumeration, which SHALL have one of the following values:

▼ **Reset** – the **SequenceNumber** is reset as shown in 1 or 2 above

▼ **Continue** – the **SequenceNumber** continues sequentially (including 3 above)

When the **SequenceNumber** is set to "0" because of 1 or 2 above, the *Sending MSH* MUST set the **status** attribute of the message to **Reset**. In all other cases, including 3 above, the **status** attribute MUST be set to **Continue.**

A *Sending MSH* MUST wait before resetting the **SequenceNumber** of a conversation until it has received all of the *Acknowledgement Messages* for Messages previously sent for the conversation. Only when all the sent Messages are acknowledged, can the *Sending MSH* reset the **SequenceNumber.** An example of **SequenceNumber** follows.

```
<eb:SequenceNumber eb:status="Reset">0</eb:SequenceNumber>
```

7.4.9   Description Element

The **Description** element is present zero or more times as a child element of **MessageHeader.** Its purpose is to provide a human readable description of the purpose or intent of the message. The language of the description is defined by a required **xml:lang** attribute. The **xml:lang** attribute MUST comply with the rules for identifying languages specified in [XML]. Each occurrence SHOULD have a different value for **xml:lang**.

7.4.10   version Attribute

The REQUIRED **version** attribute indicates the version of the *ebXML Message Service* Header Specification to which the ebXML *SOAP* **Header** extensions conform. Its purpose is to provide future versioning capabilities. The value of the **version** attribute MUST be "1.0". Future versions of this specification SHALL require other values of this attribute. The version attribute MUST be namespace qualified for the ebXML SOAP **Envelope** extensions namespace defined above.

7.4.11   SOAP mustUnderstand Attribute

The REQUIRED SOAP **mustUnderstand** attribute, namespace qualified to the SOAP namespace (http://schemas.xmlsoap.org/soap/envelope/), indicates that the contents of the **MessageHeader** element MUST be understood by a receiving process or else the message MUST be rejected in accordance with [SOAP]. This attribute MUST have a value of '1' (true).

7.4.12   MessageHeader Sample

The following fragment demonstrates the structure of the **MessageHeader** element within the SOAP **Header:**

```
<eb:MessageHeader id="…" eb:version="1.0" SOAP-ENV:mustUnder-
stand="1">
  <eb:From><eb:PartyId>uri:example.com</eb:PartyId></eb:From>
  <eb:To eb:type="someType">
    <eb:PartyId eb:type="someType">QRS543</eb:PartyId>
  </eb:To>
  <eb:CPAId>http://www.ebxml.org/cpa/123456</eb:CPAId>
  <eb:ConversationId>987654321</eb:ConversationId>
  <eb:Service eb:type="myservicetypes">QuoteToCollect</eb:Service>
  <eb:Action>NewPurchaseOrder</eb:Action>
  <eb:MessageData>
    <eb:MessageId>mid:UUID-2</eb:MessageId>
    <eb:Timestamp>2000-07-25T12:19:05Z</eb:Timestamp>
    <eb:RefToMessageId>mid:UUID-1</eb:RefToMessageId>
  </eb:MessageData>
```

```
<eb:QualityOfServiceInfo
    eb:deliverySemantics="OnceAndOnlyOnce"
    eb:deliveryReceiptRequested="Signed"/>
</eb:MessageHeader>
```

7.5   TraceHeaderList Element

A **TraceHeaderList** element consists of one or more **TraceHeader** elements. Exactly one **TraceHeader** is appended to the **TraceHeaderList** following any preexisting **TraceHeader** before transmission of a message over a data communication protocol.

The **TraceHeaderList** element MAY be omitted from the header if:

▼ the message is being sent over a single hop (see section 7.5.3), and

▼ the message is not being sent reliably (see section 9)

The **TraceHeaderList** element has three REQUIRED attributes as follows:

▼ SOAP **mustUnderstand** (See section 7.4.11 for details)

▼ SOAP **actor** attribute with the value "http://schemas.xmlsoap.org/soap/actor/next"

▼ **Version** (See section 7.4.10 for details)

In addition, the **TraceHeaderList** element MAY include an **id** attribute. See section 7.2.5 for details.

7.5.1   SOAP Actor Attribute

The **TraceHeaderList** element MUST contain a SOAP **actor** attribute with the value http://schemas.xmlsoap.org/soap/actor/next and be interpreted and processed as defined in the [SOAP] specification. This means that the **TraceHeaderList** element MUST be processed by the MSH that receives the message and SHOULD NOT be forwarded to the next MSH. A MSH that handles the **TraceHeaderList** element is REQUIRED to perform the function of appending a new **TraceHeader** element to the **TraceHeaderList** and (re)inserting it into the message for the next MSH.

7.5.2   TraceHeader Element

The **TraceHeader** element contains information about a single transmission of a message between two instances of a MSH. If a message traverses multiple hops by passing through one or more intermediate MSH nodes as it travels between the *From Party* MSH and the *To Party* MSH, then each transmission over each successive "hop" results in the addition of a new **TraceHeader** element by the *Sending MSH*.

The **TraceHeader** element is a composite element comprised of the following subordinate elements:

▼ **Sender**

▼ **Receiver**

▼ **Timestamp**

▼ **#wildcard**

In addition, the **TraceHeader** element MAY include an **id** attribute. See section 7.2.5 for details.

7.5.2.1   Sender element

The **Sender** element is a composite element comprised of the following subordinate elements:

▼ **PartyId**

▼ **Location**

As with the **From** and **To** elements, multiple **PartyId** elements may be listed in the **Sender** element. This allows receiving systems to resolve those identifiers to organizations using a preferred identification scheme without prior agreement among all parties to a single scheme.

7.5.2.1.1   PartyId Element

This element has the syntax and semantics described in Section 7.4.1.1, **PartyId** element. In this case, the identified party is the sender of the message. This element may be used in a later message addressed to this party by including it in the **To** element of that message.

7.5.2.1.2   Location Element

This element contains the URL of the Sender's Message Service Handler. Unless there is another URL identified within the *CPA* or in **MessageHeader** (section 7.4.2), the recipient of the message uses the URL to send a message, when required that:

▼ responds to an earlier message

▼ acknowledges an earlier message

▼ reports an error in an earlier message.

7.5.2.2   Receiver Element

The **Receiver** element is a composite element comprised of the following subordinate elements:

▼ **PartyId**

▼ **Location**

As with the **From** and **To** elements, multiple **PartyId** elements may be listed in the **Receiver** element. This allows sending systems to resolve those identifiers to organisations using a preferred identification scheme without prior agreement among all parties to a single scheme.

The descendant elements of the **Receiver** element (**PartyId** and **Location**) are implemented in the same manner as the Sender element (see section 7.5.2.1).

7.5.2.3   Timestamp Element

The **Timestamp** element is the time the individual **TraceHeader** was created. It is in the same format as in the **Timestamp** element in the **MessageData** element (section 7.4.6.2).

7.5.2.4   #wildcard Element

Refer to section 7.2.4 for discussion of #wildcard element handling.

7.5.3   Single Hop TraceHeader Sample

A single hop message is illustrated by the diagram below.

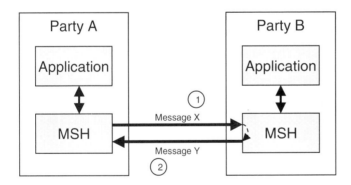

FIGURE 7-1   Single Hop Message

The content of the corresponding messages could include:

▼ Transmission 1 - Message X From Party A To Party B

```
<eb:MessageHeader eb:id="..." eb:version="1.0" SOAP-ENV:mustUnder-
stand="1">
  <eb:From>
    <eb:PartyId>urn:myscheme.com:id:PartyA-id</eb:PartyId>
  </eb:From>
  <eb:To>
```

```
      <eb:PartyId>urn:myscheme.com:id:PartyB-id</eb:PartyId>
    </eb:To>
    <eb:ConversationId>219cdj89dj2398djfjn</eb:ConversationId>
    ...
    <eb:MessageData>
      <eb:MessageId>29dmridj103kvna</eb:MessageId>
      ...
    </eb:MessageData>
    ...
</eb:MessageHeader>

<eb:TraceHeaderList eb:id="..." eb:version="1.0" SOAP-ENV:must-
Understand="1">
    <eb:TraceHeader>
      <eb:Sender>
        <eb:PartyId>urn:myscheme.com:id:PartyA-id</eb:PartyId>
        <eb:Location>http://PartyA.com/PartyAMsh</eb:Location>
      </eb:Sender>
      <eb:Receiver>
        <eb:PartyId>urn:myscheme.com:id:PartyB-id</eb:PartyId>
        <eb:Location>http://PartyB.com/PartyBMsh</eb:Location>
      </eb:Receiver>
      <eb:Timestamp>2000-12-16T21:19:35Z</eb:Timestamp>
    </eb:TraceHeader>
</eb:TraceHeaderList>
```

7.5.4 *Multi-hop TraceHeader Sample*

Multi-hop messages are not sent directly from one party to another, instead they are sent via an intermediate party, as illustrated by the diagram below:

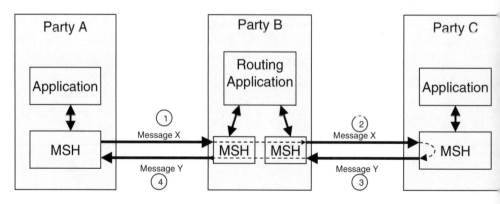

FIGURE 7-2 Multi-hop Message

The content of the corresponding messages could include:

▼ Transmission 1 - Message X From Party A To Party B

```
<eb:MessageHeader eb:id="..." eb:version="1.0" SOAP-ENV:
mustUnderstand="1">
  <eb:From>
    <eb:PartyId>urn:myscheme.com:id:PartyA-id</eb:PartyId>
  </eb:From>
  <eb:To>
    <eb:PartyId>urn:myscheme.com:id:PartyC-id</eb:PartyId>
  </eb:To>
  <eb:ConversationId>219cdj89dj2398djfjn</eb:ConversationId>
  ...
  <eb:MessageData>
    <eb:MessageId>29dmridj103kvna</eb:MessageId>
    ...
  </eb:MessageData>
  ...
</eb:MessageHeader>

<eb:TraceHeaderList eb:id="..." eb:version="1.0" SOAP-ENV:
mustUnderstand="1"
      SOAP-ENV:actor="http://schemas.xmlsoap.org/soap/actor/
next">
  <eb:TraceHeader>
    <eb:Sender>
      <eb:PartyId>urn:myscheme.com:id:PartyA-id</eb:PartyId>
      <eb:Location>http://PartyA.com/PartyAMsh</eb:Location>
    </eb:Sender>
    <eb:Receiver>
      <eb:Location>http://PartyB.com/PartyBMsh</eb:Location>
    </eb:Receiver>
    <eb:Timestamp>2000-12-16T21:19:35Z</eb:Timestamp>
  </eb:TraceHeader>
</eb:TraceHeaderList>
```

▼ Transmission 2 - Message X From Party B To Party C

```
<eb:MessageHeader eb:id="..." eb:version="1.0" SOAP-ENV:must-
Understand="1">
  <eb:From>
    <eb:PartyId>urn:myscheme.com:id:PartyA-id</eb:PartyId>
  </eb:From>
  <eb:To>
    <eb:PartyId>urn:myscheme.com:id:PartyC-id</eb:PartyId>
  </eb:To>
  <eb:ConversationId>219cdj89dj2398djfjn</eb:ConversationId>
  ...
```

```
      <eb:MessageData>
        <eb:MessageId>29dmridj103kvna</eb:MessageId>
        ...
      </eb:MessageData>
      ...
  </eb:MessageHeader>

  <eb:TraceHeaderList eb:id="..." eb:version="1.0" SOAP-ENV:
  mustUnderstand="1"
        SOAP-ENV:actor="http://schemas.xmlsoap.org/soap/actor/
  next">
    <eb:TraceHeader>
      <eb:Sender>
          <eb:PartyId>urn:myscheme.com:id:PartyA-id</eb:PartyId>
          <eb:Location>http://PartyA.com/PartyAMsh</eb:Location>
      </eb:Sender>
      <eb:Receiver>
          <eb:PartyId>urn:myscheme.com:id:PartyB-id</eb:PartyId>
          <eb:Location>http://PartyB.com/PartyBMsh</eb:Location>
      </eb:Receiver>
      <eb:Timestamp>2000-12-16T21:19:35Z</eb:Timestamp>
    </eb:TraceHeader>
    <eb:TraceHeader>
      <eb:Sender>
          <eb:PartyId>urn:myscheme.com:id:PartyB-id</eb:PartyId>
          <eb:Location>http://PartyB.com/PartyAMsh</eb:Location>
      </eb:Sender>
      <eb:Receiver>
          <eb:PartyId>urn:myscheme.com:id:PartyC-id</eb:PartyId>
          <eb:Location>http://PartyC.com/PartyBMsh</eb:Location>
      </eb:Receiver>
      <eb:Timestamp>2000-12-16T21:19:45Z</eb:Timestamp>
    </eb:TraceHeader>
  </eb:TraceHeaderList>
```

7.6   Acknowledgment Element

The **Acknowledgment** element is an optional element that is used by one Message Service Handler to indicate that another Message Service Handler has received a message. The **RefToMessageId** in a message containing an **Acknowledgement** element is used to identify the message being acknowledged by its **MessageId.**

The **Acknowledgment** element consists of the following elements and attributes:

▼   a **Timestamp** element

▼ a **From** element

▼ zero or more **ds:Reference** element(s)

▼ a REQUIRED SOAP **mustUnderstand** attribute (See section 7.4.11 for details)

▼ a REQUIRED SOAP **actor** attribute

▼ a REQUIRED **version** attribute (See section 7.4.10 for details)

▼ an **id** attribute (See section 7.2.5 for details)

7.6.1 Timestamp Element

The **Timestamp** element is a value representing the time that the message being acknowledged was received by the *Party* generating the acknowledgment message. It must conform to an [XMLSchema] timeInstant (section 7.4.6.2).

7.6.2 From Element

This is the same element as the **From** element within **MessageHeader** element (see section 7.4.1). However, when used in the context of an **Acknowledgment** element, it contains the identifier of the *Party* that is generating the *acknowledgment message*.

If the **From** element is omitted then the *Party* that is sending the element is identified by the **From** element in the **MessageHeader** element.

7.6.3 ds:Reference Element

An Acknowledgment MAY be used to enable non-repudiation of receipt by a MSH by including one or more **Reference** elements from the [XMLDSIG] namespace (http://www.w3.org/2000/09/xmldsig#) taken, or derived, from the message being acknowledged. The **Reference** element(s) MUST be namespace qualified to the aforementioned namespace and MUST conform to the XML Signature[XMLDSIG] specification.

7.6.4 SOAP Actor Attribute

The **Acknowledgment** element MUST contain a SOAP **actor** attribute with the value http://schemas.xmlsoap.org/soap/actor/next and be interpreted and processed as defined in the [SOAP] specification. This means that the **Acknowledgment** element MUST be processed by the MSH that receives the message and SHOULD NOT be forwarded to the next MSH.

7.6.5 Acknowledgement Sample

An example of the **Acknowledgement** element is given below:

```
<eb:Acknowledgment SOAP-ENV:mustUnderstand="1" eb:version="1.0"
    SOAP-ENV:actor="http://schemas.xmlsoap.org/soap/actor/next">
  <eb:Timestamp>2001-03-09T12:22:30Z</eb:Timestamp>
  <eb:From>
    <eb:PartyId>uri:www.example.com</eb:PartyId>
  </eb:From>
</eb:Acknowledgment>
```

7.7   Via Element

The **Via** element is an ebXML extension to the SOAP **Header** that is used to convey information to the next ebXML Message Service Handler (MSH) that receives the message.

Note

> This MSH can be a MSH operated by an intermediary or by the *To Party*. In particular, the Via element is used to hold data that can vary from one hop to another.

The **Via** element MUST contain the following attributes:

- ▼ **id** attribute (See section 7.2.5)
- ▼ **version** attribute (See section 7.4.10 for details)
- ▼ SOAP **MustUnderstand** attribute
- ▼ SOAP **actor** attribute

The **Via** element MUST also contain one or more of the following elements or attributes:

- ▼ **syncReply** attribute
- ▼ **reliableMessagingMethod** attribute
- ▼ **ackRequested** attribute
- ▼ **CPAId** element

The **Via** element MAY also contain the following elements:

- ▼ **Service** element
- ▼ **Action** element

7.7.1   SOAP mustUnderstand Attribute

The REQUIRED SOAP **mustUnderstand** attribute, namespace qualified to the SOAP **Envelope** namespace (http://schemas.xmlsoap.org/soap/envelope/), indicates that the contents of the **Via** element MUST be understood by a receiving process or else the message MUST be rejected in accordance with [SOAP]. This attribute MUST have a value of '1' (true). In accordance with the [SOAP] specification, a receiving *ebXML Message Service* implementation that does not provide support for the **Via** element MUST respond with a SOAP **Fault** with a **faultCode** of **MustUnderstand.**

7.7.2 SOAP Actor Attribute

The **Via** element MUST contain a SOAP **actor** attribute with the value http:// schemas.xmlsoap.org/soap/actor/next and be interpreted and processed as defined in the [SOAP] specification. This means that the **Via** element MUST be processed by the MSH that receives the message and SHOULD NOT be forwarded to the next MSH.

7.7.3 syncReply Attribute

The **syncReply** attribute is used only if the data communication protocol is *synchronous* (e.g. HTTP). It is an [XMLSchema] boolean. If the communication protocol is not *synchronous*, then the value of **syncReply** is ignored. If the **syncReply** attribute is not present, it is semantically equivalent to its presence with a value of "false". If the **syncReply** attribute is present with a value of **true,** the MSH must return the response from the application or business process in the payload of the *synchronous* reply message. See also the description of **syncReply** in the [ebCPP] specification.

7.7.4 reliableMessagingMethod Attribute

The **reliableMessagingMethod** attribute is an enumeration that SHALL have one of the following values:

▼ **ebXML**

▼ **Transport**

The default implied value for this attribute is **ebXML.**

7.7.5 ackRequested Attribute

The **ackRequested** attribute is an enumeration that SHALL have one of the following values:

▼ **Signed**

▼ **Unsigned**

▼ **None**

The default implied value for this attribute is **None.** This attribute is used to indicate to the *Receiving MSH* whether an acknowledgment message is expected, and if so, whether the acknowledgment message should be signed by the *Receiving MSH*. Refer to section 9.2.5 for a complete discussion as to the use of this attribute.

7.7.6 CPAId Element

The **CPAId** element is a string that identifies the parameters that govern the exchange of messages between two MSH instances. It has the same meaning as the **CPAId** in the **MessageHeader** except that the parameters identified by the **CPAId** apply just to the exchange of messages between the two MSH instances rather than between the *Parties* identified in the **To** and **From** elements of the **Message-Header** (section 7.4.2). This allows different parameters, transport protocols, etc, to be used on different hops when a message is passed through intermediaries.

If the **CPAId** element is present, the identified parameter values SHOULD be used instead of the values identified by the **CPAId** in the **MessageHeader** element.

7.7.7 Service and Action Elements

The **Service** and **Action** elements have the same meaning as the **Service** and **Action** elements in the **MessageHeader** element (see sections 7.4.4 and 7.4.5) except that they are interpreted and acted on by the next MSH whether or not the MSH is operated by the *To Party*.

The designer of the service or business process that is using the *ebXML Message Service* defines the values used for **Service** and **Action.**

The **Service** and **Action** elements are OPTIONAL. However, if the **Service** element is present then the **Action** element MUST also be present and vice versa.

7.7.8 Via Element Sample

The following is a sample **Via** element.

```
<eb:Via SOAP-ENV:mustUnderstand="1" eb:version="1.0"
   SOAP-ENV:actor="http://schemas.xmlsoap.org/soap/actor/next"
   eb:syncReply="false">
   <eb:CPAId>yaddaydda</eb:CPAId>
   <eb:Service>urn:services:Proxy</eb:Service>
   <eb:Action>LogActivity</eb:Action>
</eb:Via>
```

7.8 ErrorList Element

The existence of an **ErrorList** element within the SOAP **Header** element indicates that the message that is identified by the **RefToMessageId** in the **Message-Header** element has an error.

The **ErrorList** element consists of one or more **Error** elements and the following attributes:

▼ **id** attribute

▼ SOAP **mustUnderstand** attribute (See section 7.4.11 for details)

▼ **version** attribute (See section 7.4.10 for details)

▼ **highestSeverity** attribute

If there are no errors to be reported then the **ErrorList** element MUST NOT be present.

7.8.1 id Attribute

The **id** attribute uniquely identifies the **ErrorList** element within the document (See section 7.2.5).

7.8.2 highestSeverity Attribute

The **highestSeverity** attribute contains the highest severity of any of the **Error** elements. Specifically, if any of the **Error** elements have a **severity** of **Error** then **highestSeverity** must be set to **Error,** otherwise set **highestSeverity** to **Warning.**

7.8.3 Error Element

An **Error** element consists of the following attributes:

▼ **codeContext**

▼ **errorCode**

▼ **severity**

▼ **location**

▼ **xml:lang**

▼ **id** (See section 7.2.5 for details)

The content of the **Error** element contains an error message.

7.8.3.1   codeContext Attribute

The REQUIRED **codeContext** attribute identifies the namespace or scheme for the **errorCodes.** It MUST be a URI. Its default value is **http://www.ebxml.org /messageServiceErrors.** If it does not have the default value, then it indicates that an implementation of this specification has used its own **errorCodes.**

Use of non-ebXML values for **errorCodes** is NOT RECOMMENDED. In addition, an implementation of this specification MUST NOT use its own **errorCodes** if an existing **errorCode** as defined in this section has the same or very similar meaning.

7.8.3.2   errorCode Attribute

The REQUIRED **errorCode** attribute indicates the nature of the error in the message in error. Valid values for the **errorCode** and a description of the code's meaning are given in sections 7.8.5.1 and 7.8.5.2

7.8.3.3   severity Attribute

The REQUIRED **severity** attribute indicates the severity of the error. Valid values are:

- ▼ **Warning** - This indicates that although there is an error, other messages in the conversation will still be generated in the normal way.

- ▼ **Error** - This indicates that there is an unrecoverable error in the message and no further messages will be generated as part of the conversation.

7.8.3.4   location Attribute

The **location** attribute points to the part of the message that is in error.

If an error exists in an ebXML element and the element is "well formed" (see [XML]), then the content of the **location** attribute MUST be an [XPointer].

If the error is associated with the MIME envelope that wraps the SOAP envelope and the ebXML Payload, then **location** contains the `content-id` of the MIME part that is in error, in the format `cid:23912480wsr`, where the text after the":" is the value of the MIME part's `content-id`.

7.8.3.5   Error Element Content

The content of the error message provides a narrative description of the error in the language defined by the **xml:lang** attribute. Typically, it will be the message generated by the XML parser or other software that is validating the message. This means that the content is defined by the vendor/developer of the software that generated the **Error** element.

The **xml:lang** attribute must comply with the rules for identifying languages specified in [XML].

The content of the **Error** element can be empty.

7.8.4   ErrorList Sample

An example of an **ErrorList** element is given below.

```
<eb:ErrorList eb:id='3490sdo9', eb:highestSeverity="error" eb:
version="1.0"
            SOAP-ENV:mustUnderstand="1">
  <eb:Error eb:errorCode='SecurityFailure' eb:severity="Error"
    eb:location='URI_of_ds:Signature_goes_here' xml:lang="us en">
    Validation of signature failed </eb:Error>
```

```
    <eb:Error ...> ... </eb:Error>
</eb:ErrorList>
```

7.8.5 errorCode Values

This section describes the values for the **errorCode** element (see section 7.8.3.2) used in a *message reporting an erro*r. They are described in a table with three headings:

- ▼ the first column contains the value to be used as an **errorCode,** e.g. **SecurityFailure**

- ▼ the second column contains a "Short Description" of the **errorCode.**

> **This narrative MUST NOT be used in the content of the** error **element.**   **Note**

- ▼ the third column contains a "Long Description" that provides an explanation of the meaning of the error and provides guidance on when the particular **errorCode** should be used.

7.8.5.1 Reporting Errors in the ebXML Elements

The following list contains error codes that can be associated with ebXML elements:

Error Code	Short Description	Long Description
ValueNotRecognized	Element content or attribute value not recognized.	Although the document is well formed and valid, the element/ attribute contains a value that could not be recognized and therefore could not be used by the *ebXML Message Service*.
NotSupported	Element or attribute not supported	Although the document is well formed and valid, an element or attribute is present that is consistent with the rules and constraints contained in this specification, but is not supported by the *ebXML Message Service* processing the message.
Inconsistent	Element content or attribute value inconsistent with other elements or attributes.	Although the document is well formed and valid, according to the rules and constraints contained in this specification the content of an element or attribute is inconsistent with the content of other elements or their attributes.

Error Code	Short Description	Long Description
OtherXml	Other error in an element content or attribute value.	Although the document is well formed and valid, the element content or attribute value contains values that do not conform to the rules and constraints contained in this specification and is not covered by other error codes. The content of the **Error** element should be used to indicate the nature of the problem.

7.8.5.2   Non-XML Document Errors

The following are error codes that identify errors not associated with the ebXML elements:

Error Code	Short Description	Long Description
DeliveryFailure	Message Delivery Failure	A message has been received that either probably or definitely could not be sent to its next destination. **Note** If **severity** is set to **Warning** then there is a small probability that the message was delivered.
TimeToLiveExpired	Message Time To Live Expired	A message has been received that arrived after the time specified in the **TimeToLive** element of the **MessageHeader** element
SecurityFailure	Message Security Checks Failed	Validation of signatures or checks on the authenticity or authority of the sender of the message have failed.
Unknown	Unknown Error	Indicates that an error has occurred that is not covered explicitly by any of the other errors. The content of the **Error** element should be used to indicate the nature of the problem.

7.9   ds:Signature Element

An ebXML Message may be digitally signed to provide security countermeasures. Zero or more **ds:Signature** elements, belonging to the [XMLDSIG] defined namespace MAY be present in the SOAP **Header.** The **ds:Signature** element

MUST be namespace qualified in accordance with [XMLDSIG]. The structure and content of the **ds:Signature** element MUST conform to the [XMLDSIG] specification. If there is more than one **ds:Signature** element contained within the SOAP **Header,** the first MUST represent the digital signature of the ebXML Message as signed by the *From Party* MSH in conformance with section 11. Additional **ds:Signature** elements MAY be present, but their purpose is undefined by this specification.

Refer to section 11 for a detailed discussion on how to construct the **ds:Signature** element when digitally signing an ebXML Message.

7.10 SOAP Body Extensions

The SOAP **Body** element is the second child element of the SOAP **Envelope** element. It MUST have a namespace qualifier that matches the SOAP **Envelope** namespace declaration for the namespace "http://schemas.xmlsoap.org/soap/envelope/". For example:

```
<SOAP-ENV:Envelope xmlns:SOAP-ENV="http://schemas.xmlsoap.org/
soap/envelope/" …>
   <SOAP-ENV:Header>…</SOAP-ENV:Header>
   <SOAP-ENV:Body>…</SOAP-ENV:Body>
</SOAP-ENV:Envelope>
```

The SOAP **Body** element contains the ebXML SOAP **Body** extension element content as follows:

▼ **Manifest** element

▼ **StatusRequest** element

▼ **StatusResponse** element

▼ **DeliveryReceipt** element

Each is defined in the following sections.

7.11 Manifest Element

The **Manifest** element is a composite element consisting of one or more **Reference** elements. Each **Reference** element identifies data associated with the message, whether included as part of the message as payload document(s) contained in a *Payload Container*, or remote resources accessible via a URL. It is RECOMMENDED that no payload data be present in the SOAP **Body.** The purpose of the **Manifest** is as follows:

▼ to make it easier to directly extract a particular payload associated with this ebXML Message,

▼ to allow an application to determine whether it can process the payload without having to parse it.

The **Manifest** element is comprised of the following attributes and elements, each of which is described below:

▼ an **id** attribute

▼ a REQUIRED **version** attribute (See section 7.4.10 for details)

▼ one or more **Reference** elements

▼ #wildcard

7.11.1   id Attribute

The **Manifest** element MUST have an **id** attribute that is an XML ID (See section 7.2.5).

7.11.2   #wildcard Element

Refer to section 7.2.4 for discussion of #wildcard element handling.

7.11.3   Reference Element

The **Reference** element is a composite element consisting of the following subordinate elements:

▼ **Schema** - information about the schema(s) that define the instance document identified in the parent **Reference** element

▼ **Description** - a textual description of the payload object referenced by the parent **Reference** element

▼ **#wildcard** - any namespace-qualified element content belonging to a foreign namespace

The **Reference** element itself is an [XLINK] simple link. XLINK is presently a Candidate Recommendation (CR) of the W3C. It should be noted that the use of XLINK in this context is chosen solely for the purpose of providing a concise vocabulary for describing an association. Use of an XLINK processor or engine is NOT REQUIRED, but MAY prove useful in certain implementations.

The **Reference** element has the following attribute content in addition to the element content described above:

▼ **id** - an XML ID for the **Reference** element,

▼ **xlink:type** - this attribute defines the element as being an XLINK simple link. It has a fixed value of 'simple',

▼ **xlink:href** - this REQUIRED attribute has a value that is the URI of the payload object referenced. It SHALL conform to the [XLINK] specification criteria for a simple link.

▼ **xlink:role** - this attribute identifies some resource that describes the payload object or its purpose. If present, then it SHALL have a value that is a valid URI in accordance with the [XLINK] specification,

▼ Any other namespace-qualified attribute MAY be present. A *Receiving MSH* MAY choose to ignore any foreign namespace attributes other than those defined above.

7.11.3.1 Schema Element

If the item being referenced has schema(s) of some kind that describe it (e.g. an XML Schema, DTD, or a database schema), then the **Schema** element SHOULD be present as a child of the **Reference** element. It provides a means of identifying the schema and its version defining the payload object identified by the parent **Reference** element. The **Schema** element contains the following attributes:

▼ **location** - the REQUIRED URI of the schema

▼ **version** – a version identifier of the schema

7.11.3.2 Description Element

The **Reference** element MAY contain zero or more **Description** elements. The **Description** is a textual description of the payload object referenced by the parent **Reference** element. The language of the description is defined by a REQUIRED **xml:lang** attribute. The **xml:lang** attribute MUST comply with the rules for identifying languages specified in [XML]. This element is provided to allow a human readable description of the payload object identified by the parent **Reference** element. If multiple **Description** elements are present, each SHOULD have a unique **xml:lang** attribute value. An example of a **Description** element follows.

```
<eb:Description xml:lang="en-gb">Purchase Order for 100,000
widgets</eb:Description>
```

7.11.3.3 #wildcard Element

Refer to section 7.2.4 for discussion of #wildcard element handling.

7.11.4 References Included in a Manifest

The designer of the business process or information exchange that is using ebXML Messaging decides what payload data is referenced by the **Manifest** and the values to be used for **xlink:role.**

7.11.5 *Manifest Validation*

If an **xlink:href** attribute contains a URI that is a content id (URI scheme "cid") then a MIME part with that content-id MUST be present in the *Payload Container* of the message. If it is not, then the error SHALL be reported to the *From Party* with an **errorCode** of **MimeProblem** and a **severity** of **Error.**

If an **xlink:href** attribute contains a URI that is not a content id (URI scheme "cid"), and that URI cannot be resolved, then it is an implementation decision on whether to report the error. If the error is to be reported, then it SHALL be reported to the *From Party* with an **errorCode** of **MimeProblem** and a **severity** of **Error.**

7.11.6 *Manifest Sample*

The following fragment demonstrates a typical **Manifest** for a message with a single payload MIME body part:

```
<eb:Manifest eb:id="Manifest" eb:version="1.0">
  <eb:Reference eb:id="pay01"
    xlink:href="cid:payload-1"
    xlink:role="http://regrep.org/gci/purchaseOrder">
    <eb:Schema eb:location="http://regrep.org/gci/purchaseOrder/
po.xsd" eb:version="1.0"/>
    <eb:Description xml:lang="en-us">Purchase Order for 100,000
widgets</eb:Description>
  </eb:Reference>
</eb:Manifest>
```

7.12   StatusRequest Element

The **StatusRequest** element is an immediate child of a SOAP **Body** and is used to identify an earlier message whose status is being requested (see section 8.1).

The **StatusRequest** element consists of the following elements and attributes:

  ▼ a REQUIRED **RefToMessageId** element

  ▼ a REQUIRED **version** attribute (See section 7.4.10 for details)

  ▼ an **id** attribute (See section 7.2.5 for details)

7.12.1 *StatusRequest Sample*

An example of the **StatusRequest** element is given below:

```
<eb:StatusRequest eb:version="1.0" >
```

```
    <eb:RefToMessageId>323210:e52151ec74:-7ffc@xtacy</eb:RefTo-
MessageId>
</eb:StatusRequest>
```

7.13   StatusResponse Element

The **StatusResponse** element is used by one MSH to respond to a request on the status of the processing of a message that was previously sent (see also section 8.1).

The **StatusResponse** element consists of the following elements and attributes:

▼ a REQUIRED **RefToMessageId** element

▼ a **Timestamp** element

▼ a REQUIRED **version** attribute (See section 7.4.10 for details)

▼ a **messageStatus** attribute

▼ an **id** attribute (See section 7.2.5 for details)

7.13.1   RefToMessageId Element

A REQUIRED **RefToMessageId** element that contains the **MessageId** of the message whose status is being reported.

7.13.2   Timestamp Element

The **Timestamp** element contains the time that the message, whose status is being reported, was received (section 7.4.6.2.). This MUST be omitted if the message whose status is being reported is **NotRecognized** or the request was **UnAuthorized.**

7.13.3   messageStatus Attribute

The **messageStatus** attribute identifies the status of the message that is identified by the **RefToMessageId** element. It SHALL be set to one of the following values:

▼ **UnAuthorized** – the Message Status Request is not authorized or accepted

▼ **NotRecognized** – the message identified by the **RefToMessageId** element in the **StatusResponse** element is not recognized

▼ **Received** – the message identified by the **RefToMessageId** element in the **StatusResponse** element has been received by the MSH

> **If a Message Status Request is sent after the elapsed time indicated by** persistDuration **has passed since the message being queried was sent, then the Message Status Response may indicate that the** MessageId **was** NotRecognized **as the** MessageId **is no longer in persistent storage.**

Note

7.13.4   StatusResponse Sample

An example of the **StatusResponse** element is given below:

```
<eb:StatusResponse eb:version="1.0" eb:messageStatus="Received">
   <eb:RefToMessageId>323210:e52151ec74:-7ffc@xtacy</eb:RefTo-
MessageId>
   <eb:Timestamp>2001-03-09T12:22:30Z</eb:Timestamp>
</eb:StatusResponse>
```

7.14   DeliveryReceipt Element

The **DeliveryReceipt** element is an optional element that is used by the *To Party* that received a message, to let the *From Party* that sent the original message, know that the message was received. The **RefToMessageId** in a message containing a **DeliveryReceipt** element is used to identify the message being for which the receipt is being generated by its **MessageId.**

The **DeliveryReceipt** element consists of the following elements and attributes:

▼ an **id** attribute (See section 7.2.5)

▼ a REQUIRED **version** attribute (See section 7.4.10 for details)

▼ a **Timestamp** element

▼ zero or more **ds:Reference** element(s)

7.14.1   Timestamp Element

The **Timestamp** element is a value representing the time that the message for which a **DeliveryReceipt** element is being generated was received by the *To Party*. It must conform to an [XMLSchema] timeInstant.

7.14.2   ds:Reference Element

An Acknowledgment MAY be used to enable non-repudiation of receipt by a MSH by including one or more **Reference** elements from the [XMLDSIG] namespace (http://www.w3.org/2000/09/xmldsig#) taken, or derived, from the message being acknowledged. The **Reference** element(s) MUST be namespace qualified to the aforementioned namespace and MUST conform to the XML Signature [XMLDSIG] specification.

7.14.3   DeliveryReceipt Sample

An example of the **DeliveryReceipt** element is given below:

```
<eb:DeliveryReceipt eb:version="1.0">
   <eb:Timestamp>2001-03-09T12:22:30Z</eb:Timestamp>
```

```
<ds:Reference URI="cid://blahblahblah/">
    <ds:DigestMethod Algorithm="http://www.w3.org/2000/09/xmld-
sig#dsa-sha1"/>
    <ds:DigestValue>...</ds:DigestValue>
  </ds:Reference>
</eb:DeliveryReceipt>
```

7.15   Combining ebXML SOAP Extension Elements

This section describes how the various ebXML SOAP extension elements may be
used in combination.

7.15.1   Manifest Element

The **Manifest** element MUST be present if there is any data associated with the
message that is not present in the *Header Container*. This applies specifically to
data in the *Payload Container* or elsewhere, e.g. on the web.

7.15.2   MessageHeader Element

The **MessageHeader** element MUST be present in every message.

7.15.3   TraceHeaderList Element

The **TraceHeaderList** element MAY be present in any message. It MUST be present if the message is being sent reliably (see section 9) or over multiple hops (see
section 7.5.4).

7.15.4   StatusRequest Element

A **StatusRequest** element MUST NOT be present with the following elements:

▼ a **Manifest** element

▼ an **ErrorList** element

7.15.5   StatusResponse Element

This element MUST NOT be present with the following elements:

▼ a **Manifest** element

▼ a **StatusRequest** element

▼ an **ErrorList** element with a **highestSeverity** attribute set to **Error**

7.15.6   ErrorList Element

If the **highestSeverity** attribute on the **ErrorList** is set to **Warning,** then this element MAY be present with any other element.

If the **highestSeverity** attribute on the **ErrorList** is set to **Error,** then this element MUST NOT be present with the following:

▼ a **Manifest** element

▼ a **StatusResponse** element

7.15.7 Acknowledgment Element

An **Acknowledgment** element MAY be present on any message.

7.15.8 Delivery Receipt Element

A **DeliveryReceipt** element may be present on any message.

7.15.9 Signature Element

One or more **ds:Signature** elements MAY be present on any message.

7.15.10 Via Element

One-and-only-one **Via** element MAY be present in any message.

8 Message Service Handler Services

The Message Service Handler MAY support two services that are designed to help provide smooth operation of a Message Handling Service implementation:

▼ Message Status Request

▼ Message Service Handler Ping

If a *Receiving MSH* does not support the service requested, it SHOULD return a SOAP fault with a **faultCode** of **MustUnderstand.** Each service is described below.

8.1 Message Status Request Service

The Message Status Request Service consists of the following:

▼ A Message Status Request message containing details regarding a message previously sent is sent to a Message Service Handler (MSH)

▼ The Message Service Handler receiving the request responds with a Message Status Response message.

A Message Service Handler SHOULD respond to Message Status Requests for messages that have been sent reliably (see section 9) and the **MessageId** in the **RefToMessageId** is present in *persistent storage* (see section 9.1.1).

A Message Service Handler MAY respond to Message Status Requests for messages that have not been sent reliably.

A Message Service SHOULD NOT use the Message Status Request Service to implement Reliable Messaging.

8.1.1 *Message Status Request Message*

A Message Status Request message consists of an *ebXML Message* containing no *ebXML Payload* and the following elements in the SOAP **Header:**

▼ a **MessageHeader** element

▼ a **TraceHeaderList** element

▼ a **StatusRequest** element

▼ a **ds:Signature** element

The **TraceHeaderList** and the **ds:Signature** elements MAY be omitted (see sections 7.5 and 7.15.8).

The **MessageHeader** element MUST contain the following:

▼ a **From** element that identifies the *Party* that created the message status request message

▼ a **To** element identifying a *Party* who should receive the message. If a **Trace-Header** was present on the message whose status is being checked, this MUST be set using the **Receiver** of the message. All **PartyId** elements present in the **Receiver** element SHOULD be included in this **To** element.

▼ a **Service** element that contains: **uri:www.ebxml.org/messageService/**

▼ an **Action** element that contains **StatusRequest**

The message is then sent to the *To Party*.

The **RefToMessageId** element in **StatusRequest** element in the SOAP **Body** contains the **MessageId** of the message whose status is being queried.

8.1.2 *Message Status Response Message*

Once the *To Party* receives the Message Status Request message, they SHOULD generate a Message Status Response message consisting of no ebXML Payload and the following elements in the SOAP **Header** and **Body.**

▼ a **MessageHeader** element

▼ a **TraceHeaderList** element

▼ an **Acknowledgment** element

▼ a **StatusResponse** element (see section 7.13)

▼ a **ds:Signature** element

The **TraceHeaderList, Acknowledgment** and **ds:Signature** elements MAY be omitted (see sections 7.5, 7.15.7 and 7.15.8).

The **MessageHeader** element MUST contain the following:

▼ a **From** element that identifies the sender of the Message Status Response message

▼ a **To** element that is set to the value of the **From** element in the Message Status Request message

▼ a **Service** element that contains the value: **uri:www.ebxml.org/messageService/**

▼ an **Action** element that contains **StatusResponse**

▼ a **RefToMessageId** that identifies the Message Status Request message.

The message is then sent to the *To Party*.

8.1.3   *Security Considerations*

Parties who receive a Message Status Request message SHOULD always respond to the message. However, they MAY ignore the message instead of responding with **messageStatus** set to **UnAuthorized** if they consider that the sender of the message is unauthorized. The decision process that results in this course of action is implementation dependent.

8.2   Message Service Handler Ping Service

The Message Service Handler Ping Service enables one MSH to determine if another MSH is operating. It consists of:

▼ sending a Message Service Handler Ping message to a MSH, and

▼ the MSH that receives the Ping responding with a Message Service Handler Pong message.

8.2.1   *Message Service Handler Ping Message*

A Message Service Handler Ping (MSH Ping) message consists of an *ebXML Message* containing no ebXML Payload and the following elements in the SOAP **Header:**

- ▼ a **MessageHeader** element
- ▼ a **TraceHeaderList** element
- ▼ a **ds:Signature** element

The **TraceHeaderList** and the **ds:Signature** elements MAY be omitted (see sections 7.5 and 7.15.8).

The **MessageHeader** element MUST contain the following:

- ▼ a **From** element that identifies the *Party* creating the MSH Ping message
- ▼ a **To** element that identifies the *Party* that is being sent the MSH Ping message
- ▼ a **CPAId** element
- ▼ a **ConversationId** element
- ▼ a **Service** element that contains: **uri:www.ebxml.org/messageService/**
- ▼ an **Action** element that contains **Ping**

The message is then sent to the *To Party*.

8.2.2   Message Service Handler Pong Message

Once the *To Party* receives the MSH Ping message, they MAY generate a Message Service Handler Pong (MSH Pong) message consisting of an ebXML Message containing no ebXML Payload and the following elements in the SOAP **Header:**

- ▼ a **MessageHeader** element
- ▼ a **TraceHeaderList** element
- ▼ an **Acknowledgment** element
- ▼ an OPTIONAL **ds:Signature** element

The **TraceHeaderList**, **Acknowledgment** and **ds:Signature** elements MAY be omitted (see sections 7.5, 7.15.7 and 7.15.8).

The **MessageHeader** element MUST contain the following:

- ▼ a **From** element that identifies the creator of the MSH Pong message
- ▼ a **To** element that identifies a *Party* that generated the MSH Ping message
- ▼ a **CPAId** element
- ▼ a **ConversationId** element
- ▼ a **Service** element that contains the value: **uri:www.ebxml.org/messageService/**
- ▼ an **Action** element that contains the value **Pong**
- ▼ a **RefToMessageId** that identifies the MSH Ping message.

The message is then sent to the *To Party*.

8.2.3 Security Considerations

Parties who receive a MSH Ping message SHOULD always respond to the message. However, there is a risk that some parties might use the MSH Ping message to determine the existence of a Message Service Handler as part of a security attack on that MSH. Therefore, recipients of a MSH Ping MAY ignore the message if they consider that the sender of the message received is unauthorized or part of some attack. The decision process that results in this course of action is implementation dependent.

9 Reliable Messaging

Reliable Messaging defines an interoperable protocol such that the two Message Service Handlers (MSH) can "reliably" exchange messages that are sent using "reliable messaging" semantics, resulting in the *To Party* receiving the message once and only once.

Reliability is achieved by a *Receiving MSH* responding to a message with an *Acknowledgment Message*.

9.1.1 Persistent Storage and System Failure

A MSH that supports Reliable Messaging MUST keep messages that are sent or received reliably in *persistent storage*. In this context *persistent storage* is a method of storing data that does not lose information after a system failure or interruption.

This specification recognizes that different degrees of resilience may be realized depending on the technology that is used to persist the data. However, as a minimum, persistent storage that has the resilience characteristics of a hard disk (or equivalent) SHOULD be used. It is strongly RECOMMENDED though that implementers of this specification use technology that is resilient to the failure of any single hardware or software component.

After a system interruption or failure, a MSH MUST ensure that messages in persistent storage are processed in the same way as if the system failure or interruption had not occurred. How this is done is an implementation decision.

In order to support the filtering of duplicate messages, a *Receiving MSH* SHOULD save the **MessageId** in *persistent storage*. It is also RECOMMENDED that the following be kept in *Persistent Storage*:

▼ the complete message, at least until the information in the message has been passed to the application or other process that needs to process it

▼ the time the message was received, so that the information can be used to generate the response to a Message Status Request (see section 8.1)

▼ complete response message

9.1.2 Methods of Implementing Reliable Messaging

Support for Reliable Messaging MAY be implemented in one of the following two ways:

▼ using the ebXML Reliable Messaging protocol, or

▼ using ebXML SOAP structures together with commercial software products that are designed to provide reliable delivery of messages using alternative protocols.

9.2 Reliable Messaging Parameters

This section describes the parameters required to control reliable messaging. This parameter information can be specified in the *CPA* or in the **MessageHeader** (section 7.4.2).

9.2.1 Delivery Semantics

The **deliverySemantics** value MUST be used by the *From Party* MSH to indicate whether the Message MUST be sent reliably. Valid values are:

▼ **OnceAndOnlyOnce** - The message must be sent using a **reliableMessaging-Method** that will result in the application or other process at the *To Party* receiving the message once and only once

▼ **BestEffort** - The reliable delivery semantics are not used. In this case, the value of **reliableMessagingMethod** is ignored.

The value for **deliverySemantics** is specified in the CPA or in **MessageHeader** (section 7.4.2). The default value for **deliverySemantics** is **BestEffort.**

If **deliverySemantics** is set to **OnceAndOnlyOnce,** the *From Party* MSH and the *To Party* MSH must adopt a reliable messaging behavior that describes how messages are resent in the case of failure. The **deliverySemantic** value of **OnceAndOnlyOnce** will cause duplicate messages to be ignored.

If **deliverySemantics** is set to **BestEffort,** a MSH that received a message that it is unable to deliver MUST NOT take any action to recover or otherwise notify anyone of the problem. The MSH that sent the message MUST NOT attempt to recover from any failure. This means that duplicate messages might be delivered to an application and persistent storage of messages is not required.

If the *To Party* is unable to support the type of delivery semantics requested, the *To Party* SHOULD report the error to the *From Party* using an **ErrorCode** of **Not-Supported** and a **Severity** of **Error.**

9.2.2   mshTimeAccuracy

The **mshTimeAccuracy** parameter indicates the minimum accuracy a *Receiving MSH* keeps the clocks it uses when checking, for example, **TimeToLive.** Its value is in the format "mm:ss" which indicates the accuracy in minutes and seconds.

9.2.3   TimeToLive

The **TimeToLive** value indicates the time by which a message should be delivered to and processed by the *To Party*. It must conform to an XML Schema time-Instant.

In this context, the **TimeToLive** has expired if the time of the internal clock of the *Receiving MSH* is greater than the value of **TimeToLive** for the message.

When setting a value for **TimeToLive** it is RECOMMENDED that the *From Party's* MSH takes into account the accuracy of its own internal clocks as well as the **mshTimeAccuracy** parameter for the *Receiving MSH* indicating the accuracy to which a MSH will keep its internal clocks. How a MSH ensures that its internal clocks are kept sufficiently accurate is an implementation decision.

If the *To Party's* MSH receives a message where **TimeToLive** has expired, it SHALL send a message to the *From Party* MSH, reporting that the **TimeToLive** of the message has expired. This message SHALL be comprised of an **ErrorList** containing an error that has the **errorCode** attribute set to **TimeToLiveExpired,** and the **severity** attribute set to **Error.**

9.2.4   reliableMessagingMethod

The **reliableMessagingMethod** attribute SHALL have one of the following values:

▼ **ebXML**

▼ **Transport**

The default implied value for this attribute is **ebXML** and is case sensitive. Refer to section 7.7.4 for discussion of the use of this attribute.

9.2.5   ackRequested

The **ackRequested** value is used by the *Sending MSH* to request that the *Receiving MSH* returns an *acknowledgment message* with an **Acknowledgment** element.

Valid values for **ackRequested** are:

▼ **Unsigned** - requests that an unsigned Acknowledgement is requested

▼ **Signed** - requests that a signed Acknowledgement is requested, or

▼ **None** - indicates that no Acknowledgement is requested.

The default value is **None.**

9.2.6 retries

The **retries** value is an integer value that specifies the maximum number of times a *Sending MSH* SHOULD attempt to redeliver an unacknowledged *message* using the same Communications Protocol.

9.2.7 retryInterval

The **retryInterval** value is a time value, expressed as a duration in accordance with the [XMLSchema] timeDuration data type. This value specifies the minimum time the *Sending MSH* MUST wait between retries, if an *Acknowledgment Message* is not received.

9.2.8 persistDuration

The **persistDuration** value is the minimum length of time, expressed as a [XMLSchema] timeDuration, that data from a reliably sent *Message*, is kept in *Persistent Storage* by a *Receiving MSH*.

If the **persistDuration** has passed since the message was first sent, a *Sending MSH* SHOULD NOT resend a message with the same **MessageId.**

If a message cannot be sent successfully before **persistDuration** has passed, then the *Sending MSH* should report a delivery failure (see section 9.4).

9.3 ebXML Reliable Messaging Protocol

The ebXML Reliable Messaging Protocol described in this section MUST be followed if the **deliverySemantics** parameter/element is set to **OnceAndOnlyOnce** and the **reliableMessagingMethod** parameter/element is set to **ebXML** (the default).

The ebXML Reliable Messaging Protocol is illustrated by the figure below.

The receipt of the *Acknowledgment Message* indicates that the message being acknowledged has been successfully received and either processed or persisted by the *Receiving MSH*.

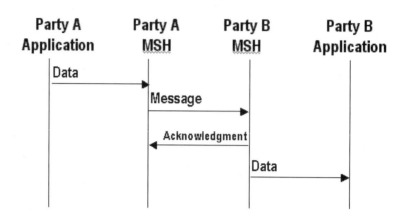

FIGURE 9-1   Indicating that a Message Has Been Received

An *Acknowledgment Message* MUST contain a **MessageData** element with a **RefToMessageId** that contains the same value as the **MessageId** element in the *message being acknowledged*.

9.3.1   Sending Message Behavior

If a MSH is given data by an application that needs to be sent reliably (i.e. the **deliverySemantics** is set to **OnceAndOnlyOnce**), then the MSH MUST do the following:

1. Create a message from components received from the application that includes a **TraceHeader** element identifying the sender and the receiver as described in Section 7.5.2 **TraceHeader** element.

2. Save the message in *persistent storage* (see section 9.1.1)

3. Send the message to the *Receiver MSH*

4. Wait for the *Receiver MSH* to return an *Acknowledgment Message* and, if it does not or a transient error is returned, then take the appropriate action as described in section 9.3.4

9.3.2   Receiving Message Behavior

If the **deliverySemantics** for the received message is set to **OnceAndOnlyOnce** then do the following:

1. If the message is just an acknowledgement (i.e. the **Service** element is set to http://www.ebxml.org/namespaces/messageService/Message-Acknowledgment and **Action** is set to **Acknowledgment**), then:

a.) Look for a message in *persistent storage* that has a **MessageId** that is the same as the value of **RefToMessageId** on the received Message

b.) If a message is found in *persistent storage* then mark the persisted message as delivered

2. Otherwise, if the message is not just an acknowledgement, then check to see if the message is a duplicate (e.g. there is a **MessageId** held in *persistent storage* that was received earlier that contains the same value for the **MessageId**)

a.) If the message is not a duplicate then do the following:

   i) Save the **MessageId** of the received message in *persistent storage*. As an implementation decision, the whole message MAY be stored if there are other reasons for doing so.

   ii) If the received message contains a **RefToMessageId** element then do the following:

      (1) Look for a message in *persistent storage* that has a **MessageId** that is the same as the value of **RefToMessageId** on the received Message

      (2) If a message is found in *persistent storage* then mark the persisted message as delivered

   iii) Generate an *Acknowledgement Message* in response (see section 9.3.3).

b.) If the message is a duplicate, then do the following:

   i) Look in persistent storage for the first response to the received message and resend it (i.e. it contains a **RefToMessageId** that matches the **MessageId** of the received message)

   ii) If a message was found in *persistent storage* then resend the persisted message back to the MSH that sent the received message,

   iii) If no message was found in *persistent storage,* then:

      (1) if **syncReply** is set to **True** and if the CPA indicates an application response is included, ignore the received message (i.e. no message was generated in response to the message, or the processing of the earlier message is not yet complete)

      (2) if **syncReply** is set to **False** then generate an *Acknowledgement Message* (see section 9.3.3).

9.3.3 Generating an Acknowledgement Message

An *Acknowledgement Message* MUST be generated whenever a message is received with:

▼ deliverySemantics set to OnceAndOnlyOnce and

▼ reliableMessagingMethod set to ebXML (the default).

As a minimum, it MUST contain a **MessageData** element with a **RefTo-MessageId** that contains the same value as the **MessageId** element in the *message being acknowledged*.

If **ackRequested** in the **Via** of the received message is set to **Signed** or **Unsigned** then the acknowledgement message MUST also contain an **Acknowledgement** element.

Depending on the value of the **syncReply** parameter, the *Acknowledgement Message* can also be sent at the same time as the response to the received message. In this case, the values for the **MessageHeader** elements of the *Acknowledgement Message* are set by the designer of the Service.

If an **Acknowledgment** element is being sent on its own, then the value of the **MessageHeader** elements MUST be set as follows:

▼ The Service element MUST be set to: uri:www.ebxml.org/messageService/

▼ The Action element MUST be set to Acknowledgment.

▼ The From element MAY be populated with the To element extracted from the message received, or it MAY be set using the Receiver from the last TraceHeader in the message that has just been received. In either case, all PartyId elements from the message received SHOULD be included in this From element.

▼ The To element MAY be populated with the From element extracted from the message received, or it MAY be set using the Sender from the last Trace-Header in the message that has just been received. In either case, all PartyId elements from the message received SHOULD be included in this To element.

▼ The RefToMessageId element MUST be set to the MessageId of the message that has just been received

9.3.4   *Resending Lost Messages and Duplicate Filtering*

This section describes the behavior that is required by the sender and receiver of a message in order to handle when messages are lost. A message is "lost" when a *Sending MSH* does not receive a response to a message. For example, it is possible that a *message* was lost, for example:

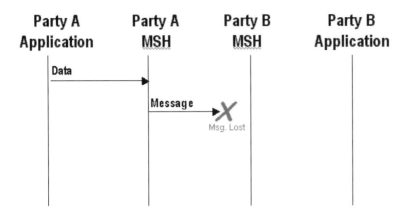

FIGURE 9-2   Undelivered Message

It is also possible that the *Acknowledgment Message* was lost, for example:

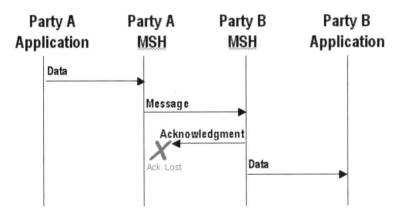

FIGURE 9-3   Lost Acknowledgment Message

The rules that apply are as follows:

1. The *Sending MSH* MUST resend the original message if an *Acknowledgment Message* has not been received from the *Receiving MSH* and the following are both true:

   a.) At least the time specified in the **retryInterval** has passed since the message was last sent, and

   b.) The message has been resent less than the number of times specified in the **retries** Parameter

2. If the *Sending MSH* does not receive an *Acknowledgment Message* after the maximum number of retries, the *Sending MSH* SHOULD notify the application and/or system administrator function of the failure to receive an acknowledgement.

3. If the *Sending MSH* detects an unrecoverable communications protocol error at the transport protocol level, the *Sending MSH* SHOULD resend the message.

9.3.5 Duplicate Message Handling

In the context of this specification, a duplicate message is:

▼ an "identical message" is a *message* that contains, apart from an additional **TraceHeader** element, the same ebXML SOAP **Header, Body** and ebXML *Payload* as the earlier *message* that was sent.

▼ a "duplicate message" is a *message* that contains the same **MessageId** as an earlier message that was received.

▼ the "first message" is the message with the earliest **Timestamp** in the **Message-Data** element that has the same **RefToMessageId** as the duplicate message.

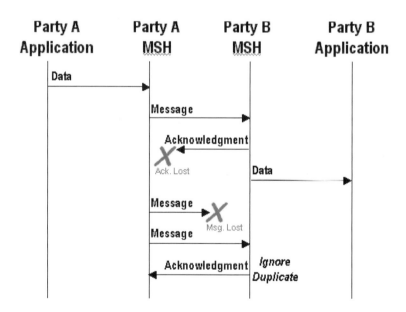

FIGURE 9-4   Resending Unacknowledged Messages

The diagram above shows the behavior that MUST be followed by the sending and *Receiving MSH* that are sent with **deliverySemantics** of **OnceAndOnlyOnce**. Specifically:

1. The sender of the message (e.g. Party A) MUST resend the "identical message" if no Acknowledgment Message is received.

2. When the recipient (Party B) of the message receives a "duplicate message", it MUST resend to the sender (Party A) a message identical to the first message that was sent to the sender Party A).

3. The recipient of the message (Party B) MUST NOT forward the message a second time to the application/process.

9.4 Failed Message Delivery

If a message sent with **deliverySemantics** set to **OnceAndOnlyOnce** cannot be delivered, the MSH or process SHOULD send a delivery failure notification to the *From Party*. The delivery failure notification message contains:

▼ a **From** element that identifies the *Party* who detected the problem

▼ a **To** element that identifies the *From Party* that created the message that could not be delivered

▼ a **Service** element and **Action** element set as described in 10.5

▼ an **Error** element with a severity of:
  ▼ **Error** if the party who detected the problem could not transmit the message (e.g. the communications transport was not available)
  ▼ Warning if the message was transmitted, but an *acknowledgment message* was not received. This means the message probably was not delivered although there is a small probability it was.
▼ an ErrorCode of DeliveryFailure

It is possible that an error message with an **Error** element with an **ErrorCode** set to **DeliveryFailure** cannot be delivered successfully for some reason. If this occurs, then the *From Party* that is the ultimate destination for the error message SHOULD be informed of the problem by other means. How this is done is outside the scope of this specification.

10 Error Reporting and Handling

This section describes how one ebXML Message Service Handler (MSH) reports errors it detects in an ebXML Message to another MSH. The *ebXML Message Service* error reporting and handling is to be considered as a layer of processing above the SOAP processor layer. This means the ebXML MSH is essentially an application-level handler of a *SOAP Message* from the perspective of the SOAP Processor. The SOAP processor MAY generate SOAP **Fault** messages if it is unable to process the message. A *Sending MSH* MUST be prepared to accept and process these SOAP **Faults.**

It is possible for the ebXML MSH software to cause a SOAP fault to be generated and returned to the sender of a SOAP *Message*. In this event, the returned message MUST conform to the [SOAP] specification processing guidelines for SOAP **Faults.**

An ebXML *SOAP Message* that reports an error that has a **highestSeverity** of **Warning** SHALL NOT be reported or returned as a SOAP **Fault.**

10.1   Definitions

For clarity, two phrases are defined that are used in this section:

▼ "message in error" - A *message* that contains or causes an error of some kind

▼ "message reporting the error" - A *message* that contains an ebXML **ErrorList** element that describes the error(s) found in a message in error.

10.2   Types of Errors

One MSH needs to report to another MSH errors in a message in error. For example, errors associated with:

▼ ebXML namespace qualified content of the *SOAP Message* document (see section 7)

▼ reliable messaging failures (see section 9)

▼ security (see section 11)

Unless specified to the contrary, all references to "an error" in the remainder of this specification imply any or all of the types of errors listed above.

Errors associated with Data Communication protocols are detected and reported using the standard mechanisms supported by that data communication protocol and do not use the error reporting mechanism described here.

10.3   When to Generate Error Messages

When a MSH detects an error in a message it is strongly RECOMMENDED that the error is reported to the MSH that sent the message that had an error if:

▼ the Error Reporting Location (see section 10.4) to which the message reporting the error should be sent can be determined, and

▼ the message in error does not have an **ErrorList** element with **highest-
  Severity** set to **Error.**

If the Error Reporting Location cannot be found or the message in error has an
ErrorList element with **highestSeverity** set to **Error,** it is RECOMMENDED that:

▼ the error is logged, and

▼ the problem is resolved by other means, and

▼ no further action is taken.

10.3.1   Security Considerations

Parties that receive a Message containing an error in the header SHOULD always
respond to the message. However, they MAY ignore the message and not respond if they consider that the message received is unauthorized or is part of
some security attack. The decision process resulting in this course of action is implementation dependent.

10.4   Identifying the Error Reporting Location

The Error Reporting Location is a URI that is specified by the sender of the message in error that indicates where to send a *message reporting the error.*

The **ErrorURI** implied by the *CPA,* identified by the **CPAId** on the message,
SHOULD be used. If no **ErrorURI** is implied by the *CPA* and a **TraceHeaderList**
is present in the message in error, the value of the **Location** element in the
Sender of the topmost **TraceHeader** MUST be used. Otherwise, the recipient
MAY resolve an **ErrorURI** using the **From** element of the message in error. If
this is not possible, no error will be reported to the sending *Party.*

Even if the message in error cannot be successfully analyzed or parsed, MSH implementers SHOULD try to determine the Error Reporting Location by other
means. How this is done is an implementation decision.

10.5   Service and Action Element Values

An **ErrorList** element can be included in a SOAP **Header** that is part of a *message*
being sent as a result of processing of an earlier message. In this case, the values
for the **Service** and **Action** elements are set by the designer of the Service.

An **ErrorList** element can also be included in an SOAP **Header** that is not being sent as a result of the processing of an earlier message. In this case, if the **highest-Severity** is set to **Error,** the values of the **Service** and **Action** elements MUST be set as follows:

▼ *The* **Service** *element MUST be set to:* **uri:www.ebxml.org/messageService/**

▼ The **Action** element MUST be set to **MessageError.**

If the **highestSeverity** is set to **Warning,** the **Service** and **Action** elements MUST NOT be used.

11 Security

The *ebXML Message Service,* by its very nature, presents certain security risks. A Message Service may be at risk by means of:

▼ Unauthorized access

▼ Data integrity and/or confidentiality attacks (e.g. through man-in-the-middle attacks)

▼ Denial-of-Service and spoofing

Each security risk is described in detail in the ebXML Technical Architecture Security Specification [ebTASEC].

Each of these security risks MAY be addressed in whole, or in part, by the application of one, or a combination, of the countermeasures described in this section. This specification describes a set of profiles, or combinations of selected countermeasures, selected to address key risks based upon commonly available technologies. Each of the specified profiles includes a description of the risks that are not addressed.

Application of countermeasures SHOULD be balanced against an assessment of the inherent risks and the value of the asset(s) that might be placed at risk.

11.1 Security and Management

No technology, regardless of how advanced it might be, is an adequate substitute to the effective application of security management policies and practices.

It is strongly RECOMMENDED that the site manager of an *ebXML Message Service* apply due diligence to the support and maintenance of its; security mechanism, site (or physical) security procedures, cryptographic protocols, update implementations and apply fixes as appropriate. (See http://www.cert.org/ and http://ciac.llnl.gov/)

11.2   Collaboration Protocol Agreement

The configuration of Security for MSHs may be specified in the *CPA*. Three areas of the *CPA* have security definitions as follows:

▼ The Document Exchange section addresses security to be applied to the payload of the message. The MSH is not responsible for any security specified at this level but may offer these services to the message sender.

▼ The Message section addresses security applied to the entire ebXML Document, which includes the header and the payload.

11.3   Countermeasure Technologies

11.3.1   Persistent Digital Signature

If signatures are being used to digitally sign an ebXML Message then XML Signature [DSIG] MUST be used to bind the ebXML SOAP **Header** and **Body** to the ebXML Payload or data elsewhere on the web that relates to the message. It is also strongly RECOMMENDED that XML Signature be used to digitally sign the Payload on its own.

The only available technology that can be applied to the purpose of digitally signing an ebXML Message (the ebXML SOAP **Header** and **Body** and its associated payload objects) is provided by technology that conforms to the W3C/IETF joint XML Signature specification [XMLDSIG]. An XML Signature conforming to this specification can selectively sign portions of an XML document(s), permitting the documents to be augmented (new element content added) while preserving the validity of the signature(s).

An ebXML Message requiring a digital signature SHALL be signed following the process defined in this section of the specification and SHALL be in full compliance with [XMLDSIG].

11.3.1.1   Signature Generation

1. Create a **ds:SignedInfo** element with **ds:SignatureMethod, ds:Canonical-izationMethod**, and **ds:Reference** elements for the SOAP **Header** and any required payload objects, as prescribed by [XMLDSIG].

2. Canonicalize and then calculate the **ds:SignatureValue** over **ds:SignedInfo** based on algorithms specified in **ds:SignedInfo** as specified in [XMLDSIG].

3. Construct the **ds:Signature** element that includes the **ds:SignedInfo, ds: KeyInfo** (RECOMMENDED), and **ds:SignatureValue** elements as specified in [XMLDSIG].

4. Include the namespace qualified **ds:Signature** element in the SOAP **Header** just signed, following the **TraceHeaderList** element.

The **ds:SignedInfo** element SHALL be composed of zero or one **ds:CanonicalizationMethod** element, the **ds:SignatureMethod** and one or more **ds:Reference** elements.

The **ds:CanonicalizationMethod** element is defined as OPTIONAL in [XMLDSIG], meaning that the element need not appear in an instance of a **ds:SignedInfo** element. The default canonicalization method that is applied to the data to be signed is [XMLC14N] in the absence of a **ds:Canonicalization** element that specifies otherwise. This default SHALL also serve as the default canonicalization method for the *ebXML Message Service*.

The **ds:SignatureMethod** element SHALL be present and SHALL have an Algorithm attribute. The RECOMMENDED value for the Algorithm attribute is:

http://www.w3.org/2000/09/xmldsig#dsa-sha1

This RECOMMENDED value SHALL be supported by all compliant *ebXML Message Service* software implementations.

The **ds:Reference** element for the SOAP **Header** document SHALL have a URI attribute value of "" to provide for the signature to be applied to the document that contains the **ds:Signature** element (the SOAP **Header**).

The **ds:Reference** element for the SOAP **Header** MAY include a **Type** attribute that has a value "http://www.w3.org/2000/09/xmldsig#Object" in accordance with [XMLDSIG]. This attribute is purely informative. It MAY be omitted. Implementations of the ebXML MSH SHALL be prepared to handle either case. The **ds:Reference** element MAY include the optional **id** attribute.

The **ds:Reference** element for the SOAP **Header** SHALL include a child **ds:Transforms** element. The **ds:Transforms** element SHALL include two **ds:Transform** child elements. The first **ds:Transform** element SHALL have a **ds:Algorithm** attribute that has a value of:

http://www.w3.org/2000/09/xmldsig#enveloped-signature

The second **ds:Transform** element SHALL have a child **ds:XPath** element that has a value of:

not(ancestor-or-self::eb:TraceHeaderList or
    ancestor-or-self::eb:Via)

The result of the first [XPath] statement excludes the **ds:Signature** element within which it is contained, and all its descendants, and the second [XPath] statement excludes the **TraceHeaderList** and **Via** elements and all their descendants, as these elements are subject to change.

Each payload object that requires signing SHALL be represented by a **ds:Reference** element that SHALL have a **URI** attribute that resolves to that payload object. This MAY be either the `Content-Id` URI of the MIME body part of the payload object, or a URI that matches the Content-Location of the MIME body part of the payload object, or a URI that resolves to an external payload object external to the Message Package. It is strongly RECOMMENDED that the URI attribute value match the xlink:href URI value of the corresponding **Manifest/Reference** element for that payload object. However, this is NOT REQUIRED.

Example of digitally signed ebXML SOAP *Message*:

```
<?xml version="1.0" encoding="utf-8"?>
<SOAP-ENV:Envelope
  xmlns:SOAP-ENV="http://schemas.xmlsoap.org/soap/envelope/"
  xmlns:eb="http://www.ebxml.org/namespaces/messageHeader"
  xmlns:xlink="http://www.w3.org/1999/xlink">
  <SOAP-ENV:Header>
    <eb:MessageHeader eb:id="…" eb:version="1.0">
    . . .
    </eb:MessageHeader>
    <eb:TraceHeaderList eb:id="…" eb:version="1.0">
      <eb:TraceHeader>
        . . .
      </eb:TraceHeader>
    </eb:TraceHeaderList>
    <ds:Signature xmlns:ds="http://www.w3.org/2000/09/xmldsig#">
      <ds:SignedInfo>
        <ds:CanonicalizationMethod Algorithm="http://www.w3.org/
TR/2000/CR-xml-c14n-20001026"/>
        <ds:SignatureMethod Algorithm="http://www.w3.org/2000/09/
xmldsig#dsa-sha1"/>
        <ds:Reference URI="">
            <Transforms>
                <Transform Algorithm="http://www.w3.org/TR/1999/
REC-xpath-19991116">
                    <XPath xmlns:dsig="http://www.w3.org/2000/09/
xmldsig#">
```

```
                                      not(ancestor-or-self::eb:TraceHeader-
List or
                                      ancestor-or-self::eb:Via)
                        </XPath>
                     </Transform>
                  </Transforms>
            <ds:DigestMethod Algorithm="http://www.w3.org/2000/09/
xmldsig#dsa-sha1"/>
            <ds:DigestValue>...</ds:DigestValue>
         </ds:Reference>
         <ds:Reference URI="cid://blahblahblah/">
         <ds:DigestMethod
Algorithm="http://www.w3.org/2000/09/xmldsig#dsa-sha1"/>
            <ds:DigestValue>...</ds:DigestValue>
         </ds:Reference>
      </ds:SignedInfo>
      <ds:SignatureValue>...</ds:SignatureValue>
      <ds:KeyInfo>...</ds:KeyInfo>
   </ds:Signature>
  </SOAP-ENV:Header>
  <SOAP-ENV:Body>
    <eb:Manifest eb:id="Mani01" eb:version="1.0">
     <eb:Reference xlink:href="cid://blahblahblah"
      xlink:role="http://ebxml.org/gci/invoice">
       <eb:Schema eb:version="1.0" eb:location="http://ebxml.org/
gci/busdocs/invoice.dtd"/>
      </eb:Reference>
     </eb:Manifest>
   </SOAP-ENV:Body>
</SOAP-ENV:Envelope>
```

11.3.2 Persistent Signed Receipt

An *ebXML Message* that has been digitally signed MAY be acknowledged with a **DeliveryReceipt** acknowledgment message that itself is digitally signed in the manner described in the previous section. The acknowledgment message MUST contain a **ds:Reference** element contained in the **ds:Signature** element of the original message within the **Acknowledgment** element.

11.3.3 Non-persistent Authentication

Non-persistent authentication is provided by the communications channel used to transport the *ebXML Message*. This authentication MAY be either in one direction, from the session initiator to the receiver, or bi-directional. The specific method will be determined by the communications protocol used. For instance, the use of a secure network protocol, such as [RFC2246] or [IPSEC] provides the sender of an *ebXML Message* with a way to authenticate the destination for the TCP/IP environment.

11.3.4   Non-persistent Integrity

Use of a secure network protocol such as [RFC2246] or [IPSEC] MAY be configured to provide for integrity check CRCs of the packets transmitted via the network connection.

11.3.5   Persistent Confidentiality

XML Encryption is a W3C/IETF joint activity that is actively engaged in the drafting of a specification for the selective encryption of an XML document(s). It is anticipated that this specification will be completed within the next year. The ebXML Transport, Routing and Packaging team has identified this technology as the only viable means of providing persistent, selective confidentiality of elements within an *ebXML Message* including the SOAP **Header.**

Confidentiality for ebXML Payloads MAY be provided by functionality possessed by a MSH. However, this specification states that it is not the responsibility of the MSH to provide security for the ebXML ````Payloads. Payload confidentiality MAY be provided by using XML Encryption (when available) or some other cryptographic process (such as [S/MIME], [S/MIMEV3], or [PGP/MIME]) bilaterally agreed upon by the parties involved. Since XML Encryption is not currently available, it is RECOMMENDED that [S/MIME] encryption methods be used for ebXML Payloads. The XML Encryption standard SHALL be the default encryption method when XML Encryption has achieved W3C Recommendation status.

11.3.6   Non-persistent Confidentiality

Use of a secure network protocol such as [RFC2246] or [IPSEC] provides transient confidentiality of a message as it is transferred between two ebXML MSH nodes.

11.3.7   Persistent Authorization

The OASIS Security Services Technical Committee (TC) is actively engaged in the definition of a specification that provides for the exchange of security credentials, including NameAssertion and Entitlements that is based on [SAML]. Use of technology that is based on this anticipated specification MAY be used to provide persistent authorization for an *ebXML Message* once it becomes available. ebXML has a formal liaison to this TC. There are also many ebXML member organizations and contributors that are active members of the OASIS Security Services TC such as Sun, IBM, CommerceOne, Cisco and others that are endeavoring to ensure that the specification meets the requirements of providing persistent authorization capabilities for the *ebXML Message Service*.

11.3.8 Non-persistent Authorization

Use of a secure network protocol such as [RFC2246] or [IPSEC] MAY be configured to provide for bilateral authentication of certificates prior to establishing a session. This provides for the ability for an ebXML MSH to authenticate the source of a connection that can be used to recognize the source as an authorized source of *ebXML Messages*.

11.3.9 Trusted Timestamp

At the time of this specification, services that offer trusted timestamp capabilities are becoming available. Once these become more widely available, and a standard has been defined for their use and expression, these standards, technologies and services will be evaluated and considered for use to provide this capability.

11.3.10 Supported Security Services

The general architecture of the ebXML Message Service Specification is intended to support all the security services required for electronic business. The following table combines the security services of the Message Service Handler into a set of security profiles. These profiles, or combinations of these profiles, support the specific security policy of the ebXML user community. Due to the immature state of XML security specifications, this version of the specification requires support for profiles 0 and 1 only. This does not preclude users from employing additional security features to protect ebXML exchanges; however, interoperability between parties using any profiles other than 0 and 1 cannot be guaranteed.

Present in baseline MSH		Persistent digital signature	Non-persistent authentication	Persistent signed receipt	Non-persistent integrity	Persistent confidentiality	Non-persistent confidentiality	Persistent authorization	Non-persistent authorization	Trusted timestamp	Description of Profile
✓	Profile 0										no security services are applied to data
✓	Profile 1	✓									*Sending MSH* applies XML/DSIG structures to message
	Profile 2		✓						✓		*Sending MSH* authenticates and *Receiving MSH* authorizes sender based on communication channel credentials.
	Profile 3		✓				✓				*Sending MSH* authenticates and both MSHs negotiate a secure channel to transmit data
	Profile 4		✓		✓						*Sending MSH* authenticates, the *Receiving MSH* performs integrity checks using communications protocol
	Profile 5		✓								*Sending MSH* authenticates the communication channel only (e.g., SSL 3.0 over TCP/IP)
	Profile 6	✓					✓				*Sending MSH* applies XML/DSIG structures to message and passes in secure communications channel
	Profile 7	✓		✓							*Sending MSH* applies XML/DSIG structures to message and *Receiving MSH* returns a signed receipt
	Profile 8	✓		✓			✓				combination of profile 6 and 7
	Profile 9	✓								✓	Profile 5 with a trusted timestamp applied
	Profile 10	✓		✓						✓	Profile 9 with *Receiving MSH* returning a signed receipt
	Profile 11	✓					✓			✓	Profile 6 with the *Receiving MSH* applying a trusted timestamp

Present in baseline MSH		Persistent digital signature	Non-persistent authentication	Persistent signed receipt	Non-persistent integrity	Persistent confidentiality	Non-persistent confidentiality	Persistent authorization	Non-persistent authorization	Trusted timestamp	Description of Profile
	Profile 12	✓		✓		✓				✓	Profile 8 with the *Receiving MSH* applying a trusted timestamp
	Profile 13	✓				✓					*Sending MSH* applies XML/DSIG structures to message and applies confidentiality structures (XML-Encryption)
	Profile 14	✓		✓		✓					Profile 13 with a signed receipt
	Profile 15	✓		✓						✓	*Sending MSH* applies XML/DSIG structures to message, a trusted timestamp is added to message, *Receiving MSH* returns a signed receipt
	Profile 16	✓				✓				✓	Profile 13 with a trusted timestamp applied
	Profile 17	✓		✓		✓				✓	Profile 14 with a trusted timestamp applied
	Profile 18	✓						✓			*Sending MSH* applies XML/DSIG structures to message and forwards authorization credentials [SAML]
	Profile 19	✓		✓				✓			Profile 18 with *Receiving MSH* returning a signed receipt
	Profile 20	✓		✓				✓		✓	Profile 19 with the a trusted timestamp being applied to the *Sending MSH* message
	Profile 21	✓		✓		✓		✓		✓	Profile 19 with the *Sending MSH* applying confidentiality structures (XML-Encryption)
	Profile 22					✓					*Sending MSH* encapsulates the message within confidentiality structures (XML-Encryption)

12   References

12.1   Normative References

[RFC2119] Key Words for use in RFCs to Indicate Requirement Levels, Internet Engineering Task Force RFC 2119, March 1997

[HTTP] IETF RFC 2068 - Hypertext Transfer Protocol — HTTP/1.1, R. Fielding, J. Gettys, J. Mogul, H. Frystyk, T. Berners-Lee, January 1997

[RFC822] Standard for the Format of ARPA Internet text messages. D. Crocker. August 1982.

[RFC2045] IETF RFC 2045. Multipurpose Internet Mail Extensions (MIME) Part One: Format of Internet Message Bodies, N Freed & N Borenstein, Published November 1996

[RFC2046] Multipurpose Internet Mail Extensions (MIME) Part Two: Media Types. N. Freed, N. Borenstein. November 1996.

[RFC2246] RFC 2246 - Dierks, T. and C. Allen, "The TLS Protocol", January 1999.

[RFC2387] The MIME Multipart/Related Content-type. E. Levinson. August 1998.

[RFC2392] IETF RFC 2392. Content-ID and Message-ID Uniform Resource Locators. E. Levinson, Published August 1998

[RFC2396] IETF RFC 2396. Uniform Resource Identifiers (URI): Generic Syntax. T Berners-Lee, Published August 1998

[RFC2487] SMTP Service Extension for Secure SMTP over TLS. P. Hoffman. January 1999.

[RFC2554] SMTP Service Extension for Authentication. J. Myers. March 1999.

[RFC2616] RFC 2616 - Fielding, R., Gettys, J., Mogul, J., Frystyk, H., Masinter, L., Leach, P. and T. Berners-Lee, "Hypertext Transfer Protocol, HTTP/1.1", , June 1999.

[RFC2617] RFC2617 - Franks, J., Hallam-Baker, P., Hostetler, J., Lawrence, S., Leach, P., Luotonen, A., Sink, E. and L. Stewart, "HTTP Authentication: Basic and Digest Access Authentication", June 1999.

[RFC2817] RFC 2817 - Khare, R. and S. Lawrence, "Upgrading to TLS Within HTTP/1.1", May 2000.

[RFC2818] RFC 2818 - Rescorla, E., "HTTP Over TLS", May 2000 [SOAP] Simple Object Access Protocol

[SMTP] IETF RFC 822, Simple Mail Transfer Protocol, D Crocker, August 1982

[SOAP] W3C-Draft-Simple Object Access Protocol (SOAP) v1.1, Don Box, DevelopMentor; David Ehnebuske, IBM; Gopal Kakivaya, Andrew Layman, Henrik Frystyk Nielsen, Satish Thatte, Microsoft; Noah Mendelsohn, Lotus Development Corp.; Dave Winer, UserLand Software, Inc.; W3C Note 08 May 2000, http://www.w3.org/TR/SOAP

[SOAPATTACH] SOAP Messages with Attachments, John J. Barton, Hewlett Packard Labs; Satish Thatte and Henrik Frystyk Nielsen, Microsoft, Published Oct 09 2000 http://www.w3.org/TR/SOAP-attachments

[SSL3] A. Frier, P. Karlton, and P. Kocher, "The SSL 3.0 Protocol", Netscape Communications Corp., Nov 18, 1996.

[UTF-8] UTF-8 is an encoding that conforms to ISO/IEC 10646. See [XML] for usage conventions.

[XLINK] W3C XML Linking Candidate Recommendation, http://www.w3.org/TR/xlink/

[XML] W3C Recommendation: Extensible Markup Language (XML) 1.0 (Second Edition), October 2000, http://www.w3.org/TR/2000/REC-xml-20001006

[XML Namespace] W3C Recommendation for Namespaces in XML, World Wide Web Consortium, 14 January 1999, http://www.w3.org/TR/REC-xml-names

[XMLDSIG] Joint W3C/IETF XML-Signature Syntax and Processing specification, http://www.w3.org/TR/2000/CR-xmldsig-core-20001031/

[XMLMedia] IETF RFC 3023, XML Media Types. M. Murata, S. St.Laurent, January 2001

12.2   Non-normative References

[ebCPP] ebXML Collaboration Protocol Profile and Agreement specification, Version 1.0, published 11 May, 2001

[ebBPSS] ebXML Business Process Specification Schema, version 1.0, published 11 May 2001.

[ebTA] ebXML Technical Architecture, version 1.04 published 16 February, 2001

[secRISK] ebXML Technical Architecture Risk Assessment Technical Report, version 1.0 published 11 May 2001

[ebRS] ebXML Registry Services Specification, version 1.0

[ebMSREQ] ebXML Transport, Routing and Packaging: Overview and Requirements, Version 0.96, Published 25 May 2000 [ebGLOSS] ebXML Glossary, http://www.ebxml.org, published 11 May, 2001.

[IPSEC] IETF RFC2402 IP Authentication Header. S. Kent, R. Atkinson. November 1998. RFC2406 IP Encapsulating Security Payload (ESP). S. Kent, R. Atkinson. November 1998.

[PGP/MIME] IETF RFC2015, "MIME Security with Pretty Good Privacy (PGP)", M. Elkins. October 1996.

[SAML] Security Assertion Markup Language, http://www.oasis-open.org/committees/security/docs/draft-sstc-use-strawman-03.html

[S/MIME] IETF RFC2311, "S/MIME Version 2 Message Specification", S. Dusse, P. Hoffman, B. Ramsdell, L. Lundblade, L. Repka. March 1998.

[S/MIMECH] IETF RFC 2312, "S/MIME Version 2 Certificate Handling", S. Dusse, P. Hoffman, B. Ramsdell, J. Weinstein. March 1998.

[S/MIMEV3] IETF RFC 2633 S/MIME Version 3 Message Specification. B. Ramsdell, Ed.. June 1999.

[TLS] RFC2246, T. Dierks, C. Allen. January 1999.

[XMLSchema] W3C XML Schema Candidate Recommendation,
http://www.w3.org/TR/xmlschema-0/
http://www.w3.org/TR/xmlschema-1/
http://www.w3.org/TR/xmlschema-2/

[XMTP] XMTP - Extensible Mail Transport Protocol
http://www.openhealth.org/documents/xmtp.htm

13 Contact Information

Team Leader

Name	Rik Drummond
Company	Drummond Group, Inc.
Street	5008 Bentwood Ct.
City, State, Postal Code	Fort Worth, Texas 76132
Country	USA
Phone	+1 (817) 294-7339
EMail:	rik@drummondgroup.com

Vice Team Leader

Name	Christopher Ferris
Company	Sun Microsystems
Street	One Network Drive
City, State, Postal Code	Burlington, MA 01803-0903
Country	USA
Phone:	+1 (781) 442-3063
EMail:	chris.ferris@sun.com

Team Editor

Name	David Burdett
Company	Commerce One
Street	4400 Rosewood Drive
City, State, Postal Code	Pleasanton, CA 94588
Country	USA
Phone:	+1 (925) 520-4422
EMail:	david.burdett@commerceone.com

Authors

Name	Dick Brooks
Company	Group 8760
Street	110 12th Street North, Suite F103
City, State, Postal Code	Birmingham, Alabama 35203
Phone:	+1 (205) 250-8053
Email:	dick@8760.com
Name	David Burdett
Company	Commerce One
Street	4400 Rosewood Drive
City, State, Postal Code	Pleasanton, CA 94588
Country	USA
Phone:	+1 (925) 520-4422
EMail:	david.burdett@commerceone.com
Name	Christopher Ferris
Company	Sun Microsystems

Street	One Network Drive
City, State, Postal Code	Burlington, MA 01803-0903
Country	USA
Phone:	+1 (781) 442-3063
EMail:	chris.ferris@east.sun.com
Name	John Ibbotson
Company	IBM UK Ltd
Street	Hursley Park
City, State, Postal Code	Winchester SO21 2JN
Country	United Kingdom
Phone:	+44 (1962) 815188
Email:	john_ibbotson@uk.ibm.com
Name	Masayoshi Shimamura
Company	Fujitsu Limited
Street	Shinyokohama Nikko Bldg., 15-16, Shinyokohama 2-chome
City, State, Postal Code	Kohoku-ku, Yokohama 222-0033, Japan
Phone:	+81-45-476-4590
EMail:	shima@rp.open.cs.fujitsu.co.jp

Document Editing Team

Name	Ralph Berwanger
Company	bTrade.com
Street	2324 Gateway Drive
City, State, Postal Code	Irving, TX 75063
Country	USA
Phone:	+1 (972) 580-3970
EMail:	rberwanger@btrade.com
Name	Colleen Evans
Company	Progress/Sonic Software
Street	14 Oak Park
City, State, Postal Code	Bedford, MA 01730
Country	USA

Phone	+1 (720) 480-3919
Email	cevans@progress.com
Name	Ian Jones
Company	British Telecommunications
Street	Enterprise House, 84-85 Adam Street
City, State, Postal Code	Cardiff, CF24 2XF
Country	United Kingdom
Phone:	+44 29 2072 4063
EMail:	ian.c.jones@bt.com
Name	Martha Warfelt
Company	DaimlerChrysler Corporation
Street	800 Chrysler Drive
City, State, Postal Code	Auburn Hills, MI
Country	USA
Phone:	+1 (248) 944-5481
EMail:	maw2@daimlerchrysler.com
Name	David Fischer
Company	Drummond Group, Inc
Street	5008 Bentwood Ct
City, State, Postal Code	Fort Worth, TX 76132
Phone	+1 (817-294-7339
EMail	david@drummondgroup.com

14   Disclaimer

The views and specification expressed in this document are those of the authors and are not necessarily those of their employers. The authors and their employers specifically disclaim responsibility for any problems arising from correct or incorrect implementation or use of this design.

Appendix A   ebXML SOAP Extension Elements Schema

The ebXML SOAP extension elements schema has been specified using the Candidate Recommendation draft of the XML Schema specification[XMLSchema]. Because ebXML has adopted SOAP 1.1 for the message format, and because the SOAP 1.1 schema resolved by the SOAP 1.1 namespace URI was written to an earlier draft of the XML Schema specification, the ebXML TRP team has created a version of the SOAP 1.1 envelope schema that is specified using the schema vocabulary that conforms to the W3C XML Schema Candidate Recommendation specification[XMLSchema].

In addition, it was necessary to craft a schema for the [XLINK] attribute vocabulary and for the XML xml:lang attribute.

Finally, because certain authoring tools do not correctly resolve local entities when importing schema, a version of the W3C XML Signature Core schema has also been provided and referenced by the ebXML SOAP extension elements schema defined in this Appendix.

These alternative schema SHALL be available from the following URL's:

XML Signature Core – http://ebxml.org/project_teams/transport/xmldsig-core-schema.xsd

Xlink - http://ebxml.org/project_teams/transport/xlink.xsd

xml:lang - http://ebxml.org/project_teams/transport/xml_lang.xsd

SOAP1.1 - http://ebxml.org/project_teams/transport/envelope.xsd

> **If inconsistencies exist between the specification and this schema, the specification supersedes this example schema.**

Note

```
<?xml version="1.0" encoding="UTF-8"?>
<schema targetNamespace="http://www.ebxml.org/namespaces/message-
Header" xmlns:xml="http://www.w3.org/XML/1998/namespace"
xmlns:tns="http://www.ebxml.org/namespaces/messageHeader"
xmlns:ds="http://www.w3.org/2000/09/xmldsig#"
xmlns:xlink="http://www.w3.org/1999/xlink"
xmlns:soap="http://schemas.xmlsoap.org/soap/envelope/"
xmlns="http://www.w3.org/2000/10/XMLSchema" version="1.0">
```

```
  <import namespace="http://www.w3.org/2000/09/xmldsig#"
schemaLocation="http://www.ebxml.org/project_teams/transport/
xmldsig-core-schema.xsd"/>
  <import namespace="http://www.w3.org/1999/xlink"
schemaLocation="http://www.ebxml.org/project_teams/transport/
xlink.xsd"/>
  <import namespace="http://schemas.xmlsoap.org/soap/envelope/"
schemaLocation="http://www.ebxml.org/project_teams/transport/
envelope.xsd"/>
  <import namespace="http://www.w3.org/XML/1998/namespace"
schemaLocation="http://www.ebxml.org/project_teams/transport/xml_l
ang.xsd"/>
  <!-- MANIFEST -->
  <element name="Manifest">
    <complexType>
      <sequence>
        <element ref="tns:Reference" maxOccurs="unbounded"/>
        <any namespace="##other" processContents="lax" min-
Occurs="0" maxOccurs="unbounded"/>
      </sequence>
      <attribute ref="tns:id"/>
      <attribute ref="tns:version"/>
      <anyAttribute namespace="http://www.w3.org/2000/10/
XMLSchema-instance"
          processContents="lax"/>
    </complexType>
  </element>
  <element name="Reference">
    <complexType>
      <sequence>
        <element ref="tns:Schema" minOccurs="0" maxOccurs=
"unbounded"/>
        <element ref="tns:Description" minOccurs="0"
maxOccurs="unbounded"/>
        <any namespace="##other" processContents="lax" min-
Occurs="0" maxOccurs="unbounded"/>
      </sequence>
      <attribute ref="tns:id"/>
      <attribute ref="xlink:type" use="fixed" value="simple"/>
      <attribute ref="xlink:href" use="required"/>
      <attribute ref="xlink:role"/>
    </complexType>
  </element>
  <element name="Schema">
    <complexType>
      <attribute name="location" type="uriReference" use=
"required"/>
```

```
       <attribute name="version" type="tns:non-empty-string"/>
    </complexType>
  </element>
  <!-- MESSAGEHEADER -->
  <element name="MessageHeader">
    <complexType>
      <sequence>
        <element ref="tns:From"/>
        <element ref="tns:To"/>
        <element ref="tns:CPAId"/>
        <element ref="tns:ConversationId"/>
        <element ref="tns:Service"/>
        <element ref="tns:Action"/>
        <element ref="tns:MessageData"/>
        <element ref="tns:QualityOfServiceInfo" minOccurs="0"/>
        <element ref="tns:Description" minOccurs="0" maxOccurs=
"unbounded"/>
        <element ref="tns:SequenceNumber" minOccurs="0"/>
      </sequence>
      <attribute ref="tns:id"/>
      <attribute ref="tns:version"/>
      <attribute ref="soap:mustUnderstand"/>
      <anyAttribute namespace="http://www.w3.org/2000/10/
XMLSchema-instance" processContents="lax"/>
    </complexType>
  </element>
  <element name="CPAId" type="tns:non-empty-string"/>
  <element name="ConversationId" type="tns:non-empty-string"/>
  <element name="Service">
    <complexType>
      <simpleContent>
        <extension base="tns:non-empty-string">
          <attribute name="type" type="tns:non-empty-string"/>
        </extension>
      </simpleContent>
    </complexType>
  </element>
  <element name="Action" type="tns:non-empty-string"/>
  <element name="MessageData">
    <complexType>
      <sequence>
        <element ref="tns:MessageId"/>
        <element ref="tns:Timestamp"/>
        <element ref="tns:RcfToMessageId" minOccurs-"0"/>
        <element ref="tns:TimeToLive" minOccurs="0"/>
      </sequence>
    </complexType>
```

```
    </element>
    <element name="MessageId" type="tns:non-empty-string"/>
    <element name="TimeToLive" type="timeInstant"/>
    <element name="QualityOfServiceInfo">
      <complexType>
        <attribute name="deliverySemantics" type="tns:delivery-
Semantics.type" use="default"
          value="BestEffort"/>
        <attribute name="messageOrderSemantics" type="tns:message-
OrderSemantics.type"
          use="default" value="NotGuaranteed"/>
        <attribute name="deliveryReceiptRequested" type="tns:signed-
Unsigned.type"
          use="default" value="None"/>
      </complexType>
    </element>
    <!-- TRACE HEADER LIST -->
    <element name="TraceHeaderList">
      <complexType>
        <sequence>
          <element ref="tns:TraceHeader" maxOccurs="unbounded"/>
        </sequence>
        <attribute ref="tns:id"/>
        <attribute ref="tns:version"/>
        <attribute ref="soap:mustUnderstand" use="required"/>
        <attribute ref="soap:actor" use="required"/>
        <anyAttribute namespace="http://www.w3.org/2000/10/
XMLSchema-instance"
          processContents="lax"/>
      </complexType>
    </element>
    <element name="TraceHeader">
      <complexType>
        <sequence>
          <element ref="tns:Sender"/>
          <element ref="tns:Receiver"/>
          <element ref="tns:Timestamp"/>
          <any namespace="##other" processContents="lax" min-
Occurs="0" maxOccurs="unbounded"/>
        </sequence>
        <attribute ref="tns:id"/>
      </complexType>
    </element>
    <element name="Sender" type="tns:senderReceiver.type"/>
    <element name="Receiver" type="tns:senderReceiver.type"/>
    <element name="SequenceNumber" type="positiveInteger"/>
    <!-- DELIVERY RECEIPT -->
```

```
  <element name="DeliveryReceipt">
    <complexType>
      <sequence>
        <element ref="tns:Timestamp"/>
        <element ref="ds:Reference" minOccurs="0" maxOccurs=
"unbounded"/>
      </sequence>
      <attribute ref="tns:id"/>
      <attribute ref="tns:version"/>
      <anyAttribute namespace="http://www.w3.org/2000/10/
XMLSchema-instance"
          processContents="lax"/>
      <!-- <attribute name="signed" type="boolean"/> -->
    </complexType>
  </element>
  <!-- ACKNOWLEDGEMENT -->
  <element name="Acknowledgment">
    <complexType>
      <sequence>
        <element ref="tns:Timestamp"/>
        <element ref="tns:From" minOccurs="0"/>
        <element ref="ds:Reference" minOccurs="0" maxOccurs=
"unbounded"/>
      </sequence>
      <attribute ref="tns:id"/>
      <attribute ref="tns:version"/>
      <attribute ref="soap:mustUnderstand" use="required"/>
      <attribute ref="soap:actor" use="required"/>
      <anyAttribute namespace="http://www.w3.org/2000/10/
XMLSchema-instance"
        processContents="lax"/>
    </complexType>
  </element>
  <!-- ERROR LIST -->
  <element name="ErrorList">
    <complexType>
      <sequence>
        <element ref="tns:Error" maxOccurs="unbounded"/>
      </sequence>
      <attribute ref="tns:id"/>
      <attribute ref="tns:version"/>
      <attribute ref="soap:mustUnderstand" use="required"/>
      <attribute name="highestSeverity" type="tns:severity.type"
        use="default" value="Warning"/>
      <anyAttribute namespace="http://www.w3.org/2000/10/
XMLSchema-instance"
        processContents="lax"/>
```

```
        </complexType>
      </element>
      <element name="Error">
        <complexType>
          <attribute ref="tns:id"/>
          <attribute name="codeContext" type="uriReference" use=
"required"/>
          <attribute name="errorCode" type="tns:non empty string"
use="required"/>
          <attribute name="severity" type="tns:severity.type" use=
"default" value="Warning"/>
          <attribute name="location" type="tns:non-empty-string"/>
          <attribute ref="xml:lang"/>
        </complexType>
      </element>
      <!-- STATUS RESPONSE -->
      <element name="StatusResponse">
        <complexType>
          <sequence>
            <element ref="tns:RefToMessageId"/>
            <element ref="tns:Timestamp" minOccurs="0"/>
          </sequence>
          <attribute ref="tns:id"/>
          <attribute ref="tns:version"/>
          <attribute name="messageStatus" type="tns:messageStatus.
type"/>
          <anyAttribute namespace="http://www.w3.org/2000/10/
XMLSchema-instance"
             processContents="lax"/>
        </complexType>
      </element>
      <!-- STATUS REQUEST -->
      <element name="StatusRequest">
        <complexType>
          <sequence>
            <element ref="tns:RefToMessageId"/>
          </sequence>
          <attribute ref="tns:id"/>
          <attribute ref="tns:version"/>
          <anyAttribute namespace="http://www.w3.org/2000/10/
XMLSchema-instance"
             processContents="lax"/>
        </complexType>
      </element>
      <!-- VIA -->
      <element name="Via">
        <complexType>
```

```
      <sequence>
        <element ref="tns:CPAId" minOccurs="0"/>
        <element ref="tns:Service" minOccurs="0"/>
        <element ref="tns:Action" minOccurs="0"/>
      </sequence>
      <attribute ref="tns:id"/>
      <attribute ref="tns:version"/>
      <attribute ref="soap:mustUnderstand" use="required"/>
      <attribute ref="soap:actor" use="required"/>
      <attribute name="syncReply" type="boolean"/>
      <attribute name="deliveryReceiptRequested" type="tns:signed-
Unsigned.type"
        use="default" value="None"/>
      <attribute name="reliableMessagingMethod"
type="tns:rmm.type"/>
      <attribute name="ackRequested" type="boolean"/>
      <anyAttribute namespace="http://www.w3.org/2000/10/
XMLSchema-instance"
        processContents="lax"/>
    </complexType>
  </element>
  <!-- COMMON TYPES -->
  <complexType name="senderReceiver.type">
    <sequence>
      <element ref="tns:PartyId" maxOccurs="unbounded"/>
      <element name="Location" type="uriReference"/>
    </sequence>
  </complexType>
  <simpleType name="messageStatus.type">
    <restriction base="NMTOKEN">
      <enumeration value="UnAuthorized"/>
      <enumeration value="NotRecognized"/>
      <enumeration value="Received"/>
      <enumeration value="Processed"/>
      <enumeration value="Forwarded"/>
    </restriction>
  </simpleType>
  <simpleType name="type.type">
    <restriction base="NMTOKEN">
      <enumeration value="DeliveryReceipt"/>
      <enumeration value="IntermediateAck"/>
    </restriction>
  </simpleType>
  <simpleType name="messageOrderSemantics.type">
    <restriction base="NMTOKEN">
      <enumeration value="Guaranteed"/>
      <enumeration value="NotGuaranteed"/>
```

```
        </restriction>
      </simpleType>
      <simpleType name="deliverySemantics.type">
        <restriction base="NMTOKEN">
          <enumeration value="OnceAndOnlyOnce"/>
          <enumeration value="BestEffort"/>
        </restriction>
      </simpleType>
      <simpleType name="non-empty-string">
        <restriction base="string">
          <minLength value="1"/>
        </restriction>
      </simpleType>
      <simpleType name="rmm.type">
        <restriction base="NMTOKEN">
          <enumeration value="ebXML"/>
          <enumeration value="Transport"/>
        </restriction>
      </simpleType>
      <simpleType name="signedUnsigned.type">
        <restriction base="NMTOKEN">
          <enumeration value="Signed"/>
          <enumeration value="Unsigned"/>
          <enumeration value="None"/>
        </restriction>
      </simpleType>
      <simpleType name="severity.type">
        <restriction base="NMTOKEN">
          <enumeration value="Warning"/>
          <enumeration value="Error"/>
        </restriction>
      </simpleType>
      <!-- COMMON ATTRIBUTES and ELEMENTS -->
      <attribute name="id" type="ID" form="unqualified"/>
      <attribute name="version" type="tns:non-empty-string"
    use="fixed" value="1.0"/>
      <element name="PartyId">
        <complexType>
          <simpleContent>
            <extension base="tns:non-empty-string">
              <attribute name="type" type="tns:non-empty-string"/>
            </extension>
          </simpleContent>
        </complexType>
      </element>
      <element name="To">
        <complexType>
```

```
      <sequence>
        <element ref="tns:PartyId" maxOccurs="unbounded"/>
      </sequence>
    </complexType>
  </element>
  <element name="From">
    <complexType>
      <sequence>
        <element ref="tns:PartyId" maxOccurs="unbounded"/>
      </sequence>
    </complexType>
  </element>
  <element name="Description">
    <complexType>
      <simpleContent>
        <extension base="tns:non-empty-string">
          <attribute ref="xml:lang"/>
        </extension>
      </simpleContent>
    </complexType>
  </element>
  <element name="RefToMessageId" type="tns:non-empty-string"/>
  <element name="Timestamp" type="timeInstant"/>
</schema>
```

Appendix B   Communication Protocol Bindings

Introduction

One of the goals of ebXML's Transport, Routing and Packaging team is to design a message handling service usable over a variety of network and application level communication protocols. These protocols serve as the "carrier" of ebXML Messages and provide the underlying services necessary to carry out a complete ebXML Message exchange between two parties. HTTP, FTP, Java Message Service (JMS) and SMTP are examples of application level communication protocols. TCP and SNA/LU6.2 are examples of network transport protocols. Communication protocols vary in their support for data content, processing behavior and error handling and reporting. For example, it is customary to send binary data in raw form over HTTP. However, in the case of SMTP it is customary to "encode" binary data into a 7-bit representation. HTTP is equally capable of carrying out *synchronous* or *asynchronous* message exchanges whereas it is likely that message exchanges occurring over SMTP will be *asynchronous*. This section describes the technical details needed to implement this abstract ebXML Message Handling Service over particular communication protocols.

This section specifies communication protocol bindings and technical details for carrying *ebXML Message Service* messages for the following communication protocols:

▼ Hypertext Transfer Protocol [HTTP], in both *asynchronous* and *synchronous* forms of transfer.

▼ Simple Mail Transfer Protocol [SMTP], in *asynchronous* form of transfer only.

HTTP

Minimum Level of HTTP Protocol

Hypertext Transfer Protocol Version 1.1 [HTTP] (http://www.ietf.org/rfc2616.txt) is the minimum level of protocol that MUST be used.

Sending ebXML Service Messages over HTTP

Even though several HTTP request methods are available, this specification only defines the use of HTTP POST requests for sending *ebXML Message Service* messages over HTTP. The identity of the ebXML MSH (e.g. ebxmlhandler) may be part of the HTTP POST request:

```
POST /ebxmlhandler HTTP/1.1
```

Prior to sending over HTTP, an ebXML Message MUST be formatted according to ebXML Message Service Specification sections 6 and **7**. Additionally, the messages MUST conform to the HTTP specific MIME canonical form constraints specified in section 19.4 of RFC 2616 [HTTP] specification (see: http://www.ietf.org/rfc2616.txt).

HTTP protocol natively supports 8-bit and Binary data. Hence, transfer encoding is OPTIONAL for such parts in an ebXML Service Message prior to sending over HTTP. However, content-transfer-encoding of such parts (e.g. using base64 encoding scheme) is not precluded by this specification.

The rules for forming an HTTP message containing an ebXML Service Message are as follows:

▼ The **Content-Type: Multipart/Related** MIME header with the associated parameters, from the ebXML Service Message Envelope MUST appear as an HTTP header.

▼ All other MIME headers that constitute the ebXML Message Envelope MUST also become part of the HTTP header.

▼ The mandatory SOAPAction HTTP header field must also be included in the HTTP header and MAY have a value of "ebXML"

SOAPAction: **"ebXML"**

▼ Other headers with semantics defined by MIME specifications, such as Content-Transfer-Encoding, SHALL NOT appear as HTTP headers. Specifically, the "MIME-Version: 1.0" header MUST NOT appear as an HTTP header. However, HTTP-specific MIME-like headers defined by HTTP 1.1 MAY be used with the semantic defined in the HTTP specification.

▼ All ebXML Service Message parts that follow the ebXML Message Envelope, including the MIME boundary string, constitute the HTTP entity body. This encompasses the SOAP **Envelope** and the constituent ebXML parts and attachments including the trailing MIME boundary strings.

The example below shows an example instance of an HTTP POST'ed ebXML Service Message:

```
POST /servlet/ebXMLhandler HTTP/1.1
Host: www.example2.com
SOAPAction: "ebXML"
Content-type: multipart/related; boundary="BoundarY";
type="text/xml";
      start=" <ebxhmheader111@example.com>"

--BoundarY
Content-ID: <ebxhmheader111@example.com>
Content-Type: text/xml

<?xml version="1.0" encoding="UTF-8"?>
<SOAP-ENV:Envelope xmlns:SOAP-ENV='http://schemas.xmlsoap.org/
soap/envelope/'
  xmlns:eb='http://www.ebxml.org/namespaces/messageHeader'>
<SOAP-ENV:Header>
  <eb:MessageHeader SOAP-ENV:mustUnderstand="1" eb:version="1.0">
    <eb:From>
      <cb:PartyId>urn:duns:123456789</eb:PartyId>
    </eb:From>
    <eb:To>
      <eb:PartyId>urn:duns:912345678</eb:PartyId>
```

```
    </eb:To>
    <eb:CPAId>20001209-133003-28572</eb:CPAId>
    <eb:ConversationId>20001209-133003-28572</eb:ConversationId>
    <eb:Service>urn:services:SupplierOrderProcessing</eb:Service>
    <eb:Action>NewOrder</eb:Action>
    <eb:MessageData>
       <eb:MessageId>20001209-133003-28572@example.com</eb:MessageId>
       <eb:Timestamp>2001-02-15T11:12:12Z</Timestamp>
    </eb:MessageData>
    <eb:QualityOfServiceInfo eb:deliverySemantics="BestEffort"/>
  </eb:MessageHeader>
</SOAP-ENV:Header>
<SOAP-ENV:Body>
  <eb:Manifest SOAP-ENV:mustUnderstand="1" eb:version="1.0">
    <eb:Reference xlink:href="cid:ebxmlpayload111@example.com"
        xlink:role="XLinkRole"
        xlink:type="simple">
        <eb:Description xml:lang="en-us">Purchase Order 1</eb:
Description>
    </eb:Reference>
  </eb:Manifest>
</SOAP-ENV:Body>
</SOAP-ENV:Envelope>

--BoundarY
Content-ID: <ebxmlpayload111@example.com>
Content-Type: text/xml

<?xml version="1.0" encoding="UTF-8"?>
<purchase_order>
  <po_number>1</po_number>
  <part_number>123</part_number>
  <price currency="USD">500.00</price>
</purchase_order>

--BoundarY--
```

HTTP Response Codes

In general, semantics of communicating over HTTP as specified in the [RFC2616]
MUST be followed, for returning the HTTP level response codes. A 2xx code
MUST be returned when the HTTP Posted message is successfully received by
the receiving HTTP entity. However, see exception for SOAP error conditions
below. Similarly, other HTTP codes in the 3xx, 4xx, 5xx range MAY be returned
for conditions corresponding to them. However, error conditions encountered

while processing an ebXML Service Message MUST be reported using the error
mechanism defined by the ebXML Message Service Specification (see section 10).

SOAP Error Conditions and Synchronous Exchanges

The SOAP 1.1 specification states:

> *"In case of a SOAP error while processing the request, the SOAP HTTP server
> MUST issue an HTTP 500 "Internal Server Error" response and include a SOAP
> message in the response containing a SOAP Fault element indicating the SOAP
> processing error. "*

However, the scope of the SOAP 1.1 specification is limited to *synchronous* mode
of message exchange over HTTP, whereas the ebXML Message Service Specification specifies both *synchronous* and *asynchronous* modes of message exchange
over HTTP. Hence, the SOAP 1.1 specification MUST be followed for *synchronous*
mode of message exchange, where the SOAP *Message* containing a SOAP **Fault**
element indicating the SOAP processing error MUST be returned in the HTTP response with a response code of "HTTP 500 Internal Server Error". When *asynchronous* mode of message exchange is being used, a HTTP response code in the
range 2xx MUST be returned when the message is received successfully and any
error conditions (including SOAP errors) must be returned via a separate HTTP
Post.

Synchronous vs. Asynchronous

When the **syncReply** parameter in the **Via** element is set to "true", the response
message(s) MUST be returned on the same HTTP connection as the inbound request, with an appropriate HTTP response code, as described above. When the
syncReply parameter is set to "false", the response messages are not returned on
the same HTTP connection as the inbound request, but using an independent
HTTP Post request. An HTTP response with a response code as defined in
"HTTP response codes," above, and with an empty HTTP body MUST be returned in response to the HTTP Post.

Access Control

Implementers MAY protect their ebXML Message Service Handlers from unauthorized access through the use of an access control mechanism. The HTTP access authentication process described in "HTTP Authentication: Basic and Digest
Access Authentication" [RFC2617] defines the access control mechanisms allowed to protect an ebXML Message Service Handler from unauthorized access.

Implementers MAY support all of the access control schemes defined in
[RFC2617] however they MUST support the Basic Authentication mechanism,
as described in section 2, when Access Control is used.

Implementers that use basic authentication for access control SHOULD also use communication protocol level security, as specified in the section titled "Confidentiality and Communication Protocol Level Security" in this document.

Confidentiality and Communication Protocol Level Security

An ebXML Message Service Handler MAY use transport layer encryption to protect the confidentiality of ebXML Messages and HTTP transport headers. The IETF Transport Layer Security specification [RFC2246] provides the specific technical details and list of allowable options, which may be used by ebXML Message Service Handlers. ebXML Message Service Handlers MUST be capable of operating in backwards compatibility mode with SSL [SSL3], as defined in Appendix E of [RFC2246].

ebXML Message Service Handlers MAY use any of the allowable encryption algorithms and key sizes specified within [RFC2246]. At a minimum ebXML Message Service Handlers MUST support the key sizes and algorithms necessary for backward compatibility with [SSL3].

The use of 40-bit encryption keys/algorithms is permitted, however it is RECOMMENDED that stronger encryption keys/algorithms SHOULD be used.

Both [RFC2246] and [SSL3] require the use of server side digital certificates. In addition client side certificate based authentication is also permitted. ebXML Message Service handlers MUST support hierarchical and peer-to-peer trust models.

SMTP

The Simple Mail Transfer Protocol [SMTP] and its companion documents [RFC822] and [ESMTP] makeup the suite of specifications commonly referred to as Internet Electronic Mail. These specifications have been augmented over the years by other specifications, which define additional functionality "layered on top" of these baseline specifications. These include:

▼ Multipurpose Internet Mail Extensions (MIME) [RFC2045], [RFC2046], [RFC2387]

▼ SMTP Service Extension for Authentication [RFC2554]

▼ SMTP Service Extension for Secure SMTP over TLS [RFC2487]

Typically, Internet Electronic Mail Implementations consist of two "agent" types:

▼ Message Transfer Agent (MTA): Programs that send and receive mail messages with other MTA's on behalf of MUA's. Microsoft Exchange Server is an example of a MTA

▼ Mail User Agent (MUA): Electronic Mail programs are used to construct electronic mail messages and communicate with an MTA to send/retrieve mail messages. Microsoft Outlook is an example of a MUA.

MTA's often serve as "mail hubs" and can typically service hundreds or more MUA's.

MUA's are responsible for constructing electronic mail messages in accordance with the Internet Electronic Mail Specifications identified above. This section describes the "binding" of an ebXML compliant message for transport via eMail from the perspective of a MUA. No attempt is made to define the binding of an ebXML Message exchange over SMTP from the standpoint of a MTA.

Minimum Level of Supported Protocols

▼ Simple Mail Transfer Protocol [RFC821] and [RFC822]

▼ MIME [RFC2045] and [RFC2046]

▼ Multipart/Related MIME [RFC2387]

Sending ebXML Messages over SMTP

Prior to sending messages over SMTP an ebXML Message MUST be formatted according to ebXML Message Service Specification sections 6 and 7. Additionally the messages must also conform to the syntax, format and encoding rules specified by MIME [RFC2045], [RFC2046] and [RFC2387].

Many types of data that a party might desire to transport via email are represented as 8bit characters or binary data. Such data cannot be transmitted over SMTP[SMTP], which restricts mail messages to 7bit US-ASCII data with lines no longer than 1000 characters including any trailing CRLF line separator. If a sending Message Service Handler knows that a receiving MTA, or ANY intermediary MTA's, are restricted to handling 7-bit data then any document part that uses 8 bit (or binary) representation must be "transformed" according to the encoding rules specified in section 6 of [RFC2045]. In cases where a Message Service Handler knows that a receiving MTA and ALL intermediary MTA's are capable of handling 8-bit data then no transformation is needed on any part of the ebXML Message.

The rules for forming an ebXML Message for transport via SMTP are as follows:

▼ If using [RFC821] restricted transport paths, apply transfer encoding to all 8-bit data that will be transported in an ebXML message, according to the encoding rules defined in section 6 of [RFC2045]. The Content-Transfer-Encoding MIME header MUST be included in the MIME envelope portion of any body part that has been transformed (encoded).

▼ The `Content-Type: Multipart/Related` MIME header with the associated parameters, from the ebXML Message Envelope MUST appear as an eMail MIME header.

▼ All other MIME headers that constitute the ebXML Message Envelope MUST also become part of the eMail MIME header.

▼ The `SOAPAction` MIME header field must also be included in the eMail MIME header and MAY have the value of ebXML:

SOAPAction: **"ebXML"**

Where Service and Action are values of the corresponding elements from the ebXML **MessageHeader**.

▼ The "MIME-Version: 1.0" header must appear as an eMail MIME header.

▼ The eMail header "To:" MUST contain the [RFC822] compliant eMail address of the ebXML Message Service Handler.

▼ The eMail header "From:" MUST contain the [RFC822] compliant eMail address of the senders ebXML Message Service Handler.

▼ Construct a "Date:" eMail header in accordance with [RFC822]

▼ Other headers MAY occur within the eMail message header in accordance with [RFC822] and [RFC2045], however ebXML Message Service Handlers MAY choose to ignore them.

The example below shows a minimal example of an eMail message containing an ebXML Message:

```
From: ebXMLhandler@example.com
To: ebXMLhandler@example2.com
Date: Thu, 08 Feb 2001 19:32:11 CST
MIME-Version: 1.0
SOAPAction: "ebXML"
Content-type: multipart/related; boundary="BoundarY"; type="text/
xml";
        start="<ebxhmheader111@example.com>"

--BoundarY
Content-ID: <ebxhmheader111@example.com>
Content-Type: text/xml

<?xml version="1.0" encoding="UTF-8"?>
<SOAP-ENV:Envelope xmlns:SOAP-ENV='http://schemas.xmlsoap.org/
soap/envelope/'
   xmlns:eb='http://www.ebxml.org/namespaces/messageHeader'>
<SOAP-ENV:Header>
  <eb:MessageHeader SOAP-ENV:mustUnderstand="1" eb:version="1.0">
```

```
      <eb:From>
        <eb:PartyId>urn:duns:123456789</eb:PartyId>
      </eb:From>
      <eb:To>
        <eb:PartyId>urn:duns:912345678</eb:PartyId>
      </eb:To>
      <eb:CPAId>20001209-133003-28572</eb:CPAId>
      <eb:ConversationId>20001209-133003-28572</eb:ConversationId>
      <eb:Service>urn:services:SupplierOrderProcessing</eb:Service>
      <eb:Action>NewOrder</eb:Action>
      <eb:MessageData>
        <eb:MessageId>20001209-133003-28572@example.com</eb:MessageId>
        <eb:Timestamp>2001-02-15T11:12:12Z</Timestamp>
      </eb:MessageData>
      <eb:QualityOfServiceInfo eb:deliverySemantics="BestEffort"/>
    </eb:MessageHeader>
</SOAP-ENV:Header>
<SOAP-ENV:Body>
  <eb:Manifest SOAP-ENV:mustUnderstand="1" eb:version="1.0">
    <eb:Reference xlink:href="cid:ebxmlpayload111@example.com"
        xlink:role="XLinkRole"
        xlink:type="simple">
        <eb:Description xml:lang="en-us">Purchase Order 1</eb:
Description>
    </eb:Reference>
  </eb:Manifest>
</SOAP-ENV:Body>
</SOAP-ENV:Envelope>

--BoundarY
Content-ID: <ebxhmheader111@example.com>
Content-Type: text/xml

<?xml version="1.0" encoding="UTF-8"?>
<purchase_order>
  <po_number>1</po_number>
  <part_number>123</part_number>
  <price currency="USD">500.00</price>
</purchase_order>

--BoundarY--
```

Response Messages

All ebXML response messages, including errors and acknowledgements, are delivered *asynchronously* between ebXML Message Service Handlers. Each response message MUST be constructed in accordance with the rules specified in the section titled "Sending ebXML messages over SMTP" elsewhere in this document.

ebXML Message Service Handlers MUST be capable of receiving a delivery failure notification message sent by an MTA. A MSH that receives a delivery failure notification message SHOULD examine the message to determine which ebXML message, sent by the MSH, resulted in a message delivery failure. The MSH SHOULD attempt to identify the application responsible for sending the offending message causing the failure. The MSH SHOULD attempt to notify the application that a message delivery failure has occurred. If the MSH is unable to determine the source of the offending message the MSH administrator should be notified.

MSH's which cannot identify a received message as a valid ebXML message or a message delivery failure SHOULD retain the unidentified message in a "dead letter" folder.

A MSH SHOULD place an entry in an audit log indicating the disposition of each received message.

Access Control

Implementers MAY protect their ebXML Message Service Handlers from unauthorized access through the use of an access control mechanism. The SMTP access authentication process described in "SMTP Service Extension for Authentication" [RFC2554] defines the ebXML recommended access control mechanism to protect a SMTP based ebXML Message Service Handler from unauthorized access.

Confidentiality and Communication Protocol Level Security

An ebXML Message Service Handler MAY use transport layer encryption to protect the confidentiality of ebXML messages. The IETF "SMTP Service Extension for Secure SMTP over TLS" specification [RFC2487] provides the specific technical details and list of allowable options, which may be used.

SMTP Model

All *ebXML Message Service* messages carried as mail in a [SMTP] Mail Transaction as shown in the figure below.

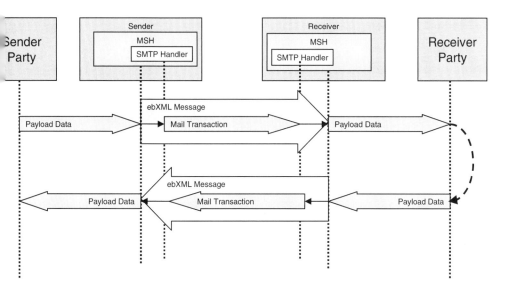

Communication Errors During Reliable Messaging

When the Sender or the Receiver detects a transport protocol level error (such as an HTTP, SMTP or FTP error) and Reliable Messaging is being used then the appropriate transport recovery handler will execute a recovery sequence. Only if the error is unrecoverable, does Reliable Messaging recovery take place (see section 9).

Glossary

v1.0
Technical Architecture Team
May 2001

TABLE OF CONTENTS

1   Status of this Document

This document is a ebXML Reference Document for the eBusiness community.

Distribution of this document is unlimited.

The document formatting is based on the Internet Society's Standard RFC format.

This version:

http://www.ebxml.org/specs/ebGLOSS.pdf

Latest version:

http://www.ebxml.org/specs/ebGLOSS.pdf

2   ebXML Participants

The editors wish to acknowledge the support of the members of the Technical Architecture Project Team who contributed to the formulation of this document.

Team Lead

    Anders Grangard

Editors

Colin Barham	TIE
Al Boseman	ATPCO
Melanie McCarthy	General Motors
Robert Cunningham	Military Traffic Management Command, US Army

3   ebXML Group and Specification/ Document Names

3.1   Technical Specifications

[ebTA] ebXML Technical Architecture Specification

[ebBPSS] ebXML Business Process Specification Schema

[ebRIM] ebXML Registry Information Model

[ebRS] ebXML Registry Services Specification

[ebREQ] ebXML Requirements Specification

[ebCPP] ebXML Collaboration-Protocol Profile and Agreement Specification

[ebMS] ebXML Message Service Specification

3.2   Technical Reports

[bpOVER] Business Process and Business Information Analysis Overview

[bpWS] Business Process Analysis Worksheets and Guidelines

[bpPATT] E-Commerce Patterns

[bpPROC] ebXML Catalog of Common Business Processes

[ccOVER] Core Component Overview

[ebCCD&A] Core Components Discovery and Analysis

[ebCNTXT] Context and Re-Usability of Core Components

[ccCTLG] Guide to the Core Components Dictionary

[ebCCNAM] Naming Convention for Core Components

[ebCCDOC] Document Assembly and Context Rules

[ccDRIV] Catalogue of Context Drivers

[ccDICT] Core Component Dictionary

[ccSTRUCT] Core Component Structure

[secRISK] Technical Architecture Risk Assessment

3.3 Reference Materials

[ebGLOSS] ebXML Glossary

4 Glossary

TERM	ACRONYM	DEFINITION	SOURCE	COMMENTS ON DEFINITIONS
ABSTRACT CLASS		A class that cannot be directly instantiated.	UML Glossary V1.3	Contrast: concrete class.
ABSTRACTION		The essential characteristics of an entity that distinguish it from all other kinds of entities.	UML Glossary V1.3	An abstraction defines a boundary relative to the perspective of the viewer.
ACTIVE CLASS		A class whose instances are active objects.	UML Glossary V1.3	
ACTOR		Someone or something, outside the system or business that interacts with the system or business.	Rational Unified Process	
AGGREGATE [CLASS]		A class that represents the "whole" in an aggregation (whole-part) relationship.	UML Glossary V1.3	
AGGREGATE CORE COMPONENT		Defines a functional unit representation form that contains embedded information entities	CC/ Core Component Terminology	

TERM	ACRONYM	DEFINITION	SOURCE	COMMENTS ON DEFINITIONS
AGGREGATION		A special form of association that specifies a whole-part relationship between the aggregate (whole) and a component part.	UML Glossary V1.3	
AGREEMENT		An arrangement between two partner types that specifies in advance the conditions under which they will trade (terms of shipment, terms of payment, collaboration protocols, etc.) An agreement does not imply specific economic commitments.	BP team Terminology	
APPLICATION		An Application is software that may implement a Service by processing one or more of the Messages in the Document Exchanges associated with the Service.	ebXML Glossary	
ARCHITECTURE		The architecture of a software system (at a given point in time) is its organization or structure of significant components interacting through interfaces	Rational Unified Process	
AUTHORISATION		A right or a permission that is granted to a system entity to access a system resource.	IETF RFC 2828	
AUTHORISATION PROCESS		A procedure for granting authorisation	IETF RFC 2828	
BUSINESS ENTITY		Something that is accessed, inspected, manipulated, produced, and worked on in the business.	UMM	

TERM	ACRONYM	DEFINITION	SOURCE	COMMENTS ON DEFINITIONS
BASIC INFORMATION ENTITY		Defines a component which contains data but which does not have embedded information entities.	CC/ Core Component Terminology	
BEHAVIOUR		The observable effects of an operation or event, including its results.	UML Glossary V1.3	
BUSINESS		A series of processes, each having a clearly understood purpose, involving more than one organization, realized through the exchange of information and directed towards some mutually agreed upon goal, extending over a period of time.	(Open-edi Reference Model Standard - ISO/IEC 14662). (MoU)	
BUSINESS LIBRARY		A repository of business process specifications and business information objects within an industry, and of common business process specifications and common business information objects that are shared by multiple industries.	TA Specification Terminology	
BUSINESS ACTIVITY		A business activity is used to represent the state of the business process of one of the partners.	BP Team Terminology	For instance the requester is either in the state of sending the request, in the state of waiting for the response, or in the state of receiving.
BUSINESS COLLABORATION		An activity conducted between two or more parties for the purpose of achieving a specified outcome.	TA Specification Terminology	

TERM	ACRONYM	DEFINITION	SOURCE	COMMENTS ON DEFINITIONS
BUSINESS COLLABORATION KNOWLEDGE		The knowledge involved in a collaboration	TA Specification Terminology	
BUSINESS CONTEXT		Defines a context in which a business has chosen to employ an information entity	CC/ Core Component Terminology	
BUSINESS DOCUMENT		The set of information components that are inter-changed as part of a business activity.	CC/ Core Component Terminology	
BUSINESS ENTITY		Something that is ac-cessed, inspected, manip-ulated, produced, and worked on in the business.	UMM	
BUSINESS INFORMATION GROUP		A set of basic and/or aggregate information entities that convey a single business function.	CC/ Core Component Terminology	
BUSINESS OPERATIONAL VIEW (BOV)	BOV	A perspective of business transactions limited to those aspects regarding the making of business decisions and commit-ments among organisa-tions, which are needed for the description of a business transaction.	TA Specification Terminology	
BUSINESS PARTNER		An entity that engages in business transactions with another business partner(s).		
BUSINESS PROCESS		The means by which one or more activities are ac-complished in operating business practices.	UMM	

TERM	ACRONYM	DEFINITION	SOURCE	COMMENTS ON DEFINITIONS
BUSINESS PROCESS INTERFACE		The definition of how to interact with one partner role in order to make partner perform a desired service.	BP Team Terminology	
BUSINESS PROCESS SPECIFICATION SCHEMA		Defines the necessary set of elements to specify run-time aspects and configuration parameters to drive the partners' systems used in the collaboration.	BP Team Terminology	The goal of the BP Specification Schema is to provide the bridge between the eBusiness process modelling and specification of eBusiness software components.
BUSINESS PROFILE		Describes a company's ebXML capabilities and constraints, as well as its supported business scenarios.		
BUSINESS RULE		Rules, regulations and practices for business.	UMM	
BUSINESS SERVICE INTERFACE		An ebXML collaboration that is conducted by two or more parties each using a human or auto-mated business service that interprets the docu-ments and document envelopes transmitted and decides how to (or whether to) respond.	BP Team Terminology	
BUSINESS TRANSACTION		A business transaction is a logical unit of business conducted by two or more parties that gener-ates a computable success or failure state.	BP Team Terminology	The community, the partners, and the process, are all in a definable, and self-reliant state prior to the business trans-action, and in a new definable, and self-reliant state after the

TERM	ACRONYM	DEFINITION	SOURCE	COMMENTS ON DEFINITIONS
				business transaction. In other words if you are still 'waiting' for your business partner's response or reaction, the business transaction has not completed.
CHOREOGRAPHY		A declaration of the activities within collaboration and the sequencing rules and dependencies between these activities.		
CLASS		A description of a set of objects that share the same attributes, operations, methods, relationships, and semantics.	Rational Unified Process	
CLASS DIAGRAM		A graphical representation that shows static structure of concepts, types, and classes.	UML Glossary V1.3	Concepts show how users think about the world; types show interfaces of software components; classes show implementation of software components.
CODE		A character string (letters, figures or symbols) that for brevity and / or language independency may be used to represent or replace a definitive value or text of an attribute.	ebXML CC Dictionary Naming Conventions	Codes usually are maintained in code lists per attribute type (e.g. colour).
COLLABORATION		Describes a pattern of interaction among objects; it shows the objects participating in the interaction by their links to each other and the messages they send to each other.	Rational Unified Process Terminology	

TERM	ACRONYM	DEFINITION	SOURCE	COMMENTS ON DEFINITIONS
COLLABORATION DIAGRAM		A graphical representation of collaboration.	Rational Unified Process Terminology	
COLLABORATION PROTOCOL		The protocol that defines for a Collaborative Process:	CPA Specification Terminology	1. The sequence, dependencies and semantics of the Documents that are exchanged between Parties in order to carry out that Collaborative Process, and 2. The Messaging Capabilities used when sending documents between those Parties. Note that a Collaborative Process may have more than one Collaboration Protocol by which it may be implemented.
COLLABORATION PROTOCOL AGREEMENT	CPA	Information agreed between two (or more) Parties that identifies or describes the specific Collaboration Protocol that they have agreed to use.	CPA Specification Terminology	A CPA indicates what the involved Parties "will" do when carrying out a Collaborative Process. A CPA must be representable by a Document
COLLABORATION PROTOCOL PROFILE	CPP	Information about a Party that can be used to describe one or more Collaborative Processes and associated Collaborative Protocols that the Party supports.	CPA Specification Terminology	A CPP indicates what a Party "can" do in order to carry out a Collaborative Process. A CPP must be representable by a Document. While logically, a CPP is a single document, in practice, the CPP may be a set of linked documents

TERM	ACRONYM	DEFINITION	SOURCE	COMMENTS ON DEFINITIONS
				that express various aspects of the capabilities. A CPP is not an agreement. It represents the capabilities of a Party.
COLLABORATIVE PROCESS		A shared process by which two Parties work together in order to carry out a process.	CPA Specification Terminology	The Collaborative Process may be defined by an ebXML Collaboration Model.
COMMITMENT		An obligation to perform an economic event (that is, transfer ownership of a specified quantity of a specified economic resource type) at some future point in time. Order line items are examples of commitments.	BP Team Terminology	
COMMON BUSINESS LIBRARY	CBL			
COMMON BUSINESS PROCESS		A business process that is used with reasonable frequency in a business community.	BP Team Terminology	For electronic business-to-business commerce, we are interested in business processes that manifest themselves in an exchange (one way, two way, or n-way) of information in electronic format between parties. Typically, Common Business Processes are defined by standards bodies or business communities that are generally perceived as defining defacto standards for business processes within their domain of specializa-

TERM	ACRONYM	DEFINITION	SOURCE	COMMENTS ON DEFINITIONS
				tion. A business process that is not defined as common by a standards body or is only used by a small business community is not a Common Business Process. The phrase "exchange of information in electronic format" includes XML messaging, EDI messaging, file transfers, and other forms of electronic data exchange. This could include facsimile, email, and phone conversations. However, it is probably important that any business process that contains a facsimile or phone conversation component also include at least one electronic message, file transfer, or the like.
COMMUNICATION PROTOCOL ENVELOPE		The outermost envelope of an ebXML Message.	Messaging Service Specification Terminology	For example: HTTP or SMTP.
CONCRETE CLASS		A class that can be directly instantiated.	UML Glossary V1.3	
CONFORMANCE		Fulfilment of a product, process or service of all requirements specified; adherence of an implementation to the requirements of one or more specific standards or technical specifications.	ISO Guide 2	

TERM	ACRONYM	DEFINITION	SOURCE	COMMENTS ON DEFINITIONS
CONSTRAINT		A condition or a restriction.	UMM	
CONTROLLING AGENCY		Agency responsible for controlling the content of a basic information entity	CC/ Core Component Terminology	
CORE COMPONENT		Generic term that covers Core Component Type, Aggregate Information Entity and Basic Information Entity.	CC/ Core Component Terminology	
CORE COMPONENT TYPE		Any Core Component that has no business meaning on its own. When they are reused in a business context, Core Component Types become Basic Information Entities.	CC/ Core Component Terminology	For example, quantity has no business meaning, but quantity shipped does.
CORE LIBRARY		Contains data and process definitions, including relationships and cross references, as expressed in business terminology that may be tied to accepted industry classification scheme or taxonomy.		
DATA TYPE		A type of data to be used to represent the content of an information entity.	CC/ Core Component Terminology	This can be specified in XML Schema or ISO 8601.
DIGITAL SIGNATURE		A digital code that can be attached to an electronically transmitted message that uniquely identifies the sender	Digital Signature Scheme ISO 9796	
DISTRIBUTED REGISTRY		Federation of multiple registries that behaves logically as one registry.	TA Specification Terminology	

TERM	ACRONYM	DEFINITION	SOURCE	COMMENTS ON DEFINITIONS
DOCUMENT TYPE DEFINITION	DTD	Allows different instances of documents of the same type to be automatically processed in a uniform way.	XMI Glossary: OMG	
DOMAIN		A district or area under someone's control, range of influence.	CC/ Core Component Terminology	
ebXML INFRASTRUCTURE		The full compliment of technical specifications encompassed within the ebXML framework.	Technical Architecture terminology	
ECONOMIC CONTRACT		A subtype of agreement between partner types that some actual economic exchanges will occur in the future.	BP Team Terminology	Contracts can have recursive relationships with other contracts, for example, yearly contracts with monthly releases and weekly or daily shipping schedules. Contracts are containers for collections of commitments. For example, a purchase order is a contract wherein the line items are commitments.
ECONOMIC EVENT		The transfer of control of an economic resource from one party to another party.	BP Team Terminology	
ECONOMIC RESOURCE		A quantity of something of value that is under the control of an enterprise.	BP Team Terminology	
ECONOMIC RESOURCE TYPE		An economic resource type is the abstract classification or definition of an economic resource.	BP Team Terminology	For example, in an ERP system, Item-Master or Product-Master would represent the Economic Resource Type that abstractly defines an Inventory item or product. Forms of

TERM	ACRONYM	DEFINITION	SOURCE	COMMENTS ON DEFINITIONS
				payment are also defined by economic resource types, e.g. currency
EDIFACT WORKING GROUP	UN/ EWG	To develop and maintain UN/EDIFACT, support of harmonised implementations and the use of multilingual terminology.	UN/EWG	
ELECTRONIC BUSINESS	eBusiness	A generic term covering information definition and exchange requirements within and between enterprises by electronic means	(MoU)	
electronic business XML	ebXML			
ELECTRONIC COMMERCE		Electronic Commerce is doing business electronically. This includes the sharing of standardised unstructured or structured business information by any electronic means.	UN/CEFACT SIMAC	
ELECTRONIC DATA INTERCHANGE	EDI	The automated exchange of any predefined and structured data for business among information systems of two or more organizations.	(Open-edi Reference Model Standard - ISO/IEC 14662). (MoU)	
ELEMENT		An atomic constituent of a model.	UML Glossary V1.3	
ENCRYPTION		Cryptographic transformation of data (called "plaintext") into a form (called "ciphertext") that conceals the data's original meaning to prevent it from being known or used.	IETF RFC 2828	If the transformation is reversible, the corresponding reversal process is called "decryption", which is a transformation that restores encrypted data to its original state.

TERM	ACRONYM	DEFINITION	SOURCE	COMMENTS ON DEFINITIONS
EXTENSIBLE MARKUP LANGUAGE	XML	XML is designed to enable the exchange of information (data) between different applications and data sources on the World Wide Web and has been standardized by the W3C.	UN/CEFACT SIMAC	
FUNCTIONAL SERVICES VIEW	FSV	A perspective of business transactions limited to those information technology interoperability aspects of IT systems needed to support the execution of open-edi transactions.	Open-edi Reference Model, ISO/IEC 14662	
FUNCTIONAL SET		A set of alternative representations for the same semantic concept.	CC/ Core Component Terminology	
IMPLEMENTATION		An implementation is the realization of a specification.	NIST	It can be a software product, system or program.
INHERITANCE		The mechanism by which more specific elements incorporate structure and behaviour of more general elements related by behaviour.	Rational Unified Process Terminology	
INSTANCE		An entity to which a set of operations can be applied and which has a state that stores the effects of the operations.	Rational Unified Process Terminology	
INTERACTION DIAGRAM		Shows how several objects collaborate in single use case.	UML Glossary V1.3	
MESSAGE ENVELOPE		A communication independent envelope, specifically MIME multipart/related, which contains	Messaging Service Specification Terminology	

TERM	ACRONYM	DEFINITION	SOURCE	COMMENTS ON DEFINITIONS
		the two main parts of an ebXML compliant message (the Header and Payload containers).		
MESSAGE HEADER		A specification of the structure and composition of the information necessary for an ebXML Messaging Service to successfully generate or process and ebXML compliant message.	Messaging Service Specification Terminology	
MESSAGING CAPABILITIES		The set of capabilities that support exchange of Documents between Parties.	Messaging Service Specification Terminology	Examples are the communication protocol and its parameters, security definitions, and general properties of ending and receiving messages.
MESSAGING SERVICE		A framework that enables interoperable, secure and reliable exchange of Messages between Trading Partners.	Messaging Service Specification Terminology	
MESSAGING SERVICE LAYER		Enforces the "rules of engagement" as defined by two Trading Partners in a Collaboration Protocol Agreement (including, but not limited to security and Business Process functions related to Message delivery).	TA Specification Terminology	
METHOD		The detailed, logically ordered plans or procedures followed to accomplish a task or attain a goal.	Rational Unified Process Terminology	

TERM	ACRONYM	DEFINITION	SOURCE	COMMENTS ON DEFINITIONS
OPEN-EDI		Electronic data interchange among multiple autonomous organizations to accomplish an explicit shared business goal.	(MoU) Check reference.	
PACKAGE		A general-purpose mechanism for organizing elements into groups.	Rational Unified Process Terminology	Packages may be nested within other packages.
PACKAGE DIAGRAM		Shows groups of classes and dependencies among them.	UML Glossary V1.3	
PARTY		A Party is an entity such as a company, department, organisation or individual that can generate, send, receive or relay Documents.	CPP & CPA Specification Terminology	
PARTY DISCOVERY PROCESS		A Collaborative Process by which one Party can discover CPP information about other Parties.	CPA Specification Terminology	
PAYLOAD		A section of data/information that is not part of the ebXML wrapping.	Messaging Service Specification Terminology	
PAYLOAD CONTAINER		An optional container used to envelope the real payload of an ebXML message.	Messaging Service Specification Terminology	If a payload is present, the payload container must consist of a MIME header portion (the ebXML Payload Envelope) and a content portion (the payload itself).
PAYLOAD ENVELOPE		The specific MIME headers that are associated with a MIME part.	Messaging Service Specification	

TERM	ACRONYM	DEFINITION	SOURCE	COMMENTS ON DEFINITIONS
REGISTRY		A mechanism whereby relevant repository items and metadata about them can be registered such that a pointer to their location, and all their metadata, can be retrieved as a result of a query.	TA Specification Terminology	
REGISTRY AUTHORITY		A super user who maintains registry.	Defined in ISO11179	
REGISTRY CLIENTS		An ebXML application that makes use of services offered by a Registry using the messaging services.	TA Specification Terminology	For example: the ebXML Registry and the ebXML messaging services
REGISTRY ENTRY		Metadata that catalogs registry item.		Cannot find source of term or definition
REGISTRY INFRASTRUCTURE PROVIDER		An entity which provides a registry/ repository to store profiles, CPPs etc.		Cannot find source of term or definition
REGISTRY INTERFACE		A set of Registry Services that provide access to Registry content to clients of the Registry is defined in the ebXML Registry Services Specification.	TA Specification Terminology	
REGISTRY ITEM		The content registered in a repository.	TA Specification Terminology	
REGISTRY SERVICE		A way of providing access to Registry content to clients of the Registry.	ebXML Registry Services Specification 222	
REPOSITORY		A location or set of distributed locations where Repository Items, pointed at by the registry, reside and from which they can be retrieved.	TA Specification Terminology	

TERM	ACRONYM	DEFINITION	SOURCE	COMMENTS ON DEFINITIONS
REPRESENTATION TYPE		Type of data to be used to represent the content of an information entity	CC/ Core Component Terminology	From ISO 11179
ROLE		The named specific behaviour of an entity participating in a particular context.	UML Glossary V1.3	A role may be static (e.g., an association end) or dynamic (e.g., a collaboration role).
SCENARIO		A formal specification of a class of business activities having the same business goal.	(ISO 19735 part I)	
SECURITY MODEL		A schematic description of a set of entities and relationships by which a specified set of security services are provided by or within a system.	IETF RFC 2828	
SECURITY POLICY		A set of rules and practices that specify or regulate how a system or organization provides security services to protect sensitive and critical system resources.	IETF RFC 2828	
SEQUENCE DIAGRAM		A diagram that shows object interactions arranged in time sequence.	Rational Unified Process Terminology	In particular, it shows the objects participating in the interaction and the sequence of messages exchanged.
SIMPLE ELECTRONIC BUSINESS (SEB)	SEB	Simple Electronic Business is the application of simplified business processes, using core application data, and new and existing standardised techniques that support paperless and efficient operations.	UN/CEFACT SIMAC	

TERM	ACRONYM	DEFINITION	SOURCE	COMMENTS ON DEFINITIONS
SIMPL-EDI		Subsets of UN/EDIFACT messages especially designed for SMEs. Simpl-EDI - Simple Electronic Business defines simplest processes and their required core data allowing the exchange of the minimum data to effect a business transaction electronically.	UN/CEFACT SIMAC	
SPECIFICATION SCHEMA		An additional view of a meta model.		
SUBMITTING ORGANISATION		Any organisation that submits a repository item to be registered in a repository.	OASIS	The Submitting Organisation will be the intellectual property owner of the repository item.
SUPPLY CHAIN		A sequence of events, which may include conversion, movement or placement, which adds value to goods, products, or services.	UN/CEFACT SIMAC	
UNIFIED MODELLING LANGUAGE (UML)	UML	A set of diagrams that communicate requirements regarding a business process.		
UNIQUE IDENTIFIER	UID	The abstract concept of utilizing a standard mechanism and process for assigning a sequence of alphanumeric codes to ebXML Registry items, including: Core Components, Aggregate Information Entities, and Business Processes		

TERM	ACRONYM	DEFINITION	SOURCE	COMMENTS ON DEFINITIONS
UNIVERSALLY UNIQUE IDENTIFIER (UUID)	UUID	An identifier that is unique across both space and time, with respect to the space of all UUIDs.	DCE 1.1: Remote Procedure Call. Open Group Technical Standard. Document Number C706. The Open Group (Reading, UK: August, 1997).	A UUID can be used for multiple purposes, from tagging objects with an extremely short lifetime, to reliably identifying very persistent objects across a network.
USE CASE		Defines a sequence of actions a system performs that yields an observable result of value to a particular actor.	UML	It is used to structure the behavioural things in a model.
USE CASE MODEL		A model that describes a system's functional requirements in terms of use cases.	UML Glossary V1.3	
VULNERABILITY		A flaw or weakness in a system's design, implementation, or operation and management that could be exploited to violate the system's security policy.	IETF RFC 2828	
WORKFLOW		The sequence of activities performed in a business that produces a result of observable value to an individual actor.	Rational Unified Process	

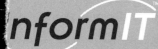